THE LETTERS OF
D. H. LAWRENCE

VOLUME II
June 1913 – October 1916

EDITED BY
GEORGE J. ZYTARUK
AND
JAMES T. BOULTON

CAMBRIDGE UNIVERSITY PRESS

CAMBRIDGE

LONDON   NEW YORK   NEW ROCHELLE
MELBOURNE   SYDNEY

Published by the Press Syndicate of the University of Cambridge
The Pitt Building, Trumpington Street, Cambridge CB2 IRP
32 East 57th Street, New York, NY 10022, USA
296 Beaconsfield Parade, Middle Park, Melbourne 3206, Australia

First published 1981

Printed in the United States of America
Typeset at the University Press, Cambridge, England
Printed and bound by Vail-Ballou Press Inc., Binghamton, New York

Library of Congress Cataloguing in Publication Data
Lawrence, David Herbert, 1885–1930
The Letters of D. H. Lawrence.
Includes index.

British Library Cataloguing in Publication Data
Lawrence, D. H.
The Letters of D. H. Lawrence.
Vol. 2: June 1913–October 1916. – (The Cambridge
edition of the letters and works of D. H. Lawrence)
1. Lawrence, D. H. – Correspondence
2. Authors, English – 20th century – Correspondence
I. Title   II. Zytaruk, George J.
III. Boulton, James T.
823'.912   PR6023.A93Z/   80–42111

ISBN 0 521 23111 6

CONTENTS

THE
CAMBRIDGE EDITION OF
THE LETTERS AND WORKS OF
D. H. LAWRENCE

THE LETTERS OF D. H. LAWRENCE

*Vol. I: September 1901 – May 1913
James T. Boulton

Vol. II: June 1913 – October 1916
George J. Zytaruk and James T. Boulton

Vol. III: 1916 – 1921
James T. Boulton and Andrew Robertson

Vol. IV: 1921 – 1924
Warren Roberts and Elizabeth Mansfield

Vol. V: 1924 – 1927
David Farmer

Vol. VI: 1927 – 1928
Gerald M. Lacy

Vol. VII: 1928 – 1930
Keith Sagar and James T. Boulton

* Already published

THE LETTERS OF D. H. LAWRENCE

ILLUSTRATIONS

ACKNOWLEDGEMENTS

The Editorial Board wishes to reiterate its thanks to all manuscript holders who have made Lawrence's letters available for the edition. The cue-titles of manuscript locations reveal those owners whose property is used in this volume.

The volume editors acknowledge the importance of advice and critical commentary they have received from fellow members of the Editorial Board. They also wish to record a profound debt of gratitude to Mr Michael Black and to his editorial staff at Cambridge University Press, while giving particular mention to the scholarly care devoted to the volume by Lindeth Vasey.

The following Libraries generously made their resources available to the editors: Beinecke Rare Books and Manuscripts Library, Yale University; the Berg Collection at the New York Public Library; Bodleian Library, Oxford; Brasenose College, Oxford; the British Library; the Humanities Research Center, University of Texas at Austin; the John Robarts Library, University of Toronto; Massey College, University of Toronto; the Nottinghamshire County Libraries; the Royal Institute of British Architects; the University of Birmingham; and the University of Nottingham.

The editors are indebted for assistance to very many individuals who have, on matters large and small, given freely of their time and knowledge to the advantage of the edition. Those who deserve mention in relation to this volume include the following: Mr Armin Arnold; Mr Peter Babando; Dr Colin Bailey; Dr Carl Baron; Dr Ben Benedikz; Professor Colin Burns; Mr W. D. S. Caird; Mr Alan Cameron; Mr John Carswell; Mr Guy Collings; Canon J. B. D. Cotter; Dr James C. Cowan; Mr Jim Davies; Professor Emile Delavenay; Mrs Katherine Delavenay; Mr John Dunlop; Dr Paul Eggert; Dr Brian Finney; Mr Nicholas Furbank; the late Dr David Garnett; Mrs Enid Goodband; Mr H. Pearson Gundy; Mr Cuthbert Gunning; Mr Michael Halls; Mrs C. Hardie; Professor James Hepburn; Mr Mark R. Hillegas; Mrs Enid Hilton; Mr Michael Holroyd; Mr William Hotten; Mr Peter Hull; Mr Fred Keay; Mr George Lazarus; Mrs Lee Mitchell; the late Professor Harry T. Moore; Mr Cyril Noall; Mr Gerald Pollinger; Dr Norbert Schuldes; Mr G. W. Slowey; Professor Alastair Smart; Professor R. Smith; Mrs Catherine Stoye; Dr Lola L. Szladits; Mr Gordon Waterfield; Mrs M. Welch; Mrs F. M. Wilkinson-Jones; Dr John Worthen. Special thanks have been earned by Dr Frank K. Robinson for his translations of letters written in German; Mrs Anne Buckley, Mrs

Deanna Hodgins and Mrs Jackie Lecour for their secretarial skills; Mrs Margaret Boulton and Mrs Marjorie Stone for their meticulous checking of every text in the volume as well as for help with proof-correcting; and Mr Peter Burbidge for his generous assistance in the preparation of the index.

George Zytaruk wishes to thank the Board of Governors of Nipissing University College for a year's sabbatical leave and the Canada Council for a Senior Leave Fellowship.

For permission to use unpublished and copyright material in the introduction and notes, gratitude is expressed to: the Berg Collection, the New York Public Library, Astor, Lenox and Tilden Foundations; Mr W. D. S. Caird; Constable & Co. Ltd; Duckworth & Co. Ltd; the late Dr David Garnett; Mr Richard Garnett; Mr R. A. Harrison; Mr Morley Kennerley; Eyre Methuen Ltd; Laurence Pollinger & Co.; the Ezra Pound Literary Property Trust, Faber & Faber Ltd and New Directions Publishing Corporation; Royal Literary Fund; Bertrand Russell Archive, McMaster University; Sidgwick & Jackson Ltd; Society of Authors; Mrs Julian Vinogradoff; Mr Gordon Waterfield.

Illustrations in this volume have been made available through the courtesy of: Mrs Annabel Anrep; Arts Council of Great Britain; Mrs Vivien Asquith; Miss Elisabeth Beresford; Mr John Carswell; Mr Peter Clayton; Mr J. Dallyn; Mr John Dunlop; Mr Luke Gertler; Mr R. A. Harrison; Harvard University; Humanities Research Center, University of Texas at Austin; the Dowager Countess of Iddesleigh; Mr Morley Kennerley; Provost and Scholars of King's College, Cambridge; Mr Edward Leigh; Lord Hutchinson of Lullington; Mr John Martin; Mrs M. Middleton Murry; National Portrait Gallery; Mr Francis Nichols; Royal Literary Fund; Dr Keith Sagar; Society of Authors; Mrs Joan Tudor; Department of Special Collections, University of Chicago Library; Van Vechten Estate; Mrs Julian Vinogradoff; Mr Gordon Waterfield.

NOTE ON THE TEXT

A full statement of the 'Rules of Transcription' and an explanation of the 'Editorial Apparatus' are provided in Volume 1, pp. xviii–xx. The reader may, however, like to be reminded that the following symbols are used:

[   ]   indicates a defect in the MS making it impossible even to conjecture what Lawrence had written. Where a reconstruction can be hazarded or a fault corrected, the conjecture or correction is shown within the square brackets.

[...]   indicates a deletion which cannot be deciphered or a postmark which is wholly or partly illegible.

TMS =   typed manuscript

TMSC =   typed manuscript copy

TSCC =   typescript carbon copy

Maps are provided mainly to show the location of places which Lawrence visited for the first time during the period covered by this volume. No attempt has been made fully to repeat information given on the maps in Volume 1.

CUE-TITLES

Cue-titles are employed both for manuscript locations and for printed works. The following appear in this volume:

A. Manuscript locations

Anderson	Dr Jack H. Anderson
Anon.	Anonymous
Bate	Mrs Elaine Bate
BL	British Library
Clarke	Mr W. H. Clarke
ColU	Columbia University
Cooney	Professor Seamus Cooney
Dunlop	Mr John Dunlop
Forster	Mr W. Forster
Garnett	The late Dr David Garnett
Harrison	Mr R. Austin Harrison
HL	Henry E. Huntington Library and Art Gallery
HU	Harvard University

IEduc	Iowa State Education Association
Jeffrey	Mr Frederick Jeffrey
KCC	King's College, Cambridge
Lazarus	Mr George Lazarus
LC	Library of Congress
Martin	Mr John Martin
McMU	McMaster University
Moore	The late Professor Harry T. Moore
NCL	Nottinghamshire County Libraries
NWU	Northwestern University
NYPL	New York Public Library
NZNL	Katherine Mansfield Papers, Alexander Turnbull Library, National Library of New Zealand
PU	Princeton University
Putt	Mr S. Gorley Putt
RLFund	Royal Literary Fund
SIU	Southern Illinois University
StaU	Stanford University
UCB	University of California at Berkeley
UChi	University of Chicago
UCin	University of Cincinnati
UCLA	University of California at Los Angeles
UIll	University of Illinois
UN	University of Nottingham
UNYB	State University of New York at Buffalo
UT	University of Texas at Austin
UTul	University of Tulsa
VC	Vassar College
Waterfield	Mr Gordon Waterfield
YU	Yale University

B. *Printed works*
(The place of publication is London unless otherwise stated.)

Asquith, *Diaries*	Lady Cynthia Asquith. *Diaries: 1915–1918.* Hutchinson, 1968
Carswell, *Adelphi*	Catherine Carswell, 'Reminiscences of D. H. Lawrence', *Adelphi*, iii (November 1931–March 1932), 77–85, 162–70, 210–18, 283–93, 387–96
Carswell	Catherine Carswell. *The Savage Pilgrimage: A Narrative of D. H. Lawrence.* Chatto and Windus, 1932
Damon	S. Foster Damon. *Amy Lowell: A Chronicle.* New York: Houghton Mifflin, 1935
Delany	Paul Delany. *D. H. Lawrence's Nightmare.* Hassocks, Sussex: The Harvester Press, 1979
Delavenay	Emile Delavenay. *D. H. Lawrence: The Man and His Work: The Formative Years, 1885–1919.* Heinemann, 1972
DHL Review	James C. Cowan, ed. *The D. H. Lawrence Review.* Fayetteville: University of Arkansas, 1968–
Draper	R. P. Draper, ed. *D. H. Lawrence: The Critical Heritage.* Routledge & Kegan Paul, 1970
Furbank	P. N. Furbank. *E. M. Forster: A Life.* 2 volumes. Secker and Warburg, 1977–8
Gransden	K. W. Gransden, 'Rananim: D. H. Lawrence's Letters to S. S. Koteliansky', *Twentieth Century*, clix (January–June, 1955), 22–32
Huxley	Aldous Huxley, ed. *The Letters of D. H. Lawrence.* Heinemann, 1932
Letters	James T. Boulton, ed. *The Letters of D. H. Lawrence*, Volume i, September 1901–May 1913. Cambridge: Cambridge University Press, 1979
Monroe	Harriet Monroe, 'D. H. Lawrence', *Poetry: A Magazine of Verse*, xxxvi (May 1930), 90–6

Moore, *Atlantic Monthly*   Harry T. Moore,'D. H. Lawrence's Letters
to Bertrand Russell', *Atlantic. Monthly*,
clxxxii (December 1948), 92–102
Moore, *Bertrand Russell*   Harry T. Moore, ed. *D. H. Lawrence's
Letters to Bertrand Russell*. New York:
Gotham Book Mart, 1948
Moore, *Intelligent Heart*   Harry T. Moore. *The Intelligent Heart:
The Story of D. H. Lawrence*. New York:
Farrar, Straus, and Young, 1954
Moore   Harry T. Moore, ed. *The Collected Letters
of D. H. Lawrence*. 2 volumes. Heinemann,
1962
Murry, *New Adelphi*   John Middleton Murry, 'Reminiscences of
D. H. Lawrence I–VII', *New Adelphi*, iii
(June–August 1930 – March 1931)
Murry, *Autobiography*   John Middleton Murry. *The Autobiography
of John Middleton Murry: Between Two
Worlds*. New York: Julian Messner, Inc.,
1936
Nehls   Edward Nehls, ed. *D. H. Lawrence: A
Composite Biography*. 3 volumes. Madison:
University of Wisconsin Press, 1957–9
Ottoline at Garsington   Robert Gaythorne-Hardy, ed. *Ottoline at
Garsington: Memoirs of Lady Ottoline
Morrell 1915–1918*. Faber & Faber, 1974
Pinto   Vivian de Sola Pinto, ed. *D. H. Lawrence
after Thirty Years, Catalogue of an Exhibi-
tion held in the Art Gallery of the University
of Nottingham, 17 June–30 July, 1960*.
Nottingham: University of Nottingham,
1960
Schorer   Mark Schorer, 'I Will Send Address:
Unpublished Letters of D. H. Lawrence',
London Magazine, iii (February 1956),
44–67
Spender   [Stephen Spender],   'D. H. Lawrence:
Letters to S. S. Koteliansky', *Encounter*, i
(December 1953), 29–35
TLS   *The Times Literary Supplement*
Zytaruk, *Malahat*   George J. Zytaruk, ed. 'D. H. Lawrence:

Zytaruk

Letters to Koteliansky', *Malahat Review*, i
(January 1967), 17–40
George J. Zytaruk, ed. *The Quest for
Rananim: D. H. Lawrence's Letters to S. S.
Koteliansky 1914 to 1930.* Montreal:
McGill–Queen's University Press, 1970

MONETARY TERMS
tanner = sixpence (6d) = $2\frac{1}{2}$p.
bob = one shilling (1/-) = 5p.
half-a-crown = 2/6 = $12\frac{1}{2}$p.
quid = £1.
guinea = £1/1/- = £1.05.

LAWRENCE: A CHRONOLOGY, 1913–1916

19 April – 1 June 1913	Lawrence and Frieda in Irschenhausen at the Haus Jaffe
17 June 1913	Leaves for England
19 June 1913	Arrives in London
19 June – 9 July 1913	Stays at The Cearne (home of Edward Garnett); several visits to London
July 1913	'German Books: Thomas Mann' in *Blue Review*
9 July 1913	Stays overnight in Hampstead en route for Kingsgate; meets Katherine Mansfield and Norman Douglas
10–29 July 1913	At Riley House, 28 Percy Avenue, Kingsgate, Broadstairs, Kent
16 July 1913	Visited by Henry Savage
20 July 1913	Introduced to Herbert and Cynthia Asquith by Edward Marsh
29 July 1913	Stays with Gordon Campbell at 9 Selwood Terrace, South Kensington, London
30 July 1913	Introduced to W. H. Davies by Edward Marsh
31 July – 2 August 1913	At The Cearne; Frieda to Germany
2–6 August 1913	Eastwood (staying with William Hopkin) for his sister Ada's marriage on Monday, 4 August
6 August 1913	To Downshire Hill (London home of Edward Garnett)
7 August 1913	To Irschenhausen
9 August – 17 September 1913	With Frieda in Irschenhausen
13 August 1913	'The Fly in the Ointment' in *New Statesman*
September 1913	'Italian Studies: By the Lago di Garda' in *English Review*
6 September 1913	'Strike-Pay I, Her Turn' in *Saturday Westminster Gazette*
13 September 1913	'Strike-Pay II, Ephraim's Half Sovereign' in *Saturday Westminster Gazette*; 'A Sick Collier' in *New Statesman*
17 September 1913	Lawrence leaves Irschenhausen for Switzerland; Frieda for Baden-Baden

18–26 September 1913	Switzerland: journey across Lake Constance, 'down the Rhine to the falls', mostly on foot from 'Schaffhausen to Zurich, Lucerne, over the Gotthard to Airolo, Bellinzona, Lugano, Como'
26 September 1913	Joins Frieda in Milan
28 September – 4 October 1913	Lerici at the Albergo delle Palme
4 October 1913 – 8 June 1914	At the Villino Ettore Gambrosier in Fiascherino on the Gulf of Spezia
18 October 1913	Frieda's divorce hearing in London
November 1913	'The Mowers' in *Smart Set*
c. 2 November 1913	Completes four stories for *English Review*; continues work on 'The Sisters'
15 November 1913	'Service of all the Dead' in *New Statesman*
29 November 1913	Visited by Wilfrid Gibson, Lascelles and Catherine Abercrombie, R. C. Trevelyan and Aubrey Waterfield
13–15 December 1913	Weekend at Aubrey Waterfield's castle in Aulla
c. 26 December 1913	Ezra Pound proposes him for the Polignac Prize in poetry
January 1914	Eight poems in *Poetry: A Magazine of Verse*
12 January 1914	Visited by Edward Marsh and James Strachey Barnes
c. 29 January – c. 7 March 1914	Visited by Constance Garnett and Vera Volkhovsky
February 1914	Article on Lawrence by W. L. George in *The Bookman*
February 1914	'Two Poems' in *English Review*
February 1914	'The Christening' in *Smart Set*
March 1914	'The Shadow in the Rose Garden' in *Smart Set*
8? March 1914	Levanto, at the home of Russian novelist Amfiteatrov
April 1914	Five poems in *Egoist*
1 April 1914	*The Widowing of Mrs Holroyd* published in New York by Mitchell Kennerley
27 April 1914	Decree absolute pronounced in Frieda's divorce case
c. 6 May – ? June 1914	Visited by Ivy Low
c. 14 May 1914	Thomas Dunlop finishes typing *The Rainbow*
16–17 May 1914	Weekend in Spezia

28 May – 1? June 1914	Aulla, with the Waterfields for 'a few days'
June 1914	'Vin Ordinaire' in *English Review*
8 June 1914	Leaves Fiascherino, Frieda to Baden-Baden
9 June 1914	Turin
10–17? June 1914	Switzerland on foot (with A. P. Lewis): Aosta, Grand St Bernard, Martigny, Interlaken and Bern
18–22 June 1914	Heidelberg (at Max Weber's) and Baden-Baden
24 June 1914	Arrives in England with Frieda
24 June – 15 August 1914	9 Selwood Terrace, South Kensington, London
27 June 1914	Introduced to Rupert Brooke by Edward Marsh
c. 28 June 1914	Meets Catherine Jackson (later Carswell)
30 June 1914	Accepts J. B. Pinker as agent and £300 advance from Methuen for *The Rainbow*
4–7 July 1914	The Cearne
13 July 1914	Marries Frieda at the Kensington Registry Office
18–23 July 1914	Ripley, Derbyshire (without Frieda) to visit his sister Ada
30 July 1914	Meets Amy Lowell, Richard and Hilda Aldington
31 July – 8 August 1914	Walking tour in Westmorland; meets S. S. Koteliansky
August 1914	'Honour and Arms' in *English Review*
5 August 1914	Barrow-in-Furness; learns that war has been declared on 4 August
c. 13 August 1914	Meets Lady Ottoline Morrell
15? August 1914 – 21 January 1915	The Triangle, Bellingdon Lane, Chesham, Bucks.
18 August 1914	'With the Guns' in *Manchester Guardian*
24 August 1914	Meets Compton Mackenzie
c. 5 September 1914	Begins 'Study of Thomas Hardy'
19–20 September 1914	London
October 1914	'The White Stocking' in *Smart Set*
16 October 1914	Receives £50 from the Royal Literary Fund
14–26 October 1914	Visited by the Murrys
29–30 October 1914	London (at Catherine Jackson's)
November 1914	'Honour and Arms' in *Metropolitan*
21–23 November 1914	London

26 November 1914	*The Prussian Officer and Other Stories* published in England by Duckworth
December 1914	Six poems in *Poetry: A Magazine of Verse*
December 1914	'Teasing' in *Poetry and Drama*
3 December 1914	'Rewriting' *The Rainbow*
5 December 1914	Sends Pinker the first hundred pages of the revised MS
6–10 December 1914	Ripley, Derbyshire; Frieda sees Ernest Weekley in Nottingham
10–12? December 1914	Stays with Edward Garnett in London
3 January 1915	First mention of founding Rananim
7 January 1915	Informs Pinker of his decision to split *The Rainbow* into two volumes
21 January 1915	To London (staying with Dr David and Edith Eder); meets E. M. Forster at Lady Ottoline's
22 January 1915	Visits Duncan Grant's studio with Forster and David Garnett
23 January – 30 July 1915	Greatham, Pulborough, Sussex (Viola Meynell's cottage)
8 February 1915	Lady Ottoline brings Bertrand Russell to Greatham
10–12 February 1915	Visited by Forster
15–16 February 1915	London: a meeting at S. S. Koteliansky's house
16–17 February 1915	Visited by Lady Cynthia
19–24 February 1915	Murry stays with the Lawrences
23–24 February 1915	Visited by Lady Ottoline
2 March 1915	Completes the MS of *The Rainbow*
6–8 March 1915	Weekend at Cambridge with Russell; meets Maynard Keynes, G. E. Moore, G. H. Hardy
20–21 March 1915	London with Frieda
1–3 April 1915	Visited by Russell
3–5 April 1915	Koteliansky and Barbara Low invited for Easter; she stays till 8 April
17 April 1915	Seven poems published in *Some Imagist Poets: An Anthology* (Boston and New York)
17–18 April 1915	Visited by David Garnett and Francis Birrell
29 April 1915	Worthing
1 May 1915	'Eloi, Eloi Lama Sabachthani' in *Egoist*
6 May 1915	Chichester
7–10 May 1915	London

10 May 1915	Examined for bankruptcy by the Registrar, Probate and Admiralty Division of the High Court, London
11–12 May 1915	Brighton with Lady Cynthia
31 May 1915	Sends the last of the revised typescript of *The Rainbow* to Pinker
5 and 19 June 1915	Visited by Lady Cynthia
12–16 June 1915	Garsington (Lady Ottoline's country house near Oxford)
19–20 June 1915	Visited by Russell
10–11 July 1915	London (staying with Dollie Radford in Hampstead)
20 July 1915	Visited by Lady Cynthia and Katharine Asquith
25 July 1915	Littlehampton with Viola Meynell to visit Lady Cynthia
30 July – 4 August 1915	At 12 Bayford Road, Littlehampton
4 August – 21 December 1915	1 Byron Villas, Vale-of-Health, Hampstead, London
5 September 1915	First mention of the *Signature* project
30 September 1915	*The Rainbow* published in England by Methuen
October 1915	'England, My England' in *English Review*
4 October 1915	'The Crown I' in *Signature*, No. 1
18 October 1915	'The Crown II' in *Signature*, No. 2
November 1915	'Service of All the Dead' and 'Meeting Among the Mountains' in *Georgian Poetry 1913–1915*
3 November 1915	Magistrate's warrant issued for suppression of *The Rainbow*
4 November 1915	'The Crown III' in *Signature*, No. 3 (last issue to be published)
5 November 1915	Lawrence and Frieda obtain passports for the USA
8–11 November 1915	Garsington
13 November 1915	*The Rainbow* on trial, Bow Street Magistrates Court, London
18 November 1915	Suppression of *The Rainbow* first questioned in the House of Commons by Philip Morrell
29 November – 2 December 1915	Garsington; meets Aldous Huxley
30 November 1915	*The Rainbow* published in America by B. W. Huebsch
1 December 1915	Second question on *The Rainbow* suppression, in the House, by Philip Morrell

6 December 1915	Elected a member of the Incorporated Society of Authors, Playwrights and Composers
21–24 December 1915	At 2 Hurst Close, Garden Suburb, London (the home of Vere H. G. Collins)
24–29 December 1915	Ripley, Derbyshire (with sister Ada)
29 December 1915	To Cornwall via London; overnight at the Eders'
30 December 1915 – 29 February 1916	At Porthcothan, St Merryn, Padstow, Cornwall (J. D. Beresford's house)
c. 9 January – 21? February 1916	Philip Heseltine (joined by Lucie Channing 26 January – 21? February) lives with the Lawrences
c. 10 January – c. 12 February 1916	Seriously ill; examined by Dr Maitland Radford
10–22 January 1916	Visited by Dikran Kouyoumdjian (Michael Arlen)
11 February 1916	First certain mention of the 'Rainbow Books and Music' publishing scheme
17 February 1916	Receives proofs of the prospectus for the 'Rainbow Books and Music'
29 February – 17 March 1916	At the Tinner's Arms, Zennor, St Ives, Cornwall
17 March 1916 – October 1917	At Higher Tregerthen, Zennor, St Ives, Cornwall
5 or 6 April 1916	Middleton Murry and Katherine Mansfield join the Lawrences to live at Higher Tregerthen
c. 19 April 1916	Begins writing *Women in Love*
ante 22 April 1916	Breaks off relationship with Philip Heseltine
6 May 1916	Five poems published in *Some Imagist Poets 1916: An Annual Anthology* (Boston and New York)
25 May 1916	Military Service Bill becomes law
c. 13–16 June 1916	Murry and Katherine Mansfield leave Higher Tregerthen for Mylor, South Cornwall
c. 15 June 1916	*Twilight in Italy* published in England by Duckworth
24 June 1916	General Conscription goes into effect
28–29 June 1916	Bodmin; medical examination for military service; granted complete exemption
c. 16 July 1916	Moves into seven-roomed cottage, formerly occupied by the Murrys, at Higher Tregerthen

July 1916	*Amores* published in England by Duckworth (in America on 25 September 1916)
22–23? July 1916	To Mylor, visiting the Murrys
c. 10–15 August 1916	Visited by Barbara Low
28 September – c. 3 October 1916	Catherine Carswell stays with the Lawrences
31 October 1916	Finishes *Women in Love* (except for 'a sort of epilogue' never completed) and sends it to Pinker for typing

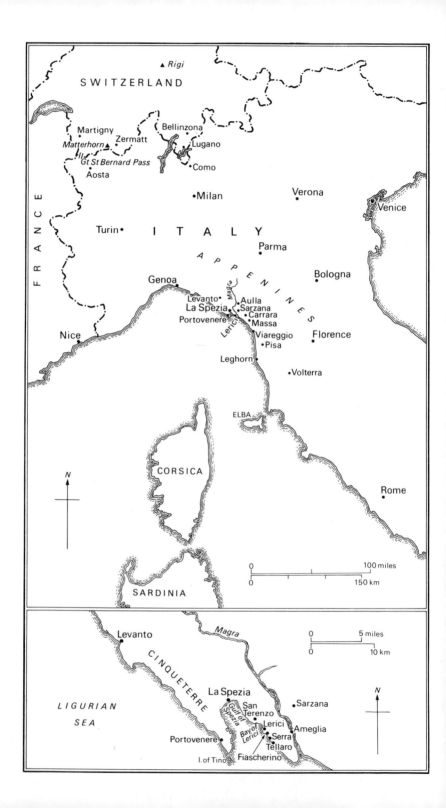

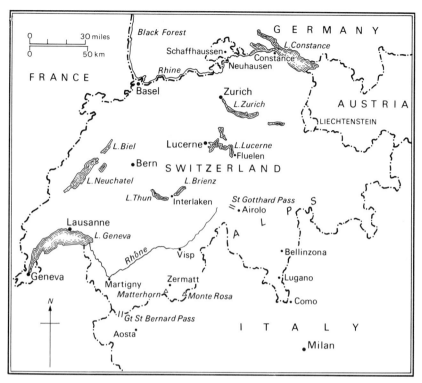

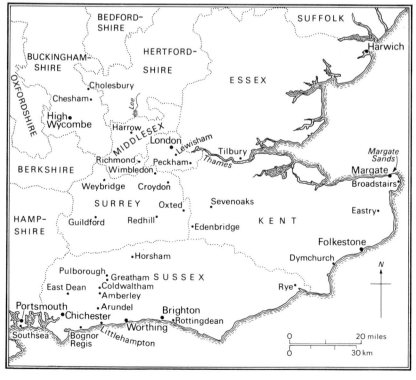

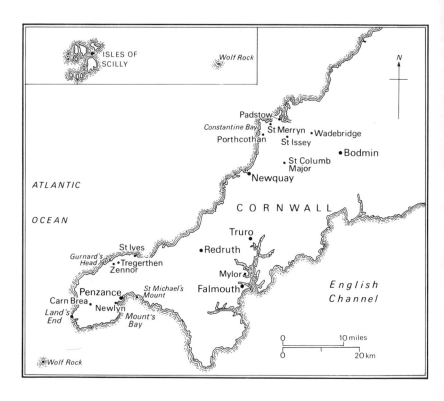

ISLES OF SCILLY

Wolf Rock

N

Padstow
Constantine Bay St Merryn •Wadebridge
Porthcothan St Issey
•Bodmin
. St Columb Major
•Newquay

ATLANTIC

C O R N W A L L

OCEAN

Truro
•Redruth

St Ives
Gurnard's Head •Tregerthen
Zennor
Mylor
Falmouth

English Channel

St Michael's Mount
Penzance
Carn Brea
Land's End Newlyn
Mount's Bay

0   10 miles
0   20 km

Wolf Rock

INTRODUCTION

With his third novel Mr D. H. Lawrence has come to full maturity as a writer...*Sons and Lovers* is so great a book that it needs sharp criticism.

Sons and Lovers is a book to haunt and waylay the mind long after it has been laid aside.

...Mr Lawrence's *Sons and Lovers*, far and away the best book he has yet written.

...we know of no active English novelist – today – who has Mr Lawrence's power to put in words the rise and fall of passion...After reading most of the more 'important' novels of the present year, we can say that we have seen none to excel it in interest and power.[1]

Such a reception of the novel published just three days before the first letter in this volume at once alerts us to expect here the letters of an author who had become publicly acknowledged. Perceptive readers, it is true, had recognised Lawrence's rare abilities at an earlier stage, but he had remained to a large degree a private man who wrote. It was now something of a pose for Lawrence to present himself merely as 'the son of a coal-miner, and very ordinary'.[2] He was an author whom readers wanted to know; they wished to exchange letters with him, to consult, even to lionise him. Ivy Low (subsequently the wife of Maxim Litvinoff, the future Soviet foreign commissar) is a case in point. She read *Sons and Lovers* in one 'all-night sitting'; the following morning she wrote postcards to her friends, particularly to Viola Meynell: '"Be sure to read *Sons and Lovers!*" "This is a book about the Oedipus complex!" "The most marvellous novel I have ever read"...Viola and I adopted D. H. Lawrence as our creed...I wrote [to him] care of his publishers.'[3] Youthful enthusiasm certainly – though Ivy Low was already the author of two novels – but it was infectious. It spread through the Meynells 'who were the nucleus of one of London's foremost literary cliques';[4] it was passed on to Catherine Jackson (later better known as Catherine Carswell, the novelist), one of Ivy's close friends; and the novel became a matter of keen discussion among Freudian psychoanalysts like Barbara Low, her aunt, and Dr David Eder, her uncle by marriage.[5] When Lawrence went to a party given by H. G. and Jane Wells, Middleton Murry,

---

[1] From reviews in *Standard*, 30 May 1913; *Westminster Gazette*, 14 June 1913; *Daily Chronicle*, 17 June 1913; *Saturday Review*, 21 June 1913. All are reprinted in Draper 58–66.
[2] Letter 598.
[3] Nehls, i. 215.
[4] Ibid.
[5] Ibid. i. 231.

who went too, was conscious of him as 'the author of *Sons and Lovers*'.[1]
And from America the publisher Mitchell Kennerley wrote to Lawrence's
patron, Edward Garnett: 'I have just finished reading *Sons and Lovers*, and
think it is the biggest novel I have read in years. If Mr Lawrence can keep
this up he will surpass all other modern novelists.'[2]

It is clear immediately, then, that the emergence of Lawrence as a writer
much discussed in private letters and conversations as well as in the press
had significant repercussions on his social life and on the range of his
correspondents. Catherine Carswell was to remain in correspondence with
him till a few months before his death; she received from him over 170
letters. Another new and important correspondent, the *grande dame* Lady
Ottoline Morrell, one of the most celebrated figures in London intellectual
society, sought him out after the appearance of *The Prussian Officer* in
November 1914. He had dined at the Morrells' house, 44 Bedford Square,
in August 1913, but it was her reaction to the volume of short stories which·
prompted her to invite him again. She wrote to Bertrand Russell – whose
mistress she then was – about the volume: 'I am amazed how good it is – quite
wonderful some of the Stories – He has great passion – and is so alive to
things outward and inward – a far better writer than [Gilbert] Cannan and
quite different from that muddled stuff of [Leonard] Woolfe.'[3] (The same
volume was considered sufficiently dangerous for Jesse Boot to refuse to
supply it to subscribers to his influential Lending Libraries.[4]) His growing
reputation promoted other friendships through the patronage of that highly
influential figure in metropolitan circles, Edward Marsh. He had included
Lawrence's poem 'Snap-Dragon' in his first volume of *Georgian Poetry*
(1912); he was to print others in two later volumes; but it was Marsh's
generosity and the introductions he provided which had the greater effect
on Lawrence's life and letters. Through him Lawrence met the Prime
Minister's daughter-in-law, (Lady) Cynthia Asquith who was to become a
significant friend and correspondent; the Oxford Professor of English, Sir
Walter Raleigh; Rupert Brooke; the painter Elliott Seabrooke; Amy Lowell
and, through her, Richard and Hilda ('H.D.') Aldington; as well as others
who, like Lawrence himself, were contributors to the *Georgian Poetry*
volumes, such as Lascelles Abercrombie, W. W. Gibson and Harold Monro.
To associate Lawrence with the 'Georgian' and 'Poetry Bookshop' circles
may now appear misleading; but not so. They consisted of congenial liberal
intellectuals whose company he obviously enjoyed – several letters testify to
it; his views on poetry did not coincide with theirs even in the early stages

[1] Ibid. i. 239.   [2] See p. 50 n. 4.
[3] See Letter 833.   [4] p. 257 n. 3.

and certainly not when he advocated a 'stark, bare, rocky directness of statement';[1] but the debates about poetic excellence carried on in letters to Marsh reveal both affection and regard for his correspondent. 'You must remain my poetic adviser', Lawrence told Marsh in March 1914: despite the touch of irony it was a genuine tribute. (He was quite prepared to accept Marsh's judgment on the appropriateness of revisions he suggested to a poem which was to appear in *Georgian Poetry 1913–1915*.[2]) Lawrence was 'moved almost to tears' by Marsh's generosity in sending £10 to ease the young writer's financial anxieties in September 1914.[3] When Marsh heard of Lawrence's plan to write what became the 'Study of Thomas Hardy' he at once sent a complete set of Hardy's works; he (together with fellow littérateurs Maurice Hewlett, Harold Monro and Gilbert Cannan) sponsored the application which obtained £50 for Lawrence from the Royal Literary Fund in October 1914; and instances of other kindnesses recur through this volume. Lawrence was capable of speaking of Marsh – as of other well-wishing friends – with great acerbity; they were critical of him; but, for the most part, they believed (as Marsh told the Royal Literary Fund trustees) that 'it would be a disaster if [his] talent were to be cramped or starved'.[4]

Evidence of this kind illustrates the sensitivity and generosity of Marsh and others; it also illuminates the vivid personal impression Lawrence made on a rapidly increasing number of people whom he met and whose presence is sensed in his letters. Most explicit about his impact was Cynthia Asquith (whom Lawrence first met when he and Frieda were staying in Broadstairs in July 1913):

I find them the most intoxicating company in the world. I never hoped to have such mental pleasure with anyone...He interests and attracts me. His talk is so extraordinarily real and living – such humour and yet so much of the fierceness and resentment which my acquiescent nature loves and covets. He is a Pentecost to one, and has the gift of intimacy and such perceptiveness that he introduces one to oneself.[5]

Comparable delight in his company was obviously experienced by people from a wide social range encountered by Lawrence and Frieda when they lived at Fiascherino in northern Italy (September 1913–June 1914) – from the local priest and schoolmistress to resident English gentry like the Cochranes 'who are rich as rich – butler and footman to serve four people at table'.[6] The reaction of the local people can be felt in Lawrence's letters; the reaction of the expatriates can similarly be felt but is also independently attested. 'The

[1] Letter 1134. [2] Letter 1001. [3] Letter 786.
[4] p. 224 n. 4. [5] Asquith, *Diaries* 18–19. [6] Letter 706.

Lawrences were all the rage in Lerici, in the English houses there': so reported Aubrey Waterfield, painter and illustrator, to the 'Georgian' poet Robert Trevelyan.[1] To take a further example, presumably it was the reputation of a man such as Cynthia Asquith described which induced the society hostess Lady St Helier to invite the Lawrences to lunch. She had been accustomed to entertaining Whistler and Millais, Tennyson and Browning; yet when the Lawrences could not accept the first invitation, they received a second.[2] Again, Bertrand Russell put on record the admiration he felt for Lawrence and the exhilaration of his company in the early days of their stormy friendship; he confessed, too, that for twenty-four hours after Lawrence denounced his brand of pacifism, in the letter of 14 September 1915, he 'contemplated committing suicide'.[3] There may be some justification for Middleton Murry's remark that Lawrence was 'perceptibly over-eager in aristocratic company'[4] – Katherine Mansfield felt it at a party given by Lady Ottoline – but manifestly this was not the whole truth. And, in any case, like Edmund Burke's, Lawrence's regard for 'aristocracy' did not necessarily extend on all occasions to the character of every aristocrat.

The period of Lawrence's life covered by this volume, then, was marked by the acquisition of new friends and correspondents striking in their variety as well as, in many cases, their social and intellectual calibre. Further examples, in addition to those already named, are S. S. Koteliansky ('Kot' as he was known), an intimate friend and collaborator from 1914 to Lawrence's death in 1930, the man to whom Lawrence wrote more frequently than to any other person; E. M. Forster; Middleton Murry and Katherine Mansfield; the novelist Gilbert Cannan and the painter Mark Gertler. There were others as diverse as Aldous Huxley and Compton Mackenzie whose significance as correspondents came much later; Thomas Dunlop, the British consul in Spezia; Irene Whittley, the daughter of Lawrence's landlord in Zennor, to whom he wrote spasmodically until 1922; or Raffaello Piccoli, Forster's friend who was then a Lecturer in Italian at Cambridge and later the Serena Professor of Italian there. (No letters to Piccoli are known; what is known, however, is that he was engaged on a comprehensive study of Lawrence at the time of his own death in 1933.) All these were new friends and acquaintances; some friendships which had been established earlier gradually faded. Both resulted from the changing needs and opportunities associated with the maturing of Lawrence's literary achievement and the growth of his reputation. Strange as it may at first appear, to set Edward Garnett beside the literary agent, J. B. Pinker in this

---

[1] From a letter dated 8 June 1914 in the possession of Mr Gordon Waterfield.
[2] Letters 705 and 743.   [3] Nehls, i. 284.   [4] Ibid. i. 240.

context proves instructive. These two men 'frame' the volume: the first letter is to Garnett about *Sons and Lovers*; the last is to Pinker about the virtually completed *Women in Love*.

No reader of Volume 1 would be surprised to find this volume opening with a letter to the man who, as Lawrence remarked, 'introduced me to the world'.[1] As 'reader' for Gerald Duckworth, Garnett had prepared the manuscript of *Sons and Lovers* for publication on 29 May 1913; he had been Lawrence's literary counsellor since their first contact in August 1911; indeed he had acted in personal matters, too, as if he were 'father and brother and all [Lawrence's] relations...except wife'.[2] The letter to Garnett on 1 June 1913 shows Lawrence continuing to rely on him, in this instance to distribute complimentary copies of the new novel and to advise about the next, 'The Sisters'. The second letter, also to Garnett, reveals a young author anxious about the novel just published; anxious, as well, about being 'cut off from [his] past life', partly at least on account of his unmarried status and Frieda's 'trouble about the children'. Naturally enough he looked to his old friend to 'stand by [him] a bit'.

Garnett did not betray Lawrence's trust. Nevertheless two factors led to a cooling in and finally to a near rupture of their friendship: both were conducive to Pinker's emergence as a significant correspondent in this volume (and beyond). First, it seems that Garnett came to find it too irksome or too complicated to be acting in a private capacity as if he were a professional literary agent. And, secondly, he gradually lost sympathy with Lawrence's development as a novelist. For his part Lawrence knew that he was changing; what he had found rewarding ceased to be so. He told Garnett in January 1914, while he was writing what was to be *The Rainbow*: 'I have no longer the joy in creating vivid scenes, that I had in *Sons and Lovers*...I have to write differently.'[3] But what replaced the stratagems of that novel did not commend itself to Garnett. He continued to expect 'the old stable ego of the character'[4] and to be highly critical when he was disappointed. Lawrence's indebtedness to Garnett made him reluctant at first forthrightly to reject the criticism. Somewhat hesitantly, in January 1914, he wrote: 'Which way I have to go, I shall go in the end I suppose – whichever way it may be'.[5] But in June he reacted much more tartly: 'I don't think the psychology is wrong...You must not say my novel is shaky – It is not perfect, because I am not expert in what I want to do. But it is the real thing, say what you like.'[6] And by the end of 1914, when he discovered that his story 'Honour and Arms' had been re-titled 'The Prussian Officer' by

[1] *Letters*, i. 16.   [2] Ibid. i. 448.   [3] Letter 700.
[4] Letter 732.   [5] Letter 700.   [6] Letter 732.

Garnett – who thereby perverted a critical scrutiny of militarism in general
into a criticism of German militarism in particular – and that title adopted
for his first collection, Lawrence was understandably furious: 'Garnett was
a devil to call my book of stories *The Prussian Officer* – what Prussian
Officer?'[1]

That riposte was directed to Pinker and, by chance, it was the same story,
'Honour and Arms', which had originally prompted Garnett himself to
propel Lawrence in Pinker's direction. Garnett knew that Pinker had offered
his professional services as a literary agent to Lawrence as early as November
1912; two months later, in evident embarrassment at the extent of the
assistance Garnett was giving him, Lawrence indirectly offered 'to shovel
all [his] stuff onto Pinker';[2] but Garnett declined. Not until July 1913 was
the decisive step taken – and it was taken by Garnett himself. In memorable
terms he wrote to engage the interest of the professional agent:

> The Cearne, Edenbridge
> July 23, 1913
>
> Dear Mr Pinker
> I am sending you herewith a very fine story 'Honour and Arms', by Mr
> D. H. Lawrence, in the hope that you will be able to place it advantageously for him.
> Of course on the usual terms.
> This study of German soldier life in my opinion is as good as Stephen Crane's
> best. In fact Crane and Conrad are the only two writers to be named in conjunction
> with this remarkable piece of psychological genius.
> If you succeed with this, there will be others to follow.
> Address me direct.
>
> Yours truly, Edward Garnett.[3]

The critical assessment here was bold as well as firm; the challenge to
Pinker's professional skill in the penultimate sentence was shrewd; Garnett
clearly wanted to be satisfied that Pinker shared his high opinion and met
the challenge before Lawrence would be encouraged to deal directly with
him. (The story was duly placed with Austin Harrison for the *English
Review*, August 1914, and with the *Metropolitan* in New York, November
1914.) Nearly a year later Lawrence still hesitated between the two men.
Symbolic of the shift from one to the other is the scene (described in a letter
of 1 July 1914) where Lawrence deliberated on the pavement outside
Garnett's office, wondering whether to go to Pinker or not. Duckworth's
refusal to match Methuen's offer of £300 for the *Rainbow* clinched it;
Lawrence needed money; so he went to Pinker and, with his advance,
opened an account at the Aldwych branch of the bank where the agent had

[1] Letter 821.   [2] *Letters*, i. 478, 501.   [3] MS NYPL.

an account. Pinker was his sponsor. Many letters in this volume attest Lawrence's continuing reliance on his judgment and generosity.[1]

To claim that Pinker's emergence as an important correspondent, as well as 'influence', was the cause of Garnett's diminishing role would be wrong. The rise of the one and the decline of the other were symptomatic of a broad truth: that Lawrence, now fully committed to the life of a professional writer (he remarked in 1916 that he would prefer even to be a soldier rather than return to teaching[2]), needed the services of a professional agent; this need coincided with his recognition that the radically innovative artist must develop complete self-reliance. The letters to Pinker are of a 'business' kind in the main and understandably lack the discursive, argumentative and personal character of those to Garnett – but in this volume Lawrence writes twice as often to the former as to the latter. Indeed he wrote as frequently to Garnett's sister-in-law and nephew, Katharine and Douglas Clayton, as to Garnett himself. The Claytons – particularly Douglas – were Lawrence's typists; they were involved in producing saleable typescripts from his manuscripts; they were therefore important in sustaining his income. And that, Lawrence was regularly exercised about: as he told Pinker in April 1914, 'I am always nearing the stony condition of a stream in summer.'[3]

Some other correspondents who were prominent in the early years also declined in importance. They included his close friend Arthur McLeod who had supplied books and news of Croydon during his first stay in Italy; but most notable, perhaps, was his younger sister Ada, the principal contact with his family. Only three letters survive to her between June 1913 and October 1916. The explanation for this is not completely apparent but part of it involved the family's actual or predictable disapproval of Lawrence's liaison with Frieda. (She did not attend Ada's wedding in August 1913 because Lawrence's 'elder sister and brother don't know about her'.[4]) What, then, served to strengthen the bonds with 'advanced' friends like Middleton Murry and Katherine Mansfield, Donald Carswell and Catherine Jackson – who, like Lawrence and Frieda, lived as man and wife but were not married – helped to distance him from his more conventional family. Nevertheless he continued to enjoy 'good old crusty Eastwood gossip': his old friends Willie and Sallie Hopkin supplied him with it.[5]

All Lawrence's relationships were subjected to intense strain following the outbreak of war on 4 August 1914 and its dreary but increasingly murderous prolongation.[6] One inevitable casualty was his friendship with Marsh who,

---

[1] E.g. see Letter 1261 for evidence of Pinker's response to Lawrence's plea for help when he had only £6 in the world. [2] Letter 1248.
[3] Letter 719. [4] Letter 608. [5] Letter 684.
[6] For a detailed investigation of this highly complex subject see Delany.

as a professional and very senior civil servant, fully identified himself with government policies. Lawrence made his own standpoint clear to Marsh before August 1914 was out: 'The war is just hell for me...I can't get away from it for a minute: live in a sort of coma, like one of those nightmares when you can't move.'[1] Frieda – divided in her loyalties because of her German origins – rallied to the attack on the view which Marsh held (with the majority of his countrymen) of the heroic grandeur of war: '*No*, it's *not* glorious; I nearly go off my head when I think of the waste and the stupidity of it.'[2] Their friendship with Marsh was unlikely to survive the joint onslaught justified though that was: whereas Lawrence had written twenty-five letters to him by September 1914, less than half that number were sent over the next two years. And while Lawrence and Frieda agreed about the 'stupidity' of war and the horror of its consequences – the principles she adumbrates in the letter just quoted parallel his own on the business of an artist in wartime expressed to Harriet Monroe two months later[3] – her natural sympathy for Germany and the Richthofen family severely taxed certain relationships. Lawrence's acquaintance with Violet Hunt, for example, was one such. A barbed conversation she had with Frieda in Spring 1915 left it in tatters.[4]

Of far greater significance was the threat posed to the central relationship between Lawrence and Frieda themselves by the psychological tensions built up in each of them during these years. Risking an over-simplification, what was endangered can be presented in terms of a letter to Murry of 3 April 1914, written from Lerici while Lawrence was at work on the novel by now re-titled 'The Wedding Ring' and soon to be re-named *The Rainbow*.[5] In this letter there is, in the comments on Murry and Katherine Mansfield, an explicit belief in the necessity to 'stick to the love you have each for the other. And one has to remember this when things go wrong.' There is, too, abundant evidence of self-criticism on Lawrence's part ('I am a tiresome thing...when one is furious with oneself, one *does* make everybody else's life a misery'); but there is also a quiet, assured confidence in the bond of love with Frieda: 'Frieda and I are really very deeply happy.' This deep fulfilment was in part dependent on and partly merged with the creative satisfaction of successful authorship: 'now, thank God, Frieda and I are together, and the work is of me and her, and it is beautiful.' Briefly glimpsed, this was the achieved and profound relationship which the war jeopardised and, on occasions, brought close to breaking-point. There were many contributory causes. They included Frieda's ever-present emotional anxiety

[1] Letter 783.   [2] Letter 787.   [3] Letter 810.
[4] See Nehls, i. 288–9.   [5] Letter 716.

about her children whom she was rarely able to see; the death of her father
in Germany and friends at the front; her alienation from her adopted country
at war with the country of her birth; as well as Lawrence's moods of black
despair, the horror he perceived in and projected on to the European conflict,
and his hatred of the militarism which sometimes had a British, sometimes
a German face. When, to take an extreme example, the liner *Lusitania* was
sunk by an enemy submarine in May 1915, Lawrence told Lady Ottoline
Morrell that he would 'like to kill a million Germans – two million'.[1] While
she might find it relatively easy to dismiss this – as she was instructed to
do – as 'extravagant talk', Frieda would not. Petty spite could also creep into
relations between Lawrence and Frieda; it does when he tells Forster that
Frieda is looking for a flat where she might live by herself in London – 'unless
a bomb has dropped on her – killed by her own countrymen – it is the kind
of fate she is cut out for'.[2] That these remarks reflect one truth about their
relationship cannot be doubted, but to represent it as the whole would be
wrong. Lawrence was equally ready to contemplate 'a new world with a new
thin unsullied air and no people in it but new-born people: moi-même et
Frieda'.[3] It was, then, a marriage fully capable of achieving the kind of deep
fulfilment already mentioned; but with 'the *difference* between us being the
adventure' (as Lawrence told Catherine Carswell), it was endangered by
circumstances which exacerbated the '*difference*', irritated it rather than
providing the tension essential to 'creative life'.[4] These circumstances the
war frequently provided.

When Lawrence applied for help from the Royal Literary Fund he was
required to explain the 'Cause of [his] Distress'. He replied: 'The War'.[5]
The letters in this volume confirm the accuracy of his cryptic statement.
Except for a period of about six weeks when the *Rainbow* prosecution and
its consequences seized his main attention, the war is rarely absent from his
letters. Images of darkness naturally occur: sometimes it is the darkness of
death which precedes re-birth ('except a seed die...'); more commonly it
is the darkness of the body 'swollen with death' or of copulating insects in
hell.[6] Not unexpectedly in the period when he produced *The Rainbow*, he
also uses images associated with Noah and the Flood; two such occasions,
the first in April 1915 and the second in October 1916, indicate the poles
between which his emotions oscillated.[7] In the first instance he tells Lady
Ottoline of the darkness of his soul, how he seems to be beneath 'a very black
flood': 'sometimes one rises like the dove from the ark: but there is no olive
branch'. The allusion to Genesis – when Noah knew 'that the waters were

[1] Letter 920. [2] Letter 932. [3] Letter 1131. [4] Letter 1263.
[5] p. 224 n. 4. [6] Letters 928, 933 and 909. [7] Letters 909 and 1293.

abated from off the earth' because the dove carried 'an olive leaf in her mouth' – conveys a mood of blank despondency. The later use of the image focuses on Noah, having survived the Flood, 'disembarking on a new world', and the emphasis here is on regeneration, resurrection. The same oscillation is further illustrated by images of the life and growth which follow destruction. They occur, for example, in a hitherto unpublished letter to the American poet and dramatist, Zoë Akins in September 1915.[1] Lawrence describes a raid by Zeppelins: these had become 'the heavenly ministers now'; 'the world's acclamation of worship' consisted of the guns firing from the ground. He describes, too, a fair with bands and swing-boats patronised by wounded soldiers, a partial but remarkable anticipation of Mark Gertler's painting, *The Merry-Go-Round*, which haunted Lawrence exactly a year later. But the letter also speaks of his determination 'to start some germ of positive belief and to work towards living, reconstructive action later on'. 'Though the skies fall...one must go on with the living, constructive spirit.'

Lawrence did not invariably succeed in holding these two opposed ideas in equilibrium. When the war pressed very close – when 'the danger of being dragged in' by conscription loomed large, for example[2] – his vilification of England and her consuming desire for self-destruction reached a crescendo. The Easter 1916 rising in Dublin shocked him as a further sign of England's decline; the rebels themselves were scathingly dismissed as 'windbags and nothings who happen to have become tragically significant in death'.[3] And the final evidence of spiritual disaster was conscription, the 'annulling' of freedom which he esteemed 'above everything'.[4] Yet his spirits revived. At the end of this volume we find him assuring Katherine Mansfield (whose brother had been killed) that 'we can build a new world...initiate a new order of life'.[5] The 'new heaven and new earth' of *Revelation* recur in the later letters. Indeed Forster's comment on Lawrence carries a central truth for the years covered by the present volume: 'The war tortured him but never paralyzed him.'[6]

The energy, both physical and psychic, which he poured into his personal relationships – through anger and frustration as well as hope and affection – and also into his writing, is the best proof of Forster's assertion. 'If one writes one must have a tough soul and put up with things, and keep grinding on. It's hellish, but it's worth it.' This previously unpublished exhortation was delivered to Henry Savage in July 1913: the determination and conviction it implies were what sustained Lawrence himself during the war years. 'There's something in hanging on like a bull-dog, because you've shut your

---

[1] Letter 993.   [2] Letter 1236.   [3] Letter 1244.
[4] Letters 1257 and 1259.   [5] Letter 1288.   [6] Nehls, i. 273.

teeth in the rear of this damned craven life. In the end one pulls it down, I think, and has a triumph.'[1] As he put it later to Murry, it is essential 'to have faith in what one ultimately is'.[2] But the support of friends was vital: 'I feel the want of friends who will believe in me a bit.'[3] These were to be the friends who would help to bring about the new world.

To this end Lawrence concentrated his immediate hopes in the founding of 'Rananim', a small, select community of 'about twenty souls' united in a single, noble purpose:

[to] sail away from this world of war and squalor and found a little colony where there shall be no money but a sort of communism as far as necessaries of life go, and some real decency...a community which is established upon the assumption of goodness in the members, instead of the assumption of badness.[4]

The cost to him was great. One facet of it emerges with sharp poignancy in a series of letters written in December 1915 from the house of his sister, Ada. In these letters he expresses the anguish experienced in being 'plunged back into the world of the past, when that past is irrevocably gone by, and a new thing far away is struggling to come to life in one'.[5] To discard what had gone 'like the love of the dead' – was essential; so was it essential to hold fast to a love which goes 'forward into the future'. That love and commitment he hoped to discover in the group of friends. The quest was agonising; there were euphoric moments of high optimism; there were others of bitter disillusion; and considerable pain was caused to all concerned.

Lawrence's correspondents especially during 1915 – what Delany calls his 'Messianic phase'[6] – had also to endure a series of bewildering shifts of political conviction. In January, as he wrote to Forster, Lawrence 'wanted a real community, not built out of abstinence or equality, but out of many fulfilled individualities seeking greater fulfilment'.[7] Early in February, in a powerful letter to Russell, Lawrence appeared to have embraced collectivism: 'There must be a revolution in the state. It shall begin by the nationalising of all industries and means of communication, and of the land – in one fell blow.'[8] The 'individualities' so highly valued in January were, by March explicitly made secondary: 'we are no longer satisfied to be individual and lyrical – we are growing out of that stage'. In art, so in life, 'the great collective experience' is the goal.[9] But in the same month an illness, a profoundly disturbing visit to Russell in Cambridge and the increasing horrors of the war massed to oppress Lawrence with a 'sense of evil in the world': 'I am struggling in the dark – very deep in the dark – and cut off

[1] Letter 589.   [2] Letter 716.   [3] Letter 723.
[4] Letter 841.   [5] Letter 1115.   [6] Delany 64.
[7] Letter 850.   [8] Letter 865.   [9] Letter 881.

from everybody and everything.'[1] The encounter with the homosexual
Keynes in Cambridge filled Lawrence with loathing: the imagery of rats
which at once follows his mention of Keynes, and of beetles in an April letter
damning David Garnett's homosexual friends (reiterated as he speaks to Kot
of 'men lovers of men'), gives the most vivid clue to Lawrence's black
melancholy.[2] It was exacerbated by the threat of bankruptcy (brought on
by the costs of Frieda's divorce proceedings); the acute strains of his marriage; even by the appearance of London which he described in terms
anticipating T. S. Eliot in *The Waste Land*: 'the traffic flows through the
rigid grey streets like the rivers of Hell through their banks of dry, rocky
ash'.[3] The gloom was unrelieved. And it was now that Lawrence's
enthusiasm for collectivism suddenly disappeared; democracy was rejected,
individualism denounced and patricianism adopted. He adjured Russell:
'You must drop all your democracy. You must not believe in "the
people"...There must be an aristocracy of people who have wisdom, and
there must be a Ruler.'[4] 'It is only the unexpected can help us now', Russell
was told. In a letter to Lady Cynthia Asquith Lawrence conveyed the
response of Russell and Lady Ottoline to his latest outburst: 'They say...I
am an exceedingly valuable personality, but that the things I say are
extravaganzas, illusions.'[5] Lady Cynthia found this letter 'very difficult to
answer'.[6]

Easier to answer was a letter written to Viola Meynell from whose cottage
at Greatham these missiles were fired at Russell, Lady Ottoline and Lady
Cynthia. Writing from Littlehampton to thank her for her generosity – Viola
Meynell had provided the cottage rent-free – Lawrence contemplates a poor
English family on the beach, 'on the edge of the water, a tiny separate
group'.[7] The scene, the imagery and the tone of lament recall Matthew
Arnold's poems such as 'Summer Night' and 'Dover Beach': 'They are all
like prisoners born in prison...It is as if all their lives were passed within
a prison-yard, and they knew their condemnation.' It comes as a relief to
find the nation, so often during the previous months viewed as an abstract
entity, now focused as a group of individuals. Lawrence's correspondent
would be the more moved by his regretful comment: 'England, the English
people, make me so sad, I could leave them for ever.'

This wish to leave became consuming as the months passed. 'Here the
whole tree of life is dying.'[8] Lawrence's energy was concentrated on a plan
to settle with a few friends – including Murry, Katherine Mansfield, Kot and
the composer Philip Heseltine ('Peter Warlock') – in Florida. Marsh was

[1] Letter 887.   [2] Letters 892, 901 and 902.   [3] Letter 920.
[4] Letter 953.   [5] Letter 970.   [6] Asquith, *Diaries* 70.
[7] Letter 964.   [8] Letter 1028.

asked for money; J ady Ottoline gave money and organised other subscriptions; Shaw contributed £5; Pinker provided letters of introduction; passports were obtained; but to leave during wartime was impossible. The plan was abandoned in January 1916. The only move Lawrence made was to a cottage at Porthcothan in Cornwall, loaned by the novelist J. D. Beresford at Murry's suggestion. Lawrence's sense of utter defeat was vividly conveyed to Murry: 'I feel absolutely run to earth, like a fox they have chased till it can't go any further, and doesn't know what to do...I must own to you, that I am beaten – knocked out entirely...I could howl with a dog's hopelessness, at nightfall.'[1] And to Lady Ottoline, probably on the same day in January, his despair and frustration were conveyed in words which seem to echo Housman's in *A Shropshire Lad*:

> Be still, be still, my soul; it is but for a season:
> Let us endure an hour and see injustice done.[2]

In Porthcothan and finally, in this volume, at Zennor, Lawrence cast himself in the role which he urged on Russell, that of 'an outlaw' awaiting the imminent collapse of the existing world-order. If he could not leave England, then he would prefer 'sulking in one of its remotest caves'.[3] The friends on whom he relied were Murry, Katherine Mansfield and Heseltine. Heseltine quickly proved treacherous, but the 'Murrys', he was sure, would be different. Only a year before, Lawrence had described Murry as 'one of the men of the future...the only man who quite simply is with me – One day he'll be ahead of me.'[4] He and Katherine Mansfield had been witnesses at Lawrence's wedding in 1914; they had participated in the abortive attempt to launch the periodical *Signature*; they were now, in February 1916, 'my only real friends in the world'.[5] One can feel the excitement in Lawrence's letters at the prospect of the Murrys' coming to Zennor to set up 'a little monastery'.[6] Frieda was equally enthusiastic. Lawrence's elastic spirits rose: 'However bad the times are, we shall pull through.'[7] Captain John Short, the owner of the Higher Tregerthen cottage at Zennor, was urged to complete the re-decorating according to the agreed colour scheme and to site the two WCs so that 'nothing disagreeable would appear'.[8] Lawrence paid a year's rent in advance; Gertler was imperiously requested to send belongings left behind in Hampstead; and the Murrys moved into their tower in early April. Lady Ottoline's offer of money was politely refused; her habit of borrowing books on her own subscription to the London Library and passing them (against the rules) on to Lawrence was gratefully encouraged.

[1] Letter 1132.　[2] p. 502 and n. 2.　[3] Letter 1158.
[4] Letter 872.　[5] Letter 1168.　[6] Letter 1196.
[7] Letter 1217.　[8] Letter 1221.

The serenity was threatened almost at once. There was considerable strain between the Lawrences; their attenuated but nonetheless valuable connection with Lady Ottoline was jeopardised by the intense jealousy reflected in Frieda's remark – 'I told her what I thought of her...inside those wonderful shawls there is cheapness and vulgarity';[1] conscription was a menace to both Murry and Lawrence; and the Murrys (by their own account) were worn 'down to the naked nerves' by the constant friction with their companions.[2] They left in June for Mylor in South Cornwall. And Lawrence had to enlist on 28 June. Though he secured complete exemption, he was humiliated by the military doctors at Bodmin. Yet, within a week, his mettle reasserted itself. 'I felt I conquered, in the barracks experience – my spirit held its own and even won, over their great collective spirit.'[3] As for Murry, Lawrence admitted that he had deceived himself: 'I am a liar to myself, about people... I give up having intimate friends at all.'[4] Yet, though Barbara Low may not have fallen into the category of 'intimate friends', he enjoyed a visit from her in August; Catherine Carswell stayed for nearly a week in late September; he had also encountered the young farmer, William Henry Hocking with whom he would establish a particularly intimate relationship.

The letters in this volume record, then, an undulating series of disasters, betrayals and black despair, alternating with periods of contentment and positive achievement, amid the pressure of events both national and local. The Lawrences' peregrinations over the same period were a severe test of their resilience. Between June 1913 and June 1914 they moved from England to Germany to Italy and again to England; during the two years following they had six different addresses (even if several brief stays elsewhere are disregarded). But Lawrence did not collapse and his literary output was astonishing. Certainly some of it represented the publication or the re-issue in collected form, of writings dating from an earlier period; but, though accurate, this obscures the real truth. *The Widowing of Mrs Holroyd*, for example, existed in an early version as long ago as 1911; the play which was published in April 1914 was the result of extensive re-writing as late as the previous September. The *Prussian Officer* volume appeared in November 1914; it included several stories which had already been published (one was first printed in 1910); but some of the best were very recent and most were heavily revised. 'Lord, how I've worked again at those stories – most of them – forging them up,' he told Marsh in July 1914.[5] And, Lawrence's first book of travel sketches, *Twilight in Italy*, related to experiences he and Frieda shared in Italy, some of them nearly four years

[1] Letter 1240.   [2] p. 608 n. 1.   [3] Letter 1253.
[4] Letter 1248.   [5] Letter 758.

before the book was published in June 1916. Several of the sketches had come out in English journals in 1913. Yet they were greatly extended and re-written for the collected volume as a series of hitherto unpublished letters to Lawrence's typist, Douglas Clayton, between August and the end of October 1915, proves conclusively.

'One sheds ones sicknesses in books – repeats and presents again ones emotions, to be master of them.'[1] Lawrence's famous remark to McLeod in October 1913 was peculiarly relevant to his predicament throughout the war years. As it had been in *Sons and Lovers*, his writing in this period, too, was in part therapeutic. But in addition it allowed him to go on to the offensive against an oppressive, disintegrating social order. An active anti-war campaign such as lost Russell his Cambridge Lectureship was not for Lawrence; he chose, for him, the more satisfying alternative of 'shooting [the social people of today] with noiseless bullets that explode in their souls... All my work is a shot at their very innermost strength.'[2]

The 'Study of Thomas Hardy' was just such a 'shot'. It is mentioned in a letter to Pinker (5 September 1914) in which the war is described as a 'colossal idiocy': here was the dynamic that provided the creative thrust for the 'Study'. Lawrence told his agent that the work would be 'queer stuff' and about almost 'anything but Thomas Hardy'. It contains, in fact, a great deal of powerful writing against the war that was a mere month old. Lawrence rejected the cant about 'a just and righteous war against Germany'; he urged, on the contrary, that the energies committed 'to risk ourselves in a rush of death' should be re-directed 'to risk ourselves in a forward venture of life'; and he underlined the lesson 'that must be learned... of reconciliation between different, maybe hostile, things'.[3] Great emphasis is laid – as so often in the eloquent letters that were written concurrently – on making conflict serve constructive, regenerative ends. The 'Study' is a highly personal response to the war; there is incoherence in it but much strenuous thought and powerful feeling besides. 'This is the real fighting line', he told Garnett, 'not where soldiers pull triggers':[4] the boast related to *The Prussian Officer*; it could be applied with equal force to the 'Study of Thomas Hardy'.

Lawrence regarded the 'Study' as his 'revolutionary utterance'.[5] The two great novels, one published and the other virtually completed in this period – *The Rainbow* and *Women in Love* – could also be properly so

---

[1] Letter 667.   [2] Letter 1174.
[3] *Phoenix: The Posthumous Papers of D. H. Lawrence*, ed. Edward D. McDonald (New York, 1936), pp. 407, 408, 512.
[4] Letter 795.   [5] Letter 880.

described. Lawrence claimed as much for the first when he answered Lady Cynthia Asquith's question about its 'message':

I don't know myself what it is: except that the old order is done for, toppling on top of us: and that it's no use the men looking to the women for salvation, nor the women looking to sensuous satisfaction for their fulfilment. There must be a new Word.[1]

Though the novel's dominant symbol is the overarching rainbow which recalls God's covenant with Noah 'from generation to generation', there is as well the unmistakable and insistent rejection of the 'old, hard barren form of bygone living'. The 'old, decaying fibrous husk' would be shattered and from it would come a 'new liberation'.[2] The blurb on the cover of the published work underlines this: '[The novel] ends with Ursula, the leading-shoot of the restless, fearless family, waiting at the advance-post of our time to blaze a path into the future.' While not fully a 'political' novel, *The Rainbow* – in its presentation of the relationship between men and women and its rejection of the old sexual order – has strong revolutionary implications. In their fumbling way Lawrence's hostile reviewers were to recognise it.

Lawrence was aware of his own outspokenness; he warned Pinker to be prepared 'to fight' for his novel. He was willing to 'take out sentences and phrases' but, unlike his former readiness to accept Edward Garnett's drastic pruning of *Sons and Lovers*, he was determined not to 'take out paragraphs or pages'.[3] The 'old order' exacted its penalty: *The Rainbow* was published on 30 September 1915 and on 13 November a court order was issued under the 1857 Obscene Publications Act for copies of the novel 'to be destroyed at the expiration of seven days'.[4] No reference had been made to the author; the publisher Methuen ('What a snake in his boiled-shirt bosom!'[5]) offered no defence. Lawrence's own reaction to the decision was pungent: 'I only curse them all, body and soul, root, branch and leaf, to eternal damnation.'[6] That his terminology was near-liturgical was highly characteristic.

The response, public and private, to the magistrate's ruling was vigorous on the part of some people like Garnett, the art critic Clive Bell, the poet John Drinkwater and, apparently, Sir Oliver Lodge, Principal of the University of Birmingham; but, to speak generally, it was muted and ineffectual. Though the Society of Authors investigated the matter, it decided not to act formally; Philip Morrell's questions in the Commons were

[1] Letter 1161.   [2] *Rainbow*, chap. 16.   [3] Letter 906.
[4] Warren Roberts, *A Bibliography of D. H. Lawrence* (1963), p. 27.
[5] Letter 1260.   [6] Letter 1042.

adroitly parried by the administration; Pinker's attempt to organise a petition seemingly evaporated; and Donald Carswell, a barrister, was prepared to fight a libel action but Morrell advised against it and Lawrence was disinclined. There was talk of issuing a private edition of the novel by subscription; Prince Bibesco (later married to Lady Cynthia's step-sister) proposed that it should be published in France; but both ideas came to nothing. A few letters have survived showing that some individuals (ranging from obscure men in Nottingham and Sheffield to the well-known Canadian bibliophile and friend of Mitchell Kennerley, Rufus Hathaway) applied for copies of *The Rainbow* to Pinker or Lawrence himself. They were informed that Huebsch's (expurgated) American edition was available. Lawrence could have extracted little comfort from their enquiries.

The Rainbow was not the only source of disenchantment in late 1915. *The Widowing of Mrs Holroyd* had caught the attention of two actor-managers very soon after publication the previous year. (An enthusiastic review in the *Times* may have provided the stimulus.) Harold V. Neilson and Lena Ashwell both expressed an interest in producing the play, at the Vaudeville and Kingsway Theatre respectively, but neither had gone further. However, in September 1915, Lawrence's hopes were raised yet again, this time by Esmé Percy who contemplated a production in Manchester (where Lawrence believed 'a good many people' cared about his work[1]), Glasgow and Edinburgh. This, too, came to naught. Percy enlisted in December 1916; eventually he did produce the play – but not until 1926.

Within two weeks of his September letter to Percy, Lawrence announced to Lady Cynthia his intention to launch with Murry a fortnightly paper for people 'who care about the real living truth of things... not people who only trifle and don't care'.[2] This was to be the *Signature*; it too was to fail.

Lawrence's own purpose in the six projected numbers of the journal was to formulate 'beliefs by which one can reconstruct the world'; Murry was to state 'his ideas on freedom for the individual soul'; and Katherine Mansfield would write some 'little satirical sketches'.[3] It was hoped that Russell (becoming notorious by his anti-war activities) and Gilbert Cannan (then a popular novelist) would also contribute. They did not. In the event only three numbers appeared; each contained a chapter of Lawrence's 'The Crown' (later published in *Reflections on the Death of a Porcupine*, 1925).

Some 250 subscriptions were required to finance this organ of bewildering though revolutionary fervour; 56 is the best estimate that can be made of subscriptions received by early October 1915; and by the end of that month

---

[1] Letter 977.   [2] Letter 979.   [3] Ibid.

the venture was abandoned. Nevertheless there are some interesting names among those who paid their half-crowns. Some were prominent in Lawrence's earlier life, like Alice Dax, Lilian Reynolds, Willie and Sallie Hopkin. Others were new friends and acquaintances including Mark Gertler; E. M. Forster and his friends Hugh Meredith and Piccoli; the poet Anna Wickham; the psychoanalyst, Dr Ernest Jones; Barbara Low; and Harriet Monroe. Still others such as the wife of the Holborn solicitor, Sir George Lewis, and Rufus Hathaway were not personally known to Lawrence (so far as can be established). Subscribers were recruited by the editors or their friends;[1] the possible clientèle was therefore severely limited; and Lawrence was financially the loser. Courageously he had been prepared for that despite his meagre resources: 'If I have nothing, I will ask people for a piece of bread. But I believe that one does not lack – it is like the prophet in the wilderness.'[2] He may have been in the wilderness but some themes and their handling in 'The Crown' were prophetic of the next great novel, *Women in Love*.[3]

Despite the frustrations and failures immediately behind him, Lawrence's confidence in his own powers rarely faltered. The evidence of the letters confirms it. Some of those printed here – holding fast to the possibility of sanity in a world gone mad – are among the most energetically brilliant of his whole career. At the end of this volume he is certain that, with *Women in Love*, he will knock 'the first loop-hole in the prison where we are all shut up...I shall do it – I feel a bubbling of gladness inside.'[4]

---

[1] This was also the case with the ill-fated 'Rainbow Books and Music' launched by Lawrence and Heseltine in February 1916.

[2] Letter 983.

[3] Henry Miller considered 'The Crown' Lawrence's 'greatest piece of writing – his central philosophy' (*Notes on Aaron's Rod*, ed. Seamus Cooney, Santa Barbara, 1980, p. 57).

[4] Letter 1293.

THE LETTERS

580. To Edward Garnett, [1 June 1913]
Text: MS NYPL; Unpublished.

Irschenhausen, (Post) *Ebenhausen*, bei München
Sunday[1]

Dear Garnett,[2]

We keep coming to the jump and balking it – I mean the coming to England. Frieda now says if she passes Baden-Baden, where her people have gone to live, and doesn't call there, she will never be forgiven. – You see what that means – that Friday is too soon for us to come. You have no idea what an awful soul-effort it means – this coming to England. And there is such an unwieldy mass of luggage. We *must* come, in the end, I suppose. If Frieda would, I would come on Friday. But she can't. So we wait another month perhaps.

And I am afraid of the expense. Here we are rent free.[3] I don't know what we shall do. I don't know. Frieda must go to Baden Baden, and we must both get ready. The moving from Italy here upset us fearfully – I am even now not quite well, nor is Frieda.

You can't curse us as much as I curse myself – though that is no good to you.

The copies of *Sons and Lovers* – save one for me, will you, for when I come. Then

1. Miss L A Lawrence,[4] Percy St, *Eastwood*, Notts.
1. G A Lawrence Esq,[5] 51 Laurel St, Dame Agnes St, Nottingham.
1. Mrs S. King,[6] 58 Pollok St, Glasgow S.8.
1. A W McLeod Esq.,[7] 5 Carew Rd, *Thornton Heath* S.E.

---

[1] On 10 June (Letter 581) DHL thanks Garnett for despatching 'the books' (copies of *Sons and Lovers*) requested in this letter: hence the conjectural date 1 June 1913 here.

[2] Edward Garnett (1868–1937), literary adviser to the publishing firm of Duckworth, and DHL's close friend and patron; see *Letters*, i. 297.

[3] DHL and Frieda were staying at the house of Dr Edgar Jaffe, Frieda's brother-in-law.

[4] DHL's younger sister, Lettice Ada Lawrence (1887–1948); see *Letters*, i. 27.

[5] George Arthur Lawrence (1876–1967), DHL's eldest brother; see *Letters*, i. 135.

[6] DHL's older sister Emily Una ('Pamela') King (1882–1962); see *Letters*, i. 36.

[7] Arthur William McLeod (1885–1956), a teacher formerly at Davidson Road School, Croydon, where DHL taught from 1908 to 1911; at this time McLeod was teaching at the Norbury Manor School; see *Letters*, i. 136.

1. Mrs J W Jones,[1] 16 Colworth Rd, Addiscombe, *Croydon.*
That is only seven, counting the one you sent me. If it is one too many, don't
keep a copy for me. – I hope it will go.

I have nearly finished The Sisters – p. 283.[2] I think the end is good. I
am rather keen to re-write it in the third person. I have worked quite hard
lately. I shall send you the remainder of the MS. next week, I hope. – It
won't be a long novel. That will please you.

Be patient with us, for God's sake.

Yours   D. H. Lawrence

When do you come back? – You say you are going away June 10th. If you
tell me a date – about the 20th – then I think we might stick to it, and
definitely come then. A fixed date not too far off is what we need. Oh curse
it all.

581. To Edward Garnett, [10 June 1913]
Text: MS NYPL; Postmark, K. B. Bahnpost 11 JUN 13; Huxley 124–5.

Irschenhausen, (Post) *Ebenhausen*, Oberbayern
Tuesday[3]

Dear Garnett,

Thanks for your letter and the reviews[4] and for sending the books off, and
for the advice you give us.

I got the first half of the Sisters returned. Did you receive the second
half? You did not mention it.

On this day week we are leaving here for England. Frieda will not wait
any longer. And she cannot come alone. I shall not mind coming with her.
We must do what we can. If you would let us have a room at the Cearne,
for not more than two weeks, we should be very glad. Then we shall go to
the sea-side, and have a room for a month or so, then, if *Sons and Lovers*
justifies it, we shall go straight to Italy. – Unless one of us is really ill, we
shall not fail to come, arriving next Wednesday[5] – What will it be, June 16th
or thereabouts?[6] I don't know the date. Frieda wants to see your brother
Robert,[7] and so on. I am doing as you say, letting her choose her own way.

---

[1] Marie Jones (1869–1950), DHL's landlady at Croydon; her husband, John William Jones
   (1868–1956), was the attendance officer for Davidson Road School; see *Letters*, i. 82.
[2] A reference to the first version of 'The Sisters' which was begun in March 1913. After
   considerable re-writing, it gave rise to two volumes, *The Rainbow* and *Women in Love*. See
   Letter 836.   [3] Tuesday] Monday
[4] Reviews of *Sons and Lovers*.   [5] Wednesday] Tuesday
[6] The correct date was 18 June; DHL and Frieda returned to England on 19 June.
[7] Edward Garnett's brother, Robert Singleton Garnett (1866–1932) a solicitor; see *Letters*, i.
   516.

But that includes my being there. And I want to help in what I can. – It is true, the trouble about the children has knocked us both a bit loose at the joints. But Frieda has stayed a day or two in Wolfratshausen alone. – There is not any definite news from anybody.

I am very anxious about *Sons and Lovers*. A friend sent me a *Standard* review, but I thought it was done by you, perhaps.[1] I have written the best short story I have ever done – about a German officer in the army and his orderly.[2] Then there is another good autobiographical story – I think it is good:[3] then there is another story in course of completion which interests me.[4] I might send them away, mightn't I. It is not fair for you to be troubled with the business. So I shall give them to you and you, perhaps, will suggest where they may go.

You are going away – is it very far? – and for a holiday or will you keep on working? You did not tell me your address.

I have been reading the *English Review*. It makes me sad that it is so piffling now.

If anything happens so that *Sons and Lovers* should not go – I was glad the libraries took it – then I shall get some work when I am in England – teaching I suppose.

I shall not change my mind about travelling next Tuesday.[5] But we shall keep it quiet, that we are in England. We might, of course, come back here in about a month's time. Professor Jaffe[6] wants us to do so. – We shan't be able to see[7] folks much in England. I *do* feel cut off from my past life – like re-incarnation.

You will come and see us when we are at the Cearne, won't you? I hope you will stand by me a bit; I haven't a man in the world, nor a woman either, besides Frieda, who will. Not that anybody else has, I suppose, who goes his own way. But I haven't yet got used to being cut off from folks – inside: – a bit childish.

How does your life of Dostoievsky go?[8] Why do you never say anything about yourself?

[1] It was probably Arthur McLeod who sent DHL the anonymous review in the *Standard* (30 May 1913), p. 5 (Draper 58–9). The author of this review has not been identified; DHL thought it was by Edward Garnett because the review was quite favourable.
[2] 'Honour and Arms', later entitled 'The Prussian Officer'.
[3] Most likely 'Once'; it was published in *Love Among the Haystacks* (Nonesuch Press, 1930).
[4] 'Vin Ordinaire', later called 'The Thorn in the Flesh'.
[5] Tuesday] Wednesday.
[6] Dr Edgar Jaffe (1866–1921), Professor of Political Economy at the University of Munich; he was married to Frieda's sister Else (1874–1973).   [7] see] visit
[8] The book which Garnett was writing was not about Dostoievsky but Tolstoy. It appeared in 1914; see *Letters*, i. 536.

The world gets a queer feel of shut-inness, as if it stifled one: the horizon being too near, and the sky too low.

If it is at all a nuisance to you, we can get a room in London. You must tell us.

This time it is really, from both of us, auf wiedersehen.

Yours   D. H. Lawrence

582. To Arthur McLeod, [11 June 1913]

Text: MS UT; PC; Postmark, Wolfratshausen 11 JUN 13; Moore, *Intelligent Heart* 150.

[Irschenhausen, (Post) *Ebenhausen*, Oberbayern]

[11 June 1913]

Thanks for the books. How rotten the *English* [*Review*] is. What do you think of *Sons and Lovers?* I am anxious to know. Have you seen any more reviews. The libraries refused it at first – then consented. I am leaving here in a week's time – probably for England. But don't say anything. Miss Mason complains you have never written her a line.[1] That is surely too bad. – Probably I shall see you before long – which is something to look forward to. I shall probably be at Garnett's – The Cearne Nr Edenbridge – in ten days time.

So auf wiedersehen   D. H. Lawrence

583. To Elizabeth Whale, [14 June 1913]

Text: MS NYPL; Unpublished.

Irschenhausen, (Post) *Ebenhausen*, Oberbayern
Saturday[2]

Dear Miss Whale,[3]

I wonder what you will say to having Frieda (she must be Mrs Lawrence)[4] and me at the Cearne for a little while. I hope you haven't got quite a bad opinion of me by now.

Mr Garnett said we might have a room any time. We are leaving here on Tuesday, but shan't get in London till *Thursday* morning – we are going Hook of Holland and Harwich – which means the Great Eastern in London, does it not? We arrive there about 8.30 in the morning. I wonder what time there is a train down to Oxted: somewhere about 10.30 from Victoria, I believe. Then we should come straight down. If the man could meet the train

[1] Agnes Mason (1871– c. 1950) had been a teacher with McLeod and DHL at Davidson Road School, Croydon, but was no longer McLeod's colleague. See p. 19, n. 7 and *Letters*, i. 194.

[2] DHL planned to leave on Tuesday, 17 June; the previous Saturday would, therefore, be 14 June 1913.

[3] Elizabeth ('Li') Whale was housekeeper for Edward and Constance Garnett at The Cearne; see *Letters*, i. 365.

[4] DHL and Frieda were not married until 13 July 1914.

in Oxted – that train which leaves London between 10.0 and eleven o'clock – if there is one – or immediately after eleven – then I should be very glad.

I am not anxious to come to England, except to see just a few of my fellow countrymen – chiefly women. But it fills my heart with relief to think of ten days or a fortnight, – not more, – at the Cearne.

I have not heard from Mr Garnett in answer to my last letter – there was scarcely time. But if he makes any arrangements, we must abide by those. I hope it will be all right, and we can stay a little while at the Cearne.

Without asking, I know you didn't like *Sons and Lovers*. But never mind my books. You must bear with me in charity.

So – auf wiedersehen. Madame sends her kind remembrances (how one has to dodge about to get a name!).

Yours Sincerely   D. H. Lawrence

584. To Edward Garnett, [16 June 1913]

Text: MS NYPL; *Frieda Lawrence: The Memoirs and Correspondence,* ed. E. W. Tedlock (1961), p. 197.

[Irschenhausen, (Post) *Ebenhausen*, Oberbayern]

[16 June 1913][1]

[Frieda Weekley begins]

Dear Mr Garnett!

So we are coming! I feel quite glad! It's like me, I ought to come in sackcloth and ashes and I feel only pleased at the thought of seeing the children! I ran away from L[awrence] for two days after having broken a plate over his head, while washing up! I was astonished I thought I was mild and good! My small nephew[2] *was* shocked at my departure, he loves L, he said: Tante Frieda, now you will get tired of this man and 3 uncles from one aunt are too much! He was distressed! However we are L and I such friends, I will wear a fragment of that plate in a locket round my neck! At first I wanted to come alone to England, but of course I am glad in a way that L. wants to come and that he cant bear to be away from me, hardly for hours you will understand rejoices my heart! Even he stays to abuse me! I shall enjoy the Cearne, I hope to see Mrs Garnett[3] and David, I want to read his novel,[4] and L. has made my mouth water with all the books at the

[1] DHL says 'It is Monday evening', which establishes the date as 16 June 1913.
[2] Else's son, Friedrich ('Friedel') Jaffe (b. 1903); see letter following.
[3] Constance Garnett, née Black (1861–1946), eminent translator of Russian literature; see *Letters,* i. 314.
[4] David Garnett (1892–1981), later novelist, editor and autobiographer; see *Letters,* i. 315. His 'novel' was untitled and never finished; see *Letters,* i. 537.

Cearne! No, no, love is no crucification, or if it is, then it will rise from the grave on the third day (after a broken plate or two!). I hope our coming is not a nuisance, deep down in me I feel that you *ought* to be cross with us, for always putting our coming off, it's not human to quite forgive us!

Auf Wiedersehen and many thanks.

Yours The one and only (Phoenix L's name for me!)

[Lawrence begins]

We arrive Thursday morning, from Harwich at about 8.30 in Paddington. – It is Monday evening and we haven't heard from you – I wonder if you didn't get my letter. – Ugh, how I hate shifting – we leave here tomorrow at noon.

585. To Friedrich Jaffe, 21 June 1913

Text: MS Jeffrey; Frieda Lawrence, *Nur Der Wind* (Berlin, 1936), p. 108.

The Cearne, Near *Edenbridge*, Kent.

21 Juni 1913

Lieber Friedel,

Hier bin ich, wieder in meinem Heimatland. Aber ich liebe es nicht. In der Ferne gibt's immer ein Dämmerung, ein Nabel und ein wenig Dunkelheit, das macht mein Herz schwer und traurig. Aber dieses Haus ist wunderschön. Die Luft duftet von Rosen, das Haus ist ganz geschmückt von viele grosse Rosen, rot, und weiss, und rose-farbe: sie kommen in die Fenstern, und oben, grosse rote Rosen-Gesichte kucken in's Schlaf-Zimmer. Heute Morgen mussten wir die Himbeeren mit grosse Netze decken, um sie von den Vogeln zu schutzen. Das war schwer, weil man müss nicht eine einzige kleine Loch lassen, die Vogeln sind so klug, sie kriechen unten, und alles fressen.

Aber ich bin noch ein wenig mude von der Fahrt. Es war sehr lang und langweilig; aber auf dem Schiff war es bequem. In Holland kam ein furchtbar Gewitter. Die Blitz war schrecklich hell, und das Donner machte grollen der Zug, als er laufte schnell über die breite Ebene. Ich glaube ein Gewitter ist viel mehr fürchtend auf einer Ebene wie in dem Gebirgen, weil es gibt kein Schutz vom Himmel. Dann war es wieder[1] still, und wir sahen die Sonne, blutrot und weit in der Ferne, gehen langsam, langsam zu Erde.

Ich dachte an dir auf dem Schiff. Da, uber das Meer, war es Vollmond und still, wir gingen sanft und süss. Ich war allein in meinem Cabin, mit vier Betten, wie vier Bretten in einem grossen Schrank. Dann dachte ich, vielleicht möchte das Friedel schlafen[2] im Bett über mir schlafen, um zu hören das Wasser rauschen, und die Maschinen schlagen lauter und weicher. Dann

[1] es wieder] es still wieder
[2] Friedel schlafen] Friedel möchte schlafen

gleich klopfte man an die Thüre, ich stand schnell auf und ging oben, und
da, niederisch und nebelisch im Morgenlicht, war England.

Montag gehen wir nach London – im vierzehn Tage an das Meer. Aber
ich möchte nicht lange Zeit in diesem England bleiben, das macht man so
schwersinnig.

Ich habe kein Wörterbuch, und die Tante Friede schläft die ganze
Nachtmittag, so sollst du mein Deutsch furchtbar auslachen. Aber das macht
nicht. Schreibe mir, in ganz deutliche Handschrift. Und grüsse von mir die
Mädel, und Peter, und Hans,[1] – viele herzliche Grüsse.

Auf Wiedersehen   D. H. Lawrence

[Dear Friedel,

Here I am, again in my native land. But I don't love it. In the distance
there's always a twilight, a mist and a bit of dimness, that makes my heart
heavy and sad. But this house is quite beautiful. The air is fragrant with roses,
the house is all adorned with many large roses, red, and white, and pink:
they come in the windows, and, upstairs, great rose-faces peep into the
bedroom. This morning we had to cover the raspberries with large nets to
protect them from the birds. That was hard, for one must not leave a single
little hole, the birds are so clever, they creep under, and eat everything.

But I am still a bit tired from the journey. It was very long and boring;
but on the ship it was comfortable. In Holland there came a frightful
thunderstorm. The lightning was terribly bright, and the thunder made the
train rumble as it ran rapidly over the broad plain. I think a thunderstorm
is much more frightening on a plain than in the mountains, because there
is no protection from the sky. Then it was still again, and we saw the sun,
blood-red and far in the distance, going slowly, slowly to earth.

I thought of you on the ship. There, over the sea, it was full moon and
still, we went gently and sweetly. I was alone in my cabin, with four beds,
like four shelves in a big cupboard. Then I thought, perhaps Friedel would
like to sleep in the bed above me, to hear the water murmuring, and the
engines throbbing louder and softer. Just then someone knocked on the door,
I got up quickly and went above, and there, low and misty in the morning
light, was England.

Monday we go to London – in a fortnight to the sea-side. But I shouldn't
like to stay a long time in this England, that makes one so melancholy.

I haven't a dictionary, and Aunt Frieda sleeps the whole afternoon, so you
shall laugh frightfully at my German. But that doesn't matter. Write me,
in quite distinct handwriting. And give my regards to the girls, and Peter,
and Hans, – many cordial greetings,

Auf Wiedersehen   D. H. Lawrence]

[1] Else Jaffe's other children: Marianne (b. 1905), Peter (1907–15) and Hans (b. 1909).

586. To Edward Garnett, 21 June 1913
Text: MS NYPL; Huxley 126–7.

The Cearne, Nr *Edenbridge*, Kent
21 June 1913

Dear Garnett,

We are here, you see, fearfully glad to be at the Cearne with Mrs Garnett and David. It is beautiful down here – I should think only England can do it. We are looking forward to seeing you on Wednesday – meanwhile the time falls softly away – we spent the morning netting the raspberries.

I liked the reviews of *Sons and Lovers*: also received cheque for £50 from Duckworth this morning.[1] I hope the book will sell. I have just had a long letter of congratulation from W. L. George.[2]

I wrote the biography, and sent it off, with what reviews of *Sons and Lovers* I had, to Mitchell Kennerley.[3] There is a letter from another American man,[4] which I shall enclose.

Then Ezra Pound asked me for some stories because 'he had got an American publisher under his wing'.[5] The tenant of Pound's wing-cover turns out to be the editor of the *American Review*[6] – a reincarnation of the *Smart Set* – and I think his name is Wright.[7] Now I have written three good short stories just before we came to England – two about German soldier life.[8] I want to know whether to send them to him or not. Then I had a letter from Austin Harrison[9] asking for stories. I shall want your advice soon. I want to send some stories out. I want to get hold of those you have in MS.

[1] Duckworth and Co. had published *Sons and Lovers* on 29 May 1913.
[2] Walter Lionel George (1882–1926), a London journalist; he had achieved success as a novelist with the publication of *A Bed of Roses* (1911), a novel about a prostitute. The letter from him has not been found.
[3] Mitchell Kennerley (1878–1950) became DHL's American publisher with the publication of *The Trespasser* in May 1912. See *Letters*, i. 430, 522, 542. Kennerley apparently wanted some biographical information to publicise the American edition of *Sons and Lovers* which was to appear on 17 September 1913. A letter dated 30 June 1913 (MS NYPL), from him to Edward Garnett, reads in part: 'Thank you for your letter of June 18th advising me that you have asked Mr Lawrence to send me his biography direct.'
[4] Unidentified.
[5] Ezra Pound (1885–1972), the American poet, was the agent in England for *Smart Set* and was eventually responsible for placing some of DHL's fiction in that magazine.
[6] The *North American Review* (see Letter 612), Boston magazine (1815–1939), which was at this time publishing the work of such writers as D'Annunzio, Maeterlinck, H. G. Wells and Henry James.
[7] Willard Huntington Wright (1888–1939), American art critic, editor, journalist and writer of detective fiction. Edited *Smart Set*, 1912–14. DHL is mistaken in his remark on Wright's connection with 'the *American Review*'.
[8] 'Honour and Arms', 'Vin Ordinaire' and probably 'Once'.
[9] The editor of the *English Review*; see *Letters*, i. 152.

and revise them. There is the *English Review*, the *Forum*,[1] *The American Review*, perhaps *The Century*.[2] I should be glad to have some stories in magazines. And do you see any reason why I shouldn't offer some poetry to the *Forum*.

Frieda wants to see your brother Robert Garnett on Monday, to talk things over with him. She has written to him.

I love the Cearne and the warm people, but the English dimness in the air gives me the blues.

We are trying to be good for David and his exam – God knows how we are succeeding – all right, I think.[3]

By the way, Pound said his wing-chicken, the editor, wanted the stuff at once.

Till Wednesday, then – riverisco.

D. H. Lawrence

Frieda sends her love and says she is so happy with Mrs Garnett.

587. To Arthur McLeod, 21 June 1913
Text: MS UT; Unpublished.

The Cearne, Nr. *Edenbridge*, Kent
21 June 1913

Dear Mac,

In England, you see! I got your letter today. We shall be down here about ten days. Now what about your seeing us. I don't want to come to Croydon, and you won't want to come here. Shall we meet somewhere in the country and have a walk and have tea out? Be nice, and arrange it – Tuesday – or Saturday or Sunday next. I'll also sign those books if you want me to, and we can manage it.[4] And I've got the Ransome for you.[5] Let me hear from you.

And auf wiedersehen   D. H. Lawrence

[1] The *Forum* (1886–1950), a monthly magazine which published discussions of contemporary problems as well as some fiction. In 1930 it absorbed the *Century* and was called *Forum and Century*.
[2] The *Century Illustrated Monthly Magazine* (1881–1930) published in New York.
[3] David Garnett was preparing for his examination for the Associateship of the Royal College of Science. See David Garnett, *The Golden Echo* (1953), p. 254.
[4] While abroad, DHL sent McLeod copies of his own publications; now he plans to autograph these for his friend; see *Letters*, i. 513, 552.
[5] On 21 May 1913 (*Letters*, i. 552) DHL promised to send 'some of Arthur Ransome's *Essays*'. He may have referred either to *The Book of Friendship* (1909) or to *The Book of Love* (1910), both edited by Arthur Ransome (1884–1967), or to his *Portraits and Speculations* (January 1913). The latter contains an essay entitled 'The Poetry of Yone Noguchi'; DHL refers to this poet in Letter 636 which may suggest that *Portraits and Speculations* was the work in question.

588. To David Garnett, [25 June 1913]

Text: MS NYPL; Unpublished.

The Cearne
Wednesday[1]

Dear Bunny,

We've been wondering about you and the Botany? – Was it decent? And what about tomorrow, and Frieda's seeing you? We shall come into town, arriving Victoria 1.30. But I have to go to the tailor's and to the photographer's,[2] so we will come to you, and enquire for you at the Students Union[3] about 3.0 oclock. –

If, however, you have written to us and made any arrangements, we will abide by *your* appointment.

Till tomorrow – much love from both of us.

D. H. Lawrence

589. To Henry Savage, 8 July 1913

Text: MS UT; Postmark, Broadstairs JY 8 13; Unpublished.

c/o Edward Garnett, The Cearne, Near Edenbridge, Kent
8 July 1913

Dear Mr Savage,[4]

Why do you say you have almost lost the vanity of wishing to see your poetry published? If one writes one must have a tough soul and put up with things, and keep grinding on. It's hellish, but it's worth it. Death is all right in its way, but one must finish one's job first. I haven't got any of Middleton's poems – I've read some of them.[5] I wish he hadn't died. Why should one

---

[1] It is presumed that DHL's meeting with Edward Garnett on 25 June, mentioned in Letter 586, would be in London; hence the conjectural date for this letter.

[2] DHL was going to have his photograph taken by W. G. Parker for the article in the *Bookman*, xlv (February 1914), 244–6, by W. L. George, where this well known portrait first appeared.

[3] The Imperial College Student Union, South Kensington (Imperial College later became part of the Royal College of Science). DHL used the Union's stationery for Letter 589.

[4] Henry Savage (b. 1881?), freelance journalist, essayist, poet and editor of the works of Richard Middleton; see *Letters*, i. 241n. He was to meet DHL on 16 July 1913 for the first time; see Letter 605.

[5] During his lifetime, Richard Barnham Middleton (1882–1911) published his work only in periodicals. He was part of a group of writers who called themselves the 'New Bohemians', through whom he got to know G. K. Chesterton and Hilaire Belloc. Middleton committed suicide by taking chloroform, when he was only twenty-nine. Savage, who was an enthusiastic admirer of Middleton at this time, later wrote a biography of Middleton called *Richard Middleton: The Man and His Work* (1922). Prior to 1913, he had edited two books of

let the cursedness of circumstances bowl one out? There's something in hanging on like a bull-dog, because you've shut your teeth in the rear of this damned craven life. In the end one pulls it down, I think, and has a triumph. (Mine hasn't turned up yet).

I am just come back from Germany – am going down to Margate for the air, for a fortnight, then returning to Bavaria, I think. I am very poor and in tight circumstances all round. But damn it all, life is like a job one has undertaken, (at the worst) and one doesn't chuck it up without owning oneself incompetent. And then life is very fine again, in a little while.

Will you send me some of your poems to read? I should like it. And if you really have a copy of Middleton's poems to spare, it would give me a good deal of pleasure to have it.[1]

I know one *does* get in a state – one foot on sea and one on shore. As you say, there's nothing but will to get us out of the state – or to hang on till we can scramble out. But then, having been through it, one is pretty strong.

Please write to me. I am a sad dog myself, pretty often: But then again, I'm not. I wish you'd send me some of your poems. Do you know mine? Things sent to this address will always find me.

Yours   D. H. Lawrence

What a miserable sheet of paper this is that I've cribbed. Folk should[2] leave better stuff than this lying about.

590. To Edward Garnett, [8 July 1913]
Text: MS NYPL; PC; Postmark, Westerham JY 8 13; Unpublished.

Cearne
– Tuesday.

Dear Garnett,

We shall be in town tomorrow (Wednesday) on our way to the sea, so I think I shall call on you at Henrietta St.[3] at about 2.0 oclock. If you're not in, just leave me a message. We may stay the night in Hampstead.

Auf wiedersehen   D. H. Lawrence

Middleton's poems, but it is more likely that Lawrence was acquainted with various poems published by Middleton in such periodicals as *Academy*, *English Review*, *Vanity Fair* and *Noelith*.

[1] *Poems and Songs* by Richard Middleton, with an Introduction by Henry Savage (1912), and *Poems and Songs* (Second Series) by Richard Middleton, with a Preface by Henry Savage (1912).   [2] should] really

[3] At the offices of Duckworth and Co.

591. To Katharine Clayton, [8 July 1913]
Text: MS NCL; Unpublished.

The Cearne
Tuesday

Dear Mrs Clayton,[1]

How are you? – jolly? We're going away to Margate tomorrow. Oh dear, oh Lord, Margate!

We have missed you – the house seems *so* much quieter since you left – although Frieda and I have quarrelled just as arduously as ever. You'll come to my funeral?

Did McLeod send on the other two stories?[2] I hope so. He is 5 Carew Rd, Thornton Heath. Tell Douglas[3] to send me the bills as soon as he's done the thing – I've got as much money now as I ever shall have. Let me have the type copies as soon as you can, please – they ought to be going out. Charge me a fair price, no humbug. I'll send you another batch from Margate.

Regards from Frieda and me.

Yours   D. H. Lawrence

And we shall see you again soon, for sure – at any rate you'll come to my funeral – no flowers, by request.

Please alter anything that seems to you wrong – these MSS are *so* slovenly.

592. To Katharine Clayton, [10 July 1913]
Text: MS Lazarus; PC; Postmark, Broadstairs JY 10 13; Unpublished.

28 Percy Avenue, Kingsgate, Broadstairs
[10 July 1913]

Dear Mrs Clayton

This is our address till July 30th. Let me have the type here, will you. We've got the jolliest little flat in Margate: I wish you'd come and see us. You got some more MS. the other day?

Regards from us   D. H. Lawrence

---

[1] Katharine ('Katie') Clayton née Black (b. 1865), was Constance Garnett's younger sister. m. Charles Clayton.

[2] Unidentified. (DHL enquired again about them nearly a year later. See Letter 741.)

[3] Douglas Clayton (1894–1960), Katharine Clayton's son. It was at Edward Garnett's suggestion that DHL approached Clayton, the result being that he typed a large number of DHL's MSS. (He was a printer in a small way, in South Croydon, throughout his life. He never married.)

593. To Edward Garnett, [10 July 1913]
Text: MS NYPL; PC; Postmark, Broadstairs JY 10 13; Unpublished.

28 Percy Avenue, Kingsgate, *Broadstairs*, Kent.
Thursday

Dear Garnett,

Here is our address. We have got a most delightful flat to ourselves – till July 31st. I will send things to you when they are typewritten – I mean just one or two things for Pinker.[1] I didn't see Hueffer – but heard about him.[2] I'll write directly.

Yrs   D. H. Lawrence

594. To Constance Garnett, [10? July 1913]
Text: MS NYPL; Unpublished.

[28 Percy Avenue, Kingsgate, Broadstairs]
[10? July 1913][3]

Dear Missis,

Here then is the coat. I put the house key into the pocket thereof. We saw Mr Garnett – and Duckworth – and Norman Douglas (I like him)[4] – and Katharine Mansfield.[5] She is (like F[rieda] and me) with Murry – a *Westminster Gazette* man – only a lad of 23.[6] He came of the common people

---

[1] James Brand Pinker (1863–1922), DHL's literary agent from July 1914 until December 1919, when DHL terminated their relationship. See Letter 743 and the letter to Pinker, 27 December 1919. (For obituary, see *Times* 10 February 1922.)

[2] Ford Madox Hueffer (later Ford) (1873–1939), founded the *English Review* in 1908 and was the first to publish DHL's poems, in November 1909. Hueffer was responsible for introducing DHL to the London literary scene. See *Letters*, i. 11–15, 138 n. 1.

[3] DHL stopped in London on 9 July 1913, on his way to Margate. This letter was probably written shortly after his arrival there.

[4] George Norman Douglas (1868–1952), b. in Austria. Educated in England and Germany, he had a brief career with the Foreign Office. Interested in music, science, and literature, Douglas published several treatises on zoology before turning to fiction; his literary reputation was established by the novel *South Wind* (1917). When DHL first met him, Douglas was Assistant Editor of the *English Review*. They met again in Capri and Italy after the war; Douglas was the model for James Argyle in *Aaron's Rod* (1921). DHL and Douglas quarrelled over the posthumous publication of Maurice Magnus' MS, published as *Memoirs of the Foreign Legion* (1924) with a lengthy introduction by DHL.

[5] Katharine Mansfield, pseudonym for Kathleen Beauchamp (1888–1923), New Zealand short-story writer; see *Letters*, i. 507.

[6] John Middleton Murry (1889–1957), journalist and critic. With Katherine Mansfield founded *Rhythm* and the *Blue Review* (see *Letters*, i, 507–8, 546); later he founded the *Adelphi*, claiming that it would provide a vehicle for DHL's views. Author of *Keats and Shakespeare* (1925), *Son of Woman, the Story of D. H. Lawrence* (1931) and *Reminiscences of D. H. Lawrence* (1933). m. (1) Katherine Mansfield, 1918; (2) Violet le Maistre, 1924; (3) Elizabeth Cockbayne, 1932?; (4) Mary Gamble, 1954.

in Peckham. Then a rich man gave him £400 a year and sent him to
Oxford – and chucked him after 4 years because he blued his exams.[1] He
has been with KM – for 16 months. Now they are bankrupt over the
Rhythm[2] – Not starving – she has some money, and he earns £7 a week. But
the bailiffs are in. It made me sad to be with them. Love and running from
husbands is desperately ticklish work.[3]

Are you thanking God without ceasing for the peace that is upon you?
Love from us both.   D. H. Lawrence

595. To David Garnett, [11 July 1913]
Text: MS NYPL; Unpublished.

28 Percy Avenue, Kingsgate, *Broadstairs*
Friday[4]

Lieber Kaninchen,[5]

We have tumbled into a most jolly little flat. The big bedroom has a
balcony that looks across the fields at the sea. Then the house has a tent,
and the way-down to the sea is just near, so one can bathe.

You'd better persuade Constanza Davidova (that how she's spelled?)[6] that
your one business in life is to study marine algae. Then you arrive down
here with a microscope and a tooth brush, and we take a bedroom upstairs
for you – et nous voilà, trois lapins dans les salades. It is sunny and I am
sleepy.

We are quite alone – the folk only let this flat. We do our own work. It
is very serene.

We must turn out on July 30th. Then I think we shall go to Irschenhausen.

---

[1] There appears to be no foundation for this statement. According to the records of Brasenose
College, Oxford, John Middleton Murry sat his Final B.A. Examinations in June 1912 and
passed with Second Class Honours. DHL's remark about a rich benefactor is contradicted
by Murry in his autobiography: 'The income from my scholarship and school exhibitions
was all I had, and it left only a narrow margin' (Murry, *Autobiography* 92). Brasenose College
records provide no evidence of other financial support.

[2] Murry recounts that at one point 'The publisher of *Rhythm* was bankrupt, or on the point
of bankruptcy.... The publisher had increased the printing order; but he had done it in my
name. I owed them £400.... It might as well have been four million.... For the moment we
temporized with the old printers, by arranging to pay them off at the rate of £100 a year:
£8. 6s. 8d. a month' (Murry, *Autobiography* 253–7).

[3] Married to George Bowden in 1909, Katherine Mansfield, like Frieda, had not yet obtained
her divorce. On 2 May 1918, the decree nisi was made absolute, six years after the original
petition; she married Murry on 3 May 1918.(See Murry, *Autobiography* 478.)

[4] Presumably written on the Friday of the first week of DHL's stay in Margate; hence, the
date 11 July 1913.

[5] 'Dear Rabbit'. David Garnett was familiarly known as 'Bunny'; see Letter 588.

[6] DHL's attempt at a Russianised form for Constance Garnett. The correct form would be
'Constanza Davidovna'.

I am too sleepy to write to you – Oh, I can't find a little story of mine, in MS, called Intimacy.[1] You might see if it's kicking round at the Cearne. Also I forgot a copy of *Sons and Lovers*. Save it for me, please, don't give it away. If you can find 'Intimacy' – send it to me here.

I take badly to new places. Now, of course, I'm hankering after the Cearne. I'm the sort of weedy plant that takes badly to removal.

Auf Wiedersehen   D. H. Lawrence

I took the *Sanine*[2] out of your bedroom. I'll send it back.

596. To Constance Garnett, [11 July 1913]
Text: MS NYPL; Unpublished.

28 Percy Avenue, Kingsgate, Broadstairs
Friday[3]

Dear Mrs Garnett,

We are here very peaceful among the holiday makers. Of course I am not yet happy in the place. There is no fault to be found with it, except that I do not belong to it at all, at all. But – ça arrivera. Soon, no doubt, I shall be here like a bird that broods on her nest. But I am sick, sick, sick of shifting.[4] I want to sit tight somewhere, and work. I am by nature not a bit of an adventurer – rather like a thing that can't leave its lair – such[5] as a cabbage.

I think it is going to be very healthy for us. We are both very sleepy. Frieda wants to write to you gratefully, but can't keep her eyes open.

I wish I was at the Cearne. It is the sort of place I fit into – something so solid and unmovable about it, something unexpected and individualised: that bare, workmanlike study, that farm-house hall, that burst into country houseism and culture in the big room, with the lapse into disgraceful, almost brutal roughness – nearly like Squire Western[6] – under the fire-place: the common place kitchen and the dejected scullery – oh Lord, I could live for ages at the Cearne, and be happy. David is a lucky devil.

I want to work, but find it rather hard to begin straight away.

Frieda will write to you soon.

---

[1] The story (first called 'Intimacy' and later 'The White Woman') was published posthumously in *Lovat Dickson's Magazine*, ii (June 1934), 697–718, under the title 'The Witch à la Mode'; it was later collected in *A Modern Lover* (1934).

[2] A Russian novel (1907) by Mikhail Petrovich Artsybashev (1878–1927). DHL probably refers to a French translation (Paris, 1911), since the first English translation (by Percy Pinkerton, with a preface by Gilbert Cannan) did not appear until 1914. The work appeared to advocate unrestrained sexual expression and revolt against all authority.

[3] The content suggests the same date as that assigned to the preceding letter.

[4] shifting] wandering.   [5] such] like

[6] In Henry Fielding's novel, *The History of Tom Jones* (1749).

Tell Mrs Clayton to send me my typed things, when you write – and give her my regards.

Frieda and I are quite aimiable.

A million thousand thanks to you. What else!

riverisco   D. H. Lawrence

597. To Ford Madox Hueffer, 11 July 1913
Text: MS NYPL; Postmark, Broadstairs JY 11 13; Unpublished.

28 Percy Avenue, Kingsgate, Broadstairs
11 July 1913

Dear Hueffer,

I was only in London a day or two, and didn't get a chance to call on you. I might have to come to Mrs Hueffer's garden party[1] – should like to have done so very much – but didn't get the invitation till too late.

Yes, I am fixed up with Duckworth for my novels. You see he advanced me £100 on *Sons and Lovers*, and I agreed to give him my next books. So it wouldn't be any use for you to see him.

We are staying here a fortnight and then going back to Germany. The air here is very fine.

Thanks ever so much for what you've done for me. My regards to Mrs Hueffer.

Yours   D. H. Lawrence

598. To Henry Savage, 12 July 1913
Text: MS UT; Unpublished.

28 Percy Avenue, Kingsgate, Broadstairs
12 July 1913

Dear Savage,

Your letter and poems and the books of Middleton have all just come.[2] Frankly I can scarcely make head or tail of you. I am by nature active, I think. I suppose you are something of a sensuous mystic – like Novalis.[3] I feel myself the appeal of 'magic' in verse – but I like things to be very human. Probably I am too gross for you. I love Burns, and ballads – but there – I love the things you have chosen also. Why should one particularise and exclude! I like any poetry, even bad poetry, but not very strutting stuff – I don't like Henley[4] very much, nor the loud trumpeters like Victor Hugo.

[1] A reference to Violet Hunt (1866–1942), who was known as 'Mrs Hueffer' but was never legally married to Hueffer; see *Letters*, i. 144 n. 1.   [2] See p. 29 n. 1.
[3] The pseudonym of the German writer Friedrich Ludwig von Hardenberg (1772–1801).
[4] William Ernest Henley (1849–1903).

Today, when I am very miserable, I hardly dare read Middleton. Lord, what a shadow he had on him.

I don't know why your poetry reminds me a bit of Novalis. I suppose you don't like his hymns[1] particularly? – One wants to read more of you before one judges. I can't get the run of 'The Last Confession'.[2] You must come and read it to us.

Come and see us. We've got a quiet little flat to ourselves. Come as soon as you can. We are nearer, I think, to Margate station than to Broadstairs. Only let me know when you will come, and we can meet you – my wife and I.

It is a queer life. I am a bad philosopher. As for your dissipating – you are too moral – unless you mean excess – which is a pity, because one should not abuse neither one's soul nor one's body. I am quite improper, because my wife was (or is – one gets so mixed up) – the legal wife of another man. But that is private news, please. I can't philosophise – only rage and gnash my teeth.

You needn't fear that we are bookish. I am the son of a coal-miner, and very ordinary. I should probably pass as a 30/- clerk.

I shall be glad to see you. I wish God would give his mills a rest – I hate being eternally, slowly ground.[3]

Greetings then from us both.

Yours   D. H. Lawrence

But how should I know you if I came to meet you at the station?
Many many thanks for the books.

599. To Edward Marsh, 12 July 1913
Text: MS NYPL; Huxley 127.

28 Percy Avenue, Kingsgate, Broadstairs
12 July 1913

Dear Mr Marsh,[4]

What joy to receive £3 out of the sweet heavens![5] I call that manna. I

[1] Probably a reference to his *Hymnen an die Nacht* (1800). The character of these 'Hymns to the Night' is perhaps suggested by this sample passage: 'My whole being awakes. I am thine, and thou art mine. Night has roused me to life and manhood. Consume my earthly frame, draw me into deeper and closer union, and may our bridal night endure for ever' (*Novalis, His Life, Thoughts and Works*, ed. M. J. Hope, 1891, p. 240).
[2] This poem by Savage was later published in his volume *Escapes and Escapades* (1915), pp. 63–4. DHL was reading Savage's poem in MS.
[3] Cf. Longfellow, 'Poetic Aphorisms' ('Retribution').
[4] (Sir) Edward Howard Marsh (1872–1953), editor (of *Georgian Poetry*, 1912–22), author and civil servant; see *Letters*, i. 459 n. 2.
[5] Contributors to *Georgian Poetry* – the first volume (December 1912) included DHL's 'Snap-Dragon' – received a royalty. The basis of the calculation is explained in Letter 603.

suppose you're the manipulating Jehovah. I'll sing you a little Te Deum.[1]

I wish you had the publishing of one's work – soon I should have a fur-lined coat.

I should like to see you very much. I suppose you won't be Margate way?[2] (Dont be insulted, at any rate). If you are, I wish you'd come and see us. But I think I shall be in London again in the very beginning of August. Are you then still in town. At any rate I'll write to you when I am coming up.

And many thanks   D. H. Lawrence

600. To Constance Garnett, [13 July 1913]
Text: MS NYPL; Postmark, Broadstairs JY 14 13; Unpublished.

Riley House, Percy Avenue, Kingsgate, *Broadstairs*
Sunday

Dear Mrs Garnett,

Thanks for your letter and forwardances. When your inquisitive eye wants to peek into any of my packages let it do so – I never have anything private. (No impudence here).

> Integer vitae scelerisque purus
> Non eget...[3]

Henry Savage sent me two vols of Richard Middleton's poems and a vol of the same author's short stories.[4] It is rather interesting. – Then he sent me some of his own poems that are beyond me. He seems a queer fish – not wonderful – just stupid in his own special philosophic–poetic style. He is coming, I think to see us. If he is any good I will move him on to you. McLeod's address is 5 Carew Rd, Thornton Heath S.E. He says he won't write to you. I expect he's shy of you, you Newnham Missis.[5]

I found the story I asked David for, mingled up with Frieda's underclothing. I at once changed its title, 'Intimacy', in order to get it out.[6] Tell the rabbit I'm sorry I bothered him.

[1] The opening words of the ancient liturgical hymn 'Te deum laudamus' ['Thee, God, we praise'].
[2] By coincidence, Marsh had an invitation to visit Herbert and Cynthia Asquith in Kingsgate during July; thus it was that DHL met Marsh and the Asquiths. See Marsh's letter to Rupert Brooke, 20 July 1913 (Nehls, i. 199).
[3] Horace, *Odes* I. xxii. 1–2. ['The man whose life is pure and untouched by crime...']
[4] See p. 29 n. 1. Savage had also edited Middleton's *The Ghost Ship and Other Stories* (1912).
[5] Constance Garnett had been educated at Newnham College, Cambridge.
[6] See p. 33 n. 1.

Will you send me the typewritten copies of the stories. If you had a little drawer in which I, poor hole-less fox and nestless sparrow,[1] – could leave my MS, I should once more call blessings on your wise and venerably translating head.

I would have snared those rabbits if you'd had faith as big as a grain of mustard seed.[2] Now they can gorge your carrots till they're giddy, and I shall only say 'go it, old fellow'. –

I am glad Lye[3] is back to take the sad burden of housekeeping off your neck. Oh Lord, these burdens of fair women – soup once a day – my God! Give Lye my love. Frieda says she says (I mean Lye) – that I'm cold. Tell her I'll black her eye to prove it.

There's an armistice at present between me and my Bellona.[4]

Love to Bunny.

Yours   D. H. Lawrence

It was a woman sent the telegram – the one whose letter on the lawn gave F. such fright of Ernst and pistols.[5] We didn't get the wire at all.

DHL

There's no ink.

601. To Katharine Clayton, [13 July 1913]

Text: MS NCL; Moore 212.

Riley House, Percy Avenue, Kingsgate, Broadstairs
Sunday[6]

Dear Mrs Clayton,

Here's another story.[7] Mrs Garnett said some typed MS had got to the Cearne, so it will soon come on here. Thanks very much.

I think we are here till the 30th. It is a nice flat we have got, but the place *bores* me. What have I to do with fat fatherly Jews and their motor cars and their bathing tents.

Frieda and I are having a lull in the storm. I've no doubt the tempest will rage again soon.

---

[1] Cf. Matthew viii. 20.   [2] Matthew xvii. 20.
[3] See p. 22 n. 3.   [4] *Macbeth* I. ii. 54.
[5] Ernest Weekley (1865–1954), University Professor and etymologist; husband of Frieda; see *Letters*, i. 374 n. 5. No record of this incident has been found; the woman has not been identified.
[6] Clearly written on the same day as Letter 600.
[7] Probably 'Intimacy'.

I've got no ink and it is Sunday. So pardon the pencil.
My thanks to Douglas.

Auf Wiedersehen   D. H. Lawrence

602. To Katharine Clayton, [14 July 1913]
Text: MS NCL; PC; Postmark, Broadstairs JY 14 13; Unpublished.

[Riley House, Percy Avenue, Kingsgate, Broadstairs]
[14 July 1913]

Dear Mrs Clayton,
   Four of the typed MS have come. They *do* look nice. Thanks very much – also for the suggestions. Yes, we'll leave the 'New Eve' for the present. – Send me the other things when they're ready, will you – But I should be glad if you could drop the MS itself into a spare drawer. It is such a nuisance carting the lumber about – send me the typed things only.

Yours   D. H. Lawrence

603. To Edward Garnett, [14 July 1913]
Text: MS NYPL; Postmark, Broadstairs JY 15 13; cited in Carolyn G. Heilbrun, *The Garnett Family* (New York, 1961), p. 157.

28 Percy Avenue, Kingsgate, Broadstairs
Monday

Dear Garnett,
   The typed stories are beginning to come now – they look nice. When the rest arrive I shall send them out. I haven't got an address of the *New Statesman* nor of the *Outlook*;[1] I must go to Margate and see if I can get the papers there. Then I've got some more things from my sister,[2] some of which I think you have never seen. I shall give them to you, all together, to send to Pinker.
   Mrs Clayton said she thought the story I called ' The New Eve ' – previously I think 'Renegade Eve' – that is the one where the telegram comes 'Meet me Marble Arch 7.30 Richard' – was unworthy of me, and so Douglas didn't type it.[3] Perhaps she's right – it amuses me.
   My sister gets married on Aug 4th.[4] But I shall only be up there for two days. I wish we could stay a day or two with you either at Downshire Hill[5]

---

[1] *Outlook* (1898–1928), a London periodical.   [2] Ada Lawrence.
[3] The incident occurs in 'New Eve and Old Adam'.
[4] Ada Lawrence was married to William Edwin Clarke on 4 August 1913.
[5] Garnett's London address.

or the Cearne. We don't really want to go back to Germany till about Aug 10th.

Do you know Edward Marsh actually sent me £3, as being $\frac{1}{17}$ of the profits of the *Georgian Poetry*. Dont you think that was nice? He writes nicely too.

I suppose you can't come down to Margate to see us. We are in a little flat to ourselves, and you might like it. But no – even I feel horribly out of place among these Jews' villas, and the babies and papas.

I am drudging away revising the stories.[1] How glad I shall be when I have cleared that mess up! I *will* keep a list.

Love from us   D. H. Lawrence

I dreamed of you last night, that you were laughing and saying very witty things to somebody I could not see – and for no reason whatever I was awfully anxious about you. And I spend the morning wondering how you can possibly have a lion in the path.

Do you know Colette Willy, a French woman. Her novels are jolly good *La Vagabonde*, for instance.[2]

604. To Edward Marsh, 14 July 1913
Text: MS NYPL; Huxley 127–8.

Riley House, Percy Avenue, Kingsgate, Broadstairs
14 July 1913

Dear Mr Marsh,

How clever of the Gods to move you down here! I wonder how long you are staying in Kingsgate. Will you come in for tea on Sunday – about 4.0? But choose your own time if you would rather.

Will the enclosed autograph do for W. H. Davies?[3] By the way, I should like to meet him – he feels so nice in all his work. Do you think it possible sometime.

adieu till Sunday.

Yours   D. H. Lawrence

My wife is looking forward to seeing you, also.

[1] They might include: 'The Fly in the Ointment' (published in *New Statesman*, 13 August 1913; see p. 64 n. 3); 'Strike-Pay I, Her Turn' (*Saturday Westminster Gazette*, 6 September 1913); 'Strike-Pay II, Ephraim's Half Sovereign' (*Saturday Westminster Gazette*, 13 September 1913); 'A Sick Collier' (*New Statesman*, 13 September 1913; see Letter 607); 'The Christening' (*Smart Set*, xiii, February 1914; see p. 41 n. 1); and 'The Shadow in the Rose Garden' (*Smart Set*, xiii, March 1914).

[2] Sidonie-Gabrielle Willy, née Colette (1873–1954), French novelist. *La Vagabonde* (1910) was translated into English by E. M. McLeod (1911).

[3] William Henry Davies (1871–1940), who published his first book of verse, *The Soul's Destroyer and Other Poems* in 1905. His *Autobiography of a Super Tramp* (1908) secured his reputation as a writer. (See also Letter 668.)

605. To Henry Savage, [15 July 1913]
Text: MS UTul; PC; Postmark, Broadstairs JY 15 13; Unpublished.

Broadstairs
[15 July 1913]

Dear Savage,

I have just got your letter – delighted to see you tomorrow. But you don't say what time you will come. However, we'll stay in during the morning – You take a tram from Margate Station to the Wheat Sheaf, and then walk down to Kingsgate – not far. The house is called Riley House.

à demain   D. H. Lawrence

606. To Katharine Clayton, [15 July 1913]
Text: MS NCL; PC; Postmark, Broadstairs JY 15 13; Unpublished.

Kingsgate
[15 July 1913]

Dear Mrs Clayton,

The 3 things came today.[1] How nice they look! Many thanks for them. We are doing well.

Yrs   D. H. Lawrence

607. To Edward Garnett, [16 July 1913]
Text: MS NYPL; Moore 213–14.

28 Percy Avenue, Kingsgate, Broadstairs
Wednesday[2]

Dear Garnett,

Fussy old woman in the *Nation*![3] But I *did* touch her up, at any rate. Do *you* think the second half of *Sons and Lovers* such a lapse from the first, or is it moralistic blarney? Frieda agrees with them that Miriam and Clara and Pauls love affairs weren't worth writing about.

Shall I send these Syndicate[4] people some of my short things. You don't

[1] Typescripts of three unidentified short stories.
[2] The reference to Marsh's visit on Sunday, 20 July, establishes the date of this letter as Wednesday, 16 July 1913.
[3] This review of *Sons and Lovers* appeared in the *Nation*, xiii (12 July 1913), 577–8. The concluding statement was: 'But, remembering all that *Sons and Lovers* gives us, we are glad to forget Paul and his "failures", his "test on Miriam", his further test (though not this time so labelled) on Clara, his "question, which was almost a lamentation, '*Why* don't they hold me?'"…to forget, in short, that half the book is against the grain, and remember gratefully and glowingly those earlier chapters which keep faith with life' (Draper 72). The reviewer was Ethel Colburn Mayne; see p. 47 n. 3.
[4] The Northern Newspaper Syndicate.

know how nice they look, and how convincing, now I have revised them and they are type-written.

They haven't all come yet, and so I can't send them out for a day or two. – I thought I might let this Syndicate have 'A Sick Collier', and perhaps 'The Bakers Man' – the one where they christen the illegitimate child.[1] I re-wrote the end and made it good.

The Society of Authors wants me to be a member.[2] Does one not bother?

Why don't you come here? – it might do you good. But certainly we might meet at Downshire Hill or the Cearne, from the 29th till Aug 2nd or 3rd. You must decide as pleases you best.

I don't think Collette Willy is improper – particularly.

Edward Marsh is coming to see us on Sunday. He is Winston Churchill's secretary[3] – and is coming down here to stay with the Herbert Asquiths, who live at the end of the avenue.[4]

I am swotting away at the short stories – and shall be so glad to get them done.

A man called Henry Savage is coming to see us today – a sort of amateur poet – the man who got Unwin to publish Richard Middleton's stuff. I'll tell you about him later.

Frieda will like the novel.[5] Thanks for the *Nation*.

Yours   D. H. Lawrence

608. To Sallie Hopkin, 17 July 1913
Text: MS NCL; cited in Paulina S. Pollak, *Journal of Modern Literature*, iii (February 1973), 28.

28 Percy Avenue, Kingsgate, Broadstairs
17 July 1913

Dear Mrs Hopkin,

It is awfully good of you to take me in for my sister's wedding. Frieda

---

[1] The incident takes place in 'The Christening', where the father of the illegitimate child is the 'Baker's man at Berryman's'. The story was first entitled 'A Bag of Cakes' and then 'Pat-a-Cake, Pat-a-Cake, Baker's Man'.

[2] DHL did not join the Society of Authors until the banning of his novel *The Rainbow* in November 1915. See Letter 1047.

[3] (Sir) Winston Spencer Churchill (1874–1965). Though later to be Prime Minister (1940–5, 1951–5), at this time he was First Lord of the Admiralty (1911–15).

[4] Herbert ('Beb') Asquith (1881–1947), m. 1910, Cynthia (1887–1960), née Charteris (daughter of Lord and Lady Elcho). Asquith, second son of Herbert Henry Asquith (1852–1928), the Prime Minister (1908–16), was a barrister by profession. He saw active service in France and Flanders, 1914–18; he wrote *Poems 1912–1933* (1934) and a number of novels. Lady Cynthia (she acquired the title when her father became 11th Earl of Wemyss on 30 June 1914) was the author of several autobiographical works – *Remember and be Glad* (1952) contains a memoir of DHL – and her *Diaries 1915–1918* (1968).

[5] Unidentified.

would like to come, but she can't because my elder sister[1] and brother[2] don't know about her. She would like to see you, and I shall be so glad – Don't tell Mrs Dax I am coming, will you.[3] I don't want to see many people.

We are staying here till July 30th. I think I shall come up to Eastwood on the Saturday – is that Aug 2nd? Then we are going back to Bavaria immediately – on Aug 5th, I think.

What a lot of things we shall have to say – dear Lord, what a year of living this has been! I shall tell you all about it. I hope you are well, fairly strong just now. How are Mr Hopkin and Enid?[4]

But we'll talk about everything when I come.

Love from us both – auf wiedersehen.

D. H. Lawrence

609. To Constance Garnett, [18? July 1913]
Text: MS NYPL; Unpublished.

28 Percy Avenue, Kingsgate, Broadstairs
Friday[5]

Dear Mrs Garnett,

Having paid Robert Garnett[6] and Mrs Clayton and one or two other people I find I shall – or may – be short of money. Will you send me a cheque for £6 14 0. That will leave £38 0 0 in the bank, I think. At any rate you know how that stands. Don't be out of patience with me for the bother.

Frieda *might* go straight to Germany from here. But that is uncertain, and, I think unlikely.

Our love – and auf wiedersehen   D. H. Lawrence

610. To Henry Savage, [18? July 1913]
Text: MS Anderson; Unpublished.

28 Percy Avenue, Kingsgate, Broadstairs
Friday[7]

Dear Savage,

Thanks very much for the books. Frieda is set up indeed. There is some interesting stuff. I have only looked at Casanova,[8] but he'll suit me.

---

[1] Emily Una King. [2] George Arthur Lawrence.
[3] Alice Mary Dax (1878–1959). DHL had had an affair with her and did not want to see her now that he was living with Frieda. See *Letters*, i. 2, 44 n. 3.
[4] William Edward Hopkin (1862–1951); m. Sallie, née Potter (d. 1923); their daughter Enid was born in 1896. William and Sallie were leading figures in Eastwood's political and intellectual life, and among DHL's closest friends. See *Letters*, i. 3, 176 n. 2.
[5] Possible dates are 18 or 25 July 1913. DHL's uncertainty about Frieda's going to Germany, suggests a date more than three days before the 28th when her intention was clear. Hence the choice of 18th.
[6] DHL refers to legal fees incurred in connection with Frieda's divorce proceedings.
[7] This appears to be DHL's first letter to Savage following the latter's visit to Kingsgate on 16 July 1913. [8] The book is unidentified.

We were awfully glad to see you. But you shouldn't be such a sad dog, you really shouldn't. One's soul needs a stomach of bronze, to digest this dammed life. But it's all right really. You did make us miserable too.

I think it is well to be mystic when things go too far. – But there, I don't know what to say, I simply dont.

But I think if I had a child coming, I think I should be happy too. Because if one is careful – if the mother is careful – I think[1] all the world starts again, right clean and jolly, when a child is born. One should be happy, I think, when a child is coming, because the mother's blood ought to run in the womb sweet like sunshine. Because we must all die, whereas we *mightn't* have been born. And when a child comes, something is which might never have been And if it was my child I should be glad, whoever died, being old, or being in a cul de sac.

Come and see us again while we are in England. Write to me about your poetry. Don't be an amateur – it is so damnable. Take the thing seriously, your writing.

Don't mind my wise preaching, will you?

I think we should like your wife.

Did you catch that train?

We thought there'd be a note in with the books, but I couldn't find one. Both our thanks to you, and regards

Yours   D. H. Lawrence

611. To Henry Savage, [20 July 1913]
Text: MS UCLA; cited in Harry T. Moore, *Yale University Library Gazette*, xxxiv (1959), 26.

28 Percy Avenue, Kingsgate, Broadstairs
Sunday[2]

Dear Savage,

Many thanks for the copy of my own poems.[3] But why, man, why in the name of fortune, did you spend money on me like that. No, you shouldn't do those things.

We had Marsh in this morning (of the *Georgian Poetry*) and he was inquiring for new poets. We give your name. Only I didn't show him those poems you copied out for me, because they're not the best.

We still remember you and the exciting debauch with pleasure. But you

---

[1] MS reads 'thing'.

[2] The reference to Marsh's visit 'this morning' establishes 20 July 1913 as the date of this letter. Cf. Letter 604.

[3] *Love Poems and Others*, which Duckworth published in February 1913.

know quite well we shan't be in London till the 30th, and you'll be gone away then, so don't be so rash with your invitations.

My respects to Mrs Savage. Madame joins me in regards to yourself.

Yours   D. H. Lawrence

612. To Edward Garnett, 20 July 1913
Text: MS NYPL; Unpublished.

Ripley House, Percy Avenue, Kingsgate, Broadstairs
20 July 1913

Dear Garnett,

I've sent two of the mildest stories to Northern Newspaper Syndicate (one you haven't seen).[1] Three I've sent for the *N[orth] American Review*.[2] Three I keep (short ones) for the *New Statesman*.[3] These two I send you, for Pinker or the *Eng[lish] Review* – which do you think? I am just having 'Two Marriages' typed again.[4] I re-wrote a good deal of it – also 'Love Among the Haystacks'.[5] Then there are two more little things I find.[6]

What will the *Forum* have, do you think?[7] Why did they send me a May number? I can send things straight to Pinker, if you give me his address. I am sick of messing with these short things. But I shall soon have done.

I think we shall leave here on the 29th – at any rate the 30th. We should love to come to the Cearne. I must go to Eastwood on the Saturday 2nd Aug. We are to go to Germany when we like – the house is ready.[8]

My love to Mrs Garnett. I hope it was nice for her at Tilbury Docks. Why hasn't David written to us?

It is a very sunny day. – See you in a week. Regards to Li.

D. H. Lawrence

Should I write to Mitchell Kennerley personally and send him a story.

You could give Norman Douglas the stories, if you thought them good for the *English*.[9]

[1] 'A Sick Collier' and 'The Christening': see Letter 635.
[2] 'Once' and two others unidentified; see Letter 659.
[3] 'The Fly in the Ointment', 'The White Stocking' and 'The Witch à la Mode' (formerly 'Intimacy').
[4] 'Two Marriages', an early version of 'The Daughters of the Vicar', had first been typed by Arthur Stanley Corke in October–November 1911. (See *Letters*, i. 168 n. 4, 309.)
[5] This story – written in October–November 1911 and now revised – was published in the posthumous collection, *Love Among the Haystacks and Other Pieces*, With a Reminiscence by David Garnett (1930). (See *Letters*, i. 323.)
[6] Perhaps 'Strike Pay' and 'Her Turn'.
[7] DHL's story 'The Soiled Rose' was published in the *Forum*, xlix (March 1913), 324–40; but the periodical accepted nothing else of his.
[8] DHL and Frieda were invited to stay at Irschenhausen at Edgar Jaffe's house. Cf. p. 19 n. 3.
[9] Norman Douglas was Assistant Editor of the *English Review*. The two stories referred to here and in the opening paragraph were 'Vin Ordinaire' and 'Honour and Arms', which the

613. To Douglas Clayton, [20 July 1913]
Text: MS NCL; Unpublished.

28 Percy Avenue, Kingsgate, Broadstairs
Sunday[1]

Dear Mr Clayton,

Many thanks for the MS. I shall be so glad if you'll pitch these in a drawer – except the one tied up in string 'Daughters of the Vicar'. Will you type me that, please, and send me the proof.

Yours – much obliged   D. H. Lawrence

614. To John Middleton Murry, [22 July 1913]
Text: MS NYPL; Murry, *New Adelphi* 264–5.

28 Percy Avenue, Kingsgate, Broadstairs
Tuesday[2]

Dear Murry,

Oh but why didn't you come and let us lend you a pound. I think when times have been so rough, you shouldn't bring about a disappointment on yourselves, just for the money. That seems to me wrong. We could just as well lend you five pounds as have it in the bank – if you want it. I consider now that your not coming on Sunday was a piece of obtuseness on your part. You are one of the people who *should* have a sense of proportionate values; you ought to know when it is worth while to let yourself borrow money, and when it isn't. Because you *must* save your soul, and Mrs Murry's soul, from any further hurts, for the present, or any disappointments, or any dreary stretches of misery.

When Marsh said on Sunday, because we couldn't understand why you hadn't come: 'I suppose they hadn't the money for the railway tickets', I thought it was stupid, because you seemed to me rich, because you can earn so much more than I can. I had no idea.

So now I think you'd better come down for the week-end. Come on Saturday and stay till Monday morning. We can put you up. Don't on any account bring chickens or such-like rubbish from town. We can get them down here. Though perhaps they are cheaper in town. Bring one if you like.

Come for the week-end, and bathe. We've got a tent in a little bay on the

---

English Review published in June 1914 and August 1914, respectively. Garnett decided to send the second to Pinker to whom he wrote on 23 July 1913 (MS NYPL): see Introduction p. 6.
[1] A note on the back of the MS, obviously by Douglas Clayton, reads: 'Type only "The Daughters of the Vicar"' and records the date on which this letter was received as 22 July 1913.
[2] The reference to Marsh's visit on 20 July fixes the date of this letter as 22 July 1913.

foreshore, and great waves come and pitch one high up, so I feel like Horace, about to smite my cranium on the sky.[1] I can only swim a little bit and am a clown in the water, but it is jolly. So you come, and bathe on Saturday. It'll be high tide then about 5.0. And bathe on Sunday, and bathe on Monday morning. Then you'll feel much jollier.

I am not poor, you know. But I didn't know you were really stoney. Only I have to watch it, because Frieda doesn't care.

Harold Hobson *might* be here – but you'd like him.[2]

Regards to you both   D. H. Lawrence

Let us know by what train you'll come on Saturday.

What a shame for Mrs Murry to have had such a chase. – I put in a sovereign. Will she give Monty half a sovereign if she can – if not, give me the money back when you like.[3]

DHL

615. To Ernest Collings, 22 July 1913
Text: MS UT; Huxley 129–30.

28 Percy Avenue, Kingsgate, Broadstairs
22 July 1913

Dear Collings,[4]

There – we are in England – came a little while ago, stayed a few days at the Cearne, and came down here for the air. We are staying till the 29th, then going to London for a day or two. Might I not see you one day – either the Wednesday 30th, or the Thursday? Or are you going away immediately.

I was glad to hear from you. If I can get a chance I will go and see that exhibition – your drawings would interest me, so would some of the other things.[5] I went one day into the Academy,[6] but was simply bored. It is the utter paucity of conception that is so disheartening. The poor devils have got nothing inside 'em – they've only got rather clever fingers.

[1] See Horace, *Odes* I. i. 35–6.
[2] Harold Hobson (1891–1974), consulting engineer; a close friend of David Garnett and of DHL; see *Letters*, i. 443 n. 3, 489 n. 1.
[3] Katherine Mansfield was acting as a go-between for Frieda and her son Montague Weekley who recalls that 'Katherine Mansfield delivered messages from my mother to us children,...' (Nehls, i. 198).
[4] Ernest Henry Roberts Collings (1882–1932), artist and illustrator; see *Letters*, i. 468 n. 1.
[5] The exhibition was that of the Allied Artists Association held in the Royal Albert Hall. (For an account of it see *The Art Chronicle*, 11 July 1913.) Known as the 'Sixth London Salon', this exhibition contained 1,300 works; yet the *Art Chronicle* reviewer felt it appropriate to make specific reference to Collings' contributions: 'Ernest Collings is a decorator with a style and will all his own; they would make or kill a room, no half measures being possible.'
[6] Royal Academy, Burlington House.

I liked the woodpecker[1] – not quite so much as some of yours – but it seemed fresh. What are you doing now.

Sons and Lovers has been well received, hasn't it? I don't know whether it has sold so well. The damned prigs in the libraries and bookshops daren't handle me because they pretend they are delicate skinned and I am hot. May they fry in Hell.

I don't like England very much, but the English *do* seem rather lovable people. They have such a lot of gentleness. There seems to be a big change in England, even in a year: such a dissolving down of old barriers and prejudices. But I look at the young women, and they all seem such sensationalists, with half a desire to expose themselves – Good God, where is there a woman for a really decent earnest man to marry. They don't want husbands and marriage any more – only sensation.

Though why I talk like this to you I don't know. Try and see us some time next week in London – We go back to Bavaria about Aug. 8th.

> Yours   D. H. Lawrence

616. To Arthur McLeod, 22 July 1913

Text: MS UT; Postmark, Broadstairs JY 22 13; Moore, *Intelligent Heart* 152.

> 28 Percy Avenue, Kingsgate, Broadstairs
> 22 July 1913

Dear Mac,

Thanks for the reviews[2] – yes they are flattering. I saw the *Nation*. Dear old lady – it was an Irish spinster, a clever woman called Miss Mayne, I believe – not old, for that matter.[3]

Oh, before I forget – send me a *New Statesman*, will you. I want to send them some sketches. Send me an old copy or just the address, anything. Don't be impatient with me, either.

The *Blue Review* is dead – died this month.[4]

We leave here on the 30th – going to the Cearne for a few days. I want to see you then. We go back to Germany about Aug. 8th – I suppose you couldn't run down here and see us. We should love it.

[1] 'The Woodpecker' by Collings was an illustration for the cover of George A. B. Dewar's *Wild Birds Through the Year* published in June 1913.

[2] Presumably of *Sons and Lovers*, but the specific reviews cannot be identified.

[3] Ethel Colburn Mayne (187?–1941), novelist, short story writer, literary historian and translator, who contributed fiction to the *Yellow Book* and was a reviewer for *Nation*, *Daily News* and *Daily Chronicle*. In 1912 she published her study of Byron, which was very favourably received. (See Letter 607 and n. 3).

[4] Murry records that 'In July 1913, *The Blue Review* came to an end. After three months it was evident that it could not pay its way; and Katherine and I were no longer quite so innocent as we had been. We had no intention of piling up another debt' (Murry, *Autobiography* 260).

We are quite swells. Edward Marsh came on Sunday (he is the *Georgian Poetry* man – and Secretary in the Admiralty to Winston Churchill) – and he took us in to tea with the Herbert Asquiths – jolly nice folk – son of the Prime Minister.[1] Today I am to meet there Sir Walter Raleigh.[2] But alas, it is not he of the cloak.

I have been grubbing away among the short stories. God, I shall be glad when it is done. I shall begin my novel again in Germany.

We bathe, and I write among the babies of the foreshore: it is an innocent life, and a dull one.

Poor Philip.[3] He'll soon be like Alexander, with no more worlds to conquer.[4] But I wouldn't like touring Europe with no German and Italian, and yet watching the pence filter out.

Frieda sends warm greetings – une bonne poignée.[5]

D. H. Lawrence

Come and see us if you can. When do you break up?

[Frieda Weekley begins]

Yes, do come! I want to see something of you too!   F.

617. To Else Jaffe, [22? July 1913]
Text: MS UT; Unpublished.

[28 Percy Avenue, Kingsgate, Broadstairs]
[22? July 1913]

[Frieda Weekley begins]

Liebe Else!

Ernst's 'verfaulte Leiche' liegt mir noch in den Knochen! Aber es ist etwas daran – Für ihn ist die Liebe tot und unerfreulich tot – Aber es ist unglaublich, daß er *so* an eine Mutter schreiben kann – Er beruhigt sich aber – Ich bin immer noch wie etwas das durch das 'Nichts' saust – Und die Kinder! – Mama's Brief freut mich sehr – Er tat mir gut – Äußerlich

---

[1] Herbert Henry Asquith was Liberal Prime Minister (1908–15); he headed the Coalition Government May 1915–December 1916. cr. Earl of Oxford and Asquith in 1925.

[2] Sir Walter Alexander Raleigh (1861–1922), Professor of English Literature and Fellow of Magdalen College, Oxford.

[3] Philip F. T. Smith (1886–1961), headmaster of Davidson Road School, Croydon (1907–13) where DHL taught; from April 1913, headmaster of Norbury Manor School to which McLeod had also transferred. See *Letters*, i. 84 n. 1.

[4] The allusion to Alexander the Great's famous remark ironically conveys DHL's irritation at Smith's frequently reiterated love of European travel ('so lordly and continental', *Letters*, i. 464).

[5] 'cordially yours' (literally 'a firm handshake').

geht's mir gut – L, nachdem er *recht* elend war die Tage hier, erholt
sich – Man macht viel Getu um ihn – Hier haben wir uns mit den Herbert
Asquiths, er ist der Sohn des Primeminister angefreundet; die Luft wird
freier in der Welt, ich bin auch ein 'success' – Gott, es ist einem so wurscht,
wenn man auch froh ist, ein wenig von sich loszukommen, und zum Glück
besitzen wir Richthofens die Gabe uns in andern verlieren zu können. Wenn
ich L. mit den andern vergleiche, sehe ich, daß er eine eigne, innere,
unabhängige Aktivität besitzt; er ist so viel mehr als man zuerst denkt – Aber
mich jetzt innerlich von den Kindern loszureißen ist entsetzlich – den
täglichen Kontakt, es ist wie wenn lebendige Stücke Fleisch von einem
gerissen werden, zum Glück denk ich die Kinder fühlen es nicht *so*. Ich
denke, wenn E. erst *geschieden* ist, beruhigt er sich mehr und mehr – Genieß
Deine Kinder nur recht, Friedel, solche Liebe, man nimmt's so hin, und
weiß nicht den Wert – Es ist auch für L. gut gewesen, daß wir nach England
kamen, Geld und Menschen u.s.w. – Wenn seine Gesundheit reicht, bringt
er's noch weit, man merkt es – Einer, der wirklich aus sich heraus leistet,
ist merkwürdig selten – Soviel ist bagatelle – Unser Leben könnte so
erfreulich sein, wenn die Tragödie nicht wäre – Mrs Murry[1]

[Lawrence begins]
28 Percy Avenue, Kingsgate, Broadstairs – acht und zwanzig – not 38 as you
put. We are here till the 30th. then the Cearne. – Yes, we get all the letters
sent on.

[Dear Else,
    Ernst's 'decayed corpse' still lies in my bones! But there is something to
that – For him love is dead and unpleasantly dead – But it is incredible that
he can write to a mother like *that* – He'll calm down, though – I am still like
something that whizzes through 'Nothingness' – And the children! –
Mama's letter made me very happy – It did me good – Outwardly I'm
doing well – L[awrence], after being *thoroughly* miserable the days here,
is recovering – Much to-do is being made over him – Here we have become
friends with the Herbert Asquiths, he is the son of the Prime Minister; the
air is getting freer in the world, I too am a 'success' – God, it makes so little
difference to one, if at the same time one is glad to get away from oneself
a little, and luckily we Richthofens possess the gift of being able to lose
ourselves in others. When I compare L. with the others, I see that he
possesses his own, inner, independent activity; he is so much more than one
at first thinks – But now inwardly to tear myself loose from the children is

[1] The MS is incomplete.

horrible – the daily contact, it is as when living pieces of flesh are torn from one, luckily I think the children do not feel it *so* much. I think once E. is *divorced*, he will calm down more and more – Enjoy your children thoroughly, Friedel, such love, one accepts it so matter-of-factly, and doesn't realise the value – It has also been good for L. that we came to England, money and people etc – If his health holds out, he'll go far, one notices it – One who really achieves out of himself is remarkably rare – So much is a bagatelle – Our life could be so pleasant if it weren't for the tragedy – Mrs Murry]

618. To Henry Savage, [28 July 1913]
Text: MS UCLA; Unpublished.

28 Percy Avenue, Kingsgate, Broadstairs
Monday[1]

Dear Savage,

It is awfully good of you to offer us a room. I hope you'll always be so kind. But we are only in town for two nights – so are staying in Kensington. We go in tomorrow after lunch – have a dinner engagement in the evening – and are full up for Wednesday. But I think Mrs Lawrence goes away by the night train, to Germany, on Thursday. So we might see you that day. Write to me at c/o Mrs Murry, 8 Chaucer Mansions, Queens Club Gardens, W. Kensington – and say if we can see you. I shall bring back your books – or post them.[2] In hope of a meeting, greetings from us

D. H. Lawrence

619. To Edward Garnett, [28 July 1913]
Text: MS NYPL; Moore 216–17.

28 Percy Avenue, Kingsgate, Broadstairs
Monday[3]

Dear Garnett,

Thanks for the cheque and the letter.[4]

We are coming up to town on Tuesday, and shall stay with Gordon

---

[1] DHL visited London on 29 and 30 July; hence Monday would be 28 July 1913.
[2] See Letter 598.
[3] Dated with reference to DHL's visit to London.
[4] Garnett may have forwarded a letter from Mitchell Kennerley, dated 18 July 1913 (TMS NYPL), which reads in part: '...I have just finished reading *Sons and Lovers*, and think it is the biggest novel I have read in years. If Mr Lawrence can keep this up he will surpass all other modern novelists.'

Campbell[1] – an Irish barrister whom the Murrys brought down on Saturday –
a most delightful man, to my thinking.

Frieda is very sad because Mrs Murry went to St Pauls to see Monty,
and he sent word by another boy 'that he was not to talk to people who came
to the school to see him'. So she – Frieda – thinks they have brought all kinds
of pressure to bear, and have instilled all kinds of horror into the lad. God
knows. But Weekley is an unutterable fool. He wrote the most hideous letter
to the Frau Baronin[2] – is altogether acting the maniacal part of the 'mari
trompé'.

So Frieda wants to go to Germany straight from London, on Thursday.
God knows whether she will get off. I at any rate shall come to the Cearne
on Thursday – thanks very much for having me.

I think we dine with W L George at the Murrys on Tuesday (not certain
though) – and we lunch with Davies[3] at Edward Marshs on Wednesday.

We have had a good time down here (now and then). The Asquiths have
been awfully nice – so were Sir Walter Raleigh (Lady Raleigh invited us to
Oxford – I suppose we still look innocent) – and Lord Elco[4] (Mrs Asquiths
people). Frieda is quite set up at this contact with the aristocracy – of course
I am quite superior.

I am just sending off the last of my sketches – have no news.

I shall be glad to be at the Cearne, where I feel at home – the only place
where I do feel at home. Perhaps Frieda will come with me. I shall come
at any rate on Thursday. If she must go by the night train, I may be a bit
late. But if I can I shall come for lunch.

Thank Mrs Garnett for her letter – she's awfully good to us.

Auf wiedersehen   D. H. Lawrence

620. To Edward Marsh, [28 July 1913]
Text: MS NYPL; Huxley 130.

28 Percy Avenue, Kingsgate, Broadstairs
28 July

Dear Marsh,

Mrs Lawrence and I will come to Raymond Buildings[5] at 1·45 on
Wednesday. We are awfully keen to see you again, and to meet Davies.

---

[1] Charles Henry Gordon Campbell (1885–1963), later 2nd Baron Glenavy of Milltown. He
was educated at Charterhouse and at the Royal Military Academy. A barrister by profession,
he served in the Ministry of Munitions (1915–18). DHL stayed in Campbell's house at 9
Selwood Terrace, South Kensington, London S.W., when he and Frieda returned to England
in 1914 to be married.   [2] Frau Baronin] Frieda   [3] W. H. Davies.
[4] Cynthia Asquith's father, Hugo Charteris, Lord Elcho (1857–1937), later 11th Earl of
Wemyss.   [5] Marsh's residence in Gray's Inn.

It was nice of you to introduce us to the Asquiths – we have enjoyed so much talking to Mrs Asquith, during the week. We hear quite a lot about you from her.

Yours sincerely   D. H. Lawrence

621. To Douglas Clayton, [28 July 1913]
Text: MS NCL; Moore 216.

Kingsgate
Monday[1]

Dear Mr Clayton,

Thanks for your letter. I am glad you are more appreciative than your mother, who treats me so harshly.

I send you here another story, 'The Primrose Path'. If you don't like the title, try and think of something better, will you? I loathe finding titles. – The MS. is very shocking – but I hadn't an inch of paper when I began.

We leave here tomorrow – Tuesday – and are staying two nights in London. Then I think Mrs Lawrence is going straight to Germany, on Thursday, while I am going to the Cearne. But tell Mrs Clayton nothing is sure about Frieda till it is done, and then it's a dead cert. – But she wants to see her people before they go back to Baden-Baden.

I believe the stories will come filtering in, still one or two.

I may see you towards the week end. Hope the processing was great. I thought Mrs Clayton sounded a bit tired. Regards to her from us.

Yours   D. H. Lawrence

622. To The Editor of the *New Statesman*, 28 July 1913
Text: MS Lazarus; Unpublished.

c/o Edward Garnett, The Cearne, Nr *Edenbridge*, Kent
28 July 1913

The Editor of the *New Statesman*
10 Great Queen St., Kingsway W.C.

Dear Sir,

I offer you the enclosed sketch,[2] for the *New Statesman*.

Since *Sons and Lovers*, my last novel, has quite a considerable success, and the *New Statesman* was kindly disposed to it, I am in hopes that your generosity may wax to printing an occasional sketch of mine.

Yours faithfully   D. H. Lawrence

[1] A typed entry on the MS indicates that it was received on 29 July 1913.
[2] 'The Fly in the Ointment'.

623. To Ernest Collings, [28 July 1913]
Text: MS UT; Unpublished.

28 Percy Avenue, Kingsgate, Broadstairs
Monday[1]

Dear Collings,

I think the best time to see you would be Wednesday evening. Come to the Murry's for tea – at 8 Chaucer Mansions, Queens Club Gardens, West Kensington. You'll be there soon after 5.0, wont you? Then we can talk away.

The Murrys are Katherine Mansfield and J M Murry.

I am going away on Thursday.

Auf wiedersehen   D. H. Lawrence

624. To Harold Monro, 1 August 1913
Text: MS IEduc; Unpublished.

c/o Edward Garnett, The Cearne, Nr *Edenbridge*, Kent
1 Aug 1913

Dear Mr Monro,[2]

I have copied out three poems for you, choosing those which I thought you might find futuristic, though I don't know whether I have been successful.[3]

I shall be awfully glad for you to have the verses if you want them. But do you pay for contributions? Because I am woefully poor, and I might get a chance of selling the poems elsewhere.

Don't be offended by this – it is mere necessity.

Yours Sincerely   D. H. Lawrence

625. To Edward Marsh, 1 August 1913
Text: MS NYPL; Unpublished.

The Cearne, Nr *Edenbridge*, Kent
1 Aug 1913

Dear Marsh,

It was an awfully nice lunch we had in your flat. Mrs Lawrence and I liked it frightfully. I do hope if you're in Italy during the winter you'll come and see us. I shall occasionally drop you a letter, if it won't bore you.

[1] DHL's presence in London, on Wednesday, 30 July 1913, establishes Monday, 28 July 1913, as the date of this letter. In addition, the MS is endorsed: 'Answd. EC [Ernest Collings] 28/7/13'.

[2] Harold Edward Monro (1879–1932), poet; author of *Poems* (1906), *Children of Love* (1914), *Trees* (1916), etc. He was better known as the proprietor of the Poetry Bookshop and as the editor of *Poetry and Drama* (1913–14), which published the work of T. S. Eliot and Ezra Pound, among others.

[3] *Poetry and Drama*, ii (December 1914), 354–5, published DHL's poem 'Teasing' (later re-titled 'Tease' in *Amores*, 1916). For an early version see *Letters*, i. 246. The other two poems have not been identified.

I am staying with Edward Garnett a day or two. He is frightfully interested in your pictures. He is keen just now on a painter whose name is Nellie Heath – admires her work very much.[1] I think she does some awfully original things. Do you know her at all? – I think she has some reputation.

Commend me to Mrs Asquith and Mr Asquith, when you see them – also, if you please, to Miss Stanley.[2]

Be kindly disposed towards me, will you, and do tell people to buy my books.

Yours   D. H. Lawrence

I'm going to tea with W H Davies today.

626. To Walter de la Mare, 1 August 1913
Text: MS UN; Unpublished.

c/o Edward Garnett, The Cearne, Nr *Edenbridge*, Kent
1 Aug 1913

Dear de la Mare,

I shall be in England another week, and should very much like to see you before I leave. Do you still go to the café where I saw you last year? Could I find you one afternoon next week, Wednesday or Thursday. But don't let me be a nuisance.

I was delighted with some of the poems in your last book.[3]

Yours   D. H. Lawrence

627. To Else Jaffe, [2 August 1913]
Text: MS Jeffrey; PC v. Knole Garden, South View; Postmark, Nottingham AU 2 13; Unpublished.

[2 August 1913]

Now I am in the train going to Nottingham. Today is a great scuffle, so perhaps I can't write you a letter. But I'll tell you all the news from Eastwood. Garnett was awfully nice, but I don't like Mrs G. and I hated her cold

[1] Ellen Maurice Heath, painter, was the daughter of Richard Heath, engraver. The Heaths were neighbours of the Garnetts at the Cearne, and Nellie Heath was 'practically one of our family'; she studied painting in Paris, and was much influenced by Sickert (Garnett, *The Golden Echo*, pp. 48–9). Some of her landscape paintings and portraits are reproduced in her book *Thirty Paintings* with a foreword by Edward Garnett (1935), including portraits of Joseph Conrad, Edward and David Garnett.
[2] Hon. Beatrice Venetia Stanley (1887–1948), daughter of Edward Stanley, 4th Baron Sheffield, and a close friend of Cynthia Asquith. 1915 m. Rt Hon. Edwin Samuel Montagu, P.C., M.P. (1879–1924), who was Financial Secretary to the Treasury, 1914–16.
[3] *Peacock Pie: A Book of Rhymes* (June 1913).

blooded sister from Ceylon.[1] The Murry's remain fearfully nice. The *Westminster* [*Gazette*] has accepted the two sketches.[2] – I may go by boat from London to Rotterdam on Thursday – I shall write and tell you. It is all [relative?] like a sleep. I think it is good for me. I wonder how you are.

My Love   DHL

628. To Edward Garnett, [5 August 1913]

Text: MS NYPL; PC; Postmark, Eastwood AU 5 13; Unpublished.

Eastwood –
Tuesday

Dear Garnett,

I shall come to Downshire Hill tomorrow evening at about 8.0 oclock, – straight from Kings X. Have you remembered the play?[3]

DHL

629. To Katharine Clayton, [7 August 1913]

Text: MS NCL; Unpublished.

Hampstead N.W.
Thursday[4]

Dear Mrs Clayton,

I have been in such a whirl lately I hardly know where I am. Tonight I go to Germany

address: Irschenhausen, (Post) *Ebenhausen*, bei München.

I get there tomorrow night.

– The wedding went off all right at Eastwood.[5] But I do miss Frieda.

Many thanks for 'The Primrose Path', and the notes. Tell Douglas I think he is wrong in his bill. I have not paid for 'Daughters of the Vicar', nor had any bill for it, have I. But will he wait just a little longer, and send me a larger bill – to Germany – there are more short stories to come.

I enclose a bit of poetry for the magazines. Will Douglas print each poem

---

[1] Constance Garnett's younger sister Grace Black (b. 1863), m. Hugh Holman, an engineer who became head of a technical college in Ceylon.

[2] 'Strike-Pay I, Her Turn' and 'Strike-Pay II, Ephraim's Half Sovereign' (see p. 39 n. 1).

[3] *The Widowing of Mrs Holroyd* (see Letter 633). Mitchell Kennerley wrote to Edward Garnett on 6 March 1913 asking to see the play in MS and by this time would have returned it to Garnett. See *Letters*, i. 542 n. 2.

[4] DHL left for Germany on 7 August 1913.

[5] See p. 38 n. 4.

pretty well on a separate page – except those Rose poems, which are a set.[1] – And will he send the typed MS. to

Ezra Pound Esq, 10 Church Walk, *Kensington* W.

enclosing also this letter which I put in for Pound.[2]

It seems a shame I did not come to see you, but I am so worn out with whirling round, I shall not budge once I get to Germany.

Thanks to Douglas – my warm regards and thanks to you.

D. H. Lawrence

630. To Walter de la Mare, [7 August 1913]
Text: MS UN; PC; Postmark, Hampstead 7 AUG 13; Unpublished.

[Hampstead N.W.]
Thursday

Dear de la Mare,

I am awfully sorry I shan't see you. I go away to Germany tonight.

Do you happen to know anything of those two sketches on the Tirol which the *W[estminster] Gazette* did not print.[3] They say they have not got them – and certainly they never sent them back to me. I should be sorry to lose them: they were so jolly.

My address is Haŭs Jaffe, Irschenhausen, post *Ebenhausen*, bei München. Best wishes to you.

D. H. Lawrence

631. To William Hopkin, [9 August 1913]
Text: MS NCL; PC; Postmark, München 9 8. 13; Unpublished.

Haus Jaffe, Irschenhausen, (Post) *Ebenhausen*, bei München
[9 August 1913]

Well I am here and we are together again – for which I am thankful. It is pretty in the garden too, and such a big wide country. I think how Mrs Hopkin will like it when she comes. – You were *awfully* good to me, and I thank you from the bottom of my heart. Frieda thanks you too, and sends love with mine –   DHL

How is that young fellow, Enid Hopkin?[4]

---

[1] Three poems, entitled 'River Roses', 'Roses on the Breakfast Table', and 'Gloire de Dijon', were published in *Poetry*, iii (January 1914) under the single title, 'All of Roses'.

[2] DHL's letter to Pound has not been located.

[3] The 'jolly' sketches of the Tirol probably were 'A Hay Hut Among the Mountains' and 'A Chapel Among the Mountains'. See Letter 635.

[4] Enid Hilton, née Hopkin, recalls that she applied for a job in a bank: 'I was accepted and so became the first, and for about a year, the only woman employed in the Nottingham and Notts Bank, at the head office, in Nottingham.' (Letter to the Eds.) Hence the reference to 'that young fellow'.

632. To William Hopkin, 11 August 1913
Text: MS NCL; Huxley 130–1.

Irschenhausen, (Post) *Ebenhausen*, bei München
11 Aug 1913.

We are settled down again here now. Frieda is getting better of her trouble about the children, for the time being, at least. And I am glad we are together again. We think of staying here till the end of September, and of then going to Lerici, on the east coast of Italy, not far from Pisa. That would, I think, be ideal, if only we had the money and could get a place there.

It is lovely to be in Germany again, for the climate. Here everything looks so bright and sharply defined, after England. The mountains twenty miles away look much, much nearer than Crich Stand[1] at home. One can see fold after fold of the Alps, all varying with the changing light. It is very beautiful, and it makes me so much more cheerful after England, where everything is dim and woolly, and the sky hangs low against ones head.

We have had half a dozen children here today. They are wild young things, full of life. It is such fun to see them racing about the woods and the grass in their striped bathing suits. They do it for the freedom of it, and call it taking a 'Luft Bad' – an air bath. It is a very wild time we have with them.

Oh but I am glad to be again in this great wide landscape where one can breathe, and where one's head does not feel tightened in.

It will be lovely, if we go to Lerici, for Mrs Hopkin to come there. There will be the Mediterranean, and the mountains, and my beloved Italy. It would not be so very dear. I hope we shall have some luck, and can get there. We should be so delighted for you to come.

I have written today my first sketch – on Eastwood.[2] It interests me very much. I propose to do a bookful of sketches – publish them in the papers first. You, Willie Hopkin, must tell me all the things that happen, and sometimes send me a Rag.[3] And remember I am going to do an article on the Artists of Eastwood. I do the Primitive Methodist Chapel next.

It is Frieda's birthday today. Her little niece came crowned with flowers, her little nephews in white, carrying a basket of peaches, and of apricots, and sweets in boxes, and perfumes, and big bunches of flowers, and other presents, walking in procession up the path through the meadow. Frieda stood on the verandah, dressed in Bavarian peasants dress, and received

---

[1] An old tower which stands on a high cliff near the small Derbyshire village of Crich about sixteen miles from Eastwood.
[2] This sketch on Eastwood has been lost; the others on 'the Artists of Eastwood' and on 'the Primitive Methodist Chapel' may not have been written at all.
[3] The local newspaper, the *Eastwood and Kimberley Advertiser*, in which Hopkin wrote a weekly column. See *Letters*, i. 233.

them. Then Peter, aged seven, recited some birthday verses, and Friedel blew
on a mouth organ. I wanted to laugh, and to hide my head. We've had quite
a feast.

We both send our love to you. Again thank you for having me at
Devonshire Drive.¹ I kiss my hand to that haughty Enid.

Yours   D. H. Lawrence

633. To Edward Garnett, 13 August 1913
Text: MS NYPL; Huxley 132–3.

Irschenhausen, (Post) Ebenhausen, Oberbayern
13 Aug 1913.

Dear Garnett,

So we are settling down again, Frieda and I, and we are going to be very
happy again. I can't tell you how glad I am to be out of England again.
Everything seems so living: so quick. I rather love my countrymen. But isn't
it queer, I feel as if not once, all the time I was in England, had I really
wakened up. Everything seems to have been ravelled and dull and woolly – no
sharp contact with anything. But, by God, it is good to breathe again, out
here. So dark and woolly everything in England seems. You should see the
mountains go up and down across the sky, twenty miles away.

I have been very busy reading the play to Frieda. It wants *a lot* of altering.
I have made it heaps better. You must by no means let the MS. go to the
printer before I have it – neither here nor in America. What a jolly fine play
it is, too, when I have pulled it together. I shall be glad if you'll send me
the typed copy when you can, so I may alter it. Must I find another title?
The Widowing of Mrs Holroyd describes it, but doesn't sound very well.

The Northern Syndicate sent back the two stories as not being of the right
length. I think I shall give one to the *New Statesman*, and one Pinker can
have.² I don't know Pinker's address. The *Smart Set* has just sent me $36
for 'Kisses in the Train' and 'Violets' – good.³ Wright, the editor, has been
ill, and so some delay. I have just got proofs of Italian sketches from the
English [*Review*].⁴ I am working hard at clearing things up. I am working
very hard. As soon as possible I begin The Sisters. I am ready for it.

---

¹ William Hopkin's residence in Eastwood.
² The *New Statesman* published 'A Sick Collier' on 13 September 1913. Letter 635 suggests
that David Garnett rather than Pinker sent 'The Christening' to the *Smart Set* where it was
published in February 1914. (See also Letter 607 and n. 1.)
³ The two poems appeared in the *Smart Set* in September 1913.
⁴ The *English Review*, xv (September 1913), 202–34, published 'Italian Studies: By The Lago
di Garda' in three parts: 'I. The Spinner and the Monks', 'II. The Lemon Gardens of the
Signor Di P.', and 'III. The Theatre'.

We think of going to Lerici for the winter. It is on the Mediterranean just above Leghorn. Mrs Garnett will come and see us there – if we get there. Already I am thinking it will be glorious.

I wish you gave me your address when you go away. But you will write to me notwithstanding.

The *Westminster Gazette* say they sent to the Cearne, last year, two sketches of the Tirol, which Frieda loves so much, and which they could not use. I wonder if you can remember anything of them.

Let me hear from you. I feel so busy.

Viele herzliche Grüsse   D. H. Lawrence

634. To Douglas Clayton, 13 August 1913
Text: MS NCL; Unpublished.

Irschenhausen, Post *Ebenhausen*, Oberbayern
13 Aug 1913.

Dear Mr Clayton,

Many thanks for doing the poems.[1] I guess they looked nice. I enclose for you 28 Mark .50. A Mark is equivalent to a shilling, so I hope they won't pay you anything less than 28/–.

There will be more things to type later. I shall send them on.

We are happy to be in Bavaria again – it is so clear and beautiful. The Alps, twenty miles away, shine morning and evening, and the pine woods smell fresh. But it rains pretty often.

My wife sends love to Mrs Clayton – With regards from myself – and to you.

D. H. Lawrence

Don't bother with a formal receipt – a post-card is quite enough. The money comes separate – through foreign post.

635. To David Garnett, [13? August 1913]
Text: MS NYPL; Tedlock, ed., *Frieda Lawrence: The Memoirs and Correspondence*, pp. 198–9.

[Irschenhausen, (Post) Ebenhausen, bei München]
[13? August 1913][2]

[Frieda Weekley begins]

Dear Bunny,

A big bunch of 'Alpenrosen' I had given me reminded me of you and the microscope! Were you glad to get back to it? We will find flowers for

[1] See Letter 629.
[2] The contents of this letter suggest a date between 11 and 13 August 1913.

you. L[awrence] and I are friends at present and the Lord has been good
to me in letting me not be so miserable any more about the children. I *do*
enjoy things again – I am sorry you saw me so much steeped in misery and
I think you helped me over it a bit, I don't understand how, but you did – Yes,
you would enjoy being here so big everything seems, there is breathing space
and nothing to make one feel *not* oneself – What's the novel doing? I am
quite in love with my niece Anita, she is a beautiful big creature, something
so strong and fresh and simple about her – She is only 12, but seems quite
womanish – Edgar[1] is here, we see a great many more people than we used
to last year, it's rather jolly – Edgar sends his love, he has just brought me
a pair of gorgious sandals, I have just danced in them, knocked my heel and
ooh, it hurts still! And my sister gave me a new bavarian dress, gorgeous
bright colours – I *am* grand – I wanted to write a *nice* letter to you and now
it does'nt seem a very exciting one after all – I am glad you had a good time
camping – The Isar is *so* green, this place of Edgar's is so nice – good-bye
and good luck to you – write to me if the spirit moves you – Is Harold[2] cross
with us? He wanted to come to Margate then never wrote and never came – (L
asks whether I want to send this 'lot of stuff' as manuscript –

Love F –

[Lawrence begins]

Dear Bunny,

It seems an awful shame to make use of you like this. I shall send you
half a crown for stamps. You won't mind. After a day or two, everybody
will write direct here to me. – The two MS that the Northern Syndicate sent
back – will you send 'The Sick Collier' to the *New Statesman* – 10 Great
Queen St, Kingsway W.C. – and 'A Christening', to Ezra Pound – 10
Church Walk, Kensington, W.[3] I enclose a note for the *New Statesman*. –
Then the *Westminster Gazette* says that last year they sent back a couple of
sketches of Frieda and me in the Tirol,[4] to the Cearne. I have seen nothing
of them. I wonder if they are at the Cearne, and if you could send them to
me. They are two short sketches – rather good. Frieda is frightfully keen on
them, and desolated for fear they are lost.

I am working like a nigger here. Lord, but I mean to get some work done,
this autumn. It is a pity you can't come here. You could have had a bed – and
it is *so* jolly. We think of staying till the end of Sept., then going to Italy,
on the coast above Leghorn. I hope it comes off and is a success. What a

[1] Edgar Jaffe.   [2] Harold Hobson.
[3] Pound...W.] Pinker, the agent – I don't know his address.
[4] See Letter 630 and n. 3.

lovely place for your mother to come and see us. Where we next go, I want
to get a more or less permanent abode.

Tell Constanza Davidovna I am sorry she is so pestered by my letters
continually arriving. Soon they will stop.

Send the note to your father.[1]

Love   D. H. Lawrence

636. To Edward Marsh, 18 [–20] August 1913

Text: MS NYPL; Postmark, Ebenhau[sen] 21 AUG 13; Huxley 135.

Irschenhausen, Post *Ebenhausen*, Oberbayern
18 Aug 1913

Dear Marsh,

I was glad to get your letter. Here it does nothing but rain. It is enough
to make one's verse as sloppy as Lamartine.[2]

– I think you will find my verse smoother – not because I consciously
attend to rhythms, but because I am no longer so criss-crossy in myself. I
think, don't you know, that my rhythms fit my mood pretty well, in the
verse. And if the mood is out of joint, the rhythm often is. I have always
tried to get an emotion out in its own course, without altering it. It needs
the finest instinct imaginable, much finer than the skill of the craftsmen. That
Japanese Yone Noguchi tried it.[3] He doesn't quite bring it off. Often I
don't – sometimes I do. Sometimes Whitman is perfect. Remember skilled
verse is dead in fifty years – I am thinking of your admiration of Flecker.[4]

Thanks very much for saying nice things about *Sons and Lovers*. I am
sure you'll help.

I want Davies to come out to Germany for a while, if we can manage it.
We move to Italy in about a month's time. My wife wants to go with her
people to Baden-Baden – then we're off. I shall be glad – it rains so much here.

Do you mind posting this letter to Mrs Asquith.[5] For the second time
I have lost her address. I don't know if one does write The Honorable. If
not, put it in another envelope, will you. – And tell me.

My wife sends greetings.

Yours   D. H. Lawrence

[1] This note has not been found.
[2] Alphonse-Marie-Louis de Prat de Lamartine (1790–1869), French Romantic poet.
[3] Yone Noguchi (1875–1947), Japanese poet. A two-volume collection of his poems called *The Pilgrimage*, written in English, was published in 1909. Cf. p. 27 n. 5.
[4] Marsh had included two poems by James Elroy Flecker (1884–1915) in *Georgian Poetry 1911–1912*. Flecker had published *Forty-Two Poems* (1911), *The Golden Journey to Samarkand* (1913), etc.
[5] For some reason this letter was left unfinished until DHL wrote to Cynthia Asquith two days later, on 20 August (the letter following); this final paragraph to Marsh was then added and the two letters posted together on 21 August.

637. To Cynthia Asquith, [20 August 1913]
Text: MS UT; Huxley 133–4.

Irschenhaŭsen, Post *Ebenhaŭsen*, Oberbayern
Wednesday Aug. 17th or thereabouts[1]

Dear Mrs Asquith,

Suddenly we've got a fit of talking about you and your skirt with holes in and your opal brooch. And again we are in the little cove by the sea – and it's absolutely heart-breaking to hear us singing the duet 'What are the wild waves saying'.[2] I think I'm the living spit and image of Paul Dombey grown up, and Frieda – well, the less said about her the better.

You were awfully nice to us at Kingsgate. But that your Marylands[3] was such a joy, I might have found myself hurrying over the edge of the cliff in my haste to get away from that half-crystallised nowhere of a place – Kingsgate. Kingsgate – oh God! The last was a pathetic little bill for one and fourpence, the dregs and lees of our housekeeping down there: I believe it was the baker. But it dogged our footsteps, and ran us down here. So I made a little boat of it, and set it afloat. 'Cast thy bread upon the waters',[4] I cried to the baker, 'and send thy bills out after[5] it'. Far down the dancing Danube, and over Hungaria's restless plains, my baker's bill on its bobbing course goes seeking the golden grains. – Ask Mr Marsh if *that* isn't perfect Flecker-rhythm. *The Golden Journey to Samarkand.* You knew it climbed Parnassus *en route?* I shall write a book called 'The Poet's Geographer' one day. – By the way, Mr Marsh will hold[6] it as a personal favour if I will take more care of my rhythms. Poor things, they go cackling round like a poultry farm. – But he told it me – I mean Eddie-dear – in a letter. He thinks I'm too Rag-Time: not that he says so. But if you'll believe me, that 'Golden Journey to Samarkand' only took place on paper – no matter who went to Asia Minor.

I hope you don't mind if my letter is rather incoherent. We live in a little

---

[1] As suggested in the previous note, it is clear that this letter was sent to Cynthia Asquith via Marsh. DHL also refers in this letter (as he does in Letter 638) to the market at Wolfratshausen which must have taken place on Sunday, 17 August. It is therefore assumed that DHL was accurate about the day, Wednesday (20 August), rather than about the date.
[2] The title of a song by Joseph Edwards Carpenter (1813–85), which begins as follows:

> What are the wild waves saying
> Sister, the whole day long,
> That ever amid our playing,
> I hear but their low, lone song?

The song was composed in response to Paul Dombey's experiences in Dickens' *Dombey and Son* (1846–8); see chaps. viii, xvi.
[3] The house in Kingsgate, where the Asquiths stayed when DHL first met them.
[4] Ecclesiastes xi. 1.   [5] out after] to follow   [6] hold] take

wooden house (but genuine Dürer engravings[1] and Persian rugs) in a corner of a pine forest. But it rains–oh Lord!–the rain positively stands up on end. Sometimes one sees the deer jumping up and down to get the wet out of their jackets, and the squirrels simply hang out by their tails, like washing. I take one morning run around the house in my bathing suit in lieu of a shower bath.

It's Frieda's brother-in-law's house. He's staying here now and then. He's a professor of political economy, among other things. Outside the rain continues. We sit by lamplight and drink beer, and hear Edgar on Modern Capitalism. *Why* was I born? It was Markt in Wolfratshausen on Sunday. But there was nothing to buy but Regenschirme and Hosenträger and Lebkuchen.[2] I wanted to buy a Herzkuchen[3] with 'Frieda' on, but there was such a mob of young gents eagerly sorting them out – one wanted Tauben mit Emilie[4] and another Vergissmeinnicht und Creszenz,[5] that I never got a look in. I am born to be elbowed out.

We are not going to Italy for a month or so. Then we think of Lerici, somewhere near Leghorn – Shelley and Byron tradition.[6] It might be good for my rhythms.

We had an awfully jolly lunch at Marsh's. Dont tell him what I say about the 'personal favour'. He is simply sweet as Maecenas[7] (how *do* you spell it?) – sweet is the only word. I liked it ever so much.

How are you and where are you? Would you like any German books – you can have some from here if you would. – That was simply the best melon I've ever tasted, the one you gave us. German books reminded me of it.[8]

How is the fat and smiling John? May I be remembered to Mr Asquith.[9] My respects to the gallant Sir Walter and his lady,[10] if ever you see them, – and to Miss Stanley and to Miss Asquith.[11]

> Viele Grüsse   D. H. Lawrence

Are you Honorable or aren't you? How does one address your letter.

[1] Albrecht Dürer (1471–1528). German painter, designer of woodcuts and engraver.

[2] 'umbrellas and braces and gingerbread'.

[3] 'heart-shaped gingerbread'. (Frieda's birthday was on 11 August.)

[4] 'doves with "Emilie"'.   [5] 'forget-me-nots and "Creszenz"'.

[6] Byron and Shelley both lived in Italy at various times. At the time of his drowning, Shelley's residence was the Casa Magni near the tiny hamlet of San Terenzo on the Gulf of Spezia, not far from Fiascherino where DHL moved in October 1913.

[7] Maecenas] Meca, Masc, Mecaenas, Macaenas. Gaius Cilnius Maecenas (c. 70–8 B.C.), Roman statesman and patron of letters. He was a trusted friend and counsellor to Emperor Augustus, a benefactor of Virgil and Horace. The allusion to Maecenas is appropriate in view of Marsh's role as a patron of the arts.   [8] it] melons.

[9] Cynthia Asquith's son John (1911–37) and husband.   [10] See p. 48 n. 2.

[11] Either Elizabeth Asquith (1897–1945) who, in 1919, m. Prince Antoine Bibesco (1878–1951), or Violet Asquith (1887–1969) who, in 1915, m. Sir Maurice Bonham Carter (1880–1960), private secretary to the Prime Minister, 1910–16.

[Frieda Weekley begins]

Dear Mrs Asquith,

Yes, you were kind to us at Margate, we just talked of the teas at your house and the cinematographic procession of people – L[awrence] has written so much and most frivolous and unrespectful, no 'nice' young man in early Victorian times would have written like that to a 'patroness'. But there 'times have changed', I wonder if they are expected to sit down with folded hands, poor times – Are you doing much? How's the quilt? Kind regards to the Manly John and Mr Asquith and you –

Yours sincerely   Frieda Lawrence

638. To Douglas Clayton, [21 August 1913]
Text: MS NCL; Unpublished.

Irschenhausen, Post *Ebenhausen*, Oberbayern

Thursday[1]

Dear Clayton,

I'm glad you got the money all right. Here it is always raining. I want to go to Italy – it is *too* wet.

On Sunday it was Market in Wolfratshausen. All the peasant people were in. They do look queer folk.

I send you another story.[2] I want it to go to Pinker, the agent. But I don't know his address. Mr Garnett does. Perhaps he'd give the thing in. – Tell me if you like this story.

I am busy now. One of the sketches was printed in the *New Statesman* last Saturday.[3] Did you see it.

How is Mrs Clayton – still rejoicing in frocks and shoes. I hope you are keeping well. My wife send regards to Mrs Clayton. – Don't hurry with the story if you're busy.

Yours   D. H. Lawrence

By the way, *did* you get the money. Frieda says there was a post card from you. I never saw it, and she doesn't know what was on it. Still, that's what you would send a p.c. to say –

DHL

639. To Arthur McLeod, [21 August 1913]
Text: MS UT; PC v. München, Karlstor; Postmark, Ebenha[usen] 21 AUG 13; Unpublished.

Irschenhausen, (Post) *Ebenhausen*, Oberbayern.

[21 August 1913]

[1] '21 Aug 1913' is written here in another hand; it is also typed on the back of the MS.
[2] Most likely 'The White Stocking'.
[3] 'The Fly in the Ointment', *New Statesman*, 13 August 1913.

Dear Mac,

You see we are back again. I was frightfully disappointed not to meet you again – so was F[rieda] – By the way, did you see my sketch in the *New Statesman* of last week – the 16th. You'll remember it. – Write to us, will you. We are here for about a month longer. I was not sorry to leave England, but am anxious to go back to Italy.

Regards from F. and me.

D. H. Lawrence

640. To Edward Garnett, 24 August 1913

Text: MS NYPL; Postmark, Ebenhausen [...]; Huxley 136–7.

Irschenhausen, Post *Ebenhausen*, Oberbayern
24 Aug 1913

Dear Garnett,

I was glad to hear from you again – your Wales sounds all right for you – but I know and hate its black rock and its atmosphere of slate and gloom.[1] Give me Bavarian highlands when the sun shines, and the pine woods are dark, with glittering flakes, and suddenly the naked, red-skinned[2] limb of a pine tree throws itself into the heat, out of the shadow, and deer go trotting through the sun-dapplings: where in the upland meadows, the autumn crocuses stand slim, a great many each standing single, in the intense green of the cut grass, lovely slender mauve-pink things, balancing their gold in the centre, while a butterfly[3] comes and goes: where the chicory bushes glimmer so blue, they seem to tremble with sources of[4] light beside the pond, as[5] the white ducks go in a row: and where far off, the golden coloured mountain tops look out of heaven, over the shoulders of the dim-radiant ranges in front. So!

I send the revised MS of the play to Duckworth.[6] It is pretty much altered, and much improved. If Kennerley has printed, I must have the MS back to correct proofs by.

Douglas Clayton will also send you another story directly. – I don't know what new MS. you were expecting from me.

I enclose the letter from the Northern Syndicate. I think they might take 'Two Marriages' – now called 'Daughters of the Vicar' – which they might

[1] Garnett was staying at Dinas Cross, Pembrokeshire.
[2] red-skinned] bruised
[3] butterfly] moth
[4] tremble with sources of] give off
[5] as] where
[6] *The Widowing of Mrs Holroyd.* (Mitchell Kennerley published the play on 1 April 1914.)

easily split up to a three-part serial.[1] Is it at Pinker? Could you get it from him and send it at once – or let him send it for me – but *privately*? – I reckon *you* ought to take the 10% commission, not him.

Harrison, I am thankful to say, is giving me £25 for 3 Italian sketches, in the Sept. *English*.[2]

We are here for another month. I hope the Tirol articles aren't lost – they are beloved of Frieda. When you have seen Pinker, give me his address so I can write him direct and save you bother.

We are going in 3 weeks I think, to Italy. The Sisters is the devil – I've made two false starts already – but it'll go –

Yrs   D. H. Lawrence

Regards from Frieda, who has bucked up.

641. To Austin Harrison, 25 August 1913
Text: MS Harrison; Moore 221–2.

Irschenhausen, (Post) *Ebenhausen*, Oberbayern
25 Aug 1913.

Dear Harrison,

Yes, you are very bountiful to print thirty four pages of me at a bang – and the twenty-five pounds will be as welcome as sunshine. That's a good soldier story too – I'm glad it'll come in the *English*.[3]

My poetry! – well, I don't write much long stuff, and you say you don't like short things. But that 'Ballad of a Wayward Woman' was good.[4] I don't believe you ever read it – sent it back without looking at it, because you felt I was coming on like the Deluge. I shall send you one more long poem, – not just yet.

It is jolly nice to be out here again – München ist so frei und lebendig[5] – out here it is so fine. We had a party in the pine wood last night – Abendessen[6] by candle-light, with the big tree-trunks standing round half present, half gone. The Herbst Zeitlosen[7] are out in all the cut grass. Do you know those exquisite autumn crocuses?

---

[1] The story was never serialised; it was first published in its entirety in *The Prussian Officer and Other Stories* (Duckworth, 1914).   [2] See p. 58 n. 4.
[3] 'Vin Ordinaire'. It is presumed that whereas Garnett had asked Pinker to place 'Honour and Arms' (see p. 6), he had himself handled 'Vin Ordinaire' and sent it direct to the *English Review*.
[4] Retitled 'Ballad of a Wilful Woman', the poem was not published until its inclusion in *Look! We Have Come Through!* (1917). (It exists under the original title in MS in NYPL.)
[5] 'Munich is so easy-going and lively'.
[6] 'supper' or 'dinner'.   [7] 'meadow saffron'.

I suppose you got the proofs of the Italian sketches. I believe the maid posted them.

Remembrances to Mr Douglas.

Viele Grüsse   D. H. Lawrence

642. To Edward Garnett, 4 September 1913
Text: MS NYPL; cited in Heilbrun, *The Garnett Family*, p. 157.

Irschenhausen, (Post) Ebenhausen, Oberbayern
4 Sept 1913

Dear Garnett,

Your letter made me very sad. It was mean of that *Daily Mail* crew. But do you think they might get the column through on the strength of the play, when it comes. That is of the same industrial interest, and they might easily work it up with *Sons and Lovers*.[1]

Will Kennerley send me proofs, by the way? I hope so. But I have heard nothing yet. You will ask Pinker to send the 'Daughters of[2] the Vicar' to those Northern Syndicate people – who will refuse it. As for that other Soldier Story[3] – or the 'Primrose Path' – might not the *Forum* take one. Wright – of the *Smart Set* – found the stories I sent him too hot[4] – they were pretty much so – but would consider something else. He might have one – say 'Primrose Path'. Ezra Pound is his English agent: 10 Church Walk, Kensington.

Frieda abused my articles in *The English* [*Review*] but I think they are all right for magazine stuff.

I am sorry *Sons and Lovers* has gone down so – God grant it may pick up – though that is not what things usually do. The *Westminster* [*Gazette*] is publishing some more of my sketches.[5] I will do what you say, and leave short stories for a while.

I shall not be able to settle down here to work, I know. We move on the 23rd of this month. Frieda is going to Baden Baden shortly. Her people are very friendly again. I should like to walk down to Italy, across Switzerland, but am not sure it is possible.

The Sisters has quite a new beginning – a new basis altogether. I hope

---

[1] Though 'the play' was *The Widowing of Mrs Holroyd* (also referred to in the first sentence of the next paragraph), DHL's general point is obscure.
[2] MS reads '&'.   [3] 'Vin Ordinaire'.
[4] One of these stories was 'Once' (see p. 82).
[5] A reference to 'Strike-Pay I, Her Turn' and 'Strike-Pay II, Ephraim's Sovereign' published in the issues for 6 and 13 September, respectively.

I can get on with it. It is much more interesting in its new form – not so damned flippant. I can feel myself getting ready for my autumn burst of work.

We have been afflicted with many visitors and so on – It is beautiful here, but one feels transitory.

Excuse the pencil. Frieda sends love.

Are you all right – By the way, Marsh said he'd like to see you and talk about Miss Heaths pictures.[1] Perhaps you'd better drop him a line.[2] His address is Edward Marsh Esq, Admiralty Whitehall. I've lost the address in Gray's Inn. He is going away on the 14th to Spain. He is nice. I should say you could get him to buy. I must write him too.

auf wiedersehen   D. H. Lawrence

643. To Ernest Collings, 4 September 1913
Text: MS UT; Huxley 137–8.

Irschenhausen, (Post) *Ebenhausen*, Oberbayern

4 Sept 1913

Dear Collings,

I was awfully pleased to get the little book, and your letter, and sketches for Elegies.[3] The latter book – of mine – is not likely to come yet, because the *Love Poems* were not a success. However in God's good time. – I am glad also to hear of you in Monro's magazine.[4] He asked me for some things, but I want paying, and I don't think he likes the idea. Or perhaps he just didn't like what I sent him. At any rate, you've got a pull of me this time. I must ask somebody to send me a copy of the *Poetry and Drama*, that has you in.

I don't like the Boucher cover design nearly as much as your other work.[5] It does not seem beautiful. It is interesting, the blanking out of the face. It achieves the high-light effect, which attracts attention straight away. But I

[1] Nellie Heath (cf. p. 54 n. 1).

[2] Edward Garnett appears to have acted at once on DHL's suggestion. In an undated letter (MS NYPL) to Marsh – written probably c. 6 September 1913 – Garnett paraphrases DHL's remarks and adds: 'I should be delighted to make your acquaintance.'

[3] In February 1913 DHL had recorded his admiration for Collings' cover design for *Poems to Pavlova* by A. Tulloch Cull. He added casually, perhaps even jocularly: 'My next book of poems will be a book of Elegies...If ever I bring it out, will you help me to design a cover?' (*Letters*, i. 519). Collings had taken the remark seriously and produced some sketches.

[4] The third number of *Poetry and Drama*, September 1913, pp. 309–11, included three poems by Collings under the general title 'Love Poems': 'Prelude', 'Adventure' and 'The Return of Love'. DHL had seen the last two in MS; for his comments see *Letters*, i. 472.

[5] Though the cover design does not wholly conform with DHL's remarks, perhaps the book in question was Catherine Mary Bearne's *A Court Painter and his Circle. François Boucher, 1703–1770*, published in September 1913. If so, then the design merits DHL's hesitant reaction.

don't like this cover very much. It does not seem beautiful[1] to me, though it is interesting. Have you read the text of the book? It is a joy.

We were awfully pleased with your drawings when we saw them. I am sure, too, this is your time for colour. You have got it in your blood. One could feel it when you were there. You are more interested in it at present than in line, I think. That is because it is more passionate, voluptuous, I suppose – and this is your hour.

As for Monro and his feminine signature, I think he is a bit of a fool.

I was in Munich the other day, at a great Exhibition of pictures and sculpture – German Spanish Italian Russian Swedish and so on.[2] I wish you could go. Some time you must come to Munich, it is such a town of pictures. The Russians interested me very much – there is more life in their things. The Germans are vigorous, and brutal, and get[3] simply amazing technical effects, but the real feeling is not there. The French are thin. Very interesting people are the Swedes – and I love that mellow colouring of Spanish pictures – dark and mellow like golden plums in the shade.

We are thinking of moving, about the 22nd of this month, down to Italy – I don't know exactly whither. So far I am restless, waiting to go. There I shall settle down to work again. This country is beautiful – far off, the high, cool, blue mountains, with a luminous air between, and dark pinewoods. That is not your style, really: too cool. You like hotter colours. You ought to go to Italy in *Autumn* – end of October. That is your time, when the dark-crimson fig-trees hang like blood on the grey rocks, and vines simply flare their yellow under a scabious blue sky.

I am having a play published directly. If I can I will send you a copy. It is pretty good, I think.

Have a good time in Cornwall. Write us again when anything is doing.

Yours   D. H. Lawrence

My wife sends her regards and best wishes for your holiday.

644. To Henry Savage, 4 September 1913

Text: MS Martin; Unpublished.

Irschenhausen, (Post) Ebenhausen, Oberbayern

4 Sept 1913

Dear Savage,

Your letter was huge. It amused us for God knows how long. But don't

---

[1] beautiful] interesting.

[2] The 'great Exhibition' occupied over fifty rooms in Munich's Glaspalast, 1 June – 31 October 1913. In addition to the countries named by DHL, Belgium, Denmark, France, Norway, Romania and Turkey exhibited works of art.   [3] get] have

get such a damned low opinion of me. I don't care about form, in a letter.
I just like people to give me a real bust of themselves. As for poetry, people
are always rapping my knuckles for my faults and transgressions. You should
hear 'em.

I don't think *Sjanin*[1] is very good – but very interesting. It has got too
much 'Tendenz'[2] – is a bit too much of an illustrated idea of how one should
behave – exactly like the novels to promulgate virtue. If it weren't that it
is bossed so much by the idea, it might be better, but it would probably fall
to pieces.

Have you got anything else interesting to read? I don't mean a great fat
parcel of books – rather a fourpence-ha'penny thing I needn't send back.
German is such a heavy language.

Did you see my Italian Sketches in this month's *English Review*? They
might amuse you, but more probably wouldn't.

By the way, what about your wife. Is she all right? You might have the
decency to mention her.

This is a beautiful place, but you set my heart hankering after Dymchurch.[3]
Sometimes that old English atmosphere appeals to me till I could weep for
it. Here we sleep on the balcony, and hear the deer crying in the woods, and
look out at the long ranges of mountains stretching under the dawn, which
comes up green like wine. The woods – mostly pine, go for miles and miles,
away at the back of the house. One can go and feed oneself on wild
raspberries.

At present I am unsettled. We are moving to Italy in about three weeks
time – the 23rd I believe – so I feel impatient now to be *en route*. God knows
what sort of place we shall find down there in the south. But if we have any
luck, I hope you'll come and see us. I should love to set off now on foot,
and walk right across the Alps, to Milan. But Frieda won't be left behind,
and we are short of money, and walking is not very cheap. Also she must
go first to see her people in Baden-Baden. So that here I remain, chewing
my impatience, and getting no milk from it.

But the place is really beautiful. The heather is in bloom in the open
places between the pines, and a beautiful purple gentian in the cool places,
while all the meadows are full of autumn crocuses: mauve-pink things, very
exquisite. I ought not to grumble. And I don't, really.

Are you any more cheerful? We have been having bad times with one
another. You know, my whole working philosophy is that the only stable

---

[1] See p. 33 n. 2.   [2] i.e. bias or propagandist inclination.
[3] There are two English villages with this name: one on the Kent coast; the other in
Warwickshire.

happiness for mankind is that it shall live married in blessed union to woman-kind – intimacy, physical and psychical[1] between a man and his wife. I wish to add that my state of bliss is by no means perfect.

I shall leave this space for Frieda to fill.

Une bonne poignée   D. H. Lawrence

[Frieda Weekley begins]

You are a difficult person to unravel, I think, but awfully interesting – It is queer to see L[awrence] and you not understanding each other a bit – Of all people in the world L. is the last to ask for form – Only in your poetry he thought that the form of rythm and words did not always express the inner form that is the meaning – You are really a moralist, you are seeking a form of life instead of living off your own bat and looking and waiting what the Lord will do – Its not safe like that – but one must swim without the lifebuoy – One has got one's 'form' inside one just as a pinetree has, it does not suddenly grow into an apple tree – But there I am what L calls 'chuffing'. Dont wait for outside things to happen, you have got it *inside* you, the life and the good things – We liked the idea of your wife and the infant – Good-bye write us another letter soon – I could'nt *quite* make out, what you are after –

Yours with much good luck.

Frieda L –

645. To Mitchell Kennerley, 8 September 1913
Text: MS VC; Huxley 138–9.

Irschenhausen, Post *Ebenhausen*, Oberbayern
8 Sept 1913.

Dear Mr Kennerley,

I am very sorry to have caused trouble by coming in so late with my revision of the play *The Widowing of Mrs. Holroyd*. The MS. had lain with Mr Garnett for nearly two years: he had had it typed, and I had seen nothing of it till I asked for it a week or two back. Then I saw how it needed altering – refining. Particularly I hated it in the last act, where the man and woman wrangled rather shallowly across the dead body of the husband. And it seemed nasty that they should make love where he lay drunk. I hope to heaven I have come in in time to have it made decent. The MS. forwarded you by Mr Duckworth, revised by me, looks rather messy, but I am sure is perfectly easy for a printer to decipher – He can correct from that copy. There is not, after all, such a great amount of alteration.

---

[1] psychical] physical

I wish I could have the proofs here. But if it is very late for you, your own proof-reader might do the corrections, because I went over that MS. very carefully.[1]

The two stories which Mr Wright returned did not come to me, but went to London.[2] If you would care to see them, I will have them sent on. I am very glad that you are so friendlily disposed to my work, and grateful also. A good deal of my hope rests on you.

Yours Sincerely   D. H. Lawrence

P.S. I don't know what you think of the title – *The Widowing of Mrs. Holroyd*. Garnett said it wasn't good. I suggested 'Afterdamp' on the last MS., but am by no means keen on it. It would do exceedingly well, in idea, but I don't like the word. I wish it were the German: 'Schlagender Wetter'.

646. To William Hopkin, [c. 15 September 1913]
Text: MS NCL; Unpublished.

[Irschenhausen, Post Ebenhausen, Oberbayern]
[c. 15 September 1913][3]

We're moving to Switzerland on Tuesday – I'll send address.[4]

647. To Henry Savage, [15 September 1913]
Text: MS YU; Moore, *Yale University Library Gazette*, xxxiv, 28–9.

Irschenhausen, Post Ebenhausen, Oberbayern
Monday.[5]

Dear Savage,

Thanks for bothering about me. I was pretty ill two years[6] ago – six months before I met Frieda – with pneumonia – which was the third time I'd had it. So that my lungs are crocky, but I'm not consumptive – the type, as they say. I am not really afraid of consumption, I don't know why – I

---

[1] Probably referring to this letter, Mitchell Kennerley wrote to Edward Garnett on 22 September 1913 (TMS NYPL): 'I have just received a letter from Mr. Lawrence from Germany explaining all about *The Widowing of Mrs. Holroyd*. I am now making all the changes and corrections he desires, and shall shortly send to him a revised proof. Of course this will delay the publication of the book, but this hardly matters, as a play can only sell a few copies at most.'   [2] See p. 67 n. 4.

[3] Apparently Frieda was to accompany DHL to Switzerland, but in Letters 647 and 648 the plans have changed, and DHL is to go there by himself, while Frieda goes to Baden-Baden.

[4] This brief note is written on the title page of a copy of Swinburne's *Atalanta in Calydon and Lyrical Poems*, Selected, With an Introduction, By William Sharp (Leipzig: Bernhard Tauchnitz, 1901). The volume is inscribed: 'W. E. Hopkin from D. H. Lawrence'.

[5] The letter appears to have been written on the Monday following DHL's birthday, 11 September 1913.   [6] two years] two and a half years

don't think I shall ever die of *that*. For one thing, I am quite certain that when I have been ill, it has been sheer distress and nerve strain which have let go on my lungs. I am one of those fools who take my living damnably hard. And I have a good old English habit of shutting my rages of trouble well inside my belly, so that they play havoc with my innards. If we had any sense we should lift our hands to heaven and shriek, and tear our hair and our garments, when things hurt like mad. Instead of which, we behave with decent restraint, and smile, and crock our lungs. – Not that I've anything so tremendous and tragic in my life, any more than anybody else. Only I am so damnably violent, really, and self destructive. One sits so tight on the crater of one's passions and emotions. I am just learning – thanks to Frieda – to let go a bit. It is this sitting tight, and this inability to let go, which is killing the modern England, I think. But soon you will see a bust, I believe.

I am glad 'Barber's Bun' is going.[1] Are you satisfied with it? I hope you'll grip Harrison really hard. I should like to see it published. With a bit of luck, it might go. – I wonder rather at your being anxious to show Raynes Park 'that you can do it'.[2] I suppose I'm so damned conceited in my belief in myself – it doesn't seem to be myself, really – I think 'here you are, I tell you the truth' – that I don't care whether I impress my neighbours or not – not much. It is a queer little ambition of yours. You are a man I can't understand as Frieda tells me. If I had been putting you in a novel, I should have made you not care a damn about Raynes Park. I suppose you are, as Frieda says, a moralist – in the bad sense of the word (I say). And a moralist is always a moral for other people, and not for himself. – And you would be a moral for Raynes Park. Then by reflex a moral for yourself. But what does it matter. – You see I'm quarrelling with you. I can't understand you. Why don't you hate Raynes Park and say to it 'Go to Hell' – no, you write it a 'Barber's Bun' and say 'Ecco'! Can you tell me, what it is on the face of earth that[3] is of supreme importance to you – and what in the name of heaven: I can't get the clue to you.

I never thought before I was patriarchal. That amuses me. I dont quite know what it means. Do you know, – another curious thing – I find your language hard to understand. We are rather foreign one to the other. I begin to feel I don't adapt myself very well to the terms of life. I feel a bit queer

[1] Harry T. Moore has suggested that this may be a reference to Savage's 'Tale in Rhyme', which appeared in the *Academy* (1915) as 'Carber's Cruise' (Moore 227). See also Letters 678, 730.
[2] Savage's address was 45 Lambton Rd, Raynes Park, Wimbledon, London, S.W.
[3] that] and

and foreign – as if I couldn't speak any language particularly – and I seem
to stutter with my mouth full. I feel a bit smock-ravelled – don't know where
the east is, nor the north and west.

Thanks for the books. I have been reading Wells.[1] I am fond of him – I
am not deeply moved by him – I don't think he means much. He is really
a writer of books of manners. He seizes the typical manners of a class. His
folk have no personality – no passion. The feeling in the book wanders
loose – like a sauce poured over it – Sehnsucht und Wehmut.[2] The people
are smothered in this sauce like shrimps in a mayonnaise – they arent much.
But still I like the sensation – warm, small, human longing for something,
an infant crying in the night, which one gets from Wells. He is like Dickens.
Not one of his characters has got a real *being* – Wesen[3] – *is* a real being –
something never localised into a passionate individuality.

I am a rotten critic, however. Many thanks for the books. They came on
my birthday, and I was quite set up.

On Thursday, Frieda is going to see the Frau Baronin, her mother, in
Baden Baden – and I am going to Constance – then walking down to
Basel – where we meet, on our way to Italy. Don't write, or don't post, till
you get an address from us.

Don't mind me – don't ever be hurt by anything I say – I don't use
language very well, in private. – Commend me to the gnädige Frau[4] – your
wife. I'm half inclined to think she's got more sense than you.

I am alone today. Frieda is in Wolfratshausen, the rest in Munich. I lie
and write in the wood – just squirrels and sunshine on the moss, and a
shadow of a bird, crossing, and sometimes a brown leaf falling on the paper.

Come and see us when we are settled in Italy.

Addio   D. H. Lawrence

648. To Edward Garnett, [15 September 1913]
Text: MS NYPL; Huxley 139–40.

Irschenhausen, (Post) *Ebenhausen*, Oberbayern
Monday[5]

Dear Garnett,

I enclose a letter from Pound.[6] You will advise me.

The Sisters is going well. I've done a hundred pages. I wonder what you'll
think of it. It is queer. It is rather fine, I think. I am in it now, deep.

---

[1] It is impossible to identify which book by H. G. Wells is in question: if it were Wells'latest
     novel, then DHL had read *The Passionate Friends*, published in September 1913.
[2] 'desire and melancholy'.   [3] 'essence or entity'.   [4] 'gracious madam'.
[5] Dated with reference to DHL's birthday.
[6] There is an undated letter (TMS NYPL) which is likely to be the one in question here. With

We are going away on Wednesday – Frieda to Baden Baden for some days.[1] I am walking a week in Switzerland – meeting her in Basel – then we go to Italy. Don't write to me till you get an address. I shall take the Sisters in a Rucksack.[2]

I shan't do anything but the Sisters now. I hope to have it done in a month. I *do* wonder what you will think of it.

We are glad you'll come to Italy to see us. Frieda says you're the only person who understands me at all. But she is a bit cross with you, because you are cross with her. She says I've ruined her in everybody's estimation, by abusing her. I say I've only ruined myself.

But I'll put her on a pedestal again. – Lord God, what a bloody time this has been. I think it will be better in Italy. At any rate, now I work myself blind.

I wrote to Mitchell Kennerley.

I haven't got any news. I'm 28 now. How slowly one gets old, in comparison.

It's a weird novel you'll get from me this time: but *perfectly* proper. The libraries will put it in their Sunday School prize list. – I shall send you my address soon. My love to Mrs Garnett. Frieda is in Wolfratshausen.[3] Good-bye.

D. H. Lawrence

Love to David – he writes splendid letters. But is he in love? What's got him? He's suddenly developed a responsible vein. He takes the world seriously, my hat, and grieves over the shallow and unprofitable asphodel[4] as if he were the Apostle [...] John in embryo.

---

it Pound sent payment presumably for DHL's poem 'The Mowers' which was to appear in the *Smart Set* in November 1913.

10 Church Walk, Kensington, W.

Dear Lawrence,

    S[mart] Set.

These people are slower than coal-tar about the stories. Enc. cheque for a poem.

Max Goschen (20 Great Russell St., W.C.) want to know what you'll take for a volume of short stories.

I dont know how sound they are. They are bringing out Hueffer, and probably me. You'd better write direct to them. I can't be responsible. They are interested and would like to do the collection of stories. That's all I can say about it.

Yours sincerely   E Pound

[1] some days.] a time.
[2] DHL did not take the MS with him as planned; he had it sent from Munich; see Letter 660.
[3] Staying with her sister Else Jaffe (see *Letters*, i. 413).
[4] Cf. *Letters*, i. 451.

649. To Enid Hopkin, [18 September 1913]

Text: MS UCLA; PC v. Überlingen Franziskanerstram Barrussertor; Postmark, Konstanz 18. 9. 13; Huxley 140.

[Konstanz]
[18 September 1913]

What jolly news, that you've got through Oxford and are swotting Matric at Nottingham.[1] I think it is good to swot while one is young – don't you slack. I liked your letter very much – it was handed in at Munich just as I left, and I read it in the train. I am at present on a steamer on the Lake of Constance going from Überlingen to Constance. I love these old towns with roofs sticking up so high, and tiles all colours – sometimes peacock blue and green. – I am going tomorrow to Schaffhausen then walking to Zurich and Lucerne and the Gotthard.

Love to your father and mother. Good luck to you.

D. H. Lawrence

650. To Edward Garnett, [19 September 1913]

Text: MS NYPL; PC v. Rheinfall und Schloss Laufen; Postmark, Neuhausen 19. IX. 13; Unpublished.

[Neuhausen]
[19 September 1913]

I came across Lake Constance yesterday and today down the Rhine to the Falls. It is *very* fine on the river. I am going on foot to Zurich and then to Lucerne. I shall be in Lucerne in five days time – that is next Wednesday. If you have anything to write me, address it Hauptpostlagernd, Lucerne. I join Frieda there on Thursday.[2] She is in Baden Baden. I am travelling on three shillings a day – jolly. I do a bit of The Sisters en route.

D. H. Lawrence

651. To Arthur McLeod, [19 September 1913]

Text: MS UT; PC v. Rheinfall und Schloss Laufen; Postmark, Neuhausen 19. IX. 13; Unpublished.

[Neuhausen]
[19 September 1913]

I have come over Lake Constance yesterday – today down the Rhine to the falls. It is *very* delicious, the last. Now I am on foot to Zürich and

---

[1] Enid Hopkin had passed the Oxford Senior Examination, a test of general knowledge used to determine the student's readiness for taking the London Matriculation Examination for which she was now preparing herself.

[2] DHL met Frieda in Milan as Letter 654 suggests.

Lucerne – where I meet Frieda. Isn't it jolly. Send me a card Hauptpost-lagernd, Lucerne, wilI you? I shall be there on Wednesday. I shall send you our Italian address when we get one. Your cards of Devonshire *were* pretty.

DHL

652. To May Holbrook, [22 September 1913]
Text: MS UN; PC v. Luzern mit dem Pilatus; Postmark, Luzern 22. IX. 1913; Nehls, iii. 628.

[Lucerne]
[22 September 1913]

I hope you got my letter from Wolfratshausen.[1] God knows where my own letters are wandering now. I am going across Switzerland on foot. Came over the Rigi today to Lucerne, and now am going down the Lake to Fluelen. When I get an address, in Italy, I will send it you.

Love to both   DHL

653. To Mitchell Kennerley, [25? September 1913]
Text: Moore, *Intelligent Heart* 157.

[25? September 1913][2]

[DHL wrote to Kennerley concerning the publication in America of *The Widowing of Mrs Holroyd*.]

It pleases me very much to think the play will be published one day.... I do hope also that you may find my writing a good speculation. But I think you will. My thanks for advertising *Sons and Lovers* so widely. I do like the reviews. But – bisogna dar tempo al tempo.[3]

654. To Edward Garnett, [25 September 1913]
Text: MS NYPL; PC v. Lago di Lugano; Postmark, Lugano 25 IX 1913; Unpublished.

[Lugano, Switzerland]
[25 September 1913]

I got your letter here. I have written to Kennerley to send me the revised MS[4] to Lerici. You send me the proofs there also:

Lerici, Golfo della Spezia, Italy.

We are going there – arrive on Sunday. Prof Jaffé is staying there, and

[1] The letter has not been found.
     Muriel May Holbrook, née Chambers (1883–1955), sister of Jessie Chambers, m. William Holbrook (1884–1960) in 1906; see *Letters*, i. 32.
[2] The conjectural date is based on DHL's statement in the next letter about his having written to Kennerley.   [3] 'wait and see' (literally 'we must give time time').
[4] *The Widowing of Mrs Holroyd*.

looking for a house for us. I will make as little alteration in the proofs as possible – except deletions, which dont matter, do they? But I *will* have the revised MS. There is one speech in it which I could not create again, and it is the keystone of the play, and I *will* have it in. It is a frightful shame you are so bothered. I meet Frieda in Milan tomorrow evening. I have walked right across Switzerland.[1] Excuse post card.

Love   D. H. Lawrence

655. To Edward Garnett, 30 September 1913
Text: MS NYPL; Huxley 141–2.

Albergo delle Palme, *Lerici*, Golfo della Spezia, Italy.
Tuesday 30 Sept. 1913

Dear Garnett,

I am so happy with the place we have at last discovered, I must write smack off to tell you. It is perfect. There is a little tiny bay half shut in by rocks, and smothered by olive woods that slope down swiftly. Then there is one pink, flat, fisherman's house. Then there is the villino of Ettore Gambrosier, a four-roomed pink cottage among a vine garden,[2] just over the water, and under the olive woods. There, D.V., is my next home. It is exquisite. One gets by rail from Genoa or from Parma to Spezia, by steamer across the gulf to Lerici, and by rowing boat round the headlands to Fiascherino, where is the villino which is to be mine. It is L 60 a month – 60 lire, that is – furnished – and 25 lire for the woman who does all the work and washing and sleeps in Tellaro, the fishing village twenty minutes off: in all, 85 francs a month. You run out of the gate into the sea, which washes among the rocks at the mouth of the bay. The garden is all vines and fig trees, and great woods on the hills all round. – Now you will come and see us – and so will Constanza Davidovna – she promised – she would be so happy. Yellow crocuses are out, wild. The Mediterranean washes softly and nicely, with just a bit of white against the rocks. Figs and grapes are ripe. You will come and see us – and David too – it is a perfect place for him. Think, we can sit round the open chimney in the kitchen at night, and burn olive wood, and hear the sea washing. I want to go tomorrow. But the proprietor remains in possession still another eight days, for the crops. I feel I can't wait: though this is a delicious hôtel – 6 francs a day pension, jolly good food, wine and all included – a big bedroom with a balcony just over the sea, very beautiful. But I want to go to my villino.

---

[1] For a detailed account of DHL's walk see Armin Arnold, 'In the Footsteps of D. H. Lawrence in Switzerland: Some New Biographical Material', *Texas Studies in Literature and Language*, iii (Summer 1961), 184–8.   [2] MS reads 'gardens'.

I haven't got much money left. The cheque from the *New Statesman* hasn't come yet – but it will eventually wander here, I suppose. Perhaps you could send me £10 from what I have left. Send it me in notes here, to this Albergo.

I walked all the way from Schaffhausen to Zürich, Lucerne, over the Gotthard to Cirolo, Bellinzona, Lugano, Como. It was beautiful – Switzerland too touristy, however – spoilt.

Don't ask me anything about literature this time.

Frieda's mother gave her a lot of this paper – please excuse it.[1]

Love from both   D. H. Lawrence

656. To Henry Savage, [4 October 1913]
Text: MS Cooney; PC; postmark, Lerici 4 10 13; Unpublished.

Villino Ettore Gambrosier, *Lerici*, per Fiascherino, *Golfo della Spezia*, Italy.

[4 October 1913]

Dear Savage,

We've got a place at last – a lovely little 4 roomed cottage on a tiny little bay – very beautiful. When we're settled you must come and see us. We've scuffled about awfully – I shall be glad to get settled. Write to us – it will be nice to hear from you in this strange place. And when we've had time to breathe, I'll send you a letter.

It is wonderful weather here on the Mediterranean - like midsummer.

Our regards to you and your wife.

D. H. Lawrence

657. To Edward Garnett, [4 October 1913]
Text: MS NYPL; PC; Postmark, Lerici 4 10 13; Unpublished.

Villino Ettore Gambrosier, *Lerici*, per Fiascherino, *Golfo della Spezia*, Italy.

[4 October 1913]

Dear Garnett,

Here is the address – we move in today. It *is* the most delicious place. You absolutely must come as soon as you can – and Mrs Garnett too.

I got the proofs of the *Widowing of Mrs Holroyd* this morning. I will have a go at them tomorrow.

It is the most wonderful weather – the Mediterranean is a miracle of blueness and sunshine. Tell David we'll write to him when we have time to draw a breath.

Yours   D. H. Lawrence

[1] The notepaper has the Richthofen coat of arms embossed on it.

658. To Mitchell Kennerley, 5 October 1913

Text: MS VC; Huxley 142–3.

Villino Ettore Gambrosier, *Lerici*, per Fiascherino, *Golfo della Spezia*, Italy

5 Ottobre 1913

Dear Mr Kennerley,

I got your letter of the 19th ult. this morning at last, and rejoiced exceedingly over it. Mr Garnett had sent me the proofs of the play a few days before, and I had wrestled with them, then given them up to await the arrival of the MS. from you. Instead I hear that Mr. Björkman will correct for me in America, and I am very glad.[1] Mr Garnett said you might legitimately send me a heavy bill for alterations,[2] and I was afraid you were displeased. However all goes well. I am glad Mr Björkman will see to the revision. He will [...] use his discretion over any little point that may arise. I like to think he will look after the thing for me. Of course I take unto myself all the beautiful and laudatory things he says about me in the preface: they seem to me very just.[3] I never did read Freud, but I have heard about him since I was in Germany.

As for *Sons and Lovers*, its star is already sinking from my sky, now I am well on into another very different novel.

We have got a tiny four-roomed cottage among the vines, on a little rocky bay down here. The Mediterranean is very warm, so I am always trying to drown myself. We've got a barefoot servant of sixty, who kisses my wife's hand and calls all the blessings of heaven on her. So we manage to live on about 130 francs a month. Felice, the woman, is wizened but triumphant. She marches like a queen with a dozen kilos of charcoal on her head. She lifts her hands and laments over our bathing in such a 'mare grosso'. Publish me something in the *Forum* if you can, will you. I am horribly afraid of not

---

[1] Edwin August Björkman (1866–1951), a Swedish-born novelist and critic, published his first book *Is There Anything New Under the Sun?* in 1911. He edited the *Modern Drama Series* (1912–15) which included the work of such dramatists as Strindberg, Björnson and Schnitzler.

[2] 'But I always remember how, in a cottage by the sea, in Italy, I re-wrote almost entirely that play, *The Widowing of Mrs. Holroyd*, right on the proofs which Mitchell Kennerley had sent me. And he nobly forbore with me' ('The Bad Side of Books', in Edward D. McDonald, *A Bibliography of the Writings of D. H. Lawrence*, Philadelphia, 1925, p. 11).

[3] The Preface by Björkman appeared in both the American and English editions of *The Widowing of Mrs Holroyd*. DHL is described as 'a man gifted with a strikingly original vision, a keen sense of beauty, an equally keen sense of verbal values, and a sincerity which makes him see and tell the truth where even the most audacious used to falter in the past. Flaubert himself was hardly less free from the old curse of sentimentalizing compromise – and yet this young writer knows how to tell the utmost truth with a daintiness that puts offence out of the question' (p. vii).

Despite his approval of Björkman's Preface here and in Letter 702, DHL later expressed annoyance at this evaluation of him as a writer. See Letter 726.

being able to pay Felice her wages, and she is my first servant, and I feel frightfully responsible for her. Her husband – ah, il poverino – died four years ago.

This is really to tell you my address. I shall be delighted to hear from Mr. Björkman, if ever he should find occasion to write.

One can hear the sea all the time. It is very beautiful here. The figs are bursting after a day's rain. Many thanks for your courtesy.

Yours Sincerely   D. H. Lawrence

We stay here at least six months – until April.

The men and women in Italy are natural enemies – it is very queer.

659. To Edward Garnett, 6 October 1913

Text: MS NYPL; Postmark, Lerici 6 10 13; Huxley 143–4.

Lerici, per Fiascherino, Golfo della Spezia

6 Ottobre 1913

Dear Garnett,

I enclose you a letter from Harrison.[1] It seems to me pretty fair. What do you think? As I am pretty badly off for money, I am jolly glad of the offer. I suppose you could get back from Pinker the one story[2] – would you?

---

[1] The typed, unsigned letter (now at NYPL) came from the *English Review*, on behalf of Austin Harrison, the Editor:

THE ENGLISH REVIEW

17–21 Tavistock Street, Covent Garden, London, W.C.

D. H. Lawrence, Esq.,
3rd October, 1913.
Lerici,
Golfo Della Spezia, Italy.

Dear Mr. Lawrence,

Mr. Harrison likes your Military story very much. He also likes the second one that was sent in by Mr. Pinker. In fact, he likes them both so much that he wants two more, and his idea is to advertise them largely and, in fact, do as much as possible for the advancement of them and their author. He is ready to pay £15 a piece, and the crux of the question is this, that if they are to be sent to him through Mr. Pinker he fears that his offer of £15 each will not be acceptable. Therefore, he wishes to know: –

(i) Can you give him two, or at least one, more story on similar lines in addition to those that he already possesses.

(ii) Can you withdraw the second story from Mr. Pinker's hands, and failing that:

(iii) Will you be disposed to instruct Mr. Pinker that he is to be satisfied with the payment of £15 for any such stories of yours as we may care to accept through him?

As you know, the financial position of this *Review* is not such as it might, and should, be. It is for this reason that Mr. Harrison cannot afford to offer you more than the sum I have named. At the same time, he thinks that four stories on those lines, duly advertised and published by us and afterwards reprinted in book form by yourself, would go far to consolidate that reputation which your literary work is deservedly procuring for you. Please let me know about this.

[2] 'Honour and Arms'. See p. 44 n. 9 and Letter 664.

Perhaps you will see Norman Douglas at lunch one day, and can tell him. I have asked Ezra Pound to forward to the *English Review* two stories he had, which were returned from the *Smart Set*. One of them 'Once', if Harrison dare print it, would go excellently well with the two soldier stories.[1] You remember, it is the tale of a woman who was loved by a young officer – he threw roses on her – one night in an hotel. What do you think of the chances of that? For a fourth, I think I would write one I have had in my mind for a long time.[2]

Then Mitchell Kennerley wrote me a fearfully nice letter in answer to one of mine from Irschenhausen. He says that Björkman will correct the proofs of the play from the revised MS. of mine – which is rather nice. So I needn't bother about the proofs from you.

Did you say Mrs Garnett posted a cheque for £4 from the *New Statesman*, to Irschenhausen? It hasn't turned up yet. The letters have been zigzagging about horribly. But perhaps I shall get it ultimately.

Kennerley also sent me a copy of his *Sons and Lovers*, and a *New York Times* with a very laudatory notice.[3]

I am working away at The Sisters. It is *so* different, so different from anything I have yet written, that I do nothing but wonder what it is like. When I get to page 200 I shall send you the MS. for your opinion.

It is very lovely here. I sit on the rocks against the sea all day, and write. I tell you it is a dream. Figs are ripe in the garden – they are delicious. Frieda and I eat hundredweights.

We've got a servant called Felice. She is a rum creature – about sixty, and wizened, and barefoot. She goes barefoot, walks with a half a hundredweight of charcoal on her head, like a queen wearing a crown, and whistles her acquiescence when you ask her to do anything. She is a jewel. You *must* come and see her.

Frieda and I are being very happy here. But the letters take the devil of a time.

                                                        Love from us to you.   D. H. Lawrence

We haven't got any money. Did you send the £10? What an awful nuisance I am to you. Never mind, you come here and stay with us, and be happy. – It is an easy place to get apartments in, quite cheap, if you know anyone wanting a resting place in Italy – I mean Lerici. – But you come and stay here with us in Fiascherino.

---

[1] 'Honour and Arms' and 'Vin Ordinaire'.   [2] Probably 'The Mortal Coil'.
[3] Signed with the initials L.M.F. (Louise Maunsell Field), the review was published in the *New York Times Book Review*, 21 September 1913. The reviewer called the book 'one of rare excellence'. (See Draper 73–4.)

I've only 50 francs in the world.

Did you say Mrs Garnett forwarded a cheque from the *New Statesman* to Irschenhausen? It has never come to me. God knows if it is lost.

Did you ever just glance round to see if the MSS of those Tirol sketches were at the Cearne?

660. To Edward Garnett, [12 October 1913]
Text: MS NYPL; PC; Postmark, Tellaro 13. 10. 13; Unpublished.

Lerici, per Fiascherino, Golfo di Spezia
Sunday

Dear Garnett,

I got the letter with the enclosures[1] all right. Many thanks. The letter from the *New Statesman* has not come: the MS. of the Sisters, which I left in Munich to be forwarded, registered, is wandering the face of the earth – I am in a rage with the damned post here. – I will write Pinker and the *New Statesman* today.[2]

Yours   D. H. Lawrence

661. To Walter de la Mare, [12? October 1913]
Text: MS UN; Unpublished.

Lerici, per Fiascherino, Golfo Della Spezia, Italy.
Sunday.[3]

Dear de la Mare,

I never got a chance of seeing you after all – and you are one of the people of whom it is difficult to believe they are real, and not like a rumour in the land. – Which is a finely affected sentence: true, though.

I wanted to ask you if you happened to look for those Tirol sketches[4] of mine, at your place. The W[estminster] G[azette] says they sent them to Garnett, Garnett says they didn't. Would you mind having a look for them. They are not of any great value, but I was fond of them, and they might bring me in a few guineas.

I wonder if you would give the *W.G.* my address, in case they need it. And if you see J. M. Murry, ask him why in the name of fortune we've not heard from him.

[1] Unidentified.
[2] Perhaps DHL's letter to Pinker was delayed: see Letter 664. The letter to the *New Statesman* has not been found.
[3] This letter must follow DHL's receiving a reply to Letter 659 in which Garnett denied having the 'Tirol sketches'.   [4] See p. 56 n. 3.

We've got a delicious little pink house here on the Mediterranean – my wife and I, and an oddity of an Italian maid. It is a rocky little bay with a decent strand, and only two houses: one belonging to a peasant, and this. The hills are all olives and vines, with some pine trees. It is lovely. I must fetch the letters from Tellaro, twenty five minutes away; and there is no road, either here or to Tellaro, that a horse or mule can take – so many steps. Everything must go by boat, on calm, calm days.

So you see it is rather nice. Shelley's San Terenzo is on Lerici bay. If you are coming to Italy, come and see us, will you, because it is so nice. We have got a room you could have, and we would leave you alone. I think you might like it rather a lot. I think I shan't be so badly off this winter, if nothing goes wrong.

It is wonderful weather, dawn a great puff of rose, and olive trees shimmering in the sun all day, the vines going red, the sea misty blue and motionless, evening coming fierce with colour, red light on the olive trees, and islands like blackish amethysts upon a flaming sky and sea. – Another gorgeous sentence to offend your taste.

One breathes so much freer out of London. When I see a red butterfly settle on a fallen, bursten fig, and breathe with its wings slow, full, as if it respired sunshine – that's how one feels in Italy, I think.

There are flies and fleas into the bargain, and the villages stink. But here the worst is the trodden grape skins, that smell acid to make the eyes water.

Regards to you.   D. H. Lawrence

662. To Edward Marsh, 14 October 1913
Text: MS NYPL; Postmark, Tellaro 15. 10. 13; Huxley 145–6.

Fiascherino, *Lerici*, Golfo di Spezia. Italy.

14 Ottobre 1913

Dear Marsh,

Don't think that it is because your last letter offended me at all, that I don't write: In reality, I quite agreed with what you said. I know my verse is often strained and mal-formed. Whether it gets better I don't know. I don't write much verse now. I've got to earn my living by prose. One day I'll copy you out some of my later things, if you'd care to see them.

We've been on the move since God knows when. That is why I haven't written. When we left Bavaria, I walked across Switzerland to Italy. Switzerland is rather banal. Then we have prospected here and there to find a spot for the winter. Now we are settled in Fiascherino. It is an hours walk from San Terenzo, Shelley's place. We've got a little pink cottage among vines and olives. I also just caught a flea, and am in a rage because it leapt from my fingers out again into the infinite. What a glorious flying jump a flea can take! The full moon shines on the sea, which moves about all glittering among black rocks. I go down and bathe and enjoy myself. You never saw such clear, buoyant water. Also I don't swim more than a dozen yards, so am always trying to follow the starry Shelley, and set amid the waves. I don't work much, and don't want to work. If I'd got the smallest income I should be delighted to loafe for ever. But now I watch the servant, Felice, and my heart goes down plump. She is delighted to serve such grand and glorious people as we are. She is sixty, very wrinkled, but full of gusto. She strides up to the little arbour they call the Belvedere – it is impossible to think it only means Bellevue – bearing the soup-tureen as if she were the Queen of Sheba taking spice to Solomon:[1] barefoot, she comes, with her petticoats kilted up, and a gleam of triumph in her eye. Think if I couldn't afford to pay her wages. I would take my last bathe. Don't mind my lapsing into pounds shillings and pence. If I die rich, I shall order my tombstone to be a big gold sovereign, with me for king – Fidei Defensor, etc, round the rim.[2] – I caught the flea, by the way. One can be so keen in the chase. – Figs are falling with ripeness in the garden. I am trying drying some – you dip them in boiling water. But I am in such a rage that the bright and shiny flies hover so thick about them when they are spread out, that they can't really get enough sun to dry them: always clouded with shadow.

How did you like your walk in Spain? I try to think of you, but can't quite see you. I suppose it would be rather fine. How did you like Lascelles Abercrombie?[3] You will introduce me to him when there is an opportunity, will you not? Davies says he'll come here in the spring.[4] I can see his one eating, gnawing anxiety is to write. God help us, when a poet must hunt his muse like Tartarin de Tarascon the one remaining hare.[5] We take ourselves too seriously, nous autres poètes.

Write me a letter, and tell me all that is happening in the world of rhyme, will you. If anything good comes, let me know and I'll try to get it. Remember me to Gibson, if you see him.[6] Tell Davies he ought to come before Spring,

---

[1] See 1 Kings x. 10.
[2] The title of 'Defender of the Faith' was given to Henry VIII and has been assumed by all succeeding monarchs; it is to be found in its Latin form (now abbreviated) on all coins.
[3] Lascelles Abercrombie (1881–1938), after a period of literary journalism, became Professor of English Literature at the University of Leeds (1922–9), and Goldsmith's Reader in English at Oxford (1935–8). He published verse drama, poetry and criticism. m. Catherine Gwatkin.
[4] W. H. Davies.   [5] See p. 537 n. 1.
[6] Wilfrid Wilson Gibson (1878–1962), poet. Like Abercrombie, Davies and DHL, he was a contributor to *Georgian Poetry 1911–1912*.

but we'll be glad to see him then if he can't get before. – I have to go to Telaro for the letters – it is a little sea-robbers nest still inaccessible – and I feel so disgusted when, after hunting down the post-master – today he was helping the priest to tack up trimmings in the church – I get only a broad smile and a wave of the hand that implies a vacuum in space, and a 'niente, signore, niente oggi, niente, niente'.[1] It is nearly half an hour's walk too. So when the post-master is forced to follow at my heels up the cobbly track, humbly to deliver me my letter, I am justified.

Many greetings from us to you.

D. H. Lawrence

663. To Arthur McLeod, [17 October 1913]
Text: MS UT; PC; Postmark, Lerici 17. 10. 13; Huxley 146–7.

Lerici, per Fiascherino, Golfo della Spezia, Italy
[17 October 1913]

Dear Mac,

I can't remember whether I wrote to you or not. I *think* I did, but you don't write to me. I have got so mixed up in everything, I scarcely know where I am.

But we've got a beautiful place – a little pink cottage on the Mediterranean among vines and olives. It isn't far from Shelley's San Terenzo – one can see his house across the bay at Lerici – but our position is a million times prettier. You have no idea – how delightful it is. You must come in the spring. [Frieda Weekley interjects: at Xmas] Perhaps we can keep this place.

The play is coming out soon. I shall send you a copy. I believe the *English Review* is going to publish me a series of four short stories.[2] That is all my literary news.

I am glad you liked *Sons and Lovers* on re-reading. I feel, somehow, as if you had not been pleased with the thing – nor with me as author of it. Don't find fault with me.

Send us a little book, will you – something that costs nothing. This is a wilderness. I have to walk two chilometri up the sea's edge to Telaro for letters every day. There is no road – everything must come by boat from Lerici – see how we are lost to the world. But one can go out of the house and bathe – I like it. Write me a letter.

D. H. Lawrence

[1] 'nothing, sir, nothing today, nothing, nothing'.
[2] See p. 81 n. 1 and 82 n. 1. The *English Review* published two stories only.

664. To J. B. Pinker, [19 October 1913]
Text; MS UT; PC; Postmark, Tellaro 19. 10 13; Unpublished.

Lerici, per Fiascherino, Golfo della Spezia, Italy
[19 October 1913]

Dear Mr Pinker,

I should be glad if you would let the *English Review* have the soldier story you sent them – 'Honour and Arms' I believe – for fifteen pounds. I have accepted Mr Harrison's offer for four stories at that price. Perhaps Mr Garnett wrote you a line.

Excuse my writing on a post card – I haven't got any stamps, and it is such a long long way to get any.

My thanks to you for looking after my stories.

Yours faithfully   D. H. Lawrence

665. To Katharine Clayton, [23 October 1913]
Text: MS NCL; PC; Postmark, Tellaro 23. 10. 13; Unpublished.

Lerici, per Fiascherino, Golfo della Spezia, Italy.
[23 October 1913]

Dear Mrs Clayton,

I was awfully glad to hear today from Mrs Garnett of Pat's success[1] – it really is something good to hear. You'll see now, how the jolly things will come cropping out of life for you.

We have got a delicious little pink house, here quite alone on the Mediterranean, with an oddity of an Italian maid. It is very jolly. I am always wishing I could have lots of people here, it is so nice. But how dirty – how you would hold up your hands! Ellide has never seen a scrubbing brush used, so behold me on my hands and knees, trying to get to the bottom of the dirt.

I am afraid I have nothing more for Douglas to type just now. But would you ask him to post to Edward Marsh, 5 Raymond Buildings, Grays Inn, just four poems – the 3 Rose Poems – 'By the Isar, in the twilight', and the other two – then 'Green', then 'Illicit': 'In front of the sombre mountains' – then 'The Wind, the rascal' – that is six little pieces and not four.[2] I don't know how much I owe – he must tell me.

We are very glad of your good news – our regards.

D. H. Lawrence

[1] The Claytons' second son, Patrick Andrew Clayton (1896–1962). Commissioned in the Royal Field Artillery in 1916; served in Greece and Turkey. 1920–38, Inspector of Desert Surveys in Egypt; assisted in the formation of the Long Range Desert Group in 1940. Awarded DSO and MBE. m. Ethel Williamson Wyatt, 1927. (See *Times* obituary, 19 March 1962.)

[2] In *Poetry*, January 1914, DHL's three 'Rose Poems' were published (see p. 56 n. 1) together with the other three poems mentioned here.

666. To Cynthia Asquith, 23 October 1913
Text: MS UT; Huxley 147–9.

Lerici, per Fiascherino, Golfo della Spezia, Italy
23 Oct 1913

Dear Mrs Asquith,

I have been wanting to write to you for such a long time. But we have been 'on the way' here. It is ages since we left Bavaria. Frieda went to her people in Baden-Baden, which I didn't want to do. So I walked across Switzerland – and am cured of that little country for ever. The only excitement in it is that you can throw a stone a frightfully long way down – and that is forbidden by law. As for mountains – if I stick my little finger over my head, I can see it shining against the sky and call it Monte Rosa. No, I can't do with mountains at close quarters – they are always in the way, and they are so stupid, never moving and never doing anything but obtrude themselves.

Then I got to beastly Milano, with its imitation hedge-hog of a cathedral and its hateful town Italians all socks and purple cravats and hats over the ear, did for me.

But we've got an adorable place here: a little four – – a beautiful palazzina in large grounds, that descend in terraces to the sea – that's the Italian for it. I call it a little, pink, four-roomed cottage in a big vine-garden, on the edge of a rocky bay. Frieda calls it a pink-washed sepulchre, because it is – or was – so dirty inside. Lord what a time we've had, scrubbing it. It was no use calling on Ellide, the girl. She had never seen a scrubbing brush used. So I tied my braces round my waist and went for it. Lord, to see the dark floor flushing crimson, the dawn of deep red bricks arise from out this night of filth, was enough to make one burst forth into hymns and psalms. 'Ah', cries Ellide, 'l'aria e la pulizia' – 'air and cleanliness are the two most important things in this life'. She might as well have said nectar and ambrosia, for all she knew of 'em.

But the Italians don't consider their houses, like we do, as being their extended persons. In England, my house is my outer cuticle, like a snail has a shell. Here, it is a hole into which I creep out of the rain and the dark. – When they eat, the Capitano and his wife – the place belongs to them, she inherited it, but they let it and live in town – they fling all their scraps and 'bouts de vin' on the floor, unceremoniously, and the cats and the flies do the war dance about them.

It is a lovely position – among the vines, a little pink house, just above a rocky bay of the Mediterranean. One goes down in a towel to bathe. *And* the water is warm and buoyant – it *is* jolly. I wish you could try it too.

We live awfully cheaply – I know these things interest you more than eternal truths – house, 60 francs a month, maid 25, and vegetables in abundance, cheap as dirt. And in the morning one wakes and sees the pines all dark and mixed up with perfect rose of dawn, and all day long the olives shimmer in the sun, and fishing boats and strange sails like Corsair ships come out of nowhere on a pale blue sea, and then at evening all the sea is milky gold and scarlet with sundown. It is very pretty.

Did you make your dash to Venice – and did it stink. Lord, but how Italy can stink. We have to fetch the letters from Tellaro – twenty five minutes upstairs and downstairs on the sea-edge, an inaccessible little sea-robber's place – and my dear heart, but it *is* dirty.

I hope you are pretty well – are you? But isn't it a bit much, to go dashing to Venice and back in a week? Why don't you go to Margate again. I think it makes an awful difference, when one is happy in a place. How is the jonquil with the golden smile.[1] Is Mr Asquith making heaps of money at the Bar? I believe I'm going to get about £150 this winter, which will be rolling wealth for us here.

We heard from Eddie Marsh yesterday – such a heavy acorn fell on my head at this moment – now that is an omen – are you any good at sooth saying? – He is fearfully warm and generous, I think. I think I was wrong to feel injured because my verse wasn't well enough dished-up to please him.

The Mediterranean can get *very* cross. Today the wind is the Maestrale, and the sea is showing its teeth in an unbecoming fashion.

I'm going to have a play published – The black hen has just come home. She went lost. Ellide is waving her hands with joy. – A very decent play. They won't give me any copies or I'd send you one. But you must read it.

My regards to Mr Asquith and to the Jonquil and to you.

Yours Sincerely   D. H. Lawrence

667. To Arthur McLeod, [26 October 1913]
Text: MS UT; Postmark, Tellaro 27. 10 13; Huxley 149–51.

Lerici, per Fiascherino, Golfo della Spezia, Italy
Sunday.

Dear Mac,

Your letter, with the cutting, came yesterday, and today the books. You are a decent chap. Frieda wanted to read *Anne Veronica*.[2] I have read it, and

---

[1] Most likely a reference to the two-year old John Asquith.

[2] *Ann Veronica: A Modern Love Story* by H. G. Wells (1909). DHL read it, probably in January 1910, and thought it 'not very good'. See *Letters*, i. 154 and 339.

found it rather trashy. I love _Tristram Shandy_.[1] But the book on _Art and Ritual_ pleases me most just now.[2] I am just in the mood for it. It just fascinates me to see art coming out of religious yearning – one's presentation of what one wants to feel again, deeply. But I haven't got far in. As for the divorce, it is curious how at first it upsets me, and then goes off, and matters no more. I have found that one has such a living social self. I am sure every man feels first, that he is a servant – be it martyr or what – of society. And if he feels that he has trespassed against society, and it is adverse to him, he suffers. Then the individual self comes up and says 'You fool'. Now again, only the sea – it is rather dark today, with heavy waves – and the olives matter to me. London is all smoke a long way off. But yesterday I was awfully grateful to you for your sane and decent letter. You must continue to believe in me – I don't mean in my talent only – because I depend on you a bit. One doesn't know, till one is a bit at odds with the world, how much one's friends who believe in one rather generously, mean to one. – I felt you had gone off from me a bit, because of _Sons and Lovers_. But one sheds ones sicknesses in books – repeats and presents again ones emotions, to be master of them.

I did send some verse the other day to the _English_ [_Review_], but I think Harrison doesn't want to publish my poetry[3] – he wants my prose more. He has got three Soldier Stories, which he is going to publish in a sort of series – perhaps four – so he says – which will make a book afterwards.[4] I hope they'll go all right. I have been so much upset, what with moving and Friedas troubling about the children – you know she has three – and what not, that I haven't been able to work. It is no joke to do as Frieda and I have done – and my very soul feels tired. But here it is going to pick up again and I am going to work like a brick.

It is very warm and beautiful here – and we bathe in a warm, bright sea. This afternoon we have been making a visit to the contadini laggiù.[5] They have the only other house on the bay – and a lot of garden and vines going up in terraces. The kitchen is the top room in the house – and wherever you sit, if you look at the window, you see the sea moving. It is very queer. I have never been in such a house. They are awfully nice people. I want you to come here, if you can – either at Christmas or Easter. It is so beautiful. Perhaps we shall keep the cottage too for next winter. Do try and come.

---

[1] Published 1759–67, by Laurence Sterne (1713–68).
[2] Jane Harrison, _Ancient Art and Ritual_ (July 1913).
[3] Harrison published two of DHL's poems – 'Twilight' and 'Meeting among the Mountains' – in _English Review_, xvi (February 1914), 305–7.
[4] See Letter 659. There is no record of why the offer to publish four stories was not fulfilled.
[5] 'the local inhabitants over the other side'.

I should like an Ernest Dowson, if you would lend me him.[1] I will send him back carefully. I only know one or two things of his and he interests me.

Don't mind what Miss Corke[2] says. If one is more or less in love with a woman whom one knows one can't love altogether, nor really, then what shall one do but take the moment – Carpe diem, if you can't gather an eternity in your fist. She is explaining how she and I failed.

You didn't tell me very much news. Write to me again and let me know about folk – Aylwin and Humphreys[3] and so on.

Frieda is going to write to you.

Love   D. H. Lawrence

How are you and what are you doing and what do you think of things nowadays?

If your mother happens to have a recipe for marrow jam – Frieda wants to make some with pumpkins. Send it me when you write, will you?

DHL

668. To Edward Marsh, 28 October 1913
Text: MS NYPL; Postmark, Tellaro 31. 10. 13; Huxley 151–3.

Lerici, per Fiascherino, Golfo Della Spezia, Italy.

28 October 1913

Dear Marsh,

We were awfully pleased with your letter – it was so full of things. Your trip in Spain sounds finer even than Italy. But Jim Barnes[4] must be a rum chap, for I can't see how politics has got much to do with poetry: – no, you say 'letters'. Letters might mean Cicero and Arthur Balfour,[5] so I suppose

[1] Ernest Dowson (1867–1900), poet. See Letter 680.
[2] Although an attempt was made to obliterate the name in the MS, the identity of the person is not in doubt. Helen Corke (1882–1978) and McLeod were both teachers in the Croydon district; they were known to one another; and they would certainly discuss DHL. (On Helen Corke see *Letters*, i. 129 n. 2.)
[3] Robert Henry Aylwin (1885–1931) and Ernest Arthur Humphreys (b. 1882), two of DHL's colleagues at Davidson Road School, Croydon. See *Letters*, i. 194 nn. 4, 6.
[4] James Thomas Strachey Barnes (1890–1955). b. India; brought up in Florence; educated at Eton and King's College, Cambridge. 1914–18 served in the Guards and Royal Flying Corps. Returned to live in Italy and became a naturalised Italian. Developed an admiration of Fascism and friendship with Mussolini. Published *The Universal Aspects of Fascism* (1928), and a two-volume autobiography, *Half a Life* (1933) and *Half a Life Left* (1937). (Obituary in *Times*, 29 August 1955.)
    Marsh and Barnes had been on a walking-tour in Spain, 6 September–5 October 1913; in January 1914 they were to go to Italy where they met DHL on 12th (Letters 695, 699; Christopher Hassall, *Edward Marsh*, 1959, pp. 249–64). Barnes refers to this meeting and records his impressions of DHL in *Half a Life*, pp. 137–8.
[5] Arthur Balfour (1848–1930), statesman and author. He became leader of the Conservative Party and served as Prime Minister 1902–5.

they do more or less flirt with politics. But I love the idea of a reformer. Tell me next time his chief dream.

I must write to Gibson. What an absolutely perfect husband he should make![1] I think I remember seeing Miss Townsend in the Poetry Bookshop[2] – rather lovable and still, one of those women that make a perfect background. They ought to be happy as birds in a quiet wood. – But probably I have got hold of quite the wrong woman, and that Miss Townsend is a Walküre. 'Twould be a pity.

The Abercrombies sound nice. But I don't like the idea of L[ascelles] A[bercrombie]'s never finishing anything. But if they are coming to Italy in November, I think either they might come this way, or we might go to Florence for a day or two.[3] I must write to Gibson. – No, I did not see the 'Solway Firth' in the *English* [*Review*].[4]

Poor Davies – he makes me so furious, and so sorry. He's really like a linnet that's got just a wee little sweet song, but it only sings when it's wild. And he's made himself a tame bird – poor little devil. He makes me furious. 'I shall be all right now the winter is coming', he writes, 'now I can sit by the fire and work'. As if he could sing when he's been straining his heart to make a sound of music, for months. It isn't as if he were a passionate writer, writing his 'agon'. Oh my God, he's like teaching a bull-finch to talk. I think one ought to be downright cruel to him, and drive him back: say to him 'Davies, your work is getting like Birmingham tinware; Davies, you drop your h's, and everybody is tempering the wind to you, because you are a shorn lamb; Davies, your accent is intolerable in a carpeted room; Davies, you hang on like the mud on a lady's silk petticoat.' Then he might leave his Sevenoaks room, where he is rigged up as rural poet, proud of the gilt mirror and his romantic past: and he might grow his wings again, and chirrup a little sadder song.

And now I've got to quarrel with you about the Ralph Hodgson poem:[5] because I think it is banal in utterance. The feeling is there, right enough – but not in itself, only represented. It's like 'I asked for bread, and he gave me a penny'.[6] Only here and there is the least touch of personality in the poem:

---

[1] William Wilfrid Gibson had just married Gertrude Townsend, secretary to Harold Monro.
[2] The Poetry Bookshop was established by Monro and Gibson at 35 Devonshire Street, near Gray's Inn, London.
[3] See Letter 677.
[4] The correct title of Gibson's poem is 'Solway Ford', *English Review*, xv (October 1913), 321–3.
[5] 'The Song of Honour' (in *Saturday Review*, cxvi, 11 October 1913), by Ralph Hodgson (1871–1962), another contributor to Marsh's *Georgian* volumes. (For the two extracts DHL quotes later, see Hodgson's *Collected Poems*, 1961, pp. 71, 72.)
[6] Cf. Matthew vii. 9.

it is the currency of poetry, not poetry itself. Every single line of it is poetic currency – and a good deal of emotion handling it about. But it isn't really poetry. I hope to God you won't hate me and think me carping, for this. But look

> 'the ruby's and the rainbow's song
> the nightingale's – all three'

There's the emotion in the rhythm, but it's loose emotion, inarticulate, common – the words are mere currency. It is exactly like a man who feels very strongly for a beggar, and gives him a sovereign. The feeling is at either end, for the moment, but the sovereign is a dead bit of metal. And this poem is the sovereign. 'Oh, I do want to give you this emotion', cries Hodgson, 'I do'. And so he takes out his poetic purse, and gives you a handful of cash, and feels very strongly, even a bit sentimentally over it.

> '…the sky was lit
> The sky was stars all over it,
> I stood, I knew not why'

No one should say 'I knew not why' any more. It is as meaningless as 'yours truly' at the end of a letter.

You *can* come this way to Rome. There is one train – about 7.0 in the morning from Milan, comes[1] Milan, Parma, *Sarzana*, Pisa, Rome – a direttissimo. Also Spezia is on the main line Genoa to Rome. But you could *easily* come via Sarzana – which is the station for Lerici. Do bring us Jim Barnes. We could put you up for a night or two. My wife is afraid because everything is so rough – but you wouldn't mind.

Did you see about the divorce,[2] and that Frieda and I are really scapegoats still. It seems queer. We have been together nearly two years. We feel a bit upset, for fear we sort of gained a false entry in Margate – with you and Mr Asquith. If you feel displeased about it, don't bother to answer the letters.

I send you some bits of poetry. Nobody will publish it. It is good, if it isn't perfect. It is not like so much poetry, good imitation only. I asked the type writer to send you one or two bits he had typed for the *English Review*.[3]

I am doing a novel for next spring.[4] I am having a play published very shortly, and, I think, a series of three or four short stories in the *English Review* – I don't know when. But they are good. You must read them.

[1] comes] leaves
[2] The hearing took place in the High Court, Probate Divorce and Admiralty Division on 18 October 1913.
[3] The six poems referred to in Letter 665.   [4] 'The Sisters'.

Frieda wrote you a letter – if I can find it again. She wrote it before we knew the divorce was heard.

a rivederla   D. H. Lawrence

I've copied you out quite a lot of poems.[1] Tell me if you like them. If you know anybody who is dying to publish such wonderful work, you may as a great favour offer him this. Don't put my 'Ballad of a Wayward Woman'[2] lightly aside. It is woman trying the various ideals – Aphrodite, Apostle John etc.

669. To Henry Savage, [31 October 1913]

Text: MS YU; Postmark, Tellaro 3.11.13; Moore, *Yale University Library Gazette*, xlvi (1972), 264–6.

Lerici, per Fiascherino, Golfo della Spezia.
Friday

Dear Savage,

We were glad to get your letter and the book.[3] The latter interests me – the things are nice and slight. Frieda thinks they are stupid – Middleton's essays – particularly about women. I think myself he was stupid about women. It seems to me silly to rage against woman – as Sphinx, or Sphinx without a secret, or cunning artist in living – or in herself.[4] It seems to me that the chief thing about a woman – who is much of a woman – is that in the long run she is not to be had. A man many bring her his laurel wreaths and songs and what not, but if that man doesn't satisfy her, in some undeniable physical fashion – then in one way or other she takes him in her mouth and shakes him like a cat a mouse, and throws him away. She is not to be caught by any of the catch-words, love, beauty, honor, duty, worth, work, salvation – none of them – not in the long run. In the long run she only says 'Am I satisfied, or is there some beastly unsatisfaction gnawing and gnawing inside me.' And if there is some unsatisfaction, it is physical at least as much as psychic, sex as much as soul. So she goes for man, or men, after

[1] They must have included 'Purity' (see Letter 674) which was later named 'Paradise Re-Entered', as well as the 'Ballad' named in this paragraph.
[2] See p. 66 n. 4.
[3] *Monologues* by Richard Middleton (October 1913) contains several essays on women, among them 'Why Women Fail in Art' and 'The New Sex'. Middleton's views of women are extremely conservative compared with those of DHL.
[4] In 'Why Woman Fail in Art', Middleton writes: '"Women", said Wilde, "are sphinxes without secrets". But he didn't give them sufficient credit for their skill in the construction of sphinxes. We simpler minded men may well lament over the subtlety of woman, when in all her wakeful life she has laboured day by day and year by year on that delightful work of art, herself' (*Monologues*, p. 129).

her own fashion, and so is called a Sphinx, and her riddle is that the man wasn't able to satisfy her – riddle enough for him: And an artist – a poet – is like a woman in that he too must have this satisfaction. There is that much life in him, more than in other people, which will not let him be. He must get his bodily and spiritual want satisfied in one and the same draught. So he must endlessly go for women, and for love. And I reckon an artist is only an ordinary man with a greater potentiality – same stuff, same make up, only more force. And the strong driving force usually finds his weak spot, and he goes cranked, or goes under. Middleton seems to me to have been wrongly directed. I think if you could have made him simply voluptuous, that would have been his salvation. He hated his flesh and blood. His life went on apart from his own flesh and blood – something like a monk who mortifies the flesh. It is a curious thing how poets tend to become ascetics, in the last sense of the word. Even a debauch for them is a self-flagellation. They go on the loose in cruelty against themselves, admitting that they are pandering to, and despising, the lower self. The lower self is the flesh, and the physical sensation, which they hate even when they praise it. For it is so much more difficult to live with one's body than with one's soul. One's body is so much more exacting: what it won't have it won't have, and nothing can make bitter into sweet. And this inexorable stubbornness of his body, that doesn't really care about little mistresses even when they are flung to it, that *isn't* satisfied even with debauch, makes a poet hate his body. He should submit to it, but he wants to be master of it. So Middleton was an ascetic who bitterly disbelieved in asceticism. But that, by training, was the only way he could work – by denying he'd got a body. He despised his own flesh and stamped it out of life, before he died. We are all alike. – You should watch the free Italians, then you'd know what we've done. We've denied the life of our bodies, so they, our bodies, deny life unto us. Curious, dried people we've become, always submitting ourselves to some damned rigid purpose, some idea, instead of fructifying in the sun while it shines.

Which is a beautifully long tirade, that you needn't read. Frieda says I'm always stupid when I'm didactic. I suppose I am – it doesn't bother me – I dont believe it – I'm only clumsy.

I retract what I say against Dickens characters – I am jealous of them. But there is something fundamental about *him* that I dislike. He is mid-Victorian, he is so governessy towards life, as if it were a naughty child.[1] His God is a Sunday-School Superintendent, on the prize-giving day, and he is the mistress of the top class. Curse him.

[1] governessy...child.] much bigger than Life, with his precepts.

It is really wonderfully beautiful here – wonderful. Sometimes the thought of the English autumn comes strangely to me, here where the sunshine is so fine, and evenings¹ such magnificent coloured things. It makes me feel as if autumn and gossamer were only painted on the air, at England, and that you² might look through like through a window, to things out here, into space and sunshine. And I seem to be able to look far down the brightness here, and see little, blue-grey, wistful-tender England.

But we've both had rotten bad colds, and have lazed about. I wish I'd got some money, and needn't work. I am feeling afraid of idling any more.

Send me a book now and then, will you – any rubbishy thing – it is so grateful. I can read Philpotts or Gissing³ – though I've read most of him – or anybody.

I hope your wife will go on all right. I don't agree with you about our separation from women. The only thing that is very separate – our bodies – is the via media for union again, if we would have it so. Nous pauvres Anglais – we've puritanised ourselves almost out of physical existence. It is so wrong.

I shall send you a copy of my play, when at length it comes out.

Our regards to you and to your wife. Come and see us then, after Christmas. All joy to the child.

D. H. Lawrence

Tolstoi – *Kreutzer Sonata* 4½d.⁴

[Frieda Weekley begins]⁵
Dear Mr Savage,

I wish I could help you but I am not good at expressing myself – But I can just say one or two things – I get so *cross* with Middleton when he hates his body, God made it and even if it was'nt Apollo like it *must* have been a lovable one – What this really means is that no woman ever loved it, if a woman had, he would not have killed himself and he would have been a very great man – It was really sex – unsatisfied sex – that killed him. – In a big soul man like Middleton *every*thing is strong, so of course the sex, that's why

---

¹ evenings] nights   ² that you] one
³ Eden Phillpotts (1862–1960) and George Gissing (1857–1903): DHL's early letters reveal a wide acquaintance particularly with the second of these novelists. See *Letters*, i. 107, 172, 203, etc.
⁴ A number of translations of Leo Tolstoy's *Kreutzer Sonata* (1889) had appeared in English though none is known at the price DHL mentions.
⁵ Frieda's letter is undated but its contents link it intimately with those of DHL's; it is presumed that the two letters were posted together. The text of Frieda's comes from MS Martin.

you say he was like a madman when in love – On the other hand he despised
and hated women, quite right from his point of view, because he had so much
to give to a woman and the fools had'nt the wit to take him – Perhaps they
took him physically, that does'nt matter but Middleton the *whole* of him they
did not take of that I am certain, a woman could have *made* him live, I loathe
my sex sometimes for being cowards and fools – He is right in his article
on the new sex, I think women should be satisfied to *be* and let the men *do*.
We can *do* so much more *that* way – I hate the women for not having enough
pride to be themselves just their own natural selves, they must wrap
themselves in false morals, do tricks in which all the time they believe in
more or less – When M. talks of women and art he is'nt quite fair, if a woman
looks on herself as a work of art why belittle it? Is'nt that a form of aspiration,
of perfecting herself, she may be stupid about it, but anyway she *tries*. But
then, poor devil, he cant have met a girl, that was equal to him – I wish I
had the poems here – I think he was eminently a lyric, and I believe for those
comes a critical time when the first youth is over and the man's period should
begin, o dear, it makes one so damned miserable that the best always seem
to snap the chord so easily – He fought so bravely for his ideals, he helped
so much but he had suffered of the sins of his contemporaries himself – He
accuses Shaw and Galsworthy[1] for sacrificing beauty to morals and yet he
had such an abstract conception of beauty himself – It makes me cross
'beauty, beauty', it's become so cheap, what does it mean – Hunting beauty,
Murillo I think made a fine picture of a boy hunting a flea[2] (there are so
many here!) He was never quite able to shake off Midvictorian middle class
– There I have jawed and very likely been no use! But it's gorgeous here,
lazy and serene, L[awrence] does'nt want to work, it seems like wasting one's
time to work, and intellectual stuff seems the Devil himself – It is so much
more satisfactory to watch the waves lap at the stones, the big rocks –
sometimes high and sometimes low, we are so happy with our little house
and all this loveliness round us – You ought to come – I suppose the infant
has arrived – I hope it will make you happy, it *ought* – I envy your wife for

---

[1] In his essay 'Traitors of Art' Middleton asserts that the 'dissatisfaction with the purely
honourable task of creating beautiful things' infected the leading writers of his time. It led
Shaw to spoil *Mrs Warren's Profession* with an excess of didacticism; 'it has damned Mr
H. G. Wells, soured Mr John Galsworthy, and made Mr Chesterton frequently tiresome'
(*Monologues*, p. 86; see also pp. 101–2, 185).

[2] The painting alluded to, by the Spanish painter Bartolomé Esteban Murillo (1617–82), must
be that in the Louvre entitled *Le Jeune Mendiant* (c. 1645–55) which portrays a boy in squalid
surroundings searching for lice under his ragged clothes. There are several copies in existence;
one is particularly worthy of note since it was offered for sale in Munich in 1911 (*Murillo.
Des Meisters Gemälde in 287 Abbildungen*, ed. August L. Mayer, Stuttgart and Berlin, 1913,
p. 289). That 'replica' may have been the version seen by Frieda.

it – I have just revelled in J. J. Rousseau's *Confessions*[1] which I adore, he is so awfully lovable, I really think genius consists in a great lovableness, but then, that is the woman's point of view – My regards to your wife, I felt so flattered, when you told me 'my wife would like you', it also showed me that you think more of her than you know, so there –

L. sends love, I do hope your 'Cruise' will be successful both in print and in person –

Your with very kind regards

Frieda – at present I have not other name I believe –

670. To Edward Garnett, [31 October 1913]
Text: MS NYPL; Postmark, Tellaro 1.11.13; Unpublished.

Lerici per Fiascherino, Golfo della Spezia, Italy
Friday.

Dear Garnett,

Write and tell us how the play went off.[2] I hope it had a success: am keen to hear. We had a letter today from Frieda's theatrical friend in Germany. He is very much excited at present over the production of his translation of Galsworthy's *Joy* in Mannheim.[3] We shall be able to get his attention really, later on.

I wrote to the *English Review* and to Pinker.[4] The latter writes to me about novels, saying that he hears I am not engaged as he had believed, to Duckworth. I don't know why he said that. A man Curtis Brown[5] wrote offering me 'a considerable advance on a 20% royalty' – for America, and so for England. I told him I was due to you and Kennerley for novels: that I *might* give him a book of stories. That's all. It bores me to write to Pinker saying nothing.

I got this letter from W L George today. I shall send him the particulars he wants. One of the photos I had in the summer has not been published – so it could be copyright if he wanted, couldn't it. It is the one with the full

[1] Jean-Jacques Rousseau's *Confessions*, first published 1781–8.
[2] Edward Garnett's play *The Trial of Jeanne d'Arc* (1912) was first performed on 26 October 1913 at the Ethical Church, Bayswater, London. See *Letters*, i. 469 n. 4.
[3] A German translation of *Joy* was made by Dr Ernst Stahl; it was produced (date unknown) by Dr Geyers at Haus Zum Löffel in Freiburg. It is assumed that Stahl's is the translation referred to here. (Galsworthy's play was first produced in London in 1907 and published in 1909.)
[4] These letters do not appear to have survived.
[5] Curtis Brown (1866–1945) was to become DHL's literary agent in 1921.

face – at the Cearne.[1] Or ought I to have another done? – Is it worth much, the *Bookman* article?[2]

I haven't heard just lately from Kennerley. He said he was sending a cheque for £25, to you, for me on acc. of *Sons and Lovers*. It hasn't reached you, has it? I have received nothing. – I am going to open a current account with a Spezia bank.

I have been doing the stories for the *English* – am just finishing the last:[3] I hope they're all right.

I haven't got on a bit with the Sisters. It always takes me so long to settle down in a place. I doubt if it'll be done by Christmas. You needn't swear at me – you've been disagreeable enough lately to last you quite a long time.

And don't ever think I shall be trafficking with agents – I shan't do anything without telling you –

It is delicious here. I am just getting sufficiently inrooted to begin work again. I was a fool to move in the midst of a flow. If the Sisters is late, it'll be my fault this time.

I hope the new house is jolly. The *English Review* hasn't answered me about the stories. Tell me about Joan[4] – I hope *she* won't leave you in the lurch.

Our love to you.   D. H. Lawrence

If you don't want to give George the poems, I've got a spare copy.

671. To Edward Garnett, [2 November 1913]

Text: MS NYPL; Unpublished.

Lerici, per Fiascherino, Golfo della Spezia, Italy
Sunday

Dear Garnett,

On getting your letter I wrote to Kennerley as you suggested.

I enclose the American reviews – I'm afraid I've lost some – if they turn up I'll send them later. Don't bother to return these.

I've finished the last of the *English Review* stories, and started the Sisters. It is going along now. We won't forget the *Jeanne D'Arc*.

This isn't a letter, because I'm working and just want to give the girl the post.

---

[1] The photograph was taken by W. G. Parker on 26 June 1913; the original is inscribed 'To Edward Garnett'. It is reproduced in this volume.

[2] See p. 28 n. 2.   [3] See p. 82 n. 2.

[4] The heroine of Garnett's play.

You'll come here in spring? The robins are singing now, and the leaves are falling from the fig-trees.

Love from us.   D. H. Lawrence

W L George says he's fixed up the *Bookman* article with the editor for February – and with you for the photograph.

672. To Ada Clarke, [5 November 1913]

Text: MS Clarke; PC v. Golfo di Spezia, Fiascherino; Postmark, Lerici, 5 11 [...]; Unpublished.

[Lerici, per Fiascherino, Golfo della Spezia, Italy]
[5 November 1913]

This is one side of our little bay – the view is taken from our garden – but it is really *much* prettier.

Are you writing to me soon? – You are at home now for good. Are you all right?

Could you hunt round for me and see if you can find an old little college note book in which I have written my poems – the first I ever wrote – a little hard bound book with the college badge on it.[1] I looked when I was in England but couldn't find it. See if you can come across it. I am perhaps bringing out another volume of poetry in America.

Are you saving up to come and see us?

Much love from us.   D. H. Lawrence

673. To Henry Savage, [15? November 1913]

Text: MS YU; Moore, *Yale University Library Gazette*, xlvi. 266–7.

Lerici, per Fiascherino, Golfo della Spezia, Italy
Saturday[2]

Dear Savage,

Don't mind if I write pencil. – Do send us some books – we've had, in French from you, only Casanova 1 vol,[3] *Ame d'Enfant*,[4] and Ekhoud.[5] – I've

---

[1] This notebook is described by Vivian de Sola Pinto in 'D. H. Lawrence, Letter Writer and Craftsman in Verse', *Renaissance and Modern Studies*, i (1957), 10–11.

[2] The date of this letter is established by its relation to Letter 669, 31 October 1913 and Letter 678, 2 December 1913. In the latter, DHL reports having 'liked *Kreutzer Sonata*', a book which he requested from Savage in Letter 669 and appears now to have received.

[3] Giacomo Casanova de Seingalt (1725–98) was an Italian adventurer, who published his memoirs in French (12 vols, Paris, 1826–38). The specific volume read by DHL has not been identified.

[4] *Ame d'Enfant* (Paris, 1894) by Paul Margueritte (1860–1918).

[5] George Eekhoud (1854–1927), a Flemish writer who wrote in French.

not read either of the things you mention. I've not read *Kreutzer Sonata*.[1]
I should rather like a *Mill on the Floss* or else *Adam Bede*, to read again.[2]
But *don't buy things*. What you send, we can save and you can take back.

About Middleton – he annoys me by never saying[3] what he wants to say.
He is Douglas' 'This is deep Hell to be expressionless'.[4] He only talks
intellectually – the deep things he never got out. He was an unsounded well,
from which we only had skimmings. Perhaps there was something obstructing
him, in his soul – and probably it was his sex. A[5] big man is big because
his power, his horse-power or vital-power, is great – even Shelley and Keats,
had terrific vital power. Some men could catch up their sex and everything
into their heads – but poets not. Most poets die of sex – Keats, Shelley,
Burns. I cant understand it myself, not a bit. But study Burns a bit, or
Verlaine, to grasp Middleton – and Baudelaire. They've all – not Burns –
Baudelaire Verlaine and Flaubert – got about them, the feeling that their own
flesh is unclean – corrupt. And their art is the art of self hate and self-murder.
Flaubert gashed himself deliberately with every stroke of the pen. He hated
himself. His mind was free of ideals of chastity, and his body supplied him
with nothing but disgust. When he had a woman, he was never satisfied. It
left a residue inside him, which went corrupt. The old artist burned up this
residue to Almighty God. What is offered to God in all time is largely
unsatisfied sex. Flaubert wouldn't have any God outside himself – and so
he only felt himself inside unclean – full of rottenness – and he tried to burn
himself up in a slow fire, as one might burn a thing one hates.

It is all much too hard for me to understand. But they denied God – if
you read David['s][6] Psalms, you will see that God is to him like a great woman
he adores – they denied God in heaven, they would not throw out their
unsatisfaction like a dove over the waters. They denied love, and lived by
hate – hate is the obverse of love, the recoil of unsatisfied love. They *wanted*
to love themselves in the flesh – their intellectual dogma said so 'We are God,
all there is of him'. And love is a going out, so it was impossible – But to
understand Middleton you must understand the whole suicidal tendency that
has overspread Europe since 1880 – half Sweden commits suicide – a great
deal of Germany and France – it is the Northern races – Madam Bovary is
Flaubert suiciding his soul.

[1] See p. 96 n. 4.
[2] These two novels by George Eliot (especially *The Mill on the Floss*) had been among DHL's
favourite reading in his youth. See *Letters*, i. 88.
[3] saying] speaking
[4] From the poem 'Silence' by Lord Alfred Douglas (1870–1945). Cf. *Letters*, i. 180.
[5] A] In a
[6] DHL inserted 'Psalms' as an afterthought but omitted to make an adjustment to 'David'.

Don't misinterpret me [...] in my use of 'Sex'. Sex is the fountain head, where life bubbles up into the person from the unknown – you conduct life further and further from sex – it becomes movement – expression – logic. The nihilists – Tolstoi was really one, or nearly one – never tried to love – Middleton didn't, really – he was profoundly a nihilist – he should have uttered nihilism, but he was English, and hadn't the courage, so he kept one flag – Beauty. You might as well try to keep the bloom on the peach, and throw the peach in the fire, as talk about Beauty. It is a cant phrase of those who lack courage to say 'we don't believe in anything anything'! Middleton only really expressed himself once – when he killed himself.[1] For all his clap trap about suicide being an act of faith, it was an act of avowal of sheer lack of belief, touched with hate. You see a poet *must* love – or hate, which is the same thing. There is nothing to love – so he hates himself.

It is much too difficult for me. I'm not sure if there isn't a modern weariness. As you say, spirit and flesh should be finely balanced. They aren't. The flesh has been starved, denied, and impoverished, till it *is* weary, stiff, moribund. So the spirit is cynical – fancy asking a spirit to live with a half corpse of a body. And nobody helped Middleton to release his body from the deadness, the cerements. God, but all Englishmen are swathed in restraint and puritanism and anti-emotion, till they are walking mummies. Lay an Englishman on his back, and he is a mummy. Don't you see, centuries of Puritanicalism, and feeding the mind and soul at the expense of the body, has done for us.

Remember Wells' future men – large globulous heads with shreds of body.[2]

My God, what fools we are – what fools – not incarnate – excarnate.

D. H. Lawrence

674. To Edward Marsh, [18 November 1913]
Text: MS NYPL; Postmark, Lerici 19.11.13; Huxley 153–7.

Lerici, per Fiascherino, Golfo della Spezia, Italy
Tuesday

Dear Marsh,

You *are* wrong. It makes me open my eyes. I think I read my poetry more

[1] See p. 28 n. 5.
[2] Probably a reference to the Martians' 'heads' and 'tentacles' in *The War of the Worlds* (1898) by H. G. Wells: 'huge round bodies – or, rather, heads – about four feet in diameter, each body having in front of it a face....In a group round the mouth were sixteen slender, almost whiplike tentacles, arranged in two bunches of eight each' (Bk. II, chap. 2).

by length than by stress – as a matter of movements in space than footsteps
hitting the earth.

> Just a few of the roses we gathered by the Isar
> Are fallen, and their blood-red petals on the cloth,
> Float like boats on a river, waiting
> For a fairy wind to wake them from their sloth.[1]

I think more of a bird with broad wings flying and lapsing through the air,
than anything, when I think of metre. – So I read

I wonder if that is quite unintelligible. I am sure I am right. There is a double
method of scanning verse – if you'll notice it.

> I have / forgòt / much/, Cỳnara! / gòne with the / wìnd
>
> Flung ròses/, roses / riòtously / with the / thròng /
>
> Dàncing / to pùt / thy pàle, / lost lìl/ies òut / of mìnd;
>
> But Ì / was dès/olàte/, and sìck / of an òld / pàssion/,
>   Yea, all the time because the dance was long:
> I have been faithful to thee Cynara, in my fashion.[2]

Would you scan like that? I hate an on-foot method of reading. I should
go

[1] From the version of 'Roses on the Breakfast Table' that was published in *Poetry*, iii, January
1914 (see p. 56 n. 1). DHL introduces one change: the printed version reads 'mauve-red'.
[2] Ernest Dowson, 'Non sum qualis eram bonae sub regno Cynarae', ll. 13–18.

It all depends on the *pause* – the natural pause, the natural *lingering* of the
voice according to the feeling – it is the hidden *emotional* pattern that makes
poetry, not the obvious form.

$$\smile \;\; \smile \quad \smile \smile \quad \text{——} \quad \text{——}\smile\smile \quad \text{——} \quad \smile \quad \smile \quad \text{——}$$
I have forgot much, Cynara, gone with the wind

It is the lapse of the feeling, something as indefinite as expression in the voice,
carrying emotion. It doesn't depend on the ear, particularly, but on the
sensitive soul. And the ear gets a habit, and becomes master, when the ebbing
and lifting emotion should be master, and the ear the transmitter. If your
ear has got stiff and a bit mechanical, *don't* blame my poetry. That's why
you like *Golden Journey to Samarkand* [1] – it fits your habituated ear, and your
feeling crouches subservient and a bit pathetic. 'It satisfies my ear' you say.
Well, I don't write for your ear. This is the constant war, I reckon, between
new expression and the habituated, mechanical transmitters and receivers
of the human constitution.

I can't tell you what *pattern* I see in any poetry, save one complete thing.
But surely you don't class poetry among the decorative or conventional arts.
I always wonder if the Greeks and Romans really did scan, or if scansion
wasn't a thing invented afterwards by the schoolmaster. – Yet I seem to find
about the same number of long, lingering notes in each line. – I know
nothing about it. I only know you aren't right.

You are wrong, I think, about the two rhymes – why need you notice they
are rhymes? [2] – you are a bit of a policeman in poetry. I *never* put them in
because they are rhymes.

'Drearisome' [3] I am guilty of – peccavo.

'Sloth' I feel a *bit* guilty about – not quite so guilty as you would have
me. I'm not sure about 'Purity' [4] – I always felt suspicious of [5] it, and yet
I am inclined to think it is good.

'The land of her glad surmise' is a penny, not a sovereign. I always knew
it was shocking bad. – I must think about that ballad. [6]

[1] See Letter 637 and p. 61 n. 4.
[2] 'cloth' and 'sloth' in his own verse above.
[3] DHL uses the word in his poem 'The Wind, The Rascal' which had been sent to Marsh
(see Letter 665).   [4] See p. 94 n. 1.   [5] of] about
[6] Marsh was apparently critical of DHL's poem 'The Ballad of a Wayward Woman' (see
Letter 668). The quotation is from the following stanza:

> He puts his surf-wet fingers
> Over her startled eyes,
> And asks if she sees the land, the land,
> The land of her glad surmise.

I rather suspect you of being a young Philistine with the poetry of youth on you, and the –

But I *am* being a David that throws stones.[1]

Don't mind me. I find it frightfully easy to theorise and say all the things I don't mean, and frightfully difficult to find out even for myself, what I do mean.

I only *know* that the verse you quote against me is right, and you are wrong. And I am a poor, maligned, misunderstood, patronised and misread poet, and soon I shall burst into tears.

But thanks be to God above, my poetry doesn't stick to me. My wife has a beastly habit of comparing poetry – all literature in fact – to the droppings of the goats among the rocks – mere excreta that fertilises the ground it falls on.

I think I came a *real* cropper in my belief in metre, over Shelley. I tried all roads to scan him, but could never *read* him as he could be scanned. And I thought what bit of Latin scansion I did was a *horrible* fake: I never believed for an instant in the Sapphic form[2] – and Horace is already a bit of a mellow varsity man who never quite forgot Oxford.

I'm frightfully furious today. I rose at six and caught the steamer for Spezia – *very beautiful* the dawn on the water and rocks that are afire and yet dont burn. But in Spezia the bank hadn't done what I wanted, and the picture framer hadn't done *anything*, and the pianoforte man hadn't got ready and I cursed the Italians right and left. I hate them and want to stamp on them.

Don't talk to me any more about poetry for months – unless it is other men's work. I really love verse, even rubbish. But I'm fearfully busy at a novel, and brush all the gossamer of verse off my face.

Non sum qualis eram bonae sub regno Cynarae. – I read that when I lift my eyes, and immediately feel inclined to weep. Why have we lost the luxury of tears. It is well done to call a good wine Lacrimae Christi.

Frieda is grilling a nice little steak over a wood fire. I think it's rough, when I've just eaten a lot of carrots in butter, and can't eat no more: then she discovers that nice little steak.

We are exceedingly anxious for you to come at Christmas. I was thinking today how I would take you (I've got a fearful desire to play 'mine host' –) on the steamer and over our gallant hills – you and Jim Barnes. Tell us *when*

---

[1] See 1 Samuel xvii. 40–50.

[2] A stanzaic pattern deriving its name from the Greek poetess Sappho, who wrote love lyrics c. 600 B.C. The form consists of three verses of eleven syllables each, and a fourth verse of five.

you'll come – come a bit earlier than the 21st if you can – and stay – it sounds
very magnificent – *two* nights, will you. This terrific burst of hospitality on
our part will surprise you. But you might be happy for two days, and dying
of boredom the third. – It's like a beautiful lady I know – very slightly.[1]
'Ah – I never stay with a man more than a fortnight, neither my clothes nor
my conversation will hold out any longer'.

It is very beautiful, and the robins sing all day among the red leaves of
the vine etc etc etc.

This coruscating notepaper was given to my wife by her mother: you must
hold us guiltless.[2]

This is a long letter. I am getting more aimiable.

Say how you'll come here, and when – whether to Sarzana or to Spezia.
Sarzana is quicker – you sit in a broken-down omnibus for an hour. Spezia
has a beautiful ride on a dirty steamer for 40 minutes across the bay.

Many thanks for giving the poem to the *New Statesman*.[3] It's a poem that
would stand printing in a weekly paper.

Many warm regards from us.

D. H. Lawrence

Your letter was jolly good to me *really* – I always thank God when a man
will say straight out to me, what he has to say. But it's rare when one will.
I call it affectionately – not anything else.

DHL

We've got in 25 litres of wine – I wonder what you'll think of it when
you come. I am fearfully proud of it – I stand and gloat over the rush-wrapped
fat bottles.

DHL

675. To Cynthia Asquith, [25 November 1913]
Text: MS UT; Huxley 161–3.

Lerici, per Fiascherino, Golfo della Spezia, Italy
Tuesday Nov? 1913[4]

Dear Mrs Asquith,

Because I feel frightfully disagreeable, and not fit to consecrate myself
to novels or to short stories, I'll write a letter. I like to write when I feel
spiteful: it's like having a good sneeze. Don't mind, will you.

[1] Unidentified.   [2] Cf. p. 79 n. 1.
[3] DHL's poem 'Service of all the Dead' appeared in the *New Statesman*, ii, (15 November
1913), and Marsh reprinted it in his *Georgian Poetry 1913–1915*. DHL later re-titled the poem
'Giorno dei Morti'.
[4] Dated with reference to the wedding of the 'peasant' Ezechiele Azzarini on 29 November
1913 ('next Saturday').

You say we're happy – per Bacchino![1] If you but knew the thunderstorms of tragedy that have played over my wretched head, as if I was set up on God's earth for a lightning conductor, you'd say, 'thank God I am not as that poor man.'[2] If you knew the slough of misery we've struggled and suffocated through, you'd stroke your counterpane with a purring motion, like an old maid having muffins for tea in the lamplight and reading Stanley in Africa.[3] If ever you hear of me in a mad-house, and Frieda buried under a nameless sod, you'll say, 'Poor things, no wonder, with all they've gone through.' You talk about tears drowning the wind[4] – my God. – We are the most unfortunate, agonised, fate-harassed mortals since Orestes[5] and that gang. Don't you forget it. Put away all illusions concerning us, and see the truth.

When I had an English feel come over me, I took it frightfully badly, that we had appeared before[6] you as if we were a perfectly respectable couple. I thought of the contamination – etc etc – and I really was upset. I'm glad you didn't mind: you might with justice have taken it amiss – and then, Lord, what a state I should have been in when the English feel came over me again. Heaven be blessed, England is only a spot of grease on the soup just now.

I am sorry you've got a cold. But what do you expect, after purpling in Venice. – Frieda's been in bed for four days also – like Robinson Crusoe: 'First day I vomited————.' I wandered under the falling vines muttering 'What rhubarb, senna and what purgative drug———.'[7] It was sheer misery. We *have* had a time, between us: oh dear o' me! She is a bit better today.

I've been to Spezia – Frieda *will* hire a piano – not a hurdy-gurdy. Well, it has to come first on the workman's steamer to Lerici, then got down into a rowing boat, and rowed along the coast, past jutting rocks where the sea goes up and down to bring your heart in your mouth, finally landed onto the shingle of this little bay, and somehow got up the steeps to the house. Well the man found out what journey it was, and he clings to his piano as if it were his only child, nor could I snatch it from him today. So we fell out – and in the midst of it a man in sailor's uniform with 'White Star'[8] on his breast came and said he was English and did we want to buy Contraband English cloth. And he wasn't English – nor French, nor

---

[1] 'by Jove!'   [2] Cf. Luke xviii. 11.
[3] Sir Henry Morton Stanley (1841–1904), the famous explorer of Africa. His most frequently published book was *In Darkest Africa* (1890); his *Autobiography* appeared in 1909.
[4] *Macbeth* I. vii. 25 ['tears shall drown the wind'].
[5] Son of Agamemnon and Clytemnestra, who avenged his father's murder by killing his mother and her lover.   [6] appeared before] come it over
[7] *Macbeth* v. iii. 66 ['...senna, or...'].
[8] The name of Cunard's fleet of passenger liners.

German, nor Italian – but spoke twenty words of each. Now I might have wrested this pianoforte out of the fervent arms of Rugi Gulielmo, but for the interruption of the sailor with a sack. As it was, I returned, boat and all, empty save of curses.

'Ecco – un pianoforte – it's not like a piece of furniture – if it was a piece of furniture – hé, va bene – but – a pianoforte – hé –' I loathe and detest the Italians. They never argue, they just get hold of a parrot phrase, shove up their shoulders and put their heads on one side, and flap their hands. And what is an honest man to do with 'em? (Forget my past when I say 'honest man'). Now I shall have to go tomorrow, and pay a regiment of facchini[1] to transport that cursed pianoforte.

> 'Take it up tenderly
> Lift it with care
> Fashioned so slenderly
> Young and so fair'[2]

And it's a tin-pot thing not fit for a cat to walk up and down. And if it *does* go to the bottom of the sea – well God bless it, and peace be with it.

Frieda has got a cough, and barks like a dog fox. It's sickening.

Eddie Marsh is coming to see us. We've got in twenty five litres of red wine – how's that for a cellar? It cost about nine shillings – made of our own vines – not bad – but in certain places they make it better.

I wish she wouldn't bark. She's that proud of her cough. And it's nothing but sound and fury, signifying nought.

Here I sit by the studious lamp, with a pentola[3] bubbling over a nice wood fire, and the cat purring twenty to the dozen. But oh the skeleton in the cupboard. – I'm the cupboard, and the skeleton's inside me.

I don't know anything about my play.[4] Nobody tells me anything. But in February I'm going to be in the *Bookman* – done by W L George – and a photograph. Do you know W L George – ? he is perfect on the theme of love. He wrote some books – *A Bed of Roses*, and so on. I rather like him – honestly. But he's one of the funniest men in London: 'Ah[5] – did you see it – the snowy white neck – the beckoning of a curl – wait – wait –' – This in the Strand as an ordinary girl goes by.

[1] 'porters'.
[2] A parody of Thomas Hood's poem, 'The Bridge of Sighs', ll. 5–8 ['Take her up tenderly, / Lift her with...'].
[3] 'pot'.   [4] *The Widowing of Mrs Holroyd.*
[5] Ah] All

I suppose you are whining and grizzling in London, and Mr Asquith has got a longer face than a violoncello: just because he can't get somebody to squabble with at the Bar. I'm only too thankful when I needn't squabble. Think of that pianoforte. – And by Jove, haven't my married Sisters and my brother ridden round like very Walküre on their broomstick indignation. They've only just known about the divorce – we have been abroad these twenty months. You tell Mr Asquith that man doth not live by Briefs alone.[1] But he won't believe you. It's no use us poets waving our idealistic banners, like frantic suffragettes.

Here – I've written about enough. I suppose – 'the jonquil flaunteth a gay, blonde head.'[2]

> 'Il pleut doucement sur la ville
> Comme il pleut dans mon cœur[3]

As a matter of fact, it's a perfectly glittery and starry night, with a glow-worm outside the door, and on the sea a lighthouse beating time to the stars.

Well, adieu, fair lady – don't be cross and sad. Think that we have simply worn holes in our hankeys, with weeping.

Why should the cat sleep all night on my knee, and give me fleas to bear? Why?

There's a peasant wedding down below, next Saturday. The bride in white silk and orange blossom must clamber fearful roads, three hours there and back, to go to the Syndaco of l'Ameglia,[4] to be married. Mass at 7.30 at Tellaro – piccola colazione[5] at the bride's house at 8.30 – un boccone[6] – marriage at 10.0, at l'Ameglia – pranzo[7] down here at midday – We are invited. – But it's rather sad – he doesn't want her *very* badly. One gets married – si – come si fa![8] They say it so often: – ma – come si fa?[9]

> Il pleut doucement dans la ville
> I think I am missing a meal

> a rivederla, Signoria[10]   D. H. Lawrence

They call us 'Signoria'. How's that for grandeur! – Shades of my poor father!

---

[1] Cf. Luke iv. 4.   [2] See p. 89 n. 1.

[3] Verlaine, *Romances sans Paroles* ['Il pleure dans mon cœur / Comme il pleut sur la ville'].
   Cf. *Letters*, i. 320.   [4] 'the Mayor of Ameglia'.

[5] 'breakfast'.   [6] 'a bite'.   [7] 'lunch'.

[8] 'yes – it's expected'.   [9] 'what can you do?'.

[10] 'goodbye, your ladyship'. (When DHL uses 'Signoria' in his postscript, he intends 'lordship and ladyship'.)

676. To John Middleton Murry, [27? November 1913]
Text: MS NYPL; cited in Murry, *New Adelphi* 266.

Lerici, per Fiascherino, Golfo della Spezia, Italy.
Thursday.[1]

Dear Murry,

I am going to answer you immediately, and frankly.

When you say you won't take Katherine's money, it means you don't trust her love for you: When you say she needs little luxuries, and you couldn't bear to deprive her of them, it means you don't respect either yourself or her sufficiently to do it.

It looks to me as if you two, far from growing nearer, are snapping the bonds that hold you together, one after another. I suppose you must both of you consult your own hearts, honestly. She must see if she really *wants* you, wants to keep you and to have no other man all her life. It means forfeiting something. But the only principle I can see in this life, is that one *must* forfeit the less for the greater.[2] Only one must be thoroughly honest about it.

She must say 'Could I live in a little place in Italy with Jack, and be lonely, have rather a bare life, but be happy'. If she could, then take her money. If she doesn't want to, don't try. But don't beat about the bush. In the way you go on, you are inevitably coming apart. She is perhaps beginning to be unsatisfied with you. And you won't make her more satisfied, by being unselfish. You must say, 'how can I make myself most healthy, strong, and satisfactory to myself and to her'? If by being lazy for six months, then be lazy, and take her money. It doesn't matter if she misses her luxuries: she won't die of it. What luxuries do you mean?

If she doesn't want to stake her whole life and being on you, then go to your University abroad for a while, alone.[3] I warn you, it'll be hellish barren.

Or else you can gradually come apart in London, and then flounder till you get your feet again, severally. But be clear about it. It lies between you and Katherine, nowhere else.

Of course you can't dream of living long without work. Couldn't you get the *Westminster* [*Gazette*] to give you *two* columns a week, abroad? You must *try*. You must stick to criticism. You ought also to plan a book, either on

---

[1] Letter 716 makes it clear that this letter was followed by a long silence on Murry's part; it also seems to suggest that this letter dated from 1913. Had it been later than Letter 677, DHL would have told Murry about the visit from the 'Georgians'.

[2] less for the greater.] greater for the less.

[3] Murry had been offered a position in a German university: 'The choice was between a very meagre lektorship in a German University, and some small journalistic job in Paris' (Murry, *Autobiography* 270). He chose the latter.

some literary point or some man. I should like to write a book on English heroines. You ought to do something of that sort, but not so cheap. Don't try a novel – try Essays – like Walter Pater[1] or somebody of that style. But you *can* do something *good* in that line: something concerning *literature* rather than life. And you must rest, and you and Katherine must heal, and come together, before you do *any serious* work of any sort. It is the split in the love that drains you. You see, while she doesn't really love you, and is not satisfied, *you* show to such frightful disadvantage. But it would be[2] a pity not to let your mind flower – it might, under decent circumstances, produce beautiful delicate things, in perception and appreciation. And *she* has a right to provide the conditions. But not if you don't trust yourself nor her nor anybody, but go on slopping, and pandering to her smaller side. If you work yourself sterile to get her chocolates, she will most justly detest you – she is *perfectly* right. If you tell her, pandering to her uncertainty in you, that in time of great stress, you could let her go to a man like a prostitute, for money, you are a fool. You *couldn't* do it, without some violation to your soul, some rupture that would cripple you for ever. Then why don't you say 'no'. She wants to be sure that she is worth it to you, and you, instead of saying yes, sort of sacrifice yourself to her. She doesn't want you to sacrifice yourself to her, you fool. Be more natural, and positive, and stick to your own guts. You spread them on a tray for her to throw to the cats.

If you want things to come right – if you are ill, and exhausted, then take her money to the last penny, and let her do her own house-work. Then she'll know you love her. You can't blame her if she's not satisfied with you. If I haven't had enough dinner, you can't blame *me*. You've got it in you to be enough for her. But you fool, you squander yourself, not for *her*, but to provide her with petty luxuries she doesn't really want. You insult her. A woman unsatisfied must have luxuries. But a woman who loves a man would sleep on a board.

It strikes me you've got off your lines, somewhere. You've not been man enough: you've felt it rested with your honor to give her a place to be proud of. It rested with your honor to give her a man to be satisfied with – and satisfaction is never accomplished even physically without the man is strongly and surely himself, and doesn't depend on anything but his own *being* to make a woman love him. You've tried to satisfy Katherine with what you could earn for her, give her: and she will only be satisfied with what you *are*.

And you don't know what you are. You've never come to it. You've always

---

[1] Walter Horatio Pater (1839–94), essayist and critic.   [2] would be] would not be

been dodging round, getting *Rhythms* and flats and doing criticism for money.[1] You are a fool to work so hard for Katherine – she hates you for it – and quite right. You want to be strong in the possession of your own soul. Perhaps you will only come to that when this affair of you and her has gone crash. I should be sorry to think that – I don't believe it. You must save yourself, and your self-respect, by making it complete between Katherine and you – if you devour her money till she walks in rags, if you are both outcast. Make her certain – don't pander to her – stick to *yourself* – do what you *want* to do – don't *consider* her – she hates and loathes being considered. You insult her in saying you wouldn't take her money.

The University idea is a bad one. It would further disintegrate you.

If you are disintegrated, then *get integrated* again.[2] Don't be a coward. If you are disintegrated your first duty is to yourself, and you may use Katherine – her money and everything – to get right again. You're not well, man. Then have the courage to get well. If you are strong again, and a bit complete, *she'll* be satisfied with you. She'll love you hard enough. But don't you see, at this rate, you distrain on her day by day and month by month. I've done it myself.

Take your rest – do *nothing* if you like for a while – though I'd do a *bit*. Get better, first and foremost – use *anybody's* money, to do so. Get better – and do things you like. Get yourself into condition – it drains and wearies Katherine to have you like this. What a fool you are, what a fool. Don't bother about her – what she wants or feels. Say 'I am a man at the end of the tether, therefore I become a man blind to everything but my own need'. But keep a heart for the long run.

Look. We pay 60 Lire[3] a month for this house: 25 Lire for the servant: and food is *very* cheap. You could live on 185 Lire a month, in plenty – and be greeted as the 'Signoria' when you went out together – it is the same as 'Guten Tag, Herrschaften'.[4] That would be luxury enough for Katherine.

Get up, lad, and be a man for yourself. It's the man who dares to take, who is independent, not he who gives.

I think Oxford did you harm.

It is beautiful, wonderful, here. A ten pound note is 253 Lire. We could get you, I believe, a jolly nice apartment in a big garden, in a house alone for 80 Lire a month. Don't waste yourself – don't be silly and floppy. You know what you *could* do – you *could* write – then prepare yourself: and first

---

[1] DHL alludes to the magazines that Murry and Katherine Mansfield had founded, *Rhythm* and the *Blue Review*.   [2] again.] enough.

[3] Three times in this sentence and the next DHL first wrote 'francs' and each time altered it to 'Lire'.   [4] 'Good day, ladies and gentlemen'.

make Katherine at rest in her love for you. Say 'this I will certainly do' – it would be a relief for her to hear you. Don't be a child – don't keep that rather childish charm. Throw everything away, and say 'Now I act for my own good, at last'.

We are getting gradually nearer again, Frieda and I. It is very beautiful here.

We are awfully sorry Katherine is so seedy. She ought to write to us. Our love to her and you.

D. H. Lawrence

If you've got an odd book or so you don't want to read, would you send it us. There is nothing for Frieda to read – and we like anything and everything.

677. To Edward Marsh, [29 November 1913]

Text: MS NYPL; PC; Postmark, Pisa-Genova 29. NOV. 13; Unpublished.

Fiascherino
[29 November 1913]

Dear Marsh,

I'm too much out of breath to say any more – but it's horrible that you're not coming for Christmas. Here we are

Wilfrid [Gibson]
Lascelles A[bercrombie]
R. C. Trevelyan
Catherine Abercrombie
D. H. Lawrence
Frieda Lawrence[1]

678. To Henry Savage, 2 December 1913

Text: MS YU and Moore AMSC; Postmark, Tellaro 2 12 13; Moore, *Yale University Library Gazette*, xxxiv. 29–31.

Lerici, per Fiascherino, Golfo della Spezia, Italia
2 Dec 1913

Dear Savage,

I've just come from rowing on the sea – one of those oily, thin-skinned, muscular seas, that are quiet and yet in powerful motion. So the world goes

---

[1] The 'Georgian party' found DHL 'attending a peasant wedding in patent-leather boots and a black suit. Though a little put out at first, DHL enjoyed the situation' (Hassall, *Edward Marsh*, p. 261). The text of the card is in DHL's hand; it is signed by each person individually. Aubrey Waterfield was of the party but was not a signatory. For a vivid description of their visit to DHL, see Lina Waterfield's *Castle in Italy* (1961), pp. 134–5.

up and down, and I feel like embracing the ilex tree. It'll be no sort of a letter, but bear with me.

The James Stephens interested me very much to start with, and ended by making me cross and impatient.[1] Nothing *happens* – I think the girl in the Charwomans story is an awfully tame bit of crimped white paper – it's a lie. The innocence I can stand, but the swiss milk sweetening, no. And the *Crock of Gold*[2] – I love him when the wife nags, and the philosopher buzzes like a top and drops dead. I love the idea of Pan and Angus Og having a talk – but poor, poor Pan, he must be in his second childhood if he talks as he does via Stephens. Fancy the God from Greece uttering such arguments for his own existence. No, it's belittling a great theme by a small handling: let him stick to little girls with beads and belts. I knew he was a little sickly man – that's why he liked that huge policeman so much, and gave himself the crown – the crinkled paper little girl – because he has more spirit. I'm sure he has more spirit than the fat policeman, but *he* isn't sure, and he envies the fat policeman painfully. As for his knowledge of women – it is so tame and trite. As you say, it's the savants' knowledge of the savage: deduction. He's a little man who has never entered into the fray, but sings 'Buttercups and Daisies'.[3] Then for God's sake let him sing 'Buttercups and Daisies', and leave the Great God Pan alone, and above all, refrain from handling Woman en gros.

I should love *Fumeurs d'Opium*[4] – they are the books that fascinate me – the raw material of Art. That's why I liked *Kreutzer Sonata* – it is exactly what Tolstoi *thought* he experienced – and jolly truthful too – but not art. But it interests me. I love travels and rather raw philosophy and when you can lend me books about Greek religions and rise of Greek Drama, or Egyptian influences – or things like that – I love them. I got a fearful lot out of a scrubby book *Art and Ritual*[5] – one of the Universal Knowledge Shilling series. It is stupidly put, but it lets one in for an idea that helps one immensely.

I think in Italy one is interested in different things from in England – one can't stand so much woolliness, and fluffiness, as there is in Stephens.

[1] DHL had been reading the novel, *The Charwoman's Daughter* (1912) by James Stephens (1882–1950).
[2] Stephens' novel *The Crock of Gold* (1912) is divided into six books: I – The Coming of Pan; II – The Philosopher's Journey; III – The Two Gods; IV – The Philosopher's Return; V – The Policeman; and VI – The Thin Woman's Journey and the Happy March.
[3] Stephens had published a poem entitled 'The Daisies', but DHL is referring to a poem which he probably knew as a child, by Mary Howitt (1799–1888), called 'Buttercups and Daisies' in a collection of verses entitled *Birds and Flowers and Other Country Things* [1855].
[4] Either *Les Fumeurs d'Opium en Chine* by Dr Henri Adolphe François Libermann (Boulogne, n.d.) or *Fumeurs d'Opium* by Jules Boissière (Paris, 1896).
[5] See p. 90 n. 2.

We don't see the *English Review*, so I cant tell you about the Middleton play.[1] I shall send you the books back in a while – you don't mind how long I keep them?

It interests me, about Middleton's *work*. I think he always felt some obstruction. I think one has as it were to fuse ones physical and mental self right down, to produce good art. And there was some of him that wouldn't fuse – like some dross, that hindered him, that he couldn't grip and reduce with passion. And so again he hated himself. Perhaps if he could have found a woman to love, and who loved him, that would have done it, and he would have been pure. He was always impure. I can't explain the word impure, because I don't know what it means.

It seems to me a purely lyric poet gives himself, right down to his sex, to his mood, utterly and abandonedly, whirls himself round like Stephens philosopher till he spontaneously combusts into verse. He has nothing that goes on, no passion, only a few intense moods, separate like odd stars, and when each has burned away, he must die. It is no accident that Shelley got drowned – he was always trying to drown himself – it was his last mood.

Then there is the half lyric poet, like Middleton. His lyrics are far, far before his prose, of course. But he had exhausted most of his moods: his one-man show was over: it needed to become a two person show. That heavier, more enduring part which wasn't a lyric poet but a man with dramatic capabilities, needed fertilising by some love. And it never was fertilised. So he destroyed it, because perhaps it had already begun to corrupt. I believe, he would have loved a man, more than a woman: even physically: like the ancients did. I believe it is because most women don't leave scope to the man's imagination – but I don't know. I should like to know why nearly every man that approaches greatness tends to homosexuality, whether he admits it or not: so that he loves the *body* of a man better than the body of a woman – as I believe the Greeks did, sculptors and all, by far. I believe a man projects his own image on another man, like on a mirror. But from a woman he wants himself re-born, re-constructed. So he can always get satisfaction from a man, but it is the hardest thing in life to get ones soul and body satisfied from a woman, so that one is free from oneself. And one is kept by all tradition and instinct from loving men, or a man – for it means just extinction of all the purposive influences. And one doesn't believe in one's power to find and to form the woman in whom one can be free – and one shoots oneself, if one is vital and feels powerfully and down to the core.

[1] 'The District Visitor', One Act, in *English Review*, xv (November 1913), 497–505.

Again I don't know what I'm talking about.

It *is* beautiful here. The sun is just setting over the sea, – and such a long gold shaky road between the milky waves.

The other day, when we were at a peasants wedding, Lascelles Abercrombie and W W Gibson and Trevelyan and another man suddenly appeared.[1] It was queer. And they seemed so shadowy and funny, after the crude, strong, rather passionate men at the wedding. I feel always top heavy with these vague countrymen of mine, though one stands steady enough with the common Italians. One man, a real type with black brows and long teeth under a black moustache, got drunk, and very queer. It is very interesting. Gibson wouldn't interest me as much in twenty years, as Severino did that evening. Modern Geniuses are so tame: and so good, and so generous. I really do love Gibson, and Abercrombie. They make me feel ashamed of myself, as if my human manners were very bad.

Your poem wasn't bad, but as you say, a little bit facile. It's as if you can't grip yourself to get at the reality.

You must come out here in the Spring. How is the Cruise?[2] What funny names for the boy. If I had a son, I wonder what I should call him – something exciting like Severino or Benedetto. The last bit of the sun has gone, and the evening wind is at once touched with snow from the Appenines.

It's a stupid letter – but bear with it. What about your dramatic critic job? I *would* get something to do, if I were you – I don't believe it matters very much what.

Love to the son – regards to Mrs Savage.

Yours   D. H. Lawrence

[Frieda Weekley begins]

Dear Mr. Savage,

If you knew how *lovely* it was to find your literature when I have climbed to Telaro (our postoffice) then to sit on the rocks and unwrap the literature (yours and the books) you wouldn't mind all the bother we are – I am lying in my hammock looking over Porto Venere, how you would love it – If you could see it, you would – but you simply *must* come, beg or borrow or steal – Abercrombie, Gibson – Trevelyan turned up the other day, when we were at the peasant's wedding here, they were so English, but lovable,

[1] Robert Calverley Trevelyan (1872–1951), poet, playwright and translator. At this time he was living in Boccaccio's villa near Florence (Hassall, *Marsh*, p. 241). Gibson and the Abercrombies were staying with him. The unnamed man was Aubrey Waterfield (d. 1944), painter and illustrator; he lived in the Castle of Aulla (about twenty miles from Spezia) from 1903. m. Lina Duff Gordon (b. 1874), 1902. See Lina Waterfield's autobiography, *Castle in Italy*.   [2] See p. 73 n. 1.

especially Trevelyan's eyes seem to shine with kindness. L[awrence] is lazy, I am glad, we are so happy on the water too in our boat with real Turner sunsets in the flesh – Your boy – *do* enjoy him, when I think of the joy mine gave me and now I have'nt got them – Is he like either you or your wife? Is he an anxiety? Don't let him be, with a first one never knows what to do; I am feeling so beautifully stupid today – I never saw Middleton's play, we have *no* paper of any sort, what you send us, is all we have read, since we are here – I just read some [Lawrence interjects: Ernest] Dowson, he is another melancholy blighter – I dont believe you are decadent, it's only a phase –

Goodbye in the sunshine, my love to the wife and the infant –

Yours Frieda L—

Bring your wife in the spring! Awfully many thanks!

679. To J. B. Pinker, 2 December 1913
Text: MS UNYB; cited in Moore, *Intelligent Heart* 158.

Lerici, per Fiascherino, Golfo della Spezia, Italia
2 Dec 1913

Dear Mr Pinker,

Thanks for your letters. God knows what I am to answer to them. *Sons and Lovers* does not seem to have done wonders, but I believe Duckworth and Mitchell Kennerley advertised it pretty well. As for giving you a novel – I can't in decency, in the near future. Later on I will if I can. I shall be glad enough for you to talk of me in America. In the spring, when I am in England, I shall come and talk to you. For the present, what is the good of promising, when I am not sure. – And I only write one novel a year.

But talk of me if you will.

Yours Sincerely   D. H. Lawrence

680. To Arthur McLeod, 2 December 1913
Text: MS UT; Postmark, Tellaro 2.12.13; Huxley 163–5.

Lerici, per Fiascherino, Golfo della Spezia, Italia
2 Dec 1913

Dear Mac,

We were awfully glad to have the Dowson, but I was disappointed.[1]

---

[1] *The Poems of Ernest Dowson*, with a memoir by Arthur Symons, Four illustrations by Aubrey Beardsley, and a Portrait by William Rothenstein (1905).

I only knew the Cynara poem, and the verse, which ran in my mind

> 'We are not long for music and laughter
> Love and desire and hate
> I think we have no portion in them, after
> We pass the gate'.[1]

That always haunted me. But I had remembered it wrong – I always remember poetry wrong. I thought he was a simple, rather restrained poet – and I find him translating Verlaine very badly. It's a shame. And yet he is a poet – I rather love him. The playlet is piffle[2] – but some of the songs – I hate the Beardsley illustrations. – I shall send you the book back soon – with many many thanks.

We have been reading James Stephens – another disappointment.

Did you see my poem in the *New Statesman*, a fortnight or so back? Some people loved it – as for me – I got a guinea for it.[3]

The other day, suddenly descended upon us Lascelles Abercrombie and W W Gibson and Trevelyan and a man called Waterfield. We were at a peasant wedding at a house on the bay, dressed in our best clothes in honor of the bride, and having an awfully good time: Gibson is a really lovable fellow – so is Trevelyan – and Abercrombie one of the sharpest men I have ever met. But it was so queer, to leave the feast and descend into the thin atmosphere of a little group of cultured Englishman. At the upper room where the feast was spread were twenty five people. There were nine fowls killed for the feast – and the next course was octopuses – (quite big ones, with arms half a yard long – I saw Ezzechiele bring them in from the sea, with their stony eyes open – and they nearly made me sick.) – The wine was running very red – then suddenly we must descend to these five English poets. It was like suddenly going into very rare air. One staggered and I quite lost my bearings. Yet they are folk I am awfully fond of.

W H Davies is coming in the Spring – oh, lots of folk. How are you going on. You don't tell us much news about yourself.

I am writing my novel slowly – it will be a beautiful novel – when it's

[1] 'Vitae summa brevis spem nos vetat incohare longam', ll. 1–4:

> They are not long, the weeping and the laughter,
>   Love and desire and hate:
> I think they have no portion in us after
>   We pass the gate.

[2] *The Pierrot of the Minute: A Dramatic Phantasy in One Act* (1897).
[3] See p. 106 n. 3.

done. But here, it is so beautiful, one can't work. I was out rowing on the sea all afternoon – and the sea *did* heave – the sky is still coming up and down. There is a new moon among a miracle of a sunset, a sea all gold and milk white, with a train of fire – ah, you should come here.

Some time, send me just a newspaper, will you. Don't send books, they are so costly.

You have no idea how much I got out of that *Ritual and Art* book – it *is* a good idea – but a school marmy woman who writes it.

It is dark. Elide must go to Tellaro – io devo finire.[1]

a rivederla   D. H. Lawrence

681. To Edward Marsh, 17 December 1913
Text: MS NYPL; Postmark, Tellaro 18.12.13; Huxley 165–7.

Lerici, per Fiascherino, Golfo della Spezia, Italy
Dec. 17. 1913

Dear Eddie,

We were awfully sorry to think of Jim Barneses appendix, as you may imagine. By this time he should be getting quite well again – is he? You seem to take appendicitis lightly[2] – which of course scares me. I think one ought to say 'he's sure to die', then perhaps he'll get better quick. We don't mind waiting if you will really come. But I hope he is well again, or on the way there, now.

I think of us driving in a carriage, glorious and resplendent, over the Magra from Sarzana to La Serra. But we must walk from Serra down here – about a mile – down paths as slippery and dangerous and beautiful as the road to hell. So don't bring your bigger luggage, because this place is nearly inaccessible.

We were to have other visitors,[3] but they won't come because of their little baby, which they daren't leave with the Irish nurse in London. So we are mourning our neglected state. I do hope that appendix will consent to abdicate peacefully. Try to stay two nights – wring them out of somebody else. Otherwise the time would be so short.

Did the poets tell you how they came and found me in patent leather boots and black suit, playing Signore at the wedding? It *was* a shock. But we went back to the feast, and had high jinks.

I loved Gibson still more than Abercrombie – perhaps because I know him better. But I think Gibson is one of the clearest and most lovable

---
[1] 'I must stop now'.
[2] lightly] quite lightly   [3] Henry Savage and his wife.

personalities that I know. Abercrombie *is* sharp – he is much more *intellectual* than I had imagined: keener, more sharp-minded. I shall enjoy talking to him. We both loved Mrs Abercrombie: she's not a bit like a Madonna, neither the Raphael nor Botticelli sort, so you're wrong there, Sir. But she's most awfully jolly, and a fine true-metal sort that I love. They invited us to go and stay with them, both the Abercombies and Gibson, with such warm generosity: and I shall kick my heels with joy, to go.

About metres, I shall have to pray for grace from God. But (scissors?) I think Shelley a million thousand times more beautiful than Milton.

I send you a poem which you ought to like. If you do, give it to somebody to publish, when you've got an easy leisurely occasion.[1]

The poets let us in for society. They brought Waterfield from Aulla, he brought Mrs Huntingdon, she brought Mrs Pearse,[2] and the plot thickens. We were the week-end at Aulla with Waterfield, who has quite a wonderful castle, in a sort of arena, like the victim, with the Appenines all round. It is a wonderful place, but it gives me the creeps down my back, just as if one sat in a chair down in the middle of the amphitheatre at Verona, and the great banks of stone took no notice, but gathered round.[3]

Only when we were coming away, at the station, there were four men emigrating to Buenos Ayres, and two young wives looking bewildered, then tears, and Frieda howling on my left hand, and the emigrants on my right, till I can tell you, I felt in the middle of a cyclone. It affects me yet.

We are just going to Mrs Pearse's for tea and last time they came here, we rowed them home. But coming back, Frieda and I fell out so frightfully – we were rowing one oar each, – that the boat revolved on its axis, and seriously thought of diving under water out of our way. So today Madam must walk, whether she will or no.

Barrie – I remembered to put Dear Sir James Barrie, when I answered – I nearly put Dear Sir James Barrie Bart – wrote me a nice little note, and was generous enough to say he was going to be proud of me.[4] – He hasn't seen me – the bel pezzo[5] that I am.

Perhaps I shan't write to you any more before Christmas. All Greetings

---

[1] The poem, 'Grief', was published entire in *Poetry*, v (December 1914). However, a poem entitled 'Twilight', which incorporates parts of 'Grief', appeared in the *English Review*, xvi (February 1914), 305.

[2] The Huntingdons and Pearses were English families living near Lerici.

[3] For further details see Lina Waterfield, *Castle in Italy*, chap. 14 and two pictures by Aubrey Waterfield reproduced facing pp. 184 and 185.

[4] This exchange of letters between DHL and Barrie has not survived. (Barrie had been made a baronet in the Birthday Honours List on 14 June 1913.)

[5] 'fine fellow'.

and Good Wishes! How did you look, futuristically? Lord, you're a bit of a jig-saw puzzle to start with, mixing poets and pictures, the Admiralty and what-not, like somebody shuffling cards.

a rivederci – auf wiedersehen – au revoir – jamque vale!

D. H. Lawrence

To Eddie Marsh, with much affection, this poem for a Christmas card, which, albeit, a trifle lugubrious, pray God may go daintily to his ear.

Grief.

The darkness steals the forms of all the queens,
But oh, the palms of his two black hands are red!
    It is death I fear so much, it is not the dead,
Not this grey book, but the torn and bloody scenes.

The lamps are white like Snowdrops in the grass,
The town is like a church-yard, all so still
And dark now night is here, – nor will
Another torn red sunset come to pass.

And so I sit and turn the book of grey,
Feeling the darkness like a blind man reading,
All fearful lest I find some new word bleeding –
    – Nay, take my painted missal book away.[1]

David Herbert
Son of Arthur John Lawrence
wrote this poem:
December 16 – 1913
Requiescat in pace.

[Sketch][2]

682. To Aubrey Waterfield, [17? December 1913]

Text: Waterfield, *Castle in Italy*, p. 138.

[Lerici, per Fiascherino, Golfo della Spezia, Italy]
[17 December 1913][3]

[DHL wrote to Aubrey Waterfield to express 'fulsome praise of his paintings and said he had found them inspiring'.]

[1] l. 7 is here,] has come,
[2] A sketch in pen-and-ink of a man and woman, both naked and with heads bowed, on either side of a setting sun.
[3] This letter and the next were probably written following the weekend referred to in the previous letter to Edward Marsh.

683. To Lina Waterfield, [17? December 1913]
Text: Waterfield, *Castle in Italy*, p. 140.

[Lerici, per Fiascherino, Golfo della Spezia, Italy]
[17? December 1913]

[DHL wrote to Lina Waterfield to convey his impression of their 'Fortezza'. 'He described his first impression when he walked in the roof-garden one evening and looked at the mountains. It seemed to him as though wild beasts were circling round a fire and he was filled with a feeling of apprehension.']

684. To William Hopkin, 18 December 1913
Text: MS NCL; Huxley 168–70.

Lerici, per Fiascherino, Golfo della Spezia, Italia
18 Dec. 1913.

Dear Will,

I *was* glad to get that letter from you, full of good old crusty Eastwood gossip. Always write to me like that.

And don't wonder at what I write now, for Felice is rattling away like a hail-storm in Italian, just near my left ear, and Frieda, with her usual softness of heart (and head now and then), is letting herself in for things that will need the courage of St. George to extricate her from.

We *have* got a beautiful place here (and don't lose the address). It is a little pink cottage of four rooms, under great hills of olive woods, just over the sea. We have a great vine garden, all shut in, and lemons on the wall, and today, with a wind from the Appenines, the big, heavy oranges swing gold in their dark green leaves. We've only one orange tree, but it is a beauty.

There is no road here, that carts may pass – not even a mule road. Everything must go by rowing boat on the sea, that is not carried on the heads of the peasants. They carry, women and all, masses of stuff on their heads. It is supposed to give them a beautiful carriage, but that is a lie. It presses in the loins in a most curious fashion.

At this time of the year all the women are out in the olive woods – you have no idea how beautiful olives are, so grey, so delicately sad, reminding one constantly of the New Testament. I am always expecting when I go to Tellaro for the letters, to meet Jesus gossiping with his disciples as he goes along above the sea, under the grey, light trees. Now, the hills are full of voices, the peasant women and children all day long and day after day, in the faint shadow of olives picking the fallen fruit off the ground, panier after panier full. Our village is Tellaro. It grows sheer out of the rocks of the sea, a sea-robbers nest of 200 souls. The church is over the water. There is a tale that once in the night the church bell rang – and rang again. The people got up in terror – the bell rung mysteriously. Then it was found that the bell rope had fallen over the edge of the cliff in among the rocks, and an octopus had got hold of the end, and was drawing it. It is quite possible. The men go fishing for the octopus with a white bait and a long spear. They get quite big ones, six or seven pounds in weight sometimes – and you never saw anything so fiendishly ugly. But they are good to eat. We were at a peasant wedding the other day, and a great feast – octopus was one of the dishes: but I could not fancy it: I can eat snails all right, but octopus – no. We can have the boat belonging to the peasants on the bay, when we like, and row out on the sea. The Mediterranean is quite wonderful – and when the sun sets beyond the islands of Porto Venere, and all the sea is like heaving white milk with a street of fire across it, and amethyst islands away back, it is too beautiful.

I am very fond of the Italians. We have a little oddity of a maid called Elide – 25 years old. Her old mother Felice is quite a figure. They are very funny and ceremonious – when Elide has put the soup on the table she says 'a rivederci, eh?', before she can leave us. There is only one other house on this bay – only one other house within nearly a mile – and that is the peasants down on the beach. They are cousins of Elide. Sometimes they come and play and sing with us at evening – bringing the guitar. It is jolly. Luigi is very beautiful – and Gentile is a wild joy. How happy you would be with these people – and Mrs Hopkin with the country. The wind is now cold – there is snow on the mountains over Carrara – but still at night a glow-worm shines near the door, and sometimes a butterfly, a big black and red one, wanders to the remaining flowers – wild pinks and campanulas. – I love living by the sea – one gets so used to its noise, one hears it no more. And the ships that pass, with many sails, to Sardinia and Sicily, and through the gates of Porto Venere to Genova, are very beautiful. Spezia is Italy's great naval arsenal. Right in the harbour lie her war-ships: and she wastes such a lot of powder with their rattling cannon. The men of the villages go into Spezia to work. The workmen run the only steamers across the bay. They are interesting.

And now, after all this, you must come – you and Mrs Hopkin at least – and Enid if she can. You can get here cheap, some way or other – perhaps by sea to Genoa or to Leghorn – or by trips. We shall be here, I think, till June. So make up your minds, and scrape together. I want you – we both *want* you to come – and it is the most beautiful place I know.

I am laughing at your swotting with Willie Dunn.¹ – We send heaps of good wishes for Christmas. Write to me oftener. And make up your minds to come – Mrs Hopkin promised us last spring.

Love from Frieda and me to you three.

                                              Yrs   D. H. Lawrence

684A. To W. H. Davies, 18 December 1913
Text: MS Forster; Unpublished.

                           Lerici, per Fiascherino, Golfo della Spezia, Italy
                                                          18 December 1913

Dear Davies,

After that last letter of mine, I wanted to kick myself.² What right have I to talk to you from the top of a stool. Don't bear me a grudge, will you. I do wish things could go well with you.

We shall be here till the end of May, I think, and shall be frightfully glad when you come. You would travel, by the ordinary route, over Paris, Milan, Parma, Spezia – and it costs about £4. But you could come by ship to Genoa or to Leghorn – they are both fairly near. You must think about it, whether you would like to come on sea or on land. We should like to come to England in June, I think, by ship from Genova – I should like the voyage. You might go back with us, unless you want to walk in the Appenines.

We haven't got anybody coming for Christmas, but we shan't be lonely. The Italians are *very* jolly – they come and play with us, and sing to the guitar at evening. You must learn some Italian when you come. And here in the harbour there is Italy's biggest naval arsenal – war-ships with search lights and cannon at night, and submarines nosing up and down. It is really jolly. The country is quite wild behind, really wilder than Wales, but not so gloomy.

You didn't tell me how the work was going. I hope you'll have a good time in Wales. All good wishes from both of us.

                                              Yours   D. H. Lawrence

---

¹ William Hopkin was employed at this time by his father Henry Hopkin, who was the subpostmaster of Eastwood. According to Mrs Olive Hopkin: 'For some reason or other it was made into a Crown Office – It was then essential for him [William Hopkin] to have passed the Post Office examinations – So under the tutelage of Willie Dunn, the son of a family friend, he studied for the exam and passed' (Letter to Eds.).
² DHL's earlier letter has not been found; its tenor may be indicated by his remarks about Davies in Letter 668.

685. To Katharine Clayton, 19 December 1913

Text: MS NCL; cited in Pinto 20.

Lerici, per Fiascherino, Golfo della Spezia, Italy
19 Dec 1913

Dear Mrs Clayton,

Don't think because we are so long that we forget to answer your letter. I shall tell you all the news. – But first I asked my Aunt[1] to send Douglas the 10/– which I owe him – I hope she has done so. Then we're so glad about Pat, and hope he's flourishing like the green bay tree.[2]

As for us – I'll satisfy your housekeeping soul. The Cottage is pink outside, with a red roof – and standing above the vines, against grey olive trees, it looks awfully pretty. It has got four rooms – two up, two down. The sala (dining room) is quite pretty now, with red curtains and whitewashed walls. It has a great open fireplace – an open chimney. At evening we burn olive logs, and are happy. In the kitchen are enormous wine barrels which are a nuisance. There is also a big open chimney, but the base is as high – oh, not quite so high as a low table – and one cooks on fornelli – little square pockets full of charcoal – and one uses earthenware to cook in – earthen casseroles [sketch] and earthen pentolas [sketch] and other things [sketch of circular pot] – and then the pots in which one brings fire to the table to keep things hot, or a boiling sauce [sketch]. Everything is just red earthenware, roughly glazed, and one can cook in them beautifully, on charcoal. The biggest pentola, that holds a gallon of soup, only costs 5d. We eat quantities of soup – the Italians themselves have only two meals a day – midday polenta made of maize flour boiled to a stiff porridge that one cuts in slices with string, and eats with salt and on Sundays with a bit of meat – evening soup, full of some sort of pasta – macaroni, vermicelli, – there are hundreds of sorts. I love Italian cooking when there isn't too much oil. We get queer vegetables – cardi – like thistle stalks, very good – and heaps of fresh sardines – $1\frac{1}{2}$d a pound. One can live quite cheap. We pay 60 Lire a month house (a lire is about $9\frac{3}{4}$d – 10d) – 25 for Elide – then we burn paraffin, – and charcoal – not very dear – wood rather dear. We've got an enormous garden, full of vines with nothing on them – one big orange tree with *very* big oranges, all golden now and swinging slowly in the wind – one lemon tree against the wall with many lemons and flowers and buds – exquisite lemons.

The people are fearfully nice – In Tellaro – the tiny village where the post comes from – we went to a wedding of a peasant, and I was witness. The

---

[1] Ada Rose Krenkow (1868–1944), the sister of DHL's mother, who lived in Leicester. m. Fritz Johann Heinrich Krenkow (1872–1953). See *Letters*, i. 7–8, 46 n. 2.

[2] Psalms xxxiv. 36.

bride walked down in her white silk, with the bridegroom in black broad cloth, then Frieda and me, as guests of honor, then the rest. The service was at 7.30 – in a church over the sea, and the waves humming in the tower. A church is a free place like a public square. The service went on in a corner, the children clicker clackered in and out, in their wooden sandals – zoccoli – boys climbed the public steps, a fat priest dodged through the service. The church is in absolute neglect in Italy. The young peasants scoff at it – nobody goes to confession but children who are forced, and old people – the very priests themselves are atheists. After a wedding breakfast that nearly killed us, we set off in a troup, bride in white silk, with bridegroom, leading, and climbed and climbed up slippery goat roads, getting higher and higher and higher over the sea till we came to the ridge, then we had to slip down again to the Magra valley, to go to Ameglia, the village of the commune where the official wedding takes place. And the children of the village swarm round like wolves yelling.

> Evviva i Sposi – Evviva i Sposi[1]
> Vun ò du
> E poi non più
> One or two
> And then no more.

They are yelling for sweets. The bride must carry a white bag full, and she throws them handfuls. Sweets are very dear in Italy – common ones, 2/- a pound.

We have been spending the week-end with an Englishman who has got a fine old castle about 10 miles inland – a wonderful place guarding two river courses, and with the Appenines all round. But we were glad to get back to our sea, with the quiet of the olive hills and the full light and the noise from the water.

I want to row Frieda to Lerici, but she says there's too much wind.

All good wishes for Christmas.

D. H. Lawrence

686. To Edward Garnett, 21 December 1913
Text: MS NYPL; Huxley 170–1.

Lerici, per Fiascherino, Golfo della Spezia, Italy.
21 Dec 1913

Dear Garnett,

I got the registered letter from the *Smart Set* – It had £10 enclosed for

---

[1] 'Long live the bride and bridegroom.'

a very short story called 'Shadow in a Rose Garden', which I think you never saw.[1] As for the 'Primrose Path' — who *would* print it.[2] I heard from Harrison he is going to print the 4 soldier stories soon.[3] But he is very vague — and common, I don't like him with his half lewd, cheap suggestions. By the way, they haven't paid me yet for those Italian Sketches that came out in August.[4] Dont you think it is time they did? I asked Harrison about it, but anything he does not want to answer, he calmly ignores.

I had a letter from the secretary of the Stage Society today, saying that Arnold Bennett had recommended the committee to consider any work of mine I might bring out, and asking me if I cared to submit the MS.[5] But the MS is in such a state they could not read it – and I have no duplicate proofs – I said I would send them a copy of the play as soon as I had one. Kennerley said he would mail me them about Jan 1st.

The novel goes slowly forward. I wonder what you'll think of it. In a few days time I shall send you the first half of the MS.

Christmas is nearly here. I feel late, and frightfully busy. – We have had to pay visits lately. This last week end we were three days at Aulla – 12 miles inland, staying with an English artist who has an Italian fortress there. It is a wonderful place: a squat, square castle on a bluff of rock, with all the jagged Appenines prowling round, two rivers creeping out of the fastness to meet at the foot of the fortress, where is a tiny town, then flowing on, red-blazing in the sunset, into the black hills towards the sea. And when one is on the roof, and the dawn comes driving rosy across the mountain tops, it is wonderful. Day seems to stay a little while pale in the valley, then comes the sunset all gorgeous flaming, clashing back the red to where the dawn came from, and the eastern peaks are alive and rosy above the gathering dusk of the valley. You must come here – it is a most wonderful place.

You will bring out the play in February? – that is the *Bookman* month. Harrison ought to be ready with the first story by then.

Our best wishes for your Christmas – I hope nice things will happen to you. I wish I were at the Cearne for a day or two with you, in spite of our wonderful emerald sea and gorgeous sunsets behind the islands.

Love   D. H. Lawrence

Send me the 'Primrose Path' here, some day when it is convenient, please.

DHL

[1] The story appeared in *Smart Set*, xlii (March 1914).
[2] It was included by DHL in *England, My England and Other Stories* (New York, 1922).
[3] See Letter 659.
[4] They appeared in the *English Review* in September 1913.
[5] The Stage Society secretary was Allan Wade. The Society performed *The Widowing of Mrs Holroyd*, but not until December 1926.

687. To Cynthia Asquith, [21 December 1913]
Text: MS UN; Huxley 171–2.

[Lawrence begins]

Lerici, per Fiascherino, Golfo della Spezia, Italy
The shortest day

[Frieda Weekley begins]   (his temper short as well)

Dear Mrs Asquith,

You wrote me such a frightfully nice letter, dont be too sympathetic, I warn you, or I shall come and weep to you, when we are in England. – Dont be too sorry either, after all we are very happy too, [Lawrence interjects: I'm not   DHL] and I believe in the miracle too; [Lawrence interjects: I don't   DHL] only it's hard, I miss them so, like one would miss a leg [Lawrence interjects: one wouldn't after a fortnight.] It's still gorgeous here – [Lawrence interjects: It isn't – it's cold and dark.] I know such a lovely little 'villa' with a 'torrino'[1] here with a beautiful beautiful view for you – We hear of you through Eddie Marsh, a Kipling performance was the last – Barrie wrote such a nice letter to L– [Lawrence interjects: he didn't.] This is to wish you all three a Merry Xmas – L. must write, being an 'autore' he does it so much better than yours [Lawrence interjects: what a hateful way of ending]

Frieda L–

[Lawrence continues]

Dear Mrs Asquith,

You never answered my highly diverting and beautiful letter, only shed a tear over Frieda – which I call skimpy. So I refuse to write you a letter. I'd send you a visiting card if I'd got one, with 'All seasonable greetings' written on it.

How is the winter treating you? – if badly, you'd better come here and set up in a beautiful little tower over the pine wood and the sea – for 140 francs a month.

We went to a castle the last week end – ancient Italian fortress, walls three yards thick. There it sits keeping an eye on the two rivers that come crawling insidiously out of the jaggy Apennines, as if expecting them to pounce. But they don't – they only swallow each other and go with trailing skirts haughtily through the mountain doors to the sea. But the castle watches, whether or not. And it gives one the fidgets. And the artist gentleman painted

---

[1] 'small tower'.

in the manner of various defunct gentleman artists – their ghosts haunted his canvases like the ghosts of old dead soldiers his castle hall. And the servants crouched in a corner of the great dark kitchen, making polenta cakes –

A Merry Christmas – though you don't deserve it, for sending Frieda only a little bottle of tears and me not even a sugared almond. – Also a Merry Christmas to Don John, and to Mr Asquith.

Yours   D. H. Lawrence

688. To Henry Savage, 22 December 1913
Text: MS YU; Moore, *Yale University Library Gazette*, xxxiv. 32–3.

Lerici, per Fiascherino, Golfo della Spezia, Italy
22 Dec 1913

Dear Savage,

What a rum chap you are. Now you're discovering Whitman and humanity. But don't you see, he says all men are my brothers, and straightway goes into the wilderness to love them. Don't let yourself in for a terrific chagrin. But I'm glad you've discovered Humanity: it is fearfully nice to feel it round one. If you read my poetry – especially the earlier rough stuff which was published in the *English Review*, and isn't in the book of poems, you would see how much it has meant to me. Only, the bitterness of it is, that while one is brother to all men, and wrote *Macbeth* with Shakespeare and the Bible with James the First's doctors, one still remains Henry Savage or D. H. Lawrence, with one's own little life to live, and one's own handful of thoughts to write. And it is so hard to combine the two, and not to lose oneself in the generalisation, and not to lose the big joy of the whole in being narrowly oneself. Which is a preach. But perhaps you, like Whitman or Christ, can take the Church to bride, and give yourself, bodily and spiritually, to the abstract. The fault about Whitman is, strictly, that he is too self-conscious to be what he says he is: he's not Walt Whitman, I, the joyous American, he is Walt Whitman, the Cosmos, trying to fit a cosmos inside his own skin: a man rongé with unsatisfiedness not at all pouring his seed into American brides to make Stalwart American Sons, but pouring his seed into the space, into the idea of humanity. Poor man, it is pathetic when he makes even an idea of his own flesh and blood. He was a martyr like Christ, in a slightly different sort. – I don't mind people being martyrs in themselves, but to make an idea of the flesh and blood is wrong. The flesh and blood must go its own road. There is something wrong with Whitman, when he addresses American women as his Stalwart brides in whom he is to pour the seed for Stalwart Sons. One doesn't think like that. Imagine yourself addressing English women like that, in the mass. One *doesn't* feel like that – except in the moments of wide, gnawing desire when everything has gone wrong. – Whitman is like a human document, or a wonderful treatise in human self revelation. It is neither art nor religion nor truth: Just a self revelation of a man who could not live, and so had to write himself. But writing should come from a strong root of life: like a battle song after a battle. – And Whitman did this, more or less. But his battle was not a real battle: he never gave his individual self into the fight: he was too much aware of it. He never fought with another person – he was like a wrestler who only wrestles with his own shadow – he never came to grips. He chucked his body into the fight, and stood apart saying 'Look how I am living'. He is really false as hell. – But he is fine too. Only, I am sure, the generalisations are *no good* to the individual: the individual comes first, then the generalisation is a kind of game, not a reality: just a surplus, an excess, not a whole.

About spiritual pride, I think you are right. I can't understand you when you think so much of books and genius. They are great too – but they are the cake and wine of life – there is the bread and butter first, the ordinary human contact, the exchange with individuals of a bit of our individual selves, like beggars might exchange bits of crust on the road side. But Whitman did not take a person: he took that generalised thing, a Woman, an Athlete, a Youth. And this is wrong, wrong, wrong. He should take Gretchen, or one Henry Wilton. It *is* no use blanking the person out to have a sort of representative.

A harangue, all for Christmas. I wish I could send you some little thing, you have been so good for me – we are [...] very grateful. Soon my play will come, and then I shall send you a copy. – At any rate, whatever Whitman is, I hope he's really let you loose from some bondage – he can do. I am glad you will rejoice in humanity. There is something a bit Greek, and a bit Christian in it: it has produced Greek art, and Michael Angelo – but not Rembrandt. – And it is largely wrong: too much intellect, too much generalisation in it. You *should* read Gilbert Murray's Euripides translations – I wish I'd got some to give you.[1] – Abel Torey wrote to me – I like him.[2] Tell me how things are going with you – I hope you are keeping up. Best wishes for Christmas – also to Mrs Savage and to the boy – Good luck – many many warm regards from Frieda and me. Write to me – tell me how you are going on.

Yrs   D. H. Lawrence

[1] Murray's translations gave DHL great pleasure. See *Letters*, i. 261.
[2] Unidentified.

689. To Edward Marsh, [23 December 1913]
Text: MS NYPL; PC; Postmark, Tellaro 23. 12. 13; Unpublished.

Fiascherino
[23 December 1913]

Caro Eddie,

Non so se va Venire dopo Natale[1] – but if you are – and surely you are – bring me a Fountain pen for 10/6 – that's good enough for me – medium nib – Swan make or any you like: and smuggle me half a pound of quite ordinary tea: it will be the work of a Christian. It doesn't matter if it is troppo disturbo[2] – don't take trouble for it.

It is 20 days before you come – I think Jim Barnes must be getting better. Think of us sitting in a Carrossa[3] driving from Sarzana over to our side of the sea. The dawn puffs up all pink, and a sharp, bright blue day vanishes into a red sunset, with amazing quickness. One ought to live to be 1000, at the rate of these days.

A rivederla – buon reposto e sia buona.[4]

D. H. Lawrence

690. To Ezra Pound, 26 December 1913
Text: MS Bate; cited in Jane Lidderdale, *Dear Miss Weaver* (New York, 1970), p. 82.

Lerici, per Fiascherino, Golfo della Spezia, Italy
26 Dec 1913

Dear Pound,

I will ask Duckworths to send you three or four copies of my book of poems. I don't know what the Polignac award is, but I shall be very glad to have it, when the sun opens flowers of fortune.[5]

I don't know who Preston[6] is, or what is *The Egoist*.[7] I am a little bit afraid

[1] 'I don't know whether you intend to come after Christmas.'
[2] 'too much trouble'. [3] 'carriage [Carrozza]'.
[4] 'Goodbye – have a nice break [riposo] and be good.'
[5] The Polignac Prize was established by the Royal Society of Literature from a sum of money provided in 1911 by Princesse Edmond De Polignac (1865–1943). £100 was awarded each November for a work of imagination that had appeared in the previous year. Walter de la Mare was the first winner in 1911, followed by John Masefield (1912) and James Stephens (1913). Ezra Pound 'roundly declared that Lawrence was a much better poet than Masefield ever would be and that he deserved recognition for his *Love Poems and Others*...in November 1914 Ralph Hodgson, not Lawrence, was the Academic Committee's choice' (Michael de Cossart, *The Food of Love*, 1978, p. 107). [6] Unidentified.
[7] The *New Freewoman* – the periodical founded by Harriet Shaw Weaver and Dora Marsden – was about to change its name. The new name, *The Egoist*, had been announced in the periodical itself on 15 December 1913; it was first formally adopted in the issue of 1 January 1914. Pound was closely associated with the editors of and tended to adopt a proprietorial attitude towards the *Egoist*.

that the poor critics or whoever they are might seize on 'Once' as a flagrant
example of my indecency, once it were published and so proceed to chase
me out of the herd – or try to. *But* if *The Egoist* is not likely to get me into
trouble by publishing 'Once', and if I am not likely to get the *Egoist* into
trouble by offering them the story, then I don't see why they shouldn't have
it, for as much as they can afford.[1] I will try and look up some poetry[2] – here
I am so lazy, and am supposed to be grinding my nose off on the mill-stone
of a novel,[3] when I'd rather row a boat on the sea.

I told the *Smart Set* Wright I didn't like his terms of payment. But wait
a while – I'll make them print me and pay me, yet.

You sound a little bit at odds with the world. Why don't you take it more
calmly.

All good wishes for the New Year from us two.

                                                         Yours   D. H. Lawrence

Is the *Egoist*, then, French–English, or what.

691. To Edward Garnett, 30 December 1913
Text: MS NYPL; Huxley 172–3.

                               Lerici, per Fiascherino, Golfo della Spezia, Italy
                                                                30 Dec 1913

Dear Garnett,

In a few days time I shall send you the first half of the Sisters – which
I should rather call The Wedding Ring – to Duckworths. It is *very* different
from *Sons and Lovers*: written in another language almost. I shall be sorry
if you don't like it, but am prepared. – I shan't write in the same manner
as *Sons and Lovers* again, I think: in that hard, violent style full of sensation
and presentation. You must see what you think of the new style.

I wish you would send to Ezra Pound – 10 Church Walk – Kensington
W – three or four copies of my poems, and send me the bill for them.[4] I
owe him something like a sovereign, which the *Smart Set* sent him as
commission, for getting them my two stories.[5] This commission he sent on
to me 'as being averse from returning anything to the maw of an editor, and
unable to take commission on my work'! – I didn't want Pound's pound of
commission. So now he says he would like 3 or 4 copies of the poems, to
get them into the hands of the members of the Polignac Prize committee,
or some such reason. The Hueffer-Pound faction seems inclined to lead me

---

[1] 'Once' was not accepted by the *Egoist*.   [2] See p. 154 n. 4.
[3] 'The Sisters'.   [4] *Love Poems and Others* (1913).
[5] 'The Christening' and 'The Shadow in the Rose Garden'.

round a little as one of their show-dogs. They seem to have a certain ear
in their possession. If they are inclined to speak my name into the ear, I don't
care.

   We had rather a nice christmas. The peasants – 16 – came in on Christmas
Eve,[1] and we sang the Pastorella at midnight. On Christmas Day we went
to English service in the Cochranes private chapel[2] – lambs we looked I can
tell you – and lunched with the Huntingdons – *very* nice folk. Then the next
day we lunched at the Pearses – I *do* like Mrs Pearse – who have a beautiful
house where the Empress Frederick of Germany spent a winter with
them – and Count Seckendorf. The parson is out here for six months – hired
by the wealthy and impossible Cochrane, who flings gold at the Italians
around and bruises their faces. The Rev John Wood is a very decent fellow – I
like him – and he has taken a great fancy to us. – When all our dark history
comes out, I shall laugh.

   The Pearses and Huntingdons read *Sons and Lovers* with great admiration.
They have been 40 years in Italy, and are not shocked any more.

   I felt injured because you never wished me a Merry Christmas.

   Best wishes for the New Year to you and Mrs Garnett and David.

                                                    Yrs   D. H. Lawrence
Send me here 'The Primrose Path' – at your leisure.

                                                                    DHL

692. To Edward Garnett, [31 December 1913]
Text: MS NYPL; Postmark, Lerici 31 12 13; Unpublished.

                           Lerici, per Fiascherino, Golfo della Spezia, Italy
                                                    [31 December 1913]

Dear Garnett,

   I was awfully pleased with this letter.[3] I wrote them saying I should like
them to publish me, would look out my things, and then write them again.
I've got enough – quite, I think – poetry for a volume. Is it all right to let
them have it for America, and Duckworth have the English rights?

   It is just beginning to look a bit like autumn – acorns and olives falling,
and vine leaves going yellow. We've had tropical torrents of rain for two days.
Now again perfect sunshine. I shall work at length.

                                                    Vale!   D. H. Lawrence

   I haven't heard from Kennerley, either about the play or the cheque, have
you?

                                                                    DHL

---

[1] Christmas] New Years   [2] In their house at Pugliola.
[3] The letter has not been preserved.

693. To Ernest Collings, [31 December 1913]
Text: MS UT; PC; Postmark, Lerici 31 12 13; Unpublished.

Lerici, per Fiascherino, Golfo della Spezia, Italy
[31 December 1913]

Dear Collings,

It is abominable the way I have neglected writing to you – but one's correspondence gets so bewildering.[1] I liked that card you sent me – was it a Russian Greek priest?

We have got a lovely little house here on the Mediterranean – quite an ideal spot. But just now it is rather cold. Many thanks for the promise of the book of drawings – I look forward to it.[2] Who is bringing it out? When is it coming? Is it black and white only, or also colour? I am interested to hear of it.

I am working away at a novel, being all behind-hand this year, after having moved about to so many places. And here is a bad place for work – one is so happy doing nothing.

Many, many good wishes from us two for the New Year.

Yours   D. H. Lawrence

694. To Edward Garnett, 6 January 1914
Text: MS NWU; Unpublished.

Lerici, per Fiascherino, Golfo della Spezia, Italia
6 Gennaio 1914

Caro Garnett,

I send you today the first half of the Sisters – re-christened – provisionally – The Wedding Ring. You will see the whole scheme of the book is changed – widened and deepened. But, I think you will be able to gather how it is going on. There may be some small weeding out to do – but this will be the final form of the book. I really think it is good. You may not find it as exciting as you expected – but I hope you'll like it. – I think I shall finish it in six weeks – perhaps in eight. If you like I'll send you the pages per 100 as I do them – then you can find any faults, and we can get them

---

[1] DHL last wrote to Collings from Irschenhausen on 4 September (Letter 643) telling him of the expected move to Italy later that month. It was only by applying to Edward Garnett for DHL's address – as he did on 10 December (MS NYPL) – that Collings was able to write the card which prompted this response.

[2] Collings' book, *Outlines: A Book of Drawings*, published in April 1914, carries the dedication: 'To D. H. Lawrence'. (It was published from Collings' home address, 24 Gorst Road, London S.W.)

settled, and rush quick into print if the hour seems to have come. My reputation is new-born and wants skilful handling, I think: but it is born.

The sales of *Sons and Lovers* are rather disappointing. I am having letters from agents[1] who say 'that fine novel hasn't had the success it deserved', and offering me £200 down for my next, on the behalf of the best established publishers in England and America – but chi va piano arriverà.[2] I hope you'll like The Sisters.

When will Duckworth bring out the play? – in Feb?[3] Can you work the *Daily Mail*, to put me a column, do you think? Harrison is publishing some poetry for that month.[4] I suppose the *Bookman* is safe?[5]

I have written to Harrison about the cheque, having occasion to write him, because of the poems. When I have done the novel I shall do some articles, and earn some money quick. Don't send the £8, I am not in need yet.

We are always having visits or visiting here – such beautiful houses too. You must come and see.

Did you send Ezra Pound the 3 or 4 copies of the *Love Poems* – Send me the bill for them – or pay them out of the £8, by cheque – it is so easy.

Are you really coming to see us this spring, as you promised? I think we shall be here till May or June 1st.

In haste   D. H. Lawrence

695. To Arthur McLeod, 10 January 1914
Text: MS UT; Postmark, Lerici 10 1 14; Huxley 173–5.

Lerici, per Fiascherino, Golfo della Spezia, Italia
10 Gennaio 1914

Dear Mac,

We owe you heaven knows how many thanks for the books at Christmas and for the newspapers. I love the *Morning Post*, it is so fat. The Italian newspapers are ha'penny thin miserable things – all alike, from the *Corriere della Sera* and the *Secolo* downwards.[6] It is lovely suddenly to flounder among English news and book reviews and articles. I hope it isn't an awful nuisance – if not, do keep it up and send us the *Morning Post* as you have

---

[1] agents] publishers. The agents have not been identified, but see Letter 718 for references to Pinker and Curtis Brown.

[2] 'he who goes gently will get there'.

[3] Duckworth published *The Widowing of Mrs Holroyd* from Kennerley sheets in April 1914.

[4] See p. 90 n. 3.

[5] A reference to the article about DHL by W. L. George.

[6] Both were published in Milan.

been doing. – We had fearful discussions on the Gilbert Murray. He is *very* interesting: just a bit conceited, but interesting right through. *Rhesus* I didn't think up to much.[1] – And it is queer how uninteresting Davies is in Italy. His *Nature Poems*, which I loved in England, seem so thin, one can hardly feel them at all.[2]

I wonder if you liked that picture of the old seigneurie.[3] I am afraid not much. I rather liked it – out here. But in England perhaps it set your teeth on edge. – All the houses here are pink like that.

You will find me next month – I expect – in the *Bookman*; also some poetry in the *English Review*, which I hope you will like. What do you think of the latest Masefield?[4]

I am awaiting the coming of my play from America: it is being published first out there. It is good, I think. The Sec. of the Stage Society wrote me and said Arnold Bennett had told them, if I ever published drama, they must get hold of it.[5] I shall send them a copy.

I have nearly finished my novel – it is a weird production. It is quite quite different from *Sons and Lovers*, much quieter. I shall not write quite so violently as *Sons and Lovers* any more. I wonder what you'll say to my new work.

We are so busy here, with visitors. There are some English people on the hills – and an English chaplain[6] – so that we are always out to tea, or having visitors. Which is very odd. I am expecting Edward Marsh – the *Georgian Poetry* man – and Jim Barnes, on Monday – they are calling on their way home from Rome – I wonder if Marsh is projecting another *Georgian Poetry* issue – I must ask him. Have you ordered the Abercrombie–Gibson–Brook–Drinkwater: *New Numbers*.[7] Gibson says he'll send it me soon. I wonder why we can't establish a real poetry number among all of us – we should do well enough if we but hang together.

Won't you come out here and stay with us a while this spring? Miss Mason *promises* to come for Easter.[8] Whether she will fulfil is another matter. Surely you might manage for Whitsuntide.[9] Why don't you want to?

---

[1] *The Rhesus of Euripides*, Translated into English Rhyming Verse, With Explanatory Notes by Gilbert Murray (1913).
[2] W. H. Davies, *Nature Poems and Others* (1908).
[3] Perhaps a postcard sent by DHL to McLeod.
[4] John Masefield's *The Daffodil Fields* (October 1913).
[5] See p. 127 n. 5.
[6] See Letter 691.
[7] A periodical issued by Lascelles Abercrombie, W. W. Gibson, John Drinkwater and Rupert Brooke, to publish their poems. Only nos 1–4 appeared, February–December 1914.
[8] See p. 22 n. 1.
[9] McLeod's school would probably be closed for the week following Whit Sunday, 31 May 1914.

Yesterday I was out with the peasants picking olives. They knock all the olives from the trees with long canes, then gather them from the ground. The picking has been going on 3 months already, and will last another 3 months. All the women are out all day. And they chatter and sing, and sometimes a man or two is with them, and it is jolly. On Wednesday I went with the chaplain on the English collier ships in Spezia harbour. They *are* rum men. But one must love Englishmen, somehow. They are so definitely resistant – they've got so much personality – and so much back bone, and are so aware of another person – more than Italians are. They felt rather brotherly, to me, those colliers on the ship. One writes stories. He is going to send me his latest to criticise. He is not a Joseph Conrad, however.

Tanti saluti affettuosi – and from Frieda –

D. H. Lawrence

696. To Henry Savage, [19 January 1914]
Text: MS YU; Postmark, Spezia 19 1 14; Moore 241–2.

Lerici, per Fiascherino, Golfo della Spezia
Monday

Dear Savage,

I wonder how long it is since we heard from you, and since I wrote. It isn't so long as it seems, I hope. We have been going for Whitman – he is quite great. But I'd rather be alive in my own way, than in Whitmans.

I am writing on the steamer, going to Spezia. It is a[1] wonderful morning, with a great, level, massive blue sea, and strange sails far out, deep in a pearl glow, and San Terenzo all glittering pink on the shore. It is so beautiful, it almost hurts: so big, with such a massive dark sea and such endless, pearl white sky far away and level with ones eyes. On the sea, looking at the horizon, I never know whether I shall feel a sensation of gradual, infinite up-slope, or of slow, sure stooping into the spaces.

We seem to have been very busy, I writing away at my novel, then visits to pay and to receive. I have done 340 pages of my novel. It is very different from *Sons and Lovers*. The Laocoon[2] writhing and shrieking have gone from my new work, and I think there is a bit of stillness, like the wide, still, unseeing eyes of a Venus of Melos.[3] I am still fascinated by the Greek – more, perhaps, by the Greek sculpture than the plays, even though I love the plays. There is something in the Greek sculpture that my soul is hungry for – something of the eternal stillness that lies under all movement, under

---

[1] a] quite a
[2] DHL's interest in the legend, and the statue (in the Vatican) based on it, was several years deep. See *Letters*, i. 5, 136–7.
[3] The well known *Venus de Milo*, found on the island of Melos, now in the Louvre.

all life, like a source, incorruptible and inexhaustible. It is deeper than change, and struggling. So long I have acknowledged only the struggle, the stream, the change. And now I begin to feel something of the source, the great impersonal which never changes and out of which all change comes. I begin to feel it in myself – so much one has fought and struggled, and shed so much blood and made so many scars and disfigured oneself. But all the time there is the unscarred and beautiful in me, even an unscarred and beautiful body. And at moments, it is seen almost pure, I think. As a rule one sees only the intertwining of change and a distortion of half made combinations, of half resolved movements. But there is behind every woman who walks, and who eats her meal, a Venus of Melos, still, unseeing, unchanging, and inexhaustible. And there is a glimpse of it everywhere, in somebody, at some moment – a glimpse of the eternal and unchangeable that they are. And some people are intrinsically beautiful – most are pathetic, because so rarely they are their own true beauty. And some people are intrinsically [...] fearful, strange forms half-uttered. And all any man can do is to struggle to be true to his own pure type. And some men are intrinsically monkeys, or dogs – but they are few, and we must forget them, once they are muzzled.

I think I cant express myself. I shall stop.

The mountains of Carrara are white, of a soft white like idelweiss, in a faint pearl haze – all snowy. The sun is very warm, and the sea glitters. We are passing a battle ship, a shadowy, bluey, rather shapely thing.

Soon I shall send your books back. I have enjoyed the *Pater* so much.[1] We have lent your books about, that is why we have kept them so long.

Love   D. H. Lawrence

697. To Arthur McLeod, [21 January 1914]
Text: MS UT; PC; Postmark, Lerici 21 1 14; Unpublished.

Fiascherino
[21 January 1914]

Dear Mac,

There is an American magazine, or review, called *Poetry*. It is published in Chicago. I don't know whether you have ever seen it – I never have. But this month – January – it contains some of my work – at least they've sent me a cheque for £20 for what they have published.[2] I wish you would get

---

[1] The particular work read by DHL has not been identified.

[2] *Poetry*, iii (January 1914), 115–25, published the following poems by DHL: 'Green', 'All of Roses', 'Fireflies in the Corn', 'A Woman and Her Dead Husband', 'The Wind, the Rascal', 'The Mother of Sons', 'Illicit' and 'Birthday'. See p. 167 n. 1.

me a copy of the paper, and tell me how much it costs. My things are getting more and more beyond my control. I have no idea what these people have put in their paper – of mine – only they have paid me fabulously, don't you think?

Look for me in February's *Bookman* – and *English* [*Review*].

Tante belle cose da noi[1]   D. H. Lawrence

698. To Constance Garnett, 23 January 1914

Text: MS NYPL; Postmark, Spezia 23.1.14; Unpublished.

Lerici, per Fiascherino, Golfo della Spezia, Italy

23 Jan 1914

Dear Mrs Garnett,

We have just got your letter – and shall be delighted if you come with Mademoiselle Vera – I forget the Russian name.[2] Frieda was horrified for fear it might be Tony – whom she doesn't like.[3] I *knew* it wasn't Tony. We should have loved you to stay in the house.

It isn't very cold here – Some days, a chill wind comes from the mountains, which are under snow. But down by the sea, here and also at Lerici, one scarcely feels it: and at the hôtel, one can sit till half past four, on a little balcony outside in the sun – and it is *very* beautiful. Do come – you are sure to love it. The hôtel as I said, is only 6 francs a day including everything. They don't speak English – but there are staying there a Mr and Mrs Wood. He is the clergyman – chaplain for Cochrane. You would like him – they are quite ordinary and nice. Then there are the Pearses and the Huntingdons whom you would like very much, I think, who have houses here. Do come, and see how beautiful it is. Yesterday I found the first wild narcissus – those little white ones with yellow hearts. And the sun already has a touch of spring.

– The hôtel is *good* – simple, perfectly clean, and perfectly warm – with one of the loveliest views in the world. The food is simple and good, too.

Tell me when you will come, and I will meet you in Spezia or in Sarzana. You can come Paris, Turin, Genoa Spezia Rome: or Paris Milan Parma

---

[1] 'All the best from us'.

[2] Vera Volkhovsky, daughter of Felix Volkhovsky (1846–1914), a Russian émigré living in London. Her story 'The Idealist' was published in the same issue of the *New Statesman* (13 August 1913) as DHL's story 'The Fly in the Ointment'. She translated Gorky's *The Outcasts and Other Stories* (1902) and *Fables* by Shchedrin [Mikhail Saltykov] (1931).

[3] Antonia ('Tony') Almgren, née Cyriax (1881–1927), m. Swedish painter, Per Johan Hugo Almgren. She stayed near DHL and Frieda when they were at Gargnano, March–April 1913. See *Letters*, i. 520 n. 2.

Spezia, or Paris Milan Parma Sarzana. It is quite a simple journey. – There
are boats from Spezia to Lerici at 10·0, 12·0, 5·0, and 7·0, in the day. From
Sarzana you drive. Either is quite easy. But tell me, so that I can meet you.
It will be fearfully jolly if you come. And you will please yourself, whether
you stay with us, or with your friend. We should be awfully glad to have
you, remember. – The telegraph address is Fiascherino, Lerici, Genoa. –
A letter is rather slow: see, I got yours only this morning – Friday. But we
are going now to Spezia to the dentist, so this should catch the night mail.

Many warm greetings from us.

D. H. Lawrence

Bring *very* warm hat and shoes – and very strong, without nails, for
walking.[1]

699. To Edward Marsh, 24 January 1914
Text: MS NYPL; Postmark, Tellaro 25.1.14; Huxley 175–7.

Lerici, per Fiascherino, Golfo della Spezia, Italy
24 gennaio 1914

Dear Eddie,

That *Georgian Poetry* book is a veritable aladdin's lamp.[2] I little thought
my 'Snapdragon' would go on blooming and seeding in this prolific fashion.
So many thanks for the cheque for four pounds, and long life to *G.P.*

We are still trying to get over the excitement of your rush through
Fiascherino. I still think with anguish of your carrying your bag up that
salita[3] from Lerici – don't remember it against me. I have received one or
two more apologies from Severino,[4] for his having taken us for the three
saltimbanchi:[5] the latter, by the way, gave a great performance in Tellaro,
at the bottom there by the sea, on Sunday. They performed in the open air.
Elide assisted at the spectacle, but confessed to disappearing into church
when the hat came round: along with three parts of the crowd. The poor
saltimbanchi were reduced to begging for a little bread, so stingy was Tellaro.

The night you went, was a great fall of snow. We woke in the morning
wondering what the queer pallor was. And the snow lay nearly six inches
deep, and was still drifting finely, shadowily, out to the sombre-looking sea.

Of course, no Ellide appeared. I got up and made a roaring fire and
proceeded to wash the pots, in a queer, silent, muffled Fiascherino; even the
sea was dead and still.

---

[1] The postscript is written on the envelope.
[2] See p. 35 n. 5.   [3] 'slope'.
[4] A member of an Italian family in Fiascherino.   [5] 'acrobats'.

It looked very queer. The olives on the hills bowed low, low under the snow, so the whole slopes seemed[1] peopled with despairing shades descending to the styx. I never saw anything so like a host of bowed, pathetic despairers, all down the hillside. And every moment came the long creak – cre-eak of a tree giving way, and the crash as it fell.

The pines on the little peninsula were very dark and snowy, above a lead grey sea. It was queer and Japanesy: no distance, no perspective, everything near and sharp on a dull grey ground. The water cut out a very perfect, sweeping curve from the snow on the beach.

The Mino – the cat – had been out at night as usual. He appeared shoulder deep in snow, mewing, terrified – and he wouldn't come near me. He knows me perfectly. But that sudden fall of deep snow had frightened him out of his wits, and it was a long time before we could get him to come in the house.

At Midday appeared Ellide with her older brother, Alessandro. *And* there was an outcry. Alessandro stood in the doorway listening to the trees cracking, and crying, ma dio, dio – senti Signore, senti – Cristo del mondo – è una rovina.[2] All Tellaro was praying to the Vergine in the church: they had rung a special appeal at 9·30, and the old women had flocked in. Ellide looked once more at the driving snow-flakes, stamped her foot like a little horse, and cried defiantly 'Ma se il Dio vuol mandare il fino del mondo – *che* lo manda'.[3] She was ready. – Meanwhile Allesandro moaned, 'una rovina, un danno'![4]

It really was a ruin. Quite half the trees were smashed. One could not get out of our garden gates, for great trees fallen there. No post came to Tellaro – nothing happened but moaning. – And the third day, in lamentation, they brought a commission to see the damage and to ask to have the taxes remitted. Now they are quite happily chopping up the ruin, crying 'Ora si puo scaldarsi'.[5]

Another excitement! Luigi, down at the house on the bay here, the evening of your departure came home pale with excitement, found our Felice, and said, hoarsely 'Ma zia, io ho una brutta notizia da portare. Quelli due Inglesi del signore erano arrestati stasera, al pontino di Lerici'.[6] Loud, loud lamentations from Felici, Ellide maintaining stoutly 'forse mancava qualche

[1] so the whole slopes seemed] looking like slopes
[2] 'O God, God – hear us, O Lord, hear us – O Christ (lord) of the world – it's a disaster.'
[3] 'If God wants to send the end of the world – *let* him send it.'
[4] 'disaster, ruin'.
[5] 'Now we can warm ourselves.'
[6] 'Aunt, I have bad news to bring. Those two Englishmen of the master's [i.e. DHL] were arrested this evening at the bridge in Lerici.'

carta – di certo è una cosa di niente'.¹ *Think* how you let us in for it –
between strolling players and arrests.

There was also a great argument between Felici and Ellide, as to which
of you was the more beautiful. Ellide said Jim Barnes, Felici said you – and
they got quite cross.

Addio   D. H. Lawrence

700. To Edward Garnett, 29 January 1914
Text: MS NYPL; Postmark, Tellaro 29. 1. 14; Huxley 177–8.

Lerici, per Fiascherino, Golfo della Spezia, Italy.

29 Gennaio 1914

Dear Garnett,

I am not very much surprised, nor even very much hurt by your letter – and
I agree with you. I agree with you about the Templeman episode.² In the
scheme of the novel, however, I *must* have Ella get some experience before
she meets her Mr Birkin.³ – I also felt that the character was inclined to fall
into two halves – and gradations between them. It came of trying to graft
on to the character of Louie⁴ the character, more or less, of Frieda. That
I ought not to have done. To your two main criticisms, that the Templeman
episode is wrong, and that the character of Ella is incoherent, I agree. Then
about the artistic side being in the background. It is that which troubles me
most. I have no longer the joy in creating vivid scenes, that I had in *Sons
and Lovers*. I don't care much more about accumulating objects in the
powerful light of emotion, and making a scene of them. I have to write
differently. I am most anxious about your criticism of this, the second half
of the novel, a hundred and fifty pages of which I send you tomorrow. Tell
me *very* frankly what you think of it: and if it pleases you, tell me whether
you think Ella would be possible, as she now stands, unless she had some
experience of love and of men. I think, impossible. Then she must have a
love episode, a significant one. But it must not be a Templeman episode.

I shall go on now to the end of the book. It will not take me long. Then
I will go over it all again, and I shall be very glad to hear *all* you have to

---

¹ 'perhaps some document was missing – certainly it's a trivial matter'.
² In this early version of *The Rainbow*, the heroine was named Ella (later Ursula Brangwen).
  A MS of *The Rainbow* (now at the Humanities Research Center, University of Texas) contains
  a section in which the character appears. The 'experience' for Ursula comes from her affair
  with Anton Skrebensky.
³ Rupert Birkin, one of the main characters in *Women in Love*.
⁴ Louisa ('Louie') Burrows (1888–1962), to whom DHL was engaged December 1910–February
  1912; see *Letters*, i. 29 n. 3.

say. But if this, the second half, also disappoints you, I will, when I come
to the end, leave this book altogether. – Then I should propose to write a
story with a plot, and to abandon the exhaustive method entirely – write pure
object and story.

I am going through a transition stage myself. I am a slow writer, really – I
only have great outbursts of work. So that I do not much mind if I put all
this novel in the fire, because it is the vaguer result of transition. I write with
everything vague – plenty of fire underneath, but, like bulbs in the ground,
only shadowy flowers that must be beaten and sustained, for another
spring. – I feel that this second half of the Sisters is very beautiful, but it
may not be sufficiently incorporated to please you. I do not try to incorporate
it very much – I prefer the permeating beauty. It is my transition stage – but
I must write to live, and it must produce its flowers, and if they be frail or
shadowy, they will be all right if they are true to their hour. – It is not so
easy for one to be married. In marriage one must become something else.
And I am changing, one way or the other. – Thank you for the trouble you
take for me. I shall be all the better in the end. Remember I am a slow
producer, really.

Yours, D. H. Lawrence

Mrs Garnett is here – we are *very* pleased to see her. I think she will be
happy here. I like Miss Volkhovsky too – very much.

I shall be all right as regards writing. Which way I have to go, I shall
go in the end I suppose – whichever way it may be.

Frieda thanks you for the book.[1] I read some of it. It is written by
somebody I don't like.

Miss Volkhovsky has lent me Tagore.[2] I don't think *so* much of the
translations – they have some beauty. I think, in this novel of mine, is some
of the same sort of feeling as in Tagore. He is[3] very popular, too, isn't he?
That is hard to understand.

I wish the play would come along from America.

I've got just over £50 now, in the bank. It must last into May – before
May I shall not need money from anybody.

I am going to give up writing about the lower middle classes: manners
and circumstance and scenes dont interest me any more.

DHL

[1] Unidentified.
[2] Rabindranath Tagore (1861–1941), Indian writer, painter, educator and musician. He visited
England in 1912, when *Gitanjali* was published. He won the Nobel Prize in 1913. *The Crescent
Moon* (1913) and the translation of his play *Chitra* (1913) were works available in English.
[3] is] was

701. To Edward Marsh, [31 January 1914]
Text: MS NYPL; PC v. Aulla il Castello; Postmark, Lerici 31 1 14; Unpublished.

[Lerici, per Fiascherino, Golfo della Spezia, Italy]

[31 January 1914]

Dear Eddie,

Do you see that little American magazine of verse called *Poetry*, published in Chicago for 15 cents. There are in it some things of mine, this month (January) – I should like to know what you think of them.

DHL

702. To Mitchell Kennerley, 7 February 1914
Text: MS HL; Unpublished.

Lerici, per Fiascherino, Golfo della Spezia, Italia

7 febraio 1914

Dear Mr Kennerley,

I am looking forward to seeing the play – soon the six copies will come. I should think Duckworth's won't think your price too high – if they do, one can't help it – come si fa! – As for their giving me a royalty, if they can't afford it, they can't. Don't you think it is rather a beautiful play, as it stands? Did W. L. George give you that article on me, which appears in this month's *Bookman*? He said he might. It isn't bad, – but it hasn't Mr Bjorkman's strong flavour.[1]

The novel – I had nearly finished it – and then I knew it wasn't *quite* there. And so I have begun it again. It is – or will be – it *is* really, a very beautiful novel, I think. – I think I will have it typed as I do it, and send you the first half when it is ready. God help me – I hope I shall be able to pay the type-writer. I've always sent in my things in[2] Manuscript, before. But somehow, the money seems to turn up, from odd ends of the earth, just enough to get along with: and I am not very afraid. –

The poems I shall leave till you *want* them: till you think a good moment has come. – And when you ask me to send you duplicates of my things, do you mean also of short stories? – It is bad luck, that Mr Wright has left the *Smart Set*.[3] – – And I hate feeling that people might publish me at a loss – I do hope I shall turn out all right for you. – I am very grateful to you for

---

[1] A reference to Edwin Björkman's preface to DHL's play, *The Widowing of Mrs Holroyd*. See p. 80 nn. 1 and 3.

[2] in] from

[3] W. H. Wright relinquished the editorship of *Smart Set* in 1914 and was succeeded by Henry Louis Mencken (1880–1956) and George Jean Nathan (1882–1958) who were joint editors until 1923.

setting up the play at all that expense you took: I should have felt so hollow-hearted about it had it come out in its first bad form. Now I am pretty sure of it.

Many thanks for the Zoë Atkins *Amorality*.[1] It is full of life and go. If only it could have developed, one act from the other, instead of being in three rather jingly parts. But I suppose she is an erratic young lady. If the iron had bitten a *little* deeper into her soul, and that play had had the one strong impulse, and the submission of the young lady to the impulse – how I should have loved it. It is a perfect Utopia, the world she creates, – if she had but admitted the pain somewhere, under the flippancy.[2] The daughter Chloe seems to me pretty real.

It is very beautiful here. I have been out on the sea all afternoon, prodding into the rocks deep under water, for fish. And the noise of the waves in the hollows, and the lift of the boat, and the sun and the smell of the things from under the sea seem to me so real; and it always hurts one inside ones chest to have to sit down and harass about books that pay and don't pay. Why are there always two halves to the world, always a wolf near the door, wherever one build ones house. – But I suppose I *really* ought not to grumble – having so much.

tanti saluti   D. H. Lawrence

I don't think *Papa* is a *social satire* at all. – I *do* think it is full of go and jolliness and life. My wife loves it.

Garnett was asking me why he had heard nothing from you of the play.

703. To Edgar Jaffe, [8 February 1914]

Text: MS UCB; Unpublished.

[Lerici, per Fiascherino, Golfo della Spezia, Italy]
Sunday[3]

Dear Edgar,

We have been out all afternoon getting shell fish in the bay – had a glorious time. It reminded me of the Sunday afternoon when we arrived at Lerici by the Vaporino and saw you paddling in the boat with your little sinner.[4] How is she, by the way? We've never heard of her. – We've got Mrs Garnett

---

[1] Zöe Akins (1886–1958), American poet and dramatist. The title of the play is *Papa: An Amorality in Three Acts* (New York: Mitchell Kennerley, 1913). The play was not produced until 1919.

[2] flippancy] laughter.

[3] Dated with reference to DHL's remark in the preceding letter about being 'out on the sea all afternoon, prodding...for fish'.

[4] Presumably the Jaffes' only daughter, Marianne.

and a Russian girl here – at the Albergo delle Palme – and live in a whirl
of visits and visitings. Sometimes we dine at the hôtel with the ladies – then
Francesco asks after you. Evidently you made a great impression on them
all. When are you coming? When Else comes, with the children, there is Mrs
Pearse's lovely tower. – One does love this place more and more as one stays.

a rivederla   D. H. Lawrence

704. To Arthur McLeod, 9 February 1914
Text: MS UT; Postmark, Lerici 9. 2. 14; Huxley 178–80.

Lerici, per Fiascherino, Golfo della Spezia, Italy
9 February 1914

Dear Mac,

I must thank you first for the books. I think Crosland's *Sonnets* are
objectionable – he is a nasty person.[1] I think Hilaire Belloc is conceited, full
of that French showing-off which goes down so well in England, and is so
smartly shallow.[2] And I have always a greater respect for Mark Rutherford:
I *do* think he is jolly good – so thorough, so sound, and so beautiful.[3]

Tell me, when you write, what you thought of the poems in *Poetry* and
in the *English* [*Review*]. I am glad you sent me the former. In England[4] people
have got that loathsome superior knack of refusing to consider me a poet
at all: 'Your prose is so good', say the kind fools, 'that we are obliged to
forgive you your poetry'. How I hate them. I believe they are still saying
that of Meredith. – In America they are not so priggish conceited.

I have begun my novel again – for about the seventh time. I hope you
are sympathising with me. I had nearly finished it. It was full of beautiful
things, but it missed – I knew that it just missed being itself. So here I am,
must sit down and write it out again. I know it is quite a lovely novel
really – you know that the perfect statue is in the marble, the kernel of it.
But the thing is the getting it out clean. I think I shall manage it pretty well.
You must say a prayer for me sometimes.

Mrs Garnett is staying at the hôtel in Lerici, with a Russian girl. She was

[1] Thomas William Hodgson Crosland (1868–1924), a prolific journalist and author. The book
to which DHL objects, *Sonnets* (1912), was very fulsomely dedicated to several people.
[2] Anglo-French poet, novelist, and essayist, Hilaire Belloc (1870–1953). M.P. 1906–10.
McLeod might have sent DHL one or more of Belloc's books of essays: *On Nothing and
Kindred Subjects* (1908), *On Everything* (1909) and *On Anything* (1910).
[3] Pseudonym of William Hale White (1831–1913), novelist and critic. In November 1912
McLeod had sent Rutherford's well-known *Revolution in Tanner's Lane* (1887) and received
an enthusiastic response from DHL (*Letters*, i. 481–2). What he had now sent is not known.
[4] In England] The English

speaking of you the other day, how sorry she was she did not see anything of you. Why don't you go and see them sometimes?

Kennerley says they[1] have sent me my plays from New York, but they haven't come yet. I look forward to having them. You must have patience with my promise of one. – By the way, what a frightfully *decent* paper the *Morning Post* is. The more I read it, the more I think it is worth while to be a gentleman and to have to do with gentlemen. Their reviews of books, their leaders, and all, have such a decent, honorable tone, such a relief after the majority of newspaper filth.

We have got spring coming in already. I have found a handful of the little wild narcissus, with the yellow centres, and a few sweet violets, and a few purplish crimson anemones with dark centres. And one can drift about all afternoon in the boat, getting shell fish from off the rocks under water, with a long, split cane. You know that warm, drowsy uneasy feel of spring, when scents rouse up. It is already here. And the lizards are whipping about on the rocks, like a sudden flicking of a dried grass blade.[2] And one is wakened in the morning by the birds singing. They are almost brave – they sing aloud as the sun comes up, in spite of the bold Italian cacciatore who, in full costume and a long slim gun, stalks shadowily through the olive trees in quest of wrens and robins.[3] When I walked in Switzerland, and came across a colony of Italians in a public house –

'L'Italia – ah che bel sole! – e gli uccellini — !!' 'Oh Italy – such a beautiful sun – and the little birds – aren't they *good*!' – the cry of the exile.

Frieda sends warmest regards – une bonne poignée.

D. H. Lawrence

705. To Lady Mary St Helier, 17 February 1914
Text: MS UT; Unpublished.

Lerici, per Fiascherino, Golfo della Spezia, Italy
17 February 1914

Dear Madam,[4]

I am sorry that I am too far away to accept your invitation to lunch. I

---

[1] Kennerley says they] They   [2] blade.] stalk.
[3] Cf DHL's essay on this subject, 'Man is a Hunter', written in November 1926 (*Phoenix*, ed. Edward D. McDonald, 1936, pp. 32–4).
[4] Lady Mary St Helier (c. 1845–1931) was the eldest daughter of Keith Stewart Mackenzie of Brahan Castle. m. (1) 1871, Col. the Hon. John Stanley (2) 1881, Francis Jeune, cr. Lord St Helier (d. 1905). Known for her philanthropy, she was particularly famous for her brilliant art of entertaining: Whistler and Millais, Tennyson and Browning were among those who gathered at her house. A frequent contributor to leading reviews, she was the author of *Memories of Fifty Years* (1909).

feel so embedded in this lazy little bay that an invitation to Portland Place[1]
quite scares me, it feels so strenuous. I think I shall be in London for three
or four months of the summer. If ever you should remember to ask me again,
during that time, I shall be very pleased to come.[2]

I have just escorted to the garden gate a little priest student of twenty
four years, who had this one day off from his seminary in Sarzana, and came
to see his folk and his friends in Tellaro – a tiny village a mile away. So they
all gave him wine, and he couldn't see his way back to the seminary, and
was in a very pathetic state. Now he has wandered forth into the hands of
God, renewed by a little strong coffee – poverini.[3]

Forgive me if I don't know how to address you fittingly.

Yours Sincerely   D. H. Lawrence

706. To May Holbrook, [22 February 1914]
Text: MS UN; Postmark, Tellaro 24.2.14; Nehls, iii. 628–9.

Lerici, per Fiascherino, Golfo della Spezia, Italia
domenica – 22 febbraio

My dear May,

Why dont you write me a proper letter and tell me about Will's going
to Canada.[4] You know right well I want to hear. Is he going anywhere
definite? – is he going with the boys? – I don't like the idea of their staying
at Doncaster. It is the same here, the vineyards and the terraces are falling
into disuse, while the men go to America to work in the factories, or they
go as stokers on board ship. Here almost every man has spent his time in
America – seven years in Buenos Ayres, or in the United States. They will
not stay any longer in Italy to be peasants without money. – You know that
here they work the land on the 'half' system. There is no rent. The peasant
takes the land, works up the olives and the wine, takes half the crop for
himself, gives half to the landlord: half the wine, half the oil, half the wood,
and half the maize. And the system no longer holds. In some parts the peasant
only gets a third. They work and slave, they make a living, and save a little.
But in ten years of America they can save as much as in a hundred years
of Italy. And the men can't settle any more. They seem to have a nostalgia

[1] 52 Portland Place, Lady Mary's residence.
[2] DHL went to lunch at Lady Mary's on 30 June 1914. See Letter 743.
[3] 'poor fellows' ('poverino', poor fellow).
[4] Her husband William Holbrook left for Canada on 21 March 1914; May followed him in 1915.
They took up homesteading in Mervyn, Saskatchewan, where May Holbrook was a teacher.
See *Letters*, i. 499 and n. 2.

of restlessness. Italy is a country on the change, and suffering it acutely. Fifty years ago, almost every man was a peasant. In one generation it has all changed. So that now the conditions are strange, there is a queer lethargy among the women, and a queer, sad, gnawing restlessness among the men. They leave their wives for seven years at a time – it is a queer business altogether. It is queer how the old, unconscious carelessness and fatalism of indisposition is working rapidly, decomposing, making the nation feverish and active. There is no religion to speak of. Catholicism is in disrepute. It is a queer country. When I think how practically seven men out of ten emigrate from the villages round about, go for seven years at least – then the stability of the world seems gone. What is England and Italy and America, when they mix their populations as they do.

Here it is as beautiful as ever. There is a big, big bowl of violets on the table. In the rocks by the sea the little white and yellow narcissus, such as one buys off Rowley's greengrocer cart in Eastwood, are twinkling away in the sunshine. Down the steep slopes there are many magenta coloured little anemones. – They are beating down the olives with long canes, and all the ground is sprinkled with the little black fruit like damsons. And all the mills by the little streams are grinding away, the peasant women are carrying great paniers of olives on their heads down to the village. It is all wonderful and sunny and beautiful. But it is all threaded through with this same absence and unsureness of emigration.

We have heaps of friends here. This morning early came a little priest from the Seminary at Sarzana, to bring us a little music: the school-mistress[1] from Tellaro will come this afternoon to tell us of her love affair with Luigi, who is the handsomest man I have ever seen handle a guitar, and who makes love very badly with the Maestra: yesterday we spent the day at the Cochranes, who are rich as rich – butler and footman to serve four people at table – tomorrow we go to the Pearses at Marigola, with whom the Empress Frederick stayed for a winter. It is a mixed life – and we have it pretty well both ways. I like people as people anywhere.

I think we come to England in June, when we shall be married. But I want to come back here in the autumn, to this beloved, beautiful little cottage.

The sea is rough today, no boating among the rocks. It is a sad sound, the waves all the time broken in the rocks and caves.

Please ask Will to write to me, and write to me also yourself. I am sorry you have been ill. I was hoping that there, happy again in the little country

[1] Signorina Eva Rainusso, who taught DHL Italian; see Nehls, iii. 747 n. 97.

school, you would be well.¹ – Tell me news of J[essie] and the boys and your
mother and father, will you.² Tell me all about them. And if there is anything
you want to know,³ just tell me.

                                        tanti, tanti saluti from us both.   D. H. Lawrence

707. To Harold Monro, 27 February 1914
Text: MS IEduc; Unpublished.

                    Lerici, per Fiascherino, Golfo della Spezia, Italia
                                                        27 febbraio 1914

Dear Mr Monro,

   I send you here four poems, which perhaps you may like to print in *Poetry
and Drama.*⁴ I don't know whether they are quite your line, or if they lack
the particular quality you admire. But it is easy to send them back. Only
don't tell me you don't think the 'Ballad of Another Ophelia' is good.⁵ It
is wonderfully good.

   It is the rainy season here. I wonder that all the olives, and the violets
and the narcissus aren't washed clean away into the sea. But there they sit
and twinkle, the flowers, when the rain moves away a little. But I can't bear
the post to be disagreeable when it rains so much.

                                        Yours Sincerely   D. H. Lawrence

708. To Edward Garnett, [March? 1914]
Text: MS NYPL; Tedlock, ed., *Frieda Lawrence: The Memoirs and Correspondence,* pp. 202–3.
[Frieda Weekley begins]

                                                        Fiascherino
                                                        [March? 1914]⁶

Dear Mr Garnett,

   I have been so cross with you! You attacked me in your letter and I was
cross but I am afraid you were right and made me realise my wrongs in a
way – I had'nt cared twopence about L[awrence]'s novel; Over the children

---

¹ well] happy and well
² For the Chambers family see an illustration in *Letters,* i. Jessie Chambers (1887–1944) was
  the model for Miriam in *Sons and Lovers:* see *Letters,* i. 22 *et passim.*
³ know] ask
⁴ The poems are unidentified; Monro accepted none of them for *Poetry and Drama.*
⁵ It was first published in *Some Imagist Poets: An Anthology* (Boston and New York, 1915).
⁶ Written during Constance Garnett's stay, c. 29 January – c. 6 March 1914. The somewhat
  delayed arrival of a copy of the February issue of the *Bookman* suggests a fairly late point
  in her stay.

I thought he was beastly, he hated me for being miserable, not a moment
of misery did he put up with; he denied all the suffering and suffered all
the more – like his mother before him; how we fought over this! In revenge
I did not care about his writing. If he denies my life and suffering I deny
his art, so you see he wrote without me at the back of him. The novel is
a failure but you must feel something at the back of it struggling, trying to
come out – You see I dont really believe in *Sons and Lovers* it feels as if there
were nothing *behind* all those happenings as if there were no 'Hinterland der
Seele'[1] only intensely felt fugitive things – I who am a believer though I dont
know in what, to me it seems an irreligious book – It does not seem the
deepest and last thing said, if for instance a man loves in a book the pretty
curl in the neck of 'her', if he loves it ever so intensely and beautifully, there
is some thing behind that curl, *more* than that curl, there is *she*, the living,
striving *she* – Writers are so beside the point not *direct* enough – I am going
to throw my self into the novel now and you will see what a 'gioia'[2] it will
be – There is one triumph for us women, you men cant do things alone – Just
as little as we can *live* alone. I have got over the worst, terrible part with
E[rnest] and the children, so I shall enjoy L. writing – So dont pitch into
me anymore, I have suffered very much for the love of men! You ought all
to be frightfully nice to me! It is jolly to have Mrs Garnett here, I go to
her and pour out my Lawrence woes to her and she listens patiently and
feelingly, so I never feel I am disloyal to L – It's *pouring* with rain, I wonder
if Mrs Garnett will move on – She said she might – I think it is rather nice
of L. and intelligent to accept your criticism as he does, because it is not
easy to swallow criticism, but you need never be afraid and mind what you
say, he would always much rather you said it! You mustn't *mind* saying it
because you are really the only man he has any opinion of[3] – I do think you
are good to him, only your second letter was too cross, perhaps it was a good
thing too! Thank you for the book![4] I was so glad to get it. Something 'goy'
in it pleased me very much – Cannot you come out soon, when I think how
you sit in Henrietta Street and how you would enjoy the sunshine and the
sea, you ought to come!

    Good-bye – Yours with love   Frieda

[Lawrence begins]

Dear Garnett,

    I didn't send those other pages,[5] because I thought I'd do the whole thing
again. We'll see how it turns out.

---

[1] 'unknown reaches of the soul'.   [2] 'joy'.
[3] MS reads 'off'.   [4] Unidentified.   [5] See Letter 700.

Mitchell Kennerley wrote to me he'd offered Duckworth some sheets of the play. You must tell me how it is decided.

Thanks for the *Bookman*. W L George had already sent it on. They are exclaiming here on the truth of what he says. But the truth of what is said about oneself, one can never see so completely.

The Consul in Spezia[1] is typing my new novel – for fun. Kennerley asked me for a copy, so I shall be able to send him one direct.

It is sunny again today.

Yours   D. H. Lawrence

709. To Edward Marsh, [5 March 1914]
Text: MS NYPL; PC; Postmark, Tellaro 5. 3. 14; Unpublished.

Fiascherino
[5 March 1914]

Dear Eddie,

I send you here the only copy of the play which has as yet come to me from America. I have asked them for some more, and if they come, I'll send you one on. – The Stage Society asked me for the proofs. I gave them. That is all that I have done as regards production. I should be very glad if your friend[2] put the thing on the stage. The Stage Society is not much of a go anyhow. But probably you won't care for the play – have a try: I am anxiously awaiting a *New Numbers* – I sent the sub., but have heard nothing.[3]

Saluti.   D. H. Lawrence

710. To Henry Savage, 7 March 1914
Text: MS YU; Postmark, Spezia 8. 3. 14; cited in Moore, *Yale University Library Gazette*, xxxiv. 27.

Lerici, per Fiascherino, Golfo della Spezia, Italy
7 March 1914.

Dear Savage,

It must be a long time since I wrote to you. I sent you some of your books back the other day. The others will follow, if you wait patiently. Don't mind that we keep you so long.

---

[1] (Sir) Thomas Dacre Dunlop (1883–1964), b. Belfast, educated at King's College, London. Began his Civil Service career on the staff of the Admiralty; entered H.M. Consular Service 1907; served in Egypt, Uruguay and Italy. He was the British Consul in Spezia in 1913, when DHL first knew him. Inspector-General of Consular Establishment from 1922 until retirement in 1943. Made a CMG in 1930 and was created KCMG in 1939. m. Margaret ('Madge') Morris, 1911.   [2] Unidentified.   [3] See p. 136 n. 7.

We have had two people here – Mrs Garnett – who translates the Russian books – and a young lady who is still with us.[1] And my dear God, how weary I am of women, women, eternal women. Do you know, there are here, in Lerici at present, seven mortal English women, and I the only man under fifty five. And a man of fifty five to me is more or less of a matron. Dear heaven, I should like to join the army, or go into a monastery.

And there isn't any news, except that we are eternally going out to lunch or dinner when we don't want to, and amusing rather elderly, but very nice people whom we don't want to amuse.

I began my novel for about the eleventh time.[2] It is on its legs and is going strong, but I shall be glad when it is finished.

I got one copy of my play the other day – and news that others are coming along. So you will get one soon.[3] It will come out in England directly, I believe.

It is so beautiful here now, with violets and wild narcissi, and anemones and primroses, such lovely sundowns and such a foamy sea and such white moonlight. I wish to God I needn't write and needn't do anything. Oh it is such beautiful spring: I wish I could just walk out of the house and into the hills, and on and on at my own sweet will. – Yesterday we climbed the hills above the sea, and looked over the river at Carrara, at the white great slits of the quarries and the ragged snowy peaks. And then we saw the sea coast curve in a fine, fine line far away into the heavens, with towns like handfuls of shells, Massa, Viareggio, and ships like butterflies in mid-air. Oh, and I wanted to go off Southwards. I never want to go north, but south I should love to go, walking. I stood and talked with the charcoal burners beside the smoking mound, up there in the wild, bosky hillside. One was old and very quiet: and he said he slept up there under a little lean-to of branches. And I wished I were there, to sleep there too. And one was young, a big, handsome fellow heavy with perfect health. He said he went with the mules down to the shore. But he too was restless. Soon he was going to America. I felt like addressing him as comrade, in the Whitman manner.[4] – It is the piggling niggling of life that I hate. Oh my God, one must trim one's speech and bring proof of one's statements. I wish we were not with so many people here, I want to feel freer.

How are you, how is your poem,[5] how are your spirits. Does the spring

---

[1] Vera Volkhovsky.

[2] 'The Wedding Ring' (in May renamed *The Rainbow*).

[3] DHL presented Savage with an inscribed copy of the London edition (2nd issue) of *The Widowing of Mrs Holroyd*. It is now at Yale. See *Yale University Library Gazette*, xxxiv. 19.

[4] DHL may have had in mind 'O camerado close!' from the concluding lines of Walt Whitman's 'Starting from Paumanok'.

[5] Not identified.

unsettle you as it does me? Oh, the spring in Italy is the devil. You can feel the earth working with birth, and one's flesh is restless the same, and ones soul is worse.

Good night and good luck to you.

D. H. Lawrence

711. To Edward Marsh, 14 March 1914
Text: MS NYPL; Postmark, Lerici 15 3 14; cited in Huxley 181–2.

Lerici, per Fiascherino, Golfo della Spezia, Italia

14 Marzo 1914

Caro Edoardo,

You'll see this letter from this man, and my answer.[1] I want you to post it on to him, if you will, and if you approve. I want you to have the stuff of mine you like for your next *Georgian* issue.[2] Advise me, please, if you don't approve of my answer to this man. And don't be bored by my bothering you. You must remain my poetic adviser.

When you do tell me what you want for your 1914–15 edition, tell me the faults you find and I will try to put them right. I was surprised that you liked 'Meeting in the Mountains'. The man, as a fact, was a man *extraordinarily* like Frieda's husband: I met him just as the poem says, in the Tirol, three months after we had come away from England. Frieda's husband was one of the[3] professors under whom I studied in Nottingham college: and I had liked him, and he had liked me. So that the poor devil suffered. It seems queer and unreal now.

There will be some of my poems in a magazine I have never seen, called the *Egoist* – next month I believe.[4] Some of them you don't know at all. One you might like – I think you might. Tell me – I always want to hear what you say.

I suppose the play was too sordid for you, was it? I want to hear from you about it. I am sorry we shall not see you at Easter. If we were well enough off, we too would go to Florence that week. Remember me to Jim Barnes. will you – I don't care for Lascelles in *New Numbers*. Wilfrid is jolly

---

[1] Unidentified; DHL's letter has not been found.
[2] *Georgian Poetry 1913–15* (1915) included DHL's two poems: 'Service of All the Dead' and 'Meeting Among the Mountains'.
[3] the] my
[4] The *Egoist*, i (April 1914), 134–5, published 'Song', 'Early Spring', 'Honeymoon', 'Fooled' and 'A Winter's Tale'. The titles of some of these poems were changed subsequently: see Warren Roberts, *A Bibliography of D. H. Lawrence*, p. 252.

good – one poem of Rupert Brooke I like – the others aren't up to much. Drinkwater isn't bad, I think.[1]

Tanti saluti D. H. Lawrence

712. To Arthur McLeod, 14 March 1914

Text: MS UT; Postmark, Tellaro 16. 3. 14; Huxley 180–1.

Lerici, per Fiascherino, Golfo della Spezia, Italia
14 Marzo 1914

Dear Mac,

Thanks for the *House of the Dead*.[2] We have begun reading it, but I don't like it *very* much. It seems a bit dull: so much *statement*.

It reminds me that the other Sunday we went to the house of a very popular modern Russian novelist, Amphiteatroff,[3] at Levanto. It *was* a rum show: twenty six people at lunch, a babble of German English Russian French Italian – a great fat laughing man, the host, carefully judging the Cinque Terre wine: a drawing room, clever, highly educated wife at the head of the table, a peasant sculptor in a peasants smock at the foot, and in between, a motley of tutors and music teachers for the children – an adopted son of Maxim Gorky, little, dark, agile, full of life,[4] and a great wild Cossack wife whom he had married for passion and had come to hate – then a house full of scuffling servants and cultured children – no, it was too much – You have no idea how one feels English and stable and solid in comparison. I felt as if my head were screwed on tighter than the foundations of the world, in comparison. I must say, in one way, I loved them – for their absolute carelessness about everything but just what interested them. They are fine where we have become stupid.

---

[1] DHL is commenting on the first issue of *New Numbers* (February 1914), since the second was not published until April 1914. The poem by Abercrombie is 'The Olympians'; W. W. Gibson's poem is 'Bloodybush Edge'; Brooke's poems are 'Sonnet', 'A Memory (from a sonnet-sequence)', 'One Day', and 'Mutability'; Drinkwater's contributions are 'The Poet to His Mistress', 'The New Miracle', 'Boundaries', 'A Town Window' and 'Memory'.

[2] F. M. Dostoievsky's *The House of the Dead* was available in Everyman's Library, trans. H. S. Edwards (1911).

[3] Aleksander Valentinovich Amfiteatrov (1862–1923) was a prolific Russian novelist, playwright and journalist.

[4] Zinovii Alekseevich Peshkov (formerly Zinovii Mikhailovich Sverdlov) was known, incorrectly, as Gorky's 'adopted son'. He had taken Gorky's name, Peshkov, when he was christened in order to enter the Imperial Philharmonic School. (Gorky himself lived on Capri from 1906 till December 1913.)

Oh it is so beautiful here, I feel as if my heart would jump out of my chest like a hare at night – it is such lovely spring. The sea is blue all day, and primrose dusking to apricot at evening. There are flowers, and peach trees in bloom, and pink almond trees among the vapor grey of the olives.

Today we have been a great picnic high up, looking at the Carrara mountains, and the flat valley of the Magra, and the sea coast sweeping round in a curve that makes my blood run with delight, sweeping round, and it seems up into the vaporous heaven with tiny scattering of villages, like handfuls of shells thrown on the beach, right beyond Viareggio. – I could not tell you how I could jump up into the air, it is so lovely. I want at this time to walk away, to walk south, into the Appenines, through the villages one sees perched high up across the valley.

My novel goes on slowly. It ought to be something when it is done, the amount of me I have given it.

I think there will be some of my poems in a paper called the *Egoist*. I don't know anything about it. Ezra Pound took some verses, and sent me £3..3 – . Try to get a copy, will you – I believe it will be next month – it might be this, but I think not. But unless I can get hold of a copy I absolutely dont know what they have published.

I wish you could come here – why don't you try.

Many regards from us both. Don't you keep on sending us things, it seems such an imposition. Did you get the copy of the play, I sent you – Tell me what you think of it – I wait to hear –

tanti saluti   D. H. Lawrence

713. To Ernest Collings, 22 March 1914
Text: MS UT; Huxley 182–5.

Lerici, per Fiascherino, Golfo della Spezia, Italia
22 marzo 1914

Dear Collings,

This morning has arrived your book of drawings.[1] It *was* an unexpected pleasure to get it. You have done me too much honor in inscribing it to me.

I am really delighted with the book, for all that. How much better your things look now they are gathered together. Now at last one is able to get

---

[1] A copy of *Outlines: A Book of Drawings* (1914) arrived on 22 March and DHL began this letter of acknowledgement on the same day, but, as Letter 714 shows, after writing a critique of four pages, he stopped. It is assumed that DHL decided to write briefly (Letter 714) on 24 March and to complete this letter at his leisure. Collings' note on the MS, 'Answd E C 4/4/14' suggests that it was posted perhaps as much as a week after Letter 714 though begun two days before it.

something like a real impression of your [. . .] work. I must confess you puzzle me. You are a queer man. I think if you persist you will one day have a real boom. Because people will think you are an esoteric wonder-freak, and it will be a kind of aesthetic qualification to know you, as it was to know Beardsley, and is rather now, to know Alastair.[1]

I wish you would tell me what you feel is your aim. Because you are, Frieda says, absolutely unemotional. But I suppose it is a form of emotion to which we are not accustomed. But *what* are you trying to interpret, I wonder. I will not say that for me your work is unemotional, because some of the pictures really move me – how, I can't say. I am always puzzled to know how I feel or what I feel. I suppose you rouse very mixed feelings. I often notice you start[2] some response in me, and then rebuff me, as in the picture 'Hill',[3] where I cannot, after answering to the figure and the clouds, receive the hard conical thrust of the jagged lines at the figures *head*. It seems to me rather as if you did not bring your two strong motions together, so that they meet and clinch and are together, but as if they lose each other. It seems to me, in the figure, you have a motion of *offering* – to the sky, from the body straight out at right angles; and then the shoot of the hill is at the head of the figure, so that I feel the picture like this[4] – no, I cant draw it – but concentrating at the *head*, when surely the hill offers to the sky a great, primitive *body*. It is this I can't understand – what you mean us to feel. Am I to believe that a hill culminates in what corresponds to the human [. . .] head (brain, – intellect) – and in the hill the human head (brain or intellect) lies forever fixed, under a sky that disregards it. Because we are so used to the mythical idea of the earth's fruitful body, or to the rocks representing the chained body, that I cannot, cannot feel them representing the head sealed down and rigid and scarcely[5] to be liberated. – You must please help me to understand. – Then in 'homage to Ivan M[ĕstrović]'[6] – I cannot understand the significance of the high wings of the sphinx. When I say understand, I mean they baffle my feeling. They don't answer to the woman-figure – or I can't see the connection. You see they have an emotional

---

[1] Aubrey Beardsley (1872–98) and, most likely, Aleister Crowley (1875–1947).

[2] start] set

[3] The drawing entitled 'Hill' (*Outlines*, p. 15) pictures the upper part of a female nude incorporated into the slope of a hill.

[4] Here DHL begins an illustration of a hill, but then crosses it out.

[5] scarcely] never

[6] A drawing of a female nude with a sphinx in the background (p. 9). Ivan Mĕstrović (1883–1962) was a Yugoslavian sculptor; he went to Paris in 1911, where he mainly worked independently; he won a prize in the 1911 International Exhibition in Rome; he exhibited his works in England and France during World War I (see Letter 947).

force. But I *cannot* feel how it relates to the other emotional force – the woman-figure. – Don't tell me it is merely beautiful form and space-filling: that means tour de force. – The thing must be the expression of some strong emotion or idea. And I can't grasp it. You are not intelligible to me. And I want to understand. – *What* do you want to convey? – I shall look at these drawings a hundred times, and try to find it. – You don't use the human figure to express any individual emotion – not dramatically – Don't say it is just a decorative use. – Look at your 'Head of a Woman'.[1] There is something – something big and looming and blanched that is very character-istic of you – a sort of looming of the brain pan big over everything, so that features, emotions are insignificant – only this big, blanched, almost blank something that is like the intellectual ego, something frozen like death which survives life, and knows nothing of life or resurrection – I don't know what it is. – I like very much 'Après Midi D'un Faune'[2] – but there again, the blanked out figures of the women, and then the over-solid figure of the man rather destroy each other – they don't seem to be in the same picture. The man's figure is not good. What do you mean by your blanked out figures. If you can tell me, then I can either see you are right, or else see where you are wrong. – I think 'Tragédie de Salome' *very* good – right proportion of blank and black[3] – Elide, the maid, says, 'Come è bella!' – 'how beautiful it is.' I think it very good indeed. Perhaps there one might find out how you use substance and blank – some relation of the human to the elements – but I dont know.

It seems to me you have two, or three styles: the marionette, and then the strong line flowing and embracing a blank, then the sort of Indian. Of the three styles, I think I like best your strong line embracing a blank – like 'Dancer' (33)[4] – That is one of the best drawings. What do you use the background lines for? the / / / / / / / / / lines? They express motion in a certain direction, I expect – then they have a tone value – and then a static value, a sort of standing value. But I don't always see *how* you have used them. In 'Youth' (47) you get a jolly good motion by means of them. I like that drawing – Frieda likes it best. Perhaps of them all I like 'The Masquers' (41) most. You've used the lines, upright and horizontal, rather well there. But *what* do you mean by your white shadows. Do you know, I think they are the most interesting thing about you. But what do you quite mean to suggest by them? I think it needs a subtler handling of the hachure lines

[1] *Outlines*, p. 11.
[2] 'Prelude à l'Après-Midi d'un Faune (Russian Ballet)', p. 13.
[3] The full title is 'Karsavina in "La Tragédie de Salome" (Russian Ballet)', p. 17.
[4] *Outlines*, p. 33.

or whatever you call them, to bring the thing home. The same in the Velasquez motiv.[1] I feel as if the lady were not in quite the right setting, and yet I have not a notion of what I would alter. Perhaps the lines and accessories, like the chequer and curtain, should suggest what you have left out of the figure: as the slanting lines in the last picture convey the eager, storm-like travelling of Youth. Then you would want to suggest, by your surrounding of your shadow lady, some essential quality of hers and her sort, by which they live almost impersonally, as the forces of nature – or a force of nature.[2]

I am afraid I am obscure. But I think, unless one is so pure[3] by instinct that one does the right thing without knowing, then one *must* know what [...] one is after. And I cant make out what you are after, however I try. You want to use the human body to express – what? – something elementary in nature, something non organic, or of the realm of physics – what? What property of the human soul[4] do you want to express? – the mechanicalness of thought, as one of the natural forces? – the natural torrent of youth? what? – I think if there had been just a bit more intensity got into 'Youth', that might have been very beautiful.

But I shall stop talking now, or I shall never have done, and I get no further.

It is very beautiful here now the spring is here with all the sunshine. The sea is rough and bursting in foam all along the shore. I am getting on with a novel – I have been lazy this last year. There will be a drama of mine published shortly. If I can get hold of any copies, I will send you one. We are thinking of staying here till the end of May, and then to England for a while. I shall see you then.

I have no other news. Tell me about your aim. The book is very interesting to us – and we thank you for it, very much.

a rivederla   D. H. Lawrence

714. To Ernest Collings, [24 March 1914]
Text: MS UT; PC; Postmark, Tellaro 24. 3. 14; Unpublished.

Fiascherino
[24 March 1914]

Dear Collings,

I *was* delighted to get the book of drawings. It made a great impression

---

[1] The title of this drawing is 'Echo of Velasquez', p. 37.

[2] DHL is referring to 'Echo of Velasquez' which depicts a silhouette of a lady in elaborate dress against a background of strong vertical black and white lines.

[3] pure] quick   [4] soul] body

on me. I am getting used to it, then I am writing to you fully about it. I have written four pages, but haven't finished yet.¹ The things look awfully well, I think, printed as they are: and a bookful helps one to get an impression. But I haven't yet got the real hang of you. I try to find out what you're after – it is not easy.

It is too flattering of you to inscribe the book to me.² Many many thanks –
                                                                    D. H. Lawrence

715. To Ivy Low, [c. April 1914]
Text: Harper's Bazaar, no. 2818 (October 1946), 412.
                              [Lerici, per Fiascherino, Golfo della Spezia, Italy]
                                                                    [c. April 1914]

Don't let the crest upset you³ – my wife's father was a baron,⁴ and we're just using up old note paper.

716. To John Middleton Murry, 3 April 1914
Text: MS NYPL; cited in Murry, New Adelphi 266, 275.
                              Lerici, per Fiascherino, Golfo della Spezia, Italia
                                                                    3 aprile 1914.

Dear Murry,

Well, your letter *was* unexpected. I thought that you and Katherine held me an interfering Sunday-school Superintendent sort of person who went too far in his superintending and became impossible: – stepped the just too far, which is the crime of crimes. And I felt guilty. And I suppose I am guilty. But thanks be to God, one is often guilty without being damned.

I quite agree with you that telling is absolutely of no use for enlightenment, it only gives one something to hang on to, occasionally: rouses some dull little instinct and gives it a stimulation. At present, I do believe in trying to give what moral support one can. I call it, helping people to have *faith*. I am rather great on faith just now. I do believe in it. We are so egoistic, that we are ashamed of ourselves out of existence. One ought to have faith

---

¹ See p. 156 n. 1.   ² See p. 134 n. 2.
³ Ivy Teresa Low (1889–1977) eldest daughter of Walter Low. m. 1916, Maxim Litvinoff (1876–1951), later Soviet foreign commissar (1930–9). Friend of Catherine Carswell and Viola Meynell, she first visited DHL in the spring of 1914. By the time she met DHL, she had published two novels: *Growing Pains* (1913) and *The Questing Beast* (January 1914). (For obituary see the *Times*, 30 April 1977.)
⁴ Catherine Carswell recalls that DHL repeated this remark in a second letter 'upon coroneted notepaper' to Ivy Low which 'made us smile' (Carswell 4).

in what one ultimately is, then one can bear at last the hosts of unpleasant things which one is en route. I seem to spend half my days having revulsions and convulsions from myself. But I do know that Frieda knows I am really decent, and so I depend on her. – It is so horribly difficult not to betray oneself, somehow, with all the different people.

I did think you didn't want to write to me any more – that I'd trampled in forbidden places. But it doesn't matter, does it? – I mean I think I did trample in forbidden places.

I'am glad you and Katharine are all right. I know and did know that you would both of you only be negative sort of things once you'd split. Whatever happens and doesn't happen, I know you should stick to the love you have each for the other. And one has to remember this when things go wrong.

Frieda and I are really very deeply happy. I am a tiresome thing to myself and to everybody. Somehow, I find it so difficult to live proportionately: to keep a proportion, a reserve. So I am always going in headlong and crawling out ignominious and furious, mostly with myself. But when one is furious with oneself, one *does* make everybody else's life a misery.

Don't mind what Eddie Marsh or Campbell say of me: it sounds as if they said unpleasant things. 'Be all things to all men.'[1] That isn't my ideal, it seems like my fate. But really, one *can* only be towards each person that which corresponds to him,[2] more or less. And one might as well talk to a daisy by the path, as be one's further self with Marsh. – Campbell ought not to misunderstand me.

Yes, you *do* need to write your own personal stuff, otherwise you can't be yourself. And if you can't be yourself, how can any woman love you. I'm glad you've come through all right. Oh, I think to myself, if only one could have a few real friends, who will understand a bit along with one. They are all against one. I feel Marsh against me with the whole of his being: and Campbell would like to be, for he is a perverse devil.

What is your work? I should like to hear about that.

Oh, I tried so hard to work, this last year. I began a novel seven times. I have written quite a thousand pages that I shall burn. But now, thank God, Frieda and I are together, and the work is of me and her, and it is beautiful, I think. I have done two-thirds. Tell me what yours is.[3]

Don't say it's a prosy history, yours. The only history is a mere question of ones struggle inside oneself. But that is the joy of it. One need neither

1 Corinthians ix. 22 ['I am become all things...'].
him] them
Murry was then working on his first novel called *Still Life* (1916): it 'was to fall dead-born from the press when it was at last published' (John Carswell, *Lives and Letters*, 1978, p. 86).

discover Americas nor conquer nations, and yet one has as great a work as Columbus or Alexander, to do. So I flatter myself.

I'm getting rather sermony. – But I say, we'll all get on, and we'll have enough money for our purposes, and we'll be jolly. I do look forward to the time when we can all be jolly together. I'm fed up with miseries and sufferings.

It is spring, with puffs of pear blossom among the olive trees. But I know your war-cry now is work.

I want to get somewhere about Frieda's children. Her old figurehead of a husband plays marionette Moses, then John Halifax Gentleman,[1] then Othello, then a Maupassant hero tracking down his victims, one stock piece after another with amazing energy. He is a fool. I wish the worms would eat him up. I would curse his wooden soul if I could. There is no living, flexible *man* in him, only, I tell you, this series of tableaux vivants. And it is so wearying, I would curse him to infinity, if it were any good.

Give my regards to Katharine. I suppose we've all abused each other, but it doesn't really matter, does it. – Frieda is out just now with her sister,[2] or she'd add a line.

D. H. Lawrence

– I am awfully glad you wrote.

717. To Arthur McLeod, 16 April 1914
Text: MS UT; Postmark, Spezia 16. 4. 14; Huxley 187–9.

Lerici, per Fiascherino, Golfo della Spezia, Italy
16 April 1914

Dear Mac,

I feel a fearful pig when the newspapers come so regularly. Are you *sure* it isn't an imposition on you. Don't send them so regularly, it makes me feel guilty. What a beast of a[3] paper is the *Egoist*. I wouldn't have given them those verses had I known. And there were 7 misprints – swine, swine.[4] I shall not easily forgive them those misprints. – Did you see in Good Friday's *Morning Post*, that the curves in Greek architecture were *not* after all to give the illusion of straight lines?[5] I remember what an impression it made on

---

[1] The eponymous character in the best known novel (1857) of Dinah Maria Mulock (1826–87).
[2] Else Jaffe.   [3] MS reads 'the'.
[4] See p. 154 n. 4. Because DHL later revised all the poems for re-publication, only six misprints can be definitely ascertained: 'notes' for 'motes' (l. 8), 'loosing' for 'loosening' (l. 12) and 'woods' for 'words' (l. 13) in 'Early Spring'; 'chouch' for 'crouch' (l. 16) and 'be' for 'me' (l. 31) in 'Honeymoon'; and 'hasted' for 'hastened' (l. 9) in 'Fooled'.
[5] The *Morning Post* (10 April 1914), p. 3, carried an article entitled 'The Curves in Greek Building', a review of a new, illustrated edition of *The Works of Man* by Lisle M. Phillip

me, when you said they were. I wonder which is right. I would rather the first were right, that the curves were made to give the temple a look of being actually straight.

We are awfully excited today because a lawyer says that a boy has a right to elect his own guardian at the age of 14. Frieda's boy is 14 in July. Weekley, who is gone mad on his injuries and his rights, raves about shooting the miserable me and himself and other vague people, if there is any mention of Frieda's even seeing the children.[1] So that we feel we have got a pull over him. I hope it will come out all right. The decree absolute should soon be pronounced. Look in the law intelligence for it, will you?[2] Then we can be married in London this summer. I shall ask you to be a marriage witness – my wedding guest – like the Ancient Mariner. You won't have to refuse. Then if Frieda can have her children for a week or two, won't it be blessed for her?

There is a great disturbance in the house today because the priest is coming on Sunday to bless the house. These people don't really *believe* any more, but they go on with the old performances. And the church ritual is very real today. 'Eh', said Achille, on Good Friday morning (the Church makes Christ die on Thursday, to have time to perform their businesses by Easter Sunday, Felice says) – 'Eh', said Achille, when Elide went for the bread, 'we can sin as much as we like today – the Signore is dead, and he won't see us.' And they half mean it. Isn't it queer? In their heads, they don't believe a thing. A man Gamba, was saying to me yesterday that the Latin nature is fundamentally *geometrical*: its deepest aspiration is essential geometry – Form. He says that is the real meaning of the Renaissance – Geometrical Form, in contrast to Mediaeval Mysticism. In the Renaissance, he says, the Roman spirit appeared again, materialistic, mathematic, individualistic, and over-threw the Germanic mediaeval influence. Does that interest you? I am trying to swallow it, to digest it. It doesn't go down very easily. Because if the nature of the Italian is rationalistic and materialistic, what about the procession I tell you of now? – and yet it *is* rationalistic and materialistic.

We went on Good Friday eve to see the procession of Jesus to the tomb. The houses in Tellaro are stuck about on the rocks in a tiny opening. It was a still night with a great moon, but the village deep in shadow, only the moonlight shining out at sea. And on all the window sills were rows of candles trembling on the still air, long rows in the square, big windows, very golden in the blue dark shadow under a lighted sky.[3] Then the procession came out

Ernest Weekley had applied for, and obtained custody of the three children.
It was pronounced on 27 April 1914; the *Times* Law Report included it ('Weekley *v.* Weekley and Lawrence') on 28 April.
dark shadow under a lighted sky.] grey night.

of church, the lads running in front clapping wooden clappers, like those
they scare birds with at home. Such a din of clappers. And the noise means
the grinding of the bones of Judas. Then came the procession – a white bier
with drawn curtains, carried high on the shoulders of men dressed all in
white, with white cloths on their heads – a weird chanting noise broken by
the noise of the sea, and candles fluttering as the white figures moved, and
two great, gilt rococco lanterns carried above. Then, with all the clatter and
the broken mournful chanting and the hoarse wash of the sea, they began
to climb the steep staircase between the high, dark houses, a white, ghostly
winding procession, with the dark dressed villagers crowding behind. It was
gone in a minute. And it made a fearful impression on me. It is the *mystery*
that does it – it is Death itself, robbed of its horrors, and only Fear and
Wonder going humbly behind. – *You* must come to Italy. Soon all this will
be gone – the Church is nearly dead.

Auf wiedersehen   D. H. Lawrence

718. To Edward Garnett, 22 April 1914
Text: MS NYPL; Postmark, Tellaro 23. 4. 14; Huxley 189–91.

Lerici, per Fiascherino, Golfo della Spezia, Italy
22 April 1914

Dear Garnett,

I send you by this post as much of the Wedding Ring as the Consul has
as yet typed.[1] I have only some 80 pages more to write. In a fortnight it
should be done. You will perhaps get it in three weeks' time, the whole.

From this part that I have sent you, follows on the original 'Sisters' – the
School inspector, and so on.[2]

I am sure of this now, this novel. It is a big and beautiful work. Before
I could not get my soul into it. That was because of the struggle and the
resistance between Frieda and me. Now you will find her and me in the novel,
I think, and the work is of both of us.

I am glad you sent back the first draught of the Wedding Ring, because I
had not been able to do in it what I wanted to do. But I was upset by the
second letter you wrote against it, because I felt it insulted rather the thing
I *wanted* to say: not me, nor what I had said, but that which I was trying
to say, and had failed in.

In the work as it stands now, there will, if anything, be only small
prolixities to cut down.

[1] See p. 152 n. 1.   [2] Rupert Birkin is the School Inspector in *Women in Love*

I hope you will like it. It is a big book now that I have got it down. I hope it will have a good sale. Both Pinker and Curtis Brown write to me definitely making offers authorised, they insist, by leading publishers in England and America – definite offers. It was horrid to receive the accounts of *Sons and Lovers*, and to see that Duckworth has lost a number of pounds on the book – fifteen or so, was it. That is very unpleasant. Because I only had a hundred pounds even then – and I have had £35 from Kennerley.[1] If a publisher is to lose by me, I would rather it were a rich commercial man such as Heinemann. You told me in your last letter that I was at liberty to go to any other firm with this novel. Do you mean you would perhaps be relieved if I went to another firm? Because if you did not mean that, wasn't it an unnecessary thing to say? You know how willing I am to hear what you have to say, and to take your advice and to act on it when I have taken it. But it is no good unless you will have patience and understand[2] what I *want* to do. I am not after all a child working erratically. All the time, underneath, there is something deep evolving itself out in me. And it is *hard* to express a new thing, in sincerity. And you should understand, and help me to the new thing, not get angry and say it is *common*, and send me back to the tone of the old Sisters. In the Sisters was the germ of this novel: [. . .] woman becoming individual, self-responsible, taking her own initiative. But the first Sisters was flippant and often vulgar and jeering. I had to get out of that attitude, and make my subject really worthy. You see – you tell me I am half a Frenchman and one-eighth a Cockney. But that isn't it. I have very often the vulgarity and disagreeableness of the common people, as you say Cockney, and I may be a Frenchman. But primarily I am a passionately religious man, and my novels must be written from the depth of my religious experience. That I must keep to, because I can only work like that. And my cockneyism and commonness are only when the deep feeling doesn't find its way out, and a sort of jeer comes instead, and sentimentality, and purplism. But you should see the religious, earnest, suffering man in me first, and then the flippant or common things after. Mrs Garnett says I have no true nobility – with all my cleverness and charm. But that is not true. It is there, in spite of all the littlenesses and commonnesses

And that is why I didn't like the second letter you wrote me about the failed novel, where you rubbed it in: because you seemed to insult my real *being*. You had a right to go for my work, but in doing that, you must not

---

[1] DHL seems to have forgotten receiving this money from Mitchell Kennerley when, in 1924, he wrote: 'America has had [*Sons and Lovers*] for nothing' ('The Bad Side of Books' in McDonald, *A Bibliography of the Writings of D. H. Lawrence*, p. 12).

[2] understand] try

make *me* cheap in your own eyes. You can be angry with a person without holding him cheap, and making him feel cheap. You believe too much in the Frenchman and the Cockney. Those are the things to criticise in me, not to rest your belief on.

Soon I shall want some money. Perhaps you might send me the little I left in Mrs Garnett's bank – is it seven pounds or so? Don't bother if it is any trouble. I have a little still in the bank here. So I can use cheques.

If Duckworth [...] is not really *keen* on this novel, we will give it to Pinker without its coming back here. I dont think I want to sign an agreement with Duckworth for another novel after this. I did not like to see he had lost on *Sons and Lovers*. And I *must* have money for my novels, to live. And if the other publishers definitely offer, they who are only commercial people, whereas you are my friend – well, they may lose as much as they like. For I don't want to feel under an obligation. You see I can't separate you from Duckworth and Co, in this question of novels. And *nobody* can do any good with my novels, commercially, unless they believe in them commercially – which you dont very much.

Will you also tell me who makes the agreement with Kennerley for USA publication, and what is the agreement made.

I see that *Mrs Holroyd* is coming out.[1] Do you give me any copies? Tell me about it, will you.

We think of staying here till the end of June, perhaps. I don't know whether we shall come straight to England, or go to Germany first. We want to be married this summer, if the decree absolute is declared all right. Then we think of coming back here for the winter. We have an invitation to the Abbruzzi, to the Baronessa di Rescis,[2] in September, and I want to go to the Abbruzzi.

I am always grateful to you, and if Duckworth could have my novels and all of us be satisfied, I should be glad. But I am sure we are none of us very well satisfied with the result of *Sons and Lovers*.

I shall be glad if you like the novel now – but you will tell me. Frieda sends her regards.

Yours   D. H. Lawrence

719. To J. B. Pinker, 22 April 1914
Text: MS UT; Unpublished.

Lerici, per Fiascherino, Golfo della Spezia, Italy
22 April 1914

Dear Mr Pinker,

Thank you for selling 'The White Stocking' to the *Smart Set*.[3] I suppose

---

[1] See p. 135 n. 3.   [2] Unidentified.
[3] 'The White Stocking' was published in *Smart Set*, xliv (October 1914).

£18 is as much as one can get out of them nowadays. When the cheque comes, send it on to me, please. I am always nearing the stony condition of a stream in summer.

In answer to your question about agreements, I don't think I have agreed for anything to anybody, after this present novel which I am this week sending in to Duckworth and to Kennerley. I believe I am free, certainly I am *legally* free, to do as I like with subsequent work. It is a question of gratitude, or perhaps of moral obligation, that is all.

But I will let you know after this novel is out.

Yours sincerely   D. H. Lawrence

I hope I shall be in London early in July. Then I shall call on you, if you are not away.

DHL

720. To Constance Garnett, 6 May 1914

Text: MS NYPL; Postmark, Tellaro 7. 5. 14; Unpublished.

Lerici, per Fiascherino, Golfo della Spezia, Italy
6 May 1914

Dear Mrs Garnett,

First of all the address of *Poetry* – is Harriet Monroe, Editor of *Poetry* – 543 Cass St, Chicago.[1] I believe she is a rather nice woman. Soon I shall send her some more things.

As for me, I had bottled myself up with all kinds of steams, and I had to let it off. Now I am quite decent again, and hoping I haven't hurt anybody.

I have nearly nearly finished the novel. When it is done I shall write to Mr Garnett again. I do want you to like that novel. I have worked at it hard and taken it seriously and put my best work into it, I think. Try and like it.

We had Herbert Trench here yesterday.[2] He is just moving to Florence. We are booked to stay with them in September. He is very nice. He says how splendid he thinks your translations. He wrote a letter about them to one of the big papers.

We are thinking of leaving here about June 14th – coming to London – staying three weeks to get married – a friend in Hampstead has invited

[1] Harriet Monroe (1860–1936), American poet and editor, founded *Poetry: A Magazine of Verse* (1912) and became a leading champion of the new poetry. She wrote several volumes of verse; *Poets and Their Art* (1926); and her autobiography, *A Poet's Life* (1938).

[2] Frederic Herbert Trench (1865–1923), an Irish-born poet and playwright. His volumes *Deirdre Wed and Other Poems* (1901) and *New Poems* (1907) established him as a poet. He was director of the Haymarket Theatre 1909–11. A student of Russian, he translated Merezhkovsky's *The Death of the Gods* (1901). He spent his retirement at Settignano near Florence.

us[1] – then Frieda will try to see the children. The Decree Absolute was pronounced the other day. Weekley is still raving, but slightly abated. I have hopes. Frieda and I get gradually better – Oh my God, what a time it's been! But it is nearly over, and I am getting quite decently normal – so is she.

It is wonderful here – such a sea of emerald and purple and blue. There are myriads of wild orchids – and wild gladioli, rose coloured – and trees of acacia like moonlight. The vines are in leaf and the figs quite big. The anemones we planted are gay in flower – and many roses.

We were at the Huntingdons yesterday to lunch. The Cugina[2] was asking after you very warmly, and saying she must write to you soon. She has not been well – she seems in that sizzing state of people who have lost their energy and cant rest. I think she and Huntingdon aren't friends just now – he is often at the Cochranes. The Woods are doing Florence and Rome, he much bored, but she a spark on the wheel.

Miss Low – Ivy Low – is staying with us a short time. We like her very much.[3]

The Dunlops know about the divorce, and take it very nicely. We get many visits from the Levanto Russians.[4]

The Cochranes are always inviting us – 'and do stay the night'. We go sometimes. They aren't nearly so bad as they seem. Even La Cugina has been rather ungenerous about them. Mrs Pearse is semper eadem[5] – she had an interesting Italian aristocrat at Easter.[6]

I hope you'll have us a little while at the Cearne – we'll promise to be good for a few days. I couldn't find any diseased anemones for Bunny – and the flowers aren't as remarkable as they ought to be.

It is supper – such a beautiful evening. The fireflies drift like sparks, wonderful, many, coming and going, under the vines. The orange tree is in full flower, and smells sweet all day long.

You didn't tell us about the Cearne garden – our roses are lovely.

Love from Frieda and me.   D. H. Lawrence

Many regards to Bunny.

721. To Henry Savage, 7 May 1914

Text: MS Martin; Postmark, Lerici 8. 5. 14; Unpublished.

Lerici, per Fiascherino, Golfo della Spezia, Italia.

7 maggio 1914

[1] Gordon Campbell.   [2] 'female cousin'.
[3] For an account of her stay with DHL and Frieda, see Nehls, i. 215–22.
[4] Maxim Gorky's 'adopted son' and Amfiteatrov; see Letter 712.
[5] 'always the same'.   [6] Perhaps the Baronessa di Rescis mentioned in Letter 718.

Dear Savage,

     Soon I suppose we shall see you again. We propose to leave here at the
end of this month, to come to England and be married. The decree absolute
was pronounced the other day. Then Frieda will try to see her children.
Perhaps when she is legally the wife of somebody else, Weekley will be able
to see her more objectively, not entirely as a monstrous iniquity against
himself, and he may let her see the children. We must try what we can do.

     Your mother is dead – at least that is over. It is no good talking. The dead
have to bury their dead.[1] But you must do something. Isn't literature almost
like a sickness with you? Why don't you chuck the thought of it away
altogether? *Why* do you want to impress Raynes Park? If you go away from
Raynes Park, then Raynes Park wouldn't exist any more.[2] Wouldn't you like
some sort of editorial work: or even publisher's reading? I think you ought
to remain among books, but rather as a soldier of literature than a writer.
Then the writing itself could come when it would. If I were you I would
throw myself into the host of books and try and help forward the stuff you
believe in. And that one does in England more by being in among all the
busy publishing and reviewing world of London, than in any other way.
Surely you could get some sort of job as a reader – and you could do
reviewing, and all the literary day-work. I believe you'd be happy. Why don't
you try. You ought to have to go into the Strand and Covent Garden
battlefield of books every day, and fight the long fight for the good stuff. Why
don't you? It seems to me that would be your best way of getting at
yourself: – by *fighting* all the other devils whom you think wrong about
books. Why don't you do that?

     There is scarcely time now for you to come out here. I have been rather
seedy this last fortnight – and I am finishing my novel. I want you to care
for that novel, when it does come. It is so different from *Sons and Lovers*,
that I believe folk won't want to accept it at all – and of course, it is what
they call improper. – I am finishing it this week. I expect it will be out in
September.[3] I want you to like it, and to stick up for it. I know it is good.
And I feel miserable sending it out into the world, because somehow I feel
as if it would be rejected – I don't mean by the publishers – you understand.

     We have got Ivy Low staying with us for a few days. She is rather a nice
girl.

     I am not quite sure where we shall stay when we are in London, but
probably in Hampstead. We shall be in London some three weeks – perhaps

---

[1] Matthew viii. 22 ['Let the dead bury...'].   [2] See Letter 647.
[3] The novel did not appear until September 1915, when it was finally published as *The Rainbow*.

a month. After that, I don't know. Perhaps we shall go into the country for a month – perhaps we shall go to Germany. We intend to return to Italy at the end of September. I never want to stay long in England – it feels so stifling.

I shall leave the middle pages for my wife. You know you always have my real sympathy – don't doubt me.

                                                  Yrs   D. H. Lawrence

[Frieda Weekley begins]
Dear Mr Savage,

I wish you could be here and see that you are alive yourself, after all – Death is not *so* terrible only the dying – I love the world so much, and I think I would love it all the more if somebody I loved were buried in it – It will also be nice to have a talk with you – L[awrence] is such a jawer but then it makes him happy but dont take him au grand sérieux always –

Good-bye and let the spring soak into your bones –

                                                              Frieda –

722. To Harriet Monroe, 8 May 1914

Text: MS UChi; Postmark, Tellaro 9. 5. 14; cited in Monroe 91.

                              Lerici, per Fiascherino, Golfo della Spezia, Italia
                                                          8 maggio 1914.

Dear Madam,

I send you a set of verses which perhaps you may like for *Poetry*.[1] You put me a fine big batch in the January issue, and when I got your cheque, I gasped, seeing it was in payment of mere verse: I felt my fortune was made in a stroke.

Please don't fight shy of these poems. A friend of mine who puts upon his visiting cards 'connoisseur de poésie'[2] said he couldn't make head or tail of the best things I send you here. I do hope it's not my fault. To me image on image and word on word holds good, for the *meaning*. But perhaps the meaning is in too tabloid a form.

Sometimes I get *Poetry* out here, and always enjoy it. I only wish one thing – that each poem had a page to itself.

                                          Tanti Saluti   D. H. Lawrence
Madame Harriet Monroe
Poetry – Chicago

---

[1] *Poetry*, v (December 1914), 102–6, printed the following: 'Grief' (the version in Letter 681), 'Memories', 'Weariness', 'Service of all the Dead', 'Don Juan' and 'Song'.
[2] Perhaps Herbert Trench.

723. To John Middleton Murry, 8 May 1914
Text: MS NYPL; cited in Murry, *New Adelphi* 266, 273.

Lerici, per Fiascherino, Golfo della Spezia, Italia
8 maggio 1914

Dear Murry,

I wrote to Katharine yesterday, but don't know if she'll get the letter, as the address is different.[1]

As a matter of fact, all you ought to do is to get well physically, and let everything else go. You say you are patient – now use your patience for letting your soul alone and making your body well. You make one as miserable as miserable. Do for God's sake lie down and leave everything to other people just now. Don't bother – things are all right, really. Let them work out themselves. Don't give up feeling that people *do* want to hear what you say: or rather, they dont *want* to hear, but they need to, poor things. Don't be so miserable. Have patience with yourself most of all. Don't be miserable. You've used too much of your strength, and now you're weak, and will have to depend on other people for a bit. But I am *sure* you are the best critic in England: I'm *sure* you can help terrifically to a new, cleaner outlook. But you can't do anything if you squander yourself in these miseries. Do consent to be poor and dependent – what does it matter?

The play – well, it's not bad. I don't set great store by it. I will send you a copy when Duckworth will give me some. I will write and ask him to send you a copy.[2] It isn't worth 3/6 of your money, at any rate.

Four days, and I shall have finished my novel, pray God. Don't get sick and leave me in the lurch over it. Can you understand how cruelly I feel the want of friends who will believe in me a bit. People think I'm a sort of queer fish that can write: that is all. And how I loathe it. There isn't a soul cares a damn for me, except Frieda – and it's rough to have all the burden put on her.

We are coming to London in June. Till the divorce was pronounced, and till Weekley wrote a little saner, we only allowed a mere possibility of England this summer. We thought of going to Germany from here. But now Frieda is set on England in June – we shall come in about a month's time. For what will happen then, we must pray heaven. – But I only decided to come two days ago.

I'm glad I shall see you again soon. We must try and be decent to each other all round. I wish you had come out here instead of going to Paris. Never mind. Do get better, and leave things.

Frieda sends many sympathies – We shall see you soon –

Yrs   D. H. Lawrence

---

[1] The letter has not been found.   [2] No such letter to Duckworth has survived.

724. To Aubrey and Lina Waterfield, [8 May 1914]
Text: MS Waterfield; Postmark, Lerici 8. 5. 14; Waterfield, *Castle in Italy*, pp. 142–3.
[Frieda Weekley begins]

Fiascherino, Lerici
[8 May 1914]

Dear Mrs and Mr Waterfield,

Every day we have thought of you, the anemones have come, first blue ones, but now they are just a joy of red and blue and cream with stripes – They are just lovely under the young vine leaves and the orange-blossom is out in myriads of blossoms and the scent! It seems too horrible to think, that *your* castle will go from you, I have connected it so with you and how you must feel it yourselves! It is too bad – The rich wretches would be bored to death as well, tell your man he is an ass[1] – But we hope to see you, do come – We can put you up, both, *very* humbly as you know – Do you know of any cottage that we could have for July August and September, it would be so good that air for L[awrence] and Margate is really too dreadful – If you know of anything *cheap* do let us know – I cannot imagine what impression *Sons and Lovers* made on you, did'nt you find it very brutal? We are cooking out of Mrs Waterfield's book[2] – I will leave this page for L. With very kind regards and auf Wiedersehen.

Frieda Lawrence

[Lawrence begins]
Dear Waterfield,

We were waiting till the anemones were really in full show, to write to you. They are just on the eve. They are very pretty indeed, and we didn't have to pay not a penny for them. They are pink and pale blue and purple and scarlet and white and black – very gay and fluttering in the early morning under the very green vine shoots. You have no idea what excitement it has been, going out to watch them every morning, and watering them every night. The ranunculi are in bud, the gladioli are long spears, and we are waiting.

We leave here either in the beginning or the middle of June. My wife wants to spend three months in England – but I don't know if we shall be there

[1] The owner of Aulla, Montagu Brown, had warned the Waterfields that he might have to ask them to leave. He planned to modernise the castle, furnish it more sumptuously and let it to rich tenants (*Castle in Italy*, p. 142).
[2] The book is *Home Life in Italy: Letters from the Appenines* by Lina Duff Gordon, with thirteen illustrations by Aubrey Waterfield (1908). Mrs Waterfield devotes a chapter to 'Italian Foods – Some Recipes'.

so long. I would rather be in Bavaria or the Black Forest than in England. We have an invitation to the Abruzzi for September – and to Florence for the first weeks of October. About the middle of October we return here. That is the idea. I wonder how long you are being in Aulla. The man is a fool, who wants to make it grand. Nobody but rather solitary people able to live and work by themselves would live there, and these don't want palaces. The world is full of fools.

Herbert Trench was here two days last week. How decent he is. He was speaking *very* warmly of you. It is he who has invited us to Florence. Sometimes we stay with the Cochranes – how rum they are! Mrs Huntingdon doesn't seem very well – Mrs Pearse about the same. – I wonder if you *will* come and stay here: we should love it, but it is so uncompromisingly crude. Many salutations to Mrs Waterfield – I hope we *may* meet.

                                                      – Ciau!   D. H. Lawrence

725. To Edward Garnett, 9 May 1914
Text: MS NYPL; Postmark, Tellaro 9. 5. 14; Huxley 193.
                    Lerici, per Fiascherino, Golfo della Spezia, Italia
                                                           9 maggio 1914

Dear Garnett,

Many thanks for your other letter with the cheque for £5. from Duckworth. Will this do as the receipt? I am surprised that the papers are going on at such length about the play.[1] I hope you will really like the novel. You will swear when you see the length. It's a magnum opus with a vengeance. I have got about three thousand more words to write – two more days, and then basta. Frieda wants the novel to be called *The Rainbow*. It doesn't look it at first sight, but I think it is a good title. I like it better than the Wedding Ring. Dunlop will have finished the typing by next Thursday. I hope you'll have the MS. by Monday week. I have been a bit seedy lately.

Don't you give me any copies of the play? I haven't had not one from England. Please send me four to here, and if you are not giving me any, make them out to my account. And will the clerk please send one copy to J. M. Murry Esq – 102 Edith Grove, Chelsea – and if six copies are due to

---

[1] An enthusiastic review of *The Widowing of Mrs Holroyd*, entitled 'A Fine Play', appeared in the *Times*, 24 April 1914: '...this play has the qualities of finished craftsmanship...the dialogue is packed with significance and suggestion...As to the form of the play as a single work of art, it is finely built and perfectly shaped. It rises to a great height of emotion, and sinks from it swiftly into a quiet and mournful close.' *TLS* reprinted the review *verbatim* on 30 April 1914.

me, then that they send the last copy to Aubrey Waterfield Esq, North-bourne Abbey, Eastry, Kent. – We shall come to England in June. Today a letter from Weekley – much milder. He will come round in the end. The divorce is a load off him, I suppose.

I shall write you a proper letter when the novel is done.

– Yours affectionately   D. H. Lawrence
Regards from Frieda.

726. To Edward Garnett, [16 May 1914]

Text: MS NYPL; Postmark, Spezia 16. 5. 14; Moore 276–8.

Lerici, per Fiascherino, Golfo della Spezia, Italia
Saturday

Dear Garnett,

The novel is finished, and I have gone through the sheets. I can't send it off, I am afraid, until Monday, because we are staying the week end in Spezia. I am rather proud of it now. I really think *The Rainbow* is a better title than the Wedding Ring, for the book as it is.

Yes, thanks, I got the £7 cheque from you, and the letter. I am sorry I forgot to mention it. I hope it was no nuisance to you – and I hope above all that it *was* as much as seven pounds which remained to me.[1] Kennerley sent me a £10 cheque, making up *Sons and Lovers* accounts. They refused to cash it in London so I had to return it to him. I haven't yet heard from him, but then he is always many weeks in replying, because he always posts by parcel mail. I also got the four English copies of the play. I wish you hadn't included Björkman's filthy little notice on me.[2] But I like the blue cover. I suppose, as you say, plays never sell. The notices were very good.

You will get the *Rainbow* – alias Wedding Ring – on Wednesday, I should say – and then tell me what you think of it. Here is a letter which Pinker sent me, offering me £300 for English volume rights. There is another definite letter, later, which I have lost, saying, 'will you accept a three hundred pound advance on account of royalties in England.' Another agent writes me the same thing. I do not know who it is that is willing to put down so much on me – but it is a pretty figure that my heart aches after. It is wearying to be always poor, when there is also Frieda. I suppose Duckworth can't afford big risks. – I wonder what you will think of the prospects for the *Rainbow* – sales, I mean. It's a hopeful title at any rate.

---

[1] See Letter 718.
[2] This statement should be contrasted with DHL's remarks in Letter 658.

We shall probably come home from Genova by ship. I wish Kennerley would return me his cheque – it is high time – because otherwise it will be a scramble to get home. Probably we shall leave Genoa on June 7th. and get to Southampton about 16th. – I am not sure. If the sea trip does not come off like that, probably Frieda will go to Baden-Baden on her way to London, and I shall get a tramp steamer. Then we should arrive somewhere the third week in June. We are going to stay in the Campbells' house – 9 Selwood Terrace, South Kensington. His wife is going to Ireland to have her second child born, and he will be alone. But he will not be in London all the time. Perhaps you would like to meet him.

I think we shall stay in London a month. – Many thanks for asking us to the Cearne. We should have felt frightfully hurt if we had not come. Then perhaps Frieda will go to her children, if the fates are kind – and perhaps I shall stay with Wilfrid Wilson Gibson and the Abercrombies for a while – I don't know. Perhaps I shall want to stay in London longer, to read in the British Museum, for my next novel. I don't know. But we shall leave England in August for Germany en route to Italy.

I have not begun to work again yet, only to think of a new novel which has been lying very small in my mind these three months.[1] I ought to do some Ligurian sketches – I have some lovely matter – but just yet I don't want to.

May is very flowery and abundant now. I wish Mrs Garnett saw the rose coloured gladioli and lovely monthly roses, all wild. Mrs Huntingdon is taking us over to the Island of Tino – the lighthouse island – for a farewell picnic. Mrs Pearse also is giving a dinner and a bust-up – also the Cochranes. We heard from Tony – rather heavy, but pretty much herself, I think.[2] Harold wrote us from Middlesboro.[3] *The English Review* publishes me a story next week.[4] We feel queer and loose at the roots, in prospect of leaving our Fiascherino – and now this long novel is done. I shall be glad to see you again – very.

D. H. Lawrence

727. To Edward Garnett, [17 May 1914]
Text: MS NYPL; PC; Postmark, Tellaro 18. 5. 14; Unpublished.

Fiascherino
Sunday

Dear Garnett,

I send you now the MS of the novel – by this post. Could you have sent for me a copy of *Sons and Lovers*, and a copy of *The Trespasser*, to

[1] The reference is obscure.   [2] Antonia Almgren.   [3] Harold Hobson.
[4] 'Vin Ordinaire', *English Review*, xvii (June 1914), 298–315.

T. D. Dunlop Esq – Consule Brittannico – Casa Alberto, Spezia – Italy. I
should be very much obliged.

Yrs   D. H. Lawrence

728. To Edward Marsh, 24 May 1914
Text: MS NYPL; Postmark, Tellaro 25 5 14; Huxley 193–5.

Lerici, per Fiascherino, Golfo della Spezia, Italia
24 maggio 1914

Dear Eddie,

It seems a long time since I wrote to you – things go on so monotonously
here. I have worked away at my novel, and finished it, and now I am getting
ready to depart from here: that is all.

The other day I got the second *New Numbers*.[1] I was rather disappointed,
because I expected Abercrombie's long poem to be great indeed.[2] I can't
write to Wilfrid because I think I have never seen him to worse advantage
than in this quarter.[3] And it is no good your telling me Lascelles' 'End of
the World' is great, because it isn't. There are some fine bits of rhetoric,
as there always are in Abercrombie. But oh, the spirit of the thing altogether
seems mean and rather vulgar. When I remember even H G Wells'
'Country of the Blind', with which this poem of Abercrombies had got
associated beforehand in my mind, then I see how beautiful is Wells'
conception, and how paltry this other.[4] Why, why, in God's name, is
Abercrombie messing about with Yokels and Cider and runaway wives? No,
but it is *bitterly* disappointing. He who loves *Paradise Lost*, must don the
red nose and the rough-spun cloak of Masefield and Wilfrid. And you
encourage it – it is too bad. Abercrombie, if he does anything, surely ought
to work upon rather noble and rather chill subjects. I hate and detest his
ridiculous imitation yokels and all the silly hash of his bucolics; I loathe his
rather nasty efforts at cruelty, like the wrapping frogs in paper and putting
them for cart wheels to crush;[5] I detest his irony with its clap-trap solution
of everything being that which it seemeth not; and I hate that way of making

[1] Published in April 1914.
[2] Abercrombie's verse play is entitled 'The End of the World'. (It was reprinted in his *Four Short Plays*, 1922.)
[3] W. W. Gibson's contributions to this issue of *New Numbers* were 'A Catch for Spring', 'The Tram', 'The Greeting', 'Hampstead Heath', 'The Ice' and 'The Gorse'.
[4] H. G. Wells published his story in *The Country of the Blind and Other Stories* (1911).
[5] DHL has in mind this passage from 'The End of the World':

> ...when I was young
> My mother would catch us frogs and set
> them down
> Lapt in a screw of paper, in the ruts,

what Meredith called cockney metaphors: – moons like a white cat and
meteors like a pike fish. And nearly all of this seems to me an Abercrombie
turning cheap and wicked. What is the matter with the man? – there's
something wrong with his soul. *Mary and the Bramble* and *Sale of St Thomas*
weren't like this.[1] They had a certain beauty of soul, a certain highness which
I loved: – though I didn't like the Indian horrors in the *St Thomas*. But
here everything is mean and rather sordid, and full of rancid hate. He talked
of *Sons and Lovers* being all odi et amo.[2] Well, I wish I could find the 'Amo'
in this poem of his. It is sheer Odi, and rather mean hatred at that. The
best feeling in the thing is a certain bitter gloating over the coming
destruction. What has happened to him? Something seems to be going bad
in his soul. Even in the poem before this, the one of the Shrivelled Zeus,
there was a gloating over nasty perishing which was objectionable.[3] But what
is the matter with him? The feelings in these late things are corrupt and
dirty. What has happened to the man? I wish to heaven he were writing the
best poems that ever were written, and there he turns out this.

I am coming soon to London. We leave here about June 14th I think.
My wife wants to go to her people in Baden Baden, I want to come straight

---

> And carts going by would quash 'em,
> and I'ld laugh,
> And yet be thinking, "Suppose it was
> myself
> Twisted stiff in huge paper, and wheels
> Big as the wall of a barn treading me flat!" (pp. 64–5)

[1] *Mary and the Bramble* (1910) and *The Sale of St Thomas* (1911). Marsh had included the
latter – Act I of a play Abercrombie later extended to six acts – in *Georgian Poetry 1911–1912*.

[1] A reference to Abercrombie's review of *Sons and Lovers* in *Manchester Guardian*, 2 July 1913,

[2] which begins: '"Odi et amo" should have been on the title-page of Mr. D. H. Lawrence's
Sons and Lovers'. (See Draper 67.)

[3] DHL has in mind the description of Zeus in Abercrombie's poem 'The Olympians' (in *New
Numbers* no. 1):

> 'She scurried to him; and a grim thing lay
> For her to see; no baby, but a man
> Unbelievably withered into age,
> The cinder of a man, parcht and blasted
> To smallness like a baby, puny and dried
> His body all drawn up into a fist;
> The pined legs, crooked as burnt candle-
> wicks,
> So taut with perisht sinews that their
> knees
> Thrusted the shrivelled belly; and his
> arms
> Hugg'd his chest with little graspless
> hands.' (pp. 39–40)

to England by sea – in a tramp steamer if I can. That idea pleases me. Italy is just beginning to get hot, and I am just ready to move.

We shall stay in London about a month, I think: to get married by the registrar. Perhaps Lascelles would like to write a long poem called the Poets Wedding, upon the subject. We shall stay with G H Campbell – an Irish barrister – a *very* nice man – do you know him? We shall see you, shall we not? I want to see Mrs Asquith also.

Oh, then I have a friend here – rather rich people who have a big house and a big garden on the hill behind Lerici. She – Mrs Cochrane – wants very much to be able to meet a certain Augustin Edwards, Envoy extraordinary – a man at the Legation who has something to do with Chili.[1] Do you know how she could get an introduction? She is very nice, and paints beautifully in water-color. The Cochranes – he is rather impossible – will be at the Alexandra Hôtel, Hyde Park Corner, from June 2nd till the tenth. If you could advise me what to tell Mrs Cochrane, or even if you could advise her yourself, I should be very grateful. She wants to do something about some land in Chili. I am afraid this is trespassing on you rather – but it is only a little thing, isn't it?

I look forward to seeing you again. Write me a line here within the next fortnight, will you?

Tanti saluti di mia moglie[2] –

Yours   D. H. Lawrence

729. To Edward Garnett, [28 May 1914]
Text: MS NYPL; PC; Postmark, Spezia 28 MAG 14; Unpublished.

Aulla
[28 May 1914]

Dear Garnett,

We are staying here in the Castle with the Waterfields for a few days, so I don't know when I shall get your letter. The cheque for £10 from Duckworths came safely. Many thanks and many regards.

Yrs   D. H. Lawrence

730. To Henry Savage, 2 June 1914
Text: MS YU; Postmark, Lerici 4 6 14; Unpublished.

Lerici, per Fiascherino, Golfo della Spezia, Italia
2nd June 1914

Dear Savage,

We are leaving here on the 8th – next Monday – and are all in the upset

---

[1] Agustin Edwards (1878–1941) had been Vice-President of Chile, 1901–2; 1910–25 he was Envoy Extraordinary and Minister Plenipotentiary to the Court of St James; and he was later the Chilean Ambassador (1935–8).   [2] 'Kindest regards from my wife.'

of departure. Frieda is going to Baden-Baden to stay with her people for a while: I am still uncertain how I shall come to England. I want to come by ship, but it is not easy to get anything but the usual course – half dress for dinner business – which would bore me.

However, I expect both Frieda and I will be in London by the 23rd or so. We are staying in the house of a very nice man – Gordon Campbell – 9 Selwood Terrace – South Kensington. Perhaps we shall be in London a month or so – there is the marriage. I don't care a button about the impressiveness or solemnity of the business: it is after all only an impersonal matter, not a ceremony, but a mere legal contract. Perhaps we shall stay longer in England, in case Frieda wants to do something about her children. We must yet see what can be done. But in case we stay, we shall find a country lodging. Certainly we shall come back to Italy in September: perhaps we go to Germany in August.

I shall write to you when we get to London, and we shall come to Wimbledon, or you must come to see us. I like the idea of a few days of walking. And I like the idea of Rye, where you were last year. Campbell asks us to go to West Ireland: that I should love. But all is on the knees of the Gods.

I am very lazy at present. I don't do anything. The days are very long, and full of strong light. I shall be glad to come to England for a while, where the sky is more restful.

You say you couldn't go into harness – I think that would be the best thing you could do. I think the very best thing for you is that you should feel yourself in the control of some duty. Then your real self might have a chance to get on its legs. Your programme of paying for the publication of your poems, thereby gaining enough reputation to make your subsequent writings saleable, seems to me a poor way out. Even if you had a regular job, you could do as much. I don't believe you are a writer, in the first place. Look at the way you got Middleton's things through.[1] You ought to be sur le champ – fighting the Cause for the books and ideas and men whom you believe in, hand to hand, not making books yourself: – except, perhaps, out of the result of your fight. By God, if anything happened to me, that I couldn't write any more, wouldn't I come to London and fight hand to hand, and make way for myself and the ideas I champion. And a jollier life it would be than this of slowly putting words together in this remoteness.

But we'll have plenty of talks when we are in London. I *should* like to see a few decent men enlist themselves just as fighters, to bring down this old régime of dirty, dead ideas and make a living revolution. But you would

[1] See p. 29 n. 1.

rather write 'Carber's Cruise',[1] and I would rather write dull stories, instead of taking up a gun and a bayonet and ramming holes in the bundled enemy.

Au revoir, for a little time. I will let you know where I am.

Yrs   D. H. Lawrence

731. To Arthur McLeod, 2 June 1914
Text: MS UT; Postmark, Lerici 4 6 14; Huxley 195–7.

Lerici, per Fiascherino, Golfo della Spezia, Italia
2 Junio 1914

Dear Mac,

I never thanked you for the Meredith poems.[2] I was very glad indeed to get them – and a bit disappointed in them. They aren't what I want just now, I suppose.

I have been interested in the futurists.[3] I got a book of their poetry – a very fat book too[4] – and . book of pictures[5] – and I read Marinetti's and Paolo Buzzi's manifestations and essays – and Sofficis essays on cubism and futurism. It interests me very much. I like it because it is the applying to emotions of the purging of the old forms and sentimentalities. I like it for its saying – enough of this sickly cant, let us be honest and stick by what is in us. Only when folk say, 'let us be honest and stick by what is in us' – they always mean, stick by those things that have been thought horrid, and by those alone. They want to deny every scrap of tradition and experience, which is silly. They are very young, infantile, college-student and medical-student at his most blatant. But I like them. Only I don't believe in them. I agree with

---

[1] See p. 73 n. 1.

[2] This volume has not been certainly identified. McLeod might have sent a copy of *Selected Poems* published by Constable in April 1914 at a shilling.

[3] The Futurists were so named because they repudiated the past and glorified youth and the future. In the arts their ideas led directly to dadaism, cubism, and surrealism; in politics they anticipated Fascism. Filippo Tommaso Marinetti (1876–1944) was an Italian dramatist, novelist, poet and critic, who launched the Futurist movement by publishing his celebrated 'Manifeste du futurisme' in *Figaro* (Paris, 20 February 1909). Paolo Buzzi (1874–1956) was an Italian free-wordist poet. Born in Milan, he was influenced by Gabriele D'Annunzio (1863–1938) and joined the Futurists in 1909. His volumes of poetry *Aeroplani* (1909) and *Versi liberi* (1913) are written in the Futurist style. Ardengo Soffici (1879–1967) was an Italian painter who in 1913 helped to found the periodical *Lacerba*, which became the principal art publication of the Futurists. In 1915 Soffici broke with the Futurists and adopted a more conservative style.

[4] With the exception of some translations of the Futurists into English by Harold Monro, which appeared in *Poetry and Drama*, i (September 1913), 301–4, the work of the Futurists was not available in English. As DHL's next letter makes clear, he read the Futurists in Italian. The 'fat book' was *I Poeti Futuristi, con un proclamo di F. T. Marinetti e uno studio sul verso libro di Paolo Buzzi* (Milano, Edizione Futuristi di 'Poesia', 1912), 428 pp. It consists mainly of Italian poetry, essays by Marinetti and Buzzi (i.e. 'manifestations and essays') and some poetry in French.

[5] Ardengo Soffici's *Cubismo e futurismo* (Firenze, Libreria della Voce, 1914).

them about the weary sickness of pedantry and tradition and inertness, but I don't agree with them as to the cure and the escape. They will progress down the purely male or intellectual or scientific line. They will even use their intuition for intellectual and scientific purpose. The one thing about their art is that it *isn't* art, but ultra scientific attempts to make diagrams of certain physic or mental states. It is ultra-ultra intellectual, going beyond Maeterlinck and the Symbolistes, who are intellectual.[1] There isn't one trace of naïveté in the works – though there's plenty of naïveté in the authors. It's the most self conscious, intentional, pseudo scientific stuff on the face of the earth. Marinetti begins 'Italy is like a great Dreadnought surrounded by her torpedo boats'.[2] That is it exactly – a great mechanism. Italy has got to go through the most mechanical and dead stage of all – everything is appraised according to its mechanic value – everything is subject to the laws of physics. This is the revolt against beastly sentiment and slavish adherence to[3] tradition and the dead mind. For that I love it. I love them when they say to the child 'all right, if you want to drag nests and torment kittens, do it, lustily'. But I reserve the right to answer 'all right, try it on. But if I catch you at it you get a hiding.'

I think the only re-sourcing of art, re-vivifying it, is to make it more the joint work of man and woman. I think *the* one thing to do, is for men to have courage to draw nearer to women, expose themselves to them, and be altered by them: and for women to accept and admit men. That is the only way for art and civilisation to get a new life, a new start – by bringing themselves together, men and women – revealing themselves each to the other, gaining great blind knowledge and suffering and joy, which it will take a big further lapse of civilisation to exploit and work out. Because the source of all life and knowledge is in man and woman, and the source of all living is in the interchange and the meeting and mingling of these two: man-life and woman-life, man knowledge and woman-knowledge, man-being and woman-being.

Which is a sermon on a stool. We are leaving here on the 8th – next Monday. Frieda goes to Baden Baden for about 10 days. I am coming to England by ship. We are staying with Gordon H Campbell in 9 Selwood Terrace, Sth Kensington. I shall write to you as soon as we arrive. I shall be 8 or 9 or 10 days at sea, I think.

---

[1] Maurice Maeterlinck (1862–1949), Belgian dramatist, philosopher and essayist; winner of the Nobel Prize for literature (1911). His dramas were closely associated with the Symbolist movement in France. (Cf. *Letters*, i. 237 n. 1.)

[2] From the 'Manifesto tecnico della letteratúra futurista', issued in Milan, 11 May 1912, and printed in *I Poeti Futuristi* (p. 12), which begins: 'L'Italia ha oggi per noi la forma e la potenza di una bella dreadnought con la sua squadriglia d'isole torpediniere'.

[3] MS reads 'to to'.

We are all upset, moving. – I want to write an essay about Futurism, when I have the inspiration and wit thereunto.[1]

Many regards from us – and auf wiedersehen.

D. H. Lawrence

732. To Edward Garnett, 5 June 1914
Text: MS NYPL; Postmark, Tellaro 6. 6. 14; Huxley 197–9.

Lerici, per Fiascherino, Golfo della Spezia, Italia
5 junio 1914

Dear Garnett,

First let me remember to thank you for letting the two books be sent to the Consul in Spezia.[2]

About Pinker, I will do as you say, and tell him that the matter of the novel is not settled, and I will call on him in some fifteen or twenty days.

I don't agree with you about the Wedding Ring. You will find that in a while you will like the book as a whole. I don't think the psychology is wrong: it is only that I have a different attitude to my characters, and that necessitates a different attitude in you, which you are not as yet prepared to give. As for its being my *cleverness* which would pull the thing through – that sounds odd to me, for I don't think I am so very clever, in that way. I think the book is a bit futuristic – quite unconsciously so. But when I read Marinetti – 'the profound intuitions of life added one to the other, word by word, according to their illogical conception, will give us the general lines of an intuitive physiology of matter'[3] I see something of what I am after. I translate him clumsily, and his Italian is obfuscated – and I don't care about physiology of matter – but somehow – that which is physic – non-human, in humanity, is more interesting to me than the old-fashioned human element – which causes one to conceive a character in a certain moral scheme and make him consistent. The certain moral scheme is what I object to. In Turguenev, and in Tolstoi, and in Dostoievski, the moral scheme into which all the characters fit – and it is nearly the same scheme – is, whatever the

---

[1] Apart from the extended discussion of Futurism in the next letter, no such essay appears to have been written.   [2] See Letter 727.

[3] DHL translates a passage from Marinetti's 'Manifesto tecnico' (*I Poeti Futuristi*, p. 20): 'Le intuizioni profonde della vita congiunte l'una all'altra, parola per parola, secondo il loro nascere illogico, ci daranno le linee generali di una FISICOLOGIA INTUITIVA DELLA MATERIA.' DHL's reading of Marinetti's 'FISICOLOGIA' as 'physiology' is probably accurate, since the original appears to be a printer's error for the word 'fisiologia', or 'physiology'. Unfortunately, most reprintings of Marinetti's text in Italian use the word 'psicologia', thus prompting the inaccurate English translation 'psychology'. Despite the apparently paradoxical notion, it would have been quite appropriate for a Futurist writer to speak of 'an intuitive physiology of matter', an idea which obviously appealed to DHL.

extraordinariness of the characters themselves, dull, old, dead.[1] When Marinetti writes: 'it is the solidity of a blade of steel that is interesting by itself, that is, the incomprehending and inhuman alliance of its molecules in resistance to, let us say, a bullet. The heat of a piece of wood or iron is in fact more passionate, for us, than the laughter or tears of a woman '[2] – then I know what he means. He is stupid, as[3] an artist, for contrasting the heat of the iron and the laugh of the woman. Because what is interesting in the laugh of the woman is the same as the binding of the molecules of steel or their action in heat: it is the inhuman will, call it physiology, or like Marinetti – physiology of matter, that fascinates me. I don't care so much about what the woman *feels* – in the ordinary usage of the word. That presumes an *ego* to feel with. I only care about what the woman *is* – what she *is* – inhumanly, physiologically, materially – according to the use of the word: but for me, what she *is* as a phenomenon (or as representing some greater, inhuman will), instead of what she feels according to the human conception. That is where the futurists are stupid. Instead of looking for the new human phenomenon, they will only look for the phenomena of the science of physics to be found in human being. They are crassly stupid. But if anyone would give them eyes, they would pull the right apples off the tree, for their stomachs are true in appetite. You mustn't look in my novel for the old stable ego of the character. There is another ego, according to whose action the individual is unrecognisable, and passes through, as it were, allotropic states which it needs a deeper sense than any we've been used to exercise, to discover are states of the same single radically-unchanged element. (Like as diamond and coal are the same pure single element of carbon. The ordinary novel would trace the history of the diamond – but I say 'diamond, what! This is carbon.' And my diamond might be coal or soot, and my theme is carbon.)

You must not say my novel is shaky – It is not perfect, because I am not expert in what I want to do. But it is the real thing, say what you like. And

[1] For a detailed analysis of DHL's attitude to the works of Tolstoy and Dostoievsky see George J. Zytaruk, *D. H. Lawrence's Response to Russian Literature* (The Hague, 1971).

[2] From Marinetti's 'Manifesto tecnico' (p. 18): 'E la solidità di una lastra d'acciaio, che c'interessa per sè stessa, cioè l'alleanza incomprensibile e inumana delle sue molecole o dei suoi elettroni, che si oppongono, per esempio, alla penetrazione di un obice. Il calore di un pezzo di ferro o di legno è ormai più appassionante, per noi, del sorriso o delle lagrime di una donna'. The translation given in *Marinetti: Selected Writings*, ed. R. W. Flint, New York, 1972, p. 87, reads: 'The solidity of a strip of steel interests us for itself; that is, the incomprehensible and nonhuman alliance of its molecules or its electrons that oppose, for instance, the penetration of a howitzer. The warmth of a piece of iron or wood is in our opinion more impassioned than the smile or tears of a woman.'

[3] as] being

I shall get my reception, if not now, then before long. Again I say, don't look for the development of the novel to follow the lines of certain characters: the characters fall into the form of some other rhythmic form, like when one draws a fiddle-bow across a fine tray delicately sanded, the sand[1] takes lines unknown.[2]

I hope this won't bore you. We leave here on Monday, the 8th. Frieda will stay in Baden Baden some 10–14 days. I am not going by sea, because of the filthy weather. I am walking across Switzerland into France with Lewis, one of the skilled engineers of Vickers Maxim works here.[3] I shall let you know my whereabouts.

Don't get chilly and disagreeable to me.

Au revoir   D. H. Lawrence

Please keep this letter, because I want to write on futurism and it will help me. – I will come and see Duckworth. Give *Bunny* my novel – I want *him* to understand it.

I shall be *awfully* glad to see Bunny again – and Mrs Garnett and you.

733. To Ada Clarke, [10 June 1914]
Text: MS Clarke; PC v. Lago dei morti; Postmark, Aosta 10. 6. 14; Ada Lawrence and G. Stuart Gelder, *Young Lorenzo* (Florence, [1931]), p. 113.

[Aosta]
[10 June 1914]

Tonight I sleep in Aosta – tomorrow we are going on foot over the St. Bernard pass. I shall be a week or so in Switzerland, then to London. Write me a p.c to *Interlaken*, Switzerland – poste restante, and tell me any news there is. – It is very beautiful in the Alps, but cold, after Italy. In Turin yesterday there was a great strike commotion whilst we were there – [4]

Love   D. H. Lawrence

---

[1] sand] tray
[2] For an elucidation of this image and an explanation of the theory of physics behind it, see C. P. Ravilious, 'Lawrence's "Chladni Figures"', *Notes and Queries*, xx (September 1973), 331–2.
[3] A. P. Lewis: in August 1914, he may have accompanied DHL on a memorable walk in Westmorland. Lewis joined the army later, and when DHL started the *Signature* in 1915 his address was 19 The Drive, Golders Green, London. See Letter 1014. (The records of Messrs Vickers Ltd provide no further information about Lewis.)
[4] The strike witnessed by DHL preceded the Italian General Strike called on 10 June 1914. On 11 June the *Times* reported the disturbances as follows: '...in Turin, where the rioting on Tuesday [9 June] led to three deaths and to the wounding of some forty persons,... the city yesterday looked, as our Correspondent tells us, like a "city of the dead".'

734. To Ada Clarke, [11 June 1914]

Text: MS Clarke; PC v. Hospice du Grand St. Bernard – Départ d'une Caravane; Postmark, Grand St Bernard 12. VI. 14; Lawrence and Gelder, *Young Lorenzo*, p. 114.

[Grand St Bernard]

[11 June 1914]

Today we have struggled up here from Aosta – the last part climbing up the face of the snow, which is more than a yard deep here. You have no idea how beautiful it is. Tonight I sleep in the monastery – such a lovely little panelled room – and tomorrow on again. I love it dearly.

Love to you and Eddie – [1]   D. H. Lawrence

735. To Edward Marsh, [13 June 1914]

Text: MS NYPL; PC v. Zermatt-Riffelsee und Matterhorn (Cervin); Postmark, Visp 13 VI. 14; Unpublished.

[13 June 1914]

Dear Eddie,

We have just walked over the Great St Bernard down here – a metre deep of snow on the pass – very fine. We shall be in London on the 20th, staying with Gordon Campbell. I look forward very much to seeing you –

Herzliche Grüsse   D. H. Lawrence

736. To David Garnett, [13 June 1914]

Text: MS NYPL; PC v. Zermatt–Riffelsee und Matterhorn (Cervin); Postmark, Visp 13 VI. 14; Unpublished.

[13 June 1914]

I have just walked from Aosta over the Gd St Bernard to Martigny. It was splendid – one day you just do it. There is a metre deep of snow on the pass. We slept the night in the Hospice – very fine – the monks so hospitable and courteous. I am walking now down to Interlaken. We shall be in London by the 20th. I am looking forward very much to seeing you.

Viele grüsse   D. H. Lawrence

737. To Edward Garnett, [18 June 1914]

Text: MS NYPL; Postmark, Heidelberg 18 6 14; Unpublished.

Darmstädter Hof, Heidelberg
Thursday

Dear Garnett,

I thought to be in London by Saturday, but Frieda is not quite well, so she will stay on in Baden until Monday or Tuesday – We shall be in England

---

[1] Ada's husband.

next Wednesday – 23rd – or Thursday. Did you write to me? – about the play? – if so the letter will have gone to Baden Baden.

We have wandered over Switzerland – mid snow and ice, like Excelsior[1] – finishing up with Exhibitions in Bern[2] – and now I am with Prof Weber in Heidelberg hearing the latest things in German philosophy and political economy.[3] I am like a little half fledged bird opening my beak *Very* wide to gulp down the fat phrases. But it is all very interesting.

I shall be very glad to see you again. Here in Heidelberg I feel a foreigner. It is not Italy. I cant remember your other London address.[4] My regards – Very warmly to Mrs Garnett and Bunny.

                                          Yrs   D. H. Lawrence

738. To Edward Marsh, [25 June 1914]
Text: MS NYPL; Unpublished.

                              9, Selwood Terrace, South Kensington, S.W.
                                                          Thursday[5]
Dear Eddie,

We got here yesterday – I've had no address for some three weeks – walking. We shall be awfully glad to come to lunch at the Moulin D'Or on Saturday – I like seeing you again. We want to meet Rupert Brooke.

                                          Yours   D. H. Lawrence

739. To Arthur McLeod, 26 June 1914
Text: MS UT; Postmark, Chelsea S.W. 27 Jun 14; Unpublished.

                              9, Selwood Terrace, South Kensington, S.W.
                                                          26 June 1914
Dear Macl.

So we have arrived at last in England. I am rushing round doing business. I am trying to get my new novel away from Duckworth for Methuen, who

[1] Longfellow, 'Excelsior', l. 3.
[2] Other than the small displays organised by booksellers in Bern, the only substantial exhibition was of the Kunstmuseum's permanent collection of modern pictures (housed in a special gallery of the Museum). DHL may well have seen this. (Unfortunately the Museum kept no record of changes made to its display; consequently which pictures were on show in June 1914 is not known.)
[3] Dr Alfred Weber (1868–1958), Professor of Sociology and Political Science at the University of Heidelberg. Frieda's sister, Else, was generally known to be his mistress. On their relationship see Martin Green, *The Richthofen Sisters* (New York, 1974), pp. 225–36.
[4] It was 14 Pond Place, Fulham Road, London S.W. (This letter was sent to Garnett c/o Duckworth.)
[5] Dated with reference to the following entry in Marsh's journal: 'Saturday June 27th [1914]. Lunched at the Moulin d'Or with D. H. and Mrs Lawrence and Rupert [Brooke], all to Allied Artists at Holland Park' (Nehls, i. 227). (Artists from more than twenty countries exhibited at the Allied Artists Association 'London Salon' in Holland Park Hall. *Times*, 14 March 1914.)

offers me £300 down.[1] Duckworth is half afraid to risk so much money, and is rather keen on a book of short stories. I am going to give him one. I wonder if you could help me. I haven't got a single solitary copy of any of my published stories. Have you any proofs or anything you could lend me – or the *English Reviews* or *Smart Sets*? I really don't know what stories I've published and what I haven't – God help me. If you would give me the pages out of the *English Reviews*, I will give you the book of stories instead: or if you don't like tearing up the magazines, just lend them to me and I'll have the stories typed out. I am so busy and breathless. When are you in town? Will you come and see us here, or would you rather come to the Cearne. We shall be down there next week-end with my sister, I think. This is the little house of a barrister, G. H. Campbell. His wife is away in Ireland for the summer,[2] he is alone, and he invites us to stay in his house. He is never at home in the day-time, and he's a very nice fellow, so you'll call any time, day or evening, that you're in town, won't you? You might telephone, or send us a post card. – We got here the day before yesterday. – I think a man – Neilson[3] of the Vaudeville Theatre – is going to do my play. I want to see you, do come – Frieda sends manifold regards.

D. H. Lawrence

Don't tear pages out of your magazines – it is a vandalistic idea.

DHL

740. To Catherine Jackson, [29 June 1914]
Text: MS YU; cited in Carswell, *Adelphi* 164.

9, Selwood Terrace, South Kensington, S.W.
Monday[4]

Dear Mrs Jackson,[5]

I must tell you I am in the middle of reading your novel.[6] You have very

---

For *The Rainbow*, which Methuen eventually published.
Beatrice Campbell, later Lady Beatrice Glenavy, recalled: 'In the early summer of 1914 I again went to Dublin... into a nursing-home for the birth of my baby girl "Biddy"' (Beatrice Lady Glenavy, *Today We Will Only Gossip*, 1964, p. 77).
Probably Harold V. Neilson (1874–1956), actor and manager. He began his acting career with F. R. Benson's company at the Theatre Royal, Manchester. In 1902 he went into management and toured with a variety of plays including some by Shaw, Ibsen and Maeterlinck.
Dated with reference to DHL's arrival in London on Wednesday, 24 June 1914 and Catherine Carswell's remark that 'it was still June when I received his first letter' (Carswell 17).
Catherine Roxburgh MacFarlane (1879–1946) m. (1) 1903, Herbert P. M. Jackson (marriage annulled, 1908) (2) 1915, Donald Carswell. A Scottish writer, she worked as reviewer and dramatic critic for the *Glasgow Herald* (1907–11). Author of *Open the Door!* (1920), *The Camomile* (1922), *The Life of Robert Burns* (1930), and *The Savage Pilgrimage: A Narrative of D. H. Lawrence* (1932). She and DHL had met as a result of her friend Ivy Low's having written to the young man who, in their view, was producing work of greater importance than that of any other writer (Carswell 4–5).
Published under the title *Open the Door!*

often a simply *beastly* style, indirect and roundabout and stiff-kneed and stupid. And your stuff is abominably muddled – you'll simply have to write it all again. But it is fascinatingly interesting. Nearly all of it is *marvellously* good. It is only so incoherent. But you can easily pull it together. It *must* be a long novel – it is of the quality of a long novel. My stars, just you work at it, and you'll have a piece of work you never need feel ashamed of. All you need is to get the whole thing under your control. You see it takes one so long to know what one is really about. Your Juley is a fascinating character – not quite understood sufficiently – not quite. Ruth is good. Leave the other children sketchy.

When I've finished it – tomorrow or Wednesday – we must have a great discussion about it. My good heart, there's some honest work here, real.

I must go to Croydon tomorrow afternoon. But I'll ring you up when I've finished.

Yours   D. H. Lawrence

You must be willing to put much real work, hard work into this, and you'll have a genuine creative piece of work. It's like Jane Austen at a deeper level.

741. To Arthur McLeod, [29 June 1914]
Text: MS UT; Postmark, South Kensington 29 JUN 14; Unpublished.

9, Selwood Terrace, South Kensington, S.W.
Monday

My dear Mac,

We shall be awfully glad to see you on Wednesday afternoon – Come to lunch if you have time – it will be a very unsubstantial meal. I'm too exhausted to write any more.

Yrs   D. H. Lawrence

Bring me those two stories, will you.[1]

742. To Catherine Jackson, [30 June 1914]
Text: MS YU; cited in Carswell, *Adelphi* 165.

9, Selwood Terrace, South Kensington, S.W.
Tuesday[2]

Dear Mrs Jackson,

I've just finished your novel. I think it's going to be something *amazingly* good. But it means work, I can tell you. – I've put thousands of notes and comments and opinions in the margin, out of my troubled soul.[3] I hope they'll help. I wonder if you could come to lunch tomorrow. Come about

---

[1] Unidentified.

[2] Dated with reference to DHL's promise in Letter 740 to finish reading the novel 'tomorrow or Wednesday'.

[3] The MS of the novel with DHL's comments has not survived.

mid-day, and we'll have a real go at this MS. I hope you can come. Ring us up. If you are not free in the morning, we have the afternoon till four oclock. I want to settle it with you before we go away.

Yours   D. H. Lawrence

743. To Edward Garnett, 1 July 1914

Text: MS NYPL; Huxley 199–200.

9, Selwood Terrace, South Kensington, S.W.
1 July 1914

Dear Garnett,

I am awfully sorry I was precipitate at the last moment. I called to see you before I went to Pinker. Then you weren't in. And I hung a few moments on the pavement outside, saying 'Shall I go to Pinker?' And there was very little time, because we had to lunch with Lady St. Helier.[1] And Frieda was so disappointed she couldn't have any money. And most of all, I remembered Mr Duckworth on Saturday.

'Well?' he said when I came in.

'Pinker offers me the £300 from Methuen', I said.

'He does?'

'Yes.'

'Then', he said, as if nettled, 'I'm afraid you'll have to accept it.'

Which rather made me shut my teeth, because the tone was peremptory. So I went to Pinker, and signed his agreement, and took his cheque, and opened an[2] acc. with the London County and Westminster Bank – et me voilà.[3]

I am sorry. Shall I see you at the Cearne –

Yrs   D. H. Lawrence

744. To Mitchell Kennerley, 1 July 1914

Text: MS NYPL; Unpublished.

9, Selwood Terrace, South Kensington, S.W.
1 July 1914

Dear Mr Kennerley,

I suppose you will hear directly from Mr Pinker. I had to put myself into an agent's hands – living in Italy, I get into such a muddle with my affairs. Methuen will publish my next novel. Mr Duckworth did not see his way

---

[1] See Letter 705.   [2] MS reads 'and'.

[3] National Westminster Bank Ltd confirms that DHL opened an account at the Aldwych branch of the London County and Westminster Bank on 30 June 1914; Pinker, now his agent, who also had an account at the branch, introduced him; and DHL appears to have maintained the account until his death.

to make the same offer Methuen made, so he will accept a book of short stories in place of the novel.

I have heard nothing at all from you for some months now – I don't know why. Did you get the MS. of the novel I sent you from Fiascherino? – I have received no acknowledgment.[1] And did you get the cheque for £10, which the bankers refused to cash for me? I sent it back to you many weeks ago, but have heard nothing of it.[2] It was the cheque for the *Sons and Lovers* account. I wish you would write to me and tell me what you want to do about the novel – The Wedding Ring, otherwise the *Rainbow* – . And tell me also what you think of the book.

Yours Sincerely   D. H. Lawrence

745. To Douglas Clayton, 2 July 1914
Text: MS NCL; Unpublished.

9, Selwood Terrace, South Kensington, S.W.
2 July 1914

Dear Clayton,

I am making a book of short stories, and I find some of the MS. missing. I wonder if you have got, and if you could let me have at once, the MS. of 'Love Among the Haystacks', and 'The Old Adam and the New Eve', or a story with a title something like that,[3] also of 'The White Stocking', and if you could send me *typed* copies of 'Once' and 'A Sick Collier'.[4] The first MS I want to go over before it is typed. I hope you have it by you. I don't think I owe you anything, do I? If so, send me a bill. And let me have these things as soon as you can: I must get this stuff ready for a volume.

My wife and I are at this address for about three weeks. I hope we shall see Mrs Clayton whilst we are in England. On Saturday we go down to the Cearne for the week-end. I am looking forward very much to that. London nearly does for me just now.

Many regards to Mrs Clayton – tell her to write us a line.

Yours   D. H. Lawrence

[1] This very important MS has not been found and there is no record in the existing letters that it was ever returned to DHL by Kennerley. It included both the *Rainbow* section and the *Women in Love* section of the novel, since DHL did not decide to split the novel into two parts until 7 January 1915 (see Letter 836). In the event B. W. Huebsch, not Kennerley, published the American edition of *The Rainbow*.   [2] See Letter 726.
[3] DHL is apparently trying to recall the title of the story 'New Eve and Old Adam' (see Letter 603).
[4] 'The White Stocking' and 'A Sick Collier' were included in DHL's next volume, *The Prussian Officer and Other Stories*. 'Love Among the Haystacks' was the title-story of a collection published posthumously in 1930; 'Once' first appeared in the same volume.

746. To Thomas Dunlop, 7 July 1914
Text: MS Dunlop; Huxley 202–4.

The Cearne, Nr *Edenbridge*, Kent
7 July 1914

Dear Dunlop,

I was glad to get your still sad letter, and sorry you are so down yet. I can't help thinking that you wouldn't be quite so down if you and Mrs Dunlop didn't let yourselves be separated rather by this trouble.[1] Why do you do that? I think the trouble ought to draw you together, and you seem to let it put you apart. Of course I may be wrong. But it seems a shame that her one cry, when she is in distress, should be for her mother. You ought to be the mother and father to her. Perhaps if you go away to your unhealthy post, it may be good for you. But perhaps you may be separating your inner life from hers – I don't mean anything actual and external – but you may be taking yourself inwardly apart from her, and leaving her inwardly separate from you: which is no true marriage, and is a form of failure. I am awfully sorry; because I think that no amount of outward trouble and stress of circumstance could really touch you both, if you were together. But if you are not together, of course the strain becomes too great, and you want to be alone, and she wants her mother. And it seems to me an awful pity if, after you have tried, you have to fail and go separate ways. I am not speaking of vulgar outward separation: I know you would always be a good reliable husband: but there is more than that: there is the real sharing of one life. I can't help thinking your love for Mrs Dunlop hasn't quite been vital enough to give you yourself peace. One must learn to love, and go through a good deal of suffering to get to it, like any knight of the Grail, and the journey is always *towards* the other soul, not away from it. Do you think love is an accomplished thing, the day it is recognised. It isn't. To love, you have to learn to understand the other, more than she understands herself, and to submit to her understanding of you. It is damnably difficult and painful, but it is the only thing which endures. You mustn't think that your desire or your fundamental need is to make a good career, or to fill your life with activity, or even to provide for your family materially. It isn't. Your most vital necessity in this life is that you shall love your wife completely and implicitly and in entire nakedness of body and spirit. Then you will have peace and inner security, no matter how many things go wrong. And this peace and security will leave you free to act and to produce your own work, a real independent workman.

---

[1] The 'trouble' was most likely Margaret ('Madge') Dunlop's pregnancy. Her second son, John, was born on 6 January 1915.

You asked me once what my message was. I haven't got any general message, because I believe a general message is a general means of side-tracking ones own personal difficulties: like Christ's – thou shalt love thy neighbour as thyself[1] – has given room for all the modern filthy system of society. But this that I tell you is my message as far as I've got any.

Please don't mind what I say – you know I don't really want to be impertinent or interfering.

Mrs Huntingdon is coming over to England this month. Probably she would bring Mrs Dunlop. But perhaps Noémi would be better.[2] I am sorry Paddy is still so seedy.[3] He is a strange boy. I think he will need a lot of love. He has a curious heavy consciousness, a curious awareness of what people feel for him. I think he will need a lot of understanding and a lot of loving. He may, I think, have quite an unusual form of intelligence. When you said he might be a musician, it struck me. He has got that curious difference from other people, which may mean he is going to have a distinct creative personality. But he will suffer a great deal, and he will want a lot of love to make up for it.

I think our marriage comes off at Kensington registrar's office on Saturday. I will try to remember to send you the *Times* you asked for. When I get paid for my novel, I want to send you a small cheque for doing the novel. You will not mind if it is not very much that I send you.

We are very tired of London already, and very glad to be down here in the country. Probably we are going to stay in Derbyshire – and then for August going to the west of Ireland. But I shall write and tell you. Don't be miserable – I have you and Mrs Dunlop rather on my conscience just now – I feel as if you were taking things badly. But dont do that –

auf wiedersehen   D. H. Lawrence

Remember me to Mrs Dunlop.

747. To Henry Savage, [8 July 1914]

Text: MS UCLA; Postmark, South Kensington 8 JUL 14; Moore 286.

9, Selwood Terrace, South Kensington, S.W.

Wednesday

Dear Savage,

We have been rather lax. We have been in town a week, but *so* much to do, *such* a rush – I wanted to get some of the turmoil over. We stayed a long while in Germany en route.

---

[1] Mark xii. 31.

[2] The Dunlop family's nurse-maid who travelled the world with them.

[3] Dunlop's eldest son, Maurice Hamilton ('Paddy') Dunlop (1912–32).

Come up here and see us – if you can come tomorrow, come early after lunch – We are out to tea and dinner. Friday we are pretty free. Come any time then. We are getting married on Sat. or Monday. Frieda doesn't want to stay any more in London. We want to see you – we were talking of you last night in the train –

au revoir   D. H. Lawrence

748. To J. B. Pinker, 8 July 1914
Text: TMSC NWU; cited in Carswell 19.

9, Selwood Terrace, South Kensington, S.W.
8 July 1914.

Dear Pinker,

The man in Nisbet's, Bertram Christian, has been asking me would I do a little book for him[1] – a sort of interpretative essay on Thomas Hardy, of about 15,000 words. It will be published at 1/- net. My payment is to be 1½d. per copy, £15 advance on royalties, half profits in America. It isn't very much, but then the work won't be very much. I think it is all right, don't you? When the agreement comes I will send it on to you, and we need not make any trouble over it.

Have you seen Methuen, and have you got the MS. of the novel,[2] and is everything all right?

Yours   D. H. Lawrence

749. To Arthur McLeod, [8 July 1914]
Text: MS UT; Postmark, London SW 9 JUL 14; Unpublished.

9 Selwood Terrace, S. Kensington, SW
Wednesday

Dear Mac,

I was awfully sorry not to get back last week. But Wyndham Lewis came in, and there was a heated and vivid discussion – you will understand.[3] Don't hold it against me, will you.

Bertram Christian (1870–1953) was a director of the publishing house, James Nisbet and Co. Ltd. He was the literary editor of the *Daily News* until 1913. (Obituary in *Times*, 5 November 1953.) Nisbet had launched a series called 'Writers of the Day'.
The Rainbow.
Percy Wyndham Lewis (1884–1957), novelist, essayist and painter. He had just published – in June 1914 – the first issue of the periodical which he, with Ezra Pound, founded and edited: *Blast: Review of the Great English Vortex.* It established him as a leader of the Vorticist movement. Among his later works were *Tarr* (1918), *Time and Western Man* (1927), *The Apes of God* (1930) and his autobiography, *Blasting and Bombardiering* (1937).

I have got your photographs of Switzerland for you. They will be good for school illustration. I think they are pretty.

I am going to do a little book of about 15000 words on Thomas Hardy. What do you think of that. Later on I shall ask you to lend me some Hardy books. And you're going to send me 'Vin Ordinaire'?

When I can lay hands on a square envelope, I shall send you your photos. But won't you come in again and see us? Come on Saturday afternoon – You are sure to be free. Soon we are going to Derbyshire to my sister.[1]

auf wiedersehen   D. H. Lawrence

750. To Douglas Clayton, [8 July 1914]
Text: MS NCL; PC; Postmark, London S.W. 9 JUL 14; Unpublished.

Selwood Terrace
[8 July 1914][2]

Dear Clayton,

Many thanks for the MS.[3] sent to the Cearne. Will you let me have a typed copy of the 'Shadow in a Rose Garden'. I'm *awfully* sorry we missed the trains on Sat. and gave Mrs Clayton all the trouble for nothing.

regards   D. H. Lawrence

751. To Douglas Clayton, [9 July 1914]
Text: MS NCL; PC; Postmark, South Kensington 9 JUL 14; Unpublished.

9 Selwood Terrace
[9 July 1914]

Dear Clayton,

Send me the MS of the story, will you.[4] I may as well revise it before it is typed – it looks better.

Yrs   D. H. Lawrence

752. To Edward Marsh, [10 July 1914]
Text: MS NYPL; Unpublished.

9, Selwood Terrace, South Kensington, S.W.
Friday[5]

[1] Ada Clarke.
[2] The postal frank reads: '4 AM 9 JUL 14'. The card was therefore almost certainly written on 8 July.
[3] Probably 'Love Among the Haystacks'; see Letter 745.
[4] 'The Shadow in the Rose Garden'.
[5] Dated with reference to DHL's marriage on 13 July 1914.

Dear Eddie,

Will you address and post this letter to Sir James Barrie.[1] My wife is absolutely intent on seeing him – won't be put off at the sword's point.

We were with Lady Cynthia yesterday – very glad to see her look so well. Many regards from her to you.

Are Rupert Brooke and Jim Barnes still with you. We are disappointed not to have seen either of them again.

I wonder if you would be a witness at my marriage on Monday – some time between 10 and 5.0 – if you have time – at Kensington.[2]

Love from us   D. H. Lawrence

753. To Edward Marsh, [11 July 1914]
Text: MS NYPL; Unpublished.

9, Selwood Terrace, South Kensington, S.W.
Saturday

Dear Eddie,

Thanks for your letter. You will excuse my not putting a stamp on Barrie's letter – I hadn't got one.

We have fixed the wedding for 10.30 Monday morning. I am very sorry it is the wrong time for you. It is at the registrars office, Marloes Rd, off Kensington High Street. You must bless us from afar, that is all.

Love from us   D. H. Lawrence

754. To Arthur McLeod, [11 July 1914]
Text: MS UT; Unpublished.

9 Selwood Terrace, S. Kensington
Saturday

Dear Mac,

Here are your photographs. They aren't much – only pretty.

The wedding – or marriage, – is on Monday morning at 10.30. I wanted you to be a witness, but you will be in school. I am sorry.

Next week we are making awful struggles to see the children. It hangs over us like a cloud – can you understand – and paralyses us somehow. But I suppose it will pass away.

We must see you again before we go to Ireland – which wont be till the end of the month.[3]

Yours   D. H. Lawrence

The letter to Barrie has not come to light.
The two witnesses at DHL's wedding proved to be John Middleton Murry and Gordon Campbell.
The trip to Ireland did not materialise.

755. To Catherine Jackson, [12 July 1914]
Text: MS YU; PC; Postmark, Chelsea 13 JUL 14; Carswell, *Adelphi* 165.

9 Selwood Terrace
[12 July 1914]

I'm awfully sorry we couldn't come tonight. I poor devil am seedy with neuralgia in my left eye and my heart in my boots. Domani sono i nostri matrimonii – alle 10½. Povero me, mi sentio poco bene.[1] – Frieda says will you meet her on Tuesday morning – and will you ring us up –

Yrs   D. H. Lawrence

756. To Sallie Hopkin, 13 July 1914
Text: MS NCL; Huxley 205.

9, Selwood Terrace, South Kensington, S.W.
13 July 1914

Dear Mrs Hopkin,

Frieda and I were married this morning at the Kensington registrar's office. I thought it was a very decent and dignified performance. I don't feel a changed man, but I suppose I am one.

We are struggling this week to see the children. It is pretty difficult.

On Saturday I think we are going to Ripley for a few days. I don't think we shall come out to Eastwood – But you *must* come over to see us – you and Mr Hopkin and Enid. I *must* see you.

We have been so busy seeing people and doing things here in London. I am getting so tired of it. We are going to the West of Ireland for August. Write and tell us your news.

love – au revoir   D. H. Lawrence

757. To Edward Garnett, [14 July 1914]
Text: MS NYPL; Huxley 201–2.

9 Selwood Terrace, South Kensington
Tuesday[2]

Dear Garnett,

I send you herewith another batch of the short stories. There remains only one to send – one story. It is the German Soldier Story that came in last months *English Review*.[3] I find it wants writing over again, to pull it

---

[1] 'Tomorrow it is our wedding at 10.30. Poor me, I don't feel very well.'
[2] DHL finished revising 'Vin Ordinaire' by Friday 17 July 1914 (see Letter 759); therefore, the date here would be 14 July 1914.   [3] 'Vin Ordinaire'.

together. I have gone over the stories very carefully.[1] I wish you would go through the selection I have sent in, and see if there is any you would leave out, and any you would like putting in. I think all the stories have been already printed, except 'Daughters of the Vicar'.[2] I would like them arranging so.

		about
1.	'A Fragment of Stained Glass' –	6,000 words
2.	'Goose Fair'.	6,000
3.	'A Sick Collier'.	2,500
4.	'The Christening'.	3,300
5.	'Odor of Chrysanthemums'	8,000
6.	'Daughters of the Vicar'	18,980
7.	'Second Best'.	5,000
8.	'The Shadow in the Rose Garden'	6,000
9.	'The Dead Rose'.	7,000
10.	'The White Stocking'	8,000
11.	'Vin Ordinaire'	9,500
12.	'Honor and Arms'	9,600

Which makes it about 88.000 words. If you would like any more, please tell me. And which of the titles will you choose for a book-title? 'Goose Fair'?[3]

I will send in the last story – 'Vin Ordinaire' – within a day or two. Tell me if this lot is all right.

We are an[4] irrefutable married couple, now. Does it seem dull to you, to be so respectable. The trouble about the children is very acute just now. We

---

[1] For an analysis of the revisions to the stories, see Keith Cushman, *D. H. Lawrence at Work: The Emergence of 'The Prussian Officer' Stories* (Charlottesville, 1978).

[2] J. B. Pinker had submitted 'Daughters of the Vicar' along with 'The White Stocking' to the *Smart Set*, but it was rejected (letter from the magazine's Managing Editor, Norman Boyer to Pinker, 12 March 1914, MS NYPL).

The other stories first appeared in periodicals as follows: 'A Fragment of Stained Glass', *English Review*, ix (September 1911), 242–51; 'Goose Fair', *English Review*, iv (February 1910), 399–408; 'A Sick Collier', *New Statesman*, i (13 September 1913), 722–4; 'The Christening', *Smart Set*, xlii (February 1914), 81–5; 'Odour of Chrysanthemums', *English Review*, viii (June 1911), 415–33; 'Second Best', *English Review*, x (February 1912), 461–9; 'The Shadow in the Rose Garden', *Smart Set*, xlii (March 1914), 71–7; 'The Dead Rose' was retitled 'The Shades of Spring' and had appeared under the title 'The Soiled Rose' in *Forum*, xlix (March 1913), 324–40 and in *Blue Review*, i (May 1913), 6–23; 'The White Stocking', *Smart Set*, xliv (October 1914), 97–108; 'The Thorn in the Flesh', under the title 'Vin Ordinaire', in *English Review*, xvii (June 1914), 298–315; 'Honour and Arms', retitled 'The Prussian Officer', appeared under the original title in *English Review*, xviii (August 1914), 24–43 and in *Metropolitan* (November 1914), 12–14, 61–3, with illustrations by Harry E. Townsend.

[3] For DHL's reaction to the choice of volume-title – *The Prussian Officer and Other Stories* – see Letter 821.   [4] are an] are again an

are having scenes with indignant aunts, and so on. I suppose time will finish this, along with everything else.

Many regards   D. H. Lawrence

I sent the first batch of stories in to Mr Duckworth a week ago on Thursday.

758. To Edward Marsh, 15 July 1914
Text: MS NYPL; Huxley 205.

9, Selwood Terrace, South Kensington, S.W.

15 July 1914

Dear Eddie,

Have you got Lascelles Abercrombie's book on Thomas Hardy; and if so, could you lend it me for the space of, say, six weeks; and if so, do you mind if I scribble notes in it?[1] And if you've got any of those little pocket edition Hardy's, will you lend me those too. I am quite a reliable man to lend books to – I send them back safely. – I am going to write a little book on Hardy's people. I think it will interest me. We are going to Ireland at the end of this month. I shall do it there. I have just finished getting together a book of short stories. Lord, how I've worked again at those stories – most of them – forging them up. They're good, I think.

Has the Lady Cynthias baby come?[2]

We had Campbell and Murry as witnesses at the marriage. I wish you'd been there.

Saluti di cuore   D. H. Lawrence

759. To Edward Garnett, [17 July 1914]
Text: MS NYPL; Postmark, Chelsea, S.W. 18 JUL 14; cited in Delany 11, 21.

9, Selwood Terrace, South Kensington, S.W.

Friday.

Dear Garnett,

I have finished the story 'Vin Ordinaire'. I think you'd better read it through before you put it first.[3] We don't want them to sneeze at the first

---

[1] *Thomas Hardy: A Critical Study* (1912). (This copy is now in the library of the University of New Mexico, Albuquerque, New Mexico.) DHL had read Abercrombie at an earlier stage (see *Letters,* i. 544 n. 4).

[2] Lady Cynthia Asquith's second son, Michael, b. 25 July 1914 (d. 1960). On 25 July 1915 she recorded: 'The Lawrences came to Michael's birthday tea...' (Asquith, *Diaries* 58).

[3] The first story in the collection proved to be 'Honour and Arms' under its new title 'The Prussian Officer'.

whiff. I thought I might call it, in its present form, instead of 'Vin Ordinaire', which I only called it because I thought it *was* vin ordinaire, 'The Thorn in the Flesh' – which applies direct to most of the stories, I think. Do you think that would be a good title for the book – 'The Thorn in the Flesh'.

I'm sorry I can't come to Pond Place on Tuesday evening. I am just going up to the Midlands to my sister, and am staying till Wednesday night. I *do* want to see you again. I want you to come in here if you can to evening meal one day. Let me know when you can.

Frieda isn't going with me to my sister's. She is persisting in her efforts to get hold of the children. She has seen them – the little girls[1] being escorted to school by a fattish white unwholesome maiden aunt who, when she saw their mother, shrieked to the children – 'Run, children, run' – and the poor little things were terrified and ran. Frieda has written to her mother to come. I *do* hope that old Baroness will turn up in a state of indignation. Then we shall see sparks fly round the maggoty Weekley household – curse the etiolated lot of them, maggots.

I am going to fill in my next few weeks writing a little book on Thomas Hardy which a man asked me to do for him.[2] I *wonder* what sort of a mess I shall make of it. However it doesn't very much matter.

Our love to Mrs Garnett and you.   D. H. Lawrence

760. To Edward Marsh, 17 July 1914
Text: MS NYPL; Huxley 206.

9, Selwood Terrace, South Kensington, S.W.
17 July 1914

My dear Eddie,

But what a shock I got when the books came.[3] I began to yell – 'but I didn't *ask* him for them' – and I rushed round the room almost cracked, between shame of having made it possible, and horror at your spending so much money on me, and joy of having the books. Frieda was getting in my way crying 'Never mind – never mind – take them – how lovely – oh how I shall revel – let him give them you –'. I still feel shaken. I've never had such a lot of books in my life. I tell you the selfish motive is triumphing,

---

[1] Frieda's two daughters, Elsa Agnes Frieda (b. 1902) and Barbara Joy (b. 1904).
[2] See Letter 748.
[3] Marsh 'acted on a hint of Lawrence's that he was contemplating a critical study of Hardy and sent him the complete works' (Hassall, *Edward Marsh*, p. 288).

and I'm rejoicing in the land. I'm *awfully* excited about it. So is Frieda. If
my book – a tiny book – on Hardy comes off and pleases me, and you would
like it, I dedicate it to you with a fanfare of trumpets.[1]

Thank you a million times.

D. H. Lawrence

761. To Sallie Hopkin, [17 July 1914]
Text: MS NCL; Unpublished.

9, Selwood Terrace, South Kensington, S.W.

Friday

Dear Mrs Hopkin,

I'm going to Ripley tomorrow afternoon. Frieda can't come this time – the
children. I am staying till Wednesday afternoon. We'll make arrangements
to have a day together – I must keep straight with my sister – daren't make
arrangements by myself.

Love   DHL

762. To J. B. Pinker, [18 July 1914]
Text: MS Forster; Unpublished.

9, Selwood Terrace, South Kensington, S.W.

Saturday

Dear Pinker,

I had the agreement, signed it and sent it back immediately.[2] I even had
a p.c. acknowledging its receipt by you. It must be somewhere about. – I
am going to the Midlands now till Thursday – but my wife stays here and
will forward a letter – or if you want another[3] agreement signed, I am

c/o Mrs L A Clarke, Grosvenor Rd, *Ripley*, Derby.

But I suppose the first will turn up at your place.

Yours   D. H. Lawrence

763. To J. B. Pinker, 23 July 1914
Text: TMSC NWU; Unpublished.

9, Selwood Terrace, South Kensington, S.W.

July 23 – 1914

Dear Pinker,

Did you exchange the agreements with Methuen, and did he give you the
cheque for me? I wish he would, for I am again at my last pennies. Tomorrow

---

[1] The 'Study of Thomas Hardy' was not published in DHL's lifetime, and the promise of
the dedication was not fulfilled.
[2] The agreement with Methuen for the publication of *The Rainbow*.
[3] another] the

I am going to see Lena Ashwell[1] about the play.[2] It looks as if it might be produced. I send the man Neilson along to you as soon as anything is decided that way.[3]

Yours   D. H. Lawrence

764. To Douglas Clayton, [25 July 1914]
Text: MS NCL; Unpublished.

9, Selwood Terrace, South Kensington, S.W.
Saturday[4]

Dear Clayton,

Do you wonder what has become of me? Will you send a typed copy of 'Once' and 'A Primrose Path' to J B Pinker Esq, Talbot House, Arundel St, Strand, W.C. You might make a carbon copy of both, and keep that.

– We leave London on Friday, but shall be back in September.[5]

Many regards   D. H. Lawrence

765. To J. B. Pinker, [25 July 1914]
Text: MS UT; Unpublished.

9, Selwood Terrace, South Kensington, S.W.
Saturday

Dear Pinker,

Yes, please do send me another £50, awaiting Methuen's cheque.

I'll get you a copy of the play. I saw Lena Ashwell. She seems well inclined all round.

I send you the only story I have by me.[6] Later two more will come – in a day or so.[7]

Yours,   D. H. Lawrence

---

[1] Lena Ashwell (1872–1957), actress and later theatre manager. In 1907 she leased the Kingsway Theatre, and managed it until 1915. During 1914–18 war she organised companies for the entertainment of troops in France. The Lena Ashwell Players, as her company was called, appeared in various theatres in London after the war. Published her autobiography, *Myself a Player* (1936).
[2] *The Widowing of Mrs Holroyd.*   [3] See Letter 739.
[4] Dated with reference to a handwritten note by Clayton on the MS, which reads: 'Rec. 27 July 1914 at the Cearne. "Once" enclosed.'
[5] Presumably the previously announced journey to Ireland was still being considered (see Letter 758).
[6] Unidentified.   [7] See the preceding letter.

766. To Douglas Clayton, [27 July 1914]
Text: MS NCL; Unpublished.

9, Selwood Terrace, South Kensington, S.W.
Monday[1]

Dear Clayton,

Thanks very much for doing the stories. But you *shouldn't* have come back from the Cearne.

I send you here a sketch. Will you type it for me and send me the type script here.[2] I'll send you another such sketch tomorrow or Wednesday.[3]

Yours   D. H. Lawrence

It was right not to omit the sentences in 'Once'. An editor inserted the brackets.[4]

767. To J. B. Pinker, [27 July 1914]
Text: TMSC NWU; Unpublished.

9, Selwood Terrace, South Kensington, S.W.
Monday

Dear Pinker,

Many thanks for the cheque for £50, which has just come. It is very welcome.

I asked the type-writer to send you another couple of stories to show to the editor.

Yours   D. H. Lawrence

768. To Harriet Monroe, 31 July 1914
Text: MS UChi; cited in Monroe 91.

9, Selwood Terrace, South Kensington, S.W.
31 July. 1914

Dear Miss Monroe,

Your letter finds me just getting up to go from London.[5] I am satisfied that you take the poems you mention, and that you will publish them something in this order:

'Grief', 'Memories', 'Weariness', 'Service of all the Dead', 'Don Juan', 'Song' – : in November or *December*.[6]

[1] Clayton's note on the MS reads: 'Rec. 28 July 1914.'
[2] The handwritten note on the MS identifies the sketch: 'Enc. "A Chapel Among [the] Mountains".'
[3] 'A Hay Hut Among the Mountains'; see Letter 770.
[4] Probably Wright of the *Smart Set*.
[5] DHL was preparing to leave for a walking tour in Westmorland, 31 July–8 August.
[6] DHL's poems were published in that order in *Poetry*, v (December 1914), 102–6.

Why oh why do you want to cut off the tail of poor Ophelia's ballad.[1] Don't you see the poor thing is cracked, and she used all those verses – apples and chickens and rat – according to true instinctive or *dream* symbolism. This poem – I am very proud of it – has got the quality of a troublesome dream that seems incoherent but is selected by another sort of consciousness. The latter part is the waking up part – yet never really awake, because she is mad. No, you mustn't cut it in two. It is a good poem: I couldn't do it again to save my life. Use it whole or not at all. I return you the MS. If you don't use it, please destroy it.

I was at dinner with Miss Lowell[2] and the Aldingtons[3] last night, and we had some poetry. But, my dear God, when I see all the understanding and suffering and the pure intelligence necessary for the simple perceiving of poetry, then I know it is an almost hopeless business to publish the stuff at all, and particularly in magazines. It must stand by, and wait and wait. So I don't urge anybody to publish me.

Mrs Aldington has a few good poems.

Will you address me

    c/o Messrs Duckworth, 3 Henrietta St., Covent Garden, W.C.

I am without an address till I am back in Italy, about mid October.

'Lawrence at his best –'[4] merci Monsieur, whoever you are, and what do you know about it.

Yours Sincerely   D. H. Lawrence

---

[1] DHL's poem 'Ballad of Another Ophelia': Harriet Monroe did not publish it; Amy Lowell did, in her anthology, *Some Imagist Poets: An Anthology* (Boston and New York), 1915.

[2] Amy Lowell (1874–1925), American poet. In 1913 she became identified with the movement in poetry known as Imagism in which she was the dominant force after Ezra Pound abandoned the group. She edited the series of Imagist Anthologies. It was Michael Sadleir who instigated and Edward Marsh who arranged the meeting between her and DHL, the occasion when DHL 'was invited to support the Imagist group of poets which was soon to be actively anti-Georgian' (Hassall, *Marsh*, p. 289).

[3] Richard Aldington (1892–1962), poet, novelist and biographer, whose poetry of this period belonged to the Imagist school. In 1913 he worked as assistant editor of the *Egoist*. Among his novels are *Death of a Hero* (1929) and *The Colonel's Daughter* (1931). He became a close friend of DHL's and later wrote *D. H. Lawrence: Portrait of a Genius But...* (1950). When they first met, Aldington was married to Hilda Doolittle ('H.D.') (1886–1961), who was also closely identified with Imagism. Among her many volumes of poetry are *Sea Garden* (1916) and *Hymen* (1921). Her novel *Bid Me to Live* (1960) is a *roman à clef* of Bloomsbury life in 1917.

[4] DHL alludes to a note on the envelope in which the MSS were sent on 8 May 1914; it reads: 'In all this batch not a single instance of Lawrence at his best'. It is signed with the initials 'E.T.'. For the identification of the writer as Eunice Tietjens, see Alvin Sullivan, 'DHL and Poetry: The Unpublished Manuscripts', *DHL Review*, ix (Summer 1976), 267–8.

769. To Jane Wells, 31 July 1914

Text: MS UIll; cited in Harry T. Moore, *Poste Restante* (Berkeley and Los Angeles, 1956), p. 41.

9, Selwood Terrace, South Kensington, S.W.

31 July. 1914

Dear Mrs Wells,[1]

We are so glad that you wrote to us. Today I am going to the lake district till the 8th. Could we come and see you on the 13th[2] or 14th or 15th. We have those days free. Then I think we are going to Ireland, or to Germany. I am so tired of London.

Will you just let us know at Holly Bush House, Holly Mount, Hampstead, N.W.[3] if we shall come one of the days I mention. We count upon it as a pleasure indeed.

Yours Sincerely   D. H. Lawrence

770. To Douglas Clayton, [31 July 1914]

Text: MS NCL; Unpublished.

9, Selwood Terrace, South Kensington, S.W.

[31 July 1914]

Dear Clayton,

Will you type this sketch – 'Hay hut among the Mountains' – and send it with the other – 'Chapel Among the Mountains' – to

J Squire Esq,[4] *The New Statesman*, 10 Gt. Queen St, Kingsway, W.C.

and tell him I asked you to send them in, and if he writes to me will he address me Holly Bush House, Holly Mount, Hampstead, N.W. as I am leaving London and have no permanent address. Will you write me at the same place – friends will forward from there.

Will you let the other MS. I sent lie[5] by for a while.[6] I must work at it later.

Yours   D. H. Lawrence

771. To Douglas Clayton, [4? August 1914]

Text: MS NCL; Unpublished.

Clarkes Arms Hotel, Rampside, Nr. Barrow in Furness

[4? August 1914][7]

[1] Née Amy Catherine Robbins (1872–1927), the second wife of H. G. Wells (1866–1946), familiarly known as Jane Wells. They met in 1892, when she was a student at the University Correspondence College and he was a tutor in biology. m. 27 October 1895.
[2] 13th] 12   [3] The address of Catherine Jackson.
[4] (Sir) John Collings Squire (1884–1958), poet, critic and journalist, became literary editor of the *New Statesman* in 1913 and editor in 1917. His literary criticism was written under the pen-name of 'Solomon Eagle'. 1919–34, editor of the *London Mercury* and closely associated with the Georgian poets. He was knighted in 1933. Autobiography: *The Honeysuckle and the Bee* (1937).   [5] lie] lay   [6] Probably 'Love Among the Haystacks'.
[7] Dated in relation to Letter 772.

Dear Clayton,

I have just got your post card.[1] I received the typed copy of 'Chapel' also. Don't type it again unless you have begun. If you have done it, please send both to the *New Statesman*.[2] If you have not, please send 'Hay Hut' to me at 9, Selwood Terrace, S. Kensington. I shall be there for a few days after Saturday. And when you are at the Cearne, *don't* go away before your time, to do my typing. It is not worth it.

Many regards   D. H. Lawrence

772. To S. S. Koteliansky, [5 August 1914]
Text: MS BL; Moore 288–9.

Barrow in Furness
Wednesday[3]

Dear Kotiliansky,[4]

I just find that my wife did not go up to Hampstead. I think she is at 9 Selwood Terrace, Onslow Gardens, South Kensington. But I shall be back on Saturday and will send you a postcard. Tell Horne not to go to Hampstead.[5]

I am very miserable about the war.[6]

auf wiedersehen   D. H. Lawrence

---

[1] post card] letter

[2] Douglas Clayton must have sent 'A Chapel Among the Mountains' to J. C. Squire; it is this sketch that DHL refers to in Letter 813. The 'other half of it' referred to there would be 'A Hay Hut Among the Mountains', which DHL did not send to the *New Statesman* after all.

[3] The original postmark is obliterated but the envelope carries a second frank: London AUG 6 14.

[4] Samuel Solomonovich Koteliansky (1880–1955) b. Ukraine; he studied at the University of Kiev. He moved to England in July 1911 and lived there for the rest of his life, nearly forty years (1915–55) at 5, Acacia Road, St John's Wood. He became a naturalised British subject, 27 November 1929. 'Kot' first worked at the 'Russian Law Bureau', 212 High Holborn, and later read manuscripts for the Cresset Press. With various English authors including DHL, Kot translated many Russian works into English. The Hogarth Press of Leonard and Virginia Woolf published his translations of the work of Bunin, Chekhov, Gorky and the Countess Sophie Tolstoi. He bequeathed to the British Museum ten volumes of letters from such correspondents as Katherine Mansfield, Mark Gertler, Gilbert Cannan, Lady Ottoline Morrell and DHL. His letters from DHL number 346, the largest collection to a single recipient to be preserved intact. See Zytaruk, also Carswell, *Lives and Letters*.

[5] Probably William K. Horne who had some legal training, and, along with Koteliansky, was employed at the Russian Law Bureau, 212 High Holborn. Horne's name appears in DHL's address-book at 2 Museum Mansions, Great Russell Street. He became a bus-driver in France in April 1915 (see Letter 908), but little more is known of him. DHL had probably planned to meet him at Catherine Jackson's house in Hampstead.

[6] Great Britain declared war on Germany on 4 August 1914. DHL recalls his feelings upon hearing the news of the war in Letter 851 to Lady Cynthia Asquith.

773. To S. S. Koteliansky, [9 August 1914]
Text: MS BL; Postmark, Chelsea S.W. 10 AUG 14; Zytaruk 2.

9 Selwood Terrace, South Kensington, S.W.

Sunday

Dear Kotilianski,

Can you come round tomorrow evening about 8·30, and meet my wife. I'm sorry we can't ask you to a meal, but the man of the house has taken away all the knives and forks and things.

Our telephone number is 2153 Kensington. You might ring us up and say if you will come. I shall be glad to see you again.

Au revoir   D. H. Lawrence

P.S. I ask Horne to come also. Is his address 2 Museum Mansions? This is near S. Kensington station, off Onslow Gardens.

774. To Amy Lowell, [9 August 1914]
Text: MS HU; Postmark, Chelsea S.W. 10 AUG 14; cited in Moore, *Poste Restante*, p. 42.

9 Selwood Terrace, South Kensington, S.W.

Sunday.

Dear Miss Lowell,

I am back in London for a week or so. Will you ask my wife and me to come and see you – we should like very much to do so. And will you give the Aldingtons our address – of course I've forgotten theirs – and tell them we should like to come to tea. I am occupied Tuesday[1] and Wednesday afternoons, but otherwise we are free.

Please forgive the pencil – there is no pen and ink in the house. And we are so miserable about the war. My wife is German, so you may imagine – her father was an army officer.[2] Everything seems gone to pieces.

Yours Very Sincerely   D. H. Lawrence

775. To J. B. Pinker, 10 August 1914
Text: TMSC NWU; Huxley 207.

9, Selwood Terrace, South Kensington, S.W.

Dear Pinker,   10 August 1914.

Here is a state of affairs, – what is going to become of us? You said

---

[1] Tuesday] Monday.

[2] Baron Friedrich von Richthofen (1845–1915) became a professional soldier at the age of seventeen; wounded in the Franco-Prussian War of 1870–1, he was awarded the Iron Cross. Now in Metz, he served as a garrison administrative officer.

Methuen signed the agreement for the novel[1] – did he give you the cheque at the same time? I ask because I am wondering how I am going to get on. We can't go back to Italy as things stand, and I must look for somewhere to live. I think I shall try to get a tiny cottage somewhere, put a little bit of furniture in it, and live as cheaply as possible. But to do that even I must know there is a little money coming from somewhere. Will you let me know about Methuen? We can't stay here much longer.

Yours Sincerely   D. H. Lawrence

776. To S. S. Koteliansky, [11 August 1914]

Text: MS BL; Postmark, Chelsea S.W. 11 AUG 14; Zytaruk 2.

9 Selwood Terrace, S.W.
[11 August 1914]

Dear Kotilianski,

I wonder if you and Horne would care to meet two little friends of ours, with us, at the Café Royal tomorrow night (Wednesday) about 8.45 or 9.0 oclock.[2] Ring me up – 2153 Kensington – and leave a message if I'm not in –

Yrs   D. H. Lawrence

777. To Amy Lowell, 11 August 1914

Text: MS HU; Postmark, Chelsea S.W. 11 Aug 14; Unpublished.

9, Selwood Terrace, South Kensington, S.W.
11 August 1914

My Dear Miss Lowell,

It is very good and nice of you to ask us to dinner on Thursday. We look forward very much to coming. I suppose I needn't dress – just as you ordain. Is Mrs Russell staying with you? – I did not know.[3] My respects to her, and it is a pleasure to meet her again.

All my wails and laments I shall pour out when I come.

Küss die Hand   D. H. Lawrence

---

[1] For the terms of DHL's agreement with Methuen for *The Rainbow* see Letter 783.

[2] The meeting with Katherine Mansfield and John Middleton Murry did not take place, as Letter 794 shows. Katherine Mansfield did not meet Kot until she and Murry went to live at Rose Tree Cottage in October.

[3] Ada (Dwyer) Russell (b. 1863), a well known professional actress, was Amy Lowell's travelling companion and life-long friend. Before the dinner on 13 August (at the Berkeley Hotel), Amy Lowell had not been sure what to expect in Frieda: 'She was overwhelmed with astonishment and pleasure, however, to meet a lady of exquisite, vital presence' (Damon 235).

778. To J. B. Pinker, 16 August 1914

Text: MS UT; Unpublished.

The Triangle, Bellingdon Lane, Nr. Chesham, Bucks.

16 Aug 1914

Dear Pinker,

I write to give you my address. We have got a nice little cottage here, and are living the ultra-simple life. I wonder what is going to happen to the book trade.

Write to me here if you have anything to communicate, please.

Yours Sincerely   D. H. Lawrence

779. To David Garnett, 17 August 1914

Text: MS NYPL; Unpublished.

The Triangle, Bellingdon Lane, Nr. Chesham, Bucks.

17 Aug 1914

Dear David,

We've got our little cottage here – very pretty and nice. It belongs to a friend of Cannans.[1] It is tiny, but jolly – and 6/- a week in all. Unfortunately there is only one bedroom furnished. But I shall get a camp bed up. We are fixed here now for a while. You must let me hear from you. Remember we don't know Mrs Hepburn's[2] address, and so if the party on Sunday week is coming off, you must remind us. I presume you are at the Cearne. Our love to Mrs Garnett. Frieda is happy for the time being in her cottage. It is nice.

auf wiedersehen   D. H. Lawrence

780. To Amy Lowell, 22 August 1914

Text: MS HU; Postmark, Chesham 22 AU 14; Damon 247–8.

The Triangle, Bellingdon Lane, *Chesham*, Bucks.

22 Aug 1914

---

[1] Gilbert Cannan (1884–1955), novelist and dramatist. A friend of Murry's, he was educated at Cambridge; called to the bar (1908); dramatic critic on the *London Star* (1908–10). 1910 m. actress Mary Ansell (1867–1950), former wife of Sir James Barrie. His novel, *Mendel* (1916) has Mark Gertler as its principal character; it also includes portraits of Marsh, Dorothy Brett, Dora Carrington and Augustus John. At this time the Cannans were living in a remodelled windmill near Cholesbury, Herts. (See Diana Farr, *Gilbert Cannan*, 1978.)

[2] Edith Alice Mary Hepburn, née Harper (1884–1947); she used the pen-name Anna Wickham. b. Wimbledon but grew up in Australia. In 1905 she came to Europe to study singing. 1906 m. Patrick Hepburn (d. 1929), a solicitor by profession and an amateur astronomer who later became the president of the Royal Astronomical Society. Her main poetical works are *The Contemplative Quarry* (1915) and *The Man With a Hammer* (1916). (See David Garnett, *Great Friends*, 1979, pp. 80, 85.)

Dear Miss Lowell,

Here we are settled in our cottage, which is really very nice. I spend my days whitewashing the upper rooms, having a rare old time. Meanwhile I grind over in my soul the war news. Germany is a queer country: one can't regard it dispassionately. I alternate between hating it thoroughly, stick stock and stone, and yearning over it fit to break my heart. I cant help feeling it a young and adorable country – adolescent – with the faults of adolescence. There is no peace during this war. But I must say, my chief grief and misery is for Germany – so far.

In the poetry book, for my seven, will you please put

1. 'Ballad of Another Ophelia' – beginning 'O the green glimmer of apples in the orchard'. Harriett Monroe has got it, and wants to publish the far end of it and leave out the the first half: see her in blazes. But even if you don't like the poem, please put it in as you love me.

2. 'Illicit'[1] – beginning – I've forgotten – something about 'a faint, lost ribbon of rainbow'. It is in *Poetry*.

3. 'The Youth Mowing' – also in *Poetry*.[2]

4. 'Birthday' – also in *Poetry* – 'If I were well-to-do'.

5. Isar Rose Poems.[3]

6. 'Tired of the Boat'.⎫
7. 'Scent of Irises' ⎬ MS. enclosed

This is very roughly my selection. I'm quite amenable to change. Tell me yours, and let us compromise.[4] The MS. poems I sent you here have not been published, yes, 'Tired of the Boat', two years ago in the *English Review* – in an unrevised version.[5] Don't lose MS – of the 'Irises' poem, will you? – it is the only copy. I can't be bothered to write it out again. You might, if you like, offer these poems to Harriett Monroe: but not unless you like. I only insist on your taking the 'Ballad of Another Ophelia'.

Can't you come and see us? Can't you drive out here in your motor car – about 30 miles. Come to Chesham, through Harrow. In Chesham ask

---

[1] Published in *Poetry*, iii (January 1914); the title became 'On the Balcony' for DHL's collection *Look! We Have Come Through!* (1917). The first line reads: 'In front of the sombre mountains, a faint, lost ribbon of rainbow.'

[2] Entitled 'The Mowers', this poem was not published in *Poetry* but first appeared in *Smart Set*, xli (November 1913); included in *Look! We Have Come Through!* as 'A Youth Mowing'.

[3] 'Birthday' and 'All of Roses' (the 'Isar Rose Poems') were among those published in *Poetry*, iii (January 1914).

[4] The selection of DHL's poems which was finally agreed on and published in *Some Imagist Poets: An Anthology* (1915), pp. 67–78, was: 'Ballad of Another Ophelia', 'Illicit', 'Fireflies in the Corn', 'A Woman and Her Dead Husband', 'The Mowers', 'Scent of Irises' and 'Green'.

[5] *English Review*, vi (October 1910), 377–8.

for Elliotts farm at Bellingdon – we are 100 yards from the farm. We should be delighted to see you. Do try to come – any day, at any hour – you will eat eggs if there is nothing else in the house – and cheese and milk and bacon – perfectly rural and idyllic.

When you go to America, please abuse Mitchell Kennerley for me, and *please* make him send me some money. He owes me some, even if it were no more than the bad cheque for £10 he sent me and I sent back. Won't you drive over for the day, with Mrs Russell or the Aldingtons?

My wife and I send many regards to you and to Mrs Russell.

Yours   D. H. Lawrence

781. To S. S. Koteliansky, [23 August 1914]
Text: MS BL; Postmark, Chesham 24 AU 14; Moore 289–90.

The Triangle, Bellingdon Lane, *Chesham*, Bucks.
Sunday.

Dear Kotilianski,

I am a long time telling you our address. I have been very busy whitewashing the upper rooms. This is a delightful cottage, really buried in the country. Already my wife and I go picking blackberries, and find many.

When will you come to see us? Next Sunday we are invited out to tea and dinner in London, but cant you come one day in the week – you and Horne? On certain days one may have a cheap ticket 2/4 return from Baker St. Metropolitan. I believe one can also have cheap tickets from Marylebone – Gt. Central. Unfortunately there is only the one bed in the house, or you might have stayed. But we are writing for another bed. When you come, bring along with you my play *The Widowing of Mrs Holroyd* – my wife wants to amuse herself by translating it. You come to Chesham station – You may have to change at Chalfont Rd, – I think that's the junction on the main line. We are 3½ miles from the station – ask for Elliott's farm at Bellingdon, and we are quite near – a stone's throw. Tell Horne – I haven't the energy to write him another letter.[1] We shall be glad to see you and him again.

Vale   D. H. Lawrence

782. To Amy Lowell, [25 August 1914]
Text: MS HU; Postmark, Chesham 25 AU 14; Unpublished.

The Triangle, Bellingdon Lane, Chesham, Bucks
Tuesday

[1] No letters from DHL to Horne have been found.

Dear Miss Lowell,

What good news, to hear that you will come and see us. We shall look out for you on Thursday afternoon. Ask for Elliotts farm, Bellingdon, when you get to Chesham.

Tante belle cose from us to you and Mrs Russell.

D. H. Lawrence

783. To Edward Marsh, 25 August 1914

Text: MS NYPL; Postmark, Chesham [. . .] AU 14; Edward Marsh, *A Number of People* (1939), pp. 228–9.

The Triangle, Bellingdon Lane, Nr. Chesham, Bucks
25 Aug 1914

Dear Eddie,

Many thanks for the nice little cheque which came on here this morning. G[*eorgian*] P[*oetry*] is still the goose that lays the golden eggs. I suppose you'll leave the next issue till March or so.[1]

We have got a little furnished cottage here, quite nice, though I don't love this exhausted english countryside. Yes, the agreement with Methuen was signed. He owes me only £50 more: paying me £150 on receipt of MS., and £150 on publication. Pinker already advanced me £100 some months ago. We spent that, and are sitting here very tight on our last six pence, holding our breath.

The war is just hell for me. I don't see why I should be so disturbed – but I am. I can't get away from it for a minute: live in a sort of coma, like one of those nightmares when you can't move. I hate it – everything. I'm glad to hear you are enjoying yourself slogging at work. I've whitewashed the house.

I liked Elliott Seabrooke *very* much indeed – I *did* like him.[2] I think too that he's got it in him to do some real good work: whether it will always remain an undiscovered interior I don't know.

I met Bob Trevelyan's elder brother up there too – and rather hated him.[3] He's so God almighty serious. I reckon it's conceit to be quite so serious: as if he was the schoolmaster and all the world his scholars, poor dear.

---

[1] The next volume, *Georgian Poetry: 1913–1915*, was not published until November 1915.
[2] Elliott Seabrooke (1886–1950), painter, was educated at the City of London School and at the Slade. He was well known for his landscapes which were greatly influenced by his admiration for Cézanne. Some of his work is owned by the Tate Gallery and the Dublin Art Gallery. Edward Marsh was a close friend and patron. (See the *Times* obituary, 17 March 1950.)
[3] George Macaulay Trevelyan (1876–1962), the well known historian.

Come and see us here if ever you have time. It is not very far for you. We are quite near Gilbert Cannan: I like him. Yesterday we had in Compton Mackenzie: very flourishing and breezy: a nice fellow, I think, – for somebody other than me.[1]

I can't say we're happy, because we're not, Frieda and I: what with this war, and one thing and another. But the sun rises and sets as usual.

Au revoir   D. H. Lawrence[2]

784. To J. B. Pinker, 5 September 1914
Text: MS UNYB; Huxley 208.

The Triangle, Bellingdon Lane, Chesham, Bucks.

5 Sept 1914

Dear Pinker,

Are you better from your accident? We were sorry to hear of it. But your secretary said it was not at all serious. Will you thank her for her courteous[3] letter. I hope you are really all right now.

I am very sorry to worry you again about money. Do you think Methuen will pay up the £150 to you? I can last out here only another month – then I don't know where to raise a penny, for nobody will pay me. It makes me quite savage. Extort me my dues out of Methuen if you can, will you?

What a miserable world. What colossal idiocy, this war. Out of sheer rage I've begun my book about Thomas Hardy. It will be about anything but Thomas Hardy I am afraid – queer stuff – but not bad.

I do wish I neednt worry you – I wouldnt if I could help it.

Regards from us   D. H. Lawrence

785. To S. S. Koteliansky, [9 September 1914]
Text: MS BL; Postmark, Chesham 9 SP 14; Zytaruk 4.

The Triangle, Bellingdon Lane, Chesham, Bucks
Wednesday

Dear Kotilianski,

I wish you would come and see us on Sunday – Can you afford 2/4 in

---

[1] (Sir) Edward Montague Compton Mackenzie (1883–1972), novelist. At this time Mackenzie was the successful young author of *Sinister Street*, Vol. 1 (1913) [Vol. 2 appeared in November 1914]. For his fictional account of this visit to the Lawrences, see Nehls, i. 247–53. Later DHL presented a satirical portrait of Mackenzie in 'The Man Who Loved Islands', *Dial*, lxxxiii (July 1927), 1–25.

[2] DHL's letter coincided with a note from Maurice Hewlett to Marsh: 'D. H. Lawrence, one of your poets, is in great distress' (Hassall, *Marsh*, p. 293).

[3] courteous] kind

railway travelling? I hear from Horne you are on short wages, like the rest of us. He – Horne – is in Blackpool with his wife, is he not?

I was very cross and quite indignant that you didn't turn up the other Sunday. But I understand you didn't feel like it.

Do come on Sunday. The best train leaves Marylebone – Gt. Central – at 9.0 in the morning, and gets here at 9.55. By that train you need not, I think, change at Chalfont Rd. But ask. The next trains are 10.7 and 11.5 from Baker St. Metropolitan.

At Chesham, ask for the way to Bellingdon – it is about $3\frac{1}{2}$ miles here. We are near Elliotts farm – just down a little lane off the highroad. Elliotts farm is on your *right*, and has a red letter box in the gate. The house stands across a field. Immediately past the farm, our lane goes down to the right.

You cannot get astray. Do come, we shall be so glad to see you.

auf wiedersehen   D. H. Lawrence

786. To Edward Marsh, 13 September 1914

Text: MS NYPL; Marsh, *A Number of People*, pp. 229–30.

The Triangle, Bellingdon Lane, Chesham, Bucks.

13 Sept 1914.

Dear Eddie,

I am moved almost to tears by the letter and the money this morning.[1] It is true, we are in a poor condition. Pinker, however, promises me some money somehow: I should have waited till it came, or have asked my sister for a little. Frieda has always got money from Germany when we have been badly reduced before. Now she can't. But Mary Cannan wrote and told Alfred Sutro and Hewlett that we were very badly off.[2] If I had known, I think I would have asked her not to do it. Then Sutro sent me £10 in advance – that was on Thursday. It sort of came by magic, and I was rather taken aback. But I was glad, because I couldn't bear to be really penniless. I think he was *very* generous. I shall send it him back when I get some of my own money. And I shall keep yours till my ship is off the shallows again. She is right aground just now.

---

[1] In response to DHL's reference to his financial anxieties in Letter 783, Marsh at once sent 'a cheque for £10 with a note reaffirming his unshaken confidence in his young friend's genius' (Hassall, *Marsh*, p. 293).

[2] Alfred Sutro (1863–1933), dramatist and translator. His most recent play, *The Two Virtues*, had been published by Duckworth in March 1914. Maurice Hewlett (1861–1923), novelist, poet and essayist. Both men were known to Mary Cannan from the days of her marriage to James Barrie. For the consequences of her efforts on DHL's behalf see p. 224 n. 4.

Why should I have thought you a bad friend? I knew from Mark Gertler how busy you are.[1] It really touches me very close, when you write so warmly. After all, there is no reason why you should take thought for me. The debt of gratitude already is only mine, between us. – Gott sey Danck gesagt[2] – as it says on the little old ex-voto pictures among the mountains – for your warmness to us.

We live here very quietly. I scrub and Frieda makes blackberry-jelly, because there are so many blackberries this year. I never worry much about money. We need little and spend little and I have earned my bread and butter on earth.

Gertler says all your work makes you happy. The war, of course, makes us very unhappy. I cannot get any sense of an enemy – only of a disaster. When I hear of the Germans, it breaks my heart. They must not win, I know – because also they cannot. But they are a young, only adolescent nation, and they don't know what to do with themselves. I wish it needn't have been. Do you think it might be over soon?

With love from us –

Your affectionate friend   D. H. Lawrence

787. To Edward Marsh, [c. 13 September 1914]
Text: MS NYPL; Unpublished.

[The Triangle, Bellingdon Lane, Chesham, Bucks]
[c. 13 September 1914][3]

[Frieda Lawrence begins]

Dear Mr Marsh,

I was so distressed when Mark Gertler told me your views of the war – It is not *true* that the Germans and the Allies 'hate' each other – As individuals they *dont* – And this abstract hate of a fairytale German ogre (they used of Napoleon to say that he ate little children for breakfast,) it's mostly an artificial thing – Also in the Boer war they used to my horror tell ghastly stories of British cruelty in Germany – Of course in war all the madnesses come out in a man, that is the fault of *war* not of a *man* or a *nation*

---

[1] Mark Gertler (1892–1939), the painter, was a close friend of the Cannans and DHL doubtless met him at their Mill House. Gertler had studied at the Slade School of Art, where he got to know Dorothy Brett and Dora Carrington. He was a member of the New English Art Club 1912–14. See John Woodeson, *Mark Gertler: Biography of a Painter, 1892–1939* (Toronto, 1973).   [2] 'thanks be to God'.

[3] The allusion to Gertler's painting *Blue Flowers*, which dates from September 1914, and the reiterated reference to his information about Marsh's views on the war, both suggest a date close to that of the preceding letter.

– Think in the Belgian accusation there were only *two* violations of women, I think that's marvellously little[1] – And think, how the Belgians *must*, it's human nature, feel hostile towards the Germans every house is like a hostile fort – I hate the glorification of war – it is not *fine* but an awful necessity that these young men lose their chance of life but I think we shall be better *after* the war – Better people and wiser – I used to think war so glorious, my father such a hero with his iron cross and his hand that a bullet had torn – But I know now, that there are finer and truer things to live and die for – If people would see things more from an individual point of view and *be* more individual then they could not have a war – I think the *women* ought to kick and say, we *wont* have our men killed, it's such a job to bring up a child and then after all the bother, he is shot – *No*, it's *not* glorious; I nearly go off my head when I think of the waste and the stupidity of it – And I do think *my* lot the sinners – But they will learn their lesson – So will the English, they will have to alter their stiffness in attitude as we our mechanical ideal – You *are* not to hate the Germans, you can understand how it is, – We are frightfully nice people, but it is *so* difficult for the English to understand anything that is *not* English – That is my chief accusation against them – I suppose you are much too busy to see us here, or we could have an Anglo-German discussion à l'aimable, I hope – You must be glad to have Gertlers blue flowers, I thought they were fine[2] –

Goodbye, I hope nobody will loose too much or win too much.

Yours with kindest regards   Frieda Lawrence

I wish we could give you some blackberry and apple jelly –

[Lawrence begins]

Dear Eddie,

When Gertler does a good figure composition, like those angels in the doorway[3] – then, if it comes off, it should be very good – *much* better than the flowers, which are not extraordinary. I think he may do something valuable – he's the only man whose work gives me that feeling. But it will be those semi-realistic pictures that get some *awe* in them.

---

[1] Almost daily, English newspapers carried reports of German atrocities in Belgium; the Belgian Government also issued official accusations. Frieda's was a selective view and not calculated to persuade Marsh.

[2] Entitled *Agapanthus*, the painting dates from September 1914. 'E. Marsh bought…it for £25 in 1915. *Exh.* Friday Club Feb. 1915 as *Blue Flowers*' (Woodeson, *Mark Gertler*, p. 364). For a black and white reproduction see Woodeson's Plate 37.

[3] Probably *Abraham and the Angels*, a charcoal drawing, first exhibited by the New English Art Club in November 1915. See Woodeson, p. 365.

788. To J. B. Pinker, 15 September 1914
Text: MS ColU; Unpublished.

The Triangle, Bellingdon Lane, Chesham, Bucks
15 Sept 1914.

Dear Pinker,

I have asked my sister[1] to send you a duplicate typed copy of 'Honor and Arms'. The *English Review* made me furious by cutting the thing down.[2] However, you should have the complete MS. in a couple of days' time. I shall be glad for the story to appear in America.[3] They might take the other story, 'Vin Ordinaire', which appeared in June's *English Review*.[4] That also was of German soldiery.

I have heard absolutely nothing from or of Mitchell Kennerley. But Amy Lowell, who returned to America last week, promised to go and attack him in New York for me. I will tell you what she says.

Austin Harrison is advising me very strongly to go to

Stanley Unwin, 44 and 45 Rathbone Place, Oxford St

with some of my work.[5] Do you know anything of him. I am doing the book – more or less à propos of Thomas Hardy's characters – rum stuff – which I promised to Nisbet. I will let you see it as it gets done. If I am very badly off will you type it for me?

Yours Sincerely   D. H. Lawrence

789. To Amy Lowell, 18 September 1914
Text: MS HU; Damon 270.

The Triangle, Bellingdon Lane, Chesham, Bucks
18 Sept 1914.

Dear Miss Lowell,

I suppose by now you are at home with your dogs and your manuscripts.[6] Here it is raining, and the apples blown down lie almost like green lights

---

[1] Ada Clarke.

[2] The version of 'Honour and Arms' published in the *English Review*, xviii (August 1914), 24–43 is about 1500 words shorter than that collected and re-titled as 'The Prussian Officer'.

[3] See p. 197 n. 2.

[4] Pinker did submit 'Vin Ordinaire' to the *Metropolitan*, but it was returned on 14 October 1914 by Carl Hovey 'with regret that it is not just what we need for the *Metropolitan*' (MS NYPL).

[5] Harrison had given the same advice two years earlier. See *Letters*, i. 458 n. 4. Stanley Unwin had founded the publishing firm George Allen and Unwin Ltd in 1914.

[6] MSS of poems for the Imagist Anthology to be published in April 1915.

in the grass. Kennst du das Land, wo die Citronen blühen?[1] Yes, so do I. But now I hear the rain-water trickling animatedly into the green and rotten water-butt.

Will you send me the poems of mine that you think of including in the anthology, so that I can go over them and make any improvements I am capable of.[2]

You won't forget to go to Mitchell Kennerley for me, will you? My agent writes me that he also fails utterly to rouse any echo of response from that gentleman in New York. Tell him about the £25 cheque promised, and the £10 non-valid cheque that came and returned to him, bad penny as it was. Tell him how the hollow of his silence gets bigger and bigger, till he becomes almost a myth. Ask him if he received the MS. of my novel. And I kiss your hand, dear Miss Lowell, for being so good to me.

We are likely to stay in this cottage till I am a silvery haired old gentleman going round patting the curly polls of the cottage toddlers. Nobody will pay me any money, and nobody is good to me, and already the robins are brightening to sing, and the holly berries on the hedges are getting redder. Ahimé – ahimé![3] It's winter, and the wooden gate is black and sodden in the rain, above the raw, cold puddles. Ahimé once more. Im dunklen Laub die gold Orangen glühn.[4]

Give our very warm regards to your friend, and to you.

tante belle cose   D. H. Lawrence

My wife sends her love to you.
We've made some first rate blackberry jelly. That's my nearest approach to poetry here.

790. To Gordon Campbell, 21 September 1914
Text: MS YU; Moore 290–1.

The Triangle, Bellingdon Lane, Chesham, Bucks
21 Sept 1914

Dear Campbell,

We have been spending the week-end in London. The Murrys were nowhere to be found. We heard from them last week that they were back

---

[1] Goethe, *Wilhelm Meister* (1795–6), Bk III, chap. 1 ('Knowst thou the land where the lemon tree blows?') The translation given here and below is from the version available to DHL in Garnett's *International Library of Famous Literature*, x. 4567.

[2] See p. 209 n. 4.   [3] 'Oh dear – oh dear!'

[4] Goethe, *Wilhelm Meister*, Bk III, chap. 1 ('Where deep in the bower the gold orange grows').

in town – had quitted Cornwall – in fact I send you what is left of his letter.[1]
But I replied – his[2] letter came just a week ago tonight – and tried to get
them to come and see us in London – and called at the house on Sunday – all
a dead blank. God knows what they're up to.

The war makes me depressed, the talk about the war makes me sick, and
I have never come so near to hating mankind as I am now. They are fools,
and vulgar fools, and cowards who will always make a noise because they
are afraid of the silence. I don't even mind if they're killed. But I do mind
those who, being sensitive, will receive such a blow from the ghastliness and
mechanical, obsolete, hideous stupidity of war, that they will be crippled
beings further burdening our sick society. Those that die, let them die. But
those that live afterwards – the thought of them makes me sick.

The war doesn't alter my beliefs or visions. I am not Freudian and never
was – Freudianism is only a branch of medical science, interesting. I believe
there is no getting of a vision, as you call it, before we get our sex right:
before we get our souls fertilised by the *female*. I don't mean the feminine:
I mean the female. Because life tends to take two streams, male and female,
and only some female influence (not necessarily woman, but most obviously
woman) can fertilise the soul of man to vision or being. Then the vision we're
after, I don't know what it is – but it is something that contains awe and
dread and submission, not pride or sensuous egotism and assertion. I went
to the British Museum – and I know, from the Egyptian and Assyrian
sculpture – what we are after. We want to realise the tremendous *non-human*
quality of life – it is wonderful. It is not the emotions,[3] nor the personal
feelings and attachments, that matter. These are all only expressive, and
expression has become mechanical. Behind us all are the tremendous
unknown forces of life, coming unseen and unperceived as out of the desert
to the Egyptians, and driving us, forcing us, destroying us if we do not submit
to be swept away.

But letters are no good. Why should we drift away, if we have a bit of
hope in common, and a bit of courage. We are all struggling for the same
liberation, if not for the same ulterior purpose. We must struggle together,
and try to pull all in one direction, even if we're quite in the dark and dont
see what we're pulling at. Which is preaching enough.

Frieda says she stands with Beatrice.[4] But one must struggle on. It isn't

---

[1] Murry and Katherine Mansfield had gone to Cornwall for a holiday after Murry had
   impulsively enlisted in the army. He immediately extricated himself on medical grounds. See
   Murry, *Autobiography* 296–7.
[2] his] this   [3] emotions] small   [4] Campbell's wife.

one's *conscious* self that matters so much. We are conscious mad. But at the back of it all, we are sane and healthy and original. – I'll let you know about the Murrys – we're a bit bothered about them.

D. H. Lawrence

We are very badly off – and don't know what money will come, if any, during the winter. But it will be as it will be.

[Frieda Lawrence begins]

Do come and see us, we have got a bed – when you come – My love to you both.

Frieda

(I saw Ernst and children (not to speak to), Yes, I am more peaceful –)

791. To Harriet Monroe, 1 October 1914
Text: TMSC NWU; Huxley 208–9.

The Triangle, Bellingdon Lane, Chesham, Bucks.
1 Oct. 1914

Dear Harriet Monroe,

I'm glad to hear my 'Ophelia' shall go in whole – a great relief to me.[1] I could not bear that she should be cut through the middle, and the top half given to me and the lower half given to the world. Am I not her mother, you Solomon with the sword.[2]

Send me the draft here, to this God-forsaken little hole where I sit like a wise rabbit with my pen behind my ear, and listen to distant noises. I am not in the war zone. I think I am much too valuable a creature to offer myself to a German bullet gratis and for fun. Neither shall I go in for your war poem.[3] The nearest I could get to it would be in the vein of

> The owl and the pussy cat went to sea
> In a beautiful peagreen boat[4]

– and I know you wouldn't give me the hundred dollars.

I will let you know if I change my address.

Yours sincerely   D. H. Lawrence

---

[1] See p. 203 and n. 1   [2] See 1 Kings iii. 24–7.
[3] DHL is referring to 'the prize of one hundred dollars', offered in the September number of *Poetry* by anonymous donors, for the best war or peace poem 'based on the present European situation' (*Poetry*, v (November 1914), 93). The prize was awarded to Louise Driscoll for her poem called 'The Metal Checks' published in the November issue.
[4] The opening lines of 'The Owl and the Pussy-Cat' by Edward Lear (1812–88).

792. To S. S. Koteliansky, 5 October 1914

Text: MS BL; Postmark, Chesham 6 OC 14; Zytaruk, *Malahat* 19.

Bellingdon Lane, Chesham, Bucks
Oct 5 1914

Dear Kotilianski,

I ought to have written you before. I have been seedy and forced to stay in bed for a day or two, so I am not aimiable. It is nothing, but I hate to be unwell.

Will you really type-write me my book – which is supposed to be about Thomas Hardy, but which seems to be about anything else in the world but that. I have done about 50 pages – re-written them. I must get it typed somehow or other. Don't do it if it is any trouble – or if it is much trouble, for it is sure to be some. I should like a duplicate copy also.

When will you come and see us. The Murrys are taking a cottage two miles away.[1] I think they are coming down to stay with us for a week, whilst they make preparations. I should like to see you, and to know how you are. Frieda looks *so* nice in the shirt with the blue forgetmenots – she often wears it. Many regards from us –

auf wiedersehen   D. H. Lawrence

Remember me to Horne – How are things with him.

793. To J. B. Pinker, 5 October 1914

Text: MS UNYB; Unpublished.

Bellingdon Lane, Chesham, Bucks
5 Oct 1914

Dear Pinker,

Thank you for the cheque for £17 which came this morning. It comes just in good time.

Yours Sincerely   D. H. Lawrence

794. To S. S. Koteliansky, 8 October 1914

Text: MS BL; Postmark, Chesham 9 OC 14; Moore 292.

Bellingdon Lane, Chesham, Bucks
8 Oct 1914

My dear Kot,

We shall be glad to see you and Horne on Sunday. It is as well you didn'

[1] It was at the Lee near Great Missenden, about 3 miles away across the fields. Murry later wrote that Rose Tree Cottage 'was like a grey prison' (Murry, *Autobiography* 340).

come last week: I was in bed and very disagreeable. Now I am better and going to be quite cheerful.

I wonder what on earth you'll think of this stuff I want you to type. It will amuse me to know.

The Murrys will be here on Sunday. They will like meeting you and Horne in a quieter and more congenial place than the Café Royal.[1]

We shall expect you any time on Sunday, but dont be very late. I shall be glad to see you.

Auf wiedersehen   D. H. Lawrence

I partly agree about Gertler. It isn't potatoes, it is cooked onions: come dice lui.[2] But Frieda is very fond of him, so take care.

795. To Edward Garnett, 13 October 1914

Text: MS NYPL; Huxley 209–10.

Bellingdon Lane, *Chesham*, Bucks

13 Oct 1914.

Dear Garnett,

It is a long time since I have written, but the war puts a damper on ones own personal movement. It makes me feel very abstract, as if I and what I am did not matter very much.

What are you doing? Do you still go as usual to Duckworth's? – or is there not so much work to do?

The proofs of the stories keep on coming.[3] What *good* printers these Plymouth people are.[4] They never make a mistake. And how good my stories are, after the first two. It really surprises me. Shall they be called 'The Fighting Line'.[5] After all, this is the real fighting line, not where soldiers pull triggers.

We hear now and then from Germany: every German heart full of the altar-fire of sacrifice to the war: two of the Richthofen intimate officer-friends killed, 'der gute Udo von Henning ist am 7 Sept bei Chalons gefallen'[6] – that is the spirit. Frieda's father is very ill. She and I hardly quarrel any more.

An account of Kot's first meeting with Katherine Mansfield is given by Leonard Woolf. See Nehls, i. 258; see also Letter 776.   [2] 'according to him'.
The corrected page proofs (at NCL) show that signatures M and N are dated 12 October: these had presumably just arrived. Dates on earlier signatures suggest that DHL would probably have received six other batches of proofs since the beginning of the month.
William Brendon and Son Ltd, Plymouth.
The book referred to is *The Prussian Officer and Other Stories.*
'good Udo von Henning fell on Sept 7th near Chalons'. (On Frieda's relationship with von Henning see *Letters*, i. 404, 406.)

We have a little money – not much – *enough*. Pinker sold 'Honor and Arms' to America for £25,[1] and I had a little from the *Manchester Guardian*.[2] Here the autumn has been very beautiful. We are quite isolated, amid wide, grassy roads, with quantities of wild autumn fruit. This is curiously pale-tinted country, beautiful for the blueness and mists of autumn.

I have been writing my book more or less – very much less – about Thomas Hardy. I have done a third of it. When this much is typed I shall send it to Bertram Christian.

I wonder if you will come and see us. I should be very glad. It is not dear – there are cheap week-end tickets. And why doesn't David come?

Come for a week-end, will you? We have a bed. Any week-end after this next.

Our love to Mrs Garnett.

D. H. Lawrence

796. To S. S. Koteliansky, [14 October 1914]
Text: MS BL; PC; Postmark, Chesham 14 OC 14; Zytaruk 7.

Bellingdon
[14 October 1914]

Dear Kotilianski

I shan't come to London on Thursday, because I am still seedy. And Frieda won't come alone. So we shan't see you this week. But next week we shall most probably come for a day. Tell Horne.

au revoir   DHL

797. To Amy Lowell, 16 October 1914
Text: MS HU; cited in Damon 271–2.

Bellingdon Lane, *Chesham*, Bucks
16 Oct 1914

Dear Miss Lowell,

Over the type-writer I have got quite tipsy with joy: a frightfully heady bit of news.[3] Already my wife and I are pushing each other off the chair

---

[1] See p. 197 n. 2.
[2] DHL's contribution to the *Manchester Guardian*, 18 August 1914, was entitled 'With the Guns'. He was paid two guineas. For a detailed account and a reprinting of DHL's article, see Carl E. Baron, *Encounter*, xxxiii (August 1969), 5–6.
[3] Amy Lowell, in a letter to Harriet Monroe, 26 September 1914, explained her dilemma in wanting to assist DHL but being fearful of offending him: '...he is horribly poor, and of course he would not accept charity...I have racked my brains to think what I can do for him that he would take, and the only thing I can think of is to send him a typewriter which I am discarding, as I can make this appear that it is of no use to me, and he might just as well have it. He has not even been able to afford to buy a typewriter, which handicaps him very much in his work, as it is expensive to have typewriting done' (Damon 271).

and fighting as to who shall work it – the type-writer, I mean. I wonder when it will come: I wonder if it is already on the Atlantic: I wonder if it will be small enough for me to smuggle into Italy. I shall cherish it like a jewel. I always say that my only bit of property in the world is a silver watch – which is true. Now my realm is a type writer: I am a man of property: I feel quite scared lest I shall have incurred new troubles and new responsibilities. – But I hope it won't be very long in coming – the type writer – not the trouble – unberufen, unberufen.[1]

By the same post has come a cheque for £50, a grant to me from the Royal Literary Fund.[2] But that bores me. There is no joy in their tame thin-gutted charity. I would fillip it back at their old noses, the stodgy, stomachy authors, if I could afford it. But I can't.

We are curiously awaiting your book of poems.[3] You'll see me prowling through your verses like a beast of prey: and oh, the hyaena howl I shall send up when I seize on a lameness. You wait.

But for the Lord's sake, don't be modest, and say you'll listen to me. Disclaim me to start with, or I won't say anything at all.

And don't talk about putting me in the safe with Keats and Shelley. It scares me out of my life, like the disciples at the Transfiguration.[4] But I'd like to know Coleridge, when Chaaron has rowed me over.

It is good of you to see Kennerley. I don't want him ever to publish me anything ever any more as long as either of us lives. So you can say what you like to him. But I think that really he is rather nice. Just ask him about my things, will you: – no more. Pinker, my agent, is anxious to get me free from him, as there is an American publisher wants to make terms with Pinker for me.[5]

But I should be very glad of the short story arrangement, if Kennerley is off. I am having a book of stories published shortly by Duckworth. It will be called *The Prussian Officer and other Stories*, because it begins with that story I called 'Honor and Arms': which, by the way, is sold to the *Metropolitan Magazine*, in America. Also these stories need not go through my agent. If Houghtons would correspond with Duckworth, at 3 Henrietta

[1] 'touch wood!' (lit. 'unbidden, unbidden').

[2] This was the first grant that DHL received from the Royal Literary Fund during the war. For details regarding DHL's application to the RLF, see the next letter n. 4.

[3] *Sword Blades and Poppy Seed* (published on 22 September 1914).

[4] Matthew xvii. 2.

[5] The publisher was probably George H. Doran Company, New York. As early as 16 March 1914, the firm had confirmed its proposal to 'enter into contract for the next three books by D. H. Lawrence, terms to be £100 on account on each book, fifteen per cent to ten thousand and twenty per cent thereafter' (to J. B. Pinker, MS NYPL). In the event, Doran published none of DHL's books; see p. 610 n. 4.

St. Covent Garden – and if the Kennerley arrangement were off, then the thing could be settled most beautifully.[1]

We have had a beautiful dim autumn, of pale blue atmosphere and white stubble and hedges hesitating to change. But I've been seedy, and I've grown a red beard, behind which I shall take as much cover henceforth as I can, like a creature under a bush. My dear God, I've been miserable this autumn, enough to turn into wood, and be a graven image of myself.

I wish myself we could come in and drink wine and laugh with you, and hear some of other people's music. When I'm rich I shall come to America.

We may go back to Italy at the very end of the year, if we can get, and if I can get in a little more money, which of course I shall.

Greet Mrs Russell from us. I can feel her good will towards us very real over there.

Viele herzliche Grüsse, sehr-ge-ehrrte Frau.[2]

D. H. Lawrence

798. To Arthur Llewelyn Roberts, 16 October 1914
Text: MS RLFund; Unpublished.

Bellingdon Lane, *Chesham*, Bucks
16 Oct 1914

Dear Mr Roberts,[3]

Please let me thank the Literary Fund for the grant they have made me,[4]

---

[1] Nothing came of these tentative arrangements with Houghton Mifflin. When the *Prussian Officer* volume came out in America, it was under the imprint of Huebsch in 1916.

[2] 'Many cordial greetings, my dear madam.'

[3] Arthur Llewelyn Roberts (1855–1919), Secretary of the Royal Literary Fund from 1884 to his death. Educated at Eton and Magdalene College, Cambridge. Edmund Gosse believed that Roberts 'was singularly well fitted for the responsible position he held...he combined with real benevolence, a wide-awake shrewdness....He had the tact which perceives the nature of distress, and hastens to help, and yet not to wound, the sufferer' (Obituary, *Times* 18 October 1919).

[4] MSS in the possession of the Royal Literary Fund (and quoted here by permission) make it clear that DHL's application for financial assistance was sponsored by Maurice Hewlett. He submitted two letters (both written to himself) to reinforce his own support for DHL's case. One was from Harold Monro, editor of *Poetry and Drama*. He wrote on 12 September 1914 in the hope that DHL 'may receive some assistance as he is certainly a fine writer, and one who promises to do better and better'.

A second strong letter of support was addressed to Hewlett by Edward Marsh, also on 12 September: 'I am very glad to hear that you are trying to get a grant from the Royal Literary Fund for D. H. Lawrence. The remarkable quality of his three novels has been generally recognized. His poetry also shows an original and striking gift, and he has written a play of great promise. It would be a disaster if such a talent were to be cramped or starved I am sorry that Sir James Barrie is out of reach. He would certainly have supported the and you for the trouble you have taken on my behalf. Will you please send the books, *not* to the publishers, but here to me,[1]

Yours Sincerely   D. H. Lawrence

799. To Catherine Jackson, 21 October 1914
Text: MS YU; cited in Carswell, *Adelphi* 165–6.

Bellingdon Lane, Chesham, Bucks
21 Oct 1914

Dear Mrs Jackson,

How exciting your letter is! We are glad to hear you are going to marry Donald Carswell.[2] Your life will run on a stable pivot them, and you will be much happier. After all, one has a complete right to be happy. I only want to know people who have the courage to live. The dying resigned sort only bore me now. We are glad to have your news – soon we'll come and see you.

The Literary Fund gave me £50. I have got about £70 in the world now.

---

application, as he told me that he thought *Sons and Lovers* the best novel that he had read by any of the younger men.'

Gilbert Cannan wrote direct to the Committee: 'Mr Lawrence was on a visit to this country when the war broke out, his house being in Italy. Coming through Germany, he had left there two-thirds of a novel, a number of short stories, and a play on which he was working, meaning to pick them up on his return. He is unable to establish communications with his friends in Germany, and his relations here are poor and more likely to require help than to give it' (undated letter).

Both directly and indirectly, then, Hewlett had acted in response to Mary Cannan's supplication (see Letter 786). So had Alfred Sutro as appears in a letter (11 September) from the novelist and playwright, A. E. W. Mason (1865–1948), addressed to Llewelyn Roberts. It reads in part: 'A well-known author, D. H. Lawrence is, I understand at the present moment in some distress.

He has royalties coming to him, but has not got them yet. Mr. Sutro, realising the urgency of the case, writes to me that he has sent to him £10, since the Literary Fund Committee would not meet in time to enable them to give any assistance. Mr. Sutro asked me to look after it, but unfortunately I shall not be here, as I am going to America on Saturday. Could something be done about it?'

The application itself records that DHL's 'Present Means of Support' are 'money owed by *English Review* for an article, a sum on account from Methuen at a date uncertain and £3; 'Cause of Distress' is given as 'The War'.

[1] DHL had supplied the Royal Literary Fund with copies of his published books in support of his application for assistance. Article v of the 'Regulations in Regard to Applications for Relief' from the RLF stipulated that 'The Works upon which the Application is founded must therefore be submitted for examination'. DHL's works listed on the Application were the following: *The White Peacock* (London 1910), *The Trespasser* (London 1912), *Sons and Lovers* (London 1913), *The Widowing of Mrs Holroyd* (London 1914) and *Love Poems and Others* (London 1913).

[2] The marriage took place 'early in January' 1915 (Carswell 27).

Of this I owe £145 to the divorce lawyers, for costs claimed against me. This I am never going to pay. I also owe about £20 otherwise. So I've got some £50. If you think the other fund would give me any more – benissimo, I'll take it like a shot.[1] Have not I earned my whack – at least enough to live on – from this nation.

We should like to come to London one day next week, – say Tuesday – or Thursday – and stay one night at your house. We should like to do that very much. But tell us if it would be easy.

Oh, by the way – I was seedy and have grown a beard. I think I look hideous, but it is so warm and complete, and such a clothing to ones nakedness, that I like it and shall keep it. So when you see me don't laugh.

Many nice regards   D. H. Lawrence

800. To S. S. Koteliansky, [24 October 1914]
Text: MS BL; Postmark, Chesham 24 OC 14; Zytaruk 8.

Bellingdon Lane, Chesham, Bucks
Saturday

Dear Kot,

I am sorry you have been expecting us and we have not turned up. I am better in health, though this English autumn gives me a cough. This week we have been helping the Murrys to move in to their cottage. We have painted and plastered and distempered and God knows what. The place is

[1] On the matter of 'the other fund', Catherine Carswell later wrote: 'Donald [Carswell] was at this time on the staff of *The Times*, working in the same department with Mr. F. S. Lowndes, husband of Mrs. Belloc-Lowndes. Finding that Donald was acquainted with Lawrence, Mr. Lowndes, a kindly man, expressed great interest and, on learning that Lawrence was very hard up, great sympathy. He hinted that something further might be done out of a fund in which his wife had some say, and added that Mrs. Belloc-Lowndes would be very glad to have an opportunity of meeting this remarkable young man. On hearing all this from Donald I at once invited Mrs. Belloc-Lowndes to come to my house and meet Mr. and Mrs. D. H. Lawrence....But the literary fund which she was supposed to represent had melted in an explanatory haze. When we were left alone Lawrence indulged in some pithead language' (Carswell 25–6).

Marie Adelaide Belloc Lowndes (1868–1947), the wife of F. S. A. Lowndes (1868–1940), was the sister of Hilaire Belloc. She was a novelist and playwright. In 1914 she was also a member of the Council of the Society of Authors, and a member of its Committee of Management. She may well have known that DHL's application for assistance had come before the 'War Emergency Fund Administrative Sub Committee' and that the Society's Secretary, G. Herbert Thring, had written a letter about the application to the Secretary of the Royal Literary Fund. The Society of Authors was concerned lest 'the two Funds overlap', and by 7 October 1914 it was already aware of Alfred Sutro's donation of £10 to DHL. The Literary Fund awarded DHL £50 at its meeting on 14 October 1914; the Society of Authors was doubtless informed of that fact; and this probably explains why DHL's application failed Catherine Carswell's strictures against Mrs Belloc Lowndes were, then, perhaps unwarranted

now almost ready. They move in on Monday.[1] They have been staying here these 10 days.

Thank you very much for doing the typing. I don't want you to send the MS.[2] Either I am coming to London early next week, or you must come here. Could you not come one day during the week, and stay the night.

O, and a lady in America has sent me a type writing machine. It is now on the way from Liverpool.[3] You must tell me all about it when it comes, and when you come.

If I cant get to London next week, could you come here – Tuesday or Wed. or Thursday.

Very many regards   D. H. Lawrence

801. To S. S. Koteliansky, 26 October 1914

Text: MS BL; Postmark, Chesham 27 OC 14; Zytaruk 9.

Bellingdon Lane, Chesham, Bucks
26 Oct 1914

Dear Kot,

We are coming to London on Thursday, staying a night – or two nights – with Mrs Jackson. Ring us up at her house somewhere about tea-time on Thursday – she is at Holly Bush House, Hampstead. Then we will go to some music, if possible. I want very much to hear some music. That would be Thursday evening. Tell Horne.

I am looking forward to seeing you. I have not yet shaved. Many greetings from my wife.

Yours   D. H. Lawrence

802. To J. B. Pinker, 29 October 1914

Text: TMSC Lazarus; Unpublished.

Bellingdon Lane, Chesham, Bucks.
29 Oct. 1914.

Dear Pinker,

I don't feel quite in the humour for tackling the novel just now.[4] I suppose

---

[1] Of this move to Rose Tree Cottage Murry wrote: 'On October 26th, 1914, we moved in, without enthusiasm. It went against the grain to return to a part of the country where we had lived before' (Murry, *Autobiography* 305).

[2] See Letter 792.

[3] Amy Lowell's typewriter reached Liverpool in the care of the chief steward of *S.S. Laconia* (Damon 271). It reached DHL in early November; see Letter 806.

[4] *The Rainbow.*

it will do just as well in a months time. Then I'll go over the whole thing thoroughly.

Yes, I got £50 from the Royal Literary Fund, which will last me a while.

I have heard nothing yet from Kennerl[e]y, but I must hear in a little while from Amy Lowell, who is calling on him on my behalf in New York.

Yours sincerely   D. H. Lawrence

803. To S. S. Koteliansky, 31 October 1914
Text: MS BL; Zytaruk, *Malahat* 19–20.

Bellingdon Lane, Chesham, Bucks
31 Oct 1914

Dear Kot,

I send you some MS. You must tell me more particularly what you think of it.[1]

When I went down Wardour Street I saw a necklace I wanted to buy for Frieda. It is in a shop almost at the south end of Wardour St near Leicester Square, on the right hand side going down – S – a second hand jeweller's – a necklace of lapis lazuli set in little white enamel clasps – costs 30/-. It hangs up at eye level near the doorway. I send you a cheque. If you find the necklace, please buy it me. – round beads of lapis lazuli – you can't mistake it – marked 30/-

[drawing of necklace]

If you dont find it you can give me back the cheque.

I hope to see you soon again.

Many regards from us.   D. H. Lawrence

Mind you endorse the cheque just as I have entered it   S. Kotiliansk

804. To Catherine Jackson, 31 October 1914
Text: MS YU; cited in Carswell, *Adelphi* 167.

Bellingdon Lane, Chesham, Buck
31 Oct 19

Dear Mrs Jackson,

Thank you so much for having us down. I like to stay with you – you a a perfect hostess. Please don't think me a fool or conceited for my tirades

---

[1] DHL's book on Thomas Hardy.
[2] The occasion for one tirade might have been his meeting with Mrs Belloc Lowndes; s p. 226 n. 1.

I send you a cheque for 22/-. Please give the florin to your maid, for me, and tell her I had no change.

Tell us when you can come down to see us – we shall be glad.

tutti saluti da noi   D. H. Lawrence

805. To S. S. Koteliansky, 5 November 1914

Text: TMS BL; Postmark, [...] 5 NOV 14; Zytaruk 11.

Bellingdon Lane, Chesham, Bucks.

5 Nov. 1914

Dear Kot,

The necklace came this morning, much joy in the house. Thank you very much for getting it. Why do you never say whether you like a thing or not? I think it's pretty.

Why does my typewriter print double, have you any idea? You will see I am quite an expert typist, but very slow indeed. I, however, use all my fingers.

My typewriter is a Smith's Premier, No. 2. I think it is a good one, but it distresses me much by printing double. I suppose I tap it wrong.

I dont think Vera Volkhovsky will come on Saturday as she has not written. Will you and Horne come down for the weekend? One of you must sleep at the inn. If Miss Volkhovsky writes to say she is coming, I will let you know, and you will come only for the day, on Sunday.

What do you think of my MSS? – have you read it?

Tutti saluti dalla Frieda

Yrs.   D. H. Lawrence

806. To David Garnett, 5 November 1914

Text: TMS NYPL; Moore 293–4.

Bellingdon Lane, Chesham, Bucks

5 Nov 1914

My Dear Bunny,

I am very sorry I hadnt realised you expected us today. We cant come, because Helen Dudley is here for a couple of days.[1] DONT be angry, will you? Frieda is also sorry.

Helen Dudley, daughter of Dr Emelius C. Dudley, had had an affair with Bertrand Russell when he stayed with her parents in Chicago, May 1914. She came to England in August expecting to marry Russell, but he changed his mind. Various subterfuges were employed to break her tenuous hold on Russell and to keep her out of his way (see Ronald W. Clark, *The Life of Bertrand Russell*, 1975, pp. 236–41). David Garnett believed that Gilbert Cannan was probably instrumental in arranging for Helen Dudley to stay with the Lawrences. For a description of her by Lady Ottoline Morrell (then Russell's mistress) see *Ottoline at Garsington* 98; for Russell's own account of the relationship with Helen Dudley, see his *Autobiography*, i. 212–14.

You might like HELEN DUDLEY. She is an American girl, daughter of a very clever Chicago surgeon, and she has herself written two rather good plays.[1] She goes back to America in about a fortnight, I think, but if you have another reading before that is out, you might ask her to come. She is rather quiet in London. She is a jolly nice girl.

I want you to come here, and I very much want NEWTH to come also.[2] I suppose you couldnt come for the day on Sunday? I wish you could, you and Newth. LET me know, and if it cant be Sunday, then come one day in the week, next week.

Amy Lowell sent me this typewriter, so I amuse myself typing my letters.

We cant afford to come much to London, but we'd like to come once to your reading-club.[3] You can get a day or weekend ticket for 2/4 on SUNDAY, any train – also Tuesday and Thursday, I believe.

Much love from us   D. H. Lawrence

Miss Dudleys address is 4 Lansdowne Place, Russell Square. Send her a line if you would like to have her at your reading.

807. To S. S. Koteliansky, [8 November 1914]

Text: MS BL; Postmark, Chesham 8 NO 14; Zytaruk 12.

Bellingdon, Chesham, Bucks
Sunday

Dear Kot,

Horne and his wife and Lewis came today. Lewis made me very depressed because of the war. He is much nicer.

Horne says he will probably come next Sunday. So if you would rather come alone, choose one of the days in the week when you can get a cheap ticket – Tuesday, I think – and come down and stay a night. Decide for yourself.

---

[1] The plays have not been identified.

[2] H. G. Newth was a demonstrator in the Zoological Department at the Royal College of Science, which David Garnett attended. Garnett wrote: Newth was 'my closest friend for the rest of the time that I was at the Royal College of Science...[he] was a powerful influence in my development as a science student' (Garnett, *The Golden Echo*, p. 228). Newth had first met DHL and Frieda at a dinner given by Garnett in his father's flat at 19 Pond Place (Garnett, *The Flowers of the Forest*, 1955, p. 3).

[3] David Garnett recalled: 'Early in October 1914, we held the first of the weekly play-reading which Frankie Birrell had planned at our Cornish camp. We called ourselves the Caroline Club as, at first, we met in a little house in Caroline Place to which Hugh Popham and Brynhild Olivier had moved a year after their marriage.... We greatly enjoyed our readings. The company consisted of Hugh Popham...Arthur Waley, Justin Brooke, James Strachey, Frankie and myself. The women were my oldest friends and childhood playmates, Hugh's wife Brynhild and her three sisters, Margery, Daphne and Noel Olivier. Much of the success of the readings was due to Frankie, who had a gift for allotting the parts' (*Flowers of the Forest*, pp. 5–6).

You should have sent me your long foolish letter, as you call it. It is very weak to write a letter and then not to send it.

Write and say when you will come – any time –

Regards from Frieda and me. D. H. Lawrence

808. To S. S. Koteliansky, 11 November 1914

Text: MS BL; Postmark, Chesham 11 NO 14; Zytaruk, *Malahat* 20.

Bellingdon Lane, Chesham, Bucks
11 Nov 1914

My dear Kot,

But why this curtness? What ails you? Are you cross or offended, or have you got a 'bad mood' – which is it?

Why can't you come down? Why are you so silly? Why don't you say what's amiss? Is it Slatkowsky, or Horne, or just yourself?[1]

If I replied to you in your own terms, I should send you a letter like this:

> Bellingdon Lane
> Chesham
> Bucks
> 11 Nov. 1914
>
> My dear Kot,
>
> ?
>
> Kindest Regards from Frieda
> Yours Sincerely D. H. Lawrence

Enquire of Horne if he is coming at the week end, and if he is not, you come then. And please tell me what's amiss, and don't be a chump –

au revoir D. H. Lawrence

809. To S. S. Koteliansky, [13 November 1914]

Text: MS BL; PC; Postmark, Chesham 13 NO 14; Zytaruk 13.

Bellingdon
[13 November 1914]

Caro mio,

Ti aspetto Domenicà – tanto piacere vederti.

D. H. Lawrence

Dear Friend,

I'll see you on Sunday – so much pleasure to see you.]

R. S. Slatkowsky (d. 1918) was the proprietor of the Russian Law Bureau at 212 High Holborn; he was Kot's employer when DHL met Kot. For further details about the Russian Law Bureau, see Zytaruk xvii–xviii.

810. To Harriet Monroe, 17 November 1914
Text: TMSC NWU; cited in Monroe 91.

Bellingdon Lane, Chesham, Bucks.
17 Nov. 1914

Dear Harriet Monroe:

Yesterday came your cheque for £8. Thank you very much.

Today came the War Number of *Poetry*, for which also I thank you.[1] It put me into such a rage – how dare Amy talk about bohemian glass and stalks of flame?[2] – that in a real fury I had to write my war poem, because it breaks my heart, this war.

I hate, and hate, and hate the glib irreverence of some of your contributors – Aldington with his 'do you know what it's all about, brother Jonathan, we don't?'[3] It is obvious he doesn't. And your nasty, obscene, vulgar in the last degree – 'Hero' – John Russell McCarthy – may God tread him out – why did you put him in?[4] You shouldn't.

At least I like the woman who wrote 'Metal Checks'[5] – her idea, her attitude – but her poetry is pretty bad. I rather like the suggestion of Marian Ramie's 'Face I shall never see – man I shall never see'.[6] And 'Unser Gott' isn't bad – but unbeautifully ugly.[7] Your people have such little pressure their safety valve goes off at the high scream when the pressure is still so low. Have you no people with any force in them. Aldington almost shows most – if he weren't so lamentably imitating Hueffer.

I don't care what you do with my war poem.[8] I don't particularly care

---

[1] *Poetry*, v (November 1914) which bore the sub-title 'Poems of War'.
[2] DHL is alluding to a passage in Amy Lowell's piece of prose-poetry, 'The Bombardment'. 'Boom! The Cathedral is a torch, and the house next to it begins to scorch. Boom! The Bohemian glass on the étagère is no longer there. Boom! A stalk of flame sways against the red damask curtains. The old lady cannot walk. She watches the creeping stalk and counts Boom! – Boom! – Boom!'
[3] From Richard Aldington's poem, 'War Yawp':

Who can tell the end of this war?
And say, brother Jonathan,
D'you know what it's all about?
Let me whisper you a secret – we don't!

[4] 'The Hero' by John Russell McCarthy describes a troop of soldiers entering the house of 'a man and wife, three daughters – and a dog'. The soldiers cut the old man's throat, tie up the wife and force her to look on while they rape all three daughters. Later the mother and daughters are also slaughtered, and the soldiers take the dog with them for a mascot.
[5] By Louise Driscoll (1875–1957); see p. 219 n. 3.
[6] From the poem, 'Chant of the Shroud Maker'.
[7] By Karle Wilson Baker (1878–1960).
[8] DHL's 'war poem' was first identified as 'Eloi, Eloi, Lama Sabachthani?' published in *Egoist*, ii (1 May 1915), 75–6. (See E. W. Tedlock, Jr, 'A Forgotten War Poem by D. H. Lawrence', *Modern Language Notes*, lxvii (June 1952), 410–13.) The version which DHL sent to Harriet

if I don't hear of it any more. The war is dreadful. It is the business of the artist to follow it home to the heart of the individual fighters – not to talk in armies and nations and numbers – but to track it home – home – their war – and it's at the bottom of almost every Englishman's heart – the war – the desire of war – the *will* to war – and at the bottom of every German's.

Don't put common things in like the 'Campfollower'[1] – why do you? They are only ugly ugly – 'putrid lips' – it is something for the nasty people of this world to batten on.

I typed my poem on a typewriter Amy Lowell gave me. I think I did it quite well – and it was thrilling. I like it when you send me *Poetry*, even if it makes me rage.

Vale.   D. H. Lawrence

Take care how you regard my war poem – it is good.

811. To S. S. Koteliansky, 18 November 1914

Text: MS BL; Postmark, Chesham 19 NO 14; Zytaruk 14.

Bellingdon Lane, Chesham, Bucks
18 Nov. 1914

Dear Kot,

We may be coming up to London this week-end – Frieda *must* see the dentist. If he gives us an appointment for Saturday, as I have written to ask him to do, we shall be down till Monday. I want very much to go to the National Gallery, and, on a fine day, to the Zoo.

I hope you don't mind my tirades of Sunday. Don't say you will never abuse people any more. It is so nice when you abuse people. But don't avoid everybody, and annihilate him straight off. You must give yourself to people more, and take them as they are.

The Murrys said yesterday how much they like you. They want you to come to their Christmas party. You must come here at Christmas.

I have qualms when I think of you typing my MS. I am afraid you hate it, and I had no right to foist it on you. I am sorry. But then you don't do anything, do you, otherwise?

Monroe was, however, different from that published in *Egoist*. In the UChi *Poetry* collection is an autograph MS (probably written by Harriet Monroe) of a poem entitled 'Passages from *Ecce Homo*', which appears to be an early version of 'Eloi, Eloi, Lama Sabachthani?'. For a comparison of these two versions and the publication of the former, see Alvin Sullivan, 'D. H. Lawrence and *Poetry: The Unpublished Manuscripts*', *DHL Review*, ix (Summer 1976), 269–70.   [1] By Maxwell Bodenheim (1895–1954).

I have written my war poem, which everybody will think bosh. What do
you think of my MS?

Tante belle cose from Frieda and me.

a rivederti – D. H. Lawrence

812. To Amy Lowell, 18 November 1914
Text: MS HU; Damon 277–9.

Bellingdon Lane, Chesham, Bucks
18 Nov 1914

Dear Amy Lowell,

The type-writer has come, and is splendid. Why did you give it away? – I
am sure you must have wanted to keep it. But it goes like a bubbling pot,
frightfully jolly. My wife sits at it fascinated, patiently spelling out, at this
moment, my war poem.

Oh – the War Number of *Poetry* came – I thought it pretty bad. The
war-atmosphere has blackened here – it is soaking in, and getting more like
part of our daily life, and therefore much grimmer. So I was quite cross with
you for writing about bohemian glass and stalks of flame, when the thing
is so ugly and bitter to the soul.[1]

I like *you* in your poetry. I don't believe in affecting France.[2] I like you
when you are straight out. I really liked very much 'The Precinct,
Rochester'.[3] There you had a sunny, vivid, intensely still atmosphere that
was very true. I dont like your first long poem a bit.[4] I think 'A Taxi' is
very clever and futuristic – and good.[5] I like the one about the dog looking
[in] the window – good.[6]

Why don't you always be yourself. Why go to France or anywhere else
for your inspiration. If it doesn't come out of your own heart, real Amy
Lowell, it is no good, however many colours it may have. I wish one saw
more of your genuine strong, sound self in this book, full of common-sense
and kindness and the restrained, almost bitter, Puritan passion. Why do you
deny the bitterness in your nature, when you write poetry? Why do you take
a pose? It causes you always to shirk your issues, and find a banal resolution

---

[1] See p. 232 n. 2.

[2] In her Preface to *Sword Blades and Poppy Seed* Amy Lowell admits her 'immense debt to
the French, and perhaps above all to the, so-called, Parnassian School'.

[3] The poem first appeared in *Egoist*, February 1914. It had been reprinted in *Sword Blades
and Poppy Seed*, a copy of which Amy Lowell had sent to DHL. All the poems subsequently
mentioned in this letter were collected in that volume.

[4] 'Sword Blades and Poppy Seed' which occupied the first 25 pages of the book.

[5] 'The Taxi' (first printed in *Egoist*, August 1914).

[6] 'Fool's Money Bags'. (DHL's MS reads: 'looking the'.)

at the end. So your romances are spoiled. When you are full of your own strong gusto of things, real old English strong gusto it is, like those tulips,[1] then I like you very much. But you shouldn't compare the sun to the yolk of an egg, except playfully.[2] And you shouldn't spoil your story-poems with a sort of vulgar, artificial 'flourish of ink'. If you had followed the real tragedy of your man, or woman, it had been something.

I suppose you think me damned impertinent. But I hate to see you posturing, when there is thereby a real person betrayed in you.

Please don't be angry with what I say. Perhaps it really is impertinence.

At any rate, thank you very much for your book of poems, which I like because after all they have a lot of you in them – but how much nicer, finer, bigger you are, intrinsically, than your poetry is. Thank you also very much for the beautiful typewriter, with which both myself and my wife are for the present bewitched.

We are still staying on here – scarcely find it possible to move. It is cold, as you predict, but I think quite healthy. I am well, and Frieda is well. I am just finishing a book, supposed to be on Thomas Hardy, but in reality a sort of Confessions of my Heart.[3] I wonder if ever it will come out – and what you'd say to it.

I wonder if you saw Mitchell Kennerley. Pinker, the agent, is always worrying me about what he is to do with the American publishing of the novel Kennerley holds at present, in MS.[4] Tell me if you saw him, will you.

We are not so sad any more: it was perhaps a mood, brought on by the war, and the English autumn. Now the days are brief but very beautiful: a big red sun rising and setting upon a pale, bluish, hoar-frost world. It is very beautiful. The robin comes on to the door-step now, and watches me as I write. Soon he will come indoors. Then it will be mid-winter.

I wish the war were over and gone. I will not give in to it. We who shall live after it are more important than those who fall.

Give our very warm regards to Mrs Russell.

Saluti di cuore   D. H. Lawrence

Tante belle cose from my wife to you and to Mrs Russell.

In 'A Tulip Garden'.
The lines which might possibly have prompted this remark occur in 'The Shadow':

> With the first twilight he struck a match
> And watched the little blue stars hatch
> Into an egg of perfect flame.

See p. 243 and n. 4.
The Rainbow in its original form which DHL had sent to Mitchell Kennerley from Fiascherino.

813. To J. C. Squire, 19 November 1914
Text: MS Anon.; Unpublished.

Bellingdon Lane, Chesham, Bucks
19 Nov 1914.

Dear Squire,

Thank you for the MS of the Tyrol Sketch you sent me. I quite understand it is unsuitable: that is why I never sent you the other half of it.[1]

I have at last been moved, by [...] indignation at the usual cant, to write
a war poem.[2] And since you seem the only place where a bit of dignity
remains, I send it you. If you don't like it – it is very natural if you don't – I
am not offended. I am not very anxious for it to be published to the fools
that be.

Some time when I am in London, I will look in to your office, to see you.
I should like to.

Yours Sincerely   D. H. Lawrence

I liked Bernard Shaw's pamphlet.[3]

814. To S. S. Koteliansky, [20 November 1914]
Text: MS BL; PC; Postmark, Chesham 20 NO 14; Zytaruk 15.

[Bellingdon Lane, Chesham, Bucks]
[20 November 1914]

Arrive Baker St. at 11·43 – I shall go straight to Hornes. Frieda sees dentist
in Harley St. at 12·15.[4] She'll go there direct. Gertler will ring up Law
Bureau tomorrow afternoon to tell us about going to see his studio. We'd
like to go Sunday afternoon to tea.

Auf wiedersehen   D. H. Lawrence

815. To William Hopkin, 24 November 1914
Text: MS NCL; cited in Pollak, *Journal of Modern Literature*, iii. 28.

Bellingdon Lane, Chesham, Bucks
24 Nov 1914

---

[1] The 'Sketch' was 'A Chapel Among the Mountains', which Douglas Clayton sent to the
New Statesman. See Letter 771. The 'other half' refers to the sequel 'A Hay Hut Among
the Mountains'.   [2] See p. 232 n. 8.
[3] 'Common Sense About the War', published as a thirty-two page *Supplement to The New
Statesman*, 14 November 1914. Shaw summarised the article as follows: 'In it I point out
that if soldiers were wise they would shoot their officers and return home to mind their own
business; that if citizens were wise they would refuse to pay for diplomatic wars; and that
the possibility, however remote, of these things happening acts as an unmentioned limit to
war' (*What I Really Wrote About the War*, in *The Works of Bernard Shaw*, 1930, xxi. vii)
[4] Her dentist was Hugh T. Campkin at 71 Harley Street.

Dear Will,

We are thinking, Frieda and I, of coming to Nottingham – or to Ripley – on Saturday week, staying till Wednesday. Frieda wants to see her husband – the first one, that is. Will you ask Enid to tell us if Professor Weekley still leaves the University at 5.0 oclock on Tuesdays and Mondays, as he used. Frieda wants to meet him as he leaves in the evening.

If you are at home, we want to come and see you. We are here in this little cottage, very poor because of the war, unable to return to Italy, enduring our souls in patience. It is pretty here – and you must come to see us, or let Mrs Hopkin come if you can't. This is not too far.

Frieda sends her love, with mine, to Mrs Hopkin and Enid. Oh, by the way, I've let my beard grow – it looks hideous, but I like it. So don't be shocked at all.

Auf Wiedersehen   D. H. Lawrence

816. To S. S. Koteliansky, [27 November 1914]
Text: MS BL; PC; Postmark, Chesham 27 NO 14; Zytaruk 15.

Bellingdon
[27 November 1914]

Dear Kot,

We expect you on Saturday – stay till Monday. If it is perfectly easy will you bring my tooth-brush which I left in Horne's bedroom. If it is any trouble at all, don't bother – it is of no matter. You'll see the Murry's tomorrow.

Love   D. H. Lawrence

Excuse the post card – it is the only one I've got.[1]
Come early tomorrow afternoon.   DHL

817. To David Garnett, 30 November 1914
Text: MS NYPL; Unpublished.

Bellingdon Lane, Chesham – Bucks.
30 Nov. 1914

Dear Bun,

We were glad to hear from you. You are a scanty letter-writer.

It is probable that Frieda is going to Nottingham next Sunday, to stay until Wednesday. I shall not go.

---

[1] DHL erased his earlier, incomplete text on the postcard:

111 Arthur Street
Chelsea S.W.

October 3 1914
Dear Sir,
    Will you kindly send me more particulars on the two cottages you advertise

The Arthur Street address was where Murry and Katherine Mansfield stayed prior to their move to Rose Tree Cottage.

When are you coming to the Cannans'? I wish you would put me up for
the three nights, at Pond Place, can you?¹ If not, would Newth do you think,
now he has a flat?

If you are staying in Cholesbury over Sunday night, then I will sleep here
on Sunday and go down with you on Monday.

When you are here – I wish were you coming on Saturday – we will go
over and see the Murrys in their cottage – with Birrell.²

If Mary Cannan did not ask you for Saturday night, will you sleep here
on Saturday night, and Birrell at the Bull? That is very easy.

I was sorry you had neuralgia. Don't have neuralgia. I wish you had been
at the Horne's party that night.

Write and tell me what you are doing exactly this week-end. Frieda leaves
Sunday morning.

She sends her love – I mine. And remember us to Birrell. – I did enjoy
Newth and the Zoo.

D. H. Lawrence

Don't put yourself out for me.

818. To S. S. Koteliansky, [3 December 1914]
Text: MS BL; Postmark, Chesham 4 DE 14; Moore 295–6.

Bellingdon Lane
Thursday

Dear Kot,

I am most probably going to Nottingham with Frieda after all. I don't
think she wants to go alone.

You mustn't judge her lightly. There is another quality in woman that
you do not know, so you can't estimate it. You don't know that a woman
is not a man with different sex. She is a different world. You do not
understand that enough. Your world is all of one hemisphere.

We laughed at you for your pennyworth of good deeds which were stolen
from you.

¹ The Garnetts had moved from Downshire Hill in 1913 and taken 'a maisonette at 19 Pond
Place, Fulham Road' in South Kensington. David Garnett stated that the move was made so
that he 'could be near the Imperial College of Science' (Garnett, *The Golden Echo*, p. 235).
(This note corrects a detail in *Letters*, i. 297 n. 2.)
² Francis ('Frankie') Frederick Locker Birrell (1889–1935), a close friend of David Garnett,
and the son of the barrister, essayist and statesman Augustine Birrell (1850–1933), who was
Chief Secretary to the Lord Lieutenant of Ireland (1907–16). Francis Birrell was educated
at Eton and King's College, Cambridge. During the war he worked with the Friends War
Victims Relief Mission in France. Afterwards with David Garnett, he opened a bookshop;
then became a journalist, biographer and drama critic. Above all he was a conversationalist.
(See Garnett, *Great Friends*, pp. 83, 86–91; for obituary see *Times*, 4 January 1935.)

Do please get my typing done. If I can send it in, I may get a little money for it.

I thank you for getting Frieda into a good state of mind. She says it was absolutely the result of seeing how utterly wrong you were when you talked to her. So beware. Nevertheless things are very good again.

I am working *frightfully* hard – rewriting my novel.[1]

I shall see you very soon, even if I go to Nottingham – whence we return Wednesday night.

Love from us   D. H. Lawrence

Don't tumble out of the attic into the cellar.

By the way, the wind blew our attic window clean out – such a wind.

819. To David Garnett, [4 December 1914]

Text: MS NYPL; Unpublished.

Bellingdon Lane, Chesham, Bucks
Friday.

Dear Bunny,

Don't arrange anything for me, if you haven't yet done so. Frieda wants me to go to Nottingham with her. I'm sorry to change.

We are dining tomorrow with you at the Cannans – shall be glad to see you and Birrell there.

Love from us   D. H. Lawrence

820. To S. S. Koteliansky, 5 December 1914

Text: MS BL; Zytaruk 17.

Bellingdon Lane, Chesham, Bucks
5 Dec 1914

Dear Kot,

I send you the last of the MS.[2] Tell me if you get it all right. I am going to Nottingham till Wednesday. But probably next week we shall be coming

---

The Rainbow.

A puzzling remark. It suggests that Kot was asked to type the entire MS of the first version of the book on Hardy. But on 18 December (Letter 826) DHL tells Amy Lowell that he and Frieda 'type away at my book on Thomas Hardy'. It is therefore not clear whether Kot for some reason did not finish the typing and DHL and Frieda had to complete it; or whether DHL – fascinated by the gift from Amy Lowell – was already revising his text and using the typewriter for the purpose. If the latter was the case, the remark in this letter is no longer puzzling: it means what it obviously says.

to London for a day or two, with the Murrys, staying in Campbell's house – he is in Ireland. I'll let you know.

The weather is hideous. I've got a headache. Frieda shakes her fist in your direction. I hope you are still happy.

Many regards from us.

Yours   D. H. Lawrence

821. To J. B. Pinker, 5 December 1914
Text: MS UNYB; cited in Carswell 21, 27.

Bellingdon Lane, *Chesham*, Bucks
5 Dec 1914

Dear Pinker,

I send you the first hundred or so pages of my novel, which I am writing over.[1] It needs the final running through. It is a beautiful piece of work, really. It will be, when I have finished it: the body of it is so now.

I began to type it. But it took me hours, and I am too busy writing. So I left off. Is there any need to have it typed at all, the MS.? I never did for Duckworth. But if it must be done, will you have it done for me.

I am glad of this war. It kicks the pasteboard bottom in the usual 'good' popular novel. People have felt much more deeply and strongly these last few months, and they are not going to let themselves be taken in by 'serious' works whose feeling is shallower than that of the official army reports. Mackenzie was a fool not to know that the times are too serious to bother about his *Sinister Street* frippery.[2] Folk will either read sheer rubbish, or something that has in it as much or more emotional force as the newspaper has in *it* today. I am glad of the war. It sets a slump in trifling. If Lucas reads my novel, he ought to *know* how good it is. And he ought to respect it.[3]

I shall finish the thing by the end of January – perhaps earlier. I will send it to you as I do it – 100 pages at a time. Then, if at the end of January

---

[1] This autograph MS of *The Rainbow* is in the Humanities Research Center, the University of Texas at Austin. See David Farmer, 'A Descriptive and Analytical Catalogue of the D. H. Lawrence Collection at the University of Texas at Austin' (Unpublished Ph.D Dissertation, 1970), Item A40, p. 41.

[2] The second volume of Mackenzie's novel appeared in November 1914 (the first in September 1913).

[3] Edward Verrall Lucas (1868–1938), essayist, editor and anthologist. In 1900 he had been commissioned by Methuen to edit the works and write a life of Charles Lamb, and he became very closely associated with the publishing house, first as a reader, and later, after Sir Algernon Methuen's death in 1914, Lucas became Chairman of the firm. It was presumably on his recommendation that Methuen undertook to publish *The Rainbow*.

Methuen will give me more money, I shall go to Italy. I am tired of this country, the war, the winter.

I hope all is well with your business. I hope your son is at home with you, not joining the army.[1] I hope you are quite well.

Yours Sincerely   D. H. Lawrence

The Rainbow is a better title than The Wedding Ring, particularly in these times. Garnett was a devil to call my book of stories *The Prussian Officer* – what Prussian Officer?[2]

822. To S. S. Koteliansky, [9 December 1914]

Text: MS BL; Postmark, Ripley 9 DE 14; Moore 297.

Ripley – Derbyshire
Wednesday

Dear Kot,

We are going back to Bellingdon tonight – tomorrow we go to Garnetts for two days. We shall come to tea with you tomorrow, if we may. No, rather you come to us, at half past four, in the Green Room in Piccadilly Circus. Garnett is taking us to the theatre in the evening – has booked for us I believe. – Frieda saw her husband – he was very dull – affected – quarrelsome – nothing decided. But we'll tell you tomorrow.

Love from us   D. H. Lawrence

823. To S. S. Koteliansky, [9 December 1914]

Text: MS BL; Postmark, Ripley 9 DE 14; Zytaruk 18.

Ripley – Derbyshire
Wednesday

Dear Kot,

We have missed our train so cannot go to Chesham. We shall come down tomorrow straight to London, arriving at Marylebone at 3·0 oclock. The dentist was making an appointment for Frieda, writing to Chesham. I have asked him to ring you up and leave the time with you, so don't be surprised if he calls you up – Mr Campkin. If you aren't busy, come to the station to meet us, will you? If you are busy, then Green Tea Room at 4·30.

Love   D. H. Lawrence

---

[1] Probably the elder son Eric Pinker.
[2] Contrast DHL's inoffensive remark about the title in Letter 797 with his vehemence here.

824. To David Garnett, [9 December 1914]
Text: MS NYPL; Moore 297.

Ripley – Derbyshire
Wednesday

Dear Bunn,

Frieda saw Ernst – he very affected – penny novelette – nothing definite done. We'll tell you.

We will come tomorrow if you still expect us. We have arranged to tea with Kotilianski in the Green Tea Room in Picadilly Circus at 4.30 tomorrow – I suppose you won't be there. The tea room is near the tube – near the Criterion – near the Haymarket – somewhere there. We'll be at Pond Place 5.30 or 6.0.

love from us – à demain   D. H. Lawrence

825. To S. S. Koteliansky, [17 December 1914]
Text: MS BL; Postmark, Chesham 18 DE 14; Zytaruk 19.

Bellingdon – Chesham – Bucks
Thursday

Dear Kot,

Please will you come down to stay with us next *Wednesday*. I am so busy writing my novel, and Frieda wants you to come and help her to prepare for our party, which is on the Thursday – Christmas Eve. We look forward to it immensely – to your coming to stay with us. Do please try to come on Wednesday.

How are you? You must be quite jolly when you come – but it doesn't matter, if you're sad we'll 'plainly beat you'.

Vale!   D. H. Lawrence

I must call you – what is it – Shimiel – Schmuel – it ends in 'el' like all the Angels – Chamuel, Jophiel, Zadkiel, Uriel, Gabriel.[1]

826. To Amy Lowell, 18 December 1914
Text: MS HU; Moore, *Intelligent Heart* 171–4.

The Triangle, Bellingdon Lane, *Chesham*, Bucks.
18 Dec 1914

---

[1] Only the angels Michael, Gabriel, Raphael and Uriel are named in the Bible. DHL probably recalled the rest of the names from his reading (see Letter 828) of Mrs Henry Jenner's book *Christian Symbolism* (1910): 'Chamuel (the wrath of God), the angel who wrestled with Jacob. He carries a cup and a staff. Jophiel (the Splendour of God), the angel who guarded the gate of Paradise. He bears a flaming sword. Zadkiel (the Justice of God), the angel who stayed the hand of Abraham. He carries a sacrificial knife' (p. 70).

My dear Amy Lowell,

The day before yesterday came your letter. You sound so sad in it. What had depressed you? – Your book of poems, that they perhaps are stupid about in the papers? But there, they are always like that, the little critics. If the critics are not less than the authors they criticise, they will at once burst into equal authorship. And being less than the authors they criticise, they must diminish these authors. For no critic can admit anything bigger than himself. And we are all, therefore, no bigger than our little critics. So don't be sad. The work one has done with all ones might is as hard as a rock, no matter how much one suffers the silly slings and arrows in one's silly soft flesh.

Thank you very much indeed for going to Mitchell Kennerley for me. I hope you are not serious when you say that in so doing you have spoiled the *Forum* for yourself as a publishing field.[1] Is Kennerley indeed such a swine? As for what he owes me – he does not send it, even if it is only ten pounds. I haven't kept proper accounts with him, because Duckworths made the agreement and all that. I will write to them. I also will write to Pinker, to see what he can do. I *must* get this novel out of Kennerley's[2] hands, that he has in MS.

I am re-writing it. It will be called *The Rainbow*. When it is done, I think really it will be a fine piece of work.

My book of Short stories is out.[3] I am sending you a copy. I dont think it is doing very well. The critics really hate me. So they ought.

My wife and I we type away at my book on Thomas Hardy, which has turned out as a sort of *Story of My Heart*:[4] or a Confessio Fidei: which I must write again, still another time: and for which the critics will plainly beat me, as a Russian friend says.[5]

It is Christmas in a week today. I am afraid you may not get this letter in time: which is a pity. We shall be in this cottage. We shall have a little party at Christmas Eve. I at once begin to prick up my ears when I think of it. We shall have a great time, boiling ham and roasting chickens, and drinking Chianti in memory of Italy. There will be eight of us, all nice people.[6] We shall enjoy ourselves afterwards up in the attics – You wait. I shall spend 25/- on the spree, and do it quite rarely.

England is getting real thrills out of the war, at last. Yesterday and today

[1] Mitchell Kennerley was the publisher of *Forum*.   [2] Kennerley's] Pinker's
[3] *The Prussian Officer and Other Stories*, on 26 November 1914.
[4] See p. 239 n. 2. For DHL's view of Richard Jefferies' *The Story of My Heart*, see *Letters*, i. 337, 353.   [5] Kot.
[6] For Frieda's recollection of this party see p. 252 n. 2.

there is the news of the shelling of Scarboro.[1] I tell you the whole country is thrilled to the marrow, and enjoys it like hot punch. – I shall make punch at our Christmas Eve party, up in the attics with a Primus Stove.

We have been in the Midlands seeing my people, and Frieda seeing her husband. He did it in the thorough music-hall fashion. It was a surprise visit. When we were children, and used to play at being grand, we put an old discarded hearthrug in the wheel-barrow, and my sister, perched there in state 'at home', used to be 'Mrs Lawson' and I, visiting with a walking stick, was 'Mr Marchbanks'. We'd been laughing about it, my sister and I. So Frieda, in a burst of inspiration, announced herself to the landlady as 'Mrs Lawson'.

'You – ' said the quondam husband, backing away – 'I hoped[2] never to see you again.'

Frieda: 'Yes – I know.'

Quondam Husband: 'And what are you doing in *this* town.'

Frieda: I came to see you about the children.

Quondam Husband: Aren't you ashamed to show your face where you are known? Isn't the commonest prostitute better than you?

Frieda: Oh no.

Quon. Husb.: Do you want to drive me off the face of the earth, Woman? Is there no place where I can have peace?[3]

Frieda: You see I must speak to you about the children.

Quon. Husb.: You shall *not* have them – they don't want to see you.

Then the conservation developed into a deeper tinge of slanging – part of which was:

Q.H.: '*If* you had to go away, why didn't you go away with a *gentleman*?'

Frieda: He is a *great* man.

Further slanging.

Q. Husb.: Don't you know you are the vilest creature on earth?

Frieda: Oh no.

A little more of such, and a departure of Frieda. She is no further to seeing her children.

Q. Husb.: Don't you know, my solicitors have instructions to arrest you, if you attempt to interfere with the children.

Frieda: I don't care.

If this weren't too painful, dragging out for three years, as it does, it would be very funny, I think. The Quondam Husband is a Professor of French Literature, great admirer of Maupassant, has lived in Germany and Paris,

---

[1] German warships shelled the coastal towns of Hartlepool, Whitby and Scarborough on 16 December 1914.

[2] I hoped] I never hoped   [3] can have peace] am safe

and thinks he is the tip of Cosmopolitan culture. But poor Frieda can't see her children. – I really give you the conversation verbatim.

It is very rainy and very dark. I shall try to get back to Italy at the end of January.

Give my sincere sympathy to Mrs Russell. I hope things aren't going *very* badly with her. All Christmas greetings to you.

D. H. Lawrence

I do wish we might have a Christmas party together. I feel like kicking everything to the devil and enjoying myself willy-nilly: a mild drunk and a great and rowdy spree.

[Frieda Lawrence begins]

It was rather mean of us to ask you to see Kennerley – But he is a pig – He gave Lawrence £25 for *Sons and Lovers*, promised him another £25, then arrived the bad cheque – Dont bother anymore, only he must not have the new novel, but Pinker can see to that – L. hates the whole business so much that he shouts at me every time he thinks of it! I feel a grudge against Kennerley not only has he done me out of £25, but every time L. thinks of *Kennerley*, he gets in a rage with *me*, the logic of men and husbands – You knew about my nice children and what I have had to go through – I wish I could tell you all about, you are so bighearted, we think of you with great affection, one of the few oasis' in this desert world! We will go to Italy soon, as soon as we have a little money – I hope you received our letters, when you wrote you had not got our last – Our Italy address is:

Lerici per Fiascherino, Golfo di Spezia

[Lawrence interjects: (but we're not gone yet).] I wish you could come and see us soon!

Yours with many good wishes   Frieda L –
Poor Mrs Russell what a horrid time for her!

[Lawrence continues]

I shall get some money in January all right.   DHL

---

827. To J. B. Pinker, 18 December 1914
Text: MS Forster; Unpublished.
The Triangle, Bellingdon Lane, Chesham – Bucks.

18 Dec 1914

Dear Pinker,

I send you the next instalment of the novel. I rather enjoy writing it again.

Amy Lowell went to see Kennerley. He seems very slippery. He says he owes me only £10·7·6. But even that he won't pay me. He won't write either. He told Amy he wants the love passages toning down in the novel: he had a duplicate MS.[1] Could I not refuse to do this – and then sell the altered novel to somebody else. I *don't* want him to have it. He is a slippery devil. Amy Lowell says his reputation is very bad. She says Ferris Greenslet of Houghton Mifflin Company[2] – 4 Park St. – Boston, Mass – is very enthusiastic about my books, and she tells me to send him the book of short stories. She[3] has talked to him about the short stories and he wants to see them. What shall we do – will you write to Duckworth, or shall I?

Amy Lowell said if I would send her my contract with Kennerley, and list of accounts, she would put it into the hands of one of her lawyers. But I don't want to – I think it is hardly worth it either.

I don't know what my agreement with Kennerley is, Duckworths did it. Have you asked them?

All Christmas Greetings, if I don't write to you again before the 25th.

Yours Sincerely   D. H. Lawrence

828. To Gordon Campbell, [20 December 1914]

Text: MS UCin; Moore, *Intelligent Heart* 174–8.

The Triangle – Bellingdon – Chesham – Bucks.
Sunday 19 Dec 1914.

Dear Campbell,

I was awfully glad to hear from the Murrys of the novel.[4] They are wildly enthusiastic about it. I am very anxious for it to come. I shall be very glad when you've really got expression.

But do, for God's sake, mistrust and beware of these states of exaltation and ecstasy. They send you, anyone, swaying so far beyond the centre of gravity in one direction, there is the inevitable swing back with greater velocity to the other direction, and in the end you exceed the limits of your own soul's elasticity, and go smash, like a tower that has swung too far.

---

[1] Kennerley's request may have been prompted by a report on 'The Wedding Ring' by his reader, Alfred Kuttner who wrote on 10 November 1914: '...Mr Lawrence sees sex too obsessively. You may find it a difficult task to persuade him of this because it bites so deeply into his own character. That he is laboring under terrible sexual morbidities is hardly to be doubted after reading his "Honour and Arms"' (MS LC).

[2] Ferris Greenslet (1875–1959) had been literary adviser to Houghton Mifflin from 1907 and a director since 1910. Later he became general manager and editor-in-chief.

[3] stories. She] stories, saying

[4] Campbell's novel was never published.

Besides, there is no real truth in ecstasy. All vital truth contains the memory of all that for which it is not true: Ecstasy achieves itself by virtue of *exclusion*; and in making any passionate exclusion, one has already put one's right hand in the hand of the lie.

I was sorry your man commits suicide in a pool. It is futile. If the Bishop – I haven't got it very clearly – but if the bishop, and the young doctor, know that the great sin, or weakness – sin, I think you said – is Egotism, then is the conclusion to be that the doctor commits the final act of egotism and vanity, and commits suicide? Or is that not the end? If you are making a great book on Egotism – and I believe you may – for God's sake give us the death of Egotism, not the death of the sinner. Russia, and Germany, and Sweden, and Italy, have done nothing but glory in the suicide of the Egoist. But the Egoist as a divine figure on the Cross, held up to tears and love and veneration, is to me a bit nauseating now, after Artzibasheff and D'Annunzio, and the Strindberg set, and the Manns in Germany.[1]

I think the greatest book I know on the subject is the Book of Job. Job was a great, splendid Egoist. But whereas Hardy and the moderns end with 'Let the day perish – ' or more beautifully – 'the waters wear the stones; thou washest away the things which grow out of the dust of the earth; thou destroyest the hope of man:

Thou prevailest for ever against him, and he passeth: [...] thou changest his countenance, and sendest him away.'[2] – the real book of Job ends – 'Then Job answered the Lord and said:

I know that thou canst do everything, and that no thought can be withholden from thee.

Who is he that hideth counsel without knowledge? therefore have I uttered that I understood not: things too wonderful for me, which I knew not.

Hear, I beseech thee, and I will speak: I will demand of thee, and declare thou unto me.

I have heard of thee by the hearing of the ear; but now mine eye seeth thee.

Wherefore I abhor myself, and repent in dust and ashes.'[3]

If you want a story of your own soul, it is perfectly done in the book of Job – much better than in *Letters from the Underworld*.[4]

[1] Mikhail Petrovich Artsybashev (1878–1927), Russian novelist; Gabriele D'Annunzio (1863–1938), Italian poet, novelist and dramatist; Johan August Strindberg (1849–1912), Swedish novelist and dramatist; Heinrich Mann (1871–1950) and Thomas Mann (1875–1955), both German novelists.
[2] Job iii. 3; xiv. 19–20 (A.V.). [3] Job. xlii. 1–6 (A.V.).
[4] By Fyodor Dostoievsky, trans. Constant Garnett (1913).

But the moderns today prefer to end insisting on the sad plight. It is characteristic of us that we have preserved, of a trilogy which was really *Prometheus Unbound*, only the *Prometheus Bound* and terribly suffering on the rock of his own egotism.[1]

But the great souls in all time did not end there. In the mediaeval period, Christianity did *not* insist on the Cross: but on the Resurrection: churches were built to the glorious hope of resurrection. Now we think[2] we are very great, whilst we enumerate the smarts of the Crucifixion. We are too mean to get any further.

I think there is the dual way of looking at things: our way, which is to say '*I* am all. All things are but radiations out from me.' – The other way is to try to conceive the Whole, to build up a Whole by means of symbolism, because symbolism avoids the I and puts aside the egotist; and, in the Whole, to take our decent place. That was how man built the Cathedral. He didn't say 'out of my breast springs this cathedral'. But 'in this vast Whole I am a small part, I move and live and have my being'.[3]

I understand now your passion to face the west. It is the passion for the extinction of yourself and the knowledge of the triumph of *your own will* in your body's extinction. But in the great periods, when man was great, he has faced the *East*: christian, mohammedan, Hindu, all.

You should try to grasp, I think – don't be angry at my tone – the *Complete Whole* which the Celtic symbolism made in its great time. We are such egoistic fools. We see only the *symbol* as a *subjective expression*: as an expression of ourselves. That makes us so sickly when we deal with the old symbols: like Yeats.

The old symbols were each a word in a great attempt at formulating the whole history of the Soul of Man. They are *unintelligible* [...] except in their whole context. So your Ireland of you Irishmen of today is a filthy mucking-about with a part of the symbolism of a Great Statement or Vision: just as the Crucifixion of Christ is a great mucking about with part of the symbolism of a great religious Vision.

The Crucifix, and Christ, are only symbols. They do not mean a man who suffered his life out as I suffer mine. They mean a moment in the history of my soul, if I must be personal. But it is a moment fixed in context and

[1] *Prometheus Bound* is the first part of a trilogy by the Greek dramatist Aeschylus (525–456 B.C.); the other two parts, *Prometheus Unbound* and *Prometheus the Fire-bearer*, have been lost. In this trilogy Aeschylus treats the legend of the Titan Prometheus who stole fire from heaven and gave it to men. He thereby incurred the wrath of Zeus. *Prometheus Bound* tells of the punishment which Zeus visited on Prometheus for his defiance and of the manner in which Prometheus endured it.
[2] MS reads 'thing'.   [3] Acts xvii. 28 ['we live, and move, and have our being'].

having its being only according to context.Unless I have the Father, and the hierarchies of Angels, I have no Christ, no Crucifixion.

It is necessary to grasp the Whole. At last I have got it, grasping something of what the mediaeval church tried to express. To me, the Latin form of expression comes very natural. To you, the Celtic I should think. I think the Whole of the Celtic symbolism and great Utterance of its Conception has never been fathomed. But it must have been in accord with the Latin.

There is the Eternal God, not to be seen or known, so bright in his fire that all things pass away, evanescent at its touch. He is surrounded by the Hierarchy of the Cherubim and Seraphim, the Great Ones who partake of his being and transmit his glory: and they are *absorbed in praise eternally*. Beyond the Cherubim are the Dominions and Powers: and beyond these great ones, the Principalities, Archangels, and Angels, which come as messengers and guardians and carriers of blessing at last to mankind.

So, there are the central symbols, from the oldest vision.

Then God, in meditating upon himself, begot the Son. The Son receives the Divine Nature by Generation within the human flesh. In the Son, the human flesh is again crucified, to liberate the eternal Soul, the Divine Nature of God.

For[1] the Divine Nature of God, the Spirit of the Father procreating the human flesh forms the *ego*. And the Ego would fain absorb the position of the Eternal god. Therefore it must suffer crucifixion, so that it may rise again praising God, knowing with the Angels, and the Thrones, and the Cherubim.

And, from the mutual love of the Father and the Son, proceeds the Holy Spirit, the Holy Ghost, the Reconciler, the Comforter, the Annunciation.

It is a very beautiful, and a very great conception which, when one feels it, satisfies one, and one is at rest.

But Christianity should teach us now, that after our Crucifixion, and the darkness of the tomb, we shall rise again in the flesh, you, I, as we are today, resurrected in the bodies, and acknowledging the Father, and glorying in his power, like Job.

It is very dangerous to use these old terms lest they sound like Cant. But if only one can grasp and know again as a new truth, true for ones own history, the great vision, the great, satisfying conceptions of the worlds greatest periods, it is enough. Because so it is made new.

All religions I think have the same inner conception, with different expressions. Why don't you seek out the whole of the Celtic Vision, instead of messing about talking of *Ireland*. Beatrice was somewhere on the track: but she didn't know what she was after: so she over-humanised, that is, she

[1] For] But

made subjective the symbols she used, so spoiled them: by putting them as emanations of her own Ego, instead of using them as words to convey the great Whole of which her own Ego was only the Issue, as the Son is issue of the Father.

Probably this will seem all stupid to you, and you will feel you are grasping a finer, more difficult, elusive truth. But I don't believe your truths of egoistic ecstasy. Get the *greatest* truth into your novel, for God's sake. We need it so badly. Give us the Resurrection after the Crucifixion.

We have been reading a book on *Christian Symbolism*, which I liked *very* much, because it puts me more into order. It is a little half-crown vol. – in the *Little Books on Art* series by Methuen. This is written by Mrs Henry Jenner. If you don't know it, get it for Beatrice and you read it too. This copy isn't mine. And you understand the Celtic Symbolism in its entirety.

This is a Christmas greeting. For God's sake follow your novel to its *biggest* close – further than death, to the gladness. I cannot forget that the Cherubim who are nearest God and palpitate with his brightness are *absorbed in praise*. I don't know why, but the thought of the Great Bright Circle of Cherubim, Godly beyond measure, are absorbed forever in fiery praise.

I will send you a copy of my stories for Beatrice. I think she also, like you, but she without knowing it perhaps, magnifies the great Principle of the Ego. She must also die and be born again. But I think she is tenacious,[1] and will have no crucifixion, let alone resurrection. But how do I know about her, after all.

Many good wishes for Christmas.

Yrs.   D. H. Lawrence

829. To S. S. Koteliansky, [21 December 1914]
Text: MS BL.; Postmark, Chesham 21 DE 14; Zytaruk 20.

Bellingdon Lane, Chesham – Bucks
Monday.

Dear Kot,

We are expecting you on Wednesday. Let us know what train, and I'll come with the tub.[2] And please bring two flasks of Chianti such as you had at Horne's for your Jewish supper. I send you ten shillings in this letter.

[1] MS reads: 'tenacious, tenacious'.
[2] A small covered carriage common c. 1911; the word is probably an abbreviation of 'tub-gig'.

I must ask you please not to buy things to bring with you. It spoils my pleasure when you spend your money, because you are poor. Really, I feel a disappointment when you spend money, or when we occasion you to spend your money. Don't do it.

I've got a head that is so heavy it even makes my heart heavy. Gertler is here, very sad. We are going to tea with him.

But I look forward very much to Wednesday and Thursday. Come during the daylight on Wednesday if you can.

una stretta di mano[1]   D. H. Lawrence

I can only get 6/- in paper money so I send that.

forgotten p.o. again – send it tomorrow.   DHL[2]

830. To S. S. Kotcliansky, [21 December 1914]

Text: MS BL; Postmark, Chesham 21 DE 14; Zytaruk 21.

Bellingdon – Chesham – Bucks
[21 December 1914]

I am a dunderheaded donkey – here is the postal order for the two flasks of Chianti I want you to bring.

D. H. Lawrence

Such as we had at your Jewish Cosher Supper at Horne's.

831. To Arthur McLeod, 24 December 1914

Text: MS UT; Unpublished.

The Triangle, Bellingdon Lane, *Chesham*, Bucks
24 Dec. 1914

My dear Mac,

You must forgive me for not writing for so long. We have been about, here and there in England, but very disheartened by the war and everything, and without energy to write. But write to me again soon.

All affection and good wishes for Christmas from Frieda and me,

D. H. Lawrence

---

[1] 'warm greetings' (literally 'a handshake').
[2] This postscript was written on the verso of the envelope.

832. To S. S. Koteliansky, [3 January 1915]

Text: MS BL.; Postmark, Chesham 4 JA 15; cited in Gransden 24.

Bellingdon – Chesham – Bucks

3 Dec 1915[1]

Dear Kot,

I was sorry you did not sleep when you got back to the Bureau.[2] But we laughed at you in your letter nevertheless.

What about Rananim?[3] Oh, but, we are going. We are going to found an Order of the Knights of Rananim. The motto is 'Fier'[4] – or the Latin equivalent. The badge is So:

[Sketch][5]

[1] The address and postmark jointly confirm DHL's error.

[2] The Russian Law Bureau where Kot was employed.

Perhaps there is a hidden reference here to the Christmas party described by Frieda: 'Christmas 1915 came. We made the cottage splendid with holly and mistletoe, we cooked and boiled, roasted and baked. Campbell and Koteliansky and the Murrys came, and Gertler and the Cannans. We had a gay feast.

We danced on the shaky floor. Gilbert with uplifted head sang: "I feel, I feel like an eagle in the sky". Koteliansky sang soulfully his Hebrew song: "Ranani Sadekim Badanoi"' (Frieda Lawrence, *'Not I, But the Wind…'* (Santa Fe, 1934), p. 81).

[3] DHL's name for the new society that he wished to establish, described more fully in Letter 841. The origin of the name appears to be this Hebrew musical version of the first verse of Psalm 33 ('Rejoice in the Lord, O ye righteous') which is preserved among Kot's papers in the possession of Mrs Catherine Stoye:

Ran-na-ni Za–di–kim Za–di–kim l'A–do–noi Ran-na-ni Za–

di–kim Za–di–kim ___ l'A–do–noi Ran-na–ni Za–di–kim Za–di–kim

l'A–do–noi Ran-na-ni Za–di–kim Za–da–kim l'A–do–noi

K. W. Gransden has suggested that the word 'Rananim' may also 'be connected with the word Ra'annanim, meaning green, fresh or flourishing, an adjective (qualifying, again, sadikhim, the righteous) found in the fourteenth verse of Psalm 92' (Gransden 23–4).

[4] Proud. The Latin equivalent would be 'superbus'.

[5] The drawing is that of a phoenix rising from a nest of flames, with 'Fier' written beneath it. DHL's choice of the phoenix as his symbol may derive in part from his reading of Mrs Henry Jenner's book *Christian Symbolism*, p. 150 (see Letter 828): 'The *Phoenix*, which after death rose immortal from its ashes, was a popular myth, introduced into Christianity as early as the first Epistle of St. Clement of Rome, the second or third successor of St. Peter. As its special meaning was the resurrection of the dead and its triumph over death (and it is

an eagle, or phoenix argent, rising from a flaming nest of scarlet, on a black background. And our flag, the blazing, ten-pointed star, scarlet on a black background.

[Sketch][1]

The Murrys will tell you when is their party – perhaps next Saturday, perhaps the one following. Please buy for me *Chapman's* translation of Homer. It is published for 1/- in Everyman's library, I think: or, in two volumes, for 1/- each, in some other little edition.[2] A bookseller will tell you.

We look forward to seeing you. Remember Rananim.

Auf wiedersehen   D. H. Lawrence

Regards from Frieda.

833. To Lady Ottoline Morrell, 3 January 1915

Text: MS UT; Huxley 213.

The Triangle, Bellingdon Lane, Chesham – Bucks
3rd January 1915

Dear Lady Ottoline,[3]

I was glad you wrote and told me you like my stories.[4] One wants the

---

in this sense that St. Clement uses it), it was often associated with the palm tree on Christian sarcophagi, eloquent of that rapturous belief in immortality that is the prevailing characteristic of the catacombs. Representations of it rising triumphantly from its flaming nest and ascending towards the sun are somewhat less common, but the Phoenix in itself was a recognized emblem of the Resurrection of Christ.' Opposite page 150 is a reproduction of a 'Phoenix Rising from the Flames' taken from a thirteenth-century Bestiary in the Ashmolean Museum, Oxford. There is a strong similarity between this illustration and that drawn by DHL here.

[1] Of a flag bearing the star. The 'blazing, ten-pointed star' also appears as part of the illustration mentioned in the preceding note.

[2] The first part of the *Iliad* was published by George Chapman (c. 1560–1634) in 1598; the complete *Iliad* and *Odyssey* were issued in 1616, but his translations were not available in the Everyman's Library edition. (Everyman's published the Earl of Derby's translation of the *Iliad* and Cowper's of the *Odyssey*. The most recent cheap publication of Chapman's texts was in Newnes' 'Thin Paper Classics', 1904.)

[3] Lady Ottoline Violet Anne Morrell (1873–1938), daughter of Lieutenant-General Arthur Cavendish-Bentinck (d. 1877) and his second wife Lady Bolsover (b. 1834). (Her title derived from her being half-sister of the 6th Duke of Portland (1857–1943).) m. 1902 Philip Edward Morrell (1870–1943), Liberal M.P. for S. Oxon. (1906–10) and Burnley (1910–18). She became patroness of a distinguished intellectual circle, first at 44 Bedford Square, Bloomsbury and, from 1915, at Garsington Manor, Oxfordshire. DHL first met her at a party she gave at Bedford Square c. 13 August 1914 (Nehls, i. 240). For a detailed account of her relations with DHL and a vast array of other artists, see *Ottoline: The Early Memoirs of Lady Ottoline Morrell*, ed. Robert Gathorne-Hardy (1963) and *Ottoline at Garsington*.

[4] *The Prussian Officer and Other Stories* about which Lady Ottoline had written to Bertrand Russell, on 31 December 1914: 'I am amazed how good it is – quite wonderful some of the Stories – He has great passion – and is so alive to things outward and inward – a far better writer than Cannan and quite different from that muddled stuff of Woolfe – Did you ever

appreciation of the few. And it isn't faute de mieux, either – I am no democrat, save in politics. I think the state is a vulgar institution. But life itself is an affair of aristocrats. In my soul, I'd be as proud as hell. In the state, let there be the Liberté Egalité business. In so far as I am one of many, Liberté, Egalité – I won't have the Fraternité. The State is an arrangement for myriads of peoples' living together. And one doesn't have brothers by arrangement. – In so far as I am myself, Fierté, Inégalité, Hostilité.

It doesn't sound very French, but never mind. I think the time has come to wave the oriflamme[1] and rally against humanity and Ho, Ho, St John and the New Jerusalem.[2]

We should like very much to come and see you again. When we come to town we shall come to lunch with you. I shall let you know. We don't come very often, because of the poverty. I shake down the thermometer of my wealth, and find it just nearly at zero. But I like to be poor. I'd like to wave my rags like the feathers of a bird of paradise. But as yet, one must be decent.

How I loathe this dark weather.

My wife wants to see how you embroider – will you show her when we come? She sends her greetings, with mine,

Yours Sincerely   D. H. Lawrence

834. To Arthur McLeod, 5 January 1915
Text: MS UT; Postmark, Chesham 5 JA 15; Moore, *Intelligent Heart* 168, 179–80.

The Triangle, Bellingdon Lane, Chesham, Bucks

5 Jan. 1915.

Dear Mac,

Thank you for the two books. Palmer's *Comedy* is very interesting: I don't like *Nan.*[3] We are going to meet Palmer next week, I think. He is coming down to stay with the Cannan's who have the Mill house at Cholesbury, about a mile away. We are very good friends. The Murrys, – she is Katherine Mansfield, – if you remember, they ran *Rhythm* – have a cottage at Lee, three

read "Sons and Lovers" by him? It has been a comfort reading anything so real. All the Nottinghamshire Stories seem very familiar to me. Didn't you think "The Vicar's Daughters" very good?' (MS in the Bertrand Russell Archive, McMaster University, Canada).

[1] The ancient royal banner of France.
[2] An allusion to St John's vision of the new Jerusalem in Revelation xxi. 1–2.
[3] *Comedy* (1914) by John Leslie Palmer (1885–1944); *The Tragedy of Nan and Other Plays* (1909) by John Masefield (1878–1967).

miles off: so we are not quite isolated. In this time of flood, however, the duckpond is right across the lane, so to get to the high-road one must wade.

You must come down and see us one Saturday, and stay the night. We have somebody down constantly, and I must say I'd be much gladder if you came. It is not very far – about 30 miles from Baker St. or Marylebone – 2/4 return excursion. So you can easily come. We shall enjoy it. Then you can know the Cannan's also, if you want to.

I am still revising the *Rainbow* – putting a great deal of work into it. I have done 300 pages. It'll be a new sort of me for you to get used to.

I do wish I had a copy of *The Prussian Officer* to send you. But various thieves who call themselves friends carried off copies they could well afford to buy, and I am badly off, through the war. When I am richer I will send you a copy.

I don't know quite what we are doing. For my life, I couldn't say whether we shall be here through February or not. Viola Meynell offers us her cottage in Sussex if we can't get to Italy. But then the whole formidable and poetic Meynell family is down there in the Meynell settlement, so I am wary of accepting Viola's offer.[1] We shall see.

I don't think the *Prussian Officer* goes very well – struggles along, like all my books. I'm afraid, when Methuen gets the *Rainbow*, he'll wonder what changeling is foisted on him. For it *is* different from my other work. I am very glad with it. I am coming into my full feather at last, I think.

What do you mean by saying you'd go to war? No, the war is for those who are not needed for a new life. I hate and detest the war, it is all wrong, all foolish, all a wicked mistake. Why can't it end? We none of us want it, surely.

I suppose you still are having holidays. Do you continue to like school? I think of it always with great aversion. I'll be a beggar before I teach a class again.

I've got a cold with the horrible wetness of the earth. How are you? Frieda sends her warmest regards. You know you have mine.

Yrs   D. H. Lawrence

[1] Viola Meynell (1885–1956), daughter of the author and editor, Wilfred (1852–1948) and Alice Meynell (1847–1922), a well known poet and essayist. (Among the Meynells' friends were Tennyson, Patmore, Meredith and Francis Thompson.) The family owned an eighty acre tract of land with an old house and other buildings which the father had renovated for the various members of the family. See Viola Meynell's account of the family estate at Greatham, in *Alice Meynell: A Memoir* (1929), particularly the chapters 'Greatham' and 'The War', pp. 274–317. m. John Dallyn, 1922. Viola Meynell was herself a writer of novels, short stories, poems, etc. as well as biographies.

835. To S. S. Koteliansky, 7 January 1915
Text: MS BL; Postmark, Chesham 7 JA 15; Moore 306.

Bellingdon Lane, Chesham – Bucks.

7 Jan 1915.

Dear – Kot,

Dont be so absurd asking why I don't want to invite you to the Murrys party. Of course I want to invite you – and it's not a question of inviting, you are plainly coming. But the party *isn't* on Saturday – it is postponed to an indefinite date – probably till the 23rd.

We – Gilbert and Mary and Myself – have done a little Schnitzler play – 20 minutes – in readiness. It is funny.[1]

I am writing to Viola Meynell to say perhaps after all we will go to her cottage in Sussex, if we may. I am feeling seedy here, and I don't like this place. The Meynells are kinder. Probably we shall go. I shall let you know. At any rate you will come and see us before long. I will let you know that also. Frieda is not cross. She jumps at the thought of leaving Bellingdon. You would come just the same to Sussex.

Sia bene – a rivederti   D. H. Lawrence

836. To J. B. Pinker, 7 January 1915
Text: MS Forster; cited in Carswell 27.

The Triangle, Bellingdon Lane, Chesham – Bucks

7 Jan 1915.

Dear Pinker,

Here is another hundred pages of the novel. I am going to split the book into two volumes: it was so unwieldy. It needs to be in two volumes.[2]

Thank you for the little cheque. Why does the *Metropolitan Magazine* suddenly stump up another £5?[3]

Kennerley owes me exactly £10.7.6 – by his own computation. It isn't much but it would be worth having. Have you written to America about the book of stories.[4]

I've got a long, slow, pernicious cold. I hope you are well.

Yours Sincerely   D. H. Lawrence

[1] Arthur Schnitzler (1862–1931), an Austrian playwright, novelist and short story writer. His current dramas were *The Green Cockatoo and Other Plays* (1913), *Free Game* (1913), *Literature* (1913), *Professor Bernhardi* (1913) and *Gallant Cassian* (1914). J. M. Murry describes the drama conceived by the group and the 'play within a play' that resulted: see Murry, *Autobiography* 321.

[2] i.e. what proved to be *The Rainbow* and *Women in Love*.

[3] *Metropolitan* had published 'Honour and Arms' in November 1914. Perhaps this was an additional payment for that story.   [4] See Letter 827.

837. To S. S. Koteliansky, [9 January 1915]

Text: MS BL; Postmark, London JAN 9 1915; Zytaruk 24.

[Bellingdon Lane, Chesham, Bucks]

[9 January 1915]

Dear Kot,

Do come tomorrow. I've got a cold and cant go out, so shall be glad to see you. We are thinking of moving to Sussex – come and be told about it.

DHL

838. To Lady Ottoline Morrell, 13 January 1915

Text: MS StaU; Schorer 47.

Bellingdon Lane, Chesham – Bucks

13 Jan 1915

Dear Lady Ottoline,

I'm sorry we can't come to dinner tomorrow. I am rejoicing in two more days in bed, by reason of a still lingering miserable cold.

But we are leaving this miserable little cottage to go down to one more comfortable, not so depressing and misfitting, in Sussex. I think that we shall stay in town next Wednesday and Thursday, in transit. Then if we may, we will come and see you. Perhaps you will come down to see us in Sussex too, when we are there.

As for humanity – they say comprendre c'est pardonner: but it is really comprendre c'est vouloir pûnir.[1]

Greetings from my wife and me.

Yours Sincerely   D. H. Lawrence

839. To Edward Garnett, 13 January 1915

Text: MS NYPL; Huxley 214.

The Triangle, Bellingdon Lane, Chesham, Bucks

13 Jan 1915

Dear Garnett,

I send you the letter of this lady.[2] I dont know whether anything can be done with my grandfather's old rival, Jesse Boot.[3] You know that my mother's father and this grand-duke of drugs quarrelled and had a long war

---

[1] 'to understand is to forgive: but it is really to understand is to want to punish'.

[2] Not identified.

[3] Sir Jesse Boot (1850–1931), cr. 1st Baron Trent, 1929; founder and chairman of Boots Cash Chemists. The company operated a Lending Library in connection with its numerous chemists shops throughout the country. In February, when E. M. Forster came to visit DHL at Greatham, 'he... brought a rumour that Boot's Library were refusing to supply Lawrence's *The Prussian Officer* and that Sir Jesse Boot, when pressed about it, sent subscribers a private copy in a special binding, so that they could see how disgusting the book was' (Furbank, ii. 9).

as to which of them should govern a chapel in Sneinton, in Nottingham. My grandfather won.[1] So now, weh mir, dass ich ein Enkel bin – woe is me that I am a grandchild, for I am booted out of my place as a popular novelist.

I've got a cold and lie in bed for a day or two. It is nothing. Next week we go down to Sussex to live in a better and less crannied house than this. Of course I am happy in the prospect of being on the move again.

If you are in town next Wednesday and Thursday, I should like to see you. Will you let me know – How are Mrs Garnett and David? I have no news. I won't ask you about *The Prussian Officer*, it might make me sad.

Frieda sends her greetings – I mine.

Yours   D. H. Lawrence

840. To Edward Garnett, 15 January 1915
Text: MS NYPL; Unpublished.

Bellingdon – Chesham – Bucks
15 Jan 1915

Dear Garnett,

I hope you are not bored by this lady. Frankly, I think she is a treasure. I wrote to her pleasantly. Will you send her her enclosures, as she asks.

We leave here on Wednesday, and stay in town till Friday. Will you let me know if you are in town. Viola Meynell is lending us her cottage, at Greatham, Pulborough, Sussex. You must come and see us there. I don't know how long we shall stay. I get seedy here.

Let us know if you are in town. We shall stay with Dr Eder – 103 Hampstead Way, Hampstead Garden Suburb.[2]

Yours   D. H. Lawrence

841. To William Hopkin, 18 January 1915
Text: MS NCL; Huxley 214–15.

Bellingdon, Chesham – Bucks
Monday 18 Jan 1915

[1] DHL's maternal grandfather, George Beardsall (1825–99).
[2] Dr Montagu David Eder (1865–1936), an early Freudian psychoanalyst (a colleague of Dr Ernest Jones). He had strong socialist sympathies and contributed frequently to A. R. Orage's *New Age*. Later Eder became a leader in the Zionist movement: 1918–23 political head of the Zionist Executive in Jerusalem, and member of the World Zionist Executive, 1921–3. m. (1) Florence Murray (2) Edith Low, sister of Barbara. DHL met the Eders through Edith's niece, Ivy Low. (See *Times* obituary, 31 March 1936; *David Eder: Memoirs of a Modern Pioneer*, ed. J. B. Hobman, 1945.)

Dear Willie,

I just remember I've got this set of duplicate proofs of my stories, and perhaps you'll accept them in lieu of a bound volume.[1] If ever I rise to fame these will be unique – because there are many differences between these sheets and those revised and published – also you can have them bound into a book for a few pence. So don't grumble at them please. I remember I promised you a proper book.

We are just packing up to move again – not to Italy, alas – but to a beautiful place in Sussex – Greatham, Pulborough, Sussex is the address. It is the Meynells' place. You know Alice Meynell, Catholic poetess rescuer of Francis Thompson.[2] The father took a big old farm house at Greatham, then proceeded to give each of his children a cottage. Now Viola lends us hers. It is I think a big cottage, and everything nice and handy. It is on the L[ondon] B[righton] & S[outh] C[oast] Railway – near Arundel – on the edge of the downs – not far from Littlehampton, which is seaside.

So you must come and see us, all three of you, when we are settled and the spring is coming on. That will be just jolly.

We will also talk of my pet scheme.[3] I want to gather together about twenty souls and sail away from this world of war and squalor and found a little colony where there shall be no money but a sort of communism as far as necessaries of life go, and some real decency. It is to be a colony built up on the real decency which is in each member of the Community – a community which is established upon the assumption of goodness in the members, instead of the assumption of [...] badness.

What do you think of it? I think it should be quite feasible. We keep brooding the idea – I and some friends.

Now the weather is sunny, but I have hated it. I am glad to be going to Sussex – it is a county I like very much. I dont like this Bucks – it is meagre.

How are you and Sallie, and how is Enid. We leave here Thursday morning – stay two days in London – go to Pulborough on Saturday.

Many greetings from Frieda and me.   D. H. Lawrence

[1] These proofs (marked 'First Proofs' and dated 1–19 October 1914) are now deposited in NCL.
[2] Francis Joseph Thompson (1859–1907), poet and essayist, whose work first came to Wilfred Meynell's attention as editor of the Roman Catholic magazine *Merry England* in 1888. Thompson was destitute and discouraged to the point of attempting suicide. The Meynells rescued him, cared for him in his distress, and he became a member of their household. See *Letters*, i. 140, 145.   [3] For 'Rananim'.

842. To Edward Garnett, [18 January 1915]

Text: MS NYPL; PC; Postmark, Chesham 18 JA 15; Unpublished.

[The Triangle, Bellingdon Lane, Chesham, Bucks]

[18 January 1915]

Frieda says we can't come to London till Thursday – and we promised to lunch with Lady Ottoline that day[1] – so I wonder if you'll be gone out of town before we can come to Pond Place. I should be sorry. We might have tea somewhere if you are not gone.

Excuse the postcard – I have no stamps and it is so far to get any.

D. H. Lawrence

Bellingdon – Chesham

843. To S. S. Koteliansky, [20 January 1915]

Text: MS BL; PC; Postmark, Chesham 20 JA 15; Zytaruk 24.

[The Triangle, Bellingdon Lane, Chesham, Bucks]

[20 January 1915]

We are having rather a rush in London – Coming up Thursday to lunch with Lady Ottoline – tea with Garnett – then to the Eders. But I shall ring you up from the Eders and we'll make an arrangement. You must come to Campbell's – you must know him.

Frieda sends warm regards –

Vale   D. H. Lawrence

[Frieda Lawrence begins]

I would have written before –

Love   Frieda

844. To J. B. Pinker, 20 January 1915

Text: MS Forster; Unpublished.

Bellingdon – Chesham – Bucks

20 Jan 1915

Dear Pinker,

I send you on what pages of the novel[2] I have ready, because tomorrow we are leaving this cottage to go to one in Sussex, where the address is

c/o Miss Viola Meynell, Greatham, *Pulborough*, Sussex.

I wonder when Methuen would want to publish the book – have you any idea?

Yours Sincerely   D. H. Lawrence

---

[1] Lady Ottoline's guest-book at 44 Bedford Square confirms that DHL and Frieda were visitors there on 21 January 1915.   [2] *The Rainbow.*

845. To Catherine Carswell, [23 January 1915]
Text: MS YU; cited in Carswell, *Adelphi* 167.

[23 January 1915][1]

Dear Catherine

We are just on the way to Pulborough. It has been a rush. We never wrote to you about your wedding – but we didn't know when you are back. This little blue plate is a love token from us.[2] That it is a dragon is a fitting symbol. But I shall paint you a phoenix on a box.

With regards to Mr Carswell.

Mila cari saluti[3]   D. H. Lawrence

846. To S. S. Koteliansky, [24 January 1915]
Text: MS BL; Postmark, Cootham 25 JAN 15; cited in Gransden 24.

Greatham, Pulborough, Sussex.
Sunday

My dear Kot,

We got here safely last night, after a wonderful long drive in the motor car through deep snow, and between narrow hedges, and pale winter darkness. The Meynells are very nice – but all return to London tomorrow. The cottage is rather splendid – something monastic about it – severe white walls and oaken furniture – beautiful. And there is bathroom and all. And the country is very fine – Meynell owns a nice piece.

But the cottage is not yet quite finished – there are many things to do in the way of furnishing and so on. But this is really a place with beauty of character.

I hope you saw and liked Campbell; you must tell me what you talked about, and how it was. Please be friends with him.

I shall ask you to come and see us here before long. I wish you didnt spend so much money on us. I plainly hate it. Frieda likes the Meynells, but is a bit frightened of the cloistral severity of this place. I must say I love it.

Frieda sends warm regards.

a rivederti – sia bene   D. H. Lawrence

---

[1] This date assumes that DHL left Chesham on 21 January and stayed in London till 23rd when he and Frieda made the journey to Pulborough.
[2] Catherine Carswell recalled: 'Donald and I were married early in January and Lawrence sent me a little blue plate' (Carswell 27).
[3] 'Thousands of affectionate greetings'.

847. To E. M. Forster, [24 January 1915]
Text: MS KCC; Huxley 224.

Greatham, Pulborough, Sussex.

Sunday[1]

Dear Forster,[2]

Dont expect any sort of answer or attention from me today, because everything is so strange and I feel as if I'd just come out of the shell and hadn't got any feathers to protect me from the weather. It is very snowy here, and rather beautiful.

Will you come down next week-end and stay with us? I think nobody else will be here. As for my not listening to your answers, Ive got a deep impression that you never made any.

I've only read one or two stories of yours, and should like *very much* to have the *Celestial Omnibus*.[3]

This cottage is rather fine – a bit monastic – it was a cattle shed – now it is like a monks refectory – the whole establishment is cloistral.

I'm glad you're not really Buddhistic – everybody said you were.[4] I want somebody to come and make a league with me, to sing the Chanson des Chansons – das Hohe Lied[5] – and to war against the fussy Mammon, that pretends to be a tame pet now, and so devours us in our sleep.

But do come at the week-end.

D. H. Lawrence

848. To Lady Ottoline Morrell, 27 January 1915
Text: MS IEduc; Postmark, Cootham 28 JAN 15; Huxley 215–16.

Greatham, Pulborough, Sussex.

27 Jan 1915

---

[1] This letter precedes Letter 850 which repeats DHL's invitation, and would therefore have been written on the Sunday immediately following DHL's arrival at Greatham.

[2] Edward Morgan Forster (1879–1970), novelist, critic, essayist and biographer. DHL met him at Lady Ottoline Morrell's lunch party on 21 January 1915. On his relations with DHL at this time see Delany 50–7, and Furbank, ii. 4–13.

[3] Some of Forster's short stories were collected in *The Celestial Omnibus and Other Stories* (1911). As a reader of the *English Review*, DHL may have seen 'Other Kingdom', *English Review*, ii (July 1909), 651–72; 'The Point of It', *English Review*, ix (November 1911), 615–30; and 'Co-operation', *English Review*, xi (June 1912), 366–72.

[4] Perhaps with reference to Forster's visit to India, 1912–13. See 'Adrift in India', Furbank, i. 220–54.

[5] 'Song of Songs'.

Dear Lady Ottoline,

I have burnt your letter about Duncan Grant.[1] (He looks as if he dissipates, and certainly he doesn't enjoy it. Tell him to stop.) We liked him very much – I *really* liked him. Tell him not to make silly experiments in the futuristic line, with bits of color on a moving paper. Other Johnnies can do that. Neither to bother making marionettes – even titanic ones.[2] But to seek out the terms in which he shall state his whole. He is after stating an Absolute – like Fra Angelico in the *Last Judgment*[3] – a whole conception of the existence of Man – creation, good, evil, life, death, resurrection, the separating of the stream of good and evil, and its return to the eternal source. It is an Absolute we are all after, a statement of the whole scheme – the issue, the progress through Time – and the return – making unchangeable eternity.

In a geometric figure one has the abstraction ready stated △ so, or ○ so. But one cannot build a complete abstraction, or absolute, out of a number of small abstractions, or absolutes. Therefore one cannot make a picture out of geometric figures. One can only build a great abstraction out of concrete units. Painting is *not* architecture. It is puerile to try to achieve architecture – third dimension – on a flat surface, by means of 'lines of force'. The architecture comes in, in painting, only with the suggestion of some whole, some conception which conveys in its own manner the whole universe. Most puerile is this dabbing geometric figures behind one another, just to prove that the artist[4] is being abstract, that he is[5] not attempting representation of the object. The way to express the abstract-whole is to reduce the object to a unit, a term, and then out of these units and terms to make a whole statement. *Do* rub this into Duncan Grant, and save him his foolish waste. Rembrandt, Corot, Goya, Monet have been preparing us our instances – now for the great hand which can collect all the instances into an absolute statement of the whole.

---

[1] Duncan James Corrowr Grant (1885–1978), the Scottish painter. Studied at the Westminster School of Art, at the Slade, in Italy and Paris. A member of the 'Bloomsbury group', he was a close friend of Lady Ottoline. With Forster and David Garnett, DHL had visited Grant's studio on 22 January: he was savagely critical of Grant's painting and strongly resented his sexual mores.

[2] DHL may be referring to the kind of marionettes which Grant designed for one of the Bloomsbury parties: '...the guests all went up to witness a performance of Racine's *Berenice*, acted by three huge puppets eight feet tall, painted and cut out of cardboard by Duncan Grant' (Michael Holroyd, *Lytton Strachey: A Critical Biography*, 1968, pp. 135–6).

[3] Guido di Pietro Angelico (1387–1455), usually known as Fra Angelico, the celebrated Italian painter of religious subjects. DHL may have seen *The Last Judgment*, c. 1435, at the Convento di San Marco, Florence. See Jeffrey Meyers, 'The Rainbow and Fra Angelico', *DHL Review*, vii (Summer 1974), 139–55 (a reproduction of the painting, now in the Museo di San Marco, Florence, appears on p. 145).   [4] the artist] one

[5] that he is] and

I hope you aren't bored – but do tell this to Duncan Grant.

We have got a beautiful cottage here – long and narrow – it was a long barn – it is like the refectory of a little monastery. The country is beautiful. When will you come and see us? Choose your own time. And will you bring Cendrella – I don't know her name.[1] We have got spare bedrooms, if you come.

a rivederci   D. H. Lawrence

We should be very glad to see Philip Morrell, if a member of Parliament and an energetic landowner has any time to waste.[2]

849. To S. S. Koteliansky, [28 January 1915]
Text: MS BL; Postmark, Cootham 28 JAN 15; Zytaruk 26.

Greatham, Pulborough, Sussex.
Thursday

Dear Kot,

Will you come down on Saturday – write and tell us the train. I think only Viola Meynell will be here. I will walk down to meet you – but *come in the daylight*.

Don't bring anything – I do dislike it when you buy things to bring.

I shan't write a letter because I am very busy –

au revoir   D. H. Lawrence

[Frieda Lawrence begins]

Dear Kot,

Do come – and as the fare is so dear you are *not* to bring us anything – We are rich here, no rent, Viola wont even let us pay the servant – there is just the food, that's all – You will love it, it is so beautiful and white – I am glad you liked Campbell –

Bring me one of those cakes that you brought for Xmas – they last so well –

Auf Wiedersehen   Frieda

---

[1] According to Mrs Julian Vinogradoff (Lady Ottoline's daughter), 'Cendrella' was a familiar name for Marie Juliette Baillot, her Swiss governess (m. Julian Huxley, 1919).

[2] In addition to being M.P. for Burnley, he also supervised the farm work at Garsington which the Morrells had purchased on 15 March 1913. (They were not to take possession of the manor house on the estate until May 1915.)

850. To E. M. Forster, 28 January 1915
Text: MS KCC; Furbank, ii. 6–7.

Greatham, Pulborough, Sussex.
Thursday 28 Jan 1915

Dear Forster,

Very well, come when you can. I am so obsessed by the idea that you are always in the National Gallery, like an attendant or a recording angel, that I can't conceive you free during the week.[1] Come tomorrow or Monday or Tuesday or Wednesday or when you will – and stay one or two nights – as you will. Only let me know, and say if you can walk 4 miles – and I'll meet you at Pulborough.

I don't belong to any class, now. As for your class, do you think it could tempt me? If I'm one of any lot, I'm one of the common people. But I feel as if I'd known all classes now, and so am free of all. Frieda is a German of good family – in Germany she thinks herself very aristocratic. I have known Lady Ottoline's servants – gate keepers and cooks – at home, who have served in Welbeck.[2] Now I know Lady Ottoline. And whether I sit at tea with Mrs Orchard, who had been an under servant at Welbeck, and who had erysipelas in her hands, and who was glad when I sat and talked to her for hours, when I was a lad – and she didn't light the gas, for economys sake, but we looked into a red, low fire – she with her hands wrapped up, and her curious servants' face 'glotzend'[3] in the firelight, and her eyes fixed and her mouth talking, talking about the Duke and Lord Henry[4] and Lady Ottoline – or whether I sit with Lady Ottoline and talk about the war, or about people – what is it, after all? One is only going down different avenues to the same thing. One is only tracking down the secret of satisfaction for the individual – the naked, intrinsic, class-less individual. What is class, at its best, but a method of living to one's end! It doesn't *really* alter the end. And for each class, the other class seems to hold the secret of satisfaction. But no class holds it.

It is time for us now to look all round, round the whole ring of the horizon – not just out of a room with a view;[5] it is time to gather again a

[1] Forster was employed as a part-time cataloguer at the National Gallery, September 1914 – October 1915. See Furbank, i. 259–60.
[2] Welbeck Abbey, the Portland family seat near Worksop, Notts., inherited by the 6th Duke of Portland, Lady Ottoline's half-brother. Lady Ottoline went to live there in December 1879. See Gathorne-Hardy, *Ottoline: The Early Memoirs*, pp. 69–88.
[3] 'staring'.
[4] The eccentric 5th Duke of Portland and Lord Henry Bentinck, Lady Ottoline's half-brother.
[5] An allusion to Forster's novel *A Room With a View* (1908).

conception of the Whole: as Plato tried to do, and as the mediaeval men –
as Fra Angelico–a conception of the beginning and the end, of heaven and
hell, of good and evil flowing from God through humanity as through a
filter, and returning back to god as angels and demons.

We are tired of contemplating this one phase of the history of creation,
which we call humanity. We are tired of measuring everything by the human
standard: whether man is the standard or criterion, or whether he is but a
factor in the Whole whose issue and whose return we have called God.

I am tired of class, and humanity, and personal salvation. What care I
whether my neighbour feels he is saved or not – saved, completed, fulfilled,
consummated? I am tired to death of the infant crying in the night.[1] I am
sick of protesting Job, cursing his birth and his begetting.[2] Is he so
important, or his sufferings of such moment? Let him have done.

In my Island,[3] I wanted people to come without class or money, sacrificing
nothing, but each coming with all his desires, yet knowing that his life is
but a tiny section of a Whole: so that he shall fulfil his life in relation to
the Whole. I wanted a real community, not built out of abstinence or
equality, but out of many fulfilled individualities seeking greater fulfilment.

But, I can't find anybody. Each man is so bent on his own private
fulfilment – either he wants love of a woman, and can't get it complete, or
he wants to influence his fellow men (for their good, of course), or he wants
to satisfy his own soul with regard to his position in eternity. And they make
me tired, these friends of mine. They seem so childish and greedy, always
the immediate desire, always the particular outlook, no conception of the
whole horizon wheeling round.

What do you want for yourself? You used to want the fulfilment of the
natural animal in you – which is after all only an immediate need. So you
made an immediate need seem the Ultimate Necessity – so you belied and
betrayed yourself. I don't know where you've got to after *Howards End.*[4]

Don't think this priggish and conceited. I do feel every man must have
the devil of a struggle before he can have stuffed himself full enough to have
satisfied all his immediate needs, and can give up, cease, and withdraw
himself, yield himself up to his metamorphosis, his crucifixion, and so come
to his new issuing, his wings, his resurrection, his whole flesh shining like
a mote in the sunshine, fulfilled and now taking part in the fulfilment of the
Whole.

---

[1] Tennyson, *In Memoriam*, liv. 18.   [2] See Job iii. 3.
[3] The plans for Rananim at this time envisaged a remote island as the site of DHL's ideal
society. See Murry, *Autobiography* 322.
[4] Forster's novel was first published in October 1910. See *Letters*, i. 278.

So I feel frightfully like weeping in a corner – not over myself – but perhaps my own resurrection is too new, one must feel if the scars are not there, and wince – and one must see the other people all writhing and struggling and unable to give up.

How can there be a *Celestial Omnibus*? Is that satire? – like the spiritual perambulators of a parson I knew[1] – 'All of you want wheeling to heaven in a spiritual perambulator', he said.

You are to take all this quite seriously.

Yours   D. H. Lawrence

[Frieda Lawrence begins]

This is a very angelic letter but I know the flapping of wings wont quite make you overlook the little twisted horns and the hoof – I thought you were 'good' to people – You listen so carefully, it frightened me, because so many things are said thoughtlessly – And you still listen with the whole of you – It is good of you – I have only read your *Where angels fear to tread*[2] I felt like turning somersaults and loved it – So you will come soon – I am quite miserable over the Brontë sisters that I am reading[3] – How fond they were of each other –

Yours sincerely   Frieda Lawrence

851. To Lady Cynthia Asquith, [31 January 1915]
Text: MS UT; Huxley 217–19.

Greatham, Pulborough, Sussex.
Sunday 30 Jan 1915[4]

Dear Lady Cynthia,

We were very glad to hear from you. I wanted to send you a copy of my stories at Christmas, then I didn't know how the war had affected you – I knew Herbert Asquith was joined[5] – and I thought you'd rather be left alone, perhaps.

We have no history, since we saw you last.[6] I feel as if I had less than no history – as if I had spent those five [...] months in the tomb. And now, I feel very sick and corpse-cold, too newly risen to share yet with [...]

---

[1] Unidentified.   [2] Published October 1905.
[3] Frieda may have been reading May Sinclair's *The Three Brontës* (1912).
[4] Sunday was 31 January 1915.
[5] Lady Cynthia's husband, Herbert Asquith, enlisted and was commissioned in the Royal Field Artillery in 1914.
[6] The last recorded meeting was that on 9 July 1914; see Letter 752.

anybody, having the smell of the grave in my nostrils, and a feel of grave clothes about me.

The War finished me: it was the spear through the side of all sorrows and hopes. I had been walking in Westmoreland, rather happy, with water-lilies twisted round my hat – big, heavy, white and gold water-lilies that we found in a pool high up – and girls who had come out on a spree and who were having tea in the upper room of an inn shrieked with laughter. And I remember also we crouched under the loose wall on the moors and the rain flew by in streams, and the wind came rushing through the chinks in the wall behind one's head – and we shouted songs, and I imitated music hall turns, whilst the other men crouched under the wall and I pranked in the rain on the turf in the gorse, and Kotilianski groaned Hebrew music – Ranani Sadekim Badanoi.[1]

It seems like another life – we *were* happy – four men.[2] Then we came down to Barrow in Furness, and saw that war was declared. And we all went mad. I can remember soldiers kissing on Barrow station, and a woman shouting defiantly to her sweetheart 'When you get at 'em, Clem, let 'em have it', as the train drew off – and in all the tram-cars 'War'. – Messrs Vickers Maxim call in their workmen[3] – and the great notices on Vickers' gateways – and the thousands of men streaming over the bridge. Then I went down the coast a few miles. And I think of the amazing sunsets over flat sands and the smoky sea – then of sailing in a fisherman's boat, running in the wind against a heavy sea – and a French onion boat coming in with her sails set splendidly, in the morning sunshine – and the electric suspense everywhere – and the amazing, vivid, visionary beauty of everything, heightened up by immense pain everywhere.

And since then, since I came back, things have not existed for me. I have spoken to no one [...] I have touched no one, I have seen no one. All the while, I swear, my soul lay in the tomb – not dead, but with the flat stone

---

[1] 'Ranani Zadikim Zadikim l'Adonoi': see p. 252 n. 3.

[2] Some doubt exists about the identity of the 'four men'. Harry T. Moore, without citing any evidence, says 'a Russian lawyer, R. S. Slat[k]owsky' was among the walkers (Harry T. Moore, *The Priest of Love*, New York, 1974, p. 205); but because of Kot's antipathy towards Slatkowsky, this is unlikely. John Carswell believes that the party included 'two men from the Russian Law Bureau called Farbman and Horne' (*Lives and Letters*, p. 96). Horne was almost certainly present: he was a close friend of Kot's and – from references to him in several letters – was clearly well liked by DHL. There is no firm evidence for Farbman; nor for A. P. Lewis even though, in a letter to Kot on 18 December 1925, DHL recalled visiting Lewis' house. Lewis was employed by Vickers and lived in or near Barrow; to call on him does not necessarily make him one of the party. The 'four men' were, therefore: DHL, Kot, probably Horne, and either Lewis or Farbman.

[3] Vickers Maxim manufactured armaments, particularly machine guns.

over it, a corpse,[1] become corpse cold. And nobody existed, because I did not exist myself. Yet I was not dead – only passed over – trespassé. And all the time I knew I should have to rise again.

Now I am feeble[2] and half alive. On the downs on Friday I opened my eyes again, and saw it was daytime. And I saw the sea lifted up and shining like a blade with the sun on it. And high up, in the icy wind, an aeroplane flew towards us from the land – and the men ploughing, and the boys in the fields on the tablelands, and the shepherds, stood back from their work and lifted their faces. And the aeroplane was small and high in the thin, ice cold wind. And the birds became silent and dashed to cover, afraid of the noise. And the aeroplane floated high out of sight. And below, on the level earth away down, were floods and stretches of snow – And I knew I was awake. But as yet my [...] soul is cold and shaky and earthy.

I dont feel so hopeless now I am risen. My heart has been as [...] cold as a lump of dead earth, all this time, because of the war. But now I don't feel so dead. I feel hopeful. I couldn't tell you how fragile and tender the hope is – the new shoot of life. But I feel hopeful now about the war. We shall all rise again from this grave – though the killed[3] soldiers will have to wait for the Last Trump.

There is my autobiography – written because you ask me, and because, being risen from the dead, I know we shall all come through, rise again and walk healed and whole and new, in a big inheritance, here on earth.

It sounds preachy, but I dont quite know how to say it.

Viola Meynell has lent us this rather beautiful cottage. We are quite alone. It is at the foot of the downs. I wish you would come and see us, and stay a day or two. It is quite comfortable – there is hot water and a bathroom, and two spare bedrooms. I dont know when we shall [...] be able to come to London. We are too poor for excursions. But we *should* like to see you, and it *is* nice here.

auf wiedersehen   D. H. Lawrence

852. To S. S. Koteliansky, [1 February 1915]

Text: MS BL; Postmark, Cootham 1 FE 15; Zytaruk 27.

Greatham, Pulborough, Sussex
Monday

My dear Kot,

We were disappointed not to see you – the country is so beautiful, and you will like this cottage.

---

[1] a corpse,] and   [2] feeble] faint   [3] killed] dead

If you go to Glasgow, will you see my elder sister, who lives there, and take her my love?[1] She is a queer creature, she loves me very much, though. And she is sad up there, and rather poor. They have a little dairy shop (she is not beautiful either).

     Mrs S. King, 5 Harley St., Ibrox, Glasgow
is the address. I shall tell her perhaps you will see her. She has one little girl of about five, Margaret, my niece, of whom I am very fond.[2] If you took the mother and child out to tea one day, to some pleasant restaurant, it would be a nice thing.

When are you going to Glasgow? We have had today Lady Ottoline Morrell down for the day – I like her very much. You must meet her.[3] You will like her.

I shall after all send you some requests, you see. Send us one or two boxes, will you – round ones

        [Sketches]

We expect you in about a fortnight, seeing you are free then.

       Herzliche Grüsse D. H. Lawrence

Look after the Murrys a bit – their condition is I think crucial.[4]

853. To J. B. Pinker, 1 February 1915
Text: MS UNYB; Huxley 219.

           Greatham, Pulborough, Sussex.
                 1st Feb. 1915

Dear Pinker,

I wish I had done that novel, I seem so long. But it will certainly be done by the end of this month, February. For I have done 450 pages out of 600 or so. Therefore tell Methuen if he asks that the whole will be sent in by the end of the month, and that there shall be no very flagrant love-passages in it (at least, to my thinking).

---

[1] Emily Una King. See *Letters*, i. 416n.

[2] Margaret Emily King (b. 1909).

[3] According to a note among the Koteliansky Papers in the BL, Kot first met Lady Ottoline on 15 February 1915. See also Letter 867.

[4] Their relationship was under severe strain; Katherine Mansfield's attention was focused on Paris and the author Francis Carco (François Marie Alexandere Carcopino-Tussoli), (1886–1958), with whom she subsequently had a brief affair. (See Carswell, *Lives and Letters*, pp. 100–6.) There is irony in DHL's suggestion since Kot was himself to fall deeply in love with Katherine Mansfield.

Viola Meynell would like to type the MS. for me, and I think perhaps it would be safer. Will you send it to her

Miss Viola Meynell, 2A Granville Place, Portman Square, W.

I should feel safer if there were two copies extant of the manuscript.

Here it is rather beautiful – in fact very beautiful, and I am getting better. I was seedy in Bucks, and so black in spirit. I can even hope beyond the war now. Some day the world will come through, I think, and in the end will be cleaner.

I hope I'm not a great deal of trouble to you with this novel.

Yours Sincerely   D. H. Lawrence

Did you write to America about the book of short stories – or to Kennerley.[1]

854. To Lady Ottoline Morrell, 1 February 1915

Text: MS UT; Postmark, Cootham 2 [...] 15; cited in O.M. [Lady Ottoline Morrell], 'D. H. Lawrence, 1885–1930', *Nation and Athenaeum*, xlvii (22 March 1930), 860.

Greatham, Pulborough, Sussex
Monday 1 Feb 1915

Dear Lady Ottoline,

I must write you a line when you have just gone, to tell you how my heart feels quite big with hope for the future. Almost with the remainder of tears and the last gnashing of teeth,[2] I could sing the 'Magnificat'[3] for the child in my heart.[4]

I want you to form the nucleus of a new community which shall start a new life amongst us – a life in which the only riches is integrity of character. So that each one may fulfil his own nature and deep desires to the utmost, but wherein the[5] ultimate satisfaction and joy is in the completeness of us all as one. Let us be good all together, instead of just in the privacy of our chambers, let us know that the intrinsic part of all of us is the best part, the believing part, the passionate, generous part. We can all come croppers, but what does it matter. We can laugh at each other, and dislike each other, but the good remains, and we know it. And the new community shall be established upon the known, eternal good part in us. This present community consists, as far as it is a framed thing, in a myriad contrivances for preventing

---

[1] See Letter 836.
[2] Cf. 'weeping and gnashing of teeth', Matthew viii. 12 *et al.*
[3] A song of thanksgiving, based on Luke i. 46–55, which forms part of Evening Prayer in the Book of Common Prayer.
[4] A reference to DHL's dream of a new society, 'Rananim'.   [5] MS reads 'the the'.

us from being let down by the meanness in ourselves or in our neighbours. But it is like a motor car that is so encumbered with non-skid, non-puncture, non-burst, non-this and non-that contrivances, that it simply can't go any more. I hold this the most sacred duty – the gathering together of a number of people who shall so agree to live by the *best* they know, that they shall be *free* to live by the best they know. The ideal, the religion, must now be *lived, practised.* We will have no more *churches.* We will bring church and house and shop together. I do believe that there are enough decent people to make a start with. Let us get the people. Curse the Strachey who asks for a new religion – the greedy dog.[1] He wants another juicy bone for his soul, does he? Let him start to fulfil what religion we have.

After the war, the soul of the people will be so maimed and so injured that it is[2] horrible to think of. And this shall be the new hope: that there shall be a life wherein the struggle shall not be for money or for power, but for individual freedom and common effort towards good. That is surely the richest thing to have now – the feeling that one is working, that one is part of a great, good effort or of a great effort towards goodness. It is no good plastering and tinkering with this community. Every strong soul must put off its connection with this society, its vanity and chiefly its fear, and go naked with its fellows, weaponless, armourless, without shield or spear, but only with naked hands and open eyes. Not self-sacrifice, but fulfilment, the flesh and the spirit in league together, not in arms against one another. And each man shall know that he is part of the greater body, each man shall submit that his own soul is not supreme even to himself. To be or not to be is no longer the question. The question now, is how shall we fulfil our declaration 'God is'. For all our life is now based on the assumption that God is not – or except on rare occasions.

Campbell's address is

C. H. G. Campbell, 9 Selwood Terrace, South Kensington.

We must go very, very carefully at first. The great serpent to destroy, is the Will to Power: the desire for one man to have some dominion over his fellow man. Let us have *no* personal influence, if possible – nor personal magnetism, as they used to call it, nor persuasion – no 'Follow me' – but only 'Behold'. And a man shall not come to save his own soul – let his soul

[1] Lytton Strachey (1880–1932). In December 1914 he completed his biography of Cardinal Manning (later collected in *Eminent Victorians* 1918); he had read it out to friends and showed the typescript to Virginia Woolf in January 1915; so its contents became widely known. It is in part an attack on the Church and may have prompted some remarks by Lady Ottoline to which DHL responds here.   [2] is] will be

go to hell. He shall come because he knows that his own soul is not the be-all and the end-all, but that all souls of all things do but compose the body of God, and that God indeed Shall *Be*.

I do hope that we shall all of us be able to agree, that we have a common way, a common interest, not a private way and a private interest only.

It is communism based, not on poverty, but on riches, not on humility, but on pride, not on sacrifice but upon complete fulfilment in the flesh of all strong desire, not on forfeiture but upon inheritance, not on heaven but on earth. We will be Sons of God who walk here [...] on earth, not bent on getting and having, because we know we inherit all things. We will be aristocrats, and as wise as the serpent in dealing with the mob. For the mob shall not crush us nor starve us nor cry us to death. We will deal cunningly with the mob, the greedy soul, we will gradually bring it to subjection.

We will found an order, and we will all be Princes, as the angels are.

We must bring this thing about – at least set it into life, bring it forth new-born on the earth, watched over by our old cunning and guarded by our ancient, mercenary-soldier habits.

My wife sends her greetings and pledge of alliance. I shall paint you a little wooden box.[1]

Au revoir   D. H. Lawrence

855. To Gordon Campbell, [2 February 1915]

Text: MS UCin; Moore, *Intelligent Heart* 180–1.

Greatham, Pulborough, Sussex.

2 Feb. 1914

My dear Campbell,

Here we are settled in our new cottage. It is really beautiful – and really comfortable – even a bath with beautiful hot water. We are quite isolated – much lonelier than in Bucks, save for the Meynell houses. And the Meynells are all in London.

We are only a mile from the foot of the downs – half an hour from the top, where one sees all the land and sea. Really, I like it very much.

Yesterday Lady Ottoline Morrell came down – she is going to bring Bertrand Russell, the philosophic-mathematics man.[2] I talked to her about

---

[1] DHL painted a phoenix on the cover of a small round box (now in the possession of Mrs Julian Vinogradoff).

[2] Bertrand Arthur William Russell (1872–1970), mathematician and philosopher. Grandson of the 1st Earl Russell, he succeeded his brother as 3rd Earl in 1931. Privately educated, he went to Cambridge where he studied mathematics and moral sciences; became a Fellow of Trinity College in 1895. During the First World War he was a leading pacifist; in consequence

you, and she said she would ask you to go and see her. Dont refuse, because she is *really* nice – somebody to know in this scant world: though I don't like her parties.

Oh, one of my characters in my novel – minor – is a subaltern in the Engineers – does one say Royal Engineers? – he is 21 years old, son of a parson, not poor.[1] What would he be? What would he earn? What would he do? Where would he live? Have patience, and tell me.

I want you and Beatrice to come for a week-end directly. We haven't got all the things in the cottage yet. And it is such a long way from the station – 4 good miles – otherwise there is that very good 2/6 excursion on Sundays. I should like to see you soon, though.

How are the Murrys. They seem a bit upset. Please be decent to them, and don't be tiresome.

How did you get on with Kotiliansky? He says of you 'He is quite simple, really, a simple man. When he is cynical, it is nothing. He knows – he knows.'

Greetings to Beatrice Campbell. Good wishes to you.

D. H. Lawrence

856. To Lady Ottoline Morrell, [3 February 1915]
Text: MS StaU; Schorer 50.

Greatham, Pulborough, Sussex.
Wednesday[2]

My dear Lady Ottoline,

We shall be glad to see you on Saturday, if you can really come. I am still a bit scared of Mr Russell – I feel as if I should stutter.

Please don't hold too big an idea of me – for it will be your idea which is big, more than[3] me. And then I shall be to you like the corn on the rocky ground.[4] Take warning by your past experiences. You are too generous in your estimations, as you well know.

---

he was temporarily deprived of his Fellowship and imprisoned for a time. A voluminous writer, his most famous work, written with A. N. Whitehead, is *Principia Mathematica* (1910–13). Russell became Lady Ottoline's lover in 1912, but it is not clear whether DHL knew this. DHL's first meeting with Russell took place on 8 February 1915. Lady Ottoline recalled: 'On one of my visits to Greatham I took Bertrand Russell with me and it appeared a great success. From the first these two passionate men took to each other and Bertie Russell, as we drove away, exclaimed, "He is amazing; he sees through and through one"' (Gathorne-Hardy, *Ottoline: The Early Memoirs*, p. 273). For Russell's description of his relationship with DHL see his *Autobiography*, ii. 20–4. The first version, which was more complete, was published by Russell in *Harper's Magazine*, ccxi (February 1953), 93–5.
[1] The character is Anton Skrebensky (who is Ursula Brangwen's lover) in *The Rainbow*.
[2] Dated with reference to Letter 855 in which DHL first mentions a forthcoming visit by Russell, here planned for Saturday, 6 February 1915 but eventually postponed until Monday, 8 February; see Letter 860.   [3] more than] and not   [4] Cf. Mark iv. 5–6.

I send you your box, that I painted for you. The phœnix on the bottom is my badge and sign. It gives me a real thrill. Does that seem absurd? Greetings from my wife.

a rivederci   D. H. Lawrence

If the time is rather short, perhaps you would send a post card to the Station Hotel Pulborough for a fly to meet your train. If you let us know by Saturday morning that is time enough for us. I wish it would be a fine day.

857. To E. M. Forster, [3 February 1915]
Text: MS KCC; Furbank, ii. 8.

Greatham, Pulborough, Sussex
Wednesday[1]

Dear Forster,

Thank you very much for the books.[2] We are waiting for you to follow them. If you will let me know what time you get to Pulborough, I will walk down and meet you, as it is a long way and you can take a short cut.

I have just read the 'Story of a Panic'.[3] You with your 'Only Connect' motto,[4] I must say that you reach the limit of splitness here. You are bumping your nose on the end of the cul de sac.

My angels and devils are nothing compared with your Pan.[5] Don't you see Pan[6] is the undifferentiated root and stem drawing out of unfathomable darkness, and my Angels and Devils are old-fashioned symbols for the flower into which we strive to burst. Now no plant can live towards the root. That is the most split, perverse thing of all.

You see I know all about your Pan. He is not dead, he is the same forever. But you should not confuse him with universal love, as you tend to do. You are very confused. You give Pan great attributes of Christ.

All that dark, concentrated, complete, all-containing surge of which I am the fountain; and of which the well-head is my loins, is urging forward, like a plant to flower or a fountain to its parabola. And my angels and devils are a sort of old-fashioned flowering. I am just in love with mediaeval terms, that is all – Fra Angelico and Cimabue[7] and the Saints.

---

[1] Since Forster's visit to Greatham took place on 10 February 1915, it seems logical to date this letter on the preceding Wednesday.

[2] Forster had sent DHL copies of *Howards End* and *The Celestial Omnibus and Other Stories*.

[3] Included in *Celestial Omnibus*.

[4] The epigraph of *Howards End*.

[5] In his previous letter, DHL referred to 'angels and demons', and Forster seems to have objected to these terms; a discussion of Pan appears in 'Story of a Panic'.

[6] Pan] your   [7] Giovanni Cimabue (1240–1302), Florentine religious painter.

But your Pan is a stooping back to the well head, a perverse pushing back the waters to their source, and saying, the source is everything. Which is stupid and an annihilation – but very stupid. In these books, these last, you are intentional and perverse and not vitally interesting. One must live from the source, through all the racings and heats of Pan, and on to my beloved angels and devils, with their aureoles and their feet upon the flowers of light, and with their red-mouthed despairs and destructions. However, we wait till you come. Don't be alarmed – I seem to 'stunt' because I use old terms for my feeling, because I am not inventive or creative enough.

auf wiedersehen   D. H. Lawrence

858. To S. S. Koteliansky, [5 February 1915]
Text: MS BL; cited in Gransden 24.

Greatham, Pulborough, Sussex.
Friday[1]

Mein lieber Kot,

Thank you very much for sending the wooden-box list. Get me one or two of 11, 12, and 13 flat shape, and one or two 6, 7, 8 tall shape – I would like six flat ones and three or four tall ones.

I keep wondering when you will go to Glasgow, if ever. It will be an experience for you.

I have got into the stride of my novel, and am working gallantly. But I doubt I shall be too late for spring publication. However, I don't care. What is the use of giving books to the swinish public in its present state.

I continue to love this place. This long room with its untouched beams is not so very severe – beautiful, I think it. You are sure to like it. Lady Ottoline says that on her estate are some monkish buildings she is eager to make into a cottage for me and Frieda.

I have got a new birth of life since I came down here. Those five months since the war have been my time in the sepulchre. Do you remember coming down to Barrow-in-Furness and finding war declared? – I shall never forget those months in Bucks – five months, and every moment dead, dead as a corpse in its grave clothes. It is a ghastly thing to remember. Now I feel the waking up, and the thrill in my limbs, and the wind blows ripples on my blood as it rushes against this house from the sea, full of germination and quickening.

Tomorrow Lady Ottoline is coming again and bringing Bertrand Russell – the Philosophic-Mathematics man – a Fellow of Cambridge University

---

[1] Dated with reference to Russell's visit planned for Saturday, 6 February 1915.

F.R.S. – Earl Russell's brother.[1] We are going to struggle with my Island idea – Rananim – But they say, the island shall be England, that we shall start our new community in the midst of this old one, as a seed falls among the roots of the parent. Only wait, and we will remove mountains and set them in the midst of the sea.[2]

You will let us know when you can come down.

This week they have killed Hildas[3] brother at the war. She came running in as if she were shot 'Oh Mam, my poor brother's killed at the war –' I feel so bitter against the war altogether, I could wring the neck of humanity for it.

Mais – nous verrons.

Je te serre la main.[4]

D. H. Lawrence

I will take you to Lady Ottolines later.[5]

859. To E. M. Forster, [5–6 February 1915]
Text: MS KCC; Furbank, ii. 8–9.

Greatham, Pulborough, Sussex.

[Frieda Lawrence begins]

Friday[6]

Dear Mr Forster,

Thank you for *Howard's end* – It got hold of me and not being a critical person I thank the Lord for it, and what he gives me. Only perhaps the end – broken Henry's remain Henry's[7] as I know to my cost – It's a beautiful book, but now you must go further – We had violent discussions over your letters, L[awrence] and I – (Three cheers for the 'firm').[8] What ails you modern men is that you put too high a value on [Lawrence interjects: ready-made] 'consciousness' on the revealed things; Because you cannot utter the 'unutterable' you are inclined to say it does not exist – Hope and that sort of thing is *not* your strong point – You are so frightened of being

---

[1] John Francis Stanley, 2nd Earl Russell (1865–1931).
[2] Matthew xxi. 21; Mark xi. 23.
[3] The Meynells' servant who looked after the main house.
[4] 'But – we shall see. All good wishes' (literally 'I shake your hand').
[5] See p. 270 n. 3.
[6] Forster was to visit DHL on Wednesday, 10 February 1915, hence the conjectural dates of the two parts of this letter.
[7] Henry Wilcox, one of the main characters in *Howards End*.
[8] Forster objected to joint letters from the Lawrences: 'A double act on the part of man and wife did not suit Forster, and he replied tartly, refusing to "have dealings with a firm"' (Furbank, ii. 7).

let down, as if one couldn't get up again! – As to the firm you *did* hit a little sore point with me – Poor author's wife, who does her little best and everybody wishes her to Jericho – Poor second fiddle, the surprise at her existence! She goes on playing her little accompaniment so bravely! Tut-Tut, tra la-la! Thank you again for *Howard's end*, it had a bucking-up effect on me!

Yours sincerely   die zweite Flöte[1] –

And come soon –

[Lawrence begins] [6 February 1915]
Saturday

Very good, I will meet the 1.34 at Pulborough next Wednesday. Don't miss the connection – but in case you do, wire to Lawrence, Greatham, *Amberley* – only I shall leave here at 12.30, so don't wire if it is no use. We will have no other visitor (D V). You will stay till when? a couple of days at any rate.

DHL

860. To Lady Ottoline Morrell, [6 February 1915]
Text: MS StaU; Unpublished.

Greatham, Pulborough, Sussex.
Saturday night[2]

Dear Lady Ottoline

We shall be most glad to see you on Monday. The thought of Mr Russell is rather alarming – I wish one were born comfortably acquainted with everybody.

You will find a fly or a motor-car at the station to meet you, as it is too far to walk. Just say 'for Gretham'.

I hope this reaches you in time. The fly will meet the 11.57.

I hope it will be sunny.

a rivederci   D. H. Lawrence

861. To J. B. Pinker, [7? February 1915]
Text: MS Forster; Unpublished.

Greatham, Pulborough, Sussex.
Sunday–Feb 1915

---

[1] 'the second flute'.

[2] The visit had been planned for Saturday, 6 February 1915; therefore, this letter postponing it by two days was written on 6 February.

My Dear Pinker,
    Thank you for your letter about Kennerley.
    I did have one cheque for £25 from him – about fifteen or sixteen months ago.[1] Whether it came through Duckworth I am not quite sure – but I think so. The second, non-valid cheque for £10 came to me direct in Italy.[2] That is all I know of the monetary part of the business.
    At least you will get the novel[3] away from him, which is the biggest thing. I should indeed be happy if he *did* have to pay me something – I shall soon be penniless again. But we will see –
Yours   D. H. Lawrence

862. To E. M. Forster, [8 February 1915]

Text: MS KCC; Unpublished.

Greatham, Pulborough, Sussex.
Monday

Dear Forster,
    On Wednesday, if it rains much, I shan't walk down, and you must take a fly – either at the station or at the Station Hôtel opposite. If it doesn't rain I shall walk down. In any case we expect you.
Au revoir   D. H. Lawrence
You got the other letter?[4] – the girl wasnt quite sure what she did with it.

863. To Barbara Low, [11 February 1915]

Text: MS UT; Nehls, i. 272–3.

Greatham, Pulborough, Sussex.
Thursday[5]

Dear Barbara Low,[6]
    You heard how my bee-box all went wrong:[7] and Ivy blackened the other

[1] See Letters 670, 718.
[2] See Letter 726.
[3] The *Rainbow* MS.
[4] Presumably Letter 859.
[5] Forster's 'going away in the morning' – Friday, 12 February 1915 – confirms the date of this letter as 11 February.
[6] Barbara Low (1877–1955) was the aunt of Ivy Low, who had visited DHL in Lerici in April 1914, and the sister-in-law of Dr David Eder. She was a pioneer in psychoanalysis in England and the author of *Psycho-Analysis: A Brief Outline of the Freudian Theory* (1920). (For obituary see the *International Journal of Psycho-analysis*, 1956, pp. 473–4.)
[7] The nature of the 'bee-boxes' which DHL decorated appears to be clarified in Maurice Maeterlinck's *Life of the Bee*, trans. Alfred Sutro (1901), pp. 71–2: 'I...have more than once had impregnated queens sent me from Italy...It is the custom to forward them in small, perforated boxes. In these some food is placed, and the queen enclosed, together with a certain number of workers.' DHL enjoyed decorating such boxes and presenting them as small containers (for studs etc.) to his friends. See Letter 1004.

long one, when she was here – only for one day – so now I am waiting till Kotiliansky sends me another box before I can paint you one. I really want it to be a nice one. Not the spoiled bee-box. I shall do it immediately when it comes.

Forster is here. He is very nice. I wonder if the grip has gone out of him.

I get a feeling of acute misery from him – not that he does anything – but you know the acute, exquisite pain of cramps – I somehow feel that. I think I must get it by transference from him. He is going away in the morning. We have talked so hard – about a revolution – at least I have talked – it is my fate, God help me – and now I wonder, are my words gone like seed spilt on a hard floor, only reckoned an untidiness there. I must tell you I am very sad, as if it hurt very much.

You are one of the very few people who listen to me. You see I do believe some things. It is not myself. But Mrs Eder doesn't listen to me. She makes me a *Wunderkind*.[1] It is not *I* who matter – it is what is said through me.

When will you come and see us. We will talk then. My heart feels like a swelling root that quite hurts.

Don't you be sad about your life. Soon we will put our own immediate lives away, we will devote them to that which is to be done. We must revolutionise this system of life, that is based on *outside* things, money, property, and establish a system of life which is based on *inside* things. The war will come to an end, and then the Augean stables are to be cleansed.

Come any time – but if it is to stay a night, let us know, because of other people. But every Sunday there is a 2/6 Angler's excursion from Victoria, comes down early. Take that *any* Sunday.

My novel is getting along. I hope the publishers will not think it impossible to print it as it stands. Forster brought down a ghastly rumour of the *Prussian Officer*'s being withdrawn from circulation, but order of the police.[2] God save us – what is the country coming to. But it probably is not true.

Dont be miserable, because there is so much to be done, soon.

auf wiedersehen   D. H. Lawrence

864. To Lady Ottoline Morrell, [11? February 1915]
Text: MS UT; cited in Sandra Jobson Darroch, *Ottoline: The Life of Lady Ottoline Morrell* (New York, 1975), pp. 148–9.

[Greatham, Pulborough, Sussex]
[11? February 1915]

[1] Literally 'an infant prodigy'.   [2] See p. 257 n. 3.

Dear Lady Ottoline,

I do hope you wont feel very resentful at Friedas request. You see for three years now this struggle for the children has gone on.[1] And a little thing might set the whole business right.

Do you think you might write to Professor Weekley, and say that you are a friend of Mrs Lawrence, and that you would like to see him, to ask[2] him if the children might come to tea at your house, and meet their mother there for an hour. He has written a book – two books – the *Romance of Words* and the *Romance of Names*.[3] I will get Forster to send you the *Romance of Names* from a bookseller. Then you might say to him it had interested you. God grant it may.

I wish you could tell him you are Lady Ottoline – the sister of the Duke of Portland. And if you said you would so like to see the children – the boy is at St Pauls School – the elder girl also at the Girls St. Pauls. – The boy is fourteen, the girls are twelve and ten respectively. Their names are Monty, Elsa and Barby.

Weekley was at Cambridge, about 18 years ago – Trinity College. He worships Cambridge lights.

You will help us with this, won't you. It has been such a struggle these three years.

I shall trust your cleverness to make a letter to him. Do keep a copy, for me to preserve for ever. And if he fights shy – I don't think he will, somehow, because I think he would like you to [...] know his children – but if he is a mere churl, you will still be the great lady.

He is a Professor of Modern Languages at Nottingham University – has been so for 15 years.

It *is* rather splendid that you are a great lady. Don't abrogate one jot or tittle of your high birth:[4] it is too valuable in this commercial-minded, mean world: and it *does* stand as well for what you really are. Because, of what other woman could we ask this? – of what other woman of rank?

I really do honour your birth. Let us[5] do justice to its nobility: it is not mere accident. I would give a great deal to have been born an aristocrat.

Forster is here. I like him. But I'm not sure his grip has not gone. I shall tell you more about him.

Since May 1912 Ernest Weekley had resisted all Frieda's attempts to make contact with her three children. On 28 July 1913 the High Court gave him custody of the children and forbade her to interfere with them.
to ask] to try
Published respectively in 1912 and 1914. (Weekley had also produced several textbooks on French grammar and composition.)
birth] standing   [5] us] us all

I shall write you an answer about Campbell and his belief in evil. He never shows that side much – or not openly – to me. I was very interested.

It was so beautiful on the downs today, with the sea so bright on one hand, and the downs so fresh, and the floods so blue on the other hand, away below, washing at the little villages. I don't know why, but my heart was so sad, almost to break. A little train ran through the floods, and steamed on so valiant into the gap. And I seemed to feel all humanity, brave and splendid, like the train, and so blind, and so utterly unconscious of where they are going or of what they are doing.

D. H. Lawrence

865. To Bertrand Russell, 12 February 1915
Text: MS UT; Moore, *Atlantic Monthly* 92–6.

Greatham, Pulborough, Sussex.
12 Feb 1915

Dear Mr Russell,

We have had E. M. Forster here for three days. There is more in him than ever comes out. But he is not dead yet. I hope to see him pregnant with his own soul. We were on the edge of a fierce quarrel all the time. He went to bed muttering that he was not sure we – my wife and I – weren't just playing round his knees: he seized a candle and went to bed, neither would he say good night. Which I think is rather nice. He sucks his dummy – you know, those child's comforters – long after his age. But there is something very real in him, if he will not cause it to die. He is *much* more than his dummy-sucking, clever little habits allow him to be.

I write to say to you that we *must* start a solid basis of freedom of actual living – not only of thinking. We *must* provide another standard than the pecuniary standard, to measure *all* daily life by. We must be free of the economic question. Economic life must be the means to actual life. We must make it so at once.

There must be a revolution in the state. It shall begin by the nationalising of all [. . .] industries and means of communication, and of the land – in one fell blow. Then a man shall have his wages whether he is sick or well or old – if anything prevents his working, he shall have his wages just the same. So we shall not live in fear of the wolf – no man amongst us, and no woman, shall have any fear of the wolf at the door, for all wolves are dead.

Which practically solves the whole economic question for the present. All dispossessed owners shall receive a proportionate income – no capital recompense – for the space of, say fifty years.

Something like this must be done. It is no use saying a man's soul should be free, if his boots hurt him so much he can't walk. All our ideals are cant and hypocrisy till we have burst the fetters of this money. Titan[1] nailed on the rock of the modern industrial capitalistic system, declaring in fine[2] language that his soul is free as the Oceanids[3] that fly away on[4] wings of aspiration, while the bird of carrion desire gluts at his liver, is too shameful. I am ashamed to write any real writing of passionate love to my fellow men. Only satire is decent now. The rest is a lie. Until we act, move, rip ourselves off the rock. So there must be an actual revolution, to set free our bodies. For there never was a free soul in a chained body. That is a lie. There might be a resigned soul. But a resigned soul is not a free soul. A resigned soul has yielded its claim on temporal living. It can only do this because the temporal living is being done for it vicariously. Therefore it is dependent on the vicar, let it say what it will. So Christ, who resigned his life, only resigned it because he knew the others would keep theirs. They would do the living, and would later adapt his method to their living. The freedom of the soul within the denied[5] body is a sheer conceit.

Forster is not poor, but he is bound hand and foot bodily. Why? *Because he does not believe that any beauty or any divine utterance is any good any more.* Why? Because the world is suffering from bonds, and birds of foul desire which gnaw its liver. Forster knows, as every thinking man now knows, that all his thinking and his passion for humanity amounts to no more than trying to soothe with poetry a man raging with pain which can be cured. Cure the pain, don't give the poetry. Will all the poetry in the world satisfy the manhood of Forster, when Forster knows that his implicit manhood is to be satisfied by nothing but immediate physical action. He tries to dodge himself – the sight is pitiful.

But why can't he act? Why can't he take a woman and fight clear to[6] his own basic, primal being? Because he knows that self-realisation is not his ultimate desire. His ultimate desire is for the continued action which has been called the social passion – the love for humanity – the desire to work for humanity. That is every man's ultimate desire and need. Now you see the vicious circle. Shall I go to my Prometheus and tell him beautiful tales of the free, whilst the vulture gnaws his liver?[7] I am ashamed. I turn my

---

[1] In Greek mythology the Titans were the old pre-Olympian gods; here, DHL alludes to Prometheus, whom Zeus chained to a rock, as punishment for stealing fire and giving it to man.   [2] fine] fit

[3] The three thousand ocean nymphs, daughters of the sea god, Oceanus, and his consort, Tethys.

[4] on] on the   [5] denied] chained   [6] clear to] towards

[7] In some versions of the myth, a vulture gnaws Prometheus's liver while he is chained (in Aeschylus's play an eagle eats his heart).

face aside from my Prometheus, ashamed of my vain, irrelevant, impudent words. I cannot help Prometheus. And this knowledge rots the core of activity.

If I cannot help Prometheus – and I am also Prometheus – how shall I be able to take a woman? For I go to a woman to know myself, and to know her. And I want to know myself, that I may know how to act for humanity. But if I am aware that I cannot act for humanity –? Then I dare not go to a woman.

Because, if I go, I know I shall betray myself and her and everything. It will be a vicious circle. I go to her to know myself, and I know myself – what? – to enjoy myself. That is sensationalism – that I go to a woman to feel[1] myself only. Love is, that I go to a woman to know myself, and knowing myself, to go further, to explore in to the unknown, which is the woman, venture in upon the coasts of the unknown, and open my discovery to all humanity. But if I know that humanity is lame and cannot move, bo[u]nd and in pain and unable to come along, my offering it discoveries is only a cynicism. Which I know and Forster knows and even Gilbert Cannan knows. 'They can't hear you', Gilbert Cannan says of the public. 'They turn you into a sensation.' So he panders to the chained Prometheus, tickles him with near sensations – a beastly thing to do. He writes *Young Earnest*.[2]

If I know that humanity is chained to a rock, I cannot set[3] forth to find it new lands to enter upon. If I do pretend to set forth, I am a cheating, false merchant, seeking my *own* ends. And I am ashamed to be that. I will not.

So then, how shall I come to a woman? To know myself first. Well and good. But knowing myself is only preparing myself. What for? For the adventure into the unexplored, the woman, the whatever-it-is I am up against. – Then the actual heart says 'No no – I can't explore.' Because an explorer is one sent forth from a great body of people to open out new lands for their occupation. But my people cannot even move – it is chained – paralysed. I am not an explorer. I am a curious, inquisitive man with eyes that can only look for something to take back with him. And what can I take back with me? Not revelation – only curios – titillations. I am a curio hunter.

Again, I am ashamed.

Well then, I am neither explorer nor curio hunter. What then? For what do I come to a woman? To know myself. And what when I know myself? What do I then embrace her for, hold the unknown against me for? To repeat the experience of self discovery. But I have discovered myself – I am not

<hr/>

[1] feel] know   [2] A novel published in January 1915.   [3] MS reads 'set set'.

infinite. Still I can repeat the experience. But it will not be discovery. Still I can repeat the experience. – That is, I can get a sensation. The repeating of a known reaction upon myself is sensationalism. This is what nearly *all* English people now do. When a man takes a woman, he is *merely* repeating a known reaction upon himself, not seeking a new reaction, a discovery. And this is like self-abuse or masterbation. The ordinary Englishman of the educated class goes to a woman now to masterbate himself. Because he is not going for discovery or new connection or progression, but only to repeat upon himself a known reaction.

When this condition arrives, there is always Sodomy. The man goes to the man to repeat this reaction upon himself. It is a nearer form of masterbation. But still it has some *object* – there are still two bodies instead of one. A man of strong soul has too much honour for the other body – man or woman – to use it as a means of masterbation. So he remains neutral, inactive. That is Forster.

Sodomy only means that a man knows he is chained to the rock, so he will try to get the finest possible sensation out of himself.

This happens whenever the form of any living becomes too strong for the life within it: the clothes are more important than the man: therefore the man must get his satisfaction beneath the clothes.

Any man who takes a woman is up against the unknown. And a man prefers rather to have nothing to do with a woman than to have to slink away without answering the challenge. Or if he is a mean souled man, he will use the woman to masterbate himself.

There comes a point when the shell, the form of life, is a prison to the life. Then the life must either concentrate on breaking the shell, or it must turn round, turn in upon itself, and try infinite variations of a known reaction upon itself. Which produces a novelty. So that *The Rosary*[1] is a new combination of known re-actions – so is Gilbert Cannan's *Young Earnest* – so is the cinematograph drama and all our drama and all our literature.

Or, the best thing such a life can do, that knows it is confined, is to set-to to arrange and assort all the facts and knowledge of the contained life. Which is what Plato did and what most of our writers are doing on a mean scale. They know that they are enclosed entirely by the shell, the form of living. There is no going beyond it. They are bound down.

Now either we have to break the shell, the form, the whole frame, or we have got to turn to this inward activity of setting the house in order and drawing up a list before we die.

The Rosary (1909) by Florence Louisa Barclay (1862–1921), her second and highly successful novel. It sold over a million copies by 1921.

But we shall smash the frame. The land, the industries, the means of communication and the public amusements shall all be nationalised. Every man shall have his wage till the day of his death, whether he work or not, so long as he works when he is fit. Every woman shall have her wage till the day of her death, whether she work or not, so long as she works when she is fit – keeps her house or rears her children.

Then, and then only, shall we be able to *begin* living. Then we shall be able to *begin* to work. Then we can examine marriage and love and all. Till then, we are fast within the hard, unliving, impervious shell.

You must have patience with me and understand me when my language is not clear.

I shall come and see you on the Sunday, March 7th, if you still invite me, because I want to meet Lowes Dickinson[1] and the good people you are going to introduce me to.

It is very nice and spring-like. The birds are beginning to sing. I laugh at them. Their voices are quite rusty and stiff with a winter of disuse. The blackbird goes at it so hard, to get his whistle clear, and the wood-pigeon is so soon disheartened.

Yours Sincerely   D. H. Lawrence

866. To Lady Cynthia Asquith, [15 February 1915]
Text: MS UT; Unpublished.

Greatham – Pulborough – Sussex
Monday[2]

My dear Lady Cynthia,

Your train, as far as I can see, leaves Portsmouth Town 11·5 arrives Pulboro. – 12·10. I know that is right. If I told you anything else I am an ass.

The return train leaves Pulborough 5·21 arrive Portsmouth Town 6·44.

So I shall meet the 12·10 in Pulboro. and you will walk up with me, unless the skies are weeping or the telegram boy rushes in.

Do you think I can remember to repeat by heart a letter I wrote to you

---

[1] Goldsworthy ('Goldie') Lowes Dickinson (1862–1932), humanist, historian and philosophical writer. He took a First in the Cambridge Classical Tripos, 1884; was elected into a Fellowship at King's College, Cambridge, 1887, and was Lecturer in Political Science 1896–1920. Among his early books *The Greek View of Life* (1896) was the most important. Though he was not a conscientious objector in 1914–18, he was devoted to the cause of preventing future wars. He helped to found the Bryce Group which became one of the nuclei of the League of Nations Union. (For obituary see *Cambridge Review*, 14 October 1932. E. M. Forster published biography in 1934.)

[2] Clearly the Monday immediately preceding Lady Cynthia's visit on 16 February.

two weeks ago?[1] Do you think it was a lyric poem in one stanza? But doesn't the Imperial Hôtel exist in Southsea.[2]

You will scarcely have time to paint another box. I was happy about one I made, of the Rose of England, but Miss Viola Meynell and some people called the Eders said how much more beautiful was plain wood. Since then I feel I ought to consider box painting as a secret vice.

Herzliche Grüsse. Auf wiedersehen   D. H. Lawrence

I though I'd give you the most resounding hôtel going – Imperial.

867. To S. S. Koteliansky, [15 February 1915]
Text: MS BL; Zytaruk 26.

[2 Museum Mansions, Great Russell Street, London]
[15 February 1915][3]

Dear Kot,

Here am I, for the night – come up in a motor car with one of the Meynells – staying with Horne – returning tomorrow early.[4] We want to have a meeting at your house tonight. Lady Ottoline may come.

au revoir   D. H. Lawrence

Come to the Imperial Restaurant – just at the back of South Kensington Station – through the Arcade and round to the right – just near – the address is Alfred Place West.

[Sketch showing directions to restaurant]

868. To Lady Ottoline Morrell, [17 February 1915]
Text: MS StaU; Schorer 49.

Greatham, Pulborough, Sussex.
[17 February 1915][5]

[Frieda Lawrence begins]

Dear Lady Ottoline,

You can have absolutely no idea, what it means to me, that you will help

See Letter 851.

Presumably Lady Cynthia was staying in Southsea to be near her husband, then stationed at Portsmouth.

The conjectural date here is based on the first meeting between Kot and Lady Ottoline, which took place on 15 February 1915; see p. 270 n. 3. Letter 868 confirms that Lady Ottoline met some people 'on Monday evening'. Although Kot's name is not specifically mentioned, it is reasonable to assume that the meeting was held at his house as requested by DHL.

DHL would have had to return in time to meet Lady Cynthia's train in Pulborough at 12.10, as he states in the previous letter.

The date of this letter is established with reference to Lady Cynthia's visit, which took place on Tuesday, 16 February 1915. She stayed overnight (see Letter 869) and would therefore have 'just gone' on Wednesday morning; hence, the date 17 February here.

me – It is so terrible to have to hurt a man as I did, because after all he did his best according to his own lights, my first husband I mean and that everybody turned against me is only natural – but it has been so killing and desperate when I felt everybody against me, even Lawrence, who was always quite genuine, but could not bear it, when I was unhappy because of the children – Even they turned against me, naturally again they only saw how I had hurt their father and them by leaving them – But all the time I *knew* I loved them and they me and that I would not give them up entirely, it is part of me – And now I am no longer alone in this battle, you have given me a generous helping hand and I am so grateful to you that I could sing – What a conflict, what a knot of conflicts life is, and alone one could do so terribly little – Your help means such hope to me – even if you are not successful it is not as important to me as your goodwill – Lady Cynthia Asquith has just gone, she is quite nice, but – I feel sorry for her – She is poor in feeling – You will come soon, and we will have lovely talks and walks – Dont write to Weekley till you feel really like it, there is no hurry –
          Good-bye and many, many thanks.   Frieda L –
   L. loves his opal, it suits him somehow, it's like him –

[Lawrence begins]

Dear Lady Ottoline,

   I hope you weren't awfully bored on Monday evening – and with that crowd. Those Irish people like Campbell and Hope Johnson[1] are too selfish and self-uncertain ever to feel anything like religious passion – they can only niggle about religious ecstasies. They make me sick. But in spite of everything, I am confident we will have our revolution. We must go on appealing to the *thinking* people, not to the emotional greedy mob – and get it so. You are *very valuable* to me to know you are in the world – it does me good to know you are within a few hours journey. It isn't a matter of ourselves and our own souls – it is a matter of a bigger hope. And you are one with us in a[2] bigger hope. How rare people are! But we will have our Revolution – my soul feels as fixed as a star in its orbit. When you come then stay the night –

                                        D. H. Lawrence

[1] John Hope-Johnstone (b. 1883) was a friend of Augustus John and had been tutor to his children (see Michael Holroyd, *Augustus John*, 1975, ii. 20–2. See also Compton Mackenzie, *My Life and Times: Octave Five*, 1966, p. 89).   [2] a] the

869. To Barbara Low, [19 February 1915]
Text: MS UT; Nehls, i. 274–5.

Greatham, Pulborough, Sussex.

Friday[1]

Dear Barbara Low,

Thank you very much for sending the paints to my little niece,[2] and the brush and paints to me. The brush was just what I wanted – thank you very much. But *please* send me the bill – I would rather.

Here is your box – B's for Barbara. Not very profound in symbolism. But I think the box is a success; don't you?

Why do you feel shy about coming down here? That is absurd. Come one day and stay the night. Then we can really have a talk – when the lamp is lighted and neither place nor time endure. Come when you like.

I shall be in London on March 5th or 6th I think. I promised to go and stay the week-end at Cambridge with Bertrand Russell, the mathematics-philosophy man. I don't feel quite sure if I shall go – but probably. Then I shall stay a night in town en route – I will let you know.

Frieda thanks you for your letter. Lady Ottoline Morrell is going to try to help her with the children. She is become quite a real friend of us both, Lady Ottoline. We had Lady Cynthia Asquith down for the night on Tuesday. But she wearies me a bit. Now Murry is with us. Katharine Mansfield has gone to Paris for a visit.[3] He will probably stay till she comes back. But you are not shy of him, so you can come whilst he is here.

Already we have found a few primroses and violets, and the birds sing hard at evening, in the wet bushes. I am happy in this place – in so far as the place matters – which is a good bit. Many regards to you from us both.

D. H. Lawrence

870. To S. S. Koteliansky, [19 February 1915]
Text: MS BL; Postmark, Cootham 19 FEB 15; Unpublished.

[Greatham, Pulborough, Sussex]

[19 February 1915]

[Frieda Lawrence begins]

Dear Kot,

Thank you for the cake, it was good, but I hardly like it, when you give

---

Written soon after Lady Cynthia's departure (on 17 February) and during Murry's visit (19–24 February), the letter must be dated Friday, 19 February 1915.   [2] Margaret King. She went to Paris in order to meet Francis Carco on 16 February 1915; see *The Journal of Katherine Mansfield* (1954), p. 74.

me things – because you don't really like me – I was not *cross*, when you did
not come with me to Golder's Green, but I could not help thinking if
L[awrence] had been there, you *would* have come – Also I think, L. would
be fonder of you, if I were not there; your attitude to me is not really and
truly a good one – I can feel it – You think I do not count besides Lawrence,
but I take myself, my ideals and life quite as seriously as he does his – This
you will not allow, and it is our quarrel, you think I am conceited, I cant
help that – but it hurts me very much when you think I do not count as a
human being – But you do not think much of women, they are not human
beings in your eyes – It's *your* fault, not mine – You will not have me for
a friend – Yes I like Katherine, there is something exquisite about her mind
and body – and a great power for affection – You were not nice or patient
with her – Will you come for the week-end? Jack is here – Dont mind what
I say, it is better to be honest –

Fried.

[Lawrence begins]

   Venga domani.[1]

DHL

871. To S. S. Koteliansky, [22 February 1915]
Text: MS BL; Postmark, Cootham 22 FEB 15; Moore 321–2.

Greatham, Pulborough, Sussex
Monda

My dear Kot,
   You are a great donkey, and your letters to Frieda are ridiculous – Wh
the hell do you make such a palaver to her? She was cross with me – at such
times she is indignant with you for your imagined adoration (as she puts it
of me. You are an ass to make so many postures and humilities and so forth
about it. Next time, for God's sake write – 'My dear Frieda – Thank you
for your letter – e basta'.
   And if you're going to come and see us, why for Heaven's sake don't you
come – fidgetting and fuming and stirring and preparing and communing
with yourself and reading the portents – it is preposterous. If you are coming
come, and have done. If you have anything to say, say it, and have done.
But *don't* be so queasy and uneasy and important – Oh damn. Plainly I do
not like you.
   Murry is here – I don't know when he is going away. It is possible Barbara
Low may come this week-end. There is still room for you if you'll come

---

[1] 'Come tomorrow.'

But I suppose you'd rather come when we are alone. I will let you know if Barbara is coming. If she is not, then fidget no more, but come on Saturday. If she is coming, then you please yourself.

We shall be in London on March 6th. I am going to Cambridge for the week-end.

Now I hope you'll be in a good and careless state of soul after this abuse. Be *careless*, damn it – not so careful.

auf wiedersehen   D. H. Lawrence

872. To Lady Ottoline Morrell, [22 February 1915]

Text: MS StaU; Postmark, Cootham 22 FEB 15; Schorer 48.

Greatham, Pulborough, Sussex.
[22 February 1915]

Dear Lady Ottoline,

We shall be so glad to see you tomorrow. But I shan't know in time to order the carriage – Will you wire for it? I shan't walk to the station because I've got a bad cold and must sing slow for five minutes. Frieda also has a bad cold. But we're on the turn to recovery. We shall be most glad to see you. There must be a great talk. I want to hear about your estate in Oxford, and the cottage, the cottage, the cottage.[1]

Murry is here because Katharine has gone to Paris. He is one of the men of the future – you will see. He is with me for the Revolution. He is just finishing his novel – his first – *very* good.[2] At present he is my partner – the only man who quite simply is with me – One day he'll be ahead of me. Because he'll build up the temple if I carve out the way – the place.

How big we talk.

à demain   D. H. Lawrence

873. To E. M. Forster, [24? February 1915]

Text: MS KCC; cited in Furbank, ii.11.

Greatham, Pulborough, Sussex.
Wednesday[3]

Dear Forster,

I send you back the book of Woolf.[4] It was interesting, but not *very* good – nothing much behind it.

Lady Ottoline planned to provide the Lawrences with a cottage at Garsington; see Letter 858.   [2] See p. 161 n. 3.

It appears from Letter 871 that DHL had only recently become certain about his visit to Cambridge 6–8 March. This makes 24 February the most likely Wednesday.

Delany conjectures that 'the book' was an advance copy of Virginia Woolf's novel *The Voyage Out* (1915) which Forster reviewed in the *Daily News* on 8 April 1915 (see Delany 51). It was more likely to be Leonard Woolf's first novel, *The Village in the Jungle* (1913).

I have been cross with you. Some things you should not write in your letters.[1] But I am tired of being cross, and feel very friendly again.

I hope you weren't angry with me for shouting about you to Lady Ottoline. She is too good to be affected wrongly.

I only want you to stick to the idea of a social revolution, which shall throw down artificial barriers between men, and make life freer and fuller. Any big vision of life must contain a revolutionised society, and one must fulfil ones visions, or perish.

I hope we shall see you again soon. We are away March 6th–9th. And at the week end there are generally people here.

Frieda sends her regards.

Yours   D. H. Lawrence

874. To Mary Cannan, 24 February 1915
Text: MS Lazarus; Moore 322–3.

Greatham, Pulborough, Sussex.
24 Feb. 1915.

My dear Mary,

We were awfully glad to get your letter. Why didn't Gilbert put a word in?

When are you coming to see us? The days are getting longer, I have found a few primroses and violets, the birds are very gaudy and beginning to sing. Now is your time to come.

Murry has been staying with us this last week. He seems much better in spirit, in being and in belief.[1] He has come to himself at last. We have changed our island scheme. After all it was a sort of running away from the problem. Since I have been here, it has come upon me that we must have a social revolution, after the war. Private ownership of land and industries and means of commerce shall be abolished – then every child born into the world shall have food and clothing and shelter as a birth-right, work or no work. A man shall work to earn the things beyond, if he wants them. Ask Gilbert if he doesn't agree.

We must form a revolutionary party. I have talked about it with various people – also Bertrand Russell. I am going to stay with him in Cambridge March 6th–8th. Then we shall go into it more thoroughly. The book I wrote – mostly philosophicalish, slightly about Hardy – I want to re-write

---

[1] 'Forster, on his return home, wrote the Lawrences a tough and rather rude letter, saying he had not enjoyed his stay' (Furbank, ii. 11).   [2] belief] spirit.

D. H. Lawrence, 1913, from a photograph by W. G. Parker

Henry Savage,
from a portrait by
John Flanagan

Katharine Clayton,
1926, from a photograph
by Howard M. King

Edward Marsh, 1912,
from a photograph by
Elliott Seabrooke

Katherine Mansfield and John Middleton Murry, c. 1914

Lady Cynthia Asquith,
1916

Austin Harrison, 1915,
from a photograph by
Reginald Haines

Mitchell Kennerley, c. 1925,
from a photograph by
Arnold Genthe

J. B. Pinker, c. 1900

Aubrey Waterfield, c. 1915

Lina Waterfield, c. 1914

W. H. Davies, 1918, from
a portrait by
Augustus John

Harriet Monroe, 1923

Catherine Carswell, c. 1914
(*right*)

Thomas and Madge Dunlop, 1915

S. S. Koteliansky, 1917, from
a portrait by Mark Gertler

Philip Morrell, 1902

Lady Ottoline Morrell, 1912,
from a photograph by Baron de Meyer

A. Llewelyn Roberts

Viola Meynell, c. 1914, from a photograph by Sherril Schell

E. M. Forster, 1915

Bertrand Russell, 1916,
from a photograph by
Hugh Cecil

Dollie Radford

Eleanor Farjeon, c. 1916

Zoë Akins,
from a photograph by
Carl Van Vechten © 1935

Herbert Thring,
from a portrait by
William Rothenstein

Robert Nichols, c. 1930,
from a portrait by
C. Dodgson

Marie Belloc Lowndes,
from a photograph by
Elliott and Fry

Dikran Kouyoumdjian, Philip Heseltine and D. H. Lawrence,
1915, at Garsington

J. D. Beresford and Walter de la Mare, 1920

Mark Gertler, 1920, from a self-portrait

Captain John Short

'The Rainbow', a drawing by Lawrence
sent to Viola Meynell on 2 March 1915

and publish in pamphlets.[1] We must create an idea of a new, freer life, where men and women can really meet on natural terms, instead of being barred within so many barriers. And if the money spirit is killed, and eating and sleeping is free, then most of the barriers will collapse. Something must be done, and we must begin soon. Tell Gilbert to roll his sleeves up for a fight with the cursed, tame Mammon we are saddled with. Come and see us and let us talk about it.

We had E. M. Forster here for a day or two. I liked him, but his life is so ridiculously inane, the man is dying of inanition. He was very angry with me for telling him about himself.

Get the motor car ready and come down – I shall be so glad to see you again – so will Frieda. She is sad, having news that her father is dead. And we have got bad colds.

When you come, could you bring the type-writer, do you think – and the ½ doz. knives we left behind.

Love from us both to you both   D. H. Lawrence

[Frieda Lawrence begins]

Much love to you both! We also forgot 2 books – An Egyptian one[2] and *Christian Symbolism*[3] – I would be glad of them. Lady O[ttoline] left this morning, she was also sad but nice!

Auf Wiedersehen   Frieda

875. To J. B. Pinker, 24 February 1915
Text: MS UNYB; Huxley 222.

Greatham, Pulborough, Sussex.
24 Feb. 1915.

My dear Pinker,

Do be getting me some money, will you? I heard the wolf scratch the door today.

I am very, very near the end of the novel. But Miss Meynell is somewhat behind with the typing.[4] Is it definitely too late for Spring publication? I

The proposal to re-write 'Study of Thomas Hardy' (or 'Le Gai Savaire', Letter 876) for publication in pamphlet-form led to *The Signature* – published with Murry and Katherine Mansfield – which ran for three numbers, October–November 1915. Each number carried a section of DHL's 'The Crown'.
Unidentified.   [3] See Letter 828.
DHL prevaricates here. Letter 879 shows that Viola Meynell did not begin typing the *Rainbow* until after 2 March 1915. At this point, she was certainly 'behind with the typing' since DHL had not finished the writing, and she had not started typing the MS.

hear how phenomenally well novels are doing. For my own part, I always shrink from having my work published. I hate the public to read it.

I send you a letter from an American.[1] You must tell me if it is worth answering.

Do you think Methuen is ready to back up this novel of mine? He must make some fight for it. It is worth it, and he must do it. It will never be popular. But he can make it known what it is, and prevent the mean little fry from pulling it down. Later, I think I must go and see him. There will be a bit of a fight before my novels are admitted, that I know. The fight will have to be made, that is all. The field is there to conquer.

I hope your son hasn't gone to the war.

Yours Sincerely   D. H. Lawrence

876. To Bertrand Russell, 24 February 1915
Text: MS UT; cited in Moore, *Atlantic Monthly* 96.

Greatham, Pulborough, Sussex.

24 Feb. 1915

Dear Bertrand Russell,

Your letter was very kind to me, and somehow made me feel as if I were impertinent – a bit. You have worked so hard in the abstract beyond me, I feel as if I should never be where you have been for so long, and are now – it is not my destiny. And if you are there beyond me, I feel it impertinent to talk and write so vehemently. I feel you are tolerant when you listen. Which is rather saddening. I wish you'd tell me when I am foolish and over-insistent.

I have only to stick to my vision of a life where men are freer from the immediate material things, where they need never be as they are now on the defensive against each other, largely because of the struggle for existence which is a real thing, even to those who need not make the struggle. So a vision of a better life must include a revolution of society. And one must fulfil ones vision as much as possible. And the drama shall be between individual men and women, not between nations and classes. And the great living experience for every man is his adventure into the woman. And the ultimate passion of every man is to be[2] within himself the whole of mankind – which I call social passion – which is what brings to fruit your philosophical writings. The man embraces in the woman all that is not himself, and from that one resultant, from that embrace, comes every new action.

[1] Possibly B. W. Huebsch, who published *The Rainbow* in 1916.
[2] be] realise (DHL wrote 'be' above 'realise' but did not cross out the latter.)

Apart from this, a man can only take that which is already known, hold it to himself, and say 'this is good – or true – and this is not good, not true'. But this is only the sifting or re-stating of that which is given, it is not the making of a new movement, a new combination.

I hope this doesn't sound all foolish to you.

I wrote a book about these things – I used to call it *Le Gai Savaire*.[1] I want now to re-write this stuff, and make it as good as I can, and publish it in pamphlets, weekly or fortnightly, and so start a campaign for this[2] freer life. I want to talk about it when I come to Cambridge. I want to come – I want to come on the 6th and stay to the 8th – but are the two nights too long? I don't want you to put up with my talk, when it is foolish, because you think perhaps it is passionate. And it is not much good my asking you about your work. I should have to study it a long time first. And it is not in me. I feel quite sad, as if I talked a little vulgar language of my own which nobody understood. But if people all turn into stone or pillars of salt,[3] one must still talk to them. You must put off your further[4] knowledge and experience, and talk to me my way, and be with me, or I feel a babbling idiot and an intruder. My world is real, it is a true world, and it is a world I have in my measure understood.[5] But no doubt you also have a true world, which I can't understand. It makes me [. . .] sad to conclude that. But you must live in my world, while I am there. Because it *is* also a real world. And it is a world you can inhabit with me, if I can't inhabit yours with you.

I hope I shall see Lowes Dickinson too.

D. H. Lawrence

---

877. To S. S. Koteliansky, [25 February 1915]
Text: MS BL; PC; Postmark, Cootham 25 FEB 15; Zytaruk 31.

[25 February 1915]

We shall have no visitors whatsoever this week-end, so that you will find

---

[1] The idea for a book on Thomas Hardy to be published by Nisbet (Letter 748) evolved into 'Le Gai Savaire', or 'Le Gai Saver' (Letter 880). DHL continued to revise his 'philosophy', and his interim titles were 'The Signal', 'The Phoenix' and 'Morgenrot' (Letters 880, 882, 896); this work was finally published as 'The Crown' in the *Signature* (p. 293 n. 1). Chapter III from the 'Le Gai Savaire' typescript, prepared by Kot, was published as 'Six Novels of Thomas Hardy and the Real Tragedy' in the *Book Collector's Quarterly*, ii (January–March 1932), 44–61 and the complete work as 'Study of Thomas Hardy' in McDonald, ed. *Phoenix* (1936). 'Savaire' is derived from the Provençal 'saber' (knowledge, skill, or reason). The 'Gai Saber' was the art of the troubadours codified in early fourteenth-century Provence. DHL may have heard the term used by Pound; but more probably was thinking of its appropriation by Nietzsche, as in his *Die fröhliche Wissenschaft* (1882–7).

[2] this] my   [3] Cf. Genesis xix. 26.
[4] further] greater   [5] and it . . . understood.] my heart knows it.

us quite by ourselves if you come. Come over the bridge in Pulboro to Cold
Waltham, and I will walk down to meet you on the way, if you let me know
your train. We stay next week with Barbara.[1]   DHL
  Greatham-Pulboro
  Katharine came back from Paris this morning – I think they have gone
to Bucks.[2] Murry returned to London last night, to meet her.

878. To Lady Ottoline Morrell, [1 March 1915]
Text: MS UT; Postmark, Cootham 2 [...] 15; Huxley 231–3.

Greatham, Pulborough, Sussex
Monday[3]

Dear Lady Ottoline,
  Please don't call me 'Mr' any more, call me Lawrence.
  I always feel very sad and guilty for trailing you so far on the downs and
making you so tired. I hope you didn't really feel any worse for it afterwards.
  We are most excited thinking of the cottage, which is to be called our
cottage.[4] I don't want actually to own it – ownership always makes me sad,
there is something so limited and jealous in it – but I want to call it mine.
But please don't let it cost you a great deal, on our behalf, or I shall be
miserable and feel responsible again.
  I have been reading Van Gogh – very sad.[5] He couldn't get out of the
trap, poor man, so he went mad. One can see it so plainly, what he wanted.
He wanted that there should be a united impulse of all men in the fulfilment
of one idea[6] – as in Giotto's and Cimabue's time.[7] But in this world there

[1] Barbara Low.
[2] Murry stated that 'Katherine Mansfield returned disillusioned to England at the end of
February [1915] and left for Paris once more in March, and again in May' (*The Journal of
Katherine Mansfield*, p. 79).
[3] Dated from DHL's reference to his forthcoming visit to London 'on Friday', 5 March and
to Cambridge on 6 March 1915.
[4] See p. 291 n. 1
[5] From the excerpts which DHL quotes later in this letter, it is possible to identify the volume
that he was reading as *The Letters of a Post-Impressionist, being the Familiar Correspondence
of Vincent Van Gogh* (Constable, 1912).
[6] Cf. one of Van Gogh's letters in the volume cited above: '...Giotto and Cimabue, like
Holbein and Van Eyck, lived in an atmosphere of obelisks – if I may use such an
expression – in which everything was arranged with architectural method, in which every
individual was a stone or a brick in the general edifice, and all things were inter-dependent
and constituted a monumental social structure' (p. 59).
[7] Angiolotto Giotto de Bondone (1276–1337), Florentine painter, sculptor, poet and architect,
generally considered the leader of the early Renaissance in Italy. He was the pupil of
Cimabue.

is as yet only chaos. So he struggled to add one more term to the disorderly accumulation of knowledge. But it was not living. It was submitting himself to a process of reduction. Which sent him mad. To live, we must all unite, and bring all the knowledge into a coherent whole, we must all set to for the joining together of the multifarious parts, we must knit all Words together into a great new utterance, we must cast all personalities into the smelting pot, and give a new Humanity its birth. Remember, it is not anything personal we want any more – any of us. It is not honor nor personal satisfaction, it is the incorporation in the great impulse whereby a great people shall come into being, a free race as well as a race of free individuals. The individual is now more free than the race. His race hurts him and cribs him in. No one man can create a new race. It needs all of us. So we must all unite for this purpose. It makes me quite glad to think how splendid it will be, when more and more of us fasten our hands on the chains, and pull, and pull, and break them apart.

One must always destroy the old Moloch[1] of greediness and love of property and love of power. But think what a splendid world we shall have, when each man shall seek joy and understanding rather than getting and having.

Don't think that *I* am important. But this thing which is of all of us is so important and splendid that the skies shiver with delight when it is mentioned. And don't be sceptical. We are the young. And it is only the young who can know a great cause.

Bertrand Russell wrote to me. I feel a real hastening of love to him. Only wait. I am coming to London on Friday – Frieda and I both – then I go to Cambridge on Saturday – Frieda stays in London – then we come back to Greatham on Monday afternoon. I will come without Frieda, to tea or to lunch one day, and she will come without me, to see you. There is no reason why we should always be a triangle.

Why don't you have the pride of your own intrinsic self? Why must you tamper with the idea of being an ordinary physical woman – wife, mother, mistress. Primarily, you are none of these things. Primarily, you belong to a special type, a special race of women: like Cassandra in Greece,[2] and some of the great women saints. They were the great *media* of truth, of the deepest truth: through them, as through Cassandra, the truth came as through a fissure from the depths and the burning darkness that lies out of the depth of time. It is necessary for this great type to re-assert itself on the face of

A heathen god whose worship involved offering human sacrifices.
Cassandra was reputed to have the gift of prophecy.

the earth. It is not the Salon lady and the blue stocking – it is not the critic and judge, but the priestess, the medium, the prophetess. Do you know Cassandra in Aeschylus and Homer? – she is one of the world's great figures, and what the Greeks and Agamemnon did to her is symbolic of what mankind has done to her since – raped and despoiled and mocked her, to their own ruin. It is not your brain you must trust to, nor your will – but to that fundamental pathetic faculty for receiving the hidden waves that come from the depths of life, and for transferring them to the unreceptive world. It is something which happens below the consciousness, and below the range of the will – it is something which is unrecognised and frustrated and destroyed.

I am glad you are going away into the country. There you must put away this temporary life, and give yourself to the dream of the new life, the dream of the greater truth, the profoundest wisdom. Because passion is not in heat, but in deep, deep strength and profundity of source. The source of passion is the burning darkness which quickens the whole ball of this earth, from the centre, it is not the bonfire built upon the surface, which is this man or that. But the dark fire, the hidden, invisible passion, that has neither flame nor heat, that is the greatest of all passion.

Please don't mind me when I am stupid or impertinent. It is all so difficult for us each one to be his intrinsic self, each one of us to be the angel of himself in a big cause. We are the animals of ourselves also, but that when we are single, not when we are together, holding hands for the big cause.

I see Van Gogh so sadly. If he could only have set the angel of himself clear in relation to the animal of himself, clear and distinct but always truly related, in harmony and union, he need not have cut off his ear and gone mad. But he said, do you remember – about 'in the midst of an artistic life the yearning for the real life remains – *one offers no resistance, neither does one resign oneself*' – he means to the yearning to procreate oneself 'with other horses, also free'.[1] – This is why he went mad. He should either have resigned himself and lived his[2] animal 'other horses' – and have seen *if his art would come out of that* – or he should have resisted, like Fra Angelico.

---

[1] DHL quotes from the following statement by Van Gogh: 'In the midst of an artistic life there arises again and again the yearning for *real* life, which remains an unrealizable ideal...One feels exactly like an old cab horse, and one knows that one must always return to the same old shafts when all the while one would so love to live in the fields, in the sun, near the river, in the country, with other horses, also free, and have the right to procreate one's kind. And I should not be at all surprised if this were whence the heart trouble comes. One offers no resistance, neither does one resign one's self' (*Letters of a Post-Impressionist*, p. 97).   [2] his] like an

But best of all, if he could have known a great humanity where to live ones animal would be to create oneself, *in fact, be the artist creating a man in living fact* (not like Christ, as he wrongly said) – and where the art was the final expression of the created animal or man – not the [. . .] be-all and being of the man – but the end, the climax. And some men would end in artistic utterance, and some men wouldn't. But each one would create that work of art, the living man, achieve that piece of supreme art, a man's life.

D. H. Lawrence

Don't bother to answer me – just say 'thank you for your letter' to show you are not offended.

DHL

879. To Viola Meynell, 2 March 1915
Text: MS Martin; Moore, *Intelligent Heart* 190–1.

Greatham, Pulborough, Sussex
2 March 1915

My dear Viola,

I have finished my *Rainbow*, bended it and set it firm. Now off and away to find the pots of gold at its feet.

I don't hear from Pinker – but from Methuen asking for 70 words descriptive for his autumn announcement. Vile that!

You will type me the MS, won't you? – and tell me the repetitions and the things I can cross out. I must cross some things out.

Will you keep the MS. at your house, and send me the typed copy in batches, so I can run through it. I am *frightfully excited* over this novel now it is done.

I am going to begin a book about Life – more rainbows, but in different skies – which I want to publish in pamphlet form week by week – my initiation of the great and happy revolution.[1]

Thank you very much for doing this MS for me.

Yours   D. H. Lawrence

Do you mind glancing through and seeing if you have the whole sequence of the MS. from the start.

Tell me which parts you think the publisher will decidedly object to.

DHL

---

[1] See p. 293 n. 1.

880. To Bertrand Russell, 2 March 1915
Text: MS UT; Moore, *Bertrand Russell* 39.

Greatham, Pulborough, Sussex.
March 2 1915

Dear Russell,

I shall come on Saturday by the train arriving Cambridge 6·2, leaving Liverpool St. 4·50. But if I can get a week-end ticket from London, and if it obliges me to come by another train, I will send you a post card on Friday night. I hope that will do.

I have finished my novel so am very glad. I am also very excited about my novel. I feel like a bird in spring that is amazed at the colours of its own coat.

Also I feel very profound about my book 'The Signal' – 'Le Gai Saver' – or whatever it is – which I am re-beginning. It is my revolutionary utterance. I take on a very important attitude of profundity to it, and so feel happy.

Also I feel frightfully important coming to Cambridge – quite momentous the occasion is to me. I don't want to be horribly impressed and intimidated, but am afraid I may be. I only care about the revolution we shall have. But immediately I only want us to be friends. But you are so shy and then I feel so clumsy, so clownish. Don't make me see too many people at once, or I lose my wits. I am afraid of concourses and clans and societies and cliques – not so much of individuals. Truly I am rather afraid.

Yours   D. H. Lawrence

Will you tell me if I need bring evening suit: don't bother to write if it is *not* necessary – but a line if it is.

881. To Gordon Campbell, [3? March 1915]
Text: MS UCin; cited in Glenavy, *Today We Will Only Gossip*, p. 98.

[Greatham, Pulborough, Sussex]
[3? March 1915][1]

Dear Campbell

You see we are no longer satisfied to be individual and lyrical – we are growing out of that stage. A man must now needs know himself as his whole people, he must live as the centre and heart of all humanity, if he is to be

---

[1] DHL planned to go to London on 5 March and to visit some friends on Saturday, 6 March, before travelling to Cambridge. It is assumed that the remark to Campbell – 'perhaps I'll see you on Saturday' – refers to this plan. By 4 March (Letter 882) he feared he might have to go direct to Cambridge: this letter must have preceded that date.

free. It is no use hating a people or a race or humanity in mass. Because
each of us is in himself humanity. You are the English nation. That which
exists as the ostensible English nation is a mass of friable amorphous
individualities. But in me, and in you, is the living organic English nation.
It is not politics – it is religion.

And art which is lyrical can now no longer satisfy us: each work of art
that is true, now, must give expression to the great collective experience, not
to the individual. So a Rembrandt picture is what each man separately sees
for himself. But a Fra Angelico *Last Judgment*[1] – or the Aeschylus trilogy[2]
is what a nation, a race sees in its greatest, collective vision. Now we need
the great, collective vision, we have accumulated enough fragmentary data
of lyricism since the Renaissance.

It is not a political revolution I want, but a shifting of the racial system[3]
of values from the old morality and personal salvation through a Mediator
to the larger morality and salvation through the knowledge that ones
neighbour *is* oneself.[4] This means instant social revolution, from indignation
with what *is*.

Old Socialism was the application of a lyrical idea and passion to an inert
object – so it was false. It is not that I care about *other people*: I know that
I am the English nation – that *I* am the European race – and that this which
exists ostensibly as the English nation is a falsity, mere cardboard. L'Etat
c'est moi.[5] It is a great saying, and should be true of every man. La
race c'*est* moi – La race humaine, c'est *moi*. Let every man say it, and be
free.

I was not hostile to you with Murry. I told him I thought you were very
sound and healthy not to want his close love.[6] But I was purple with rage
over your talk of 'religion' – as if religion were some private little concern
of your own. These private little religions, they are more dirty than a private
property.

Murray is at present *wanting* to be superior to you. He is in the position
of a jilted lover – wants to show his superiority for the moment, because he

[1] See p. 263 n. 3.
[2] See p. 248 n. 1.   [3] system] kind
[4] the old...*is* oneself.] money property to actual living experience, and this entails a revolution
   but the revolution is not the end.
[5] The boast of Louis XIV of France (1638–1715).
[6] For an analysis of Murry's friendship with Campbell and how this was related to Murry's
   problems with Katherine Mansfield, see Delany 60–4. Murry's own account has long been
   available in *Autobiography*; see, especially, pp. 326–47. His remarkable letter to Campbell,
   written on 1 February 1915, but not posted until thirty-seven years later, is published in
   Glenavy, *Today We Will Only Gossip*, pp. 63–6.

was[1] so deeply insulted and injured. But of course he is only waiting till you can be genuine, healthy friends with each other.

I really think he has burst the skin of his womb-sac and entered into his newer, larger birth. I think he does not trouble about his own immediate self any more – his private soul – or souls. His private soul will look after itself – he has something more to do than to look after it.

You see it really means something – I *wish* I could express myself – this feeling that one is not only a little individual living a little individual life, but that one is in oneself the whole of mankind, and ones fate is the fate of the whole of mankind, and ones charge is the charge of the whole of mankind. Not *me* – the little, vain, personal D. H. Lawrence – but that unnameable me which is not vain nor personal, but strong, and glad, and ultimately sure, but so blind, so groping, so tongue-tied, so staggering. You see I *know* that if I could write the finest lyrical poetry or prose that ever was written, if I could be put on the pinnacle of immortality, I wouldn't. I would rather struggle clumsily to put into art the new Great Law of God and Mankind – not the empirical discovery of the individual – but the utterance of the great racial or human consciousness, a little of which is in me. And if I botch out a little of this utterance, so that other people are made alert and active, I don't care whether I am great or small, or rich or poor, or remembered or forgotten. What is it to me. Only there is something I *must* say to mankind – and I cant say it by myself – I feel so dumb and struggling. But it is The Law we must utter – the New, real Law – not subjective experience.

You must understand me, because I don't understand myself. But I *know* it is right, what I mean.

You shouldn't think we dont like you, and things like that. We detest you sometimes, as you detest us. But I feel as if I need you, need your belief adding to me, need you to understand the things I can't understand by myself. There are very few people whom I need *extremely* – because very few could help. But Murry – and you – and perhaps E M Forster. As for Philip Morrell and Lady O[ttoline] – they are good, genuine souls – but not fighters or leaders.

You see for this thing which I stutter at so damnably I want us to form a league – you and Murry and me and perhaps Forster – and our women – and any one who will be added on to us – so long as we are centred around a core of reality, and carried on one impulse.

Perhaps I shall see you on Saturday.

D. H. Lawrence

[1] was] is

[Frieda Lawrence begins]

I think at the *bottom* he is pure, but on top not always – Beatrice[1] letter made me quite *sad.*

[Lawrence continues]

Frieda says I am vain – but it isn't true. My spirit is pure, whatever anybody says. I have my vanity – but not in this. – And I think Murry is good now – himself at last. Let us be together.

I can see nothing to begin on, but a social revolution. For I write my novels, and I write my book of philosophy, and I must also see the social revolution set going.

882. To Lady Ottoline Morrell, [4 March 1915]
Text: MS StaU; Schorer 49–50.

Greatham, Pulboro, Sussex
Thursday

Dear Lady Ottoline,

Don't expect us at all this week-end. We've both got a relapse of influenza. Frieda certainly won't come to town. If I am well enough I shall go straight to Cambridge on Saturday. I might have lunch with you as I come home.

I *hate* having influenza.

I have finished my novel. When it is typed I will give it you to read if you like. I am doing my philosophish book – called (pro tem) The Signal – or the Phœnix (which?).[2] I want you to read this. I am also doing a Van Gogh – one of those sketches in a letter, with colour directions – of a dock and raising bridge.

[sketch][3]

I will show you when it is done.

I hope you are well. We heard from Cannan. *He* says you were depressed. Why were you? Don't be depressed.

D. H. Lawrence

---

[1] Beatrice Campbell.   [2] See p. 295 n. 1.
[3] DHL's sketch clearly refers to Van Gogh's ('with colour directions') in Letter IX, reproduced in *Lettres de Vincent Van Gogh à Emile Bernard* (Paris, 1911). Facsimiles of Van Gogh's letter and his sketch appear in the appendix to that volume. (See also *The Complete Letters of Vincent Van Gogh*, trans. J. van Goch-Bonger and C. de Dood, 1958, i. 477.)

883. To S. S. Koteliansky, [4 March 1915]
Text: MS BL; PC; Postmark, Cootham [. . .] 5; Zytaruk 31.

Greatham, Pulboro
[4 March 1915]

My dear Kot,

We've both got influenza and are in bed. If I'm better I may go straight to Cambridge on Saturday, but Frieda certainly can't turn out. We've had this influenza now a week – it got better, and now is worse again. How I hate it! We are disappointed of our town visit –

D. H. Lawrence

884. To S. S. Koteliansky, [10 March 1915]
Text: MS BL; Postmark, Cootham 11 [. . .]AR 15; Moore 328–9.

Greatham – Pulborough – Sussex
Wednesday

My dear Kot,

According to my time table there is a bad[1] train leaving Victoria 1·42, arr. Pulborough 3.40. It is a slow brute of a train, but you won't mind. If London Bridge is better, you leave there 1.50 – L[ondon] B[righton] and S[outh] C[oast] station. You may have to change at Horsham – just ask.

You come out of the station and down to the high road, then turn to the left. You will see the bridge in the meadows. When you come to the Swan Hôtel, you cross the bridge, which is just on your right, and come straight forward. I shall meet you before you get to Cold Waltham Church. If I don't, in Cold Waltham is a public house – 'The Labouring Man'. Next to that is an old house below the level of the road. At the end of the land of this house is a path going across the fields on your left. Take that. It crosses the railway and brings you to our road. Turn to the left again and you come straight to Greatham. At the red house in Greatham turn to the right down the lane and the first house is ours. So – a blind man could walk here without asking a question.

If nothing happens, I shall meet you in or about Cold Waltham, on the main road.

Will you bring please two boxes like the largest you sent last time – with sliding lids.[2]

[sketch]

Frieda thanks you for the chocolates. She says – like Barbara[3] and her

---

[1] bad] good   [2] See Letter 858.   [3] Barbara Low.

wasps – that 'cats' tongues' was Freudian on your part. She says, however, peace must now be declared on both sides.

Don't be gloomy, neither defiant of all the governments and all the Fates: prison, Siberia, and the hangmans noose. But just come in a good and spring-like mood, with a 'Courage mon ami le diable est mort'.[1] So we will have a good time. I look forward to seeing you here.

Yours   D. H. Lawrence

We will paint more boxes on Saturday, shall we? – like Christmas.

The *Smart Set*, in case you haven't got it, is

John Adams Thayer Corporation, 452 Fifth Avenue, New York.

885. To Barbara Low, [10 March 1915]

Text: MS UT; Nehls, i. 290.

Greatham, Pulborough, Sussex
Wednesday[2]

My dear Barbara Low,

I went to Cambridge and hated it beyond expression.[3]

Frieda is now almost better of her influenza. I do not feel very well, and curse myself.

Thank you *very much* for the plate, which we like very much indeed. It stands on the table with oranges, but the oranges hide the beautiful whirligig in the middle and so make me angry. I must think of something else to put in.

I hope you quarrel with Kotilianski. He is a very bossy and overbearing Jew (save the race!) Please quarrel with him very much.

When are you coming down to see us? Just let us know. The primroses are in bud, and the birds are singing. I know you love songs of the city best, 'the buses are in full tilt, and the shops are closing': but never mind, give the Lord and his handiwork a look-in now and then.

I keep on owing you your money, until I see you. You are a bad moneylender, you will get no interest.

I hear the question of wasps still troubles you. But don't you know that a wasp which has stung once, dies? At that rate, will you consider yourself

[1] 'Courage, my friend, the devil is dead.' Perhaps taken from Charles Reade, *The Cloister and the Hearth* (1861), chap. 24.

[2] Presumably written on the first Wednesday following the Cambridge visit.

[3] For DHL's account of part of his Cambridge weekend, see Letter 901. In his letters to Lady Ottoline, Bertrand Russell provides some further details; see Delany 78–80. See also Clark, *Russell*, pp. 260–1 and J. M. Keynes, *Two Memoirs* (1949), pp. 78–80, 103.

a wasp? But one day I will make you a box, of honey-comb and honey bees
and flowers as sweet as spice. And it shall be brown-gold and green and pink.
And it shall be filled with little coloured sweets. And when Cerberus opens
his mouth, or when any other dog shall bark, he shall be hushed with one
of the sweets.[1]

Now find Freud in *that*.

So au revoir. If it ever comes to blows with Kot, please beat him with
the poker.

D. H. Lawrence

Warm regards from Frieda.

[Frieda Lawrence begins]

The wasps are *his* unconscious 'waspishness', *he* thought they were
bees – Kot has just sent me some 'cats tongues' so there –!

886. To S. S. Koteliansky, [11 March 1915]
Text: MS BL; Postmark, Cootham 11 MAR 15; Zytaruk 33.

Greatham – Pulboro
– Thursday

Dear Kot,

Please bring a few tubes of Rowney's Elementary Water Colour paints –
or Reeves – but better Rowneys – they are about 2d each.

2 tubes Chinese White
1   „   Emerald Green
1   „   Crimson Lake
1   „   Prussian blue

also a couple of penny pencils one HB one B.

We look forward to having you here.

Bring a 1/- pot of Cross and Blackwells Bloater Paste.

Mind you are jolly.

DHL

Bring me 2 packets ordinary envelopes. Don't be cross with all these
Commissions. I'll meet you as near Pulboro as possible.

---

[1] Cerberus was the dog of Pluto; he was the guardian of the entrance to Hades. The Sibyl
who led Aeneas through the Inferno put Cerberus to sleep by giving him cake seasoned with
poppies and honey.

887. To Bertrand Russell, [15? March 1915]

Text: MS UT; Moore, *Bertrand Russell* 41–2.

Greatham, Pulborough, Sussex.
Monday[1]

Dear Russell,

I wanted to write to you when there was something to write about: also when I could send you some of the 'philosophy'. But the time goes by, and I haven't done enough of the writing, and there isn't any news. I shall send you the philosophy when I have done these first crucial chapters. I cannot help being very much interested in God and the devil – particularly the devil – and in immortality. I cannot help writing about them in the 'philosophy'. But all the time I am struggling in the dark – very deep in the dark – and cut off from everybody and everything. Sometimes I seem to stumble into the light, for a day, or even two days – then in I plunge again, god knows where and into what utter darkness of chaos. I don't mind very much. But sometimes I am afraid of the terrible things that are real, in the darkness, and of the entire unreality of these things I see. It becomes like a madness at last, to know one is all the time walking in a pale assembly of an unreal world – this house, the furniture, the sky and the earth – whilst oneself is all the while a piece of darkness pulsating in shocks, and the shocks and the darkness are real. The whole universe of darkness and dark passions – the subterranean universe – not inferno, because that is 'after' – the subterranean black universe of the things which have not yet had being – has conquered for me now, and I can't escape. So I think with fear of having to talk to anybody, because I can't talk.

But I wanted to write this to ask you please to be with me – in the underworld – or at any rate to wait for me. Don't let me go, that is all. Keep somewhere, in the darkness of reality, a connection with me. I feel there is something to go through – something very important. It may be it is only in my own soul – but it seems to grow more and more looming, and this day time reality becomes more and more unreal, as if one wrote from a grave – or a womb – they are the same thing, at opposite extremes. I wish you would swear a sort of allegiance with me.

D. H. Lawrence

Thank you very much for the umbrella.

---

[1] Dated with reference to the return of DHL's umbrella (mentioned in his postscript) which he had presumably forgotten when leaving Cambridge on 8 March.

888. To Lady Ottoline Morrell, [c. 19 March 1915]
Text: MS StaU; Schorer 50.

[Greatham, Pulborough, Sussex]

[c. 19 March 1915][1]

I'm afraid all this may bore you very much. But if you really want the cottage to be very handy, I should like to come and see it before it is done.

I have been revising my novel – but I've only got the first 71 typed pages. It is really very good. It really puts a new thing in the world, almost a new vision of life. I shall send it you when it gets more, and perhaps you will hand it to Forster: though what *he* will say to it, God alone knows.

Then I am going to send you my philosophicalish stuff, before long. You will like that, I know.

The postman is here.

Auf Wiedersehen   D. H. Lawrence

We can talk some German to Julian in Garsington.[2]

889. To S. S. Koteliansky, [19 March 1915]
Text: MS BL; Postmark, Cootham 19 MAR 15; Zytaruk, *Malahat* 22.

Greatham, Pulborough – Sussex

Friday

My dear Kot.

We are coming to London tomorrow, arrive Victoria 1.52. I have asked Murry to meet us at the station. Will you also be there? Because I don't know what we shall do, exactly, tomorrow. On Sunday we must stay a good deal with Barbara. Tomorrow we are free of her.

You know Katharine has again fled to Paris?[3] Murry once more gloomy.

I hope you are well and cheerful. Buck up or I shall shove you under a bus as a reward for melancholy.

à demain   D. H. Lawrence

---

[1] The reference to revising the novel (*The Rainbow*) and the typing of the first 71 pp., in this fragment of a letter, suggests mid-March 1915. The conjecture is reinforced by the reference to the cottage on Lady Ottoline's estate in Letter 890.

[2] Lady Ottoline's daughter and only child, Julian (b. 1906). m. (1) Victor Goodman, 1928 (2) Igor Vinogradoff, 1942.

[3] She went to Paris again on 18 March 1915. See *Journal of Katherine Mansfield*, p. 79.

890. To Bertrand Russell, [19? March 1915]

Text: MS UT; Moore, *Bertrand Russell* 43.

Greatham – Pulborough – Sussex
Friday[1]

Dear Russell,

It is true Cambridge made me very black and down. I cannot bear its smell of rottenness, marsh-stagnancy. I get a melancholic malaria. How can so sick people rise up? They must die first.

I was too sad to write my 'philosophy' (forgive the word) any more. I can't write it when I am depressed or hopeless. But it comes back all right, the philosophy and the belief. God help us, and give us endurance.

When will you come and see us? Don't lapse back from the promise. Remember you will come and we will have a good time – vogue la galère.[2] Will you ask Mr Hardy if he will come and see us during vacation – I should be glad.[3]

You know Lady Ottoline is making us a cottage at Garsington which she will lend to us. She is so generous, one shrinks a bit. One feels one would rather give things to a woman so generous. Do you think it will make an appreciable difference to her to make the cottage? – to her weight of expenses?[4]

Do you still speak at the U[nion of] D[emocratic] C[ontrol][5] of the nations

---

[1] DHL's second letter to Russell after the Cambridge visit was probably written on the Friday following the date of Letter 887.   [2] 'come what may'.

[3] Godfrey Harold Hardy (1877–1947), the Cambridge mathematician, best known for his theory of numbers. His popular book *A Course of Pure Mathematics* (1908) exerted a wide influence. DHL 'had a long and friendly discussion' with him during his visit to Russell in Cambridge (Nehls, i. 574 n. 103).

[4] The renovation costs proved prohibitive; see Letters 903 and 904. Lady Ottoline later attributed the collapse of the project to Frieda's over-high expectations: '...when Philip [Morrell] offered to adapt the old "monastic building" here [at Garsington] for them she required so much done that it would have cost far more than we could afford' (*Ottoline at Garsington* 36). Letters 892 and 899, however, show that DHL himself made most of the suggestions regarding the proposed renovations.

[5] The Union of Democratic Control of which Lowes Dickinson was the first president and Russell a founder-member, was a pacifist organization. Russell recalls: 'A few pacifist M.P.'s, together with two or three sympathizers, began to have meetings at the Morrells' house in Bedford Square. I used to attend these meetings, which gave rise to the Union of Democratic Control' (Russell, *Autobiography*, ii. 17). He adds: 'I took to organizing a branch of the Union of Democratic Control among the dons, of whom at Trinity quite a number were at first sympathetic. I also addressed meetings of undergraduates who were quite willing to listen to me' (ii. 18). Later, Russell gave it up as too ineffectual; he wrote Lady Ottoline Morrell, 11 July 1915; 'I think I will make friends with the No-Conscription people. The U.D.C. is too mild and troubled with irrelevancies. It will be all right after the war, but not now. I wish good people were not so mild' (ii. 52).

kissing each other, when your soul prowls the frontier all the time most jealously, to defend what it has and to seize what it can. It makes me laugh when you admit it. But we are all like that. Only, let us seize and defend that which is worth having, and which we want.

Saluti di Cuore   D. H. Lawrence

891. To S. S. Koteliansky, [24 March 1915]
Text: MS BL; Postmark, Cootham 24 MAR 15; Zytaruk 34.

Greatham – Pulborough – Sussex
Wednesday

My dear Kot,

I am very glad you are quite happy again. Soon it will be your turn to shove me off a bus.

Next week Bertrand Russell wants to come, from Thursday to Saturday. Would you be sad if I asked you to come on Saturday, when we have got rid of him? Barbara also asked if she might come for Easter. Now don't be cross, and say you don't like her. I *do* rather like her. You must like her too – and have a honeymoon in the Garden Suburb.

There is a train from Victoria at 10.20 (I believe) on Saturday morning. Barbara will probably come by that. Do please be nice, and come with her. Be a good soul.

Gilbert and Mary Cannan are here. I rather love them. There is real Good – power for Good – in Gilbert. I am not very well. It is that which affects me – nothing else.

We *will* have a walk, given a fine Easter. We will set out on Saturday. I want us really to be happy then. So come and be nice. I get depressed by the sense of evil in the world.

Auf wiedersehen   D. H. Lawrence

892. To Lady Ottoline Morrell, [24 March 1915]
Text: MS UT; Huxley 237–8.

Greatham – Pulborough – Sussex
Wednesday[1]

My dear Lady Ottoline,

The plans are very fine now: how beautiful the place will be! I think an

---

[1] The mention of the visit from the Cannans (see preceding letter) and of Russell's anticipated visit 'next weekend' (which took place on 1 April) both point to Wednesday, 24 March 1915.

[...] E. window to the S.E. bedroom is *very good*: as for a N. door, that
would make natural access to the stairs for your visitors, but it is as Morrell
likes. What a good place the Monastic Buildings will be – you will be
outrivalled, in your manor. And we cuckoos, we shall plume ourselves, in
such a nest of a fine bird.

A man told me one must have 6% on house property: but it occurs to
me that this would mean 10% in rent, to cover expenses. Tell Philip Morrell
5% won't do – it is too little.

Thank you very much for the books and your letter. You shouldn't say
you are afraid of writing dull things. They are not dull. The feeling that comes
out of your letter is like a scent of flowers, so generous and reassuring. It
is no good now, thinking that to understand a man from his own point of
view is to be happy about him. I can imagine the mind of a rat, as it slithers
along in the dark, pointing its sharp nose. But I can never feel happy about
it, I must always want to kill it. It contains a principle of evil. There *is* a
principle of evil. Let us acknowledge it once and for all. I saw it so plainly
in Keynes at Cambridge, it made me sick.[1] I am sick with the knowledge
of the prevalence of evil, as if it were some insidious disease.

I have been reading Dostoievsky's *Idiot*.[2] I don't like Dostoievsky. He
is again like the rat, slithering along in hate, in the shadows, and, in order
to belong to the light, professing love, all love. But his nose is sharp with
hate, his running is shadowy and rat-like, he is a will fixed and gripped like
a trap. He is not nice.

The Cannans are here. I must say I rather love them. Strangely enough,
I feel a real, unalterable power for good in Gilbert. But he is very crude,
very shockingly undisciplined, and consequently inarticulate. He is not *very*
passionate. But he is a power for good, nevertheless, and I like him to be
with us. Mary is rather nice too: she *is* rather a dear: but shallow. I like
Gilbert, I am glad of his existence.

Bertie Russell will come next Thursday, to stay till Saturday. Will you
let us know when you will come? You choose your own day.

Love from Frieda and me.   D. H. Lawrence

---

[1] John Maynard Keynes (1883–1946), created 1st Baron Keynes of Tilton, 1942. Distinguished
economist. Fellow and Bursar of King's College, Cambridge; editor of the *Economic Journal*
(1912–45); he served in the Treasury (1915–19) and was principal representative of the
Treasury at the Paris Peace Conference (1919). Author of various works on economics, among
the best known being *The Economic Consequences of the Peace* (1919). For his memoirs, see
p. 305 n. 3.
[2] Doubtless in the translation by Constance Garnett (1913).

893. To S. S. Koteliansky, [31 March 1915]

Text: MS BL.; Postmark, Cootham 31 MAR 15; Zytaruk 35.

Greatham, Pulborough, Sussex.
Wednesday

My dear Kot,

You are commissioned please to bring two bottles of Chianti as at Christmas. We are having a dinner on Sunday evening – all the hosts of Midian present.[1]

You will come either by the train leaving Victoria at 10·20 or by the 1·42. Bring Barbara and be nice to her.

Perhaps on Monday we will set out on a walk and go to Chichester. It will be nice. Mind you are jolly. If I can, I will walk down to meet you – you won't take a carriage, will you? But come over Cold Waltham, not the same way you went last time. Bertrand Russell may be here – he goes away on Saturday.

Au revoir, mon cher   D. H. Lawrence

Don't bring anything but Chianti – and for that I pay you.

894. To Lady Ottoline Morrell, [2 April 1915]

Text: MS StaU; Schorer 51.

Greatham, Pulborough, Sussex.
Good Friday 1915

My dear Lady Ottoline,

I liked the little salve[2] box very much. I shall be fond of it always.

We have had a good time with Russell – really been people living together. He is very natural to me – sort of kinship, so we are free together.

Do come down – but not till after the middle of next week, because I want you to come when people are not here. We shall be *very* glad to have you.

I am sad now, and want to weep in my corner, but it is largely with relief. I know Russell is with me, really, now.

Viola Meynell is typing my novel, and does it slowly, so I am delayed sending it to you. But next week there will be a moderately good batch ready, which I shall send you. As for my 'Contrat Social',[3] wait, wait, wait, for I can't do it yet. Soon I shall try.

I keep wondering how Garsington is going.[4]

---

[1] See Judges vii. 8 (A.V.).   [2] MS reads 'slave'.

[3] DHL's new version of his 'philosophy' seen in relation to *Du Contrat Social* (1762) by Jean-Jacques Rousseau (1712–78).

[4] Either a reference to the renovation of Garsington Manor in preparation for the Morrells' move there, or an enquiry about the 'cottage' for the Lawrences.

I hope you are well and happy. I wish I had something to send you for Easter, but there is nothing I can find. –

Love from Frieda and me   D. H. Lawrence

I shall send you my play.[1] It [...] may be you have read it – and perhaps it isn't very good – but an author may give his own books away.

DHL

895. To S. S. Koteliansky, [8 April 1915]

Text: MS BL; Postmark, Cootham 8 APR 15; Spender 29.

Greatham, Pulborough, Sussex.
Thursday

My dear Kot,

Barbara has just gone. I like her, but she gets on my nerves with her eternal: 'but *do* you think' – 'but, look here, *isn't* it rather that – – – – – – .' I want to say: 'For Gods sake woman, stop haggling'. And she is so deprecating, and so persistent. Oh God! But – basta!

I must tell you, caro mio, that I liked you very much while you were here. You must continue to be patient with me.

But you positively *must not* be so inert. You are getting simply a monolith. You *must* rouse yourself. You *must* do something – anything. Really it is a disgrace to be as inert as you are. Really, it is unforgivable. Write for the papers, do anything, but don't continue in this negation.

I think I shall send you my philosophy to type again for me. I have begun it again. I will not tell the people[2] this time that they are angels in disguise. Curse them, I will tell them they are dogs and swine, bloodsuckers.

I will send you the *Idiot* to read.

Will you type my philosophy again? – one copy only this time, on common paper? I shall have to get it done somewhere or other. But if the burden on you, monolith, is too great, then refuse.

I have been fighting the powers of darkness lately. Still they prevail with me. But I have more or less got my head out of the inferno, my body will follow later. How one has to struggle, really, to overcome this cursed blackness. It would do me so much good if I could kill a few people.

Is Katharine at home, or have you heard from her?[3] And how is Murry? I will write to him. I feel all right again towards him. My spleen has worked itself off.

---

[1] *The Widowing of Mrs Holroyd.*

[2] MS reads 'them the people': DHL inserted 'the people' but omitted to delete 'them'.

[3] Katherine Mansfield had gone to Paris on 18 March 1915 and had not yet returned.

I am still in bed with my cold. It is a sort of cold in my inside – like a sore throat in ones stomach. Do you understand? I am going to stay in bed till it is better. Thank God Barbara isn't here to nag at me – poor thing.

My dear Kot, now that the spring has come, *do* rouse up, and *don't* be sad and inert. It is so terrible to be such a weight upon the face of the earth. But you were almost all right this time you were here. Next time you must come when nobody else is here.

Frieda sends her love, with mine. I am reading the Dostoevsky letters.[1] What an amazing person he was – a pure introvert,[2] a purely disintegrating will – there was not a grain of the passion of love within him – all the passion of hate, of evil. Yet a great man. It has become, I think, now, a supreme wickedness to set up a Christ-worship as Dostoevsky did: it is the outcome of an evil will, disguising itself in terms of love.

But he is a great man and I have the greatest admiration for him. I even feel a sort of subterranean[3] love for him. But he never, never wanted anybody to love him, to come close to him. He exerted repelling influence on everybody.

Write to me soon –

Yrs   D. H. Lawrence

896. To Lady Ottoline Morrell, [8 April 1915]
Text: MS IEduc; Postmark, Cootham 8 APR 15; Huxley 236–7.

Greatham, Pulborough, Sussex.
Thursday

Dear Lady Ottoline,

I send you so much of my novel as is typed. It is perhaps one-half or one-third of the whole – one-third, I should say.

I know you will take care of the MS. Let Russell read it if he wants to. And tell me very plainly what you think.[4] I really do like criticism.

When are you coming to see us? At last, today, all our visitors have gone

---

[1] Probably *Letters of F. M. Dostoevsky to his Family and Friends*, trans. Ethel C. Mayne (1914).
[2] introvert] egoism
[3] subterranean] wondering
[4] It is not known whether Lady Ottoline expressed her frank opinion to DHL. In her memoirs, however, she described her reaction to *The Rainbow*: 'I was shocked in reading it by what then seemed to me to be the slapdash amateurish style in which it was written, and the habit when he then first began of repeating the same word about ten times in a paragraph. I counted the word "fecund", I think, twelve times on one page...there were also passages of such intensity and such passionate beauty that they never leave one's memory' (Gathorne-Hardy, *Ottoline: The Early Memoirs*, p. 283).

away. I have been in bed for three days. My old cold that I have had so long never really gets better, and occasionally comes full tilt back again. It is a sort of cold in the stomach: it feels like a sore throat in the middle of one's belly – very horrid and tiring and irritating. I am afraid this house is damp. Frieda has had a very bad raw cold for the last two weeks again. I think soon we shall move from here – because of the dampness. When will Garsington be ready for us to come.

To-day I have begun again my philosophy – *Morgenrot*[1] is my new name for it. I feel as if I can do it now. God preserve me from getting out of my depths.

Had you read my play before I sent it you? Tell me if you like it. Nobody sends us letters nowadays.

Love from Frieda and me to you.   D. H. Lawrence

I have just read Brailsford on Shelley and Godwin – *very* good. I like Brailsford.[2] Can I meet him? I still dont like Strachey – his *French Literature* neither – words – litterateur – bore.[3]

Do you notice that Shelley believed in the principle of Evil, coeval with the Principle of Good. That is right.

Have you got a Chapman's *Homer* or a *Brothers Karamazov* to lend me.[4] I beg and implore you not to buy either if you haven't got it. I shall bring your other books to Garsington, if not to London – all of them.

My novel is so good – please have patience with it.

I have had a great struggle with the Powers of Darkness lately. I think I have just got the better of them again. Do not tell me there is no Devil. There is a Prince of Darkness. Sometimes I wish I could let go, and be really wicked – kill and murder – but kill chiefly. I do want to kill. But I want to select whom I shall kill. Then I shall enjoy it. The war is no good. It is this black desire I have become conscious of. We cant so much about goodness – it is canting. Tell Russell he does the same – let him recognise the powerful malignant will in him. This is the very worst wickedness, that we refuse to acknowledge the passionate evil that is in us. This makes us secret and rotten.

[1] A title probably modelled on Nietzsche's *Morgenröte* (*The Dawn*) (1881).

[2] Henry Noel Brailsford (1873–1958), political writer and journalist; he was a friend of Bertrand Russell and a fellow pacifist. His *Shelley, Godwin and their Circle* appeared in 1913.

[3] A reference to Lytton Strachey's book, *Landmarks in French Literature* (1912).

[4] On *Homer* see p. 253 n. 2. Dostoievsky's novel was published in Constance Garnett's translation in 1912.

897. To Dollie Radford, [9 April 1915]

Text: MS UN; Postmark, Cootham [...]5; Nehls, i. 307.

Greatham, Pulborough, Sussex.
Friday[1]

Dear Dollie Radford,[2]

Thank you very much for sending me the play.[3] Frieda and I have read it, and like it very much. I like the last act the best. There is to me something rather terrible in the idea of the chorus of unloved women chanting against the chorus of prostitutes – something really Great in the conception. That is the most splendid part of the play. I wish you could have made the Margery a sterner, more aloof, more completely abstract or generalised figure – as Antigone[4] in a Greek play – so that she is a figure of vengeance as well as of love: and the same with Carol. Those who know how to love must know how to slay. If we are not to be given up to love, then let us be given up to the contest with the dragon. If we may not kiss, then let us strike. For there is the dragon preventing us.

I have been seedy and in bed these four days with a cold in my inside. But it is getting better.

Margaret[5] is coming today. We shall see her soon. And you will be down next week.

Auf Wiedersehen, liebe Freundin   D. H. Lawrence

898. To S. S. Koteliansky, [10 April 1915]

Text: MS BL; Zytaruk 38.

Greatham – Pulborough – Sussex
Saturday[6]

---

[1] The previous letter refers to DHL's being 'in bed for three days' with a cold; in this letter the remark 'in bed these four days' strongly suggests 9 April 1915.

[2] Dollie Radford née Maitland (1864?–1920), was the wife of Ernest Radford (1857–1919), Fabian, poet and critic. Among his works are *Translations from Heine and Other Verse* (1882) and *Measured Steps* (1884). Dollie was educated at Queen's College, Baker Street, London, and was herself a poet. She met (and liked) the Lawrences while living in Rackham Cottage on the Meynell estate at Greatham. Their first meeting took place before 27 March 1915 (see Nehls, i. 291–2). Later, from December 1917 to November 1919, she lent her Hermitage cottage to the Lawrences and on a number of occasions they stayed in her London home at 32 Well Walk, Hampstead.

[3] Dollie Radford published a play called *The Ransom* in *Drama*, vi (March–April 1915), 117–53.

[4] In Greek legend, daughter of Oedipus whom she accompanied in his wanderings until his death at Colonos. Sophocles dramatised her own tragedy in *Antigone*.

[5] The younger daughter of Dollie and Ernest Radford.

[6] It is assumed that this letter was written during the same week of DHL's illness as the previous two letters.

My dear Kot,

I send you the first chapter of my philosophy so that you can get on with it when you like. Positively I know how to do it now.[1] Positively I shall say what I like, very nicely. Dont be sceptical of it. I wish I could think of a nice title – like Morgenrot in German – or – I don't know.

I got up today, this afternoon – very limp and weed-like. I wrote to Eder all my symptoms and my ailments – he must cure me.[2]

'I am weary in heart and head, in hands and feet
And surely more than all things sleep were sweet,
Than all things, save the unconquerable desire
Which whoso knoweth shall not faint nor tire.'[3]

I am so limp I could recite Swinburne. That is a sign of great maudlin. Vado in letto. Buona notte, amico.[4]

D. H. Lawrence

On this sort of paper, one copy – don't bore yourself to death doing it – plenty of time –

899. To Lady Ottoline Morrell, [15? April 1915]
Text: MS IEduc; Huxley 234.

Greatham, Pulborough, Sussex
Thursday[5]

Dear Lady Ottoline,

Thank you very much for your letter. I did not want you to think me impudent, making suggestions for the cottage. But we have by now lived in so many little houses, in England and Germany and Italy, that we know their joys and their terrors, pretty thoroughly. A bathroom is infinitely more valuable in a cottage than in a big house, because in a cottage there is so little room, and very often, no servant, so that it is well to escape the necessity of wash-stands and bath-tubs in the bedrooms. As for the work-room for me, that is mere suggestion on my part. Only, it will be difficult to heat such a large room as that will be in the cottage if it is undivided. It is very good to suggest a small rentage. I should feel much happier if I paid a 6% rent on the cost of alterations and furnishing. I presume you would prefer to

---

[1] 'Positively', like 'plainly' (Letter 846), was an expression often used by Kot.
[2] The letter to David Eder has not been found.
[3] When composing these lines, DHL probably recalled Swinburne, 'The Garden of Proserpine', ll. 9–16.
[4] 'I'm going to bed. Goodnight, my friend.'
[5] This letter appears to fall between Letters 896 and 900.

furnish the cottage: then the whole thing will be always yours, complete. And it doesn't need much: just a few very simple things. – And I will pay ten, or fifteen, or twenty pounds a year, according to the just percentage on the outlay. And on the initial cost of the buildings you will have no return: for that I am your complete debtor. I am badly off now, but the publisher will eventually pay me £200 as he has agreed.[1] Then I pay my rent. I shall always owe you a big debt of gratitude. But let that be.

We shall be most glad to have a place we can always come to. And if you have need of the cottage, you will tell us at once. I know I shall be restless all my life. If I had a house and home, I should become wicked. I hate any thought of possessions sticking on to me like barnacles, at once I feel destructive. And wherever I am, after a while I begin to ail me to go away.

I believe you, that love is all. But it is not easy. If I love a man, and a dog bites him, I must hate the dog. But if I must love the dog? And if I love my fellow-men, how must I feel, say, about Cambridge? Must I take hope and faith? But if I have toothache I don't depend on hope nor faith nor love, but on surgery. And surgery is pure hate of the defect in the loved thing. And it is surgery we want, Cambridge wants, England wants, I want. There is in us what the common people call 'proud flesh'[2] – i.e., mortified flesh: which must be cut out: it cannot be kissed out, nor hoped out, nor removed by faith. It must be removed by surgery. And it is in us now 'proud flesh'.

I thought the war would surgeon us. Still it may. But this England at home is as yet entirely unaffected, entirely unaware of the mortification in its own body. It takes a dodge to protect its own fester from being touched: preserve your ill from touch or knowledge: that is the motto.

'If thine eye offend thee, pluck it out.'[3] It has all been said before, plainly. It is all there, for every man to hear. But if no man wants to hear? – Will cajolery or the toleration of love affect him? Curse him, let him die, and let us look to the young. That is all the faith and hope one can have – or even love.

– Our love to you   D. H. Lawrence

900. To Lady Ottoline Morrell, [19 April 1915]
Text: MS UT; Postmark, Hampstead 19 APR 15; Huxley 223–4.

Greatham, Pulborough, Sussex.
Monday

[1] Methuen, the publisher of *The Rainbow*.
[2] A granulated growth or excrescence of flesh in a wound so called because of its swelling up.
[3] Mark ix. 47 (A.V.).

My dear Lady Ottoline

Today you will be going to Buxton, through this magnificent sunshine.[1] I almost wish it were my turn to rise up and depart. My soul is restless and not to be appeased. One walks away to another place, and life begins anew. But it is a midge's life.

We have had MacQueen[2] and David Garnett and Francis Birrell here for the week-end. When Birrell comes – tired and a bit lost and wondering – I love him. But my God, to hear him talk sends me mad. To hear these young people talking really fills me with black fury: they talk endlessly, but endlessly – and never, never a good or a real thing said. Their attitude is so irreverent and blatant. They are cased each in a hard little shell of his own and out of this they talk words. There is never for one second any outgoing of feeling, and no reverence – not a crumb or grain of reverence. I cannot stand it. I *will not* have people like this – I had rather be alone. They made me dream in the night of a beetle that bites like a scorpion. But I killed it – a very large beetle. I scotched it – and it ran off – but I came upon it again and killed it. It is this horror of little swarming selves that I can't stand: Birrells, D. Grants, and Keynses.

Pinker writes to me that he wants to have my novel set up in type, to avoid futile delay again. Would you send him the MS. as soon as you can, to

J. B. Pinker Esq, Talbot House, Arundel St., Strand W.C.

I should be very much obliged if you would. But read it first.

I hope you will not find Buxton too dull. You should indeed have taken your dog.

I like David Garnett – but there is something wrong with him. Is he also like Keynes and Grant. It is enough to drive one frantic. It makes me long for my Italy. Sometimes I think I can't stand this England any more: it is too wicked and perverse.

But we must fight this Baal,[3] and keep the other flag flying. Dear Lady Ottoline, remember we must stick together. It really seems to me a matter of life and death. But I am a proverbial exaggerator.

[1] Lady Ottoline Morrell recalled: 'In April [1915] I went by myself to the Hydro in Buxton to have some treatment for rheumatism...what I chiefly remember is reading the manuscript of *The Rainbow* which D. H. Lawrence sent me in detachments, also that he wrote me charming letters to cheer me and keep me company in my solitude' (Gathorne-Hardy, *Ottoline: The Early Memoirs*, p. 283).

[2] William ('Willie') MacQueen (b. 1891?) was in England after being wounded at Ypres in November 1914 as an officer in the Royal Field Artillery. He returned to France in June 1915. He was a friend of Aldous Huxley at Oxford and shared his literary interests (MacQueen matriculated at Wadham College, from Glasgow Academy, in 1909). A member of the 'Garsington circle', MacQueen signed Lady Ottoline's guest-book on 29 November 1915.

[3] The supreme god of the Phoenicians and the Canaanites; in general terms, a false god.

I will send you some of your books to Buxton, the Brailsford for example, if you would care for it.[1]

Love from Frieda and me   D. H. Lawrence

901. To David Garnett, [19 April 1915]

Text: MS Garnett D.; Postmark, [. . .] Sussex 2[. . .]5; cited in D. Garnett, 'Introductory Note' to J. M. Keynes, *Two Memoirs* (1949), p. 77.

Greatham, Pulborough, Sussex.
Monday.[2]

My dear David,

I can't bear to think of you, David, so wretched as you are – and your hand shaky – and everything wrong. It is foolish of you to say that it doesn't matter either way – the men loving men.[3] It doesn't matter in the public way. But it matters so much, David, to the man himself – at any rate to us northern nations – that it is like a blow of triumphant decay, when I meet Birrell or the others. I simply can't bear it. It is so wrong, it is unbearable. It makes a form of inward corruption which truly makes me scarce able to live. Why is there this horrible sense of frowstiness, so repulsive, as if it came from deep inward dirt – a sort of sewer – deep in men like K[eynes] and B[irrell] and D[uncan] G[rant].[4] It is something almost unbearable to me. And not from any moral disapprobation. I myself never considered Plato very wrong, or Oscar Wilde.[5] I never knew what it meant till I saw K., till I saw him at Cambridge. We went into his rooms at midday, and it was very sunny. He was not there, so Russell was writing a note. Then suddenly a door opened

[1] See p. 315 n. 2.
[2] The verso of the envelope bears a second postmark: Chichester 20 AP 15. (DHL wrote above the address: 'Absolutely Private'.)
[3] (David Garnett provided the General Editor with notes to elucidate this letter. They are the source of comments shown in quotation marks here and in footnotes which follow.) 'It is clear to me now that Ottoline must have been giving DHL a lurid account of my friendship with Francis Birrell. He was physically attracted by me, but I was unable to respond, and during our friendship which lasted from early 1914 until his death, I was quite incapable of returning his early "falling in love" with me which was rather imagined than real.'
[4] 'I lived with Vanessa [Bell] and Duncan (from 1915 to early 1919) who were lovers and I was devoted to them both.... I felt a warm affection for Maynard Keynes, founded on our mutual love for Duncan Grant and Vanessa Bell. In the same way I felt a deep affection for Lytton Strachey.... Both Maynard and Lytton liked me and were very kind to me.'
[5] Plato (?428–?348 B.C.), in fact opposed homosexuality as it was practised in Athens. Although he recognised the power of physical homosexual attraction, he called it 'unnatural'. Oscar Wilde (1854–1900), the Irish poet, dramatist and essayist, was found guilty of homosexual practices and sentenced to imprisonment (1895–7).

and K. was there, blinking from sleep, standing in his pyjamas. And as[1] he stood there gradually a knowledge passed into me, which has been like a little madness to me ever since. And it was carried along with the most dreadful sense of repulsiveness – something like carrion – a vulture gives me the same feeling. I begin to feel mad as I think of it – insane.

Never bring B. to see me any more. There is something nasty[2] about him, like black-beetles. He is horrible and unclean. I feel as if I should go mad, if I think of your set, D.G. and K. and B. It makes me dream of beetles. In Cambridge I had a similar dream. Somehow, I can't bear it. It is wrong beyond all bounds of wrongness. I had felt it slightly before, in the Stracheys.[3] But it came full upon me in K., and in D.G. And yesterday I knew it again, in B.

David, my dear, I love your father and I love your mother. I think your father has been shamefully treated at the hands of life. Though I don't see him, I do love him in my soul – more even than I love your mother. And I feel, because I love your father, that you must leave these 'friends', these beetles. You must wrench away and start a new life. B. and D.G. are done for, I think – done for for ever. K. I am not sure. But you, my dear, you can be all right. You can come away, and grow whole, and love a woman, and marry her, and make life good, and be happy. Now David, in the name of everything that is called love, leave this set and stop this blasphemy against love. It isn't that I speak from a moral code. Truly I didn't know it was wrong, till I saw K. that morning in Cambridge. It was one of the crises in my life. It sent me mad with misery and hostility and rage. Go away, David, and try to love a woman. My God, I could kiss Eleanor Farjeon with my body and soul, when I think how good she is, in comparison.[4] But the Oliviers,[5] and such girls, are wrong.

I could sit and howl in a corner like a child, I feel so bad about it all.

D. H. Lawrence

as] suddenly   [2] nasty] horrid

Most probably Lytton and James (1887–1967), the youngest of the five brothers.

Eleanor Farjeon (1881–1965), was the daughter of the English editor, novelist and dramatist, Benjamin Leopold Farjeon (1838–1903), who lived in Australia and New Zealand from 1855 onwards. She became particularly well known as a writer of works for children. Her brother was Herbert Farjeon (1887–1945), dramatist and editor of the Nonesuch Shakespeare. (See Eileen Colwell, *Eleanor Farjeon: A Biography*, 1961.) For DHL's acquaintance with her works, see Letter 921. David Garnett recalled: 'Eleanor Farjeon...did not attract me at all and was in any case in love with Edward Thomas, a great friend of mine and my father's.'

Brynhild, Daphne, Noel and Margery, the four daughters of Sir Sidney Olivier (1859–1943), 1st Lord Olivier, an early member of the Fabian Society, who later became Secretary of State for India.

322   *[19 April 1915]*

[Frieda Lawrence begins]

My dear David,

Are you getting sick of being bombarded with letters? I was so very fond of you when you were here, and I did not think you were satisfied or happy – I felt a great strength and livingness and a genuine *you*, if only you could *believe* in yourself more, in the individual bottomself of you and collect your strength and direct it – You always admire other people much too much, you are really *more* than Birrell or the others, I *know*. but you dare'nt trust yourself – I thought Ruth rather fine[1] – *for another man* – She is much too fixed in her morality, she would be your conscience-keeper and you would always want to be free – Dont marry her, David, I can see so plainly, what would happen – She would not *see* so much, that is in you and make you to ordinary tight standards – You would never come very close to her and you do want and need intimacy – And at present your vital interest is in men, just like your devotion for the Indian,[2] but you loose and forget *yourself* in other men and you have got it in you to stand for yourself and by yourself – Also I rather think the young men you know exploit you and feed on your warmth, because you are generous – I have learnt a great deal how much one has to use one's wits, and it is want of courage if we dont stick to the self, that God has given us – I think that Anna[3] you loved, but there was something hopeless in it from the beginning, that has left a lot of unbelief in you – But you do really want so much and much will come, if you only let it – Anyhow, you are my dear friend,

Yours   Frieda

[Lawrence continues]

My dear David,

Don't marry anybody. Go right away and be alone and work, and come to your real self. But do leave this group of 'friends'. You have always known the wrong people – Harolds, and Olivier girls.[4] Do go right away, right away, and be by yourself.

Love   D. H. Lawrence

---

[1] 'Ruth was the sister of Godwin Baynes, M.D. (later the translator of Jung) who "spewed me out of his mouth" when I became a conscientious objector. I broke off my abortive love affair with Ruth after that, as she was not sympathetic to my beliefs.' (On Godwin Baynes see *Letters*, i. 475.)

[2] Damodar Savarkar (see Garnett, *The Golden Echo*, pp. 144–62).

[3] See p. 208 n. 2.

[4] 'Harold Hobson and the four Olivier girls were my most intimate friends and playmates from the age of five. Noel Olivier and Harold remained my close friends until their deaths.'

902. To S. S. Koteliansky, [20 April 1915]

Text: MS BL; cited in Gransden 24.

Greatham – Pulborough – Sussex
Tuesday[1]

My dear Kot,

Thank you very much for the typewriting.[2] Soon you will be as accomplished a typist as our dear Viola.

I have not sent you any more MS: because I am very slow; and I thought you wanted to be lentissimo yourself. Herewith I forward a little more – enough to keep you from idleness and mischief.

I am at last, after swallowing various concoctions, really beginning to be better. I am 'on the mend', as they say.

We have had another influx of visitors: David Garnett and Francis Birrell turned up the other day – Saturday. I like David, but Birrell I have come to detest. These horrible little frowsty people, men lovers of men, they give me such a sense of corruption, almost putrescence, that I dream of beetles. It is abominable. To escape from visitors, I must go to Italy again. Madame Sowerby[3] has been down – and McQueen – and God knows who.

Probably we shall not have the Lady Ottoline cottage. In my soul, I shall be glad. I would rather take some little place and be by myself. We will look out for some tiny place on the sea, not too far off, shall we. I must write to the Murrys about it.

But why don't they write to us? It is their turn. Nevertheless I will write tomorrow.

I don't know when I shall come to London. But I am beginning to get unstuck from this place. There is too great a danger from invasion from the other houses. I cannot stand the perpetual wash of forced visitors, under the door. So be ready for news of our decamping: how and whither I don't as yet know: but decamp I will before very long.

Thank heaven we shall get out of the Lady Ottoline cottage. I cannot have such a place like a log on my ankle. God protects me, and keeps me free. Let us think of some place to which we can betake ourselves.

I have promised to go to Scotland in the summer.[4] We might stay there for a while.

I feel we shall be seeing you before long. I feel I am like a swallow getting my wings ready for flight.

Frieda sends her love. She will write directly.

Love from me   D. H. Lawrence

[1] The reference to the visit by David Garnett and Birrell establishes the date of this letter as 20 April 1915.   [2] See Letter 898.

[3] Olivia Sowerby, married daughter of Wilfrid and Alice Meynell; she lived in Bristol.

[4] To visit his sister, Emily King.

903. To Philip Morrell, [20 April 1915]
Text: MS StaU; Schorer 51–2.

Greatham, Pulborough, Sussex.
Tuesday[1]

My dear Morrell,

Of course the costs for the monastic house are impossible beyond all consideration. I thought that the whole thing would be done for about £200. The prices are monstrous. The only thing to do under these circumstances of war and exorbitancy is to employ the minimum of labour and do the minimum of building or alteration. Certainly it is utterly impossible to go in for these extravagances. What a vile, thieving, swindling life! What a horrible generation! One can only want to hide oneself away from its contact.

Lady Ottoline said we could have three rooms in the gardener's cottage. If we could really have those for a time, it would be quite enough. For heavens sake don't build a single brick on our account. The thought of your being swindled to this extent makes me feel I would rather be a rabbit in a rabbit-hoie, than hire a bricklayer for even half an hour. No, the only satisfaction I get is to think that, by living in the three – or two – rooms of the gardener's cottage, all that bleeding is saved. The miserable miscreant vermin, with their prices! It is too horrible and degrading.

It will be, as you say, only possible to begin on the monastic buildings when things become normal again – if ever they do. But really, if there *are* the spare rooms in the gardener's cottage, we should like to stay there for a time. It would be very disappointing not to come to Garsington at all.

These vile greedy contractors, they set my blood boiling to such a degree, I can scarcely bear to write.

But I shall be *very* glad if you are not put to much expense on our account. You are both so generous, that I could feel it only a vileness to trespass on your generosity. We shall be *very* grateful for the two or three rooms in the gardener's cottage, and always grateful for the gift of the monastic buildings. I only feel those vile sordid contractors have stolen these away from us.

Please don't think any more about *any* alterations or hired workmen on our account – a little furniture in the three rooms is more than enough.

Yours very sincerely   D. H. Lawrence

904. To Lady Ottoline Morrell, [20 April 1915]
Text: MS StaU; Postmark, [C]ooth[am] 20 [. . .]5; cited in Schorer 52.

Greatham, Pulborough, Sussex.
Tuesday. April 1915[2]

---

[1] The contents of this letter point to the same Tuesday as Letter 904.
[2] Lady Ottoline left on 19 April 1915 for Buxton; presumably this leter was written the next day.

My dear Lady Ottoline,

Morrell tells me about the estimates. It is monstrous. Not a brick nor a stone will I have laid on my account, at such prices. I would not live in such costly monastic buildings, not for a day: I should hate the place, every stroke of work that had been done, I should hate it as if it were a blow struck at me. Enough, enough – while this thievery and abomination lasts, I would not have a moment of hired work done for me. Let us have it all left until there is some decency on the face of the earth again.

We shall be quite happy in the gardener's rooms for a while – quite happy there – and we can have our good times just the same – so the vile contractors haven't really hit us. Let us forget they are so beastly, and look forward to the two or three rooms in the cottage. Perhaps we will all go to Italy in the winter. At any rate the world is ours.

I hope Buxton is making you feel better. You must let us know. Tell me if I shall send you any books.

Page 40 of my philosophy. It is very good and rather terrible, and nobody will ever publish it unless – I don't know. Tell Russell to write to Frieda, or else she feels he is trying to insult her. Everything is perfectly all right and she likes him very much. But I hope to God he's not assuming the Olympic, the high horse.

You had a beautiful day to go to Buxton – I hope you will have a good time there.

                                                             au revoir   D. H. Lawrence

905. To Lady Ottoline Morrell, 23 April 1915
Text: MS StaU; Schorer 52–3.

                                                      Greatham, Pulborough, Sussex.
                                                                          23 April 1915.

My Dear Lady Ottoline,

We were shocked about Maria:[1] it really is rather horrible. I'm not sure whether you aren't really more wicked than I had at first thought you. I think you can't help torturing a bit.

---

[1] Maria Nys (1898–1955), b. Flanders; when the Germans invaded Belgium in 1914 she fled and came to England to live with Lady Ottoline, first at 44 Bedford Square, London, and later at Garsington. m. 10 July 1919 Aldous Huxley (1894–1963), the novelist and essayist. Her suicide attempt, to which DHL alludes, has been described as follows: 'In the spring of 1915, before she ever met Aldous, there had been some kind of crisis. Ottoline was off somewhere without taking Maria, or Ottoline had been talking of sending her away for her own good; whatever it was, Maria in a moment of passionate grief swallowed some chloride. There was commotion, the doctor in the night, she was saved. They were very angry with her. . . . The wicked corrosive stuff burned her insides, possibly affected her health' (Sybille Bedford, *Aldous Huxley*, 1973, i. 80). Both Aldous and Maria Huxley became close friends of DHL in the 1920s.

But I think it [...] something – as if you, with a strong, old-developed *will* had enveloped the girl, in this will, so that she lived under the dominance of your will: and then you want to put her away from you, eject her from your will. So that when she says it was because she couldn't bear being left, that she took the poison, it is a great deal true. Also she feels quite bewildered and chaotic. I think she really does know nothing about herself, in her consciousness. Her instincts are self-defensive enough. But she has not much consciousness. We English, with our old-developed public selves, and the consequent powerful will, and the accompanying rudimentary private or instinctive selves, I think we are very baffling to any other nation. We are apt to assume domination, when we are not really personally implicated. A young foreigner can't understand this – not a girl like Maria.

Why must you always use your *will* so much, why can't you let things be, without always grasping and trying to know and to dominate. I'm too much like this myself.

There, now I'm scolding at you, even. But *why* will you use power instead of love, good public control instead of affection. I suppose it is breeding.

Don't mind what I say. – I send you another batch of MS.[1] You will forward it to Pinker, won't you, as soon as possible – J B Pinker, Talbot House, Arundel St, Strand, W C. He will get it set up in type, and then there will be no delay in publication. I am always delayed. And if you think it good, or bad, do tell me.

Be careful not to spend money on us at Garsington *now*: just the gardener's rooms, I beg you. Perhaps later on we shall all be rich.

Tell us how Buxton suits you. The days are beautiful, I hope you are having a nice time.

Still we must form the nucleus of a new society, as we said at the very first. But you use your will so much, always your will.

                                        Our love to you   D. H. Lawrence

If y[ou] haven't sent off the last MS. will you look at the last page of it and correct my numbering, as duplicate, on the new batch, for a few pages – or perhaps all through it if you would be so good. I forgot what page we had come to, so started these at 250 at random. Tell me next time you write, if you can, what is the last page of all the MS. you have – the number please.

                                                                    DHL

---

[1] Of *The Rainbow*. For a description of the typescript at the Humanities Research Center, see Farmer, 'Descriptive and Analytical Catalogue of the DHL Collection', item A41, p. 42.

906. To J. B. Pinker, 23 April 1915
Text: MS UNYB; Huxley 225.

Greatham, Pulborough, Sussex.

23 April 1915.

Dear Pinker,

Miss Meynell told me you wanted the MS of the novel. Lady Ottoline Morrell is reading it just now: she will send it on to you as she reads it.

I hope you are willing to fight for this novel. It is nearly three years of hard work, and I am proud of it, and it must be stood up for. I'm afraid there are parts of it Methuen wont want to publish. He must. I will take out sentences and phrases, but I won't take out paragraphs or pages. So you must tell me in detail if there are real objections to printing any parts.

You see a novel, after all this period of coming into being, has a definite organic form, just as a man has when he is grown. And we don't ask a man to cut his nose off because the public won't like it: because he must have a nose, and his own nose too.

Oh God, I hope I'm not going to have a miserable time over this book, now I've at last got it pretty much to its real being.

Very soon, I shall have no money. I got £25 paid in the last time at the last moment. Now it is nearly gone. I depend on you to get me something.

Yours very Sincerely   D. H. Lawrence

907. To Bertrand Russell, [29 April 1915]
Text: MS UT; Moore, *Bertrand Russell* 44.

Greatham, Pulborough, Sussex.

Thursday[1]

Dear Russell,

They are going to make me a bankrupt because I can't – and won't – pay the £150 of the divorce costs. I wouldn't pay them if I were a millionaire – I would rather go to prison. Messrs Goldberg Newall and Co, beasts, bugs, leeches, shall not have a penny from me if I can help it.[2]

---

[1] Dated with reference to the contents of this letter and those, together with the date, of the one which follows.

[2] The Registrar (Mr W. D. S. Caird) at Somerset House has provided the following information: 'In the divorce Mr Lawrence was ordered by order dated 5th December 1913 to pay Mr Weekley's costs amounting to £144 12s. 10d. Subsequently on 23rd February 1915 Mr. Lawrence was ordered to attend before one of the registrars of the then Probate Divorce & Admiralty Division of the High Court at such time and place as the registrar might appoint to be examined as to his means of satisfying the order of the 5th December 1913. I cannot trace a record of the examination, but it looks from the letters as if it is the one...on the 10th

– Today a very unclean creature came and gave me a paper, saying I must go on May 10th before the registrar and declare what debts are owing me. I'm sorry to say the publishers owe about £200, but as that is the last money I can possibly make for the next two years, they won't take it all from me.

Would you believe it, the unclean object gave me 25/-, and a paper – and I had to sign the receipt '25/- for conduct money'. What conduct? I am still gazing blankly at the golden sovereign. But I spat on it for luck.

I cannot tell you how this reinforces in me my utter hatred of the whole establishment – the whole constitution of England as it now stands. I wish I were a criminal instead of a bankrupt. But softly – softly. I will do my best to lay a mine under their foundations.

So we shall come to town on May 8th. I hope we shall be able to see you. I don't know where we shall stay, but I shall let you know.

Don't imagine I want any money – I don't. I wish I could tell the registrar I hadn't twopence – neither in hand nor owing. But I can't, because Methuen owes me £190 – to be paid when the novel is published.

I wanted to write and tell you – I don't know why. But you can't imagine[1] how it wears on one, having at every moment to resist this established world, and to know its unconscious hostility. For I am hostile, hostile, hostile to all that is, in our public and national life. I want to destroy it.

Let us know if you will be in town next week end but one.

Herzliche – no, Freundliche Grüsse,[2] Frieda says.

D. H. Lawrence

908. To S. S. Koteliansky, [30 April 1915]
Text: MS BL; Postmark, Cootham [...] 15; Moore 338.

Greatham, Pulborough, Sussex.
Friday[3]

My dear Kot,

Did I ever thank you for the collars and shirt? The shirt you should *not*

May 1915. He was ordered on 8th July 1915 to pay a further £10 15s. 2d. costs of the Petitioner. This would seem to be the costs of the examination. There is no indication on the divorce file that any further step was taken. There is not, nor would I expect to find, any record on the Court file of whether Lawrence finally paid or whether Weekley let the order go unsatisfied. The examination would have been just a question and answer exercise to enable the creditor to find out the means of the debtor so that he could decide whether it was worth proceeding further and, if so, what process of enforcement to take.' Although there is no record of payment, Letter 929 suggests that Robert Garnett was instructed to make some arrangement for payment on behalf of DHL, but no details of the amount have come to light.

[1] imagine] tell   [2] 'Cordial – no, friendly greetings'.
[3] Dated with reference to the forthcoming visit to London of 8 May 1915.

have sent. One day I shall send you a pair of spectacles, and make you wear
them, in retaliation. But thank you very much for the collars. I feel like a
winged Mercury in them – the wings slipped down to my neck, supporting
the Adam's Apple.

We are coming to London next week. I am going to be a bankrupt, because
I can't and won't pay the £150 divorce costs. I don't care a damn.

Horne writes he is going to France, to be a bus-driver. I wish I could
drive a bus, I'd go as well. He wants us to see him before he goes.

> 'Onward through shot and shell
> Onward they charge to hell
> Lorry and bus as well
> Chauffeur and stoker — —.'[1]

We might come up on Wednesday – but prefer Thursday or Friday. We shall
stay in a room in a street behind the National Gallery, which a man called
Proctor will lend us.[2] Then we are on our own.

Frieda wants a coat and skirt. If you would see your tailor, and ask him
if he could do her one, at once, and how much it would be – an ordinary
navy blue coat and skirt – and how many tryings on, it might all be settled
while we are up. We shall stay four or five days. Say we will pay him *at once*:
we will.

So au revoir   D. H. Lawrence

909. To Lady Ottoline Morrell, 30 April 1915
Text: MS UT; Postmark, Cootham 30 [...] 15; Huxley 225–7.

Greatham, Pulborough, Sussex.
30 April 1915

My dear Lady Ottoline,

Never mind the numbering of the pages of the MS. Just tell me the last
page of this secondary numbering when you write: is it 356? – and send the
batch to Pinker: Talbot House, Arundel St. Strand. I'm glad you like it.

You were quite cross with me last time, because of my 'elaborate theory'.[3]
Never mind – don't let us bother.

[1] A parody of the famous lines from Tennyson's 'The Charge of the Light Brigade', ll. 18–26.
[2] Basil Procter (1876–1943) was an architect educated at Newcastle-on-Tyne and in Paris, but
now living at 18 Whitcomb Street, Pall Mall. He designed various houses in Sussex and
Surrey. Probably his most important work was the extensive alteration to Castle Huntley,
near Loch Tay, in Scotland. He also published some humorous verse. No letters from DHL
to him have been found. (See Letter 917.)
[3] About her overpowering will; see Letter 905.

We went to Worthing yesterday on the motor bus: very beautiful: even I loved Worthing: and such light, such quantities of light beating and throbbing all round. I felt like Persephone come up from Hell. But today I would rather say like Eurydice: jamque Vale![1]

How dark my soul is! I stumble and grope about and don't get much further. I suppose it must be so. All the beauty and light of the days seems like a iridescence on a very black flood. Mostly one is underneath: sometimes one rises like the dove from the ark: but there is no olive branch.[2]

What a sentimental simile: myself as a dove: a sparrow is nearer the mark.

If you are in London next week – Wednesday till Monday – we are there then, so let us go somewhere together, shall we? – to Kew or to Hampton Court – London excursioners.

This is very beautiful weather. But it is going to rain. I can smell the soot in the chimney.

I wish I were going to Thibet – or Kamschatka – or Tahiti – to the Ultima ultima ultima Thule.[3] I feel sometimes, I shall go mad, because there is nowhere to go, no 'new world'. One of these days, unless I watch myself, I shall be departing in some rash fashion, to some foolish place.

We had promised to go to see my sister in Glasgow:[4] I have not seen her for two years: I might go there for a while, then walk in the hills.

I almost wish I could go to this war: not to shoot: I have vowed an eternal oath that I won't shoot in this war, not even if I am shot. I should like to be a bus conductor at the front – anything to escape this that is.

The death of Rupert Brooke fills me more and more [...] with the sense of the fatuity of it all. He was slain by bright Phoebus shaft – it was in keeping with his general sunniness – it was the real climax of his pose.[5] I first heard of him as a Greek God under a Japanese Sunshade, reading poetry in his

---

[1] 'And now farewell!' (Virgil, *Georgics*, iv. 497). Eurydice addressed these words to her husband, Orpheus, as she was taken from him back to Hell; Persephone, on the other hand, having been abducted by Pluto and taken to the underworld, was allowed to return to earth for six months of the year.

[2] Cf. Genesis viii. 11 (A.V.): 'And the dove came in to him in the evening; and, lo, in her mouth *was* an olive leaf pluckt off: so Noah knew that the waters were abated from off the earth.'

[3] Virgil, *Georgics*, i. 30: 'Farthest Thule', i.e. the end of the world.

[4] Emily King.

[5] DHL attributes Brooke's death to Phoebus Apollo, the sun-god, who determines the fate of various heroes in Homer's *Iliad*. Brooke actually died on a hospital ship on 23 April 1915 (see Edward Marsh, *Rupert Brooke: The Collected Poems*, 1918, pp. cl–clvi).

pyjamas, at Grantchester, at Grantchester, upon the lawns where the river goes.[1] Bright Phoebus smote him down. It is all in the saga.

O God Oh God, it is all too much of a piece: It is like madness.

Yesterday, at Worthing, there were many soldiers. Can I ever tell you how ugly they were: 'to insects – sensual lust.'[2] I like sensual lust – but insectwise, no – it is obscene. I like men to be beasts – but insects – one insect mounted on another – oh God! The soldiers at Worthing are like that – they remind me of lice or bugs: – 'to insects – sensual lust'. They will murder their officers one day. They are teeming insects. What massive creeping hell is not let loose nowadays.

It isn't my disordered imagination. There is a wagtail sitting on the gatepost. I see how sweet and swift heaven is. But hell is slow and creeping and viscous, and insect-teeming: as is this Europe now – this England.

Vale   D. H. Lawrence

910. To J. B. Pinker, 30 April 1915
Text: MS Forster; Unpublished.

Greatham, Pulborough, Sussex.
Friday 30 April 1915

Dear Pinker,

Do get me some money, will you: I am at the end. You are receiving the MS. now?[3] Lady Ottoline sent you the first batch, she says. She will send the next tomorrow. That is the first half complete. The rest won't be long. We wait only for Miss Meynell. Thank you for your assurances.

Yours   D. H. Lawrence

---

[1] DHL is recalling the well-known poem, 'The Old Vicarage, Grantchester', in which Brooke celebrates his house near Cambridge. The poem was included in *Georgian Poetry 1911–1912* to which DHL also contributed. He had doubtless heard of Brooke from Edward Marsh.

[2] An allusion to Dostoievsky's *The Brothers Karamazov:* 'I want to tell you now about the insects to whom God gave "sensual lust"…. I am that insect brother' (iii. 3), trans. Constance Garnett (1912).

[3] *The Rainbow.*

911. To Eleanor Farjeon, [1 May 1915]

Text: MS UT; cited in Eleanor Farjeon, 'Springtime with D. H. Lawrence', *London Magazine*, ii (April 1955), 57.

Greatham, Pulborough, Sussex.

[1 May 1915][1]

1. Mr McKinley[2] he aint done no wrong
   He went down to Buffalo way Michigan along
   For to lay him down, boys,
   For to lay him down.

2. Mr McKinley he went there just for fun
   An' Sholgosh 'e shot him with an Ivor Johnson
       gun,
   For etc.

3. Mrs McKinley she hollered and she swore
   When she heard her old man wasn't comin back
       no more
   For etc.

4. Sholgosh they shoved him into SingSing gaol
   And all the money in the world wouldn't get
       him out on bail
   For to etc.

5. Sholgosh they put him in the 'lectric chair
   And they shocked him so hard that they shocked
       off all his hair
   For to etc.

6. You should have seen old Satan grin
   When they opened Hell doors an' shoved old
       Sholgosh in
   For to lay him down boys, for to lay him
       do–own.[3]

---

[1] Eleanor Farjeon's statement that this was DHL's 'last note' (*London Magazine*, ii. 57), would mean that the letter should be dated after 18 May 1915; however, DHL's reference below to 'the first of May' may suggest that her memory was at fault. (Apparently she knew the tune but not the words of the song 'Mr McKinley' and had asked DHL to write out the words for her.)

[2] William McKinley (1843–1901), 25th President of the United States (1897–1901), was shot on 4 September 1901 by an anarchist, Leon F. Czolgosz (1873–1901), in the Temple of Music at the Pan-American Exposition at Buffalo. He died on 14 September 1901; 'Sholgosh' was executed for his crime on 29 October.

[3] DHL clearly relished this song. He taught it to his ten-year-old pupil Mary Saleeby, while at Greatham in 1915. See Nehls, i. 304.

Sehr-geehrte[1] Eleanor,

Thank you very much for the letter and greetings and stamps, all of which I lost. You had better have stayed at Rackham Cottage[2] – Margaret isn't so happy and Miss Paget and I only quarrel. But it's my fault – I am rude and cross.

> On the first of May
> O fatal day – make a song of it.

Heartlike greetings   D. H. Lawrence

912. To S. S. Koteliansky, 3 May 1915

Text: MS BL; Postmark, Pulborough 4 MAY 15; Zytaruk 42.

Greatham, Pulborough, Sussex.
3 May 1915

My dear Kot,

We shall come up to town either on Friday or on Saturday. I am not quite sure.

I am sorry your eyes are bad. I think it is your liver, which is sluggish, which makes them bad. Take some ordinary medicine, effervescing salts or anything, for the liver: and don't bother about the type-writing – I will get it done outside somewhere. I don't want you to trouble with it, particularly when your eyes are not good.

Does Katharine depress you.[3] Her letters are as jarring as the sound of a saw.

Au revoir   D. H. Lawrence

913. To Robert Garnett, 3 May 1915

Text: MS Forster; Unpublished.

Greatham, Pulborough, Sussex.
3 May 1915

Dear Mr Garnett,

I want to pay my debts to you. I think I remember that the bill was £2.[4] I hope I haven't delayed too long my settling up. When I am in difficulties,

---

[1] 'Dear'

[2] Rackham Cottage belonged to Percy and Madeleine Lucas (née Meynell). It was located on the Meynell estate but was some distance from the cottage occupied by DHL. Eleanor Farjeon recalls: 'In April this cottage was lent to Dolly Radford, and she invited me to spend a few weeks there with her daughter Margaret, and a Miss Paget who came to housekeep and look after things for us' (*London Magazine*, ii. 50).

[3] Katherine Mansfield was writing from Paris. See p. 296 n. 2.

[4] Probably legal fees connected with advice over Frieda's divorce.

I shall come to you again, if I may, because I know you will be good to me.
Thank you for your kindness.

Yours Sincerely   D. H. Lawrence

914. To J. B. Pinker, 4 May 1915
Text: MS UNYB; Unpublished.

Greatham, Pulborough, Sussex.
4 May 1915

Dear Pinker,

Thank you very much for the £25, which will last me for some time.

Yours Sincerely   D. H. Lawrence

915. To Lady Cynthia Asquith, [4 May 1915]
Text: Asquith, *Diaries* 16.

[Greatham, Pulborough, Sussex]
[4 May 1915]

[On 5 May 1915 Lady Cynthia Asquith received a letter from DHL 'wanting
to know what had happened since our expedition to Chichester'.]

916. To Lady Ottoline Morrell, 5 May 1915
Text: MS StaU; Unpublished.

Greatham, Pulborough, Sussex
5 May 1915

My dear Lady Ottoline,

You see I have two things to send you: the Imagiste anthology[1] and some
more MS. of the novel. If you don't like my poems, I don't mind very much.
They are old ones. I just give you the book because you might like to have
it.

I too like Gilbert's *Windmills* better, I think, than anything he has yet
done.[2]

I keep going on with my philosophy, and getting stuck. I suppose I shall
finish it some day.

I shan't write you a letter now, because I have been working sitting in

---

[1] *Some Imagist Poets* was published on 17 April 1915. DHL's misspelling may have derived
   from the title of Pound's anthology, *Des Imagistes*, published by the Poetry Bookshop a year
   earlier. (See p. 209 n. 4.)
[2] Gilbert Cannan, *Windmills: A Book of Fables* (April 1915).

the sun, and so I feel very silent. But I liked your letter very much: it was a real word to me, that was.

We will write again soon – and au revoir.

D. H. Lawrence

917. To S. S. Koteliansky, [6 May 1915]
Text: MS BL; PC; Postmark, Chichester 6 MY 15; Zytaruk 43.

Chichester –
Thursday

My dear Kot,

We go to London tomorrow afternoon, but I don't know the train. If you come round to 18 Whitcomb St. Pall Mall at about 6.0 I think we shall be there. Basil Procter is the host – a young architect.

Today I walked here from Greatham – very beautiful.

I hope you weren't seedy.

Yrs   D. H. Lawrence

918. To Lady Cynthia Asquith, 14 May 1915
Text: MS UT; cited in Huxley 227–8.

Greatham – Pulborough – Sussex
14 May 1915

My dear Lady Cynthia,

I am not in a mood to write you about John, because I feel churlish.[1] When we talked in Brighton, lying on the cliff, I did not take much notice of what I said, because my subconsciousness was occupied with the idea of how pleasant it would be to walk over the edge of the cliff. There seemed another, brighter sort of world away below, and this world on top is all torture and a flounder of stupidity.

I don't know much about John, and probably everything I say is pure bosh, a tangle of theory of my own. And you will be treating me as a sort of professional, directly, a mixture between a professor of psychology and a clairvoyant, a charlatan expert in psychiatry. You won't be able to prevent yourself. I rather resent this demand for a letter. Why can't you leave our relationship commonly[2] human, and not set me writing out prescriptions. You should listen to what I say, which comes spontaneously, and not set

---

[1] John Asquith, Lady Cynthia's eldest son, suffered from an undiagnosed case of autism. Lady Cynthia recorded in her diary on 17 May 1915: 'a very curious [letter] from Lawrence in answer to my request for a written analysis of John's character. He calls my spirit hard and stoical – a serious indictment to which I do not plead guilty' (Asquith, *Diaries* 22).

[2] commonly] purely

me deliberately dictating. I must tell you I resent it. Why do you want a letter, in what spirit do you ask?

But I will write to you because I feel a sort of love for your hard, stoical spirit – not for anything else.

I don't think John is so very extraordinary. I think, if one could consider it intrinsically, he has a sensitive, happy soul. But every soul is born into an existing world. The world is not made afresh for every new soul, as the shell for every egg. And long before John was ever born or conceived, your soul knew that, within the hard form of existing conditions, of the existing 'world', it was like a thing born to remain forever in prison: your own soul knew, before ever John was possible, that it was itself bound in, like a tree that grows under a low roof and can never break through, and which must be deformed, unfulfilled. Herbert Asquith must have known the same thing, in his soul.

Now a soul which knows that it is bound in by the existing conditions, bound in and formed or deformed by the world wherein it comes to being, this soul is a dead[1] soul. Every living soul believes that the conditions will be modified to its own growth or expression. Every living soul believes that all things rest within the scope of a Great Will which is working Itself out in all things, but also and most vitally in the soul itself. This I call a belief in God, or belief in Love – what you like. Now if a soul believes that the Great Will is working in all things, even though itself be thwarted and deformed and frustrated, that is what I call a *dead* belief: not a living belief. Because every *living* soul believes that, whatever the conditions, there will be that conjunction between the conditions and the soul itself which shall fulfil the *Great* Will. The soul which believes that the Great Will, or God, will make all things right, and that the agency of the particular soul is insignificant, this soul is an unbeliever affirming belief. Because every living soul says, 'I am[2] of God'. Then, if I am insignificant, God in me is insignificant. Which is unbelief: *much more insidious* than atheism.

Now the soul which was born into John was born in the womb of your unbelief and from the loins of its father's unbelief, the [...] unbelief affirming belief. It is born of unbelief, but into an affirmation of belief. Which is why the soul of John re-acts from your soul, even from the start: because he knows that you are Unbelief, and he reacts from your affirmation of belief always with hostility.

The nurse, being a smaller soul, has plenty of room to grow within the existing condition, as a fern in a room, where a tree would be worse than

---

[1] dead] living-dead   [2] I am] God is

dead. So she is a believer – her soul fulfils itself, because it is a good small soul and has room. John knows her, and has some inkling of belief. You are his great doubt. He knows your unbelief. He fights your affirmation of belief, when he throws down the crust.

Don't try to make him love you, or obey you – don't do it. The love he would have for you would be a much greater love than he would ever have for his nurse, or anybody else, because it would be a love born of trust and confirmation of joy and belief. But you can never fight for this love. That you fight is only a sign that you are wanting in yourself. The child knows that. Your own soul is deficient, so it fights for the love of the child. And the child's soul, born in the womb of your unbelief, laughs at you and defies you, almost jeers at you, almost hates you.

The great thing is, *not* to exert authority unnecessarily over the child – no prerogative, only the prerogative of pure justice. That he is not[1] to throw down crusts is a pure autocratic command. No[t] to throw down crusts because it is [. . .] a trouble to nurse to pick them up, is an appeal to a sense of justice and love, which is an appeal to the believing soul of the child.

Put yourself aside with regard to him. You have no right to his love. Care only for his good and well-being: make *no* demands on him.

But for yourself, you must learn to believe in God. Believe me, in the end, we will unite in our Knowledge of God. Believe me, this England, we very English people, will at length join together and say, 'We will not do these things, because in our knowledge of God we know them wrong.' We shall put away our greediness and our living for material things only, because we shall agree we don't want these things. We know they are inferior, base, so we shall have courage to put them away. We shall unite in our knowledge of God – not perhaps in our expression of God – but in our *knowledge* of God: and we shall agree that we don't want to live only to work and make riches, that England does not care only to have the Greatest Empire or the Greatest Commerce, but that she does care supremely for the pure truth of God, which she will try to fulfil.

This isn't ranting – it is pure reasoning from the knowledge of God and of truth. It is not our wickedness which kills us, but our unbelief. You learn to believe, in your very self, that we in England shall unite in our knowledge of God to live according to the best of our knowledge – Prime Ministers and capitalists and artizans all working in pure effort towards God – here, tomorrow, in this England – and you will save your own soul and the soul of your son. Then there will be love enough.

---

[1] That he is not] Not

You see this change must come to pass. But nobody will believe it, however *obvious* it is. So it almost sends me mad, I am almost a lunatic.

Please write to me and ask me anything you like – but please do believe that the thing *shall* be.

D. H. Lawrence

Remember, if you are inclined to take this half as a joke, it was an impertinence on your part to ask me for it in any but an entirely non-flippant spirit.

919. To Eleanor Farjeon, 14 May 1915
Text: MS UT; Eleanor Farjeon, *Magic Casements* (1941), p. 41.

Greatham, Pulborough, Sussex.

14 May 1915

Dear Eleanor,[1]

I'm sorry we weren't back on Tuesday, to see you before you went. But we came home by way of Brighton, staying there two days with Cynthia Asquith, who was down with her children.

We had a jolly walk to Chichester.[2] Some time, let us take another walk, shall we? The country is now very beautiful, much apple-blossom and blue-bells. I wish we were walking up that down again, or sitting in the inn at East Dean.

May I send you the MS of my 'philosophy' to type? Be sure and say no if there is anything against it.

Frieda is going to have two little rooms on Park Hill Rd, Haverstock Hill.[3] So when we are in town we shall be neighbours, and we must be neighbourly.

tante belle cose   D. H. Lawrence

920. To Lady Ottoline Morrell, 14 May 1915
Text: MS UT; Postmark, Cootham 14 MY 15; cited in Morrell, *Nation and Athenaeum*, xlvii. 860.

Greatham – Pulborough – Sussex

14 May 1915

My dear Lady Ottoline,

I wonder if you are still in Buxton, and if you got the last batch of MS.

---

[1] See p. 321 n. 4.
[2] An account of this walk occurs in Eleanor Farjeon, *London Magazine*, ii. 52. DHL 'was in his angelic, child-like mood'.
[3] Frieda wanted to be closer to her children who were at school in London; it is also clear that DHL's marriage was under considerable strain. See Letter 923.

which I sent you, enclosed with a copy of the Imagist Anthology which
contains some of my verses. If you got them, tell me, will you.

We were in London for four days: beautiful weather, but I don't like
London. My eyes can see nothing human that is good, nowadays: at any rate,
nothing public. London seems to me like some hoary massive underworld,
a hoary, ponderous inferno. The traffic flows through the rigid grey streets
like the rivers of Hell through their banks of dry, rocky ash. The fashions
and the women's clothes are very ugly.

On the way back we went down to Brighton and stayed the night with
Cynthia Asquith, who was there with her two children.[1] I am rather fond
of her. Somewhere, in her own soul, she is not afraid to face the Truth,
whatever it may be. She is something of a stoic, with a nature hard and sad
as rock. I admire her for her hard, isolated courage. She has never been in
contact with anyone. It is as if she can't. There is something sea-like about
her, cold and with a sort of passion like salt, that burns and corrodes.

Coming back here, I find the country very beautiful. The apple-trees are
leaning forwards, all white with blossom, towards the very green grass. I
watch, in the morning when I wake up, a thrush on the wall outside the
window – not a thrush, a blackbird – and he sings, opening his beak. It is
a strange thing to watch him singing, opening his beak and giving out his
calls and warblings, then remaining silent. He looks so remote, so buried in
primeval silence, standing there on the wall, and bethinking himself, then
opening his beak to make the strange, strong sounds. He seems as if his
singing were a sort of talking to himself, or of thinking aloud his strongest
thoughts. I wish I was a blackbird, like him. I hate men.

> 'The ousel cock of tawny hue
> And orange-yellow bill.'[2]

The bluebells are all out in the wood, under the new vivid leaves. But
they are rather dashed aside by yesterdays rain. It would be nice if the Lord
sent another Flood and drowned the world. Probably I should want to be
Noah. I am not sure.

I've got again into one of those horrible sleeps from which I can't wake.
I can't brush it aside to wake up. You know those horrible sleeps when one
is struggling to wake up, and can't. I was like it all autumn – now I am again
like it. Everything has a touch of delirium – the blackbird on the wall is [. . .]
delirium, even the apple-blossom. And when I see a snake winding rapidly
in the marshy places, I think I am mad.

[1] John and Michael.
[2] *A Midsummer Night's Dream*, III. i. 128 ['The ousel cock, so black of hue, | With
orange-tawny bill'].

It is not a question of me, it is the world of men. The world of men is dreaming, it has gone mad in its sleep, and a snake is strangling it, but it cant wake up.

When I read of the *Lusitania*,[1] and of the riots in London, I know it is so.[2] I think soon we must get up and try to stop it. Let us wait a little longer. Then when we cannot bear it any more, we must try to wake up the world of men, which has gone mad in its sleep.

I cannot bear it, much longer, to let the madness get stronger and stronger possession. Soon we in England shall go fully mad, with hate. I too hate the Germans so much, I could kill every one of them. Why should they goad us to this frenzy of hatred, why should we be tortured to bloody madness, when we are only grieved in our souls, and heavy. They will drive our heaviness and our grief away in a fury of rage. And we don't want to be worked up into this fury, this destructive madness of rage. Yet we must, we are goaded on and on. I am mad with rage myself. I would like to kill a million Germans – two million.

I wonder when we shall see you again, and where you are. I have promised to stay here for another month at least, to teach Mary Saleeby.[3] Her mother has a nervous breakdown, and they asked me to teach the child. I do it for the child's sake, for nothing else. So my mornings are taken up, for $3\frac{1}{2}$ hours each day.

Don't take any notice of my extravagant talk – one must say something. Write soon and tell us where you are, and how you are. I feel a little bit anxious about you, when you do not write.

Vale   D. H. Lawrence

921. To Eleanor Farjeon, 18 May 1915
Text: MS UT; Postmark, Cootham 18 MY 15; Farjeon, *Magic Casements*, pp. 41–2.

Greatham – Pulborough – Sussex
18 May 1915
My dear Eleanor,

Thank you very much for the poems.[4] I think there is *real* poetry in them.

[1] On the afternoon of 7 May 1915 the Cunard liner *Lusitania* was torpedoed by a German submarine off the Old Head of Kinsale on the south coast of Ireland, with the loss of 1,198 lives.

[2] Anti-German riots in London began on 11 May 1915. *Times* (12 May) reported: 'an apparently concerted attack was made last night on Germans in East-end districts... many shops were completely wrecked'. The riots continued for several days. 'There were further anti-German demonstrations at Tottenham last night' (*Times*, 15 May 1915).

[3] Mary Saleeby (b. 1905), the elder daughter of C. W. Saleeby and Monica Saleeby, née Meynell. Her parents were estranged before she and her mother went to live at Greatham in 1912. m. Reginald Brettauer Fisher, 1929. (See Nehls, i. 303–4.)

[4] Eleanor Farjeon says that she sent 'some serious unpublished poems' to DHL (*Magic Casements*, p. 41); she must also have included some of her published work.

It is strange, in you, that you never seem to fight things out to their last issue: and things which seem to me so amazingly potentially good. You have a far finer and more beautiful poetry in you than Margaret has,[1] even than such men as De la Mare or Davies. But they get theirs verily smelted out, and you never burn yours in the last fire. I wonder why. It is the same here as in *Kol Nikon.*[2] But these are better than *Kol Nikon*. How beautiful 'Revolt' nearly is,[3] very beautiful, but for a faint tinge of sentimentality, a dross of smallness, almost cowardice, or disbelief, that should have been burnt out.

> – but still in the cities of men
> Thou shalt spin thy thread of existence in a
> pattern not thine own.

That is very fine. But if you gave your real passion to it you would save your poems from their clichés of desolate waters and 'scale the steeps of the air'.

'Underworld' also has something very beautiful about it.

> I could believe the only voice that sings
> Is of the leafage sparkling into song.[4]

But never the last dregs of bitterness will you drink, never face the last embrace of the fire, in your poems.

I think I like the 'Sonnets' best.[5] But there is a tendency for anybody, in writing the Shakespearean sonnet, to become facile. It is a form that lends itself to facility. But there is dignity and beauty and worth in these sonnets. I wish you had never read a line of Elizabethan poetry in your life, and then we might have had pure utterance from you. But I like them, I do: 'Certain among us walk in loneliness,' and 'When all is said'.[6] 'When all is said' expresses you perfectly. It is very good. But it is not quite true. We *can* by the strength of our desires compel our destinies.[7] Indeed our destiny lies in the strength of our desires. Why are you a little cynical, or perhaps, even a little conceited. 'Destiny is the strength of our desires.' Let that be your line.

I have decided to try to type my MS. myself. When I break down I shall come to you for help.

---

[1] Margaret Radford.
[2] Eleanor Farjeon's novel, *The Soul of Kol Nikon* had appeared serially in the *Irish Review* (1914); it was published in book form in 1923.
[3] A poem in her collection *Dream-Songs for the Beloved* (1911), pp. 33–4.
[4] Ibid. p. 48.
[5] Later published as *First & Second Love: Sonnets* (1947).
[6] Sonnets XIX and XVIII.
[7] Sonnet XVIII ll. 9–10: 'We cannot by the strength of desires | Compel our destinies.'

It is sad, we have not got the Hampstead rooms: applied too late. But they were too small. We must try again.

Why don't you come down to Rackham Cottage for Whitsun, you and your brother or somebody you can choose. I wish you would.

Love from Frieda and me   D. H. Lawrence

922. To Lady Ottoline Morrell, [c. 19 May 1915]
Text: MS UT; Morrell, *Nation and Athenaeum*, xlvii. 860.

Greatham, Pulborough, Sussex.
[c. 19 May 1915][1]

My dear Lady Ottoline,

I send you the next batch of MS.[2] There will only be one more lot. I hope you will like it.

Monica has a motor-car every day to drive her out, so we go too.[3] Today we drove to Bognor. It was strange at Bognor – a white, vague, powerful sea, with long waves falling heavily; with a crash of frosty white out of the pearly whiteness of the day, of the wide sea. And the small boats that were out in the distance heaved, and seemed to glisten shadowily. Strange, the sea was, so strong. I saw a soldier on the pier, with only one leg. He was young and handsome: and strangely self-conscious, and slightly ostentatious: but confused. As yet, he does not realise anything, he is still in the shock. And he is strangely roused by the women, who seem to have a craving[4] for him. They look at him with eyes of longing, and they want to talk to him. So he is roused, like a roused male. Yet there is more wistfulness and wonder than passion or desire. I could see him under chloroform having the leg amputated. It was still in his face. But he was brown and strong and handsome.[5]

It seemed to me anything might come out of that white, silent, opalescent sea; and the great icy shocks of foam were strange. I felt as if legions were marching in the mist. I cannot tell you why, but I am afraid. I am afraid of the ghosts of the dead. They seem to come marching home in legions over the white, silent sea, breaking in on us with a roar and a white iciness.

---

[1] The official announcement regarding the Coalition Government was made by the Prime Minister in the House of Commons on 19 May 1915. DHL's remark, 'So they are making a coalition Government', suggests an adjacent date.

[2] *The Rainbow.*

[3] Monica (1880–1929), second child of Wilfrid and Alice Meynell. m. Caleb W. Saleeby, 1903. After the breakdown of her marriage she moved, with her daughter Mary, to Greatham where Wilfrid Meynell provided them with a house.

[4] craving] passion

[5] This scene, with the women fascinated by the wounded soldier, reappears in 'The Crown', chap. 5 (*Phoenix II*, ed. Warren Roberts and Harry T. Moore, 1968, pp. 401–2).

Perhaps this is why I feel so afraid. I don't know. But the land beyond looked warm, with a warm blue sky, very homely: and over the sea legions of white ghosts tramping. I was on the pier.

So they are making a coalition Government. I cannot tell you how icy cold my heart is with fear. It is as if we were all going to die. Did I not tell you my revolution would come? It will come, God help us. The ghosts will bring it. Why does one feel so coldly afraid? Why does even the Coalition of the Government fill me with terror. Some say it is for peace negotiations. It may be, because we are all afraid. But it is most probably for conscription. The touch of death is very cold and horrible on us all.

D. H. Lawrence

It is the whiteness of the ghost-legions that is so awful.

923. To S. S. Koteliansky, 19 May 1915
Text: MS BL; Postmark, Cootham 20 [...] 15; Moore 344–5.

Greatham, Pulborough, Sussex.
19 May 1915

My dear Kot,

Thank you very much for Soloviev.[1] He is interesting, very – but he never says anything he wants to say. He makes a rare mess, fiddling about with orthodox Christianity. Dostoevsky made the same mess.

There is no news from here, except that we applied too late for the rooms in Hampstead. They were too small. Friends are looking for another place for Frieda, also in Hampstead. Probably she will go and stay alone in them for some time, if she gets them. She spends her time thinking herself a wronged, injured and aggrieved person, because of the children, and because she is a German. I am angry and bored. I wish she would have her rooms in Hampstead and leave me alone.

For Whitsun, Viola is staying in this house, and Ivy Low: so we are full up in such an unwelcome fashion. Never mind – I stay here only three weeks more. Meanwhile my mornings are occupied in teaching Mary Saleeby.[2] I am typing my philosophy myself. When I read it in comparison with Soloviev, I am proud of my cleverness.

[1] Vladimir Solovyov (1853–1900), Russian philosopher. Kot most probably sent Solovyov's book, *War, Progress and the End of History: Including a Short History of the Antichrist*, trans. Alexander Bakshy (April 1915).
[2] By the time she arrived at Greatham, Mary had received no formal education. She was due to go to St Paul's Girls' School in London in September 1915: DHL gave her regular tuition in preparation for this.

I hope your eyes are getting better. Tell me any news of Murry or yourself. The country is *very* beautiful. I am happy when I am gardening
over at Rackham Cottage – only then. But then I am quite happy, with the
plants.

I hope you are well.

Let me hear from you.

Yours   D. H. Lawrence

924. To Lady Ottoline Morrell, [post 19 May 1915]
Text: MS StaU; Schorer 53–4.

Greatham, Pulborough, Sussex.
[post 19 May 1915]¹

[Frieda Lawrence begins]

Dear Lady Ottoline,

This is to welcome you at Garsington – It ought to look jolly now –
Everything looks splendid here, except the people – Monica has had a
hysterical breakdown, just flops in bed for 3 weeks, a nurse, a doctor how
cross it would make you, it does me – she has no interest at all in anything,
it's the spring, I suppose and nothing for her to do – and no man – Yes, the
war is vile and degrading – The hate of the Germans is getting so strong – It
takes one all one's time to keep on believing the best *one* knows – And the
women are as bad; this coalition business seems splendid to me, there is a
chance for a real opposition now, isn't there?² What could be done soon
seems hopeful sometimes – I am going to have a tiny flat in Hampstead, I
think, I simply must be by myself sometimes, L[awrence] is very wearing
and also I will see the children on their way to school, that they dont get
used to *not* seeing me – The war has done this for me, that it makes me see
my own misery, which at one time seemed quite phantastically horrible, quite
small, they are alive and there is all the future – But the deep rage I am in,
when I think, that this is the law of man; and if I were a prostitute the
children would be *mine* and a man would be obliged to pay me – It must

¹ Lady Ottoline's recollection of the date for the move to Garsington, 'At last on May 17th
[1915] the day arrived for us to cross the threshold of our new home' (*Ottoline at Garsington*
31); the receipt of the Solovyov book from Kot on or just before 19 May; as well as the
implication here that the Coalition Government is now official, all point to this letter being
written shortly after 19 May 1915.
² Asquith's announcement that 'steps are in contemplation which involve the reconstruction
of the Government on a broader personal and political basis', would in reality limit the scope
for the opposition.

have been strange to be in your childhood's surroundings, I think those old
atmospheres are generally very upsetting –

My love to you

L. will write, he is sending you a book by a Russian – You will like L's
philosophy!

[Lawrence begins]

Isn't it a funny thing, if a woman has got her children, she doesn't care
about them, and if she has a man, she doesn't care about him, she only wants
her children. There is something in the talk about female perversity. Frieda
only cares about her children now. It is as if women – or she – persisted in
being unfortunate and hopelessly unsatisfied: if a man wants much, she
becomes violently a mother and a man-hater, if her children want much, she
becomes a violent disciple of 'love' as against domesticity or maternity.
What a miserable creature!

I send you Soloviev – he is not very profound, but interesting as revealing
the desire of Dostoevsky's Russian, for God, and his hopeless muddle with
Christianity. When shall we see you again. One tries hard to stick to ones
ideal of one man-one woman, in love, but probably you are right, and one
should go to different persons to get companionship for the different sides
of ones nature.

I hope we shall see you soon.

D. H. Lawrence

925. To Lady Ottoline Morrell, [25 May 1915]
Text: MS UT; cited in Huxley 236.

Greatham – Pulborough – Sussex
Tuesday[1]

My dear Lady Ottoline,

I want very much to come this week-end. But I won't move from here
now until I leave for good. I look to escape during the next two or three
weeks. I want to go away. The whole Meynellàge is down here – I like
them – but they are so flusterous – and then Monica with her breakdown
takes refuge in me, and is very heavy. It is altogether a crisis. And I must
see this crisis through. Then – libre – libero – free – I rise up from another
little epoch, and depart to a new history. I shall move very soon.

---

[1] The presence of the whole Meynell family (confirmed in Letter 926) and DHL's visit to the
Cannans and Garsington in '2 or 3 weeks time' (he stayed at the latter 12–16 June) combine
to suggest 25 May as the date for this letter.

We have promised to go to the Cannans for a few days – in 2 or 3 weeks time – then may we come to Garsington. I am hoping always that things will so work out that I am free of my pupil in a week or so, and then I must come and look at Garsington. I want very much to come.

It is beautiful also here: on the top of the downs a whole fire of gorse – very fine.

I dreamed last night that all the stars were moving out of the sky. It was awful. Orion in particular went very fast, the other stars in a disorderly fashion, but all trooping out of the sky, in haste, to the left hand. And some of them, low down, took fire. I was very terrified, more terrified than I have ever been. There became a smoke and a burning.

Now read my dream, you who should be a prophetess.

D. H. Lawrence

We aren't so very badly off, yet. They didn't make me a bankrupt – it is still in the air. But I was examined – I hated it.[1] When I am in need I shall take your money – gratefully. – We didn't get the rooms in Hampstead after all.

DHL

926. To Dollie Radford, [26 May 1915]
Text: MS UN; Postmark, Cootham 26 [...] 1[...]; Nehls, i. 306–7.

Greatham, Pulborough, Sussex
Wednesday

Dear Dollie Radford,

Frieda couldn't come to London today, because Barbara Low couldn't put her up. But she thinks she will come tomorrow. She will if possible come and see you in the afternoon. I hope she will find her two little rooms in Hampstead, she is very keen on them.

It is very hot and very beautiful down here. The flowers are passing with amazing rapidity, drying up like dew, gone like a white cloud. The apple trees seem all in shadow, no blossom left.

The poor Rackham cottage was a seething pot, I tell you, six children and six grown-ups. The parent Meynells are down.[2] I rather like her. Monica gets better, but there are still great and wearying consultations. I wonder how long we shall stay now. The teaching Mary keeps me.

I hope you are well, and that Margaret keeps better. Tell her I like her at the cottage – now we don't go across. Will she come down again? Will you come? I feel everything very unsettled and critical here.

Au revoir   D. H. Lawrence

[1] See p. 327 n. 2.   [2] Wilfred and Alice Meynell.

927. To E. M. Forster, 29 May 1915
Text: MS KCC; Unpublished.

Greatham, Pulborough, Sussex.
29 May 1915

My dear Forster,

I was wondering what had happened to you. I'm glad it's no worse than chicken-pox. And is that all the news you have? And is there any connection between the rainbow and the pox.

We are here with the state of dissolution just setting in. That is, we are more or less preparing to leave Greatham: to go to the Ottoline's for a time, and then I don't know where. I feel my feet are loosened from this place – heaven knows where they intend to take me.

The spring has been very beautiful – very brilliant, upon a black undertone of the war horror. One doesn't feel expansive – there is a darkness between us all, separating us. We are all isolated.

You should tell me your news – if you have anything further. Let me know when the chicken-pox is gone. We will meet in London. Frieda is looking for a couple of rooms in Hampstead. You must come and see her there, when they are found. Tell us how you are.

D. H. Lawrence

928. To Bertrand Russell, 29 May 1915
Text: MS UT; Moore, *Bertrand Russell* 46.

Greatham – Pulborough – Sussex
29 May 1915

Dear Russell,

If they hound you out of Trinity, so much the better: I am glad.[1] Entire separation, that is what must happen to one: not even the nominal shelter left, not even the mere fact of inclusion in the host. One must be entirely cast forth.

As for political revolution, that too must come. But now, only the darkness thrusts more and more between us all, like a sword, cutting us off entirely each from the other, severing us and burying us each one separate in the utter darkness. After this we shall know the change, we shall really move back in one movement to the sun. Except a seed die, it bringeth not forth.[2]

---

[1] On 28 May 1915 Trinity College rescinded their earlier decision to appoint Russell to a Research Fellowship; instead they agreed to renew his Lectureship for 5 years. Russell was sure that the College Council had been swayed by disgust at his involvement with the Union of Democratic Control. [2] Cf. 1 Corinthians xv. 36.

Only wait. Our death must be accomplished first, then we will rise up. Only wait, and be ready. We shall have to sound the resurrection soon. Leave your Cambridge then: that is very good. And let us die from this life, from this year of life, and rise up when the winter is drawing over, after the time in the tomb. But we are never dead. When everything else is gone, and there is no touch nor sense of each other left, there is always the sense of God, of the Absolute. Our sense of the Absolute is the only sense left to us.

Soon we are leaving here. You must come and see us before we go, if you can. It is beautiful. We are one in allegiance, really, you and I. We have one faith, we must unite in one fight. Wait only a little while –

D. H. Lawrence

929. To J. B. Pinker, 29 May 1915
Text: MS Forster; Moore 345–6.

Greatham – Pulborough – Sussex.
29 May 1915

Dear Pinker,

Thank you for your letter. I will try and write a story for the *Strand*.[1] If I have a stroke of genius, I might do one. An American sent me a letter too – he seems a good man. He might publish simultaneously.

Now only vexation is coming. The MS. is being finished by Miss Meynell this very day. I have only to revise it and let you have it.

But I am in difficulty. Some lawyers called Goldberg are trying to get from me £144 for divorce costs. I had to go and declare all that is owing to me, before the Registrar at Somerset House, on May 3rd.[2] I hated it.

I have written to my solicitor – Garnett's brother – 'Robert Garnett, 36 John St., Bedford Row', – to ask him to advise me, and [...] to compound with the detestable Goldbergs.[3] If he comes to you for a copy of my agreement with Methuen, or for any information, I should be so glad if you would let him have what he wants.

I am afraid, if I hand in the MS., the Goldbergs – Goldberg, Newall, Braun and Co, solicitors in the city – will serve a summons on me and on Methuen, ordering Methuen to pay to them the £50 due to me. They can't serve the summons – or at least it is null if they do – until the debt is due. So I would like some arrangement to be made by Robt. Garnett, before I

[1] DHL's sole publication in *Strand Magazine* was 'Tickets Please' which did not appear until April 1919.
[2] According to Letter 907 DHL was ordered to appear on 10 May 1915.
[3] Neither the letter to Garnett nor details of the settlement have been found.

hand in the MS. Because, the debt to me does not fall due till I hand in the MS. to you.

You see I can't pay this £144, or I shall starve for ever. This money for the *Rainbow* is all I have to look forward to at all – and Mrs Lawrence can't get any money from Germany now. So it is a hole.

I am very sorry to trouble you. I think it will be only a little trouble – a very few days. Perhaps I shall come to town, then I shall come to see you. But I am not very well.

Please don't be angry with me for all this bother. I hate it so much.

Yours   D. H. Lawrence

930. To J. B. Pinker, 31 May 1915
Text: MS YU; Huxley 230.

Greatham – Pulborough.

31 May 1915

Dear Pinker,

In response to the wire from R. Garnett, I send you the final batch of MS. of the *Rainbow*. One or two little things: you will see the pages are not numbered: we all lost count after a certain point. Will you let somebody number the pages: also see that they run on, that none of the MS. is missing: also please to see that the chapters are correctly numbered.

I hope you will like the book: also that it is not very improper. It did not seem to me very improper, as I went through it. But then I feel very incompetent to judge, on that point.

My beloved book, I am sorry to give it to you to be printed. I could weep tears in my heart, when I read these pages. If I had my way, I would put off the publishing yet a while.

One other little thing: I want, on the fly leaf, in German characters, the

inscription 'Zu Else' – i.e. " *zu Elfn.* " Put that in

for me, will you. It is just 'To Elsa'. But it must be in Gothic letters.[1]

We shall have peace by the time this book is published.

Yours   D. H. Lawrence

---

[1] This dedication to Frieda's sister may have exacerbated the anger of officialdom to the novel.

350   *[? June 1915]*

931. To Margaret Radford, [? June 1915]
Text: MS UN; Unpublished.

[Greatham, Pulborough, Sussex]
[? June 1915]¹

My dear Margaret,

I have been reading the poems, and am more struck by those I have never seen before.² They have got the other-world in them, which is the world of poetry. They are in the otherworld. One must either be in this world or in the world beyond, in the temporal or the eternal life. One cannot have one foot on sea and one on shore. And your best poems belong to the eternal world altogether. 'Loneliness' is almost perfect.

> 'And what has the melodied soul to do
> With aught but what is blest?
> It cannot laugh, nor blame, nor teach
> Defend nor interest.'³

That is quite perfect, and a very great truth. Such loneliness, where one lives in the presence of things blest, in the knowledge of the Infinite, the Eternal, where each thing is consummate and completed, this is the very antithesis of loneliness. Loneliness is part of temporality and partiality, it has no place in eternality. Milton's God is the great Absolute, the Eternity, interpreted by us, from mortality, into loneliness. But it is just this which is *not* loneliness, which avails against all loneliness.

I want to say to you, do not force yourself to the temporal life, the incomplete life. Do not force yourself to the things that are only relative – housekeeping and so on – the eternal world is the perfect world, and you belong more to that. If you have to forfeit the mortal world somewhat, do it gladly, and live for the immortal, as the mediaeval women did, some of them. Let the world be perfect as a vision. There are two planes – the perfect and the imperfect. Some of us can only exist on the one. Speedwell⁴ is purely for the mortal, temporal, imperfect world. You are almost purely for the other. Speedwell knows her half – leave it to her. You have your half – be satisfied and glad in it. It is the confusion of the two worlds that makes so much disharmony. Let us really be pure in our being, as far as we can.

I hope you are not very unwell. – I am not.

D. H. Lawrence

Don't try and have power in the mortal world – particular personal power – leave it.

¹ Margaret Radford's book, *Poems*, was published in June 1915; it is likely that this letter was written during that month.
² Presumably DHL had seen some poems in MS on an earlier occasion.
³ See *Poems*, p. 23.   ⁴ Unidentified.

932. To E. M. Forster, 2 June 1915
Text: MS KCC; cited in Delany 109.

Greatham – Pulborough
2 June 1915

Dear Forster,

I'm sorry I can't send you the *Rainbow*, because Pinker wired for it just before your letter came: he is very anxious to set it up – so I sent it him. I can wash my hands of it. Soon after I hear from you again, I will send you some of my 'philosophy'. It is such highly debateable stuff, I am a rash man.

As for you – above all, don't read the *Crown of Hinduism*.[1] I can't tell you how I detest things Hindu and things Buddhistic – it is all such ineffable self-conceit as to be overwhelming. Better read *Tartuffe* – though why not *Le Bourgeois Gentilhomme* – no, *Tartuffe* is better.[2] Read what the devil you like. The only thing I should like to read is the death-notice of a vast number of particular people.

We should be in town probably in a fortnight. Mrs Lawrence is up there looking for her flat – unless a bomb has dropped on her – killed by her own countrymen – it is the kind of fate she is cut out for.

I'll let you know when we are in town,

D. H. Lawrence

933. To Lady Ottoline Morrell, 2 June 1915
Text: MS IEduc; cited in Delany 111.

Greatham – Pulborough
2 June 1915

My dear Lady Ottoline,

Are[3] you at the end of your painting and house preparations? I have got a respite from my pupil.[4] She has gone to the sea with her mother for 2 weeks. I shall try to get her put to school. Then can we come to Garsington? We have promised to stay with the Cannans en route. Frieda is in London looking for a little flat for herself in Hampstead – unless a vague bomb has dropped on her. I am not sure when she will be back.

I am so sorry, Pinker wired me for the rest of the MS, and I had to send it him. He was in a great hurry. But I will let you have the proofs. You did receive the second Garsington batch of MS., didn't you – where Ursula teaches in school[5] – and you sent it to Pinker. Now he has it all.

[1] John N. Farquhar, *The Crown of Hinduism* (Oxford, 1913; new edn, March 1915).
[2] Both plays are by Molière: *Le Tartuffe* (1664) and *Le Bourgeois Gentilhomme* (1670).
[3] Are] Were   [4] Mary Saleeby.   [5] See *The Rainbow*, chap. 13.

Soon I shall send you some of my philosophy. I am typing it myself – a
great work – re-composing as I go. This is my work that I give to this
crisis – my contribution. I dont know what it is, but it is all I've got. You
will like it better than the novel.

Bertie Russell is being separated out from the pack.[1] I am very glad. Soon
he will be an outlaw. I am very glad. Then we are brothers.

The days go on – my soul is only black and turgid. I feel always filled
with corrosive darkness, and cut off from everybody. There won't be an end
yet. The Belloc party says peace in two months – through negotiations.[2] I
can see only death and more death, till we are black and swollen with death.
This is no end, nor any nearing of the end. I say to myself, not yet, not yet.
But our day will come, to move. Let them die, we await our day.

Au revoir   D. H. Lawrence

934. To Bertrand Russell, 2 June 1915
Text: MS UT; Moore, *Atlantic Monthly* 96.

Greatham – Pulborough
2 June 1915

Dear Russell,

We shall be very glad to see you on June 19th – if we are still here. If
we want to go away I shall tell you.

I shall be glad when you have strangled the invincible respectability that
dogs your steps. What does it mean, really. Integer vitae scelerisque purus?[3]
But before what tribunal? I refuse to be judged by them. It is not for them
to exculpate or to blame me. They are not my peers. Where are my peers?
I acknowledge no more than five or six – not so many – in the world. But
one must take care of the pack. When they hunt together they are very strong.
Never expose yourself to the pack. Be careful of them. Be rather their secret
enemy, the secret enemy, working to split up and dismember the pack from
inside, not from outside. Don't make attacks from outside. Dont give yourself
into their power. Don't do it.

And whoever dies, let us not die. Let us kill this hydra, this pack, before
we die.

I shall be glad to see you again. I shall give you my philosophy.

[1] See p. 347 n. 1.
[2] Presumably a reference to one of the widely discussed series of weekly articles Hilaire Belloc
wrote (from 22 August 1914) on the military situation for the new periodical *Land and Water*
[3] Horace, *Odes* I. xxii. 1 ['He who is upright in his way of life'].

Hilaire Belloc says, peace in two months. All the Bellocites are convinced.
I am not. I think like you, more death, and ever more death, till the fire burns
itself out. Let it be so – I am willing. But I won't die. Let us remain and
get a new start made, when we can get a look in.

Yrs   D. H. Lawrence

935. To David Garnett, 3 June 1915
Text: MS NYPL; Moore 348.

Greatham – Pulborough
3 June 1915

My dear Bunny,

Here is your play.[1] It is hardly the kind of thing you will be able to do
anything with now – too fin de siècle, and we've got to begin a new siècle.

Do you mean you'd join the Quakers ambulancing?[2] That might be all
right. I hope you will do that. I almost wish I could do something of the
same myself. I'm afraid my health is too crachetty.[3]

We shall probably be here till towards the end of July, because I have
promised to teach Mary Saleeby to get her ready for school. Why don't you
come down here and stay with us a bit? We should be glad. Then we could
really talk about things.

I think Vera Volkhovsky is coming this week-end.

I still feel gassed by the war. Do you hear of Belloc's peace in 2 months
prophecy? I almost wish I believed it.

Come down and see us.

Yrs   D. H. Lawrence

Frieda is in Hampstead hunting rooms.

936. To Lady Ottoline Morrell, [4 June 1915]
Text: MS StaU; Schorer 54.

Greatham – Pulborough
Friday[4]

My dear Lady Ottoline,

We have a visitor this week-end, or we would have come. Suddenly I
feel careless – vogue la galère. Can we come next Friday – is it 11th – and
stay till Monday? I should like that.

---

[1] The play existed only in MS and was never published.
[2] In June 1915 David Garnett was 'far from having a conscientious objection to military service'
(Garnett, *The Flowers of the Forest*, p. 58) but, persuaded by his parents and Francis Birrell,
he joined the Friends War Victims Relief Mission and soon went to France.
[3] Nottinghamshire dialect word meaning ailing, poor or shaky.
[4] A week before Friday 11th as DHL indicates.

You hear of the little £36 a year flat right on Hampstead Heath that we have almost taken.[1] I feel that next winter I must be a good bit in London, for work. We shall ask every one of our friends to give us a tiny bit of furniture – an egg-cup or a salt-spoon – to help to furnish. What will you give us? Something *very* inexpensive, or I am cross. Then you will come and see us there. It will be fun.

I want to see Garsington very much.

Tell us at once if we can come next week-end, because then we shall go to London to whitewash the flat, if it is to be ours, in the fore part of the week.

Suddenly we shall be seeing you – it is rather nice.

D. H. Lawrence

937. To J. B. Pinker, 6 June 1915
Text: MS Forster; cited in Delany 97.

Greatham – Pulborough
6 June 1915.

Dear Pinker,

Very good, then: put the words in English 'To Else'.[2]

I haven't another copy of the novel, because this I sent you is so much altered from the original MS., that the latter is no good.

Did you arrange about the money with Methuen? Don't let those Goldberg lawyers have it, will you. One must be quick. – I want Garnett to make an arrangement with them, to pay over a term of years.[3]

I want to take a tiny flat in Hampstead. Will you give me a reference to the house-agents? I shall ask them to write to you. If ever I am too hard up, a friend will pay the rent – which is only £36 a year.

I send you a story, which England will not publish, I am afraid, but which America may.[4] I also enclose a letter from an American.[5] I will begin just now, when I have finished a book of philosophy which I am doing, to write

---

[1] The flat at 1 Byron Villas, Vale of Health, Hampstead, N.W., where he moved on 5 August 1915; see Letter 967.
[2] See Letter 930.   [3] See Letter 929.
[4] Lady Cynthia Asquith, who visited DHL on 5 June 1915, confirms that he was writing a story at this time: 'Lawrence has taken to a typewriter – there was a war story coming to life on it' (Asquith, *Diaries* 37). The story was 'England, My England', based on the Percy Lucas family, whom DHL knew at Greatham (see Letter 979). Its anti-war sentiments would explain DHL's comment. The story was published in the *English Review*, xxi (October 1915), 238–52.   [5] Unidentified.

some short stories. Shall I send you the book of philosophy, or shall I see about it myself? However, I will finish it first.

If you get the money from Methuen, – and it is very risky if you don't – will you leave it in your bank for a while, till I ask you for it?

Yours   D. H. Lawrence

938. To Lady Ottoline Morrell, [8 June 1915]
Text: MS StaU; Postmark, Coot[ham] [...] 15; Unpublished.

Greatham – Pulborough
Tuesday

My dear Lady Ottoline,

We will come on Saturday and stay till Wednesday, which is your birthday:[1] but we must leave on Wednesday afternoon. I don't know the trains to Oxford, but I will find out and let you know – we will arrive by an afternoon train in Oxford. I look forward to coming, and am very anxious to see you and Garsington.

Bertie Russell comes to us on the 19th.

Is your birthday really the 16th. That is my sister's birthday.[2] I am very fond of her.

auf baldiges Wiedersehen[3]   D. H. Lawrence

I do hope you didn't mind writing to the house agent.

939. To E. M. Forster, 8 June 1915
Text: MS KCC; cited in Furbank, ii. 12.

Greatham – Pulborough
8 June 1915

Dear Forster,

According to my promise, I send you as much as is done of my philosophy – about one/fourth. I can trust you to take me seriously, and really to read. Because whatever I may be, you *do* listen. Tell me carefully what you think, and what you have to say. And don't be against what I say, at the outset.

D. H. Lawrence

Lady Ottoline b. 16 June 1873. (The birthday party is described in *Ottoline at Garsington* 36–8.)
Ada Clarke, b. 16 June 1887.   [3] 'till we meet soon'.

940. To J. B. Pinker, [8 June 1915]
Text: MS UNYB; Unpublished.

Pulborough
Tuesday.

Dear Pinker,

Thank you for your letter. I understand that you have got £50 for me in your account – or £45 or something like that. Is that right? And did you make any arrangement with Methuen about the £150 for Sept. If that too could be paid in advance, everything would be safe. Would you mind just dropping one line to R. Garnett – 36 John St – Bedford Row, to tell him exactly what arrangement you did make with Methuen. I should be much obliged.

And thank you very much for giving a reference to the house agent.

I will write for another copy of 'The Primrose Path'.

Yours   D. H. Lawrence

941. To Douglas Clayton, 8 June 1915
Text: MS NCL; Unpublished.

Greatham – Pulborough, Sussex
8 June 1915

Dear Clayton,

If you have the MS of 'The Primrose Path', I wish you would send a typed copy to J B Pinker – Talbot House – Arundel St – Strand. He has lost the copy he had.

I do hope you are well, you and Mrs Clayton. I know you are hard at work with Murry's novel.[1] I am waiting for it to be done, so that I can read it.

With regards from my wife to Mrs Clayton and you.

Yours Sincerely   D. H. Lawrence

There is no great hurry for the story.

942. To Bertrand Russell, 8 June 1915
Text: MS UT; Moore, *Bertrand Russell* 49.

Greatham – Pulborough
8 June 1915

Dear Russell,

I send you the first quarter of my philosophy. You mustn't think it bosh

---

[1] Clayton was typing Murry's first novel, *Still Life*.

I depend on you to help me with it. Don't go against me, and say it doesn't interest you, or that there are beautiful things in it, or something like that. But help me, and tell me where I can say the thing better.

I got the *Labour Leader* with your article against Lord Northcliffe.[1] I think Lord Northcliffe wants sinking to the bottom, but you do say rash things, and give yourself away. Let me beg you not to get into trouble now, at this juncture. I do beg you to save yourself for the great attack, later on, when the opportunity comes. We must go much deeper and beyond Lord Northcliffe. Let us wait a little while, till we can assemble the nucleus of a new belief, get a new centre of attack, not using *Labour Leaders* and so on.

We are going to Garsington Saturday – Wednesday.[2] I wonder if we shall see you there. At any rate you are coming to us on the 19th. Then we will thresh out this business. I wonder if you would like to meet Murry – but not this time.

D. H. Lawrence

Don't be rash now, against Northcliffes. They will fall.

943. To J. B. Pinker, [10 June 1915]
Text: MS Forster; Unpublished.

Greatham – Pulborough
Thursday[3]

Dear Pinker,

R. Garnett says I must have the money from Methuen, otherwise those people[4] may claim it from me. Will you send me the cheque?

What a lot of bother it is.

Yours   D. H. Lawrence

Lord Alfred Harmsworth Northcliffe (1865–1922), leading newspaper proprietor who, in 1918, assumed full charge of government propaganda. Bertrand Russell's article, entitled 'Lord Northcliffe's Triumph', appeared on the front page of the *Labour Leader* (A Weekly Journal of Socialism, Trade Unionism, and Politics), xii (27 May 1915). Among other things, Russell said: 'War being good in itself, it is impossible to have too much of it. Having got war, Lord Northcliffe felt it his duty to try to prolong it'. DHL's concern about Russell's rashness is, therefore, understandable.
² Wednesday.] Tuesday.
³ Dated with reference to DHL's letter on 17 June in which he acknowledges the money requested here.
⁴ Ernest Weekley's solicitors; see Letter 929.

944. To J. B. Pinker, 12 June 1915
Text: MS UNYB; Unpublished.

Greatham – Pulborough
12 June 1915

Dear Pinker,

Thank you very much for the cheque for £42.10.0, which came this morning,

Yours Sincerely   D. H. Lawrence

945. To J. B. Pinker, 17 June 1915
Text: MS Forster; Unpublished.

Greatham – Pulborough.
17 June 1915

Dear Pinker,

Thank you very much for the cheque for £90, which I received today. If there are any enquiries, don't say anything about it, unless you need. Let it be supposed it falls due only on publication.

Yours   D. H. Lawrence

946. To Lady Ottoline Morrell, [20 June 1915]
Text: MS UT; Huxley 238–40.

Greatham – Pulborough – Sussex
Sunday

My dear Lady Ottoline,

I send you what is done of my philosophy.[2] Tell me what you think exactly.

Bertie Russell is here. I feel rather glad at the bottom, because we are rallying to a point. I do want him to work in the Knowledge of the Absolute in the Knowledge of Eternity. He *will* – apart from philosophical mathematics – be so temporal, so immediate. He won't let go, he won't act in the eternal things, when it comes to men and life. But now he will: now he is changing. He is coming to have a real, actual, logical belief in Eternity and upon this he can work: a belief in the absolute, an existence in the Infinite. It is very good and I am very glad.

---

[1] Dated with reference to Russell's visit, 19–20 June 1915; see also p. 359 n. 3.
[2] Probably the copy returned by Russell.

We think to have a lecture hall in London in the autumn, and give lectures: he on Ethics, I on Immortality:[1] also to have meetings, to establish a little society or body around a *religious belief which leads to action*. We must centre in the Knowledge of the Infinite, of God. Then from this Centre each one of us must work to put the temporal things of our own natures and of our own circumstances in accord with the Eternal God we know. You must be president. You must preside over our meetings. You must be the centre-pin that holds us together, and the needle which keeps our direction constant, always towards the Eternal thing. We *mustn't* lapse into temporality.

Murry must come in, and Gilbert – and perhaps Campbell. We can all lecture, at odd times. Murry has a genuine side to his nature: so has Mrs Murry. Don't mistrust them. They are valuable, I know.

We must have some meetings at Garsington. Garsington must be the retreat where we come together and knit ourselves together. Garsington is wonderful for that. It is like the Boccaccio place where they told all the *Decamerone*.[2] That wonderful lawn, under the ilex trees, with the old house and its exquisite old front – it is *so* remote, so perfectly a small world to itself, where one *can* get away from the temporal things to consider the big things. We must draw together. Russell and I have really got somewhere. We must bring the Murrys in. Don't be doubtful of them. And Frieda will come round soon. It is the same thing with her as with all the Germans – all the world – she hates the Infinite, my immortality. But she will come round.

I *know* what great work there is for us all to do in the autumn and onwards. Mind you keep your strength for it. And we must really put aside the smaller, personal things and really live together, in the big impersonal world as well: that must be our real place of assembly, the immortal world, the heaven of the great angels.

Send my philosophy on to Gilbert, will you. And tell me if you like it.

Don't be sad. We are only sad for a little while. At the bottom one *knows* the eternal things, and is glad.

Yesterday Cynthia Asquith came with her husband.[3] He is home slightly wounded – three teeth knocked out. But he is well. Only all his soul is left

---

Russell wrote to Lady Ottoline: 'We talked of a plan for lecturing in the autumn on his religion, politics in the light of religion & so on. I believe something might be made of it. I could make a splendid course on political ideas; morality, the State, property, marriage, war, taking them to their roots in human nature, & show how each is a prison for the infinite in us' (Clark, *Russell*, p. 261).

Giovanni Boccaccio (1313–75) whose collection of one hundred tales, *The Decameron* (written between 1348 and 1358), is represented as having been told in ten days by ten story-tellers in Florence.

Her diary for 19 June 1915 confirms this visit (Asquith, *Diaries* 45).

at the war. The war is the only reality to him. All this here is unreal, this England: only the trenches are Life to him. Cynthia is very unhappy – he is not even aware of her existence. He is spell-bound by the fighting line. He ought to die. It all seemed horrid, like hypnotism.

My love to Julian and to you. My warm regards to Morrell – remember me to Maria, and to Miss Sands and Miss Hudson.[1] I trust in you entirely in this eternal belief.

D. H. Lawrence

947. To Ernest Collings, 26 June 1915
Text: MS UT; Unpublished.

Greatham – Pulborough – Sussex
26 June 1915

Dear Collings,

Thank you very much for the card for Mestrovig.[2] I should have been very glad if I could have gone to see the works. But we were unable to come to town last week.

I was wondering how you were. I have no news of myself – I hate the war – that's all. We shall be in England for some time now, I expect. We have taken a tiny little flat in Hampstead Vale, and shall be up there in August and September, for part of the time. I hope you will come and see us.

What are you doing? Have you published any drawings since the book?[3] Has the war affected you much?

How long does the Mestrovig exhibition last? We may be in town next week-end. I should really like to see the sculptures if they are still to be seen.

Mrs Lawrence sends greetings.

Yours   D. H. Lawrence

948. To E. M. Forster, [7? July 1915]
Text: MS KCC; Unpublished.

Greatham – Pulborough
Wednesday

---

[1] 'Miss Sands was a highly cultivated New Englander, a painter and a friend of Henry James and Logan Pearsall Smith' (Russell, *Autobiography*, ii. 54). Lady Ottoline also remarked on the two women: 'Ethel Sands... came of American parentage.... When a young girl she...gracefully removed herself to Paris, where she lived with a friend, Miss [Nancy] Hudson, and worked seriously at painting... We made real friends with her, and have always remained so' (Gathorne-Hardy, *Ottoline: The Early Memoirs*, p. 129). Ethel Sands was an accomplice in the affair between Russell and Lady Ottoline (Clark, *Russell*, p. 136).

[2] Collings must have sent DHL a card announcing the opening of the exhibition of Ivan Mêstrović's sculpture which ran from 24 June to 25 August 1915 at the Victoria and Albert Museum. (Cf. p. 157 n. 6. For a review of the exhibition see *Times*, 26 June 1915, p. 11.)

[3] *Outlines*: see Letter 713.

[4] DHL told Lady Ottoline on 9 July 1915 that he had 'broken down in the middle' of his 'philosophy'; the almost identical remark in this letter strongly suggests an adjacent date.

Dear Forster,

I hope Mrs Lawrence answered your letter. Our flat is 1 Byron Villas, Vale of Health, Hampstead. She is up there now seeing to furniture etc. We move in finally on July 31st. I am here till then. I want to see you again. If you are in town, you might ring up Frieda at Mrs Radford's, 32 Well Walk, Hampstead. But when we are at our flat, then come at once, if you can.

I left off the philosophy in the middle, to think again. I will give it you later.

Au revoir   D. H. Lawrence

949. To Bertrand Russell, [c. 8 July 1915]

Text: MS UT; Moore, *Bertrand Russell* 77.

[Greatham, Pulborough, Sussex]

[c. 8 July 1915][1]

Don't be angry that I have scribbled all over your work.[2] But this which you say is *all social criticism*; it isn't social reconstruction. You must take a plunge into another element if it is to be social reconstruction.

Primarily, you must allow and acknowledge and be prepared to proceed from the fundamental impulse in all of us towards The Truth, the fundamental passion also, the *most fundamental* passion in man, for Wholeness of Movement, Unanimity of Purpose, Oneness in Construction. *This is the principle of Construction.* The rest is all criticism, destruction.

Do, do get these essays ready, for the love of God. But make them more profound, more philosophical. Make them not popular, oh, not popular. The best is[3] to attack the spirit, then proceed to the form. You call the spirit Subjectivism. Do go to the root of this: kill it at the root. Show how everything works upon this great falsity of subjectivism, now. I like it where you take them one by one, The State, Marriage etc. But you *must* put in the *positive idea*. Every living community is a living State. You must go very deep into the State, and its relation to the individual.

We shall be at 32 Well Walk, Hampstead – Mrs Radford – this week-end. must see you.

Above all don't be angry with my scribbling. But above all, *do* do these lectures.

I must lecture – or preach – on religion – give myself away.

But you must dare *very* much more than you have done here – you must dare be positive, not only critical.

D. H. Lawrence

Dated with reference to DHL's visit to London, 10–11 July 1915.
This letter accompanied DHL's pencilled comments on an outline of lectures that Russell had sent him. Russell's MS, entitled 'Philosophy of Social Reconstruction' is printed in Moore, *Bertrand Russell* 79–96.   [3] The best is] A great idea is

950. To Lady Ottoline Morrell, 9 July 1915
Text: MS IEduc; Huxley 240–1.

Greatham, Pulborough, Sussex.
9 July 1915

My dear Lady Ottoline,

I wonder if you got the boxes I sent off the other day, and if you liked them.[1] I wonder if this queer unsettled weather affects your health. I hope you are well.

I am just going to London[2] for the week-end to see about furnishing the flat. Frieda has been up for several days. We should come back on Sunday evening. I shall see Russell, and we shall talk about the scheme of lectures. He sent me a synopsis of a set of lectures on Political Ideas. But as yet he stands too much on the shore of this existing world. He must get into a boat and preach from out of the waters of eternity, if he is going to do any good.[3] But I hope he isn't angry with me.

There are 3 weeks more here: 3 weeks today and I have finished. Then I go to London, and we come to Garsington. I feel, when we leave here there is the entry upon a new epoch. I am quite afraid, I feel as if I would run away – I don't know from what. But one can't run away from fate. The thought of fate makes me grin in my soul with pleasure: I am so glad it is inevitable, even if it bites off my nose.

I have broken down in the middle of my philosophy – I suppose I shall go on later when I am freer. I am correcting the proofs of the *Rainbow* Whatever else it is, it is the voyage of discovery towards the real and eternal and unknown land. We are like Columbus, we have our back upon Europe till we come to the new world.

I must go now to teach the child[4] – in three weeks we leave here, it is finished.

Au revoir   D. H. Lawrence

951. To Lady Ottoline Morrell, [12 July 1915]
Text: MS UT; Huxley 241.

Greatham, Pulborough
Monday

My dear Lady Ottoline,

I was in London this week-end for two days. Bertie Russell told me about

---

[1] Presumably some of the boxes which DHL decorated for his friends.
[2] London] Hendon   [3] Cf. Luke v. 3.   [4] Mary Saleeby.
[5] Dated with reference to DHL's visit to London, 10–11 July 1915.

your eyes. I was *very* sorry. You must keep very still, and not think about troublesome things. I wish I could have come to Garsington. But I can't neglect my teaching, for the short time longer it lasts.

The flat will look quite nice. Frieda is still in London doing it.

Do let the Cannans have the rooms,[1] if they want them. I shall come to Garsington in August for part of the month, but if you will have me in the house it will do just as well. I cannot answer for Frieda. She may stay in her flat. But let the Cannans' have the rooms if they want them.

I rather quarrelled with Russell's lectures.[2] He won't accept in his philosophy the Infinite, the Boundless, the Eternal, as the real starting point, and I think, whosoever will really set out on the journey towards Truth and the real end must do this, now. But I didn't quarrel with him. We have almost sworn Blutbruderschaft.[3] We will set out together, he and I. We shall really be doing something, in the autumn. I want you to believe always.

As for my philosophy, I shall write it again. And we will talk about it when I see you.

Cynthia Asquith is coming here with Katherine Asquith next week.[4] You know Cynthia told me she wished you would know her.

I really think I shall give some lectures on Eternity. I shrink from it very much. I am very shy, publicly. I hate publicity of all sorts. I am safe and remote, when I write. It will be horrible to stand up and say the things I feel most vitally, before an audience. But I think it must be done. I think I shall do it. I don't know. There is a little fog between me and the autumn. I must wait for the impulse really to be born. But I think I shall be speaking. God help me, I would rather have done anything else. I would like to be remote, in Italy, writing my soul's words. To have to speak in the body is a violation to me – you don't know how much. However, anything for the new infinite relation that must come to pass.

Vale   D. H. Lawrence

Presumably the so-called gardener's rooms at Garsington, which Lady Ottoline offered to DHL instead of a separate cottage.

The substance of the controversy can be gathered from DHL's pencilled comments on Russell's lecture-outline, but the actual debate must have taken place during the meeting between the two men during the weekend in London. For Russell's version of their disagreement, see his *Autobiography*, ii. 53–4.

'Blood-brotherhood', a pledge of allegiance.

Lady Cynthia Asquith confirms that the visit took place on 20 July: 'We started off for our much anticipated and discussed visit to Lawrence at 3:30.... We found Lawrence alone, Frieda being in London...Katharine loved him' (Asquith, *Diaries* 56). Katharine Asquith was the Prime Minister's daughter-in-law; m. Raymond Asquith (1878–1916).

952. To J. B. Pinker, 13 July 1915
Text: MS UT; Unpublished.

Greatham – Pulborough.
13 July 1915

Dear Pinker,

Thank you for selling the story for me.[1] I will write some more soon. I am very busy just now – so many proofs, and other things.

I will go through the slips for modification, and let you have them tomorrow.[2]

Yours Sincerely   D. H. Lawrence

953. To Bertrand Russell, [14? July 1915]
Text: MS UT; Moore, *Bertrand Russell* 50.

Greatham – Pulborough
Wednesday[3]

Dear Russell,

Are you doing the lectures. I have dropped writing my philosophy, but I go on working very hard in my soul. I shall lift up my voice in the autumn, and in connection with you, not apart. I have been wrong, much too Christian, in my philosophy. These early Greeks have clarified my soul.[4] I must drop all about God.

You must drop all your democracy. You must not believe in 'the people'. One class is no better than another. It must be a case of Wisdom, or Truth. Let the working classes *be* working classes. That is the truth.

There must be an aristocracy of people who[5] have wisdom, and there must be a Ruler: a Kaiser: no Presidents and democracies. I shall write out Herakleitos, on tablets of bronze.[6]

'And it is law, too, to obey the counsel of one.'[7]

'For what thought or wisdom have they? They follow the poets and take the crowd as their teacher, knowing not that there are many bad and few

---

[1] 'England, My England'; see p. 354 n. 4.
[2] The 'slips' indicated changes requested by Methuen to the text of *The Rainbow*. Cf. Letters 958 and 959.
[3] DHL's statement, 'In a fortnight now I shall come to town', is echoed at the end of the (dated) letter which follows; hence the conjectural date here.
[4] DHL was reading John Burnet's *Early Greek Philosophy* (1892), from which he quotes in this letter.
[5] who] of
[6] The early Greek philosopher (c. 535 – c. 475 B.C.), who held the theory that all was subject to change and was in a constant state of flux.
[7] From Fragment 110 of Heraclitus, printed in Burnet's *Early Greek Philosophy*, p. 140.

good. For even the best of them choose one thing above all others, immortal glory among mortals: while most of them are glutted like beasts.'[1]

'They vainly purify themselves by defiling themselves with blood.'[2]

I am sure, now, that if we go on with the war, we shall be beaten by Germany. I am sure that, unless the new spirit comes, we shall be irrecoverably[3] beaten. Remember when you write your lectures, that you are a beaten nation. We are a beaten nation. It is no longer a case for satire or gibe or criticism. It is for a new truth,[4] a further belief.

Also we must unite together, not work apart.

I am rid of all my christian religiosity. It was only a muddiness. You need not mistrust me. In fact you don't.

In a[5] fortnight now I shall come to town.

Murry, on the Sunday, was himself again.

'If you do not expect the unexpected, you will not find it. For it is hard to [be] sought out, and difficult.'[6]

It is only the unexpected can help us now.

D. H. Lawrence

954. To Bertrand Russell, [16 July 1915]
Text: MS UT; Moore, *Atlantic Monthly* 98.

Greatham, Pulborough, Sussex.
Friday 15 July.

In your lecture on the State, you must criticise the extant *democracy*, the young idea. That is our enemy. This existing phase is now in its collapse. What we must hasten to prevent is this young democratic party from getting into power. The idea of giving power to the hands of the working class is *wrong*. The working man must elect the immediate government, of his [...] work, of his [...] district, not the ultimate government of the nation. There must be a body of chosen patricians. There must be woman governing equally with men, especially all the inner[7] half of life. The whole must culminate in an absolute *Dictator*, and an equivalent *Dictatrix*. There must be none of your bourgeois presidents of Republics. The women's share must be equal with the men's. You must work this out in your own way. But you must do it.

---

[1] Fragment 111, ibid. p. 141.
[2] Fragments 129, 130, ibid. p. 142.
[3] irrecoverably] *badly* (DHL wrote 'irrecoverably' above '*badly*' but omitted to delete the latter.)   [4] truth] hope   [5] In a] In about a
[6] Fragment 7, Burnet, p. 134.   [7] inner] domestic

Can't you see the whole state is collapsing. Look at the Welsh Strike.[1] This war is going to develop into the last great war between labour and capital. It will be a ghastly chaos of destruction, if it is left to Labour to be constructive. The fight must immediately be given a higher aim than the triumph of Labour, or we shall have another French Revolution. The deadly Hydra now is the hydra of Equality. Liberty, Equality and Fraternity is the three-fanged serpent. You must have a government based upon good, better and best. You must get this into your lectures, at once. You are too old-fashioned. The back of your serpent is already broken.

A new constructive idea of a new state is needed *immediately*. Criticism is *unnecessary*. It is behind the times. You *must*[2] work out the idea of a new state, not go on criticising this old one. Get anybody and everybody to help – Orage,[3] Shaw, anybody, but it must be a *new State*. And the idea is, that every man shall vote according to his understanding,[4] and that the highest understanding must dictate for the lower understandings. And the desire is to have a perfect government perfectly related in all its parts, the highest aim of the government is the highest good of the *soul* of the individual, the fulfilment in the Infinite, in the Absolute.

In a fortnight I shall come and take account of you.

DHL

955. To Lady Ottoline Morrell, [19 July 1915]
Text: MS IEduc; Huxley 235.

Greatham – Pulborough
Monday[5]

My dear Lady Ottoline,

Why then are you both so downcast, both you and Russell. What is the use of being downcast, when there is so much to be done? What ails Russell is, in matters of life and emotion, the inexperience of youth. He is, vitally, emotionally, much too inexperienced in personal contact and conflict, for a man of his age and calibre. It isn't that life has been too much for him, but too little. Tell him he is not to write lachrymose letters to me of disillusion

---

[1] The strike of the South Wales Miners' Federation lasted 15–21 July 1915.
[2] The word is heavily underlined 15 times.
[3] Alfred Richard Orage (1873–1934), journalist and editor. In May 1907, with the backing of Bernard Shaw, he took over the editing (with Holbrook Jackson) of the weekly review, *New Age*. Author of *Frederick Nietzsche: The Dionysian Spirit of the Age* (Edinburgh, 1906), etc. (See Carswell, *Lives and Letters*.)
[4] understanding,] higher understanding,
[5] DHL's promise to bring Lady Ottoline's books 'in a fortnight', c. 31 July, establishes the date here.

and disappointment and age: that sounds like 19, almost like David Garnett. Tell him he is to get up and clench his fist in the face of the world. Really, he is too absurdly young in his pessimism, almost juvenile.

I think we can come to Garsington, if not on July 31st, at least very early in August. Will you allow me a day or two, so I know how much I must do at the flat, before I definitely tell you definitely what day we will come. I want us to have a real meeting at Garsington: Russell, the Cannans, ourselves, to discuss propaganda.

I don't mean a 'tyranny' in the state: but I *don't* believe in the democratic electorate. The working man is not fit to elect the ultimate government of the country. And the holding of office *shall not* rest upon the Choice of the mob: it shall be almost immune from them.

I shall write all my philosophy again. Last time I came out of the Christian Camp. This time I must come out of these early Greek philosophers.[1] I am so sure of what I know, and what is true, now, that I am sure I am stronger, in the truth, in the knowledge I have, than all the world outside that knowledge. So I am not finally afraid of anything.

The war is resolving itself into a war between Labour and Capital. Unless real leaders step forward, to lead in the light of a wide-embracing philosophy, there will be another French Revolution muddle. We shall never finish our fight with Germany. The fight will shift to England. And we must be ready *in time* to direct the way, to win with the truth.

We shall see you in a very short time. Then we shall *begin*.

Frieda is still in town. I expect her home tomorrow.

I asked Mrs Radford to send you on your *Karamazov*. It went up with all our books. I do hope it comes at once. I will bring all the others in a fortnight. Don't be melancholy, there isn't time.

Love   D. H. Lawrence

956. To Lady Cynthia Asquith, [21 July 1915]
Text: MS UT; Huxley 243–4.

Greatham – Pulborough
Wednesday[2]

My dear Lady Cynthia,

I wish you would send me a p.c. to tell me what number you are, S. Parade Littlehampton, as I quite forget.

See p. 364 n. 4.

Lady Cynthia Asquith visited DHL on 20 July 1915; see p. 363 n. 4. He is here – the next day – making plans for his visit to Littlehampton on 25 July.

Also may we bring Viola Meynell to the tea-party, as she would like to come, because she thinks you are the most beautiful woman she has ever seen. It always irritates me, this talk of 'a beautiful woman'. There is something so infinitely more important in you than your beauty. Why do you always ignore the realest thing in you, this hard, stoic, elemental sense of logic and truth? That is your real beauty.

I think I should like Catherine Asquith *very* much. But I doubt if she's got the quality of absoluteness there is in you – or not so much of it.

I hope, after the war, we may have a real revolution. I want the whole form of government changing. I don't believe in the democratic (republican) form of election. I think the artizan is fit to elect for his immediate surroundings, but for no ultimate government. The electors for the highest places should be the governors of the bigger[1] districts – the whole thing should work upwards, every man voting for that which he more or less understands through contact – no canvassing of mass votes.

And women shall vote equally with the men, but for different things. Women *must* govern such things as the feeding and housing of the race. And if a system works up to a Dictator who controls the greater industrial[2] side of the national life, it must work up to a Dictatrix who controls the things relating to private life. And the women shall have absolutely equal voice with regard to marriage, custody of children etc.

There will inevitably come a revolution during the next 10 years. I only don't want the democratic party to get the control. We *must not* have Labour in power, any more than Capital.

I want you to agree to these things, vitally: because we must prepare the way for this in the autumn.

D. H. Lawrence

It is for these things I want you to know Lady Ottoline. So few women [...] or men – have any real sense of absolute truth, irregardless of circumstance. I do want a few exceptional women to unite for pure truth in the form of our national and social life. Does Catherine Asquith care, do you think?

DHL

And don't be conservative about land – after all, what does it matter if one *owns* land or not – the life cannot consist in ownership. Life does not consist in ownership, not for any of us, any more.

DHL

---

[1] bigger] local   [2] industrial] industrial and economic

You see men like Harold Baker are really no good¹ – they've got no going-forward in them – or has he, I might be mistaken – But I'd rather trust your husband, who is not so clever, but who has more power to change – more power to believe. But it is killing work trying to get a few people to believe – Frieda, Russell, Lady O. I've only half succeeded as yet with anybody. Yet the truth is the truth.

957. To S. S. Koteliansky, [22 July 1915]

Text: MS BL.; Postmark, Cootham 22 JY 15; Moore 355.

Greatham – Pulborough
Thursday

My dear Kot,

Forgive my not having answered your letter sooner. Even now I don't know how to answer it. My feelings are confused and suffering under various sorts of shocks in one direction and another. I hope you will not mind if we leave it for a while, this question of a relationship between us, until I am settled and dependable. Then I will answer your letter.

Yours   D. H. Lawrence

958. To J. B. Pinker, [22 July 1915]

Text: MS UNYB; PC; Postmark, Cootham 22 JY 15; Unpublished.

Greatham
[22 July 1915]

Dear Pinker,

Will you let the slips be sent on to me, then, for me to alter.²

D. H. Lawrence

959. To J. B. Pinker, 26 July 1915

Text: MS UNYB; Huxley 242.

Greatham – Pulborough
26 July 1915

Dear Pinker,

I send you back the slips and pages. I have cut out, as I said I would,

---

¹ Rt Hon. Harold Trevor Baker (1877–1960). Originally a barrister, he was Liberal M.P. for Accrington (1910–18); became member of the Army Council (1914) and Inspector of Quartermaster General Services (1916). He was a particularly close friend of Lady Cynthia and frequently appears in her *Diaries*.   ² See p. 364 n. 2.

all the *phrases* objected to. The passages and paragraphs marked I cannot alter. There is nothing offensive in them, beyond the very substance they contain, and that is no more offensive than that of all the rest of the novel. The libraries won't object to the book any less, or approve of it any more, if these passages are cut out. And I cant cut them out, because they are living parts of an organic whole. Those who object, will object to the book altogether. These bits won't affect them particularly.

Tell Methuen, he need not be afraid. If the novel doesn't pay him back this year, it will before very long. Does he expect me to be popular? I shan't be that. But I am a safe speculation for a publisher.

These slips and pages I return to you are *not revised proofs*. I am now at p. 192 of the revised proofs, the final form, and I must go on from there.

Yours Sincerely   D. H. Lawrence

960. To Katharine Clayton, 26 July 1915
Text: MS NCL; Unpublished.

Greatham – Pulborough, Sussex.
26 July 1915

Dear Mrs Clayton,

I was *very* sorry to hear Douglas had been so ill. It is hard luck. And Patrick too a soldier.[1] But he will be all right.

Is Douglas in want of any work? – if so I will send him some which I want doing rather quickly – finishing within the next 3 weeks. Will you let me know? And don't I owe you some money? Tell me what it is.

We leave here for good on Friday – first to Littlehampton, where our address is 12 Bayford Rd. We stay there till Wednesday. Then we go up to our own tiny flat, where you must come and see us.

1 Byron Villas, Vale of Health, Hampstead, N.W.

I do hope things are all right with you.

Yours   D. H. Lawrence

961. To Bertrand Russell, 26 July 1915
Text: MS UT; Moore, *Atlantic Monthly* 98–100.

Greatham – Pulborough
26 July 1915

Dear Russell,

I rather hated your letter, and am terrified of what you are putting in your lectures. I don't want tyrants. But I don't believe in democratic control. I

[1] See p. 87 n. 1.

think the working man is fit to elect governors or overseers for his immediate circumstances, but for no more. You must utterly revise the electorate. The working man shall elect superiors for the things that concern him immediately, no more. From the other classes, as they rise, shall be elected the higher governors. The thing must culminate in one real head, as every organic thing must – no foolish republics with foolish presidents, but an elected King, something like Julius Caesar. And as the men elect and govern the industrial side of life, so the women must elect and govern the domestic side. And there must be a rising rank of women governors, as of men, culminating in a woman Dictator, of equal authority with the supreme Man. It isn't bosh, but rational sense. The whole thing must be living. Above all there must be no democratic control – that is the worst of all. There must be an elected aristocracy.

As for Horace Bottomley, a nation in a false system acting in a false spirit will quite rightly choose him.[1] But a nation striving for the truth and the establishment of truth and right will forget him in a second.

I shan't come to Garsington at once, because I am not quite in the mood. We are going on Friday to the seaside, to Littlehampton for a week. Then we go to London. Then we might arrange a meeting all together at Garsington, if Lady Ottoline can do with us.

I care only about the autumn venture – that must be a real thing.

Frieda sends her Greetings.

Yours   D. H. Lawrence

We must have the same general ideas if we are going to be or to do anything. I will listen gladly to all your ideas: but we must *put our ideas together*. This is a united effort, or it is nothing – a mere tiresome playing about, lecturing and so on. It is no mere personal voice that must be raised: but a sound, living idea round which we all rally.

962. To Lady Ottoline Morrell, 29 July 1915

Text: MS IEduc; Huxley 242–3.

Greatham – Pulborough
29 July 1915

My dear Lady Ottoline,

We are going down to Littlehampton to-morrow, to the sea, for a few

---

[1] Horatio William Bottomley (1860–1933), journalist and financier. Established and edited the weekly journal, *John Bull*, 1906–29; Liberal M.P. for South Hackney, 1906–12, 1918–22. 1901–5 there were 67 bankruptcy petitions and writs filed against him; by 1915 he had begun to organise the financial ventures which, in 1922, led to his conviction for fraudulent conversion and a sentence of seven years' penal servitude; but in 1915 – as DHL knew – the Government (particularly Lloyd George and Winston Churchill) were prepared to enlist the aid of Bottomley's oratorical skills in exhorting Clydeside workers to accelerate their output of war supplies.

days. I feel I want to be blown and washed, and to forget. We were at Littlehampton on Sunday; the Radfords are there, also Lady Cynthia was there.[1] We had a very good bathe, very good indeed. There was a strong wind that never ceased, and the waves came travelling high – much water travelling heavily and swinging one away. It was very good indeed.

Berties letter chagrined me. Are we never going to unite in one idea and one purpose? Is it to be a case of each one of us having his own personal and private fling? That is nothing. If we are going to remain a group of separate entities separately engaged, then there is no reason why we should be a group at all. We are just individualists. And individuls do not *vitally* concern me any more. Only a *purpose* vitally concerns me, not individuals – neither my own individual self, nor any other. I want very much to come to Garsington if we are going to be a little group filled with one spirit and striving for one end. But if we are going to be a little set of individuals each one concerned with himself and his own personal fling at the world, I can't bear it.

Let us see what we can do, how we can do something, when we come back from Littlehampton. Our address there is 12 Bayford Rd. We shall be back in London by next Friday. There we are

      1 Byron Villas, Vale of Health, Hampstead, N.W.

The post man is here –

                          Au revoir   D. H. Lawrence

963. To J. B. Pinker, 29 July 1915
Text: MS UNYB; cited in Delany 136.

                         Greatham – Pulborough
                                29 July 1915

Dear Pinker,

Thank you for your letter and assurance concerning Methuen: also for selling the story to the *English Review*.[2]

Duckworth has asked me to give him a book of my sketches, some of which have appeared in England. I shall do this, as I always feel a sort of gratitude to Duckworth.[3] I believe my sketches may easily prove good selling stuff,

---

[1] DHL and Frieda went to Lady Cynthia's son, Michael's, 'birthday tea bringing Viola Meynell, who never moves without a copybook in which she enters notes for her novels. ...it was the least successful of all my Lawrence meetings' (Asquith, *Diaries* 58).

[2] See p. 354 n. 4.

[3] Duckworth published *The Trespasser* (1912), *Sons and Lovers* (1913) and *Love Poems and Others* (1913).

better than a novel. Also they might do very well in America, sold separately. None of them has ever appeared in the U.S.A. They are all studies in Germany or Austria or Italy, and should go specially well in this war-time.[1] Even the *Century* should be grateful for one of them.[2] However, you will know what to do with them. I shall send the MS to Duckworth direct – you can write to him about the agreement, when it is all ready. I shall send you a copy of each sketch – or essay – as I get it ready. I send you the first one now. This has appeared in a very abbreviated form in the *Westminster* two[3] years ago.[4] Could it appear again in England, now that it is more than[5] twice as long, and quite different? The title before was 'Christs in the Tyrol'.

I hope everything is well with the novel.

Yours   D. H. Lawrence

964. To Viola Meynell, 31 July 1915

Text: MS Moore; Postmark, Littlehampton 31 JY 15; Moore, *Intelligent Heart* 194–5.

12 Bayford Rd – Littlehampton

31 July 1915.

My dear Prue,

It is a grey day with many shadowy sailing-ships on the Channel, and greenish-luminous water, and many noisy little waves. It is very healing, I think, to have all the land behind one, all this England with its weight of myriad amorphous houses, put back, and only the variegated pebbles, and the little waves, and the great far-off dividing line of sea and sky, with grey sailing ships like ghosts hovering motionless, suspended with thought. If one could only sweep clear this England, of all its houses and pavements, so that we could all begin again!

We have had lunch on the beach, everybody gone away but just a youth in a cap, and a baby, and a young woman. I think they are very poor. The young father plays with the child, the mother sits very still, and they are nice and all child-like. They always keep their faces to the sea. And I think of what they represent, inland, and how nice they are, clean and isolated, on the edge of the water, a tiny separate group. England, the English people, make me so sad, I could leave them for ever. They are all like prisoners born

---

[1] The sketches were published by Duckworth as *Twilight in Italy* in June 1916.

[2] Edward Garnett had made abortive attempts, August 1911–January 1912, to place some of DHL's writings in the (American) *Century Illustrated Monthly Magazine*. None of DHL's work ever appeared in it.   [3] two] three

[4] 'Christs in the Tirol', *Saturday Westminster Gazette*, 22 March 1913. DHL changed the title to 'The Crucifix Across the Mountains' when he included the sketch in *Twilight in Italy*.

[5] more than] about

in prison, with a strange abstractness, submissiveness, and an isolation. It is as if all their lives were passed within[1] a prison-yard, and they knew their condemnation.

This is really a letter to thank you for the cottage once more. I am *very glad* you lent it to us. It has a special atmosphere, and I feel as if I had been born afresh there, got a new, sure, separate soul: as a monk in a monastery, or St John in the wilderness. Now we must go back into the world to fight. I don't want to, they are so many and they have so many roots. But we must set about cleaning the face of the earth a bit, or everything will perish.

I hope we shall see you on Tuesday. You remember our flat in 1 Byron Villas,[2] Vale of Health, Hampstead. We shall be there on Wednesday evening. Mind you come when you are up.

If you are going to town on Wednesday evening, I shall be having Charman to catch the 5.21 at Pulborough.[3] So you might come then. Will you let me know?

Love from Frieda and me   D. H. Lawrence

965. To Lady Ottoline Morrell, [2 August 1915]
Text: MS IEduc; Huxley 244–5.

12 Bayford Rd – Littlehampton
Bank Holiday Monday

My dear Lady Ottoline,

We are here till Wednesday or Friday of this week. Then we go to London, to our flat.

It is very blowy, with a heavy sea: very beautiful to see the sailing-ship beat up, with only her top-sails spread, very nervous and phantom-like, till she is in the river, safe, gliding in: and the sailors, very easy now, standing with their arms folded, leaning against the yellow timber, and looking up at the people on the banks.

We are going to Chichester today, to the cathedral. I am very fond of Sussex – it is so full of sky and wind and weather.

I think things come right, if one can manage to persist, or to keep ones soul living and unbroken. What a struggle. But we will have a meeting soon, and make a new start. It is no use meeting unless we are in a good ready

---

[1] MS reads 'with'.

[2] 1 Byron Villas] 1 Vale of

[3] John George Charman (1884?–1938), a self-employed carrier and cabman; visitors to Greatham arriving at Pulborough station either walked (4 miles) or hired his services.

spirit. When we are sure, then we will make a new start. It is to be done. We've got to get our own souls ready. I have my periods of revulsion, when I don't care a broken straw about the things I care most for, at another time. One can only say 'Now, I don't care. Very good, I don't care. If I care again, I shall care again. "Come sarà sarà".'[1] It is like a tide in one's soul. And one's will is like King Canute. Come sarà, sarà. But it will be all right.

Au revoir   D. H. Lawrence

966. To Lady Cynthia Asquith, [3 August 1915]
Text: MS UT; Huxley 245–6.

Littlehampton
– Tuesday

My dear Lady Cynthia,

We have lived a few days on the sea-shore, with the waves banging up at us. Also over the river, beyond the ferry, there is the flat silvery world, as in the beginning, untouched: with pale sand, and very much white foam, row after row, coming from under the sky, in the silver evening: and no people, no people at all, no houses, no buildings, only a haystack on the edge of the shingle, and an old black mill. For the rest, the flat unfinished world running with foam and noise and silvery light, and a few gulls swinging like a half-born thought. It is a great thing to realise that the original world is still there – perfectly clean and pure, many white advancing foams, and only the gulls swinging between the sky and the shore: and in the wind the yellow sea-poppies fluttering very hard, like yellow gleams in the wind: and the windy flourish of the seed-horns.

It is this mass of unclean world that we have super-imposed on the clean world that we cannot bear. When I looked back, out of the clearness of the open evening, at this Littlehampton dark and amorphous like a bad eruption on the edge of the land, I was so sick I felt I could not come back: all these little, amorphous houses like an eruption, a disease on the clean earth: and all of them full of such a diseased spirit, every landlady harping on her money, her furniture, every visitor harping on his latitude of escape from money and furniture: The whole thing like an active disease, fighting out the health. One watches them on the sea-shore, all the people: and there is something pathetic, almost wistful in them, as if they wished that their lives did *not* add up to this scaly nullity of possession, but as if they could not escape. It is a dragon that has devoured us all: these obscene, scaly houses, this

---

[1] 'What will be will be'.

insatiable struggle and desire to possess, to possess always and in spite of everything, this need to be an owner, lest one be owned. It is too horrible. One can no longer live with people: it is too hideous and nauseating. Owners and owned, they are like the two sides of a ghastly disease. One feels a sort of madness come over one, as if the world had become hell. But it is only super-imposed: it is only a temporary disease. It can be cleaned away.

Of course your husband will go to the war and love it much better than you, if you want him to make money. It doesn't matter whether you *need* money or not. You *do* need it. But the fact that you would ask him to work, put his soul into getting it, makes him love better war and pure destruction. The thing is painfully irrational. How can a man be so developed, as to be able to devote himself to making money, and at the same time keep himself in utter antagonism to the whole system of money. If he is in antagonism, he is in antagonism. And he will escape, with joy, from the necessity for money and the production of money, into war, which is its pure destruction.

One must destroy the spirit of money, the blind spirit of possession. It is the dragon for your St George: neither rewards on earth nor in heaven, of ownership: but always the give and take, the fight and the embrace: no more: no diseased stability of possessions, but the give and take of love and conflict, with the eternal consummation in each. The only permanent thing is *consummation* in love or hate:[1]

967. To J. B. Pinker, 5 August 1915
Text: MS UNYB; Unpublished.

1 Byron Villas, Vale of Health, Hampstead, N W

5 Aug 1915

Dear Pinker,

Will you please note that this is now my permanent address.

Yours Sincerely   D. H. Lawrence

968. To Bertrand Russell, 5 August 1915
Text: MS UT; Moore, *Bertrand Russell* 56.

1 Byron Villas, Vale of Health, Hampstead, N.W.

5 Aug 1915

Dear Russell,

We are up here now for good – in the throes of furnishing. It is a great

---

[1] The remainder of the MS is missing.

struggle. But it won't take long. When it is sufficiently done, let us go to Garsington, if Lady Ottoline is free. At present I am delivered up to chairs and tables and door-mats. You might come up and see us on Saturday if you are in town. I am *very* dislocated and unhappy in these new circumstances – but shall get all right soon. We will put our heads together directly, though.

Auf wiedersehen   D. H. Lawrence

969. To Dollie Radford, 6 August 1915
Text: MS UN; Postmark, Ha[mp]stead 6 AUG 15; Nehls, i. 318.

1 Byron Villas, Vale of Health N W
6 Aug 1915

My dear Dollie,

We are struggling along with the furnishing: got a writing desk and 2 sitting room chairs, 3 Windsor kitchen chairs – also a Chinese Coat for Frieda. It is going to look nice, our flat. But it will be nicer still when you come back to be our neighbours. I think of you in Littlehampton, and pray that Maitlands[1] coming may make things happier for you. Never mind – we had one or two good times: at Chichester, the evening in the tent, the lunch on the further shore, with a great row about the Infinite.

The infinite is now swallowed up in chairs and scrubbing brushes and waste paper baskets, as far as I am concerned. I went to the Caledonian Market this morning. That is the reverse of infinity – a chaos, an unpleasant insanity. I bought one chair. 10/-.

Thank you very much for looking after us at Littlehampton and elsewhere.

Your very finite   D. H. Lawrence

Love to Margaret.

[Frieda Lawrence begins]

Dear Dolly,

You were so good when I was in the throes, that I must tell you that my expeditions in the early morning were not in vain – Ernst's solicitor wrote begrudgingly but he *did* write that I could see the children – only for 30 min, and at his office but – I am in *bliss*. It's a beginning, the relief of it makes one quite giddy – I dont know what made E. do it, perhaps the children themselves – I shall see them on the *11th* which is my birthday – O dear, I *am* glad. I did enjoy our week – give my love to Margaret, to-morrow you will have Maitland with you –

Love F.

---

[1] Dr Maitland Radford (1884–1944), Dollie's son, now commissioned in the Royal Army Medical Corps.

970. To Lady Cynthia Asquith, 16 August 1915
Text: MS UT; Huxley 246–50.

1 Byron Villas, Vale of Health, Hampstead, N. W.
16 Aug 1915

My dear Lady Cynthia,

We also waited at the Appenrodts till 5.30: you must have gone to the wrong one.[1] Bad luck.

I am sorry that gloom tumbles on top of gloom with you. But the dead are the only people one need not fret about, nowadays.

The lectures you ask about: I don't know if they will ever begin.[2] I don't see how I am to start. Russell and I were to do something together. He was to give a *real* course on political reconstruction ideas. But it is no good. He sent me a synopsis of the lectures, and I can only think them pernicious. And now his vanity is piqued, because I said they *must* be different. He cannot stand the *must*. And yet they *must* be different, if they are to be even decent.

I am so sick of people: they preserve an evil, bad, separating spirit under the warm cloak of good words. That is intolerable in them. The conservative talks about the old and glorious national ideal, the liberal talks about this great struggle for right in which the nation is engaged, the peaceful women talk about disarmament and international peace, Bertie Russell talks about democratic control and the educating of the artizan, and all this, all this goodness, is just a warm and cosy cloak for a bad spirit. They all want the same thing: a continuing in this state of disintegration wherein each separate little ego is an independent little principality by itself. What does Russell really want? He wants to keep his own little established ego, his finite and ready-defined self intact, free from contact and connection. He wants to be ultimately a free agent. That's what they all want, ultimately – That is what is at the back of all International peace-for-ever and democratic-control talk: they want an outward system of nullity, which they call peace and goodwill, so that in their own souls they can be independent little gods, referred nowhere and to nothing: little mortal Absolutes, secure from question. That is at the back of all liberalism, Fabianism, and democracy. It stinks. It is the will of the louse. And the Conservative either wants to bully or to be bullied. And the young authoritarian, the young man who turns Roman Catholic in order to put himself under the authority of the Church, in order

---

[1] There were four Appenrodts restaurants in London. The confusion about the meeting must have arisen because one of the restaurants was located near Oxford Circus and another at 269 Oxford Street. Lady Cynthia Asquith's diary for Wednesday, 11 August 1915, reads: 'Went to tea at Appen[r]odt's for an assignation with the Lawrences, but it didn't come off' (Asquith, *Diaries* 68).   [2] See Letter 946.

to enjoy the aesthetic quality of obedience, he is such a swine with cringing hind-quarters, that I am delighted, I dance for joy when I see him rushing down the Gadarene slope[1] of the war.

I feel like knocking my head against the wall: or of running off to some unformed South American place where there is no thought of civilised effort. I suppose I could learn to ride a horse and live just by myself for myself.

But it is too bad, it is too mean, that they are all so pettily selfish, these good people who sacrifice themselves. I want them – just Russell, or Murry – anybody – to say: 'This is wrong, we are acting in a wrong spirit. We have created a great, almost overwhelming incubus of falsity and ugliness on top of us, so that we are almost crushed to death. Now let us move it. Let us have done with this foolish form of government, and this idea of democratic control. Let us submit to the knowledge that there are aristocrats and plebeians, born, not made. Some amongst us are born fit to govern, and some are born only fit to be governed. Some are born to be artizans and laborers, some to be lords and governors.' But it is not a question of tradition or heritage. It is a question of the incontrovertible soul. If we have a right spirit, even the most stupid of us will know how to choose our governors, and in that way we shall give the nucleus of our classes. There are such falsities of distinction now. Let us get rid of them.

It is a question of the spirit. *Why* are we a nation? We are a nation which must be built up according to a living idea, a great architecture of living people, which shall express the greatest truth of which we are capable. There must be King and Queen, and Lords and Ladies, and burghers and burgesses, and servants: but not King George and Queen Mary,[2] not Lord Kitchener[3] or Earl Grey[4] or Mr Asquith[5] or Lloyd George.[6] It is a question of spirit even more than of intelligence. A bad spirit in a nation chooses a bad spirit in a governor. We must begin to choose all afresh, for the pure, great truth. We must have a new King, who stands for the truth, and a new

[1] Cf. Mark v. 13.
[2] George V and Queen Mary reigned 1910–36.
[3] Horatio Herbert Kitchener (1850–1916), 1st Earl Kitchener of Khartoum and of Broome, famous general. On the outbreak of hostilities, he was appointed Secretary of State for War.
[4] Sir Edward Grey (1862–1933), cr. Viscount Grey of Fallodon, 1916; became Secretary of State for Foreign Affairs in December 1905. He resigned because of ill health in December 1916, when the Asquith ministry was superseded by that of Lloyd George.
[5] The Prime Minister.
[6] David Lloyd George (1863–1945), cr. 1st Earl, 1945; Liberal M.P.; became Minister of Munitions in July 1915 in the Coalition Cabinet under Asquith. Following Lord Kitchener's death he took over the post of Secretary of State for War (July 1916). After an internal cabinet struggle, Asquith resigned and Lloyd George became Prime Minister (7 December 1916–22 October 1922).

Queen, a house of Lords, and a house of Ladies, but Lords of the Spirit
and the Knowledge, and Ladies the same. If we have a right spirit, then our
Lords and our Ladies will appear, as the flowers come forth from nowhere
in the spring. If we continue in our bad spirit, we shall have Horatio
Bottomley for our Prime Minister before a year is out.

We must rid ourselves of this ponderous incubus of falsehood, this massive
London, with its streets and streets of nullity: we must, with one accord
and in purity of spirit, pull it down and build up a beautiful thing. We must
rid ourselves of the idea of money. A rich man with a beautiful house is like
a jewel on a leper's body. You know that. Your Stanway[1] is a jewel on a
leper's body: so near to Burslem Hanley and Stoke, and Wolverhampton.[2]
Our business is not in jewellery,[3] but in the body politic. You know that.
What good is it to a sick, unclean man, if he wears jewels.

I hope you are with me in this. Russell says I cherish illusions, that there
is no such spirit as I like to imagine, the spirit of unanimity in truth, among
mankind. He says that is fiction. Murry says that the spirit matters, but that
an idea is bad. He says he believes in what I say, because he believes in me,
that he might help in the work I set out to do because he would be believing
in me. But he would not believe in the work. He would deplore it. He says
the whole thing is personal: that between him and me it is a case of Lawrence
and Murry, not of any union in an *idea*. He thinks the introduction of any
idea, particularly of any political idea, highly dangerous and deplorable. The
thing should be left personal, each man just expressing himself. – Frieda says
things are not so bad as I pretend, that people are good, that life is also good,
that London is also good and that this civilisation is great and wonderful.
She thinks if the war were over things would be pretty well all right.

But they are all wrong.

I've got a real bitterness in my soul, just now, as if Russell and Lady
Ottoline were [...] traitors – they are traitors. They betray the real truth.
They come to me, and they make me talk, and they enjoy it, it gives them
a profoundly gratifying sensation. And that is all. As if what I say were meant
only to give them gratification, because of the flavour of personality: as if
I were a cake or a wine or a pudding. They then say, I – D.H.L. am wonderful,
I am an exceedingly valuable personality, but that the things I say are
extravaganzas, illusions. They say I cannot think.

All that is dynamic in the world, they convert to a sensation, to the
gratification of that which is static. They are static, static, static, they come,

---

[1] Stanway House, Gloucestershire, where Lady Cynthia Asquith grew up. For a description
see Asquith, *Diaries* xiv–xv; for a photograph see ibid. 108.
[2] Manufacturing towns in the Midlands (a considerable distance from Stanway).
[3] MS reads 'jewelly'.

they say to me, 'You are wonderful, you are dynamic', then they filch my
life for a sensation unto themselves, all my effort, which is my life, they
betray, they are like Judas: they turn it all to their own static selves, convert
it into the static nullity. The result is for them a gratifying sensation, a
tickling, and for me a real bleeding.

But I know them now, which is enough.

I don't know how to begin to lecture or write, publicly, these things of
the real truth and the living spirit. Everything is so awful and static, so large
and ponderous, like the physical mass of London lying on the plain of south
England. And one must shift that mass: it is the mountain which faith must
move.[1] I do believe there are people who wait for the spirit of truth. But
I think one[2] can't find them personally. I had hoped and tried to get a little
nucleus of living people together. But I think it is no good. One must start
direct with the open public, without associates. But how to begin, and when,
I don't yet know.

I hope you don't mind having all this fired off at you.[3] I half feel I ought
not to send it. But I intend to send it.

Only, I don't want any friends, except the friends who are going to *act*,
put everything – or at any rate, put *something* into the effort to[4] bring about
a new unanimity among us, a new movement for the pure truth, an
immediate destructive and reconstructive revolution in actual life, England,
now.

Yours   D. H. Lawrence

971. To Douglas Clayton, 20 August 1915

Text: MS NCL; Unpublished.

1 Byron Villas, Vale of Health, Hampstead, N W
20 Aug 1915

Dear Clayton,

Will you type this sketch for me, and make a carbon copy.[5] There is no
great hurry now – as I have been delayed. This is one of a series of sketches,

---

[1] Matthew xvii. 20.   [2] MS reads 'on'.

[3] Upon receiving DHL's letter, Lady Cynthia wrote in her diary: 'Lawrence's letter very long
and full of bitterness and diatribe – very difficult to answer. It is so difficult to know whether
he has any constructive plans which are at all applicable. I fear I am what he calls "static"'
(Asquith, *Diaries* 70).   [4] MS reads 'be'.

[5] A note by Clayton on the MS identifies the sketch: 'Rec. 21st August 1915 (with MS of
"The Spinner and the Monks"). My reply on back.' The reply reads as follows:

Croydon, 22nd August 1915.

Dear L.,

The work and letter received with thanks. Yes, I am quite ready to do them; will begin
this one on Tuesday [?morning].

Please say, when sending next lot, if the work goes straight to printer, because I will not
put into covers if so.   Yours Douglas

Also, do you want both copies sent to you or shall I keep the carbons?

to make a book. I shall send you them one by one, if you can do with them.
I hope you are pretty well. Greetings to Mrs Clayton. Tell her to come and
see us if she is in town.

Yours   D. H. Lawrence

972. To S. S. Koteliansky, [23 August 1915]
Text: MS BL; Postmark, Hampstead 24 AUG 15; Zytaruk, *Malahat* 22–3.

1 Byron Villas, Vale of Health, Hampstead
Monday

My dear Kot,

Would you mind coming on Thursday instead of on Tuesday evening?
Frieda is still in bed with her cold, which has developed into a bad one. I
am sorry to change the day – please forgive me. But it would not be so well
if you brought your friends when Frieda was laid up.

You take the tube to Hampstead station, from thence walk straight up the
hill to the Heath, and continue straight on, past the pond, along the
Spaniards Road, a little way, till you come to the public house called Jack
Straw's Castle. Across the road from this the path drops down the Heath
straight into the Vale of Health, and the road winding to the right leads you to
Byron Villas. I hope you will like our flat – I think you will.

Murry just mentioned something about the translating of my book into
Russian.[1] I should like that very much. Was that the scheme you meant?
I should be very proud to see myself in Russian, and not to understand a
single word.

I have been to see a man this afternoon who talks of producing my play
in Edinborough and Glasgow and Manchester.[2] That will be rather good
fun, seeing what the thing looks like on the stage. We shall probably have
to go to Nottingham next week for rehearsals – perhaps.

What a funny life – none of these things seem really to belong to me, and
yet I am in them.

Goodbye till Thursday   D. H. Lawrence

973. To Douglas Clayton, [23 August 1915]
Text: MS NCL; PC; Postmark, Hampstead 24 AUG 15; Unpublished.

1 Byron Villas – Vale of Health
Monday[3]

[1] Probably *The Rainbow*, but nothing came of the plan.
[2] The producer interested in DHL's play was Esmé Percy. See Letter 977.
[3] Clayton has noted on the MS: 'Rec/24 August 1915.'

Dear Clayton,

Please put the 1st copy into covers, the carbon copy not into covers.

Yours Sincerely   D. H. Lawrence

Count up the words, will you please.

974. To Douglas Clayton, [24 August 1915]

Text: MS NCL; Unpublished.

1 Byron Villas – Vale of Health, Hampstead
Tuesday

Dear Clayton,

Here is a second sketch.[1] I hope the MS. is not too dishevelled for you to decipher.

Yours   D. H. Lawrence

If you are at all hard up, I will pay you for each sketch as you do it. It is just the same to me.

975. To Douglas Clayton, 1 September 1915

Text: MS NCL; Unpublished.

1 Byron Villas, Vale of Health, Hampstead
1 Sept 1915.

Dear Clayton,

Thank you for the typing: it is very nice indeed. I like to hear what you think. I send you just the beginning of a sketch,[2] to be going on with – the rest tomorrow.

Yours   D. H. Lawrence

---

[1] Clayton's note on the MS identifies the sketch as 'Lemon Gardens'. His response to DHL's letter was as follows:

25th Aug '15

Dear Lawrence,

Thanks for the second parcel & yr letter. Don't apologise for anything! it's such a joy to get onto a piece of work that is English and grammatical! I have just been doing a novel in which there are neither capitals nor grammar; it is like a fantasia on a 1d. serial shocker. As it happens, I am fairly flush with money, but shall have to pay for a new typewriter shortly; so may I just send in an account after about five sketches etcetera.

Yours sincerely

[2] Clayton has noted on the MS: 'Rec/2nd Sept 1915 & Part III', which indicates that the sketch in question is 'The Theatre', part three of 'On the Lago di Garda' in *Twilight in Italy*.

384   *2 September 1915*

976. To Edward Marsh, 2 September 1915
Text: MS NYPL; Unpublished.

1 Byron Villas – Vale of Health – Hampstead, N.W.
2 Sept 1915

My dear Eddie,

I was glad to hear from you again. We must not cease to be friends, though all this misery separates everybody like a darkness.

Put what you like in the Anthology.[1] I only gave the 'Pro Italia' the 'Village Funeral' poem for their book.[2] Perhaps now you will like the Ophelia poem. I send you this American Imagiste book, so you can see it in print.[3] I think it is a good poem. 'The Scent of Irises' is good too; and most people *love* 'The Mower', though I'm not so very fond of it. But take what you like.

If ever you have time, come and see us. Come for an evening – any evening – to a meal or after, as you like. We have got this little flat and shall be here for a winter. I hope you can come.

Our love to you   D. H. Lawrence

977. To Esmé Percy, 3 September 1915
Text: MS Lazarus; Moore 363.

1 Byron Villas – Vale of Health, Hampstead, N W
3 Sept. 1915.

Dear Percy,[4]

Never mind about Manchester. Yes, do the play in Glasgow and Edinboro, if you will.[5] Let me know beforehand, because I think I can help you quite a lot, in both places – have connections with newspapers there, and know people. As a matter of fact, a good many people in Manchester care about my work. But no matter.

Ask Miss Graeme to come and see us when she is in town.[6]

Yours   D. H. Lawrence

[1] *Georgian Poetry 1913–1915*, edited by Edward Marsh and published in November 1915.
[2] DHL's 'Giorno dei Morti' appeared in *The Book of Italy*, ed. Raffaello Piccoli and published by Fisher Unwin for the Pro-Italia Committee in April 1916. (Contributors to the book included Sir James Frazer, Chesterton, Galsworthy, Frederic Harrison and Gilbert Murray; opposite DHL's poem appears a reproduction of Edwin Bale's picture, *Corpus Domini Procession, Como*.)
[3] 'Ballad of Another Ophelia', which appeared in *Some Imagist Poets* (1915). See p. 209 n. 4.
[4] Esmé Saville Percy (1887–1957), a distinguished actor, particularly admired for his work in Shakespeare and Shaw. His first theatrical appearance was in Nottingham in 1904. In 1911 he joined Miss Horniman's theatre company in Manchester. He was to enlist in the army in December 1915 and to remain in it until 1923.
[5] No production of DHL's play, *The Widowing of Mrs Holroyd*, was staged until 1920, but Esmé Percy eventually directed a production of the play at the Kingsway Theatre, London, in December 1926.
[6] Kirsteen Graeme with whom Percy had formed a touring theatrical company in 1913.

978. To Douglas Clayton, 5 September 1915
Text: MS NCL; Unpublished.

1 Byron Villas – Vale of Health – Hampstead, N W

5 Sept 1915

Dear Clayton,

Don't be cross, please, when you get this. But will you take out pp. 4–10 of this sketch,[1] and insert instead the pages of MS. I enclose – type these out and insert them where I have crossed out a piece. I am sorry I must make these alterations,

Yours Sincerely   D. H. Lawrence

979. To Lady Cynthia Asquith, 5 September 1915
Text: MS UT; Huxley 250–1.

1 Byron Villas – Vale of Health – Hampstead, N W.

5 Sept 1915

My dear Lady Cynthia,

I think you didn't like my last letter. But I don't know that I am any the better for your rebuke. My soul is still fizzing savagely.

We are thinking – Murry and Mrs Murry and I, primarily – of issuing a little paper, fortnightly, to private subscribers – 2/6 for 3 months (6 copies) including postage.[2] Perhaps Bertie Russell and Gilbert Cannan will come in. I don't know.

We have found a little Jew in the East End, who is engaged on the *Jewish Encyclopaedia*.[3] He will print us 250 copies, of 28 pages, of 36 lines, for £5: or 36 pages for £6. It will be about the same size as the *Mercure de France*,[4] but 28 or 36 pages thick. If it is 28 p. thick, that costs £30 for 3 months: 250 half crowns is just £31-5-0. So we must get 250 subscribers.[5] You must

---

[1] 'The Lemon Gardens', as the following note written on the MS by Clayton shows: 'Rec/7th Sept 1915/Alterations to II – The Lemon Gardens.' Two pages of typescript heavily over-written by DHL are attached to the letter.

[2] The magazine was called *The Signature*. Only three numbers appeared (4 and 18 October, and 4 November 1915). The main contributors were DHL and Murry; Koteliansky served as the business manager. For DHL's later recollections of the project, see his 'Note to The Crown' at the beginning of *Reflections on the Death of a Porcupine and Other Essays* (Philadelphia, 1925). Murry's version of the venture is given in his *Autobiography* 349–58.

[3] The *Jewish Encyclopaedia*, ed. Cyrus Adler *et al.*, first appeared in 1906 in 12 volumes. The printer's name was Narodiczky, from the Mile End Road.

[4] *Le Mercure de France* (1890–1965), founded by Alfred Vallette and a group of writers. At first it was particularly associated with Symbolism, but later featured original works by writers of all schools and nationalities.

[5] It is not known exactly how many subscribers there were; DHL recalls 'perhaps fifty' ('Note to The Crown' in *Reflections*); in Letter 1006 he mentions '£7 in subscriptions' which would mean 56.

subscribe[1] and find one or two people who care about the real living truth of things: for God's sake, not people who only trifle and don't care.

I am going to do the preaching – sort of philosophy – the beliefs by which one can reconstruct the world:[2] Murry will do his ideas on [...] freedom for the individual soul, Katharine Mansfield will do her little satirical sketches.[3] Then there is perhaps Bertie Russell and Cannan.

I hope you are interested. As for lectures, I have quarrelled in my soul with Bertie Russell – I don't think he will give his, I shall do nothing at all in that line. The sight of the people of London strikes me into a dumb fury. The persistent nothingness of the war makes me feel like a paralytic convulsed with rage. Meanwhile I am writing a book of sketches, or preparing a book of sketches, about the nations, Italian German and English, full of philosophising and struggling to show things real.[4] My head feels like a hammer that keeps[5] hammering on a nail. The only thing I know is, that the hammer is tougher than the nail, in the long run. It is not I who will break.

You will find in the *English Review* for next month a story about the Lucases:[6] you remember we passed by their cottage, and went into the garden, at Greatham, with Herbert Asquith and John. The story is the story of most men and women who are married today – of most men at the war, and wives at home. You must read it, and tell me what you think.

My novel comes out on the 30th of this month.[7] I will send you a copy. Presently you will be bored, with my I, I, and My, my.

Tell us how you are, and what you are doing. Mind you help with our paper. I think it is to be called *The Signature*.

Frieda sends her love. She hates me for the present. But I shall not go to the war.

                                                    Vale   D. H. Lawrence

980. To Bertrand Russell, 5 September 1915
Text: MS UT; Moore, *Bertrand Russell* 57.

                            1 Byron Villas – Vale of Health – Hampstead, N.W.
                                                                5 Sept 1915

[1] subscribe] get
[2] 'The Crown', which represented DHL's 'philosophy', appeared serially in the three numbers of *The Signature*, but the remaining three parts were not published until 1925 in *Reflections*.
[3] Murry's contribution, which also ran in all three numbers, was 'There Was a Little Man'; it likewise, was incomplete. See Murry, *Autobiography* 358. Katharine Mansfield's contributions, under the pseudonym Matilda Berry (see p. 393 n. 1), were the stories, 'Autumn I' and 'Autumn II' (retitled 'The Apple Tree'), and 'The Little Governess'.
[4] *Twilight in Italy*.
[5] keeps] feels
[6] 'England, My England'; see p. 354 n. 4. DHL later expressed some regret that he had written this story; see Letter 1263.
[7] *The Rainbow* was published on 30 September 1915.

Dear Russell,

We are going to start a little paper, myself and Murry and Katharine Mansfield (Mrs Murry) – and you and Cannan if you care to join.[1] We have found a little printer in the East End, who will print us a little booklet, leaves of the same size as the *Mercure de France*, on decent paper, 36 pages of 36 lines each (about 10 words a line), 250 copies for £6: or 28 pages for £5. I think we shall call it *The Signature* – which means a little booklet made out of one folded leaf – also whatever else you like. At present, we think of having 28 pages. It will be 10,000 words: that is about 3000 words each. It will come out every fortnight, and will be posted to subscribers. It is not for public sale (not at first, at any rate), but we are going to get subscribers, people who care about things, 2/6 subscription for 3 months (6 copies), postage free. I shall be the preacher, Murry will be the revealer of the individual soul with respect to the big questions, particularly he will give an account of the real freedom of the individual soul, as he conceives it, Katharine will do satirical sketches. You will do something serious, I hope, and Gilbert can flounder prehistorically.

250 half crowns are £31-5-0. That would just pay for the 6 copies of 28 pages each, and for postage.

The thing would come out the first and third Monday in every month, beginning the first Monday in October, if possible. The printer must have the copy 15 days before publication, because he does everything himself.

I only want people who really care, and who really want a new world, to subscribe. If we lose money, it can't be very much. Murry and I will share that. At any rate we shall try the three months.

I wish, if you are in town, you would come and see us.

Yours   D. H. Lawrence

981. To Douglas Clayton, 6 September 1915
Text: MS NCL; Unpublished.

1 Byron Villas – Vale of Health – Hampstead, N W
6 Sept 1915

Dear Clayton,

This is the end of the third of the Lago di Garda Sketches: 'The Theatre'.[2] I hope it is not *very* untidy and difficult for you to read. You must tell me if I am too exigeant with my scrappy MS.

Yours   D. H. Lawrence

[1] On the MS is a note, which may be Russell's: 'Ans. *Yes* as to writing, *no* as to money.' Nothing by Russell was published in *The Signature*.
[2] Clayton notes on the MS: 'Rec/8 Sept: 1915. [Page] 19 – end of "The Theatre" & III of series.'

982. To E. M. Forster, [8 September 1915]
Text: MS KCC; Unpublished.

1 Byron Villas, Vale of Health – Hampstead, N W
Wednesday[1]

Dear Forster,

I hear from Piccoli[2] you are still in England, still at the National Gallery.[3] I wish you would come and see us. Come to tea tomorrow or on Friday, if you can.

I am very busy about a little paper we are going to have – myself, J M Murry, perhaps Bertie Russell. We want to have a little club as well. Come and see us about it, will you? – quickly.

Yours   D. H. Lawrence

983. To Lady Ottoline Morrell, 9 September 1915
Text: MS UT; Huxley 251–3.

1 Byron Villas, Vale of Health, Hampstead, N W.
9 Sept. 1915.

My dear Lady Ottoline,

One can't help the silences that intervene nowadays, it must be so. But I think they are times when new things are born, and like winter, when trees are rid of their old leaves, to start again. It is the new year one wants so badly; let the old die altogether, completely. It is only the new spring I care about, opening the hard little buds that seem like stone, in the souls of people. They must open and a new world begin. But first there is the shedding of the old, which is so slow and so difficult, like a sickness. I find it so difficult to let the old life go, and to wait for the new life to take form. But it begins to take form now. It is not any more such a fierce question of shedding away.

I always want us to be friends, real friends in the deep, honorable, permanent sense. But it is very difficult for me to be clear and true to my deepest self. We must allow first of all for the extreme lapses in ourselves. But the little hard buds of a new world are not destroyed. I do believe in our permanent friendship, something not temporal.

[1] Dated with reference to Letter 983 in which DHL reports, 'Forster came to see us today'.
[2] Raffaello Piccoli (d. 1933) was appointed Lecturer in Italian at Cambridge in 1912; he taught there until c. 1915 when he returned to Italy in order to enlist in the army. After the war he taught in USA; he became Professor of English Literature at the University of Naples; and, finally, was appointed to the Serena Chair of Italian in Cambridge in 1929. The *Times* obituary (23 January 1933) states: 'At the time of his final illness he was engaged upon a comprehensive study of D. H. Lawrence.' (See also p. 384 n. 2.)
[3] See p. 265 n. 1.

Russell and I have parted for a little while, but it is only in the natural course. The real development continues even in its negation, under the winter.

For the present, Murry and I are going to start a little paper, which is to contain his ideas of immediate, personal freedom, what it means for me to feel free in my own soul, when I am alone: and I am to write my ideas of the other, the impersonal freedom, the freedom of me in relation to all the world, me and all the world, a free thing. Then Mrs Murry is to write a satirical sketch, perhaps each number.

We have found an East End printer who will do us 250 copies for £5 – little journal of 28 pages. We will produce it by *private subscription*, not expose it for public sale. It is to be sent post free to the subscriber on the first and third Monday of the month: it is a fortnightly. The subscription is 2/6 for 6 copies – that is for 3 months. We hope to cover expenses: if not, we must pay what we lack. At any rate, for 3 months the total expenditure is only £30. We begin in October.

We have taken also a large – fairly large room off Southampton Row, to use as a sort of club room.[1] It is 7/6 a week. We must have meetings there.

We begin in October. Then for 3 months I shall work hard, and not mind if people are sterile as stones. Then at the end of 3 months we shall reconsider what is done and what is to be done.

Perhaps it won't interest you very much. But it is something, a beginning. I will not merely join on to the *Cambridge Review*, as Russell will.[2] Leaving all behind, one must make a new start.

I should want you to subscribe the 2/6, and to get me anybody you know, who *cares*. I only want the people who care. It is not a matter even of making the thing pay. I am quite willing to lose. I am weary of the consideration of money. If I have nothing, I will ask people for a piece of bread. But I believe that one does not lack – it is like the prophet in the wilderness.[3]

Our coming to see you depends on us all three, you and me and Frieda. When we all want it, to make the new thing, the new world that is to be, then we will come. And I should very much like you to see our flat here.

Last night when we were coming home the guns broke out, and there was a noise of bombs. Then we saw the Zeppelin above us, just ahead, amid a

[1] The address was 12 Fisher Street, Southampton Row, W.C.
[2] Since the *Cambridge Review* (subtitled *A Journal of University Life and Thought*) was overwhelmingly concerned with the trivia of university life – clubs, sports, balls, etc. – though it had a Literary Supplement to which Russell contributed reviews, DHL is here presumably making a derogatory (and unjustified) remark about Russell's lack of adventurousness.
[3] 1 Kings xvii. 6.

gleaming of clouds: high up, like a bright golden finger, quite small, among a fragile incandescence of clouds.[1] And underneath it were splashes of fire as the shells fired from earth burst. Then there were flashes near the ground – and the shaking noise. It was like Milton – then there was war in heaven.[2] But it was not angels. It was that small golden Zeppelin, like a long oval world, high up. It seemed as if the cosmic order were gone, as if there had come a new order, a new heavens above us: and as if the world in anger were trying to revoke it. Then the small long-ovate luminary, the new world in the heavens, disappeared again.

I cannot get over it, that the moon is not Queen of the sky by night, and the stars the lesser lights. It seems the Zeppelin is in the zenith of the night, golden like a moon, having taken control of the sky; and the bursting shells are the lesser lights.

So it seems our cosmos is burst, burst at last, the stars and moon blown away, the envelope of the sky burst out, and a new cosmos appeared, with a long-ovate, gleaming central luminary, calm and drifting in a glow of light, like a new moon, with its light bursting in flashes on the earth, to burst away the earth also. So it is the end – our world is gone, and we are like dust in the air.

But there must be a new heaven and a new earth,[3] a clearer, eternal moon above, and a clean world below. So it will be.

Everything is burst away now, there remains only to take on a new being.

I look forward to seeing you again. Frieda will write to you soon. Remember me to Morrell and to Julian. Forster came to see us today: still annulled and inconclusive. But he too must come gradually to a new life.

I should like the Murrys to be with us at Garsington one day. And let us all have patience with each other: though I'm the worst for patience.

D. H. Lawrence

984. To Douglas Clayton, [11 September 1915]
Text: MS NCL; Unpublished.

1 Byron Villas, Vale of Health, Hampstead, N W
Saturday

Dear Clayton,

Here is another sketch[4] – you will have done about half now.

Yours   D. H. Lawrence

---

[1] Zeppelin airships bombed London and eastern counties on 8 September, killing 20 people.
[2] Revelation xii. 7 (cf. *Paradise Lost*, Bk. vi).   [3] Ibid. xxi. 1.
[4] A note by Clayton identifies the sketch: 'I ack[nowledged]/same day, Monday, 13tʰ Sept/1915. IV "San Gaudenzio"' (later published in *Twilight in Italy*).

985. To William Hopkin, 14 September 1915
Text: MS NCL; Huxley 254–5.

1, Byron Villas, Vale-of-Heath, Hampstead, London.
14 Sept 1915.

My dear Willie,

We have taken a little flat here, and are to spend the winter in town. If ever you can get up to London, you or Sallie, or Enid, we can rig you up a bed. We shall be very glad to see you.

I send you some leaflets about our paper. It is a rash venture. We are desperately poor, but we must do something, so we are taking the responsibility of this little journal on ourselves, Murry and I, and also we are going to have meetings in a room in town – 12 Fisher St – which we have taken. Heaven knows what will come of it: but this is my first try at direct approach to the public: art after all is indirect and ultimate, I want this to be more immediate.

Get me a few people in Sheffield, will you – people who care vitally about the freedom of the soul – a few people anywhere – but only those who really care.[1] Ask Sallie to write to Mrs Dax – I would rather not open a correspondence with her again, after so long a silence; though I like her, and always shall feel her an integral part of my life; but that is in the past, and the future is separate: yet I want her to have this paper, which will contain my essential beliefs, the ideas I struggle with. And perhaps she – Alice Dax – will ask one or two people in Liverpool, Blanche Jennings, for instance.[2] You see I want to initiate, if possible, a new movement for real life and real freedom. One can but try.

I wish we could meet and talk. Soon I shall go to Ripley. Perhaps you will come to London. I send you the proofs of a story that is coming in next month's *English Review*.

Tell Sallie I feel she *must* come and see this *tiny* flat on Hampstead Heath. Greetings from Frieda, and love from me.

D. H. Lawrence

---

[1] Hopkin was in close touch with the left-wing intelligentsia in the Sheffield area (30 miles from Eastwood); among them was Edward Carpenter (see p. 401 n. 3).

[2] Alice Dax responded on 29 September 1915: 'I shall be glad to receive copies of "The Signature" as per your circular letter of Sept. 11th and enclose P.O. 2/6 herewith. Yours truly Alice Dax (Mrs)' (MS BL among the Koteliansky Papers). Blanche Jennings' name does not appear on any of the lists of subscribers that have survived; see *Letters*, i. 2, 43 n. 2.

986. To Bertrand Russell, 14 September 1915

Text: MS UT; Moore, *Atlantic Monthly* 100.

1 Byron Villas – Vale of Health – Hampstead, N W

14 Sept 1915.

Dear Russell,

I'm going to quarrel with you again. You simply don't speak the truth, you simply are not sincere. The article you send me is a plausible lie, and I hate it.[1] If it says some true things, that is not the point. The fact is that you, in the essay, are all the time a lie.

Your basic desire is the maximum of desire of war, you are really the super-war-spirit. What you want is to jab and strike, like the soldier with the bayonet, only you are sublimated into words. And you are like a soldier who might jab man after man with his bayonet, saying 'this is for ultimate peace'. The soldier would be a liar. And it isn't in the least true that you, your basic self, want ultimate peace. You are satisfying in an indirect, false way your lust to jab and strike. Either satisfy it in a direct and honorable way, saying 'I hate you all, liars and swine, and am out to set upon you', or stick to mathematics, where you can be true. But to come as the angel of peace – no, I prefer Tirpitz a thousand times, in that rôle.[2]

You are simply *full* of repressed desires, which have become savage and anti-social. And they come out in this sheep's clothing of peace propaganda. As a woman said to me, who had been to one of your meetings: 'It seemed so strange, with his face looking so evil, to be talking about peace and love. He can't have *meant* what he said'.

I believe in your inherent power for realising the truth. But I don't believe in your will, not for a second. Your will is false and cruel.[3] You are too full of devilish repressions to be anything but lustful and cruel. I would rather have the German soldiers with rapine and cruelty, than you with your words of goodness. It is the falsity I can't bear. I wouldn't care if you were six times a murderer, so long as you said to yourself, 'I am this'. The enemy of all mankind, you are, full of the lust of enmity. It is *not* the hatred of falsehood which inspires you. It is the hatred of people, of flesh and blood.[4] It is a perverted, mental blood-lust. Why don't you own it.

Let us become strangers again, I think it is better.[5]

D. H. Lawrence

---

[1] 'The Danger to Civilization' offered as a contribution to *The Signature*, in response to Letter 980.

[2] Alfred von Tirpitz (1849–1930), German admiral, who advocated Germany's policy of unrestricted submarine warfare.

[3] cruel.] dark.   [4] of flesh and blood.] all people.

[5] Russell later recorded his reaction to this letter: 'I was inclined to believe that [DHL] had

987. To Lady Ottoline Morrell, 14 September 1915

Text: MS UT; Huxley 253–4.

1, Byron Villas, Vale-of-Health, Hampstead, London.

14 Sept 1915

My dear Lady Ottoline,

I send you a few leaflets about our paper.[1] If you or Morrell could get a few people who really care, to take it, I should be very glad. But only people who care about this life now and in the future.

Today I wrote very violently to Russell. I am glad, because it had to be said sometime. But also I am very sorry, and feel like going into a corner to cry, as I used to do when I was a child. But there seems so much to cry for, one doesn't know where to begin. And then, damn it all, why should one.

Viele Grüsse   D. H. Lawrence

Tell those two American ladies near you,[2] whom I went to see, that I expect them to have my paper, because of what it says.

988. To Harriet Monroe, 15 September 1915

Text: MS UChi; Monroe 91–2.

1, Byron Villas, Vale-of-Health, Hampstead, London.

15 Sept 1915

Dear Harriet Monroe,

How is poetry going in America? There is none in England: the muse has gone, like the swallows in winter.

This is the real winter of the spirit in England. We are just preparing to come to fast grips with the war. At last we are going to give ourselves up to it – and everything else we are letting go. I thought we should never come to this: but we are. And the war will go on for a very long time. I knew

---

some insight denied to me, and when he said that my pacifism was rooted in blood-lust I supposed he must be right. For twenty-four hours I thought that I was not fit to live and contemplated suicide. But at the end of that time, a healthier reaction set in, and I decided to have done with such morbidness' (*Autobiography*, ii. 22).

[1] The text of the leaflet (dated 11 September 1915) reads as follows: 'It is proposed to issue a small fortnightly journal, called THE SIGNATURE, which will contain a series of six papers on social and personal freedom by D. H. Lawrence and J. M. Murry, and a set of satirical sketches by Matilda Berry; also such other contributions as may be found in harmony with the general idea of the journal.

The paper will be published by subscription only, at 2/6 for the set of six copies. It will be sent post free to the subscribers on the first and third Mondays of the month, beginning in October next.'

[2] Ethel Sands and Nancy Hudson who lived at Newington House (see Gathorne-Hardy, *Ottoline: The Early Memoirs*, pp. 128–9). See p. 360 n. 1.

it when I watched the Zeppelin the other night, gleaming like a new great sign in the heavens, a new, supreme celestial body. I knew by the spirit of London – game for fight, all consideration gone – and I knew by the look of the Zeppelin, which had assumed the heavens as its own. God knows now what the end will be.

Only I feel, that even if we are all going to be rushed down to extinction, one must hold up the other, living truth, of Right, and pure reality, the reality of the clear, eternal spirit. One must speak for life and growth, amid all this mass of destruction and disintegration.

So I bring out this little paper. And will you take it too, and get one or two friends to take it – not for the money's sake, but for the spirit which is struggling in it.

Pray to heaven to keep America always out of the war.[1] God knows what will be the end of Europe.

Yours   D. H. Lawrence

989. To Amy Lowell, 15 September 1915
Text: MS HU; Unpublished.

1, Byron Villas, Vale-of-Health, Hampstead, London.
15 Sept 1915.

Dear Amy Lowell,

I wonder how you are and what you are doing. We have taken a flat here, and shall stay the winter through, I expect.

Thank you for the copy of the Imagiste.[2] It was a nice little volume, I thought. I don't know in the least how the English edition has done.

I am very busy with a lot of work – a novel coming out on the 30th of this month, a book of Italian and German studies soon. Then we are doing this little paper. It is the attempt to get at the real basis from which to start a reconstructive idea of this life of ours. I think you will be really interested. I wonder if you would care to subscribe, and to ask any serious people who care about the last questions of life to subscribe too.

At any rate, write and tell us how you are and what you are doing in America.

Yours very Sincerely   D. H. Lawrence

My wife sends greetings. I am always *very* grateful for the typewriter.

---

[1] After the sinking of the *Lusitania* (see p. 340 n. 1), when 128 American lives were lost, US sympathies gradually turned against Germany; America entered the war on 6 April 1917.
[2] See p. 384 n. 3.

990. To Douglas Clayton, 15 September 1915
Text: MS NCL; Unpublished.

1, Byron Villas, Vale-of-Health, Hampstead, London.
15 Sept 1915

Dear Clayton,
    Thank you very much for the typed MS. I enclose your account and a cheque.[1]

Yours   D. H. Lawrence

991. To Ernest Collings, [15 September 1915]
Text: MS UT; PC; Postmark, Hampstead 15 SEP 15; Unpublished.

1 Byron Villas – Vale of Health, Hampstead.
[15 September 1915]

Do come to tea on Sunday. We shall expect you about 4.0.

D. H. Lawrence[2]

992. To Arthur McLeod, 15 September 1915
Text: MS UT; Postmark, Hampstead 17 SEP 15; Huxley 255.

1, Byron Villas, Vale-of-Health, Hampstead, London.
15 Sept 1915

My dear Mac,
    At last we have come up to London, and taken a little flat here. We shall stay the winter, I expect. Now you must come and see us.
    I wonder if [you] are still interested in my work. The new novel comes out on the 30th of this month – *The Rainbow*. You must read it: it is really something new in the art of the novel, I think. There is a story to come in October's *English Review*. And then we are doing this little paper. I want you particularly to take the paper, because it contains the stuff I believe in most deeply – the philosophy. And get just one or two people who really *care* about the freedom of the soul, to subscribe, will you?
    I wonder how you are, and what you are doing. Come and see us when you are in town.
    Greetings from both of us.

Yours   D. H. Lawrence

---

[1] Clayton noted that the amount was £1 7. 8. 'Recd 15 Sept: 1915.'
[2] A note by Collings on the MS reads: '2/6 for "Signature" and prospectus of "Form" sent 21/9/15.' *Form: A Quarterly of the Arts* ran for a year from April 1916.

993. To Zoë Akins, 15 September 1915
Text: MS HL; Unpublished.

> 1, Byron Villas, Vale-of Health, Hampstead, London.
> 15 Sept. 1915

Dear Miss Zoï Atkins,[1]

Thank you very much for your letter – which I very stupidly have lost – and for the promise of the book. I hope we shall continue mutually to admire each other's work for a long while – though it's a pretty hard thing to do, I believe. I am having another novel – *The Rainbow* – out on the 30th of this month. I don't know when the American edition comes – but before long. I wonder how that book will strike you. I think a good deal of it myself.

I have come to London to do some work for the winter – *not* for the war. In the midst of all this chaos of disintegration I want if possible to start some germ of positive belief and to work towards living, reconstructive action later on. So we are having a little paper, and a club. Perhaps you would like to have the paper – would you? And if it means anything to you, perhaps you would get one or two of your friends, people who care about truth and living spirit, not only about destruction and negation, to take it too.

We have taken a flat here on Hampstead Heath for the winter. There is a fair on behalf of the wounded soldiers today, and myriads of the wounded, in their bright blue uniforms and red scarves, and bands, and swing-boats, and a whole rowdy enjoyment. It is queer.

But the war will never end. The English are just getting at it. My God, the stupendous rashness and folly of it.

The other night we watched the Zeppelin, gleaming golden like a long-ovate moon, and the faint clouds fuming round it, in the grasp of the searchlight. It looked strange, like a strange new celestial body dominating the night heavens – moon and stars passed away, and a new heaven above us. Under the long-ovate, gleaming moon, which moved very slowly, amid its halo of cloud, the shells were bursting in splashes of fire, and down below, on earth, fire seemed to leap up now and again from the fallen bombs. All the while the big guns were bellowing angrily. And everybody stood with face turned to the sky. It is a new order, a new world. These are the heavenly ministers now, and this gun-fire is the world's acclamation of worship.

Oh, it is all bad and wrong and foolish. But we shall go on and on with it, for years.

---

[1] See p. 145 n. 1.

Nevertheless, though the skies fall, or have fallen, one must go on with the living, constructive spirit – Somebody must.

Tell us who you are, will you, when you write. I am married, aged 30, a novelist of some small reputation, poor –

Yours Sincerely   D. H. Lawrence

994. To Douglas Clayton, [20 September 1915]
Text: MS NCL; PC; Postmark, Hampstead 20 SEP 15; Unpublished.

[1, Byron Villas, Vale-of-Health, Hampstead, London.]
[20 September 1915]

Thanks for the work. I'll send more soon.

D. H. Lawrence

995. To Lady Cynthia Asquith, 20 September 1915
Text: MS UT; Huxley 257.

1, Byron Villas, Vale-of-Health, Hampstead, London.
20 Sept. 1915

My dear Lady Cynthia,

We have not heard from you for a long time. I hope there is no bad news perching on your house-roof, that keeps you silent.

At last we have burst into a sort of activity. You will see by the leaflet, about the little paper we are starting. Today I have sent in the MS. of the first number.

Murry and I are doing it just off our own bat. Russell stuck by an old formula, that I hated, so I just had a violent sort of row, a thunderstorm, and went on without him. It is better so, for the present. My last letter to you was in the midst of a series of thunderstorms. Now the air is clearer, there is a sort of washed freshness in the sky, and the light is beginning to shine for a new creation, I think.

We have found a little Jew in the Mile End Rd who will print us 250 copies of our little journal at £5 a time, so we have begun: and what we lose, we lose of our own. It is a three months venture.

We have also taken two rooms in Fisher St, and are going to have little club meetings.

Don't be alarmed at the paper: my contribution is purely philosophic and metaphysical, and on these grounds sociological. Murry is purely introspective.

You must be a subscriber, and ask some of your friends, like Harold Baker and Catherine Asquith – people who care, somewhere in their souls: Perhaps even Arthur Balfour will read it.[1] It is the best I can do.

Perhaps by Christmas we shall have some little footing, and I can be reconciled to all my friends – Frieda still abhors the Ottoline, and will have no relation at all with her – and we can unite in a bigger effort, a bigger paper, and Russell give his lectures, and we have good club meetings. Perhaps – God knows. And perhaps everything will fizzle out. Then if possible we shall go abroad, and I shall have another try when the social weather is more promising.

At least tell us how you are. Frieda sends her love – I mine –

D. H. Lawrence

Eddie is coming to see us tomorrow!!

996. To J. B. Pinker, 20 September 1915
Text: MS Forster; Unpublished.

1, Byron Villas, Vale-of-Health, Hampstead, London.

20 Sept 1915

Dear Pinker,

I send you Italian Sketches for American publication. The duplicate copies I keep for Duckworth.[2] But I shan't send them him till I have the book complete. I am somewhat delayed. This, with that first sketch about Crucifixes,[3] amounts to some 30,000 words. I shall bring the total up to 50,000. Did Duckworth write you about the publication of these in vol. this autumn? What do you think? Shall I get them done for him quickly, so that he can bring them out before Christmas, or will they wait?

Of these sketches, the 1st and 4th are just right for magazine publication as they stand – the 2nd and 3rd are too long.[4] But the whole set would look nice as a serial. But I suppose nobody will want to do that. Yet it would go well, I'm sure. And there can be added on to these 26000 words, another or two other sketches, at choice.

Tell me what you think.

Yours   D. H. Lawrence

---

[1] DHL may have recalled reading A. J. Balfour's article, 'Creative Evolution and Philosophic Doubt' in the *Hibbert Journal* (October 1911); see *Letters*, i. 359. (Balfour was now First Lord of the Admiralty.)

[2] The English edition by Duckworth appeared in June 1916; B. W. Huebsch published the book in America in the same year (from the Duckworth sheets).

[3] 'The Crucifix Across the Mountains'.

[4] By 'these sketches' DHL probably meant those in the 'Lago di Garda' series recently typed by Douglas Clayton: nos 1 and 4 would therefore be 'The Spinner and the Monks' and 'San Gaudenzio', nos 2 and 3, 'The Lemon Gardens' and 'The Theatre'.

997. To Edward Marsh, 22 September 1915
Text: MS NYPL; Postmark, Hampstead 23 SEP 15; Unpublished.

1 Byron Villas, Vale-of-Health, Hampstead

22 Sept. 1915

Dear Eddie,

I altered the one verse, as you see.[1] But I haven't got the poem anywhere, so I don't know how the other verse runs. I wish you could let me see the whole poem – or all the poems – that you will print of mine. I might make a little improvement. I will let you have them back by Saturday.

Yours   D. H. Lawrence

> Still in his nostrils the frozen breath of despair
> And heart like a cross that bears dead agony
> Of naked love, clenched in his fists the shame,
> And in his belly the smouldering hate of me.

998. To Lady Cynthia Asquith, 22 September 1915
Text: MS UT; Huxley 258.

1, Byron Villas, Vale-of-Health, Hampstead, London.

22 Sept 1915

My dear Lady Cynthia,

I send you a few more leaflets, as you ask me. Let the half crowns be posted to Fisher St or to me, as you will.

But if you really do care about affirmation, in this life of negation, please do get the other people who care, to have the paper. It is really *something*: the seed, I hope, of a great change in life: the beginning of a new religious era, from my point. I hope to God the new religious era is starting into being also at other points, and that soon there will be a body of believers, in this howling desert of unbelief and sensation. Above all – no, not above all – but really I want Arthur Balfour to read it. It may mean something to him, in truth. But I don't know.

I wish you would come back to town. There are so many people, but none of them have any real *being*. They are all inconclusive and unresolved, as if they had no absolute existence at all, anywhere, but were only sorts of small relative natural phenomena, all of them, without souls.

We have only got about 30 subscribers so far. But there will be more.

---

[1] The penultimate stanza of 'Meeting Among the Mountains'. See p. 154 n. 2.

I am glad Herbert Asquith is away from the war.[1] He doesn't say any more, that a man only really lives when he is at the front, does he?[2]

Greetings from both of us   D. H. Lawrence

999. To Ernest Collings, [22? September 1915]
Text: MS UT; Huxley 259.

1 Byron Villas
[22? September 1915][3]

Dear Collings

Thanks for your Subscription. If you can get another it will be welcome. I send you back the *Form*.[4] [...] I don't think much of the drawing:[5] it is rather foolishly phallic, I think. One can't do these things deliberately, without being stupid and affected.

Yours   DHL

1000. To Edward Marsh, [24? September 1915]
Text: MS NYPL; Huxley 258.

1, Byron Villas, Vale-of-Health, Hampstead, London.
Friday[6]

Dear Eddie,

I don't believe you've seen these poems by Anna Wickham (Mrs Hepburn).[7] She is just bringing out a book, with Grant Richards: either in

---

[1] He was home on sick-leave.

[2] Lady Cynthia's recollection of 'Lawrence's statement that Beb's destructive spirit had been aroused', together with her husband's sensitivity to 'the great gulf' between the men at the front and people at home, provide some background for this remark. See Asquith, *Diaries* 80.

[3] Collings sent in his subscription on 21 September 1915; hence the date here. See p. 395 n. 2.

[4] Cf. p. 395 n. 2.   [5] Possibly a woodcut by Austin Spare.

[6] DHL had discussed his contributions to *Georgian Poetry 1913–1915*, with Marsh, on 21 September 1915; it is assumed that this letter was an afterthought. A typescript of the poems (TMSC NWU) which accompanied DHL's letter, is headed: 'Poems by Anna Wickham enclosed to E. Marsh, 17 Sep 1915': its origin and the authority for the date are not known.

[7] With one exception, the poems enclosed were subsequently published, with only minor variations, in Anna Wickham's *The Man With a Hammer* (February 1916), as follows: 'After Annunciation', p. 43; 'The Avenue', p. 54; 'The Trespasser', p. 66; 'Insensibility', p. 68; 'The Dependence', p. 71; 'The Garden', p. 72; 'My True Love Hath My Heart', retitled 'Epicurean Lover', p. 73; 'Prayer on Sunday' and (greatly modified) 'Theft' p. 92. The exception, 'Sentiments', reads:

> Windswept from where they grew
> These tender flowers lie dead.
> How many things were true
> Had they been left unsaid.

December or February. Her address is 49 Downshire Hill, N.W. I think some of these poems *very* good. You may like them for the *Georgian Poetry*.

D. H. Lawrence

1001. To Edward Marsh, [25 September 1915]
Text: MS NYPL; Unpublished.

1, Byron Villas, Vale-of-Health, Hampstead, London.
Saturday[1]

Dear Eddie,

I send you the poems. I wish I cared for 'Cruelty and Love'.[2] It doesn't interest me a bit.

If you don't like any of the alterations, alter them back to what they were.

Saluti cari   D. H. Lawrence

1002. To William and Sallie Hopkin, 25 September 1915
Text: MS NCL; cited in Pollak, *Journal of Modern Literature*, iii. 29.

1, Byron Villas, Vale-of-Health, Hampstead, London.
25 Sept 1915

Dear Willie and Sallie,

Thank you both for your letters, and the promise. If you will send Edward Carpenter a leaflet, I shall be glad: though he is not in my line.[3] But he may give the paper to some young creature.

I wish also you would send a leaflet to Jessie Chambers. It is only fair she should have access to my work, if she still has any interest in it.

This paper is not run in the least as a financial venture. I only want it to pay its way, if possible. But I do want some little seed of affirmation to start growing, if possible.

I've met all kinds of people, known and unknown: but it's devilish hard to find anybody who'll stand up for anything. I rather like young

---

[1] Dated with reference to Letter 997, in which DHL promises to return the poems offered for publication in *Georgian Poetry 1913–1915*, 'by Saturday'.

[2] DHL's poem published in *Love Poems and Others* (1913). In *Collected Poems* (1928) it was renamed 'Love on the Farm'.

[3] Edward Carpenter (1844–1929), graduated from Trinity Hall, Cambridge in 1868, where he became a Fellow and then took holy orders (soon abandoned). He made his home near Sheffield and in 1885 started the local Socialist Society. Author of *Towards Democracy* (1883), *The Intermediate Sex* (1908), *My Days and Dreams* (1916), etc. For a comparative study of his ideas and those of DHL, see Emile Delavenay, *D. H. Lawrence and Edward Carpenter: A Study in Edwardian Transition* (1971).

Massingham:[1] the father's a swine. Murry is going to be something very good. He's young yet. He's about the only man who's got a real venture in him.

I'm sorry you didn't like the story.[2]

I've just had a violent split with Bertie Russell – the Hon. Bertrand. We were working more or less together: but I can't stand the things he says, and told him so. We had a man called Meredith in last night – economist.[3] I liked him. But he says he's going mad, and I think he is. But he takes it very comfortably. I'm due to meet Bernard Shaw and Arthur Balfour directly. But I don't think that men who have had any public position for long will be any good.

Do help with the paper a little. Believe me we shall get somewhere, after a while, a real change that alters things from the bottom.

Our love to you both   D. H. Lawrence

1003. To Emily King, 27 September 1915
Text: MS Lazarus; Unpublished.

1 Byron Villas – Vale of Health, Hampstead
27 Sept 1915

My dear Sister,

I send you my new novel. I hope you will like it. The cover-wrapper is vile beyond words.[4] I think Methuen is a swine to have put it on. But then he is a swine.

The weather is cold today, and the winter is coming. I hate it so much.

---

[1] Harold John Massingham (1888–1952), journalist and critic; son of Henry William Massingham (1860–1924), editor of *Nation* (1907–23). Between 1912 and 1924 Harold Massingham was on the literary staffs of the *Athenaeum* (1912–13) and *Nation* (1917–24). (See Nehls, i. 274.)

[2] 'England, My England'.

[3] Hugh Owen Meredith (1878–1964) had been a close friend of E. M. Forster since their undergraduate days in Cambridge. (For an account of their relationship, see Furbank, i. 60–4, 97–101.) Fellow of King's College, 1903–8; Lecturer in Economic History, University of Manchester, 1905–8; Professor of Economics, Queens University, Belfast, 1911–46. Author of *Outlines of the Economic History of England* (1908). DHL later read some of Meredith's poetry; see Letter 1035.

[4] The scene on the dust-jacket of *The Rainbow* (officially published on 30 September) is sentimental, showing a man and a woman in a highly stylised embrace (from a painting by Frank Wright). On the spine is a synopsis: 'This story, by one of the most remarkable of the younger school of novelists, contains a history of the Brangwen character through its developing crises of love, religion, and social passion. It ends with Ursula, the leading-shoot of the restless, fearless family, waiting at the advance-post of our time to blaze a path into the future.' (A colour reproduction of the jacket is printed in Keith Sagar, *The Life of D. H. Lawrence*, 1980, facing p. 128.)

One always feels like dying as the winter comes on in England. It is so cold and lugubrious.

But I am very busy, always seeing people, always people coming here. I wonder how long I shall stand it.

I was very glad to hear Peggy is really better.[1] Frieda and I are all right as far as health goes, now. But my soul feels very dismal when I see the approach of the English winter. Till now I have been able to sit out of doors on the Heath every day. And it is really rather beautiful, rounded masses of trees and grassy slopes.

Don't hurry to read the novel, you probably wont like it.

Love to all.

Your brother   D. H. Lawrence

1004. To E. M. Forster, 28 September 1915
Text: MS KCC; cited in Furbank, ii. 13.

1 Byron Villas
28 Sept 1915

Dear Forster,

I send you the catalogues of the boxes, for your friend: 'Who is an officer and a gentleman'[2] also two boxes which I have by me, which I prepared with white lead, so that they will take oil color or enamel instead of water color, which wears badly. The long box makes a nice stud box. You can make a good futuristic design with studs and buttonholes. One box is for you, and one for the officer and gentleman. I think water color will go on white lead, also, if you want it to. Let me know the results.

Hugh Meredith (it is Hugh, isn't it?) came to see us.[3] He led off by saying 'I'm tired of language, both written and spoken'. Of course, after that, what was to be done. I asked him to turn cart wheels in the passage, or to gambol and bark like a dog on the rug. But he didn't rise to the occasion.

Then suddenly he appeared at eleven at night, the same night, for no reason whatever, and we talked till one oclock. He says he's going mad. I say it's very undistinguished, because most folks are. We have a fireworky sort of conversation.

---

[1] Emily King's daughter, Margaret.

[2] Ernest Altounyan (1888–1962), a half-Irish, half-Armenian doctor; he had been commissioned in the Royal Army Medical Corps. He was a close personal friend of Forster at this time and later of T. E. Lawrence. m. Dora Collingwood.

[3] 'In the autumn, when Hugh Meredith published a volume of poems, Forster sent Lawrence a copy, and on the strength of this Meredith paid Lawrence a visit in Hampstead' (Furbank, ii. 13).

There's no earthly reason why he *should* go mad, except the important one, that he wants to.

I rather liked him. Please send me his address. He is not in London nor in Belfast. But if I had his Hampstead address, it would get him.

These are fine friends you turn on to me. Perhaps the officer-and-gentleman touch is to assure us that you can do the conventional thing. But an officer-and-gentleman painting little wooden boxes – Baccholino!

I'm doing my *Signature* proofs. We've got 40 half crowns – just £5 – just not quite enough for the first number. Poveri noi.[1] But treasures in heaven – neither moth nor rust doth corrupt, nor thieves break in and steal[2] – e basta.[3]

D. H. Lawrence

I should like the catalogue of boxes back some time, if it is not too much trouble.

1005. To S. S. Koteliansky, [28 September 1915]
Text: MS BL; Zytaruk 49.

[1 Byron Villas, Vale-of-Health, Hampstead, London]
[28 September 1915][4]

18th Mrs Dollie Radford, 32 Well Walk, Hampstead. 1.
21st Miss L. Reynolds,[5] 20 Ifold Rd, Redhill, Surrey. 1.
22nd E. Collings Esq, 18 Ravenslea Rd, Balham, S.W. 1.
22 Miss Mary Phelps, 19 Temple Fortune Hill, Hendon, N.W.
23 Miss Barbara Low.
23rd Miss Louis, 7 Colehill Gardens, Fulham Palace Rd, S W.
24th E. M. Forster, Harnham, Monument Green, Weybridge, Surrey.
26 Dr. Ernest Jones, 69 Portland Court, W.
27 Miss Isabel Carswell, 43 Moray Place, Edinburgh.[6]
28 Drey.[7]

[1] 'Poor us.'
[2] Matthew vi. 20 (A.V.) ['...heaven, where neither...corrupt, and where thieves do not break through nor steal'].
[3] 'and that's it'.
[4] According to a note on the MS (obviously in Kot's hand), this list of subscribers to *The Signature* was received on '28 Sept. from DHL'. The names are in DHL's hand. Figures preceding the names presumably recorded the date when DHL received a subscription. The figure one following the first three names indicates the person had paid for a single copy.
[5] Lilian Reynolds (1877–1954) whom DHL knew as a teacher in Croydon. See *Letters*, i. 236 n. 2.   [6] See p. 617 n. 1.
[7] O. Raymond Drey, husband of Ann Estelle Rice, an artist who was a close friend of Katherine Mansfield. She later illustrated DHL's volume of poems, *Bay* (1919).

1006. To Lady Cynthia Asquith, 2 October 1915

Text: MS UT; Huxley 259–60.

1 Byron Villas – Vale-of-Health, Hampstead
2 Oct. 1915.

My dear Lady Cynthia,

Thank you for the 2/6 for the *Signature*. I have done my 6 papers[1] – but I wonder if we shall ever be able to afford to continue the paper. We've only got about £7 in subscriptions so far. We shall need £30 for the whole.

I think my papers are very beautiful and very good. I feel if only people, decent people, would read them, somehow a new era might set in. But I don't think people care. And perhaps I am too self-important. At any rate, it will be as it will be. But still, we must do our best. It is no good, if everybody leaves the doing to everybody else.

I send you my novel, and also your scarf, which I am ashamed to find still in this house. I wanted Frieda to send it you weeks ago.

Where is your husband? And when are you coming to town? What was the matter with Herbert Asquith? Give us some news of him. Queer, how one feels these returned soldiers on one's conscience. Those that are dead are all right. But those that are alive have to begin to live again. One must put away all ordinary common sense, I think, and work only from the invisible world. The visible world is not true. The invisible world is true and real. One must live and work from that.

Frieda sends her love   D. H. Lawrence

The scarf is all in holes. I am very sorry. But I think it is age. Because [...] Frieda has not used it, more than once or twice. But some holes came in the washing. I hope you dont mind.

DHL

1007. To J. B. Pinker, 2 October 1915

Text: MS Forster; Unpublished.

1, Byron Villas, Vale-of-Health, Hampstead, London.
2 Oct 1915

Dear Pinker,

I have your letter about the book of Sketches for Duckworth. I think the terms are all right, as you have arranged them. Perhaps a special format, with possible illustrations, might be rather jolly. I must get on and do more sketches now.

[1] See p. 386 n.2.

I have got the copies of *The Rainbow*. What a vile cover wrapper they have given it.

Methuens owe us £50 still, don't they? I suppose they will pay it.

The 'England My England' story is in this months *English Review*. Have you any idea when it comes in America?[1]

Yours   D. H. Lawrence

1008. To Edward Marsh, 4 October 1915
Text: MS NYPL; Huxley 260.

1, Byron Villas, Vale-of-Health, Hampstead, London.
4 Oct 1915

Dear Eddie,

Thank you for your letter. I'm glad you like the *Rainbow*. I should have sent you a copy from the publisher – but now you have one.

Do as you like about the poetry.[2] I cannot really get the hang of verses again, after I've left them for a long time.

And come and see us again one evening, wont you?

Yours   D. H. Lawrence

1009. To J. B. Pinker, 5 October 1915
Text: MS Forster; Unpublished.

1 Byron Villas – Vale of Health, Hampstead
5 Oct 1915

Dear Pinker,

Thank you for cheque for £33, from Methuen. I think he is rather stingy about the corrections of proofs.[3]

Tell me what happens to *The Rainbow*, will you – how the libraries and so on behave. If Methuen does not make his money now, he will do so later.

I enclose the signed agreement with Duckworth.[4]

Yours   D. H. Lawrence

Not until April 1917 in the *Metropolitan*.
See Letter 1001.
DHL was charged for making too many corrections as this letter, 1 October 1915, from Methuen to Pinker shows: 'We are sorry that although we did our best to keep down the printers' bill for corrections on the proofs of "THE RAINBOW" (D. H. Lawrence) we find after a careful examination of their account that there is an excess of £9. 3. 9 over the amount allowed by the terms of the agreement. We warned Mr. Lawrence in June last that we feared there would be a charge' (MS NYPL).
For the publication of *Twilight in Italy* (called, in the agreement, 'a Book of Italian Sketches').
The agreement is dated – probably by Pinker – 6 October 1915.

1010. To S. S. Koteliansky, 7 October 1915
Text: MS BL; Zytaruk 47–9.

1, Byron Villas, Vale-of-Health, Hampstead, London.
7 Oct. 1915

My dear Kot,

Will you send a copy of the *Signature* to each of the following three, from whom I have received subscriptions:

1. the Misses Fairfield, 'Fairliehope', Chatham Close, Erskine Hill, Golders Green, NW. 2/6.
1. Dr. Margaret Hogarth, 3 Albany Terrace, Regents Park, NW. 2/6.
1. M. Roth Esq., Orchestrelle Coy., Aeolean Hall, New Bond St., 2/6.

Also I have received subscriptions from the following, to whom I have *sent* the *Signature*

1. Clifford Bax Esq,[1] 1 The Bishops Avenue, East Finchley, N. 2/6.
2. J. F. Cannan Esq, 92 Furness Rd., Willesden, N.W. 2/6.
3. Mark Gertler, Penn Studio, Rudall Crescent, Hampstead. 2/6.
4. Mrs Anna Hepburn, 49 Downshire Hill, Hampstead. 2/6.
5. A. Brackenbury Esq, 14a Downshire Hill, Hampstead. 2/6.
6. Leonard Smith Esq, The Vicarage, Cholesbury, Tring, Herts 2/6.

Also I have a p. c. from Jones and Evans Bookshop, 77 Queen St, Cheapside, E C. saying they want to subscribe for 3 copies, and asking for particulars. I refer them to Fisher St. and ask them to send 7/6.

When there are letters addressed to me at Fisher St, please open them unless they are marked 'private'.

When you come to Murrys tonight, please bring for me 6 copies of the *Signature*, in their envelopes.

Yours   D. H. Lawrence

1011. To Eleanor Farjeon, 7 October 1915
Text: MS UT; Huxley 260–1.

1 Byron Villas, Vale of Health, Hampstead
7 Oct 1915

Dear Eleanor,

I mean the 'of' to be there.[2] When Christ said 'the blasphemy against the Father should be forgiven, and the blasphemy against the Son, but *not*

---

[1] DHL had met the poet and playwright Clifford Bax (1886–1962) in 1912; see *Letters*, i. 405 n.
[2] A reference to the concluding paragraph of 'The Crown' in the first issue of *The Signature*, which reads: 'And this, this last, is our blasphemy of the war. We would have the lamb roar like the lion, all doves turn into eagles.'

the blasphemy against the Holy Ghost',[1] he meant, surely, that that which is absolute and timeless, the supreme *relation* between the Father and Son, not a relation of love, which is specific and relative, but an absolute relation, of opposition and attraction both, this should not be blasphemed. And it seems to me a *blasphemy* to say that the Holy Spirit is Love. In the Old Testament it is an Eagle: in the New it is a Dove. Christ insists on the Dove: but in his supreme moments he includes the Eagle.

Can you not see that if the relation between Father and Son, in the Christian theology, were only *love*, then how could they even feel love unless they were separate and different, and if they are divinely different, does not this imply that they are divine opposites, and hence the relation *implied* is of eternal opposition, the relation *stated* is eternal attraction, love.

I hope this doesn't seem confused: I think it is quite clear really –

Yours   D. H. Lawrence

Christ himself is always going against the Holy Spirit. He must *insist* on the love, because it has been overlooked. But insistence on the one is not to be interpreted as negation of the other. In his purest moments, Christ knew that the Holy Spirit was both love and hate – not one only.

1012. To Douglas Clayton, 8 October 1915
Text: MS NCL; Unpublished.

1 Byron Villas – Vale of Health, Hampstead
8 Oct. 1915

Dear Clayton,

Here is another Lago di Garda sketch:[2] I am going on with them after an interval. Let me know if there is any news of your family: Pat or your mother,

Yours   D. H. Lawrence

1013. To S. S. Koteliansky, [10 October 1915]
Text: MS BL; Postmark; Hampstead 11 OCT 15; Zytaruk 50.

1 Byron Villas – Vale of Health
Sunday

---

[1] Cf. Matthew xii. 31–2.   [2] A note on the MS reads: 'Il Duro enclosed. No. V.'

Dear Kot,

Will you put down these names of subscribers, to whom I have *already* sent copies of the *Signature*

Lady Lewis[1] – The Grange – Rottingdean, Sussex. 5/-. Two copies

Mrs Poole, Buckless Hard, Beaulieu, Hants. 2/6.

Mrs Riviere, 10 Nottingham Terrace, York Gate, N.W. 2/6.

Tomorrow (Monday) at 8.0 oclock, we are to have a meeting at Fisher St., for discussion. Will you come? It would be nice if you were there at 7.30, as Frieda and I want to put up curtains. Then you could open us the door. We shall bring a lamp, and oil, and some sticks. Could you bring just a little bit of coal, enough just to make one fire? I'm afraid we can't carry so much.

Today we are going to Horne's to tea: but dread the Maisie.[2] I hope you don't mind my rudeness of the other evening,

Yours   D. H. Lawrence

1014. To S. S. Koteliansky, [11 October 1915]

Text: MS BL; Zytaruk 51.

1, Byron Villas, Vale-of-Health, Hampstead, London.

Monday

Dear Kot,

Thank you very much for making the room so nice, and the fire.

Did you not stay to the meeting, because you were busy, or too sorry about Katharine's brother,[3] or because you were offended with me. If you are offended, that is foolish. But you do as you like.

Three people took *Signature*s and paid me 2/6.

Percy Peacock Esq, 2 Leighton Gardens, Streatham, S.W.

A. P. Lewis Esq, 19 The Drive, Golders Green, N.W.

T. S. Knowlson Esq, Meloin Hall, Golders Green Rd, N.W.

I hope you will keep an account, of the money you have spent, for coal etc. Also I owe you for the teas of the other day. We will have a reckoning.

There is another meeting this day fortnight. I hope you will come to it.

D. H. Lawrence

The printer has not sent me my *Signature* proofs – I wonder why? I write to him now.[4]

---

[1] Wife of Sir George James Graham Lewis, Bt (1868–1927), head of Lewis and Lewis, solicitors, Holborn.   [2] Horne's wife.

[3] Katherine Mansfield's brother, Leslie Heron Beauchamp, was killed on 7 October 1915 (see *Journal of Katherine Mansfield*, p. 83). She was prostrated by the news.

[4] The letter has not been found.

1015. To J. B. Pinker, 11 October 1915
Text: MS Forster; Unpublished.

1 Byron Villas – Vale of Health, Hampstead
11 Oct 1915

Dear Pinker,

A friend[1] of mine has drawn up this letter, to send to Mudies'[2] – she will get it signed by subscribers – do you think this is all right? Tell me what you think.

Yours   D. H. Lawrence

1016. To Douglas Clayton, [12 October 1915]
Text: MS NCL; Unpublished.

1 Byron Villas – Vale of Health, Hampstead
[12 October 1915]

Dear Clayton,

Still another Italian Study.[3] When you send me the type, please tell me how many words. I must have a total of not less than 50,000 words in all. I, II, and III make about 20,000 I believe. I should think by now I have in all 40,000.

Yours   D. H. Lawrence

1017. To S. S. Koteliansky, [14 October 1915]
Text: MS BL; PC; Postmark, Hampstead 14 OCT 15; Zytaruk 52.

[1, Byron Villas, Vale-of-Health, Hampstead, London]
[14 October 1915]

Dear Kot

Please send a copy of the *Signature* to

A. Robert Mountsier Esq,[4] 36 Guildford St., Russell Square, W.C. but don't enter him as a subscriber.

Yours   D. H. Lawrence

---

[1] Unidentified; the letter has not been found.
[2] Mudie's Lending Library was the largest circulating library in London: it was founded in 1842 by Charles Edward Mudie (1818–90) and survived till 1937.
[3] Clayton's note identifies the sketch as 'Italians in Exile'. He also records: 'Rec/13th Oct 1915/Sent Ack[nowledgment]/formal and "Will send iv, v, & vi in a couple of days. Also no. of words."'
[4] Robert Mountsier, American journalist, who became DHL's literary agent in America during the period 1920–2.

Also send me, please, by post or by Murry, 4 copies of the *Signature*. Also please post one copy to C. P. Sanger,[1] 50 Oakley St, Chelsea, S.W. I have received his subscription.

DHL

1018. To Lady Cynthia Asquith, [14 October 1915]
Text: MS UT; Huxley 292–3.

1 Byron Villas – Vale of Health – Hampstead, N.W.
Thursday[2]

My dear Lady Cynthia,

I see you also are rather hostile to what I say, like everybody else. But I didn't write for 'average stupidity'. And the Lion and the Unicorn are at any rate better than 'the universe consists in a duality, but there is an initial element called polarity etc etc'. As for the *Rainbow*'s being cheerful,[3] I don't think we've any of us the right to be cheerful. I think it is a true novel, and a big one, and as for the other people, if they can't swallow it, let them spit it out. They are mostly impertinent (e.g. Eddie) if not insulting.[4] Thank goodness you weren't that – either of those.

I never said the war was a blasphemy.[5] I said 'the blasphemy of the war *is* –' just as one could say 'The blasphemy contained in Christianity is –' The war is not a blasphemy: but it contains a blasphemy.

Frieda has got a bad cold. Will you come here and see us. Come any time tomorrow, or later, if you will send a p.c. You come to the Hampstead Tube Station, walk up the hill and along past the pond to Jack Straw's Castle, drop down the heath on the path opposite the inn, at the bottom swerve round to the left right into the Vale, and there is Byron Villas before your eyes.

The only comfort, in the long run, is the truth, however bitter it be. As for the maimed and wounded and bereaved – even for them the only comfort is the utter truth – otherwise their souls are hollow.

I don't want the *Signature* to be a 'success', I want it only to rally together just a few passionate, vital, constructive people. But they must consent first

---

[1] Charles P. Sanger (1871–1930), lawyer and a close friend of Bertrand Russell.

[2] Dated with reference to Lady Cynthia's diary entry for Thursday, 14 October 1915: 'I got a rather sore letter from Lawrence. He is irritated by the criticisms of the *Signature* and *The Rainbow*' (Asquith, *Diaries* 88).

[3] Lady Cynthia's private comment on the novel was: 'a strange, bewildering, disturbing book' (Asquith, *Diaries* 86).

[4] The reference to Edward Marsh is puzzling in the light of DHL's comment in Letter 1008 on Marsh's opinion of *The Rainbow*; but see also letter 1041.

[5] See p. 407 n. 2.

to cast away all that is of no use – all that is wrong: And we have been, we are, colossally wrong, so much so, we daren't face it.

The *Signature* will get *worse*, not better, from the standpoint of comfortlessness with regard to the war etc. So please, if you think we had better *not* send it to any of your responsible addresses, let me know.

Mary Cannan is here for a day or two – no, she goes away at 2.0 oclock today.

But come and see us – Frieda wants to see you very much –

Yours   D. H. Lawrence

You can come here by bus – to Hampstead Heath terminus – then walk straight forward up the hill till you come to the finger pointing to the Vale of Health, at the very top. Bus is best.

1019. To J. B. Pinker, [17 October 1915]

Text: TMSC Lazarus; Unpublished.

1 Byron Villas, Vale-of-Health, Hampstead, London.
Sunday – Oct. 16.

Dear Pinker,

Will you be in on Wednesday or Thursday of this week? – if so, I should like to see you, particularly on Wednesday.

Yours sincerely   D. H. Lawrence

1020. To S. S. Koteliansky, [post 18 October 1915]

Text: MS BL; Zytaruk 53.

[1, Byron Villas, Vale-of-Health, Hampstead, London.]
[post 18 October 1915][1]

Please send Nos. 1 and 2 to Monroe, Calhouse, Ricketts and Tchaichowsky – No. 2 to Piccoli and de la Feld.

Miss Harriet Monroe, 543 Cass St., Chicago, U.S.A., 2/6.

Miss W. J. Calhouse, 1310 Astor St, Chicago, U.S.A., 2/6.

Raff. Piccoli, 2/6.

Count de la Feld, 2/6.

Chas. Ricketts Esq, Lansdowne House, Lansdowne Rd, Holland Park, W., 2/6.

Miss Vera Tchaichowsky, Seven Winds, Naphill, High Wycombe, Bucks., 2/6.

---

[1] Since DHL asks Kot to 'send Nos. 1 and 2' of *The Signature* to the subscribers listed, this letter must have been written after 18 October 1915 (when No. 2 was published).

Herbert Watson Esq, 13 Holly Mount, Hampstead N.W. (2 copies *already sent*) – 5/-¹

1021. To Douglas Clayton, 19 October 1915
Text: MS NCL; Unpublished.

1, Byron Villas, Vale-of-Health, Hampstead, London.
19 Oct 1915

Dear Clayton

I send you another sketch.² Will you fairly soon be letting me have some MS. for the publisher?

Yours   D. H. Lawrence

1022. To S. S. Koteliansky, 21 October 1915
Text: MS BL; Zytaruk 54.

1, Byron Villas, Vale-of-Health, Hampstead, London.
21 Oct. 1915

My dear Kot,

I send you back the letters, so that you can always check them.³ I am giving one weeks notice when I pay the rent today – so that we shall have the Fisher St rooms only for one week more, now. Everything comes to an end.

But there will be a meeting at Fisher St on Monday at 8·0 – come if you can.

I think we are going to try to get to America, Murry and I. I shall go down about a passport tomorrow. My soul is torn out of me now: I can't stop here any longer and acquiesce in this which is the spirit now: I would rather die. I will let you know what I am doing exactly, and perhaps you will come up and see us – I'll tell you when.

Yours   D. H. Lawrence

1023. To Katharine Clayton, [21 October 1915]
Text: MS NCL; PC; Postmark, Hampstead 21 OCT 15; Moore 371.

Hampstead
[21 October 1915]

Dear Mrs Clayton,

Thank Douglas for the MS. Perhaps you are right about the sketch: though

---

¹ Kot added the following names and addresses at the end of DHL's letter:
  Mrs H. Pulley, 41 Devonshire Street, Theobald's Road, W.C.
  Lieutenant Lewis, R.N.R., Armstrong College Hospital, Newcastle on Tyne.
² According to Clayton's note on the MS, the title was 'On the Road', which DHL changed to 'The Return Journey' for publication in *Twilight in Italy*.
³ i.e. letters from subscribers to *The Signature*. (Many of them are preserved among the Koteliansky Papers in the BL.)

I had not thought anybody – except you and Mrs Garnett – could recognize T[ony][1] – there are thousands of English women refugees in Italy and there was nothing that mattered. However, I can leave it as it is in the type – or just make another end. Certainly I don't want to hurt T. – Douglas, reminding me of her sketches, reminds me that she wanted to publish them as illustrations to her own letter-press:[2] but she could never write: she might like to put her pictures with my writing. I'll ask her. The publisher did say he would illustrate the book. It might be a good thing for her.

D. H. Lawrence

What is her address now? – I'll write her about the sketches.

1024. To Lady Cynthia Asquith, 21 October 1915
Text: MS UT; Huxley 261–2.

1, Byron Villas, Vale-of-Health, Hampstead, London.
21 Oct. 1915

My dear Lady Cynthia,

What can one say about your brother's death except that it *should not be*.[3] How long will the nations continue to empty the future: it is your own phrase: think what it means. I am sick in my soul, sick to death. But not angry any more, only unfathomably miserable about it all. I think I shall go away, to America if they will let me. In this war, in the whole spirit which we now maintain, I do *not* believe, I believe it is *wrong*, so awfully wrong, that it is like a great consuming fire that draws up all our souls in its draught. So if they will let me I shall go away soon, to America. Perhaps you will say it is cowardice: but how shall one submit to such ultimate wrong as this which we commit, now, England – and the other nations. If thine eye offend thee, pluck it out.[4] And I am English, and my Englishness is my very vision. But now I must go away, if my soul is sightless for ever. Let it then be blind, rather than commit the vast wickedness of acquiescence.

Don't think I am not sorry about your brother – it makes me tremble. Don't think I want to hurt you – or anybody – I would do anything rather.

---

[1] Antonia Almgren: see p. 139 n. 3. DHL used her as a model for an English 'blonde signora' in Part v, 'The Dance', of *Twilight in Italy*.

[2] She later published *Among Italian Peasants* (1919), which includes some of her own water colours.

[3] Hon. Yvo Charteris (1896–1915), Lady Cynthia's brother, was killed in action on 19 October at Loos after only three weeks in France. She wrote: 'For the first time I felt the full mad horror of the war' (Asquith, *Diaries* 90).

[4] Matthew xviii. 9 (A.V.).

But now I feel like a blind man who would put his eyes out rather than stand
witness to a colossal and deliberate horror.

Yours   D. H. Lawrence

I am so sorry for your mother, I can't bear it. If only the women would
get up and speak with authority.

1025. To Lady Ottoline Morrell, [24? October 1915]
Text: MS StaU; cited in Delany 156.

1, Byron Villas, Vale-of-Health, Hampstead, London.
Sunday[1]

My dear Lady Ottoline,

I am glad you liked the *Rainbow* better.[2] As for the *Signature*, I don't know
what to do.

When will you be in town? I should like to see you. Frieda and I will
come together, and we will all be friends. This has been a crisis which for
me is beginning to pass away, now. But I do not see that there is any hope
for this side of the world: perhaps for America, there is.

dunque – a rivederci   D. H. Lawrence

1026. To Else Jaffe, 26 October 1915
Text: MS Jeffrey; Unpublished.

1, Byron Villas, Vale-of-Health, Hampstead, London.
26 Oct. 1915

My dear Else,

I am so sorry about the death of Peter: his blue eyes so thoughtful like
flowers, and his piping voice.[3] It seems there must needs be a heaven for
the children, he would be so natural there. One can believe better in the
heaven than in this earth and this life now. It is a sacrilege to keep our
children in such a world: there is a heaven which is better for them: one
cannot help thinking it.

I am so sad about it all, that I must live in a heaven which is beyond. Here
the soul is shut out, and homeless. So it finds a place in an unearthly paradise.
Only the dead are happy with one, now. The living are like dark, oppressive

---

[1] The conjectural date takes account of the publication of *The Rainbow* (30 September 1915)
and the likelihood that two (of the three) issues of *Signature* had appeared.

[2] See p. 314 n. 4.

[3] Peter Jaffe (1907–15), Else's son by Otto Gross; see Green, *The Richthofen Sisters*, p. 59.

ghosts. To the living one has nothing to say, not one word. But with the dead one has converse, in the heaven. Life has become a shadow and a falsity, the kingdom of death endures and is real. What can one want on earth now? – We have no place now.

Somehow I think you will not be very sorrowful about Peter. For the dead there is no sorrow. But for the living children there is real anguish still to bear. You have one child at least at peace in your soul: eternal, beyond anxiety. For the rest, we must watch.

I feel so sad, I can't say any more. My love to all.

D. H. Lawrence

1027. To Douglas Clayton, 26 October 1915
Text: MS NCL; Unpublished.

1, Byron Villas, Vale-of-Health, Hampstead, London.
26 Oct. 1915

Dear Clayton,

Thank you for the MS.[1] I think it has all come now. It is all right – there has been no particular hurry. Now I can send the whole thing off to the publisher and settle with him.

I enclose cheque for the account. Is this all I owe you?

Yours   D. H. Lawrence

1028. To Harriet Monroe, 26 October 1915
Text: TMSC NWU; cited in Monroe 92.

1, Byron Villas, Vale-of-Health, Hampstead, London
26 Oct 1915

Dear Harriet Monroe

Thank you for the subscriptions to the *Signature*: the two numbers will be on their way to you by now.

Thank you also for the *Poetry* numbers.[2] I liked some things: Hermann Hagedorn, 'Fatherland', very much.[3] I should like to know him some time: my wife is German. I liked your 'Mountain Song':[4] also Nancy Campbell

---

[1] Presumably the last section of *Twilight in Italy* (see Letter 1021). Clayton noted on DHL's letter that he received, and sent a receipt for, £2 1. 0.

[2] DHL's subsequent references show that he must have received both the August and September 1915 issues of *Poetry*.

[3] Hermann Hagedorn (1882–1964), American author best known for his poems about President Theodore Roosevelt (1858–1919). 'Fatherland' appeared in *Poetry*, vi (September 1915), 280–1.   [4] In *Poetry*, vi (August 1915), 219.

'The Monkey'[1] – Agnes Lee is rather good.[2] I shall be glad when American verse develops away from European influence.

I send you the only poem I have done for a long while: and it was done in these last days. If you don't like it, wait awhile before sending it back.[3] I think I am coming to America.

I enclose also some of Anna Hepburn's poems.[4] Her book is just coming out, with Grant Richards. I think she is good. When you have to write to her, or return her manuscript, write to Mrs Hepburn, 49 Downshire Hill, Hampstead, N.W.

Probably I am coming to America. Probably, in a month's time, I shall be in New York. I hope, if I come, I can come to Chicago to see you all. Tell Amy, if you see her, I think of coming. I must see America: here the autumn of all life has set in, the fall: we are hardly more than the ghosts in the haze, we who stand apart from the flux of death. I must see America. I think one can feel hope there. I think that there the life comes up from the roots, crude but vital. Here the whole tree of life is dying. It is like being dead: the underworld. I must see America. I believe it is beginning, not ending.

I hope I shall see you all, you Chicago <i>Poetry</i> people, if I come.

Yours   D. H. Lawrence

1029. To J. B. Pinker, 26 October 1915
Text: MS Forster; Unpublished.

1, Byron Villas, Vale-of-Health, Hampstead, London.
26 Oct 1915

Dear Pinker,

I send you the rest of the Italian Studies. I have sent the complete MS. to Duckworth.

I am still thinking of going soon to America. I feel if I stay in Europe now I shall die. You must give me letters and things when I really am going.

Is there any more news from Doran?[5] Perhaps you will tell him when you write of my intention to go to New York.

[1] Ibid, vi (August 1915), 224.
[2] Agnes Lee (1868–1939), Chicago poet, author of <i>The Border of the Lake</i> (1910) and <i>The Sharing</i> (1914). Her poems 'Three Guests', 'At Dawn' and 'Long Distance Line' appeared in <i>Poetry</i>, vi (September 1915), 285.
[3] 'Resurrection' was published in <i>Poetry</i>, x (June 1917), 139.
[4] DHL might have sent Harriet Monroe the same set of poems by Anna Wickham that he gave to Edward Marsh; see Letter 1000.
[5] George H. Doran (1869–1956), American publisher. He published in U.S.A. for Hodder and Stoughton, and started his own firm in 1909. (Pinker was Arnold Bennett's agent and Doran his American publisher.)

You look saddened since I saw you last, and not so well. I hope things don't depress you too much.

Yours   D. H. Lawrence

1030. To S. S. Koteliansky, 29 October 1915
Text: MS BL; Zytaruk 55.

1, Byron Villas, Vale-of-Health, Hampstead, London.
29 Oct. 1915

My dear Kot,

I have 2/6 from this man – send him the 3 numbers on Monday:

Professor H. O. Meredith, 55 Bryansburn Rd, Bangor, Co. Down, Ireland.

You remember that the tenancy of 12 Fisher St. ends tomorrow: Can you take away all the *Signatures* to the Law Bureau: also let Narodiczky know that he must send the new number to *you*.

When we have got something a bit settled, we will have an evening together. At present all is turmoil and unrest.

Yours   D. H. Lawrence

I should also be *very much* obliged if you could carry round to the Bureau the curtains and the carpet out of Fisher St. Then I will come and fetch them.

1031. To Lady Cynthia Asquith, 29 October 1915
Text: MS UT; Huxley 263.

1, Byron Villas, Vale-of-Health, Hampstead, London.
29 Oct. 1915

My dear Lady Cynthia,

I got Frieda's passport-form handed in today – C H G Campbell vouched it. It is made out for U·S·A, like mine: Frieda Lawrence. If you didn't write to your friend in the Foreign Office,[1] I should be so grateful if you would do so. They may keep Frieda hanging round: her 'born at Metz' may worry them. And I haven't got my passport yet. You know we are perfectly straight. Why should they keep us hanging round for ever.

Your showing me that detestable Selfridge sketch of yourself reminds me that I have done a rather good word-sketch of you: in a story.[2] *I* think it

---

[1] Unidentified.

[2] The 'sketch' of Lady Cynthia may have been the drawing by Sargent which she too found offensive: 'I think the one of me presents the foulest woman I have ever seen' (Asquith, *Diaries* 174). DHL's story was 'The Thimble': see p. 420 n. 1.

good. When the story is finished, and I've got it typed, I'll give you the MS. to see what you think of your likeness.

I hope it isn't a nuisance, this our bothering you about passports. Come and see us when you can, you and Herbert Asquith.

Yours   D. H. Lawrence

I bet you my sketch of you, in words, is better than Sargent or Watts in paint.[1]

1032. To J. B. Pinker, 29 October 1915

Text: MS Forster; Unpublished.

1, Byron Villas, Vale-of-Health, Hampstead, London.
29 Oct. 1915

Dear Pinker,

I have your letter about Doran.[2] It doesn't seem to me that it is any use altering the *Rainbow* for the Americans. Curse them, what good is it to them, altered or not. Don't you think it is best to leave it – not to publish in America at all?

The book of Italian Studies is pretty well complete. America might like it as a volume.

The doctor says I mustn't go to New York for the winter. I think I shall go to the north of Spain. I have applied for a passport.

Tomorrow I will send you the first of a set of more cheerful and not at all improper stories[3] – though whether they are ideal for the *Strand Magazine* I cannot tell.

Yours   D. H. Lawrence

---

[1] John Singer Sargent (1856–1925); George Frederic Watts (1817–1904). (Lady Cynthia felt 'uneasy' at the prospect of a word-sketch of herself by DHL: she was 'dreading a minute "belly" analysis'. Asquith, *Diaries* 94; see also p. 89.)

[2] On 14 October 1915 Doran informed Pinker by cable of his reluctance to publish the *Rainbow*: 'Cannot possibly publish Lawrence's Rainbow in form submitted. Am legally advised distribution would be forbidden' (MS NYPL). He then wrote to Pinker on 22 October: 'Just to set your mind at rest on one point, in response to your cable of the twentieth, I am taking steps properly to copyright Lawrence's THE RAINBOW in the United States.

I am having a very careful study made of the possibility of making changes in the book. Frankly, the publication seems to me to be hopeless.

If I have any more encouraging word, I will cable you' (MS NYPL).

[3] Unidentified.

1033. To Lady Cynthia Asquith, 30 October 1915
Text: MS UT; Huxley 264–5.

1, Byron Villas, Vale-of-Health, Hampstead, London.
30 Oct 1915

My dear Lady Cynthia,

This is the story: I don't know what you'll think of it.[1] The fact of resurrection, in this life, is all in all to me now. I don't know what the story is like, as a story. I don't want to read it over: not yet. Send it back to me soon, will you, and tell me what you think of it. Then I can see if it is fit to be typed and offered to an editor: though who will print it, God knows. If you like – if you want the MS., when I have got typed copies, I will give it you. The fact of resurrection is everything, now: whether we dead can rise from the dead, and love, and live, in a new life, here.

I tremble very much in front of this. If it could come to pass, one would give anything. If it cannot come to pass, one must go away: you and your husband also. Having known this death, one cannot remain in death. That were a profanity. One must go away.

If the war could but end this winter, we might rise to life again, here in this our world. If it sets in for another year, all is lost. One should give anything now, give the Germans England and the whole Empire, if they want it, so we may save the hope of a resurrection from the dead, we English, all Europe. What is the whole Empire and Kingdom, save the thimble in my story. If we could but bring our souls through, to life.

So I keep suspended the thought of going away. The passports are for U.S.A, I mean the applications. Let them stand at that. If I go, I will go to America. If I go, I will see about that novel: the publisher keeps on cabling.[2] But I hope not to go.

Yet will you write to your friend and ask him will he see our passports for U.S.A. through, so I may not sit any more hours in that shed at the Foreign Office. Then I am equipped to go, if we must go.

---

[1] Lady Cynthia received 'The Thimble' on 31 October 1915. Her impression was '[It] is extremely well written, I think, though the symbolism of the thimble is somewhat obscure. I *was* amused to see the "word picture" of me. He has quite gratuitously put in the large feet. I think some of his character hints are damnably good. He has kept fairly close to the model in the circumstances' (Asquith, *Diaries* 95). The story was published in New York in *Seven Arts*, i (March 1917), 435–48. It was later re-written and published as 'The Ladybird' in the collection of stories, *The Ladybird* (Secker, 1923; published by Seltzer in New York as *The Captain's Doll*, 1923).

[2] Probably a reference to Doran who, on 27 October 1915, cabled Pinker: 'Can arrange that Huebsch publish *Rainbow*. Because precarious conditions cannot secure royalty advance. Shall I conclude' (MS NYPL). A letter of 12 November 1915 (MS NYPL) from Doran to Pinker confirms that Huebsch and Doran reached an agreement; Huebsch published an expurgated version of the novel in New York on 30 November 1915.

Let us all now conquer death and this rushing on death, if we can. Let us set hard against the war, and also against the anarchy, the breaking of all unity which is going on everywhere: this false democracy. I think Herbert Asquith is good for a new life, now, a new reality. That makes me at once not want to leave England.

Oh God, what tender timid hopes one has – then the cursed blackening frost.

Frieda sends her love.

D. H. Lawrence

1034. To Lady Cynthia Asquith, 2 November 1915
Text: MS UT; Huxley 265–8.

The Turning Back[1]

There has been so much noise
So much bleeding and shouting and dying
So much clamour of death.

There are so many dead
So many ghosts among us:
Between me and thee, so many ghosts of the slain.

Be still then, and let be.
How long shall we strike through the immutable
    ghosts of the slain?
How long shall we shriek and shout across the
    silence of ghosts?

Hush, let the silence be
For a moment over us,
Perfect and utter stillness within and without

Oh listen to the stillness of the ghosts
That press noiselessly about us, for a place
Wherein to rest, wherein to lie at peace.

Page 1 of the MS, containing parts i and ii of the poem, is missing. The text of these parts is taken from a holograph version found in a notebook and printed by David Farmer in 'D. H. Lawrence's "The Turning Back": The Text and Its Genesis in Correspondence', *DHL Review*, v (Summer 1972), 121–31. According to Farmer, the original title, 'A Plea for Peace', was changed by DHL to 'The Turning Back'. See Farmer's article for a comprehensive discussion of the poem, its publication history and relation to DHL's letters.

ii

But I have enemies, and something they want,
Houses and land and having, chattels and goods!
Say they may have it all, I give it them

They must be lords and masters over me
Bidding my outgoing and my incoming?
Say they may have it so, I yield it them.

They want my life, they want me to be dead?
Tell them they are mistaken, it is not true,
They do not want my life, me to be dead.

Yes, still they want my life, me to be dead.
Tell them to come and see that they are mistaken.
But if in the end they want it, let them take it.

For as for me, I have no enemies.
I am older than they, so I can understand
That they do evil, seeing I have done so ill.

iii

We have gone too far, oh very much too far;
Only attend to the noiseless multitudes
Of ghosts that throng about our muffled hearts.

Only behold the ghosts, the ghosts of the slain,
Behold them homeless and houseless, without complaint
Of their patient waiting upon us, the throng of the ghosts.

And say, what matters any more, what matters
Save the cold ghosts that homeless flock about
Our serried hearts, drifting without a place?

What matters any more, but only love?
There's only love that matters any more.
There's only love, the rest is all outspent.

Let us receive our ghosts, and give them place,
Open the ranks, and let them in our hearts,
And lay them deep in love, lay them to sleep.

The foe can take our goods, and homes and land,
Also the lives that still he may require,
But leave us still to love, still leave us love.

Leave us to take our ghosts into our hearts,
To lap them round with love, and lay them by
To sleep at last in immemorial love.

We let the weapons slip from out our hands,
We loose our grip, and we unstrain our eyes,
We let our souls be pure and vulnerable.

We cover the houseless dead, so they sleep in
    peace,
We yield the enemy his last demands
So he too may be healed, be soothed to peace.

For now the hosts of homeless ghosts do throng
Too many about us, so we wander about
Blind with the gossamer of prevalent death.

But let us free our eyes, and look beyond
This serried ecstasy of prevalent death,
And pass beyond, with the foe and the homeless
    ghosts.

Let us rise up, and go from out this grey
Last twilight of the gods, to find again
The lost Hesperides where love is pure.

For we have gone too far, oh much too far
Towards the darkness and the shadow of death;
Let us turn back, lest we should all be lost

Let us go back now, though we give up all
The treasure and the vaunt we ever had,
Let us go back, the only way is love.

Hampstead.
2 Nov. 1915.

My dear Lady Cynthia,

I will answer you straight away about the 'downing tools'. First of all I send you the poem, which might help to convince you.[1] You say that the war does not prevent *personal* life from going on, that the individual can still love and be complete. It isn't true. The one quality of love is that it universalises the individual. If I love, then I am extended over all people, but particularly over my own nation. It is an extending in concentric waves over all people. This is the process of love. And if I love, I, the individual, then necessarily the love extends from me to my nearest neighbour, and outwards, and outwards, till it loses itself in vast distance. This *is* love, there is no love but this. So that if I love, the love must beat upon my neighbours, till they too live in the spirit of the love, and so on, further and further. And how can this be, in war, when the spirit is against love.

The spirit of war is, that I am a unit, a single entity that has no *intrinsic* reference to the rest: the reference is extrinsic, a question of living, not of *being*. In war, in my *being* I am a detached entity, and every one of my actions is an act of further detaching my own single entity from all the rest.

If I love, then, I am in direct opposition to the principle of war. If war prevails, I do not love. If love prevails, there is no war. War is a great and necessary disintegrating autumnal process. Love is the great creative process, like Spring, the making an integral[2] unity out of many disintegrated factors. We have had enough of the disintegrating process. If it goes on any further, we shall so thoroughly have destroyed the unifying force from among us, we shall have become each one of us so completely a separate entity, that the whole will be an amorphous heap, like sand, sterile, hopeless, useless, like a dead tree. This is true, and it is so great a danger, that one almost goes mad, facing it.

That is why I almost went away, out of the country: I may still have to go: because in myself I can never agree to the complete disintegration, never stand witness to it, never.

Then the Prussian rule. The Prussian rule would be an external evil. The disintegrating process of the war has become an internal evil, so vast as to

---

[1] DHL's letter and poem did not convince Lady Cynthia: '... poor Lawrence's last extraordinary letter about the war in which, with the assistance of a poem, he tries to convince me that we ought to "down tools". He appears to think that *I* could stop the war, if only I really wanted to! He writes wildly about the disintegrating process of war, etc., and makes rather arbitrary distinctions between *in*trinsic and *ex*trinsic evil – all eloquent enough, but I'm afraid his feet quite leave the ground' (Asquith, *Diaries* 95).
[2] integral] complex

be almost unthinkable, so nearly overwhelming us, that we stand on the very brink of oblivion. Better *anything* than the utter disintegration. And it is *England* who is the determining factor for Europe: if England goes, then Europe goes: for we are at this time the vital core of the whole organism. Let the leaves perish, but let the tree stand, living and bare. For the tree, the living organism of the soul of Europe is good, only the external forms and growths are bad. Let all the leaves fall, and many branches. But the quick of the tree must not perish. There are unrevealed buds which can come forward into another epoch of civilisation, if only we can shed this dead form and be strong in the spirit of love and creation.

Besides, Germany, Prussia, is not evil through and through. Her mood is now *evil*. But we reap what we have sowed. It is as with a child: if with a sullen, evil soul one provokes an evil mood in the child, there is destruction. But no child is all evil. And Germany is the child of Europe: and senile Europe, with her conventions and arbitrary rules of conduct and life and very being, has provoked Germany into a purely destructive mood. If a mother does this to a child – and it often happens – is she to go on till the child is killed or broken, so that the mother have her way? – Is she not rather, at a certain point, to yield to the paroxysm of the child, which passes away *swiftly* when the opposition is removed? And if Prussia for a time imposes her rule on us, let us bear it, as a mother temporarily bears the ugly tyranny of the child, trusting in the ultimate good. The good will not be long in coming, all over Europe, if we can but trust it within ourselves. (This is not yielding to the child – this is knowing beyond the child's knowledge.)

I very much want you to tell me what you think, because it is a question for the *women* of the land now to decide: the men will never see it. I don't know one single man who would give the faintest response to this. But I still have some hope of the women: they should *know* that only love matters, now; that further destruction only means death, universal death, disintegration.

D. H. Lawrence

1035. To Hugh Meredith, 2 November 1915

Text: MS Putt; Postmark, Hampstead 3 NOV 15; Moore 373–4.

1, Byron Villas, Vale-of-Health, Hampstead, London.
2 Nov 1915

Dear Meredith,

Forster sent me your poems.[1] Some of them I like very much.

I hope he didn't bore you and lecture you, E.M. He is a silly. We were laughing about you, that was all.

---

[1] Perhaps a copy of *Week-Day Poems* (1911) together with others in MS.

I am bored by coherent thought. Its very coherence is a dead shell. But we must help the living impulse that is within the shell. The shell is being smashed.

Like you in your poems, I believe an end is coming: the war, a plague, a fire, God knows what. But the end is taking place: the beginning of the end has set in, and the process won't be slow. I am very much frightened, but hopeful – a grain of hope yet.

One has oneself a fixed conscious entity, a self, which one has to smash. We are all like tortoises who have to smash their shells and creep forth tender and overvulnerable, but alive.

It is no good being sexual. That is only a form of the same static consciousness. Sex is not living till it is unconscious: and it never becomes unconscious by attending to sex. One has to face the whole of ones conscious self, and smash that. This London of yours is your own overcumbered material consciousness.

It is a great struggle now, whether the whole tree of life dies now, in Europe, and crumbles down to dust: whether we are reduced to a mass of amorphous entities, sands of the desert. But that is the most wretched form of undying death. One must try to save the quick, to send up the new shoots of a new era: a great, utter revolution, and the dawn of a new historical epoch: either that, or the vast amorphous dust. – I can make nothing of the men, they are all dead. E.M. is dead und schon verweste.[1] Perhaps the women – God knows, it is enough to send one mad.

Yours   D. H. Lawrence

1036. To J. B. Pinker, 2 November 1915
Text: MS Forster; cited in Delany 157.

1, Byron Villas – Vale of Health – Hampstead
2 Nov. 1915

Dear Pinker,

I send you a story:[2] probably you can sell it, I don't know. Will you please have it typed for me, and send me back the M.S. here, as soon as it is done.

Who is Hübsch – Huebsch?[3] – you know it is the German for 'pretty'? Is he somebody disreputable, or what? And why will he publish the novel if Doran wont?

I will come and see you again soon. I will also do some more stories, even more suitable for the family,

Yours   D. H. Lawrence

[1] 'and already mouldered' ['verwest'].
[2] Probably 'The Thimble'. See p. 420 n. 1.
[3] Benjamin W. Huebsch (1876–1964) was a New York publisher. He began publishing books under his own imprint and also published *Freeman* (a weekly), 1920–4. His firm merged with the Viking Press in 1925. (See p. 420 n. 2.)

1037. To Harold Monro, 3 November 1915
Text: MS IEduc; Unpublished.

1, Byron Villas, Vale-of-Health, Hampstead, London.

3 Nov. 1915

Dear Monro,

Thank you for your letter about the chap-book.[1] I very much doubt whether I have a sufficient number of poems for your purpose: and I doubt even more whether you would think even those I have are good poems. Still, I should have been pleased to send them along had they been enough in bulk.

Yours Sincerely   D. H. Lawrence

1038. To S. S. Koteliansky, [4 November 1915]
Text: MS BL; Postmark, Hampstead 4 NOV 15; Zytaruk 56.

[1, Byron Villas, Vale-of-Health, Hampstead, London.]

[4 November 1915]

My dear Kot,

Send *Signatures* to these two people, will you? – I expect we shall see you at Brett's studio tomorrow.[2]

Thanks for p. o's last night.

D. H. Lawrence

1039. To Lady Ottoline Morrell, [5 November 1915]
Text: MS UT; cited in Morrell, *Nation and Athenaeum*, xlvii. 860.

1, Byron Villas, Vale-of-Health, Hampstead, London.

Friday[3]

My dear Lady Ottoline,

We should like to come to Garsington on Monday, and stay till Thursday. On Friday Frieda must go to the dentist.

[1] The last issue of *Poetry and Drama*, in December 1914, announced a forthcoming series of 'chapbooks and broadsides'. Monro – who had taken over Claud Lovat Fraser's Flying Fame Press – hoped to make the work of contemporary poets available in a cheap format: '"Anyone who will is supposed to be able to buy them. They're not the final form of production, but something between the periodical and the collected volume"' (Joy Grant, *Harold Monro and the Poetry Bookshop*, 1967, p. 109). Two chapbooks were issued in December 1915: Richard Aldington's *Images* and F. S. Flint's *Cadences*; each cost 8d.

[2] Hon. Dorothy Eugenie Brett (1883–1977), painter, daughter of Reginald Baliol Brett, 2nd Viscount Esher, sister of the Ranee of Sarawak. Studied at the Slade School of Art, London. Friend of Mark Gertler, Lady Ottoline Morrell, Middleton Murry, Katherine Mansfield, Beatrice Campbell and Virginia Woolf. Travelled in 1924 with DHL to New Mexico, where she made her home until her death. Her poignant memoir of DHL provides a detailed account of their relations: *Lawrence and Brett: A Friendship* (1933); reissued with an 'Epilogue' in 1974. Her portrait of DHL is in the National Portrait Gallery. When she met DHL, she had a studio in Earls Court Road. (For obituary see *Times*, 6 September 1977.)

[3] Dated with reference to DHL's visit to Garsington on Monday, 8 November 1915.

I haven't asked the Murry's, because, I think I would rather we came alone. But if you have asked them, separately, to come with us, very good.

Today I have got our passports. I feel as if really we were going to America – and *soon*. We may go to Florida for this winter. I must see if I can get some money, that is all. But I can, I think, all right.

Perhaps you would not mind sending a letter or a wire, to tell us which train it would be most convenient to you, for us to come by: because of the dog-cart. I don't mind whether we come to Oxford or Wheatley, nor at what time: just as suits you and the farm-work best.

I feel awfully queer and trembling in my spirit, because I am going away from the land and the nation I have belonged to: departing, emigrating, changing the land of my soul as well as my mere domicile. It is rather terrible, a form of death. But I feel as if it were my fate, I must: to live.

Yours   D. H. Lawrence

1040. To S. S. Koteliansky, [6 November 1915]

Text: MS BL; PC; Postmark, [...]; Zytaruk 56.

[1, Byron Villas, Vale-of-Health, Hampstead, London.]

My dear Kot,   [6 November 1915][1]

How is your head this morning?

Would you go round to Wheeler,[2] at 12 Fisher St, and ask him, will he buy the whole of the *Signature* furniture, as it stands? – and take what he will give. We paid about £3··5··0 for it.

D. H. Lawrence

1041. To Edward Marsh, 6 November 1915

Text: MS NYPL; Huxley 270.

1, Byron Villas, Vale-of-Health, Hampstead, London.

6 Nov. 1915.

My dear Eddie,

You jeered rather at *The Rainbow*, but notwithstanding, it is a big book, and one of the important novels in the language. I tell you, who know. Now the magistrates have suppressed the sale of the book, and ordered Methuen to deliver up all copies in existence.[3]

---

[1] Dated with reference to Brett's party on 5 November 1915; see Letter 1038.

[2] Probably the landlord at 12 Fisher Street.

[3] The Bow Street magistrate's warrant to seize all copies of *The Rainbow* was served on the publishers Methuen and Co. on 3 November 1915, but DHL was not informed. He learned of the suppression from W. L. George; see Letter 1057. For a detailed analysis of the legal aspects of the case, see Delavenay, *D. H. Lawrence: The Man and His Work*, pp. 235–42.

And I am so sick, in body and soul, that if I don't go away I shall die. A man said we could live on his little estate in Florida.[1] I want you, if you can, to give me a little money to go with: if you can, easily that is. God knows I don't want to mulct you. I'll give it you back if ever I have any money: I owe you £10 already. And I will give you full and final possession of some poems, when I have any you like. And I will ask you not to send me any part in the proceeds of *Georgian Poetry*. – Because if I can get a little money now, so that my wife and I can go away, I will work at anything over there. But I feel so sick, I shall never be able to get through a winter here.

Yours   D. H. Lawrence

1042. To J. B. Pinker, 6 November 1915
Text: MS UT; Huxley 269–70.

1, Byron Villas, Vale-of-Health, Hampstead, London.
6 Nov. 1915

Dear Pinker,

I had heard yesterday about the magistrates and the *Rainbow*. I am not very much moved: am beyond that by now. I only curse them all, body and soul, root, branch and leaf, to eternal damnation.

As for Hübsch, if you think it is a good and wise proceeding for him to publish the book in America, then let him publish it. But please tell him all that has happened here.

I am away from Monday to Thursday of next week. If there is anything to write to me, address me at

Garsington Manor, Near Oxford.

I will come and see you on Friday, if that suits you. Perhaps you will offer me that lunch then: otherwise one day early the next week.

I hope to be going away in about a fortnights time: to America: there is a man who more or less offers us a cottage in Florida: but nothing is settled yet. We have got passports. It is the end of my writing for England. I will try to change my public.

Yours   D. H. Lawrence

[1] Perhaps the 'Mr. Keen' mentioned in Letter 1062. Keen was an American friend of Dollie Radford's (see Nehls, i. 579 nn. 197, 202). See Letter 1044.

1043. To J. B. Pinker, 6 November 1915
Text: MS UNYB; cited in Moore, *Intelligent Heart* 199.

1, Byron Villas, Vale-of-Health, Hampstead, London.
6 Nov. 1915

Dear Pinker,

On second thoughts, I want to see you at once: on Monday morning at 11.30, if you are in. Will you ring up Mrs Dollie Radford, 32 Well Walk, Hampstead, between 10.0 and 11.0 on Monday morning, leaving a message for me, to say whether you will be in or not. Then I will come down. I am going away from Paddington at 2.30 in the afternoon.

But we must do something about this suppression business.[1] I must move a body of people, we must get it reversed.

Yours   D. H. Lawrence

1044. To Dollie Radford, 6 November 1915
Text: MS UN; Postmark, Hampstead 6 NOV 15; Nehls, i. 328.

1, Byron Villas, Vale-of-Health, Hampstead, London.
6 Nov. 1915.

My dear Dollie,

I am wondering if you have written to the man about Florida. Do, I want so much to go.

Here's another news: the authorities have suppressed the sale of *The Rainbow*, and Methuen's are under orders of the magistrate to deliver up all existing copies. Isn't this monstrous? We must do something about it. We must get a body of people to have the thing altered. Do you know what we can do? What about Bernard Shaw? I feel most awfully sick about it.

We are going on Monday to stay with Lady Ottoline Morrell
at Garsington Manor Nr. Oxford.

We shall be there till Thursday, when we are home again. My dear Dollie, this world is hellish.

My regards to Maitland – I hope he is better.

Yours   D. H. Lawrence

---

[1] Methuen and Co. were soon to make their position clear to Pinker (in a misdated letter, MS NYPL): 'It would we think, be ridiculous for us to make a public protest about a book which contains such passages. Certainly let the author do what he can. I think that as he is a member of the Authors' Society, he might persuade the society to take the matter up.' (For another letter from Methuen and Co. regarding the prosecution of *The Rainbow*, see those to G. H. Thring, Secretary of the Society of Authors, printed in *TLS*, 27 February 1969.)

1045. To Lady Cynthia Asquith, [9 November 1915]
Text: MS UT; Huxley 270–2.

Garsington Manor, Oxford
Tuesday.[1]

My dear Lady Cynthia.

I am staying here with the Ottoline till Thursday.

Your letter makes me sad. Believe me, my feet are more sure upon the earth than you will allow[2] – given that the earth is a living body, not a dead fact.

More tiresomeness is that a magistrate[3] has suppressed the sale of *The Rainbow*, and Methuens are under orders to deliver up all existing copies. This is most irritating. Some interfering person goes to a police magistrate and says: 'this book is indecent, listen here!' Then the police magistrate says: 'By jove, we'll stop that!' Then the thing is suppressed. But I think it is possible to have the decision reversed. If it is possible, and you and Herbert Asquith can help, would you do so? You know quite well the book is not indecent: though I heard of you saying to a man that it was like the second story in the *Prussian Officer*, only much *worse*.[4] Still, one easily says those things. But I never quite know where you stand: whether the[5] inner things, the abstract right as you call it, is important to you, or only a rather titillating excursus. I suppose you've got to arrange your life between the two: it is your belief – pragmatistic. I suppose it has to be so, since the world is as it is, and you must live in the world. But if you can help me about the *Rainbow*, I shall ask you to do so, because I know that the pure truth *does* matter to you, beyond the relative, immediate truths of fact.

We have got our passports: thank you very much.

When I drive across this country, with the autumn falling and rustling to pieces, I am so sad, for my country, for this great wave of civilisation, 2000 years, which is now collapsing, that it is hard to live. So much beauty and pathos of old things passing away and no new things coming: this house of the Ottolines – It is England – my God, it breaks my soul – this England, these shafted windows, the elm-trees, the blue distance – the past, the great past, crumbling down, breaking down, not under the force of the coming

---

[1] Dated with reference to DHL's stay at Garsington; see Letter 1042.

[2] DHL's remark may indicate that at least one phrase from Lady Cynthia's diary-entry about his views on the war found its way into her reply; see p. 424 n. 1.

[3] a magistrate] the magistrates

[4] The story is 'The Thorn in the Flesh'. According to Lady Cynthia's diary 12 November 1915, her comment (made to Lord Basil Blackwood) was passed on by J. M. Murry, 'that little sneak' (Asquith, *Diaries* 98).   [5] whether the] whether you think the

buds, but under the weight of many exhausted, lovely yellow leaves, that
drift over the lawn and over the pond, like the soldiers, passing away, into
winter and the darkness of winter – no, I can't bear it. For the winter
stretches ahead, where all vision is lost and all memory dies out.

It has been 2000 years, the spring and summer of our era. What then will
the winter be? No I cant bear it, I can't let it go. Yet who can stop the autumn
from falling to pieces, when November has come in. It is almost better to
be dead, than to see this awful process finally strangling us to oblivion, like
the leaves off the trees.

I want to go to America, to Florida, as soon as I can: as soon as I have
enough money to cross, with Frieda. My life is ended here: I must go as
a seed that falls into new ground. But this, this England, these elm trees,
the grey wind with yellow leaves – it is so awful, the being gone from it
altogether, one must be blind henceforth. But better have a quick of hope
in the soul, than all the beauty that fills the eyes.

It sounds very rhapsodic: it is this old house, the beautiful shafted
windows, the grey gate-pillars under the elm trees: really, I can't bear it:
the past, the past, the falling, perishing, crumbling past, so great, so
magnificent.

Come and see us when you are in town. I don't think we shall be here
very much longer. My life now is one repeated, tortured Vale! Vale! Vale!

Please burn this over-loose letter.

D. H. Lawrence

1046. To Edward Marsh, [10 November 1915]
Text: MS NYPL; Huxley 272–3.

Garsington Manor, Oxford
Wednesday[1]

My dear Eddie,

Thank you very much for your letter. Oh no, I only hoped you might
lend me £10 or £15. Twenty pounds is the outside of hope. You see I have
about £40: – about £25 for passages would leave none for the necessaries
I must buy here. Then we must have £10 each, to be allowed to land in
New York. But with £20, I think – I am sure – I shall be able to manage.
And I will give it you back, God willing, before many months are past.[2]
Thank you very much indeed for being so kind.

[1] Dated with reference to DHL's stay at Garsington.
[2] The debt was repaid seven years later as shown in a letter to Marsh, 18 September 1922.

As for the novel, I am not surprised. Only the most horrible feeling of hopelessness has come over me lately – I feel as if the whole thing were coming to an end – the whole of England, of the Christian era: as if ours was the age only of Decline and Fall. It almost makes one die. I cannot bear it – this England, this past.

I am staying with Lady Ottoline till tomorrow. Here one feels the real England – this old house, this countryside – so poignantly, I wonder if ever I shall have strength to drag my feet over the next length of journey. It isn't my novel that hurts me – it's the hopelessness of the world.

Yours D. H. Lawrence

1047. To Herbert Thring, 11 November 1915
Text: MS BL; Unpublished.

1, Byron Villas, Vale-of-Health, Hampstead, London.
11 Nov. 1915

Dear Sir,

Thank you for your letter. I wish you would propose me as a member of the Authors Society.[1] I will send the fee as soon as I hear from you.

Yours faithfully D. H. Lawrence

1048. To Edward Marsh, 11 November 1915
Text: MS NYPL; Huxley 276.

1, Byron Villas, Vale-of-Health, Hampstead, London.
11 Nov. 1915

My dear Eddie,

Thank you very much for the letter and the twenty pounds. That was a nice letter from you. Only I feel so sad, at the present time, that I cannot be optimistic. I feel as if some hope were broken in my chest, that has never been broken before.

I will write to you as we have any definite plans: it will probably be quite soon.

Yours D. H. Lawrence

[1] The Incorporated Society of Authors, Playwrights and Composers. Its President was Thomas Hardy. It published a monthly journal called the *Author*, devoted to the protection and maintenance of literary property. DHL was not elected a member until 6 December 1915. George Herbert Thring (1859–1941), a solicitor and expert on the law of copyright, was Secretary to the Society, 1892–1930. He had taken the initiative in inviting DHL to join the Society after W. L. George had requested that it should take up DHL's case (*TLS*, 27 February 1969, p. 216).

1049. To Lady Ottoline Morrell, [11 November 1915]
Text: TMSC NWU; Morrell, *Nation and Athenaeum*, xlvii. 860.

1, Byron Villas, Vale-of-Health, Hampstead, London.
Thursday.¹

My dear Lady Ottoline,

I arrived home safely, in the rain, with my Hessians and my flowers. London *does* strike a blow at the heart, I must say: tonight, in a black rain out of doors, and a tube full of spectral, decayed people. How much better and more beautiful the country is: you are very wise to be at Garsington.

Frieda is delighted with the flowers, and my wonderful boots, and with the thought of the embroidery. What queer things to come home with! I hope the Hessians are seven-leagued boots that will carry me to the ends of the earth: to the Blessed Isles to the undiscovered lands whose fruits are all unknown to us.

I am very glad I came down: it will always be a sort of last vision of England to me, the beauty of England, the wonder of this terrible autumn: when we set the irises above the pond, in the stillness and the wetness.

How cruel it is that the world should so have come to an end, this world, our world, whilst we still live in it, that we must either die or go away dispossessed, exiled in body and spirit.

Remember me to Julian and Philip. I hope all the flowers will grow and be beautiful. We shall see you again soon.

D. H. Lawrence

1050. To Herbert Thring, 13 November 1915
Text: MS BL; John Carter, 'The Rainbow Prosecution', *TLS*, 27 February 1969, p. 216.

1, Byron Villas, Vale-of-Health, Hampstead, London.
13 Nov. 1915

Dear Sir,

I should like your Committee to consider the suppression of my novel, *The Rainbow*. I'm afraid there aren't any details. The book came out on the first day of October. On the 5th of November Methuens were notified by the police that the sale was suppressed, and that all existing copies must lie untouched. I don't know any more.

But my agent,

J B Pinker, Talbot House, Arundel St, Strand

would tell you everything if you would ring him up on the telephone.²

¹ DHL returned from Garsington on 11 November 1915.
² See Pinker's letter to Herbert Thring, 16 November 1915, printed in *TLS*, 27 February 1969, p. 216.

For the rest, I think a letter is to be sent to the papers, in protest, signed by Walter de la Mare, E. M. Forster, John Middleton Murry, J. D. Beresford, Hugh Walpole, and Gilbert Cannan.[1]

Thank you very much for taking this interest in the book, which I hope indeed was written in purity of spirit.

Yours truly   D. H. Lawrence

1051. To Lady Ottoline Morrell, [15 November 1915]
Text: MS UT; Postmark, Hampstead 15 NOV 15; Moore 380.

1, Byron Villas, Vale-of-Health, Hampstead, London.
Monday.

My dear Ottoline,

I am posting to you a pack of MS, including that of *The Rainbow*. If you don't want it you can have it burnt: otherwise it might lie at Garsington till it is worth the selling. I don't want to see it any more.

We are getting ready to go. I have made all inquiries, preparatory to booking, to sail on the 24th of this month. We shall have to hurry to get things done. We shall go next Tuesday to see my people in Derbyshire, and on from there to Liverpool the next day. I feel very strange and abstracted, preparing to go.

I am writing to Russell to ask him if he will come to see us this week.[2]

Cynthia Asquith came up with her husband:[3] she says we ought not to go. She and he are very absent from each other.

I shall always look to you as being a sort of spiritual home in England, for me, for us. It makes it very much easier to go, that you are there, to be in connection with us, wherever we are, you on this shore, we on that, and the true connection between us.

You will come and see us. Frieda sends her love, with mine.

D. H. Lawrence

I owe you 10/- and Eva 6d – thank Eva for me, for posting my letters[4] – I am sending you such a lot of MS. I hope you wont mind.

I rather like Clive Bell – not deeply.[5] He says it is tragic that you can never

[1] No such letter was published.   [2] See Letter 1052.

[3] See Lady Cynthia's account of this visit (on 12 November) in Asquith, *Diaries* 97–8.

[4] Eva was Lady Ottoline's maid.

[5] Arthur Clive Howard Bell (1881–1964), art critic and writer; his book *Art* (1914), greatly influenced the public view of modern art. Bell maintained that 'significant form' is the important matter in painting and sculpture. His other writings include *Peace at Once* (1915), *Pot Boilers* (1918) and *Since Cézanne* (1922). For his connection with the Bloomsbury Group, see his son's account in Quentin Bell, *Bloomsbury* (1968). m. Vanessa Stephen, 1907.

have any *real* connection with anybody. I did not say that there *was* a real connection between you and me. Let them not know – swine. But there *is* a bond between us, in spirit, deep to the bottom.

DHL

1052. To Bertrand Russell, [15 November 1915]
Text: MS UT; Moore, *Bertrand Russell* 62.

1, Byron Villas, Vale-of-Health, Hampstead, London.
Monday¹

Dear Russell,

We want to go away to America, soon – on the 24th of this month, if possible. Will you come up and see us one day this week – Friday evening perhaps? I should be glad to see you before we go: so would Frieda. We are not really enemies: it is only a question of attitude.

I send you your book.² Thank you very much for lending it me. *Do* come and see us one day this week.

Yours   D. H. Lawrence

1053. To J. B. Pinker, 16 November 1915
Text: MS UNYB; Unpublished.

1, Byron Villas, Vale-of-Health, Hampstead, London.
16 Nov. 1915

Dear Pinker,

Shall I lunch with you on Thursday? – or shall I see you about 12·0 oclock. It doesn't matter a bit about the lunch, if you are busy – not a bit.

My wife and I intend to sail for New York, en route for a warmer climate, in about 10 days time – the 24th. You will have some letters of introduction for me, won't you? – but not sealed up, because one is not supposed to carry sealed letters.

Yours   D. H. Lawrence

1054. To Lady Cynthia Asquith, 16 November 1915
Text: MS UT; Huxley 274–6.

1, Byron Villas, Vale-of-Health, Hampstead, London.
16 Nov. 1915.

¹ Dated with reference to DHL's remark in the preceding letter about 'writing to Russell'.
² Unidentified: perhaps Russell had lent DHL a copy of his most recent work, a pamphlet published by the Union of Democratic Control: *War, the Offspring of Fear* (1915).

My dear Lady Cynthia,

We have decided to go away to America, sailing on Wednesday week, the 24th. I have made enquiries, and everything seems to be in order. But I hear the authorities seem to have an insane determination that nobody shall leave the country. Do you know whether it is necessary to get any further safeguard against their interference? It would be monstrous to be turned back, at Liverpool. We are going Second Class, by the steamer *Adriatic*, White Star Line.

Shall we see you again? – are you coming up to town? I must go to see my sister in Derbyshire: either we shall go there for the week-end – Sat. and Sunday – or we shall go there on Tuesday, on our way to Liverpool. I will let you know.

We are horribly poor. I am rather frightened about the money. But pray heaven we shall manage: if we land with about £20 or £30.

I want you to go and stay with the Ottoline. When I say she is *quite* unreal, that is wrong of me. There is an unformed reality in her, very deep. I think she is a big woman. But of course her whole effort has been spent in getting away from her tradition etc. Now she is exhausted. She has, in some sense, got away: but she has not got anywhere. She feels it bitterly. It is a bitter thing, only to have destroyed, not to have created. But she is pretty well spent now. Yet she still understands that there is the beyond. She is like an old, tragic queen who knows that her life has been spent in conflict with a kingdom that was not worth her life. Her life is in a way lost, yet not lost. She has not found the reality, because it was not to be found till she had pulled the temple down. But she has, for herself, pulled the temple down, even if she lies exhausted in the ruins.[1] It is more than remaining safe in the temple.

If you know her, be patient and go to the real things, not to the unreal things in her: for they are legion. But she is a big woman – something like Queen Elizabeth at the end. Which is my parting injunction about Ottoline.

Also – this is my parting letter – you must get the *intrinsic* reality clear within your soul: even if you betray it in actuality, yet *know* it: that is everything. And know, that in the end, always, you keep the ultimate choice of your destiny: to abide by the intrinsic reality, or by the extrinsic: the choice is yours, do not let it slide from you: keep it always secure, reserved.

I feel I must leave this side, this phase of life, for ever. The living part is overwhelmed by the dead part, and there is no altering it. So that life which is still fertile must take its departure, like seeds from a dead plant. I want to transplant my life. I think there is hope of a future, in America. I want

[1] Cf. Judges xvi. 25–31.

if possible to grow towards that future. There is no future here, only decomposition.

I want you to reserve to yourself, always, the choice, whether you too shall come to America also, at any time. You have your children. Probably you will have to rescue them from this decadence, this collapsing life. You must reserve to yourself the power, at all times, to bring them away. You must not let them be drawn into this slow flux of destruction and nihilism, *unless they belong to it*. If John becomes wicked, within the flux, then take him away into a new life: never mind how much it costs.

I will tell you all about America. I shall try to start a new shoot, a new germ of a new creation, there: I believe it exists there already. I want to join on to it. So as the years go by, I will tell you how it is. And then you will know, if you must come away, with John.

Your husband should have left this decomposing life. There was nowhere to go. Perhaps now he is beaten. Perhaps now the true living is defeated in him. But it is not yet defeated in you. You must watch your children, and the spirit of the world, and keep the choice of the right always in your own hands. Never admit that it is taken from you. Perhaps in the future Frieda and I can help you: remember we will always do so. I want to stake out an advance-post for your children to come to. Remember I am doing that, and that it is being done, unknown, without me, in America. So don't give John into this decline and fall. Give him to the *future*, if so his nature demands it: and I think it does.

I write to you about the things of the spirit. Remember Frieda and I will stand by you; and you must stand by us. Remember you keep the choice of life, for yourself and your children, and probably your husband, always in your hands: *don't* ever relinquish it up: even Herbert Asquith is probably only defeated here, in *this* flux, not in the flux of a new spirit.

                                          Yours   D. H. Lawrence

1055. To Lady Ottoline Morrell, 17 November 1915
Text: MS StaU; Postmark, London 17 NOV 15; Schorer 55.
                              1, Byron Villas, Vale-of-Health, Hampstead, London.
                                                            17 Nov. 1915.

My dear Ottoline,

I didn't want you to give so much money: it is sad that only the poor will give away their things. But never mind: I verily want you to have that manuscript,[1] and perhaps it will please you to have it.

---

[1] See Letter 1051. See Letter 1064 about the 'money'.

Now people are beginning to make a stir about the *Rainbow*. It is possible the Authors Society will take it up:[1] and that I may have to stay in England a week or two to see it through. I don't want to, really, because now I am ready to go. But I must fight for the book, if I can. If it is possible, I shall keep to my plan, and go away next Wednesday. But if the Authors Society says I must stay because they will fight for the book, I stay.

Come on Friday to lunch, will you? – and I will meet you at the tube anywhere about lunch time. Or come after lunch, if that is easier. I will wait for you at the tube, if you send me just a post card.

Bertie Russell is coming up also on Friday – perhaps to tea. I am glad.

The new stream of life has set in. I feel now, I have conquered: or that the Good has conquered, for me.

Till Friday   D. H. Lawrence

1056. To J. B. Pinker, [17 November 1915]
Text: MS YU; PC; Huxley 277–8.

Hampstead
– Wednesday[2]

Dear Pinker,

Could you send round to Phillip Morrell, 44 Bedford Square, tomorrow morning, as early as possible, a copy of my agreement with Methuen. Mr Morrell is going to ask a question tomorrow, in the House of Commons, about the *Rainbow*.[3] I can't come to lunch on Friday: I will look in tomorrow

---

[1] DHL had probably learned from Pinker that the Authors Society had decided that the 'Committee of Management...will be considering the suppression of Mr. Lawrence's book' and that they wished to 'have the fullest information as to the action taken by the publishers, and to know what defence the publishers put up and whether the author had the opportunity of being heard' (MS letter to Pinker, NYPL).

[2] Philip Morrell asked the first question in the Commons concerning *The Rainbow* on 18 November 1915: hence the dating of this postcard.

[3] Morrell asked the Home Secretary, on 18 November 1915, 'whether his attention has been called to the proceedings recently instituted by the Commissioner of Police for the suppression of a book by Mr. D. H. Lawrence, entitled "The Rainbow"; whether the police were acting with the knowledge and authority of the Home Office; and whether the author of the book had any opportunity of replying to the charge made against him?'

Sir John Simon (1873–1954), Home Secretary replied: 'My attention has been drawn to the proceedings in question, which were taken by the police in pursuance of their ordinary duty. Home Office authorisation is not required in such a case. The publishers, and not the author, were the defendants, and they had the customary opportunity to produce such evidence as they considered necessary in their defence' (Nehls, i. 333). Additional relevant excerpts from the *Parliamentary Debates*, 5th Series, lxxvi (18 November 1915) are printed in Nehls, i. 333–4.

about 12·30 or 12·45 – it doesn't matter. I promised to see the Mrs Ryan:[1]
I will be brief and discreet. Henry James might be *very* useful. Has he read
the book?[2] He might be very helpful if he could send a letter to Phillip
Morrell.

Yours   D. H. Lawrence

1057. To J. B. Pinker, 17 November 1915
Text: MS Martin; Huxley 276–7.

1, Byron Villas, Vale-of-Health, Hampstead, London.
17 Nov. 1915

Dear Pinker,

I cannot believe that the Authors Society will really do anything. If they
will, so much the better.[3]

No, I received no notice at all about the suppression of the *Rainbow* – the
first intimation was from W L George, who had phoned up Methuen to ask
why the advertisement was stopped. Then I had your letter.

You will arrange about the Italian Sketches. You know best.

I have had letters from a lot of people about the *Rainbow* – Oliver Lodge[4]
and others. I think we might make a good row.

But I wish I could go to America. I've got everything ready, and I want
to go on the 24th. Must I stay for the proceedings about the *Rainbow*? Must
I appear – Of course I want to do what I can for the book. Also I want to
go away. I will stay if it is really any good.

Yours   D. H. Lawrence

1058. To Unidentified Recipient, [17 November 1915]
Text: MS Anon; Unpublished.

1, Byron Villas, Vale-of-Health, Hampstead, London.
Wednesday 17 Nov

[1] See p. 441 n. 1.
[2] The answer to DHL's question is not known.
[3] Presumably Pinker had told DHL of his letter to Thring on 16 November, putting the facts
relating to Methuen's reluctance to defend *The Rainbow* 'or to protect the author's interest'
(*TLS*, 27 February 1969, p. 216).
[4] Sir Oliver Joseph Lodge (1851–1940), eminent scientist, important writer on psychic
phenomena and at this time Principal of the University of Birmingham. He was president
of the Society for Psychical Research (1901–4). Among his publications are *Science and
Immortality* (1908) and *Reason and Belief* (1910).

Dear Madam,[1]

I will come to see you at 12.0 oclock tomorrow morning, if that will do. If you send me a post card tonight, I shall have it in time. I sent the girl out with a telephone message to you, but heaven knows what has happened to her, she does not return.

Yours faithfully   D. H. Lawrence

1059. To Constance Garnett, 17 November 1915

Text: MS NYPL; Heilbrun, *The Garnett Family*, p. 160.

1, Byron Villas, Vale-of-Health, Hampstead, London.

17 Nov. 1915

Dear Mrs Garnett,

I was glad to hear from you. When Edward comes home, ask him to come and see us as soon as possible.

It is vile about the *Rainbow*. The book is perfectly pure. But it seems there is a good chance that the Authors Society will take up the case, to fight it: because I was condemned entirely without hearing. Methuen, the skunk, left the book entirely in the lurch: whined and puled, said not a word for it.[2] But perhaps we can get the decision reversed.

We are all ready to go to America. I cannot live here any more: and I am sure I cannot do any more work for this country. I know America is bad, but I think it has a future. I think there is no future for England: only a decline and fall. That is the dreadful and unbearable part of it: to have been born into a decadent era, a decline of life, a collapsing civilisation. We should be going to America next Wednesday: all is ready: but now I am afraid I shall have to stay to fight out this business of *The Rainbow*.

Phillip Morrell is putting a question in the House of Commons tomorrow, about the suppression of the book. Perhaps we shall get the decision reversed.

Frieda and I both send our love to you.

D. H. Lawrence

---

[1] Probably 'the Mrs Ryan' mentioned in Letters 1056 and 1064; she may have been an employee of the publisher Huebsch. DHL met her apparently to discuss the possible publication of *The Rainbow*, which she thought 'might do well in America' (see Letter 1064).

[2] Methuen and Co. did not defend the novel before the magistrate on 13 November and pleaded guilty to the obscenity charge.

1060. To Bertrand Russell, 17 November 1915

Text: MS UT; cited in Moore, *Atlantic Monthly* 100.

1, Byron Villas, Vale-of-Health, Hampstead, London.
17 Nov. 1915

Dear Russell,

I am sorry we have promised to go out to dinner on Thursday. Could you come on Friday to tea, if you wish to leave town in the afternoon. Lady Ottoline is coming I think to lunch.

Also I may have to stay in England a little longer, to fight for my novel. Yesterday I heard from the Authors Society that they will *probably* stand by me, because the book was condemned wholly without reference to me.[1] I don't want to stay, because now we are ready, quite ready, to go. But if I must stay to fight about the book, I will stay.

But you will come on Friday to see us. I shall be very glad to talk to you again, to be friends. After all, my quarrelling with you was largely a quarelling with something in *myself*, something I was struggling away from in myself.

Yours   D. H. Lawrence

1061. To Robert Nichols, 17 November 1915

Text: MS YU; Moore 383–4.

1, Byron Villas, Vale-of-Health, Hampstead, London.
17 Nov. 1915.

Dear Nicol,[2]

I went to dinner with Heseltine.[3] I like him *very* much: I think he is one of the men who will count, in the future. I must know him more.

---

[1] Thring wrote as follows on 15 November 1915 (BL Add. MS. 57181):
Dear Sir,
    I beg to thank you for your letter [13 November] and will get the fullest particulars that I can on the matter. It is of course impossible for me to say what line the Committee would adopt, but judging from the course they have taken in other matters, I think they would be inclined to support the view that it is essential that every author should have the right to appear in his own defence. I shall be much obliged if you will forward me a copy of the book.
                                                                      Yours truly

[2] Robert Malise Bowyer Nichols (1893–1944), poet and dramatist, who spent a year at Trinity College, Oxford and was then commissioned in the Royal Field Artillery. He saw service briefly on the Belgian-French front and then spent five months in hospital where Philip Heseltine took DHL to meet him. Later he served in the Ministry of Labour and on the British Mission (Ministry of Information) in New York. 1921–4 he occupied the chair of English Literature at the Imperial University, Tokyo. His principal poetic works include *Invocation* (1915), *Ardours and Endurances* (1917) and *Such was my Singing* (1942).

[3] Philip Arnold Heseltine (1894–1930), pseudonym Peter Warlock, composer, writer on music, and editor of old English airs. He was a close friend of Nichols. For further details see Cecil Gray, *Peter Warlock* (1934).

I have had a day rushing about.[1] Tomorrow Phillip Morrell is asking a question in the House of Commons, about the suppression of *The Rainbow*. Then I think the Authors Society is going to take the matter up. We must get a body of opinion behind us. If you know of anybody who will give important support, you might get them ready, for when the time comes.

All this will defer my going to America until there is some decision. I shall go then. So I expect to have time to see you more than once again. Just now I am rushed: but in a few days I will come.

I liked seeing you and knowing you very much. But I am sorry you are so much bowled over. It is a case of concussion: these cases are *frightfully* common. I have just been seeing Herbert Asquith, the Prime Ministers son. He is in the same way: he was an artillery man too. And there are so many knocked down as you are. But do try and be happier: try and trust in love: there is love still in life, and it will prevail yet. Don't *dream* of going back to the front. You must *never* go back. When you are better, go and stay with somebody who is fond of you, and learn to be still. Only learn to be still, and at peace with yourself. Give yourself up to peace, and trust in the power of love. There is so much hate and destruction and disintegration: let it all go, you do not belong to it any more. You belong now to the creative, constructive, loving side of life: believe in this, and get well, to be happy. You must learn to be happy – no sensationalism. Learn to be still and to trust yourself to the unseen loving forces of life: they are there, though the evil predominates.

I have your poetry safe.[2] (I had not read it – I began here.) The 'Fragment of a Poem of Vision' is good, and 'Marsyas'. I *don't* care for the 'Sonnet' and the 'Invocation'. The Courage of death is *no courage* any more: *the courage to die has become a vice*. Show me the courage to live, to live in spirit with the proud, serene angels. Some of 'Jerusalem' is *very good*. I think you are a poet: take care, save yourself, above all, save yourself: there is such need of poets, that the world will all perish, without them. You have a mission, to be a living poet. For God's sake fulfil it – 'Jerusalem' is very very good, at the end – the last two stanzas. I *must* get some of these printed

---

[1] Among other things, DHL had a hasty meeting with Philip Morrell in the House of Commons. Lady Cynthia reports that while she was at DHL's on Wednesday 17 November, 'a telegram came from Morrell, asking if Lawrence would come and see him at the House of Commons about *The Rainbow*. So I drove him back to London' (Asquith, *Diaries* 101).
[2] By this time, Nichols had published some poetry in *Oxford Poetry* and one volume of verse entitled *Invocation: War Poems and Others* (1915). Only 'Invocation' (pp. 11–12), 'Sonnet', in the series 'Five Sonnets Upon Imminent Departure' (pp. 15–19), and 'Before Jerusalem' (pp. 26–9) were published in this volume. 'Fragment of a Poem of Vision', 'Spring Song of Marsyas' and 'The Hill' were not available in published form and must have been read by DHL in MS. That Nichols had sent some MSS becomes clear in Letter 1063.

for you. 'The Hill' – *very* good. I must go over them with you. You are a poet, my dear fellow: I am *so glad*: the first I have found: the future. *Only be still*, be very still, and let the poetry come.

I am so glad to have found you.

D. H. Lawrence

You are a poet – 'The Hill': 'Jerusalem': they are poetry: I could sing as if the heavens had opened: a young poet at last – thank God. I only read your poems after I had begun this letter – I *must* read them with you: they are real poetry.

I couldn't tell you how glad I am to know you: only get well, and learn to be at peace, learn to love – then it will be glorious, we can create the future.

1062. To Dollie Radford, [18 November 1915]
Text: MS UN; Postmark, Hampstead 18 NOV 15; Nehls, i. 332–3.

1, Byron Villas, Vale-of-Health, Hampstead, London.
17 Nov. 1915[1]

My dear Dollie,

Thank you very much for your letter. Florida sounds *very good*: I believe it will come off. A friend[2] also has written to the musician Delius, who also has a forsaken estate in Florida.[3] What the final upshot will be I do not know. But I should like to go with you to see Mr. Keen as soon as you are back in town.

We were all ready to sail for New York next Wednesday. But now we are again held back, to fight for the *Rainbow*. I believe the Society of Authors is going to stand by me. If there is a trial, we must get Wells and Shaw and everybody on our side. You might, when you write to Jane Wells, ask her if H.G. has read the book and will help me if need be. Let us make a good little fight for it.

Today Phillip Morrell is asking a question in the House of Commons, about the suppression of the book. Perhaps something will come of it. So you see I must stay behind to see the thing through, though I am sick to get away. I want to go, I don't want to stay any more.

---

[1] DHL's reference to Morrell's question in the Commons 'today' suggests 18, not 17, November.

[2] Philip Heseltine. For his letter and the reply from Delius, which contains a description of the Florida estate ('a wilderness of gigantic weeds and plants'), see Nehls, i. 329–30.

[3] Frederick Delius (1862–1934), composer, had lived as an orange planter in Florida, 1884–5. He studied in Leipzig and then settled in France. His works include the operas, *Koanga* (1897) and *A Village Romeo and Juliet* (1901), as well as many symphonic works, songs, concertos and chamber music.

Also I have found a poet: a lad of 21 whose nerves are shattered at the war. He is a young Oxford undergraduate, artillery Lieutenant, lying now in Lord Knutsfords Hospital for Officers. You must see some of his poetry. It is beautiful. Also you must meet him later.

How are you, my dear Dollie? and how is the cloud of your troubles? I feel it is dissipating a little. Let us know as soon as you are back.

I took the machine home – the sewing machine.

Au revoir   D. H. Lawrence

1063. To Robert Nichols, 18 November 1915
Text: MS YU; Moore 387–8.

1, Byron Villas – Vale of Health, Hampstead, N.W.
18 Nov. 1915

My dear Nichols,

I have been reading your poems again. Now I send them back to you. I'll tell you how I like them.

1. 'Invocation': – I hate it. This courage of the conscious will to defeat the instincts is evil. The whole poem hits me like a newspaper cliché.

2. 'Spring Song of Marsyas': I like it, but it is in parts rather like an echo of things heard before.

3. 'Sonnet': I hate it: again the mere courage of acquiescence in death, which I think purely vicious.

4. 'Midday': Good, I like it.[1] It has not quite enough *nerve*, perhaps: all soft and warm. But then it is Midday. But surely a little too sensuous-sweet. Don't take any notice of their scansion criticisms. I think you are right every time, where they question.

5. 'Fragment of a Poem of Vision': The beginning and the middle are not so very good: the end is *very good indeed*: the last page or so. I don't think you've got the middle part, the singing part, quite *true*. I wonder if it could be altered, if you concentrated on it. The end is *so good*, I wish this were truly uttered, this middle part, after the first break. You see 'The Shining round of heavenly love' doesn't quite mean anything. 'My heart climbed like a circling dove', is very beautiful. Again

> 'Into my being stole a song
> Of unimaginable pulses born –'

---

[1] 'Midday on the Edge of the Downs', published as the second part of a three–part poem entitled 'Black Songs' in *Ardours and Endurances* pp. 170–4.

is not good. A thing which is *born* doesn't *steal*. You didn't concentrate here. I like the last page so much.

6. 'Jerusalem': is splendid, really splendid.

7. 'A Tryptych' also very good indeed.[1] These two are the best.

I must see you soon, and we will talk about these poems. I should like to talk one or two places over with you – the rhythm. Also I want you to have the MS. typed out. It would only cost a few shillings: you should have a proof copy and a duplicate, or even two duplicates, of each. If you like I will send them to my man, to have them done for you. Or you can send them yourself. My man is an excellent typist, and perfect in reliability. He is

Douglas Clayton, 54 Birdhurst Rd., *S. Croydon.*

I shall be glad when *all* this MS. is duly typed out. Then I will send 'Jerusalem' to Harrison, for the *English Review*, and one smaller one to the *Nation*, and duplicates to America.

I told you our going to America is postponed by trouble with *The Rainbow*. Did I tell you also that I asked Heseltine to write to Delius about the Florida estate? I want us all to go and live there for a while. You must get well enough, and we will all go to Florida for a year or two. What do you think of that? I think it would be splendid.

I will come to see you either Sunday or Monday – tell me which day you would rather. Perhaps my wife will come too. Let me know which day.

Yours   D. H. Lawrence

1064. To J. B. Pinker, 18 November 1915
Text: MS Forster; Huxley 277.

1, Byron Villas, Vale-of-Health, Hampstead, London.
18 Nov. 1915

Dear Pinker,

You didn't tell me about Huebsch – have you any news of him? I wanted to know. That Mrs Ryan came. I told her not to say much of the book.[2] Poor little woman, she was quite nice, but not important. But she thinks the book might do well in America, since their postal-censor man is dead.[3]

I should like to know what Henry James and Bennett say of the book.[4]

---

[1] 'A Tryptych' consisting of I. 'First Panel: The Hill'; II. 'Second and Centre Panel: The Tower'; III. 'Third Panel: The Tree', published in *Ardours and Endurances*, pp. 139–52.

[2] *The Rainbow.*   [3] Anthony Comstock (1844–1915).

[4] There is no record of James's assessment. Arnold Bennett's opinion of the novel was very high: he used it as a standard of excellence when writing to Frank Swinnerton in 1919. See *The Letters of Arnold Bennett 1916–1931*, ed. James Hepburn, iii (1970), 111.

I know Henry James would hate it. But I should like to know. And if they would like to give me a little money, I should be glad. I should be freer. But it doesn't *matter*. I was very badly off. But Lady Ottoline Morrell sent me £30, so I shall have about £60 to buy passages and go to America.[1]

I think it would be a *really good* thing to get the public protest from the authors – Bennett etc. John Drinkwater came in just now – he is anxious to do something. Very many people are in a rage over the occurrence. Will you organise a public protest, do you think? – it would be best.

Yours D. H. Lawrence

1065. To S. S. Koteliansky, [22 November 1915]
Text: MS BL; PC; Postmark, Hampstead 22 NOV 15; Zytaruk 59.

Hampstead
– Monday

Thank you very much for the Tchekhov. I am very glad to have it.[2] The first story reads *splendidly*: you have done it well. Will you send *Signatures* to:

V. H. Bischoff-Collins Esq.,[3] 2 Hurst-Close, Hampstead Garden Suburb.

I have his subscription.

When I said 8/- from the Poetry Bookshop, of course I meant 3/-. The man only wants *one* copy – I was thinking three.

Come up again soon.

Yours D. H. Lawrence

1066. To Philip Heseltine, 22 November 1915
Text: MS NWU; Unpublished.

1, Byron Villas, Vale-of-Health, Hampstead, London.
22 Nov. 1915

My dear Heseltine,

I hope you didn't mind the holding forth of last night. But do think about what we were saying, of art, and life.

It is so important that now, the great reducing, analytic, introspective

---

[1] A letter to Edward Marsh (MS NYPL) on 12 November 1915 indicates the efforts Lady Ottoline made 'to collect a sum of money for Lawrence. – To enable him to go to Florida.' She hoped to raise £40; she invited Marsh to contribute and had written to the Duke of Portland; and she asked Marsh to suggest other names. Whether the £30 mentioned here represents her own donation or contributions from several people is not known.
[2] Anton Chekhov, *The Bet and Other Stories*, trans. S. S. Koteliansky and J. M. Murry (October 1915).
[3] In Letter 1084 Bischoff-Collins is wrongly described as 'the Cambridge Press man'. In fact he was employed by Oxford University Press: see p. 483 n. 1.

process, which has gone on pure and uninterrupted since the Renaissance; – at least since Milton – should now give way to a constructive, synthetic, metaphysical process. Because now, reduction, introspection, has reached the point when it has practically no more to reveal to us, and can only produce sensationalism.

One must fight every minute – at least I must – to overcome this great flux of disintegration, further analysis, self analysis. If it continues, this flux, then our phase, our era, passes swiftly into oblivion. – In physical life, it is homosexuality, the reduction process. When man and woman come together in love, that is the great *immediate* synthesis. When men come together, that is immediate reduction: those complex states, the finest product of generations of synthetic living, are *reduced* in homosexual love, liberating a conscious knowledge of the component parts. This is like Plato. But the *knowledge* is always contained and included within the spirit, the process, of reduction, disintegration.

This may sound wild, but it is true. And it is necessary to overcome the great stream of disintegration, the flux of reduction, like a man swimming against the stream. Otherwise there is nothing but despair. This is why I am going to Florida. Here the whole flux is deathly. One must climb out on to a firm shore.

If we can pull Nichols out, then he will be a living poet. But I don't feel very hopeful about him.

Above all, be careful about losing the power to love really and profoundly, from the bottom of your soul, to love a woman – not men. Otherwise you will only feel despair. And I believe that music too must become now synthetic, metaphysical, giving a musical utterance to the sense of the Whole. But perhaps I dont know enough about it.

I am glad you are happier about the girl: and that she is happier.[1] Don't be afraid of being sentimental: it is healthy to be a little sentimental at times. Only don't be cynical and self-sufficient: your face shows traces already.

I shall ask Lady Ottoline Morrell to invite you to Garsington. She is a sister of the Duke of Portland, wife of Phillip Morrell, radical M.P. for Burnley. She has had crowds of artists at her house: often unfortunately. But she is a big woman, essentially genuine and religious. Only don't stick at the outside queernesses. You and Chrustchoff[2] must go and see her.

Yours   D. H. Lawrence

---

[1] The identity of the girl is uncertain but she presumably was the person DHL and Frieda considered suitable for either Nichols or Heseltine to marry. See Gray, *Peter Warlock*, pp. 89–90.   [2] Boris de Croustchoff, Russian bibliographer.

1067. To Lady Ottoline Morrell, 22 November 1915
Text: MS StaU; Schorer 55–6.

1, Byron Villas, Vale-of-Health, Hampstead, London.
22 Nov. 1915.

My dear Ottoline,

Yesterday I saw the sick poet in his hospital:
Robert Nichols, Lord Knutsford's Hospital for Officers,
10 Palace Green, W.

He jumped for joy at the thought of coming to see you. I like the other man, the musician, even better.

Philip[1] Heseltine, 12A Rossetti Garden Mansions, Chelsea, SW.

I wish we could all have come down together: perhaps we might. At any rate, if you ask Nichols – he is really rather seedy yet, very nervous – ask Heseltine along with him.

Also yesterday I went and chose a frame for the embroidery: dark olive green. I think it will look *very* nice. We are excited for it to come home. I want to see it done.

I talked with one man about Florida.[2] He said his place was near Fort Myers. You know the map of Florida.

[Sketch][3]

Fort Myers is about 10 miles from the sea, on a river 1 mile wide. Florida is a flat peninsula, all pine forests and orange groves. One can live there very cheaply: as cheaply as in England – perhaps cheaper. One can take a cotton boat to Jacksonville – or perhaps a phosphate boat even to Ft. Myers. Can you tell me how one finds out about ships? I don't want to go to New York – no – I want to go straight to Florida. Pinker says he will try and make my money up to £100. That would be very good: then I can go straight to Florida, without waiting in New York to get some money.

It was nice of Bernard Shaw to send £5. I am glad.

There are so many letters about *The Rainbow*, so many people wanting it. I wonder why it cant be printed privately, by subscription – I believe money could be made that way, even.

I think we shall get off all right. It will be splendid if we can gain a new footing in a freer place. Then many people will come: the truly vital people. And you will come later, with Julian: sailing in a cotton boat to these Semi-tropical seas: and you will live for a while also in Florida. Oh, life is

---

[1] Philip] Robert   [2] Moore identifies him as Dr Dudley (Moore 388).
[3] A rough map of the American coastline from New York to the Gulf of Mexico showing Florida with Jacksonville and Fort Myers.

not ended yet: these are the splendid days ahead: we will forget these past days of destruction and misery.

I liked Bertie very much on Friday: really the simple man was there for once, almost childish. And then at the end he reproached me for my letter to him, as if I had wantonly hurt him. That was not manly of him. Sometimes he begs indulgence like a child. And after all he was more simple and real on Friday than I have ever known him. So my letter must have been productive in him, liberating something.

A man came up yesterday who will take the flat, unfurnished, for a year. If we agree with him, I will send the furniture to Bedford Square, to stay in your house, may I?

I am waiting now to hear from Delius, through Heseltine, about *his* place in Florida. That is nearer to Jacksonville. If there is nothing for us, from Delius, we will go to Fort Myers.

But we shall see you again before long. I wish we could have another day or so at Garsington: I think we can.

We have got colds. Frieda thinks it is the liver. Desmond Macarthy said you had good stuff for the liver 'a large bolus' he said.[1] Can you give me the name or the prescription?

> With love from us both   D. H. Lawrence

1068. To J. B. Pinker, 23 November 1915
Text: MS Forster; Moore 388–9.

> 1, Byron Villas, Vale-of-Health, Hampstead, London.
> 23 Nov. 1915

Dear Pinker,

It would be so good if we could make up my money to £100. Then I could go straight to Florida, without going to that cursed New York: a tiny [...] town,[2] 5,000 people – by a wide river, ten miles from the sea – and living as cheap or cheaper than in England: I have talked it all over with the man. You don't know how to find out about trading ships going to Florida – to Jacksonville or Susquehanna or Fort Myers, do you?

So[3] many letters come to me about *The Rainbow* – so very many people

---

[1] (Sir) Desmond MacCarthy (1877–1952), journalist and literary critic. Dramatic critic and later literary editor of the *New Statesman* (1913–28); editor of the periodical *Life and Letters* (1928–33). Joined the Red Cross in 1914. He was a close friend of Lady Cynthia Asquith.
[2] Fort Myers, Florida; see Letter 1067.   [3] MS reads 'Such'.

wanting it. If any man were energetic enough, it would pay him to print it privately, by subscription.

As for Wells and my observation of life – if his own portrayal of life had a tithe of truth in it nowadays, he would be glad. He knows he is making a failure of himself, going to pieces, so he will see a serious piece of work with a yellow eye. He admires me really, at the bottom – too much perhaps. With Henry James it is different – he was always on a different line – subtle conventional design was his aim.

You too are depressed nowadays. But never mind, we will flourish when they are withering.

Yours   D. H. Lawrence

If you can send me some unsaleable stories of mine, I will give them to Clive Bell. Shall I? – You remember, for his private circulation venture –

1069. To Edward Garnett, [23 November 1915]
Text: MS NYPL; PC; Postmark, Hampstead 25 NOV 15; Unpublished.

Hampstead
– Tuesday

DO come to lunch tomorrow. Mary Cannan will be here, and another woman[1] – but that you'll have to put up with.

Yrs   D. H. Lawrence

1070. To John Middleton Murry and Katherine Mansfield, 25 November 1915
Text: MS NYPL; cited in Murry, *New Adelphi*, 146.

1, Byron Villas, Vale-of-Health, Hampstead, London.
25 Nov. 1915

Dear Murry and Katharine,

I got your address from Kot.

First to explain the non-meeting. I said on my card '*Unless I hear* from you, I will come at 8·30'. I got your card saying *you* would come to *us*. So I rushed home from town and we waited for you. There you are, wessel-brained[2] as usual.

How are you and what are you doing? Send me a letter.

---

[1] Unidentified.

[2] i.e. feeble-minded (dialect form probably from 'weazel', a foolish fellow).

We were all ready to sail last Wednesday, when the business of the *Rainbow* kept me: the Authors Society promising to take it up, Phillip Morrell asking a question in the House of Commons etc. But I don't know that anything will come of it. However, I am not sorry we stayed, because I am hoping to be able to sail straight to Florida, without going to New York. Oh happy prospect – if only it can be fulfilled. I heard from the American: no house on his estate: but he will give letters of introduction to Fort Myers – a little town on *West* of peninsula – 5,000 people, many niggers – 9 miles from sea, on a big river one mile wide: many fish, and quails, and wild turkeys: land flat, covered with orange groves and pine trees: climate perfect.

If only we can get there, and settle, then you will come, and we will live on no money at all. *The Rainbow* is being published in New York. Pinker will try and get me a little money to go out with. If only it will all end up happily, like a song or a poem, and we live blythely by a big river, where there are fish, and in the forest behind wild turkeys and quails: there we make songs and poems and stories and dramas, in a vale of Avalon, in the Hesperides,[1] among the Loves. Meanwhile it is very cold in London, bleak, and nothing ripens, neither good nor evil, but goes bitter on the tree, with cold slowness.

I hope all is well with you: I will let you know when something decisive happens to us.

Yours   D. H. Lawrence

1071. To Lady Ottoline Morrell, 26 November 1915
Text: MS StaU; Unpublished.

1, Byron Villas, Vale-of-Health, Hampstead, London.
26 Nov. 1915

My Dear Ottoline,

I'm sorry we can't come tomorrow, but we will come if we may on Monday, for a day or two. We must go out to dinner tomorrow and have people coming here on Sunday.

It would perhaps be nice if Heseltine came with us – just he, so that we can introduce him to you – or else he will never come at all.[2] I wonder if you would write to him:

Philip Heseltine, 13 Rossetti Mansions, Chelsea, S.W.

I'm not sure if we can persuade him to come: he says he has no right to foist himself off on people: an access of self-depreciation.

Just send us a postcard, if we shall come to Wheatley by the same train

---

[1] i.e. in an earthly paradise (the first from Celtic, the second from Greek mythology).

[2] Lady Ottoline's visitors' book shows, under 29 November 1915, that Heseltine was a guest along with the Lawrences, Aldous Huxley, Willy MacQueen and Hasan Shahid Suhrawardy.

as before. It will be so jolly: I hope the sun shines as it does today: a post-card will get us on Monday morning: it is so jolly to think of coming again at once.

Yours   D. H. Lawrence

1072. To J. B. Pinker, [26 November 1915]

Text: MS Forster; Unpublished.

1, Byron Villas – Vale of Health, Hampstead
Friday[1]

Dear Pinker,

I'm glad Doran will see the publication through.[2] He won't want alterations made, will he?

Prince Antoine Bibesco,[3] of the Roumanian Legation, says he thinks he could get the *Rainbow* published in Paris, by a man called Conard:[4] a sort of Tauchnitz.[5] Don't you think that would be rather good?

You'll let me know when there is any news for me – I am looking for a ship to Florida now.

From Monday to Wednesday night I shall be

at Garsington Manor Nr. Oxford.

Yours   D. H. Lawrence

1073. To Edward Garnett, [26 November 1915]

Text: MS NYPL; Unpublished.

1 Byron Villas – Vale of Health, Hampstead, N.W.
Friday[6]

Dear Garnett,

The Prince sent back the book. He says he could get it printed in Paris, by Conard, a sort of French Tauchnitz. Don't you think it would be nice?

You'll give me this copy back, wont you.   Yours   D. H. Lawrence

---

[1] Dated with reference to DHL's departure for Garsington 29 November 1915.

[2] See p. 420 n. 2.

[3] Prince Antoine Bibesco (1878–1951), Roumanian diplomat. m. 1919, Elizabeth Asquith (1897–1945), daughter of H. H. Asquith by his second wife, and step-sister of Herbert Asquith, Lady Cynthia's husband.

[4] Most likely the Parisian house of Editions Conard which, as the result of amalgamation, subsequently became Editions Conard–Lambert. (In 1960 it was absorbed into Librairie de l'Abbaye, 27 rue Bonaparte, Paris.)

[5] Christian Bernhard von Tauchnitz (1816–95), publisher in Leipzig. Beginning in 1841 he issued the Tauchnitz Edition of the 'Collection of British and American Authors', and in 1868 added the 'Collection of German Authors' in English translation.

[6] Dated with reference to the contents of Letter 1072.

1074. To Lady Cynthia Asquith, 28 November 1915
Text: MS UT; Huxley 278–9.

1 Byron Villas – Vale of Health, Hampstead, N.W.
28 Nov. 1915

My dear Lady Cynthia,

You ask me to send you our news: but as there isn't any, there's no excuse for writing. People are desultorily working about the *Rainbow*: I am struggling like a fly on a treacle paper, to leave this country. I am hoping to be able to scrape together a little money, so that we can go to Florida straight, instead of going first to New York. I don't want to go to New York – not yet, not now. I would like to go to a land where there are only birds and beasts and no humanity, nor inhumanity-masks.

This is the plan and the prospect. A man will find out about a trading ship going to the Gulf of Mexico. We sail in this – soon. Then, if possible, we make for our destination in Florida – Fort Myers.

[Sketch]¹

Fort Myers is a little town (5000) – half negro – 9 miles from sea, on a wide river 1½ miles wide – backed by orange groves and pine forests. An American here will give us letters of introduction to friends there. That is the plan. I hope to find the ship and to sail before Christmas. There is the other point, whether the English government will let me go. But I must go – I have had far too much already.

For the rest of the news: tomorrow we are going to the Ottoline's for a day or two. I've got a new suit and Frieda has got a new coat and skirt. I have made her a hat, a sort of Russian toque – out of bits of fur – so she looks very nice. She is also going to have a big warm coat, because it is so cold.

My heart is smashed into a thousand fragments, and I shall never have the energy to collect the bits – like Osiris – or Isis.² In Florida I shall swallow a palm seed, and see if that'll grow into a new heart for me.

I want to begin all all again. All these Gethsemane Calvary and Sepulchre stages must be over now: there must be a resurrection – resurrection: a resurrection with sound hands and feet and a whole body and a new soul: above all, a new soul: a resurrection. It is finished, and ended, and put away,

---

¹ Cf. p. 449 n. 3.
² Osiris, the Egyptian god and judge of the dead, and lord of the underworld (whom DHL uses in *The Escaped Cock*, 1929). According to myth, Osiris was killed, cut up into fourteen pieces and scattered over Egypt. His sister Isis recovered all the pieces except the phallus

and forgotten, and translated to a new birth, this life, these thirty years. There
must be a new heaven and a new earth, and a new heart and soul: all new:
a pure resurrection.

> Now like a crocus in the autumn time
> My soul comes naked from the falling night
> Of death, a cyclamen, a crocus flower
> Of windy autumn when the winds all sweep
> The hosts away to death, where heap on heap
> The leaves are smouldering in a funeral wind.[1]

That is the first poem I have written for many many a day – a bit of it – there's
much more.[2] They burn the leaves in heaps on the Heath – and the leaves
blow in the wind, then the smoke: and the leaves are like soldiers.

I don't know why on earth I say these things to you: why you sort of
ask me. But the conscious life – which you adhere to – is no more than a
masquerade of death: there is a living unconscious life. If only we would
shut our eyes: if only we were all struck blind, and things vanished from
our sight: we should marvel that we had fought and lived for shallow,
visionary, peripheral nothingnesses. We should find reality in the darkness.

Sometimes I am angry that I write these letters to you – but then I'm often
angry. I suppose you *do* really care about the difference between life and
death.

Vale   D. H. Lawrence

1075. To S. S. Koteliansky, [28 November 1915]
Text: MS BL; PC; Postmark, [...], Zytaruk 57.

Hampstead
– Sunday[3]

Dear Kot,

Will you send the 3 numbers of the *Signature* to:

Trevor Walsh Esq, Scott House, West Malling, Kent.

I have his 2/6.

If you don't come to see us tonight, don't come till the end of the week,
as we are going away, Monday till Friday.

Greetings   D. H. Lawrence

---

[1] l. 6 leaves] hosts
[2] The poem (of 77 lines) is entitled 'Resurrection'.
[3] Dated with reference to DHL's departure for Garsington on Monday, 29 November 1915.

1076. To Catherine Carswell, [29 November 1915]
Text: MS YU; cited in Moore, *Intelligent Heart* 205.

[1, Byron Villas, Vale-of-Health, Hampstead, London.]
[29 November 1915]

I called to see if you know anything about the ship.[1] Let me know at once, will you?

We are going away now to Lady Ottolines
at Garsington Manor, Nr Oxford.
We shall be back Thursday night.

D. H. Lawrence

1077. To Catherine Carswell, 29 November 1915
Text: MS YU; cited in Moore, *Post Restante*, p. 44.

Garsington Manor, Oxford
29 Nov. 1915

Dear Catherine,

Did you get my note this morning? Do ask Carswell to tell me about the ship as soon as possible.

We are talking about the *Rainbow*: we want very much to get a private edition done, by subscription. If ever Don has time, and it would interest him, would he tell us whether a private printing would be any infringement of Methuen's rights. We were suppressed by the Obscene Print Act of 1857 (Lord Campbell's act).[2] What does that mean? that the existing print is destroyed by police order, or that the book may not be published at all?

Could you send to Phillip Morrell –

44 Bedford Square, W.C.

a copy of your review in the *Glasgow Herald* (tell him if it is *Glasgow Herald* or not).[3] He is asking a longer and more important question in the House on Wednesday.[4]

[1] The ship might be the *Crown de Leon* mentioned in Letter 1084.

[2] Its correct title is the 'Obscene Publications Act' of 1857; the name attached to it is that of John Campbell, 1st Baron Campbell (1779–1861), then Chancellor of the Duchy of Lancaster and later Lord Chancellor. The Act gave magistrates power of summary jurisdiction on information from the police.

[3] The unsigned review was published in the *Glasgow Herald*, 4 November 1915, p. 4 (see Draper 100–1). It cost Catherine Carswell her job as a reviewer for the *Herald* (see Carswell 41).

[4] Philip Morrell submitted a written question to the Home Secretary, seeking to discover 'why proceedings were taken for the suppression...without any notice being given to the author', whether the Home Secretary was aware 'that no direct evidence was given by the prosecution in support of the charge', and whether the Home Secretary 'will see that no further

I hope this is not an awful nuisance to you. We shall be home on Friday – come and see us.

Yours   D. H. Lawrence

1078. To J. B. Pinker, 29 November 1915

Text: MS Forster; Unpublished.

Garsington Manor, Oxford

29 Nov 1915

Dear Pinker,

I am here with Phillip Morrell and Lady Ottoline until Friday. We are talking about printing *The Rainbow* privately, by subscription. I really think it ought to be done.

I wish you could approach Methuen – in this way – whether he intends to do any more with *The Rainbow* (clause 11 of agreement): if so whether he has any objection to the book's being privately printed: (though I don't know whether he has any further right to object): and whether he might sell the plates. – I think it ought to [be]¹ printed by subscription, so we want to form a little company, among ourselves, to do it. So tell me what you think, and what you can get out of Methuen, will you.²

Also Mr Morrell is asking another question in the House of Commons tomorrow – Wednesday. I wish you would ring him up at 44 Bedford Square, Tel. Museum 31 at 11.0 in the morning (Wednesday) to see if you could give him any helpful information. Also could you send him a copy of the review of *The Rainbow* that appeared in *The Standard*³ – that was a very

---

proceedings of this kind are taken by the police'. (The Home Office minute containing the question is reproduced in Delavenay, *D. H. Lawrence: The Man and His Work*, between pp. 160 and 161.) In the House of Commons on 1 December 1915, Sir John Simon replied that 'these proceedings were taken by the police in pursuance of their ordinary duty; the decision was a judicial decision arrived at by the chief magistrate, and was concurred in by the producers of the book'. He added that 'if an author who has a pecuniary interest in the sale of a book thinks it necessary to do so...he could stipulate that his publisher should give him notice of proceedings such as these, and the magistrate would then determine whether he could not be heard' (Nehls, i. 334–5).

¹ MS reads 'to printed'.
² Methuen informed Pinker on 9 December 1915 that 'all the copies and plates of "THE RAINBOW" which we had were taken by the Police and on the order of the magistrate have been destroyed'. As far as the copyright of the work was concerned, Methuen held that 'no copyright can exist in the book' and that 'there can be no question as to publishing or any other rights'. Since DHL was given an advance of £300 for a copyright work which he failed to deliver 'there has been a complete failure of the consideration for which we paid our money. Mr. Lawrence should now repay this sum' (MS NYPL).
³ On 1 October 1915; see Draper 89–90.

favorable review – also that of *The Observer*.[1] – We might make money out
of a private edition of the book – sure to.

Yours   D. H. Lawrence

Though I am going away as soon as I get a ship.

1079. To J. B. Pinker, 30 November 1915
Text: MS Forster; Huxley 280.

Garsington Manor, Oxford
30 Nov 1915

Dear Pinker,

Thank you very much for the £40. But where did it come from? Have
you advanced it out of your own account? You shouldn't do that.

Good about Conard.[2] I will write to Prince Bibesco.

This place is so beautiful, so complete, and so utterly past, bygone,
reminiscent, that it seems like a dying man seeing the whole of his past life
in a flash, as he dies. But I look at the ruffled turkeys on the farm – there
are wild turkeys in Florida.

Yours   D. H. Lawrence

1080. To Prince Antoine Bibesco, 30 November 1915
Text: MS Lazarus; Unpublished.

Garsington Manor, Oxford
30 Nov 1915

Dear Prince Bibesco,

I wrote to my agent Pinker about the publication of the *Rainbow* in Paris.
He knows Conard personally, so that he thinks probably he can bring the
thing off.

I should be very glad if you also would write to Conard, to persuade him,
as you said you would.

Yours Sincerely   D. H. Lawrence

1081. To S. S. Koteliansky, [30 November 1915]
Text: MS BL; Postmark, Garsington 1 DE 15; Zytaruk 58.

Garsington Manor, Oxford
Tuesday

---

[1] The *Observer* printed no review of the novel before this date. Presumably DHL was
misremembering its account of the prosecution of Methuen and Co. on 14 November 1915.
[2] See Letter 1072.

My dear Kot,

We are down here for a day or two.

Pinker – my agent – is making arrangements with Conard – a sort of Tauchnitz publisher in Paris – to publish the *Rainbow* in English there. That would be a good idea.

I wonder if you know Zenaida Vengerova's present address:[1] if you would ask her, could she let me have back the proofs of the novel, which I sent her some time ago, so that Conard could print from them. In that case it would not be necessary to tear a book to pieces.

We shall be back on Friday – come and see us during the week-end. I hope soon we shall be going to Florida.

Many Greetings from D. H. Lawrence

1082. To Lady Ottoline Morrell, 1 December 1915

Text: MS UT; Huxley 280–2.

Garsington
1st December 1915

So vivid a vision, everything so visually poignant, it is like that concentrated moment when a drowning man sees all his[2] past crystallised into one jewel of recollection.

The slow, reluctant, pallid morning, unwillingly releasing its tarnished embellishment of gold, far off there, outside, beyond the shafted windows, beyond, over the forgotten, unseen country, that lies sunken in gloom[3] below, whilst the dawn sluggishly bestirs itself, far off, beyond the window-shafts of stone, dark pillars, like bars, dark and unfathomed, set near me, before the reluctance of the far-off dawn:

the window shafts, like pillars, like bars, the shallow Tudor arch looping over between them, looping the darkness in a pure edge, in front of the far-off reluctance of the dawn:

Shafted, looped windows between[4] the without and the within, the old house, the perfect old intervention of fitted stone, fitted perfectly about a silent soul, the soul that in drowning under this last wave of time looks out clear through the shafted windows to see the dawn of all dawns taking place, the England of all recollection rousing into being:

[1] Zinaida Afanasevna Vengerova (1867–1941) was a translator mainly of plays into Russian, but also of Trotsky into English. It is possible that she had the proofs of *The Rainbow* in connection with the plan mentioned in Letter 972 to publish a Russian translation of the novel. See also Letter 1087.

[2] his] the

[3] gloom] darkness

[4] between] within

the wet lawn drizzled with brown, sodden leaves; the feathery heap of the ilex tree; the garden-seat all wet and reminiscent:

between the ilex tree and the bare, purplish elms, a gleaming segment of all England, the dark plough-land and wan grass, and the blue, hazy heap of the distance, under the accomplished morning.

So the day has taken place, all the visionary business of the day. The young cattle stand in the straw of the stack yard, the sun gleams on their white fleece, the eyes of Io,[1] and the man with side-whiskers carries more yellow straw into the compound. The sun comes in all down one side, and above, in the sky, all the gables and the grey stone chimney-stacks are floating in pure dreams.

There is threshed wheat smouldering in the great barn, the fire of life; and the sound of the threshing machine, running, drumming.

The threshing machine, running, drumming, waving its steam in a corner of a great field, the rapid nucleus of darkness beside the yellow ricks: and the rich plough-land comes up, ripples up in endless grape-coloured ripples, like a tide of procreant desire: the machine sighs and drums, wind blows the chaff in little eddies, blows the clothes of the men on the ricks close against their limbs: the men on the stacks in the wind against a bare blue heaven, their limbs blown clean in contour, naked shapely animated fragments of earth active in heaven:

coming home, by the purple and crimson hedges, red with berries, up hill over the heavy ground to the stone, old, three[2]-pointed house with its raised chimney stacks, the old manor lifting its fair, pure stone amid trees and foliage, rising from the lawn, we pass the pond where white ducks hastily launch upon the lustrous, dark grey water.

So to the steps up the porch, through the doorway, and into the interior, fragrant with all the memories of old age, and of by-gone, remembered lustiness.

It is the vision of a drowning man, the vision of all that I am, all I have become, and ceased to be. It is me, generations and generations me, every complex, gleaming fibre of me, every lucid pang of my coming into being. And oh, my God, I cannot bear it. For it is not this me who am drowning swiftly under this last wave of time, this bursten flood.

But in the farmyard up the hill, I remember, there were clusters of turkeys that ruffled themselves like flowers suddenly ruffled into blossom, and made strange, unacquainted noises, a foreign tongue, exiles of another life.

[1] Mistress of Zeus who turned her into a beautiful heifer.
[2] three] two

In Florida they will go in droves in the shadow, like metallic clouds, like flowers with red pistils drooping in the shade, under the quivering, quick, miraculous roof of pine-needles, or drifting between the glowing pine trunks, metallic birds, or perched at evening like cones on the red hot pine boughs, or bursting in the morning across open glades of sunshine, like[1] flowers burst and taking wing.

There is a morning which dawns like an iridescence on the wings of sleeping darkness, till the darkness bursts and flies off in glory, dripping with the rose of morning.

There is the soaring suspense of day, dizzy with sunshine, and night flown away and utterly forgotten.

There is evening coming to settle amid the red-hot bars of the pine-trunks, dark cones, that emit the utter, electric darkness.

Another dawn, another day, another night – another heaven and earth – a resurrection –

D. H. Lawrence

1083. To S. S. Koteliansky, [3 December 1915]
Text: MS BL; PC; Postmark, Hampstead 3 DEC 15; Zytaruk 60.

Hampstead
Friday

Come on Sunday evening instead of Saturday – will you please.

Yours   D. H. Lawrence

Bring me 2 sets of *Signatures* also, will you.

1084. To Lady Ottoline Morrell, 3 December 1915
Text: MSS IEduc and StaU; Huxley 282–3.

1, Byron Villas, Vale-of-Health, Hampstead, London.
3 Dec 1915

My dear Ottoline,

You cannot conceive how dark and hideous London is today, mouldering in a dank fog. I am glad we have let this flat. Even were we staying in England, I should have to leave London.

We were so sorry the flowers were not with the berries, in Oxford, at the station yesterday, and so glad when they came this morning. They are on

[1] like] that

the table, under your embroidery, which hangs on the wall. It is a great success, in its dark green frame. We love it: it is like a new presence in the house: it gives a new quality to the room: quite new. It is strange.

We had some fine hours, all of us together, didn't we? But there comes the inevitable friction. Frieda hates me because she says I am *a favorite*, which is ignominious (she says), also she says I am a traitor to her. But let it be – it is a bore.

This morning Prince Bibesco came to see us. He was rather nice – really concerned about the injustice to *The Rainbow*. But I liked him: his nature is really rather fresh – but not deep. Perhaps in society he is less simple.

Carswell – a new barrister – very much wants to have the case of *The Rainbow* fought out. He says there is a clear and complete case of libel against Clement Shorter[1] and James Douglas:[2] also he says, that acting on Sir John Simon's suggestion, one could have another copy of *The Rainbow* seized, and I could bring the whole matter into court, and have it threshed out.[3] – But my spirit[4] will not rise to it – I can't come so near to them as to fight them. I have done with them. I am not going to pay any more out of my soul, even for the sake of beating them.

We hear of the *Crown de Leon*, a tramp steamer sailing on the 20th of this month, to the West Indies. Probably we shall go by that. It takes a month to reach its destination. But I don't mind that. Heseltine wants to come with us, when we sail, if possible – and failing that, as soon after as he can. Suhrawardy also wants to come.[5] We shall have our little[6] colony yet – which is what I have always wanted.

I think it will be quite easy for us to get enough subscribers for a private edition of the *Rainbow*. It seems, that Methuen, in disowning the book, has forfeited all his copyright, so we are free to do as we like.[7] Only there must

[1] Clement King Shorter (1857–1926), journalist and critic; editor of the *Illustrated London News* (1891–1900); editor of the *Sketch* (1893–1900) which he founded; from 1900, editor of the *Sphere*, which he also founded. Among his publications are *Charlotte Brontë and Her Circle* (1896) and *George Borrow* (1913). His review of DHL's *The Rainbow* in the *Sphere* on 23 October 1915, was extremely hostile: 'Zola's novels are child's food compared with the strong meat contained in [*The Rainbow*]'. This opinion was quoted by the prosecuting solicitor, Herbert Muskett, in court on 13 November. (See Draper 96–7.)

[2] James Douglas (1867–1940), editor of the London *Star* and then of the *Sunday Express* (1920–31). His review of *The Rainbow* in the *Star*, 22 October 1914, p. 4, was as hostile as Shorter's; he thought the book 'has no right to exist'. (See Draper 93–5.)

[3] DHL refers to the statement in the House of Commons made by Sir John Simon on 1 December 1915: 'I imagine it will be possible, if the author thinks he has been wrongly treated, for another copy to be seized by arrangement, in order that he might defend the book' (Nehls, i. 335).

[4] spirit] soul   [5] Hasan Shahid Suhrawardy; see p. 452 n. 2.

[6] From here to the end of the letter the text derives from MS StaU.

[7] See p. 457 n. 2.

be no publicity. Prince Bibesco will send subscribers. Tonight the man Bischoff Collins, the Cambridge Press man, is coming to see us about this business of private printing. I will let you know what he says.

Thank Phillip very much for all he has done for the book. Tell him it isn't important what Pinker says – I'm glad the second question went so well.

By Monday or Tuesday I shall know finally about a ship. Then we can make last preparations. You don't think Conscription will prevent our going?[1]

Send Bertie also out to Florida, in a little while.

I like Suhrawardy and Heseltine very much.[2]

With love to you, and to the children.

D. H. Lawrence

1085. To Catherine Carswell, [c. 3 December 1915]
Text: MS YU; Unpublished.

[1, Byron Villas, Vale-of-Health, Hampstead, London.]
[c. 3 December 1915][3]

Phillip Morrell writes he will see Don, if Don will ring him up – 44 Bedford Square – tomorrow before 2.0 oclock. But he doesn't think it any good at all proceeding with the case, legally – no good at all having it come in the courts. Hope to see you soon.

D. H. Lawrence

1086. To Gustav Biart-Bellens, [3? December 1915]
Text: MS NYPL; Unpublished.

[1, Byron Villas, Vale-of-Health, Hampstead, London]
[3? December 1915]

[Lawrence responded to Biart-Bellens' enquiry as to how he might acquire a copy of *The Rainbow*, by suggesting that he should apply to J. B. Pinker for advice.][4]

---

[1] The possibility of compulsory military service was being keenly debated in Parliament and the country; it produced a serious split in the Cabinet; but finally, on 29 December 1915, the Cabinet accepted the principle of compulsion.

[2] Lady Ottoline did not share DHL's enthusiasm: she did not 'understand the Indian Sarawadi' and found Heseltine 'soft and so degenerate that he seems somehow corrupt' (*Ottoline at Garsington* 77).

[3] Dated with reference to Letter 1084, and Donald Carswell's desire to have 'the case of *The Rainbow* fought out'.

[4] The existence of DHL's letter is established by an unpublished letter from Biart-Bellens to Pinker, 8 December 1915 (MS NYPL). Nothing is known of Biart-Bellens except that he resided from 1915 to 1920 at 25 Hoole Road, Broomhill, Sheffield.

1087. To J. B. Pinker, 4 December 1915
Text: TMSC Lazarus; Unpublished.

1, Byron Villas, Vale-of-Health, Hampstead, N.W.
4 Dec. 1915.

Dear Pinker,

It seems *The Rainbow* is going to struggle out of the cloud of obscurity after all – one gleam of sunshine is enough to show a rainbow. I will let you have the galley-proofs to print from – I wish I could lay hold of the revised proofs, but I am afraid they have gone to Russia.[1]

Are you going on with the protest from the authors?[2]

I enclose a letter from Paris – nothing, I expect. Prince Bibesco came to see me – he is writing to Conard.

I will surely see you before we go away.

Yours,   D. H. Lawrence

1088. To John Middleton Murry, 4 December 1915
Text: MS NYPL; Huxley 287–8.

1, Byron Villas, Vale-of-Health, Hampstead, N.W.
4 Dec 1915

Dear Murry,

You are a miserable devil – always lamentoso. You feel sick at being ejected from your habitual surroundings – it is natural. But do look on the bright side!!

I wrote you a letter to Cook's at Marseilles.[3] I hope you got it.

As you surmise, we are still here. But we are struggling gradually free. I have let this flat – transferred the whole of the lease – unfurnished. I have got buyers for most of the furniture. So we've got to move from here. I've collected some money. I am on the track of a ship going to the West Indies. I have got letters of introduction to men in Fort Myers, Florida. And I hope to be allowed to sail on the 20th of this month, from Glasgow, by the *Crown de Leon*, going to Barbadoes, Trinidad and God knows where.

[1] See p. 459 n. 1.
[2] See Letter 1064. DHL had not left the initiative wholly in Pinker's hands. Edward Garnett wrote to Pinker, 1 December 1915 (MS NYPL): 'Mr D. H. Lawrence tells me that you are getting up a petition by the Authors against the suppression of *The Rainbow*. I shall be glad to sign this, if so. Of course the book ought to have been revised and a few passages cancelled before publication, but even so, the procedure was unjustifiable.'
[3] Thomas Cook Ltd, the travel agency. The letter referred to may have been 1070; Katherine Mansfield wrote to Kot from Marseilles on 19 November 1915.

I think France must be very bad, as far as the people go.

I wish you were sailing with us on the *Crown de Leon*: if we go off in it.

The Rainbow is probably coming out in a private edition. There is a good bit of fuss in the literary world. They want me to stay and have a lawsuit. But I'm damned if I will, if I can but get off. At any rate we leave here before the 20th.

I see you back in London, come the New Year. Perhaps we shall still be detained here – perhaps not. But of course we shall always be in connection, you and I. Only for God's sake, don't be lamentable. We will get along and have a good time yet – patience, mon ami – le diable est mourant.[1]

Thank Katharine for her cards. London is vile beyond words: a fog that hurts one's insides. Praise God that you have a clear air. We have both got heavy colds.

I have found a nice man called Heseltine who will come to Florida – a musician, 21, very nice – also an Indian – very nice. We will have a happy time yet, we will blossom like the rose. At the present it is the heaviest of winters.

Love to Katharine and you from both of us.

D. H. Lawrence

Don't come back to London – be advised – it is so wretched.[2]

1089. To Lady Cynthia Asquith, 5 December 1915
Text: MS UT; Huxley 283–5.

1 Byron Villas – Vale of Health – Hampstead, N.W.

Sunday 5 Decem. 1915.

My dear Lady Cynthia,

I am sorry we were away when you were up in town. Still, it was jolly to be at the Ottolines: it is in its way so beautiful, one is tempted to give in, and to stay there, to lapse back into its peaceful beauty of bygone things, to live in pure recollection, looking at the accomplished past, which is so lovely. But one's soul rebels.

We played and acted in the hall with the children. The Ottoline has hundreds of exquisite rags, heaps of coloured cloths and things, like an Eastern bazaar. One can dress up splendidly. I wish you were there with

---

[1] 'patience, my friend – the devil is dying'.

[2] Katherine Mansfield gave up the lease to the house at 5 Acacia Road, St John's Wood in November 1915 and went to the south of France. Murry went with her, but returned to England after three weeks. At the end of December 1915, Katherine and Murry rented the Villa Pauline in Bandol, where they stayed until April 1916.

us one time, we could all dress up. One can only be perfectly happy, now, in a world of make-belief. But that is very delightful. There was an Indian there – a lineal descendent of the Prophet, whose curse is a dreadful thing – and a young musician, and Bertie Russell. Of course we talked violently in between-whiles, politics and India and so on. I always shout too loud. That annoys the Ottoline. The Indian says (he is of Persian family): 'Oh, she is *so* like a Persian princess, it is strange – something grand, and perhaps cruel.' It is pleasant to see with all kinds of eyes, like Argus.[1] Suhrawardy was my pair of Indo-persian eyes. He is coming to Florida.

We are ready now to go, waiting for the last news of the ship, finally to book the passages. We think to go by the *Crown de Leon*, which sails from Glasgow on the 20th of this month, going to the Barbadoes, and to Trinidad, and to Demarara. She is a tramp steamer who carries a few passengers. I don't know where she will eventually land us: but I don't care. When we come ashore, we can ask 'Pray, what is this place?'[2] And no doubt at last, like the Israelites in the desert, we shall come to some Canaan. I am really bound to Fort Myers in Florida: I have the letters of introduction to the important townspeople there: but it seems only a bird can come to the town, there is no railway and no regular ship.

I want you please to write to your friend in the Foreign Office to ask him what we need to do, what other permits we need to have, over and above our pass-ports. Somebody says we must have another visa from the Foreign Office. And somebody else says I must go to a recruiting office and swear to serve my king and country, and be examined, and thus get an exemption. If I must do so I must. But it makes me angry to go and say I will serve my king and country, when, in the way of war, I won't; it makes me angry also to be stripped naked before two recruiting sergeants, and examined. But I would rather have all these things than stop here. But do you please write this one more time to your friend in the Foreign Office, so I may know exactly what to do. And please let me know at once.

We have transferred the lease of this flat to another man, and most of the furniture is sold: not gone away, only promised. But after the 20th of this month, we have no place here any more. The *Crown de Leon*: I wonder if we shall really sail by her, or by another. – You must have something from the flat, as a memento.

How are you, and how is Herbert Asquith? Is he better? I hope he remains just sufficiently unwell to be kept at home.

---

[1] In Greek legend, the guardian of Io, with a hundred eyes.
[2] Cf. *Twelfth Night* I. ii. 1: 'What country, friends, is this?'

I think that there is just a chance of peace this winter. But I think it will not be taken, that the war will go on.

The Rainbow is going to come out privately, I believe. Are you still bös, angry with everybody? I am not angry. Only I've got a cold and feel evanescent.

Yours   D. H. Lawrence

1090. To William Hopkin, 7 December 1915
Text: MS NCL; cited in Pollak, *Journal of Modern Literature*, iii. 30.

1 Byron Villas – Vale of Health – Hampstead, N.W.
7 Dec. 1915.

Dear Willie,

I was glad to hear from you, that you are still safe and sound, you three. As for the *Rainbow*, the suppression was caused by a certain league – the league for the promotion of moral purity, I believe it calls itself.[1] It is very proud of its action. What fools and cowards this world is made up of!

We are trying to get away to Florida for a while: into the sunshine and a little peace. I hope it will come off. The devils make such a fuss about a man's leaving England now. – But in any case, we shall see you soon: – before Christmas, as we shall be paying a certain visit to Ripley.

I will get you a copy of the *Rainbow* in a little while, either from the American edition, or from a set that will, I think, be printed for private circulation. So have only a little more patience. But I don't expect you to like the book very much: Sallie I know will lift an accusatory finger against me, for cruelty and what not. But it is not true: the book is a big book.

Frieda sends warm greetings, we shall be seeing you very shortly now.

Yours   D. H. Lawrence

1091. To Aldous Huxley, [7? December 1915]
Text: TMSC Moore; Moore 393.

[1, Byron Villas, Vale-of-Health, Hampstead, London.]
[7? December 1915][2]

Dear Mr Huxley,

Lady Ottoline Morrell wrote to me, that we ought to know each other.[3]

---

[1] Richard Aldington states that the 'prosecution for obscenity, [was] instigated by the self-styled Public Morality Council of London, a body of puritanical fanatics who were making themselves patriotically useful by trying to suppress anything they didn't approve' (*Life For Life's Sake*, 1968, p. 209). See DHL's similar explanation in Letter 1103. This assertion has been seriously questioned; see Delavenay, *D. H. Lawrence: The Man and His Work*, pp. 240–2.
[2] Dated with reference to the remark in Letter 1092: 'I have written to Huxley.'
[3] DHL would have met Huxley at Garsington on 29 November 1915; see p. 452 n. 2.

I should be glad if you would let me know when you come to London, so you can come and have tea with us here. I am afraid we may be going away in about a fortnight's time, so come before that is up.

Yours sincerely   D. H. Lawrence

1092. To Lady Ottoline Morrell, 7 December 1915
Text: MS UT; Huxley 285–6.

1 Byron Villas – Vale of Health – Hampstead, N.W.

7 Dec. 1915

My dear Ottoline,

I have written to Huxley to ask him to come here as soon as he is in London. I will see also if Brett will come to tea with us, without Gertler's omnipresent guardianship.

I also think, that perhaps, in a little while, I can unite with the very young people, to do something. But first let them try their teeth on the world, let them taste it thoroughly as it is, so that they shall be ready to reject it. I feel my going away will only be a sort of retirement to get strength and concord in myself. I am pretty sick also, and must get robust again in spirit. Also this country must go through some stages of its disease, till I am any good for it, or it is any good for me. It is full of unripe ulcers, that must come out, come to a head, then perhaps they can be lanced and healed. It must work out the impurity which is now deep-seated in its blood. There is no other help for it.

Why are you so sad about your life? Only let go all this will to have things in your own control. We must all submit to be helpless and obliterated, quite obliterated, destroyed, cast away into nothingness. There is something will rise out of it, something new, that now is not. This which we are must cease to be, that we may come to pass in another being. Do not struggle with your will, to dominate your conscious life – do not do it. Only drift, and let go – let go, entirely, and become dark, quite dark – like winter which mows away all the leaves and flowers, and lets only the dark underground roots remain. Let all the leaves and flowers and arborescent form of your life be cut off and cast away, all cut off and cast away, all the old life, so that only the deep roots remain in the darkness underground, and you have no place in the light, no place at all. Let all knots be broken, all bonds unloosed, all connections slackened and released, all released, like the trees which release their leaves, and the plants which die away utterly above ground, let go all their being and pass away, only sleep in the profound darkness where being takes place again.

Do not keep your will in your *conscious* self. Forget, utterly forget, and let go. Let your will lapse back into your unconscious self, so you move in a sleep, and in darkness, without sight or understanding. Only then you will act straight from the dark source of [. . .] life, outwards, which is creative life.

I tell this to you, I tell it to myself – to let go, to release from my will everything that my will would hold, to lapse back into darkness and unknowing. There must be deep winter before there can be spring.

I will let you know when anything happens to our plans.

D. H. Lawrence

Only do not struggle – let go and become dark, quite dark.

1093. To Herbert Thring, 8 December 1915
Text: MS BL; Unpublished.

1 Byron Villas – Vale of Health – Hampstead, N.W.
8 Dec. 1915.

Dear Sir,

I have your letter informing me of my election to your society.[1] I beg to enclose my subscription for the coming year.

With regard to the printing of names and addresses in *The Author*, will you please not give this address of mine, as I am leaving London immediately and am not quite sure where I shall be.[2]

Thank you also for your further letter referring to *The Rainbow*,[3]

Yours Sincerely   D. H. Lawrence

1094. To Bertrand Russell, 8 December 1915
Text: MS UT; Moore, *Atlantic Monthly* 100–2.

1 Byron Villas – Vale-of-Health – Hampstead, N.W.
8 Dec. 1915

Dear Russell,

I called to see you yesterday but you were out. I hope you will come up and see us soon. – No definite developement in our plans.

---

[1] DHL was formally elected to the Society of Authors on 6 December 1915; see *TLS*, 27 February 1969, p. 216.

[2] *The Author*, xxvi (1 January 1916), 82 reported the 'December Elections, 1915', including the name of 'Lawrence, W. H.'. No address is given.

[3] The substance of the letter was as follows: 'This matter was referred to the Committee at their meeting held yesterday, and I am asked to inform you that after full consideration of the position, and after hearing the opinion of the Solicitors in regard to the legal aspect, the Committee came to the conclusion that in the present circumstances they could not take any useful action on the general principles involved' (*TLS*, 27 February 1969, p. 216).

I have been reading Frazer's *Golden Bough* and *Totemism and Exogamy*.[1]
Now I am convinced of what I believed when I was about twenty – that there
is another seat of consciousness than the brain and the nerve system: there
is a blood-consciousness which exists in us independently of the ordinary
mental consciousness, which depends on the eye as its source or connector.
There is the blood-consciousness, with the sexual connection, holding the
same relation as the eye, in seeing, holds to the mental consciousness. One
lives, knows, and has one's being in the blood, without any reference to nerves
and brain. This is one half of life, belonging to the darkness. And the tragedy
of this our life, and of your life, is that the mental and nerve consciousness
exerts a tyranny over the blood-consciousness, and that your will has gone
completely over to the mental consciousness, and is engaged in the
destruction of your blood-being or blood-consciousness, the final liberating
of the one, which is only death in result. Plato was the same. Now it is
necessary for us to realise that there is this other great half of our life active
in the darkness, the blood-relationship: that when I *see*, there is a connection
between my mental-consciousness and an outside body, forming a percept;
but at the same time, there is a transmission through the darkness which
is never absent from the light, into my blood-consciousness: but in seeing,
the blood-percept is perhaps not strong. On the other hand, when I take a
woman, then the blood-percept is supreme, my blood-knowing is overwhelming. There is a transmission, I don't know of what, between her blood
and mine, in the act of connection. So that afterwards, even if she goes away,
the blood-consciousness persists between us, when the mental consciousness
is suspended; and I am formed then by my blood-consciousness, not by my
mind or nerves at all.

Similarly in the transmission from the blood of the mother to the embryo
in the womb, there goes the whole *blood* consciousness. And when they say
a mental image is sometimes transmitted from the mother to the embryo,
this is not the *mental* image, but the *blood-image*. All living things, even plants,
have a blood-being. If a lizard falls on the breast of a pregnant woman, then
the blood-being of the lizard passes with a shock into the blood-being of the
woman, and is transferred to the foetus, probably without intervention either
of nerve or brain consciousness. And this is the origin of totem: and for this
reason some tribes no doubt really *were* kangaroos: they contained the
blood-knowledge of the kangaroo. – And blood knowledge comes either

---

[1] Sir James George Frazer (1854–1941), Scottish anthropologist, educated at Glasgow. Fellow
of Trinity College, Cambridge. Professor of Social Anthropology at the University of
Liverpool (1907–22). Best known as author of *The Golden Bough* in 12 vols. (1890–1915).
His *Totemism and Exogamy* was published in 4 vols., 1910.

through the mother or through the sex – so that dreams at puberty are as good an origin of the totem as the percept of a pregnant woman.

This is very important to our living, that we should realise that we have a blood-being, a blood-consciousness, a blood-soul, complete and apart from the mental and nerve consciousness.

Do you know what science says about these things? It is *very*[1] important: the whole of our future life depends on it.

Yours   D. H. Lawrence

1095. To Marie Belloc Lowndes, 9 December 1915
Text: MS UT; Postmark, Hampstead 9 DEC 15; Unpublished.

1 Byron Villas – Vale of Health – Hampstead, N.W.
9 Dec. 1915

Dear Mrs Belloc-Lowndes,[2]

My wife and I will be very pleased to see you here tomorrow (Friday) evening at about six o'clock, as you say.

Yours very Sincerely   D. H. Lawrence

1096. To Aldous Huxley, [9? December 1915]
Text: TMSC Moore; Unpublished.

1 Byron Villas – Vale of Health
[9? December 1915][3]

Dear Mr Huxley,

Will you come to tea tomorrow, (Friday) at about 4.30: if not that, then tea on Saturday. We will expect you tomorrow. Come to the Hampstead Tube Station, and walk straight up the hill past the pond and along the Spaniards Road to Jack Straws Castle. Drop down the path facing the inn, straight down into the Vale, and the road to the left will bring you to the centre of the vale, where is Byron Villas.

Yours sincerely   D. H. Lawrence

1097. To Katherine Mansfield, 12 December 1915
Text: MS NYPL; Huxley 288–90.

1 Byron Villas – Vale of Health – Hampstead, N.W.
Sunday, 12 Dec. 1915

My dear Katharine,

Murry turned up on Friday,[4] to my moderate surprise. He doesn't look

---

[1] The word is heavily underlined three times.   [2] See p. 226 n. 1.
[3] In Letter 1091 DHL told Huxley that he would be 'going away in about a fortnight's time';
 this letter was probably written two weeks before his departure on 24 December 1915.
[4] See p. 465 n. 2.

well; tells us of his dreadful experience in France, and is *very* chirpy. At
the present I am not very much in sympathy with him, so I won't say any
more about it. He came yesterday with Goodyear,[1] whom I like, but who
is on the same Oxford introspective line, who has an 'inner life' to concern
himself with – which bores me. I'm sick to death of people who are wrapped
up in their own inner lives, inner selves.

We are on the point of departure, where to I don't know. We leave this
flat on the 20th; the furniture is sold, the lease transferred altogether. So
after the 20th we are free – We spend Christmas with my sister: *c/o Mrs
Clarke, Grosvenor Rd, Ripley, Derbyshire*. After that I don't know what
happens. I am afraid they will not let me leave the country, unless I get an
exemption from service, which I haven't yet got. We may go somewhere in
Somerset, or Devon, I don't know. We *may* even get off to Florida. It is
on the knees of the Gods, and I am not troubling. At any rate we leave
London permanently. I cannot live here.

No doubt you hear of Murrys scheme for publishing books, the authors'
to be publishers.[2] But what I wonder is, are there either books or authors,[3]
at the present moment. There are Gilbert Cannans and Beresfords, but I
have nothing to do with them. I intend to lie fallow for a bit. I know one
or two very young people – 20, 21, 22 – who seem to have something real
in them, for a new phase. But it is necessary that these unite together: a
perfectly new *body* of purpose, that is the only thing that will avail anything.
Perhaps it will come – but nobody can force it into being. So for the time
being, everything is unresolved, and must remain so until it resolves of itself.
Mental decisions are of no use. It is a matter of underground developement,
developement of new being in the roots of life, not in the head.

One thing I know, I am tired of this insistence on the *personal* element:
personal truth, personal reality. It is very stale and profitless. I want some
new non-personal activity, which is at the same time a genuine vital activity.
And I want relations which are not purely personal, based on purely personal
qualities; but relations based upon some unanimous accord in truth or
belief, and a harmony of *purpose*, rather than of personality. I am weary of
personality. It remains now whether Murry is still based upon the personal

---

[1] Frederick Goodyear (1887–1917) was a friend of Murry's from his days at Brasenose College,
Oxford. According to Murry, 'Goodyear, who had gone to the war, returned at this moment
on leave. He slept the night on my attic floor, and went the next day with me to see the
Lawrences' (Murry, *Autobiography* 376). He was killed in France, May 1917 (see *Times*, 27
May 1917).

[2] It may have led DHL and Heseltine to issue the *Prospectus for the Rainbow Books and Music*
in February 1916. See p. 542 n. 1. Murry was apparently offended at DHL's appropriation
of his idea.   [3] authors] publishers

hypothesis: because if he is, then our ways are different. I don't want a purely personal relation with him: he is a man, therefore our relation should be based on *purpose*; not upon that which we *are*, but upon that which we wish to bring to pass.[1] I am sick and tired of personality in every way. Let us be easy and impersonal, not forever fingering over our own souls, and the souls of our acquaintances, but trying to create a new life, a new common life, a new complete tree of life from the roots that are in us. I am weary to death of these dead, dry leaves of personalities which flap in every wind.

My dear Katharine, you know that in this we are your sincere friends, and what we want is to create a new, good, common life, the germ of a new social life altogether. That is what we want. But we must grow from our deepest underground roots, out of the *unconsciousness*, not from the conscious concepts which we falsely call ourselves. Murry irritates me and falsifies me, and I must tell him so. He makes *me* false. If that must always be so, then there is no relation between us. But we must try that there *is* a living relation between us, all of us, because then we shall be happy.

Frieda sends her love, I mine.

D. H. Lawrence

1098. To Lady Ottoline Morrell, 12 December 1915
Text: MS UT; Huxley 290–2.

1 Byron Villas – Vale of Health – Hampstead, N.W.

12 Dec. 1915

My dear Ottoline,

Thank you for the letter and the pound. The last I *did not want*.

I hear Heseltine and Kouyoumdjian[2] are coming to you tomorrow. Heseltine is a bit backboneless and needs stiffening up. But I like him very much. Kouyoumdjian seems a bit blatant and pushing: you may be put off him. But that is because he is *very foreign*, even though he doesn't know it himself. In English life he is in a strange, alien medium, and he can't adjust himself. But I find the core of him *very good*. One must be patient with his[3]

---

[1] to bring to pass] done.
[2] Dikran Kouyoumdjian (1895–1956), original name of Michael Arlen, novelist. b. Bulgaria; became a British citizen (1922); later moved to USA. His works include *The Green Hat* (1924), *Man's Mortality* (1933), *The Crooked Coronet* (1937) and *Flying Dutchman* (1939). Lady Ottoline recalls: 'Kouyoumdjian is a fat dark-blooded tight-skinned Armenian Jew, and though Lawrence believes that he will be a great writer, I find it hard to believe. Obviously he has a certain vulgar sexual force, but he is very coarse-grained and conceited' (*Ottoline at Garsington* 77).
[3] MS reads 'is'.

jarring manner, and listen to the sound decency that is in him. He is not a bit rotten, which most young cultivated Englishmen are.

Murry is back, and I am rather out of sympathy with him. Bertie came. He is growing *much better*: he is going to become young and new. I have more hopes.

Don't trust Brett very much: I think she doesn't quite tell the truth about herself to you. She is very satisfied as she is, really very satisfied. She is one of the 'sisters' of this life, her rôle is always to be a sister.

We leave here on the 20th – go to my sister's in Derbyshire for Christmas, and then I don't know where. I must say I feel again a certain amount of slow, subterranean hope. It wont put forth any leaves, nor show[1] any activity yet, I believe: but it seems to be full and nascent somewhere in the under-earth of my soul. Probably we shall go to the West – Devon, Somerset – for a while after Christmas, I don't know. I must let things work themselves into being. One can do nothing now, forcing is disastrous. I shall not go to America until a stronger force from there pulls me across the sea. It is not a case of my will.

I went to a recruiting station yesterday to be attested and to get a military exemption. But I hated it so much, after waiting nearly two hours, that I came away. And yet, waiting there in the queue, I felt the *men* were very decent, and that the slumbering lion was going to wake up in them: not against the Germans either, but against the great lie of this life. I felt all the men were decent, even the police and the officials. It was at Battersea Town Hall. A strange, patient spirit possesses everybody, as under a doom, a bad fate superimposed. But I felt the patience rested upon slumbering strength, not exhaustion, and the strength would begin before long to stretch itself [...] like a waking lion. I felt, though I *hated*[2] the situation almost to *madness*, so vile and false and degrading, such an utter travesty of action on my part, waiting even to be attested that I might be rejected, still I felt, when suddenly I broke out of the queue, in face of the table where one's name was to be written, and went out, across the hall away from all the underworld of this spectral submission, and climbed a bus, and in a while saw the fugitive sunshine across the river on the spectral, sunlit towers at Westminster, that I had triumphed, like Satan flying over the world and knowing he had won at last, though he had not come into even a fragment of his own. I feel somewhere that the triumph is mine, remote, oh very remote and buried underground, but the triumph is mine. It is only the immediate present which frightens me and bullies me. In the long run, I have the victory: for

---

[1] MS reads 'any show'   [2] The word is heavily underlined five times.

all those men in the queue, for those spectral, hazy, sunny towers hovering beyond the river, for the world that is to be. Endless patient strength and courage, that is all that is necessary – and the avoiding of disaster.

Let us only be still, and know we can force nothing, and compel nothing, can only nourish in the darkness the unuttered buds of the new life that shall be. That is our life now: this nourishing of the germs, the unknown quicks where the new life is coming into being in us and in others. I have hope of Bertie too – only patience, only patience, and endless courage to reject false dead things and false, killing processes.

With love from Frieda and me   D. H. Lawrence

I shall see Phillip on Tuesday at the House.[1]

1099. To J. B. Pinker, 14 December 1915
Text: TMSC Lazarus; Unpublished.

1 Byron Villas, Vale-of-Health, Hampstead, N.W.
14 Dec. 1915.

My dear Pinker,

I don't know what to call the book: something plain: Studies of Restless Italy – An Italian Winter – Uneasy Italy – Studies of Italian Restlessness – I can't think of anything – I like the last title best.[2]

We leave here on the 22nd, for good: going to the country for a while, then, I hope, soon to Florida.

I hear Huebsch is sailing on the Peace Ship:[3] is Doran too? When are they publishing *The Rainbow*, do you know.[4] Mountsier wrote me that the editor of *The Metropolitan Magazine* was praising the book enthusiastically – heaven knows why.

Yours   D. H. Lawrence

1100.   To Lady Cynthia Asquith, 14 December 1915
Text: Asquith, *Diaries* 111.

[1, Byron Villas, Vale-of-Health, Hampstead, N.W.]
[14 December 1915]

['The Lawrences were to have lunched with me [Lady Cynthia] somewhere, but I got a telegram to say he couldn't come – he was ill – so I lunched in.']

---

[1] i.e the House of Commons.
[2] The title selected in the end was *Twilight in Italy*.
[3] The American billionaire Henry Ford (1863–1947) chartered a 'peace ship', the *Oscar II*, in an effort to bring World War I to a peaceful settlement. It sailed from New York on 4 December 1915. B. W. Huebsch, DHL's publisher, was among the passengers. The *Times* reported (6 December 1915): 'There is no one of any prominence in American political or professional life on board.'   [4] See p. 420 n. 2.

1101. To Lady Ottoline Morrell, 15 December 1915
Text: MS StaU; Schorer 56.

1 Byron Villas – Hampstead Vale
15 Dec. 1915

My dear Ottoline,

I am laid up again with a bad cold, which I hate. I must go to a warmer place, these colds come too often.

Murry is here – homeless infant as usual. I am sure he would be very grateful if you could offer him your hospitality for Christmas. She is still in France.[1] His address is

J. M. Murry, 23 Worsley Rd, Hampstead, N.W.
Perhaps you might be able to tuck in his forlornness for a few days.

We are going to my sister's on the 23rd – leaving here on the 22nd. My sister is *Mrs Clarke, Grosvenor Rd, Ripley, Derbyshire.* It is she whom I should like you to see one day.

You hear the project of the Berkshire farmhouse, in the interim of going to Florida.[2] I think it would be well. You could drive over to see us. But I *do* want to go to Florida – when I get sick like this I know I ought to have gone before.

I shan't stay long in Ripley – the whole family will be there, and I cant bear it for long. If the Berkshire place is not available, could we come to the rooms over the bailiffs house – Berties rooms[3] – for a day or two, do you think – say from the 28th? What a wandering state we[4] are in.

Let me know how you liked Heseltine this time, and Kouyoumdjian.

With love from us both   D. H. Lawrence

Murry says he will go on with the *Signature* in January. I must have sent my MS. to you – 'The Crown IV, V, and VI.'[5] I wonder if you would look in one of the smaller parcels – any time.

---

[1] Katherine Mansfield was at the Villa Pauline, Bandol.

[2] DHL moved to Cornwall instead, but later, at Christmas 1917, he went to live in Dollie Radford's cottage at Hermitage in Berkshire. Perhaps the latter was being considered at this time.

[3] Bertrand Russell, a frequent visitor at Garsington, was having an affair with Lady Ottoline. When Philip Morrell first learned this, he imposed the condition on the two that they 'should never spend a night together' (Russell, *Autobiography*, i. 205). Russell was therefore always accommodated in rooms apart from the main house at Garsington.

[4] we] you

[5] The last three parts, which did not appear in *The Signature*.

1102. To Marie Belloc Lowndes, [15 December 1915]
Text: MS UT; Unpublished.

1, Bryon Villas, Vale-of-Health, Hampstead, London.

Wednesday[1]

Dear Mrs Lowndes,

I am in bed just now with a bad cold, so I feel it would be impolitic to promise to come to tea on Friday, though we should have liked to. Will you then please accept our thanks for the invitation, and allow us to come some later day.

Yours very Sincerely   D. H. Lawrence

1103. To Thomas Dunlop, 16 December 1915
Text: MS Dunlop; Huxley 293–5.

1, Byron Villas, Vale-of-Health, Hampstead, London.

16 Dec. 1915

Dear Dunlop,

Edward Garnett was up here the other day, talking about you. I must write you a letter for Christmas. I was glad to hear that you and Mrs Dunlop were having a good time, and that the children are all right.

We are going stormily on, as ever. Of course you heard of the suppression of the *Rainbow*. That was a ridiculous affair, instigated by the National Purity League, Dr Horton and Co, nonconformity.[2] Of course I achieved a good deal of notoriety, if not fame, am become one of the regular topics. But the whole thing is nasty and offensive. – I heard that Hatchard's[3] had sold their last copy of the *Rainbow*, sub rosa, for four guineas. So you may even have got an acquisition in that copy of yours.

The American edition will be out by now, I fancy, so we shall be able to get the book from New York.

We are leaving here directly – my proverbial restlessness. We took and furnished this little flat in June – now I have transferred the lease and sold

---

[1] Letter 1095 eliminates Friday, 10 December 1915 as the date of the invitation to tea; DHL left for Ripley on Friday, 24 December; Wednesday, 15 December therefore seems the most likely date for this letter.

[2] Robert Forman Horton, D.D. (1855–1934), Congregational minister and theological writer. Fellow of New College, Oxford, 1879–86. Minister of Congregational Church, Hampstead, 1884–1930. President of National Free Church Council, 1905. Author of over fifty publications including *An Autobiography* (1917).

[3] The London bookshop.

the furniture. I can't bear having a house on my head. I want to go to Florida for a while. This English winter suits me very badly. I think, perhaps, we shall go to Florida in a month or two's time. In the meanwhile we are taking a farm-house on the Berkshire downs, which has been turned into a country place by some friends. Heaven knows how long we shall stay there. I find it impossible to sit still in one place.

At present I am laid up in bed with a very bad sort of cold. I wish to heaven the war would cease, so that one could feel more at rest.

We seem to have lived several little lives away, since you saw us last – known streams of different people – Vanity of Vanities, saith the preacher, all is Vanity.[1] Mrs Lawrence has seen her children once or twice, and has almost ceased to fret about them. I am having a book of Italian Sketches published in January, which I will send you.

That reminds me, I have long intended to ask you if you think I could easily get my MS. verses from Tellaro. All my poems are in little University note books, and in a brown Tagebuch of Frieda's, left behind with the poor old Felice. You know that our Elide died? It made me frightfully miserable. Do you think you might write to the schoolmistress, Signorina Eva Rainusso, Lerici per Tellaro, Sarzana, and ask her to send to you all the books of MS. poems I left with Felice Fiori when I left Fiascherino? I forget how many there are – 2 or 3 black, small note-books with red backs, and a brown Tagebuch, rather bigger – the note books have the Nottingham University arms on them. If you could do this, and if you could send ten Lire for Felice, the dear old soul, I should be *so glad*. I will send you a cheque the minute you let me know. And tell the maestra I am sending her a book. If there is anything I could send for you or Mrs Dunlop, *please* let me know, I should be so glad.

With all good greetings from us for the Christmas.

                                                    Yours   D. H. Lawrence
This address will always find me.

1104. To J. B. Pinker, 16 December 1915
Text: MS Forster; Huxley 295.

                              1, Byron Villas, Vale-of-Health, Hampstead, London.
                                                                        16 Dec 1915
My dear Pinker,

I am glad to hear about the *Rainbow* in America, and very anxious to see the book, to see if they have done anything to it. I shall hate it if they have mutilated it.

---

[1] Ecclesiastes i. 2.

You know Phillip Morrell is anxious to go ahead about the private circulation in England. So you will let him know about the American sheets, wont you. Even if they have made alterations, we might buy sheets and insert just those pages that are altered – no doubt it could be done.

I haven't written a line these many weeks. It is winter with me, my heart is frost-bound. We'll thaw it out one day. If only I could go away.

Tell Arnold Bennett that all rules of construction hold good only for novels which are copies of other novels.¹ A book which is not a copy of other books has its own construction, and what he calls faults, he being an old imitator, I call characteristics. I shall repeat till I am grey – when they have as good a work to show, they may make their pronouncements ex cathedra. Till then, let them learn decent respect.

Still, I think he is generous.

I am laid up in bed with a violent cold, and wonder why one should ever trouble to get up, into this filthy world. The war stinks worse and worse.

Yours   D. H. Lawrence

1105. To Marie Belloc Lowndes, [17? December 1915]
Text: MS PU; Moore 399–400.

1, Byron Villas, Vale-of-Health, Hampstead, London.
Friday²

Dear Mrs Lowndes,

Thank you for the letter and the cutting. That was nice of Arnold Bennett.³

I am afraid I shant be out of doors by Sunday. But we shall be staying in London till Friday, then we might come to tea with you next Wednesday or Thursday, if that would do.

Yours very Sincerely   D. H. Lawrence

Today has come a copy of the *Rainbow* from America – very nice and plain – and I believe only one small passage omitted from the original.⁴ So there is no reason why we shouldn't buy sheets in New York for private publication here.

---

¹ As agent for both men, Pinker clearly acted as go-between in this critical exchange.
² Dated with reference to DHL's illness mentioned in Letter 1104.
³ Mrs Belloc Lowndes was a friend of Arnold Bennett's and probably sent DHL a copy of his long article 'In the Midlands: A Visit to the Workers', *Daily News and Leader*, 15 December 1915. In the article Bennett wrote: 'And I thought of the memorable and awful board-school scenes in Mr D. H. Lawrence's beautiful and maligned novel, *The Rainbow*.'
⁴ Huebsch published his expurgated edition in New York on 30 November 1915. The extent of his expurgations is more accurately defined in the letter following.

1106. To J. B. Pinker, [18 December 1915]

Text: MS UNYB; Moore, *Intelligent Heart* 208–9.

1 Byron Villas – Vale of Health – Hampstead, N.W.
Saturday.

My dear Pinker,

The omissions from the American *Rainbow* are not very many.

Methuen edition

p. *220*: lines 20–24 (3 lines)

(He wished he were a cat – – – her flesh)[1]

p. *300*: line 18 (Let me come – let me come)

p. *318*: lines 7–10 (4 lines)

(Ursula lay still – – – about her mistress)

p. *425*: lines 4–26 (24 lines)

(But the air was cold – – – always laughing)

p. *446*:[2] lines 10–40 (30 lines)

(She let him take her – – – house felt to her)

They are not many, yet they make me sad and angry.[3] If we buy sheets from America to bind here, we ought to print these pages and insert at the back, just saying: 'The following pages from the Methuen edition are[4] printed incomplete in the present edition'.

We might also put a report[5] of the process – the suppression – at the end of the book.

Shall I send you back this copy of the American edition, or shall I keep it?

There may be one or two small omissions, I have not searched very thoroughly, but I dont think there is much.

I am still laid up.

Yours   D. H. Lawrence

1107. To Philip Heseltine, [18? December 1915]

Text: MS NWU; Unpublished.

1 Byron Villas – Vale – Hampstead
Saturday[6]

---

[1] her flesh] let me come   [2] 446] 460

[3] There are five other omissions not noticed by DHL, e.g. Huebsch had deleted the reference to Will's nakedness in the scene in which he gets up to make breakfast for Anna on their honeymoon; two further cuts were made to the account of the relationship between Ursula and Winifred Inger.   [4] Methuen edition are] English edition were

[5] report] copy

[6] Dated with reference to the proposed move to Berkshire which was under consideration at this time.

Dear Heseltine,

Don't lapse away in the wrong direction. It is best if we try Berkshire and Florida – it is best if you come too.

If you are very fond of Mlle Baillot,[1] then marry her. I think it would be best. Have enough of the other,[2] then marry the little Swiss, properly, and she shall come too. I think probably she will suit you better than any English woman you can find. Since I have been thinking about it, I think you are right to be fond of her. She is probably your woman.

Excuse the interference – I do want a few of us to make a good thing of life, a new start. And I think we might do it together.

But always do that which you want most to do.

Come and see me some time, tomorrow if possible – also Suhrawardy.

Yours   D. H. Lawrence

1108. To Katherine Mansfield, 20 December 1915

Text: MS NYPL; Murry, *New Adelphi* 147.

1 Byron Villas – Vale of Health – Hampstead, N. W.
Monday 20 Dec. 1915

My dear Katharine,

Your letter came this morning. I am so sorry you are so ill. Yesterday Murry was here when the letter came – Kot brought it – and he was much upset.

Do not be sad. It is one life which is passing away from us, one 'I' is dying; but there is another coming into being, which is the happy, creative you. I knew you would have to die with your brother; you also, go down into death and be extinguished. But for us there is a rising from the grave, there is a resurrection, and a clean life to begin from the start, new, and happy. Don't be afraid, don't doubt it, it is so.

You have gone further into your death than Murry has. He runs away. But one day he too will submit, he will dare to go down, and be killed, to die in this self which he is. Then he will become a man: not till. He is not a man yet.

When you get better, you must come back and we will begin afresh, it will be the first struggling days of spring, after winter. Our lives have been

---

[1] Marie Juliette Baillot (1896–), who came from Switzerland to Garsington Manor as governess–companion to Julian Morrell. m. 1919 (Sir) Julian Sorell Huxley (1887–1975), the eminent biologist, brother of Aldous Huxley. 'I remember her as a singularly beautiful young woman', wrote Lady Ottoline Morrell (*Ottoline at Garsington* 34).

[2] Minnie Lucie Channing, known as 'Puma', a Soho artist's model, whom Heseltine eventually married. For her portrait see *D. H. Lawrence and His World*, ed. Harry T. Moore and Warren Roberts (1966), p. 55.

all autumnal and wintry. Now it is mid-winter. But we are strong enough to give way, to pass away, and to be born again.

I want so much that we should create a life in common, a new spirit, a spirit of unanimity between a few of us who are desirous in spirit, that we should add our lives together, to make one tree, each of us free and producing in his separate fashion, but all of us together forming one Spring, a unanimous blossoming. It needs that we be one in spirit, that is all. What we are personally is of second importance.

And it is in its inception, this new life. From the old life, all is gone. There remain only you and Murry in our lives. We look at the others as across the grave. A death, and a grave lies between us and them. They are the other side of the grave, the old, far side, these Campbells and Cannans. We must not look back. There must be no looking back. There must be no more retrospection, which is introspection, no more remembering and interpreting. We must look forward into the unknown that is to be, like flowers that come up in the spring. Because we really *are* born again.

We have met one or two young people, just one or two, who have the germ of the new life in them. It doesn't matter what they are personally. Murry dismisses them with a sneer, for all that which is the *past* in them, but I hold on by that which is the future, which is gladdening.

We give up this flat tomorrow. For Christmas we go to my sisters in Derbyshire: c/o Mrs Clarke, Grosvenor Rd, Ripley, Derbyshire. We stay there till the 29th December. Then we go to the Beresfords' cottage in Cornwall, to live there till March.[1] One or two others will come too. I want it now that we live together. When you come back, I want you and Murry to live with us, or near us, in unanimity: not these separations. Let us all live together and create a new world. If it is too difficult in England, because here all is destruction and dying and corruption, let us go away to Florida: soon. But let us go *together*, and keep together, several of us, as being of one spirit. Only let there be no *personal* obligation, no personal idea. Let it be a union in the unconsciousness, not in the consciousness. Get better soon, and come back, and let us all try to be happy *together*, in unanimity, not in hostility, creating, not destroying.
                                              Love from me   D. H. Lawrence

1109. To Lady Ottoline Morrell, [22 December 1915]
Text: MS UT; Postmark, Hendon 23 DEC 15; Huxley 297–8.
                                        2 Hurst Close, Garden Suburb, N.W.
                                                                Wednesday

---

[1] Cf. Murry, *Autobiography* 380: 'I have to go to J. D. Beresford this afternoon [19 December 1915] and see if there is a cottage for [DHL] in Cornwall.' On John and Beatrice Beresford see p. 484 n. 2.

My dear Ottoline,

We are out of the flat – staying here till early Friday morning – then to my sisters for a few days – c/o Mrs Clarke, Grosvenor Rd, Ripley, Derby. We stay there till the 29th – then to *Cornwall*. We've got a house there, and we'll go direct, for my health. I am better.

This man here is the manager – one of the managers of the Oxford University Press.[1] He gives me some of the Ajanta reproductions. They are so lovely, I *must* send you the folio.[2] He will get it me cheaper, and I shall ask Bertie to pay half. They are for Christmas for you. I love them so much. We will all put our names in, Frieda and Bertie and I. You can look at them many times and be happy whilst you see them: these Indian frescoes.

A thousand good wishes to you all, and love from Frieda and me.

D. H. Lawrence

I liked Huxley *very* much. He will come to Florida.[3]

1110. To S. S. Koteliansky, [23 December 1915]
Text: MS BL; Zytaruk 60.

103 Hampstead Way
Thursday[4]

My dear Kot,

This a handkerchief for your christmas.

I want to say to you, please gather your money during these next few months, so you can come to Florida with us. This is serious. Do make some money and save it, and come with us.

Best of greetings for Christmas from both of us.

D. H. Lawrence

---

[1] Vere Henry Gratz Collins (1872–1966) who later encouraged DHL to write *Movements in European History*, which Oxford University Press published under DHL's pseudonym, Lawrence H. Davison, in 1921. Collins was Educational Books Manager of O.U.P. until he retired in 1935. (The confusion over Collins' name – see Letter 1065 – cannot be accounted for.)

[2] See p. 488 n. 3.

[3] See Aldous Huxley's letter to Lady Ottoline Morrell, after he had visited DHL, dated Sunday 1916: 'I think there's a lot in his theory of the world being in a destructive, autumnal period. What seems to me questionable is, are you going to hustle on the spring by going to Florida to immure yourself with one Armenian, one German wife and, problematically, one or two other young people? It may be possible that some Pentecostal gift of inspiration may descend, and I suppose it's worth risking failure for that possibility. If, as seems probable, I go and visit my Texan brother [Julian Huxley was a professor at the Rice Institute at Houston, Texas, 1913–16] next year, I shall certainly join his colony for a bit. I think it might be very good to lead the monastic life for a little' (*Ottoline at Garsington* 80 1)

[4] It is presumed that this and the letter following were written the day before DHL left for Ripley on 24 December 1915. They were written from the home of David and Edith Eder.

[Frieda Lawrence begins]

Dear Kot,

I hope you like the hanky – it looks like the unutterable name of the Lord – *I* chose it –

1111. To J. B. Pinker, [23 December 1915]
Text: TMSC NWU; PC; Unpublished.

[103 Hampstead Way]
Thursday.

Dear Pinker,

Please tell Duckworth I won't have 'Hours'.[1] Let the book be called 'Italian Days', if no one else has had it.

Yours   D. H. Lawrence

My address for a week is
c/o Mrs Clarke, Grosvenor Rd., Ripley, Derbyshire.

1112. To J. D. Beresford, 24 December 1915
Text: MS StaU; Unpublished.

c/o Mrs Clarke, Grosvenor Rd, Ripley, Derbyshire
24 Dec. 1915.

Dear Beresford,[2]

We arrived here with a bit of a struggle. It is a painful thing to go back to the past, however much one may care for one's people. I shall breathe again when we are in Cornwall.

We can't go down till the 30th. Could you definitely order the conveyance for then – that 6.30 train in Padstow. We shall have to go back to London on the 29th, sleep one night there, then off to Padstow on the 30th. So that is definite.

[1] Pinker had received the following letter from Duckworth and Co. (MS NYPL): 'We have thought very carefully over the title for Lawrence's book, and for one reason or another do not find ourselves attracted by any of the titles suggested. "Restless Italy" seems to have a political significance, and the word Studies, as suggested in other titles, is hardly the right description. What do you think of "*Hours in Restless Italy*"? This seems to convey the spirit of the book and to avoid any political implications.'

[2] John Davys Beresford (1873–1947), novelist and architect. m. Beatrice Roskams. First achieved prominence through a trilogy dealing with the life of an architect: *The Early History of Jacob Stahl* (1911), *A Candidate for Truth* (1912), and *The Invisible Event* (1915). His cottage, which he lent to DHL, was at Porthcothan, St Merryn, Padstow, Cornwall. (*Times* obituary, 4 February 1947.)

Would you please order the things on the list, for us.

I can't tell you how grateful I am to you, every time I think of Cornwall.
Warm greetings from Mrs Lawrence to Mrs Beresford,

Yours   D. H. Lawrence

But you'll send me the address.

If there is anything else you can think of for the list, please put it on – or
alter –

1113. To Mary Cannan, 24 December 1915

Text: MS Lazarus; Unpublished.

c/o Mrs Clarke, Grosvenor Rd, *Ripley*, Derbyshire
24 Dec. 1915

My dear Mary,

I was so glad to get your letter, to know you were not cross with me any
more. The flat is gone, the furniture given away or sold, and all our
belongings are packed into three smallish trunks. So once more I feel free
and mobile, and I am glad. We are staying here till Wednesday with my sister
– two sisters, in fact – one has come from Glasgow.[1] How terrible it is to
turn back into the past – to turn round, to go back into the far past. One
loves ones people – but it is a pain.

You know we are going to Cornwall to the Beresfords' house, on leaving
here. This is not putting off Florida for ever – only for a few weeks – three
months or so. We shall certainly go before the summer is out. There are
several others want to go with us: we shall be a little Community – which
is what I want; a new life, a life *together*, in a new spirit. Not always this
Criticism and introspection and analysis – a new Creative unanimous life. We
shall have it, surely.

I am having a few bulbs sent to you from Hampstead, for your rockery.
I do hope they'll grow, and be nice.

Much love to you and to Gilbert from Frieda and me.

D. H. Lawrence

1114. To Catherine Carswell, 24 December 1915

Text: MS YU; cited in Carswell 41.

c/o Mrs Clarke, Grosvenor Rd, Ripley, Derbyshire
24 Dec. 1915.

My dear Catherine,

We got here with a struggle. How terrible it is to return into the past like
this – with the future quivering far off, forsaken – to turn back to the past.

---

[1] Emily King.

My sister from Glasgow is here – Harley St., Ibrox. She has a child of six who goes to an elementary school and is shockingly crammed.[1] She is a nervous overwrought thing – and can read as fluently as a child of twelve ought to read. Can you tell me if there is a Froebel school in Glasgow,[2] or a good Kindergarten school to which she might be sent. Do tell if there is – one near enough. They will kill the child with their relentless teaching.

Many warm greetings to you both   D. H. Lawrence

1115. To Lady Cynthia Asquith, [24 December 1915]
Text: MS UT; Huxley 298–9.

c/o Mrs Clarke – Grosvenor Rd, *Ripley*, Derbyshire
Thursday 24 Dec.

My dear Lady Cynthia,

We ought to have answered your letter before, and have thanked you for Frieda's 10/-. She bought herself with it a tan suède hat with a little stiff brim, from Liberty's, which suits her.

We are here till next week with my sister: both my sisters, in fact: the elder is here from Glasgow, with her child – a girl: the younger has a boy of a year.[3] It is very queer, to be here – makes me sad. I am fond of my people, but they seem to belong to another life, not to my own life. And the pathos of tiny children, in this age, is acute and painful. They are both nice children, poignant and direct; the world seems diabolical to me, with these small, new, fragile, pure children. I can't bear it that the parents should have the children. The world is *vile*, when one looks at these tiny lives, so new and clear.

But enough grizzling – I'm not going to grizzle any more, while I live. I'm not going to lament and fret over the world any more. I'm not responsible for the world, as it is.

We are not going to Florida immediately. There are several others – young men and women – who are anxious to come with us, and we shall have to wait for them: just a month or two. I am glad there are some others who want to come with us. They are all young, a new generation, a generation younger than you even. We want to make a new life in common – not a thing just for ourselves, a new life in common, a new birth in a new spirit, together. We shall do it, and we shall bring it off, and it will be good. I am going to be happy – really really happy – we all are. It is a new thing which is in its inception.

[1] Margaret King.
[2] i.e. a Kindergarten school of the kind founded by Friedrich Froebel (1782–1852), the German educationalist.   [3] Ada Clarke's son, John Lawrence (1915–42).

In the meantime of our going to Florida we have a house in Cornwall. The flat in the Vale of Health is empty, the furniture sold or given away, the lease transferred to another man. We go back there no more. Again I am Vogelfrei,[1] thank God – nothing but the trunks to bother us – no house nor possessions – thank heaven again.

The novelist J D Beresford has lent us his house near Padstow, on the sea in Cornwall. We go down there next week. Some members of our Florida expedition are coming down too – we begin the new life in Cornwall. It is real.

I saw Herbert Asquith was bringing out a book of poems.[2] I see also Mrs Asquith's law-suit. It is all very nasty.[3] I suppose you ought to be very circumspect also, not to lay yourself open to criticism.

Frieda sends her love to you, and thanks you very much for the jaunty tan hat she bought with your Christmas present.

I shall be glad when I can go away again from here – this atmosphere of my boyhood. Nothing is more painful than to be plunged back into the world of the past, when that past is irrevocably gone by, and a new thing far away is struggling to come to life in one. But there will be the new life. And this love which goes back into the past, but not forward into the future – like the love of the dead – is very painful.

With all good greetings – D. H. Lawrence

1116. To P. I. M., [post 24 December 1915]
Text: Everyman, 13 March 1930.

[c/o Mrs Clarke, Grosvenor Road, Ripley, Derbyshire]
[post 24 December 1915][4]

[P. I. M. had written to Lawrence describing *The Rainbow* as the greatest novel published in his lifetime. In reply Lawrence said 'he was coming through London and would call'.][5]

[1] 'outlawed'.   [2] *The Volunteer and Other Poems* (December 1915).
[3] Mrs Margot Asquith, wife of the Prime Minister, had brought a libel action against the owners of the *Globe* newspaper, which had alleged that she sent food and other presents to German officers who were prisoners of war. On 22 December an injunction was granted restraining the *Globe* from repeating such allegations. On 22 March 1916, the *Globe* unreservedly withdrew the allegations and agreed to pay Mrs Asquith damages of £1000 and to indemnify her for all expenses in connection with the matter.
[4] P.I.M. makes it clear that DHL's letter was written after the prosecution of *The Rainbow*. It is therefore assumed that DHL wrote following his arrival in Ripley and before his departure for London and Cornwall.
[5] P.I.M. stubbornly remains unidentified. He was the writer of 'Bookman's Diary' in *Everyman*; he referred to his brief encounter with DHL in a general critical assessment of DHL's significance, on 13 March 1930.

1117. To S. S. Koteliansky, 25 December 1915
Text: MS BL; Postmark, Ripley 25 DE 15; Zytaruk 61.

c/o Mrs Clarke, Grosvenor Rd, Ripley, Derbyshire
25 Dec 1915

My dear Kot,

Will you send copies of the *Signature* to H. Booth, the Gables, *Swanwick*, Nr Alfreton, Derbyshire. He says he sent his 2/6 and never had the book. So enter his name, will you, and see that the postage is all right.

We are here with all my people – very nice: but it is painful to go back so into the past. One's people are the past – pure, without mitigation. And it is so hard to get to the future: and one *must* look to the future: one must create the future. That is why we go to Florida: a new life, a new beginning: the inception of a new epoch.

We are coming down to London on Wednesday evening, and going on to Cornwall on Thursday morning. I'm afraid to make any appointments, it is such a rush. But we shall meet before long.

The Kümmel and the sweets are very good: but the others don't like Kümmel; it makes them cough. My sister has got a very beautiful child, a boy, a year old. There is something lovely about these pure small children. It makes one hate the cowardly suppressed grown-ups.

I hope you will make up your quarrel with Barbara.[1] I really like her, and we might as well all remain friends.

Auf wiedersehen   D. H. Lawrence

1118. To Lady Ottoline Morrell, 27 December 1915
Text: MS UT; Huxley 299–301.

Ripley – Derbyshire
Monday – 27 Dec. 1915

My dear Ottoline,

Your letter and parcel came this morning. The books are spendid: but why did you give me the book, the Shelley, you must value it.[2] It is gay and pretty. I shall keep it safe.

Did you like the Ajanta frescoes:[3] I *loved* them: the pure fulfilment – the

---

[1] Barbara Low. (See Letter 885.)

[2] The 'Shelley' was in all probability *Shelley Prometheus Unbound and Other Poems* (Oxford, 1910), in its attractive binding which qualifies as 'gay and pretty'. A copy of the book is in the library of Mrs Julian Vinogradoff. The other books are unidentified.

[3] *The Ajanta Frescoes* (Oxford, October 1915). (It contains 42 reproductions in colour and monochrome.) The book, now in the library of Mrs Julian Vinogradoff, is inscribed: 'To Ottoline Morrell from D. H. Lawrence' and 'A Merry Xmas! Frieda'. Although Bertrand Russell contributed to the cost (Letter 1119), he did not sign the book, even though DHL had duly written the instruction: 'to be signed here by Bertie'.

pure simplicity – the complete, almost perfect relations between the men and the women – the most perfect things I have *ever* seen – Botticelli is vulgar beside them. They are the zenith of a very lovely civilisation, the crest of a very perfect wave of human developement. I love them beyond everything pictorial that I have ever seen – the perfect perfect intimate relation between the men and women, so simple and complete, such a very perfection of passion, a fulness, a whole blossom. That which we call passion is a very one-sided thing, based chiefly on hatred and Wille zur Macht.[1] There is no Will to Power here – it is so lovely – in these frescoes.

We are here in Ripley – suffering rather. It is a cruel thing to go back into the past, to turn ones back on the future and go back to that which one has been. I've just been differing violently with my eldest brother, who is a radical nonconformist.[2]

Altogether the life here is so dark and violent: it all happens in the senses, powerful and rather destructive: no mind nor mental consciousness, unintellectual. These men are passionate enough, sensuous, dark – God, how all my boyhood comes back – so violent, so dark, the mind always dark and without understanding, the senses violently active. It makes me sad beyond words. These men, whom I love so much – and the life has such a power over me – they *understand* mentally so horribly: only industrialism, only wages and money and machinery. They can't *think* anything else. All their collective thinking is in these terms only. They are utterly unable to appreciate any pure, ulterior truth: only this industrial – mechanical – wage idea. This they will act from – nothing else. That is why we are *bound* to get something like Guild-Socialism in the long run.[3] Which is a reduction to the lowest terms – nothing higher than that which now is, only lower. But I suppose things have got to be reduced to their lowest terms. Only, Oh God, I don't want to be implicated in it. It is necessary to get the germ of a new developement *towards*[4] *the highest*, not a reduction to the lowest. That we must do, in Cornwall and Florida; the germ of a new era. But here, the reduction to the lowest must go on.

The strange, dark, sensual life, so violent, and hopeless at the bottom, combined with this horrible paucity and materialism of mental consciousness, makes me so [. . .] sad, I could scream. They are still so living, so vulnerable, so darkly passionate. I love them like brothers – but my God, I hate them too: I don't intend to own them as masters – not while the world stands.

---

[1] DHL alludes to the title of Nietzsche's philosophical work (*Will to Power*), published in 1906.
[2] George Arthur Lawrence. See *Letters*, i. 135 n. 1.
[3] A form of Socialism that would make trade unions (or guilds) the authority for industrial matters.   [4] *towards*] *to*

29 December 1915]

One must conquer them also – think beyond them, know beyond them, act beyond them.

But there will be a big row after the war, with these working men – I don't think I could bear to be here to see it. I couldn't bear it – this last reduction. But here they think the war will last long – they are not like London.

At last, at last, one will be able to set forth from it all, into the uncreated future, the unborn, unconceived era. One must leave all this to finish itself: the new unanimity, the new complete happiness beyond – one must be strong enough to create this –

Love from us both   D. H. Lawrence

Thank Phillip for his letter. Greet Murry from me.

We go to London on Wednesday, Cornwall on Thursday. There is the beginning.

1119. To Bertrand Russell, [29 December 1915]
Text: MS UT; Moore, *Bertrand Russell* 66.

Ripley – Derby
Wednesday

Dear Russell,

I got your letter this morning: thank you for the £2. We sent the reproductions to Lady Ottoline – they were *really beautiful*. But I haven't had the bill yet: I will straighten up with you when it comes.[1]

We go to Cornwall on Thursday – 30th. The address is c/o J D Beresford, Porthcothan, St. Merryn, Padstow, Cornwall. Come and see us there – and stay a week or so.

Don't be so despondent about your lectures.

We are waiting to go to Florida, for the others. We must go as a little body: it is not a personal matter – it is a bigger thing. There are several young people very anxious to come. I must wait for them. I can't go without them. We shall be six or seven. As soon as they are free to come, then we shall sail off. It is all so complicated, because of money and the war. They are all very young people. We can go and start a new life in a new spirit – a spirit of coming together, not going apart. Won't you come to Florida too? Do! It is hopeless to stay in England. Do you come and be president of us.

It is so queer being up here at home. The colliers are queer too. I wish you were here to have a talk. But more and more I realise it is hopeless to stay in England.

Greetings from Frieda and me   D. H. Lawrence

Thank you for sending the ticket to Barbara Low.

[1] *The Ajanta Frescoes* was published at £4 4. 0; but see Letter 1136.

1120. To S. S. Koteliansky, [30 December 1915]
Text: MS BL; Postmark, St. Merryn 30 DE 15; Gransden 25.

Porthcothan, St. Merryn, Padstow, Cornwall
Thursday 30 Dec.

My dear Kot,

We got here tonight – it is splendid – a biggish house with big clear rooms, and a good housekeeper to look after us. This is the first move to Florida. Here already one feels a good peace and a good silence, and a freedom to love and to create a new life. We must begin afresh – we must begin to create a life all together – unanimous. Then we shall be happy. We must be happy. But we shall only be happy if we are creating a life together. We must cease this analysis and introspection and individualism – begin to be free and happy with each other.

Tell Murry please to write to me – I have forgotten his address, but I want to hear from him. Tell him as soon as you can.

You also write and tell me how things are with you.

Yours   D. H. Lawrence

1121. To Lady Cynthia Asquith, [30 December 1915]
Text: MS UT; Huxley 301.

Porthcothan, St Merryn, Padstow, Cornwall.
Thursday 30 December

My dear Lady Cynthia,

We came here to night – a nice old house with large clear rooms, and such wonderful silence – only a faint sound of sea and wind. It is like being at the window and looking out of England to the beyond. This is my first move outwards, to a new life. One must be free to love, only to love and create, and to be happy. One can feel it here, that it can come to pass – one is much nearer to freedom – the freedom to love and to be completely happy.

Let us have some news of you.

Yours   D. H. Lawrence

This is the first move to Florida.

1122. To Edith Eder, 30 December 1915
Text: Hobman, *David Eder*, p. 118.

Porthcothan, Padstow, Cornwall.
Thursday, 30th Dec., 1915.

Dear Edith Eder,

We arrived here to-night – a fine large house with clear, large rooms, and such lovely silence, with a little wind and a faint sound of the sea: such peace,

I could cry. One only wants to be allowed to begin to love again – not all this friction and going apart. Only let us begin once more to love – I feel like imploring the winds and the waters. But one dare not address the people.

Thank you very much for looking after us.[1] You are really a perfect hostess – you make one feel so free and simple, when one lives in your house. Make the boys grow up quickly, so you can come to Florida with them. Murry says, '*Is* there a Florida?' There is a Florida to be – it must be so.

Frieda sends her love. We must all leave that complex, disintegrating life – London, England. Here one stands on tiptoe, ready to leap off.

Many real thanks to you.

Affectionately,   D. H. Lawrence

1123. To Lady Ottoline Morrell, 31 December 1915
Text: MS IEduc; Unpublished.

Porthcothan, St. Merryn, Padstow, Cornwall
31 Dec. 1915

My dear Ottoline,

I am so happy to be here. The house is an old farm place, with large, silent rooms full of peace. I love it.

It looks over the brow of the land at the sea, which is quite near, and sounds out night and day, through the restless wind. So there is only the clean remoteness of the Western sea, and it seems so lovely, so real and true. It seems as if the truth were still living here, growing like the sea holly, and love like Tristan,[2] and old reality like King Arthur, none of this horrible last phase of irritable reduction. You must come and stay with us. I believe we can be here about ten weeks.

Love from us both – also to Phillip and Julian.

D. H. Lawrence

1124. To Catherine Carswell, 31 December 1915
Text: MS YU; Carswell, *Adelphi* 210–11.

Porthcothan, St. Merryn, Padstow, Cornwall
31 Dec. 1915.

---

[1] See p. 483 n. 4.

[2] A legendary hero who – with his mistress, Iseult or Isolde – figures in the Arthurian cycle. DHL was acquainted with the story through Sir Thomas Malory's *Morte Darthur* (1485), Wagner's opera, *Tristan und Isolde* (1865) and Swinburne's poem, 'Tristram of Lyonesse' (1882). See references to these last works in *Letters*, i.

My dear Catherine,

Thank you for your letter and poem, which I received at Ripley.[1] Do send me news of a school for my niece, if you get any.

The poem I liked – but you had scarcely put enough into it, enough passion, to create it. It is not sufficiently fused: the heat of creation was not great enough. In the second stanza 'pale' is somehow wrong – cliché – and 'brow' is wrong – false metaphor. There is a really good conception of a poem: but you have not given yourself with sufficient passion to the creating, to bring it forth. I'm not sure that I want you to – there is something tragic and displeasing about a woman who writes – but I suppose Sapho is as inevitable and as right as Shelley – but you must burn, to be Sapho – burn at the stake. And Sapho is the only woman poet.[2]

I love being here: such a calm, old, slightly deserted house – a farm-house; and the country remote and desolate and unconnected: it belongs still to the days before Christianity, the days of Druids, or of desolate Celtic magic and conjuring; and the sea is so grey and shaggy, and the wind so restless, as if it had never found a home since the days of Iseult. Here I think my life begins again – one is free. Here the autumn is gone by, it is pure winter of forgetfulness. I love it. Soon I shall begin to write a story – a mid-winter story of oblivion.[3]

Let me hear how you go on. I wonder, will you write, turn towards that, like Sapho. It is as fate decides.[4]

Give my greetings to Carswell – Frieda sends her love to you, with mine.

D. H. Lawrence

1125. To Dollie Radford, 31 December 1915
Text: MS UN; Postmark, St. Merryn 1 JA 16; Nehls, i. 345.

Porthcothan, St. Merryn, Padstow, Cornwall
31 Dec. 1915

My dear Dollie,

We came down here yesterday, and we love it. It is quite a big house looking down on a cove of the sea: an old farmhouse with space and largeness and a sort of immemorial peace, a calm that belongs to the earth. It does one good. We can see the sea, and hear the sound of it, and the wind is strong and fierce, it booms all the while in the chimney.

---

[1] The poem has not been identified.   [2] Sappho: see p. 105 n. 2.

[3] Almost certainly the story published as 'Samson and Delilah', *English Review*, xxiv (March 1917), 209–24. (The MS bears the title, 'The Prodigal Husband'.)

[4] decides.] decides. I would rather that they

This country is bare and rather desolate, a sort of no-man's-land. For that I love it: it is not England. And there is no war – since Tristran of Lyonesse died, from these parts.

We have a good housekeeper,[1] native of the village, and all at last is well.

I hope things are going decently with you. I asked Margaret[2] to get me some bulbs, and to send them to Mary Cannan. I wonder if she did so. I would not have troubled her, but I thought perhaps it might please her, to choose the bulbs. Do let me know, if she bought them, how much they cost

I am going to begin to write again soon – a story I am thinking of. Perhaps I shall begin it tomorrow, which is New Years day.

Frieda sends her love – with mine –

D. H. Lawrence

1126. To J. B. Pinker, 1 January 1916
Text: MS UN; Huxley 302.

Porthcothan, St. Merryn, Padstow, Cornwall
1 Jan 1916

Dear Pinker,

This is the new address for the time being. J. D. Beresford has lent us his house: for which may the Gods shower blessings and much money on him.

Already, here, in Cornwall, it is better: the wind blows very hard, the sea all comes up the cliffs in smoke. Here one is outside England, the England of London – thank God.

Will Duckworths call the book 'Italian Days'?[3] It is by no means a brilliant title, but I should think it will do.

I got your letter too late to send you the American *Rainbow*, and now I have lost it – don't know *where* it can be. Perhaps you will have got one by now. Let me know, will you, what is to be done about it – re-publication.

If Duckworths hate Italian Days – they might like Italian Hours – which is detestable, but for some reason, catchy, I believe. At least several women said to me: 'I should *want* to buy a book called Italian Hours'. My God, what objectionable things people are.

But it is better in Cornwall.

Yours   D. H. Lawrence

---

[1] Emma Pollard (d. c. 1921), the Beresfords' housekeeper. (See Letter 1133.)
[2] Margaret Radford.
[3] On 30 December 1915, Duckworth wrote to Pinker (MS NYPL): 'I have your letter with regard to Mr. Lawrence's "Italian Sketches". We will call the book "Italian Days", as suggested. I do not find that this title has been used.' Despite this assurance, the title chosen was *Twilight in Italy*.

1127. To J. D. Beresford, 5 January 1916

Text: MS StaU; *A Letter from Cornwall*, Yerba Buena Press, 1931.

Porthcothan, St. Merryn, Padstow, Cornwall

5 Jan. 1916.

Dear Beresford,

We have been here a week, so I must report myself to you.

We *love* being here. There have been great winds, and the sea has been smoking white above the cliffs – such a wind that it made one laugh with astonishment. Now it is still again, and the evening is very yellow.

The house is always peaceful and a real delight. We live in the dining room, and don't use the drawing room, at present. Emma is excellent, I think. We have a fine time, with her cakes and bread and puddings. And most of the people seem nice – really very nice. There is a rare [...] quality of gentleness in some of them – a sort of natural, flowering gentleness which I love. But then, alas, there is Hawken, whom I don't like.[1] He came in – with his small eyes and his paunch – talking about how he turned the old woman out of this house, for he couldn't have a tenant like her – and about his property Truro way. But we have known the peasant type before – mean and stupidly cunning and base – so everything went off affably. One can't take offence at a *type* – it's no use. The offensiveness isn't really individual.

We have walked to Padstow – the Lowestoft fleet going out is so pretty – and to the next bay north – and today right up on the downs, looking upon the country, upon St Columb and beyond Wadebridge. I do like Cornwall. It is still something like King Arthur and Tristan. It has never taken the Anglo Saxon civilisation, the Anglo Saxon sort of Christianity. One can feel free here, for that reason – feel the world as it was in that flicker of pre-Christian celtic civilisation, when humanity was really young – like the *Mabinogion* – not like *Beowulf*[2] and the ridiculous Malory, with his Grails and his chivalries.

But the war has come. Derby's scheme has wrung their withers.[3] They

---

[1] Not identified.

[2] *The Mabinogion*, a collection of medieval Welsh tales which deal with Celtic legends and mythology, in which magic and the supernatural abound. *Beowulf*, the eighth-century Anglo-Saxon epic poem.

[3] Edward George Stanley, 17th Earl of Derby (1865–1948) was made Director General of Recruiting on 11 October 1915. The 'Derby Scheme' was his plan to step up recruiting for the armed services. Under it men were asked voluntarily to attest their willingness to serve and then to await call-up. The scheme caused a temporary boom in recruiting, but it was soon considered a failure and the Bill for introducing compulsory military service for single men was brought in by the Prime Minister on 5 January 1916. The Bill received its third reading on 24 January 1916.

are very sad. Emma was telling us of her sister-in-law, who had just been stitching the *armlet* on her husbands sleeve.

'It's come now', she said. 'We've never had it till now, but it's come now. I'm sure, when I look at these buttons, I think "We've got the Kaiser to thank for these." Every stitch I put in goes through my heart.'

Which I think is rather beautiful, showing sincere gentleness and a power of love. The English women stitch armlets on freely enough: they have lost the power of love. But it does linger here.

I think I shall begin to write again here – it is so congenial to me. I must always thank you again for letting us come here – it was such a blessing to me.

Best greetings from my wife and me, to Mrs Beresford and the boy[1] and you.

Yours Sincerely   D. H. Lawrence

1128. To Barbara Low, 5 January 1916
Text: MS UT; Nehls, i. 345–6.

Porthcothan, St. Merryn, Padstow, Cornwall
5 Jan 1916

My dear Barbara,

We have been here nearly a week – and we like it very much. The sea has been storming high, bursting up the cliffs in whiteness and smoke, such a wind. Now it is quiet. Today we have been on the downs – I like Cornwall *very* much: it is so uncivilised, unchristianised – in spite of the churches. It is always King Arthur and Tristan for me. I see them coming in their boats round the rocks, and riding along the muddy grass over the bare, sky-pressed upland. I am very fond of that pre-christian Celtic flicker of civilisation. But I hate Malory: I hate the Grail and chivalry – lies.

There isn't any real news. Heseltine wandered down on Saturday – Kouyoumdjian is coming next Monday. We are trying to think of a plan of getting out of the country on a ship. I wish we could do it – nicely and romantically. I wish I knew just *how* to do it.

I am once more beginning to write a sort of philosophy:[2] a maturer and more intelligible *Signature*. At last, this time, I have got it: the fifth time of writing. I think it will come off: though I don't know if the people will ever be born, who are to read it.

There is some war here now – the Derby scheme did it. But at last I have found a place where some of the men and women really love each other – with

---

[1] John Tristram Beresford (b. 1914).   [2] See p. 558 n. 4.

a fine softness and rareness that delights me. The women are so soft and so wise and so attractive – so soft, and unopposing, yet so true: a quality of winsomeness and rare, unconscious Female soothingness and fertility of being. I would marry a Cornish woman.

But some of the men are detestably small-eyed and mean – real cunning nosed peasants mean as imbeciles.

My dear Barbara, I hope you are well and not tired. I hope you will come to Florida, when at last we can sail away. I count you as one to come.

Frieda sends her love, I mine. I wish you were not in that vile school.[1]

Yours   D. H. Lawrence

1129. To Thomas Dunlop, 5 January 1916
Text: MS Dunlop; Huxley 304.

Porthcothan, St. Merryn, Padstow, Cornwall
5 Jan. 1916

Dear Dunlop,

I got your letter here, where we are staying for some weeks. It is a very jolly house on the sea – J D Beresford lent it us – do you remember his novel that you liked – *The House in Demetrius Rd.*[2] I like him better than his books – he's a nice man.

We shall be here at least till March – then I don't know where we go.

I was glad to hear such good news of you and Mrs Dunlop. Don't get sent to Salonika, however: there seems to be a down on consuls there, just now.[3]

The Cornish sea is rather lovely, so wild. It makes me think of Fiascherino here – another such a small rocky bay looking west. But oh Heaven, what a difference also!

Don't, my dear Dunlop, be persuaded into Roman Catholicism. For an Englishman that is such a piece of retrogressive sentimentalism. I have ordered the two books by Carmichael to be sent to you, however, from Bumpus in Oxford St.[4] I expect they will arrive duly. Only don't, for God's sake, slither into the easy slough of the Roman religion.

---

[1] She was teaching at the Hackney Downs Boys' School, London.

[2] Published in 1914.

[3] In retaliation for a bombing raid on Salonika by German aircraft, the commander of French troops there arrested the German, Austrian, Turkish and Bulgarian consuls on 31 December 1915; the Norwegian consul was arrested on 3 January 1916. The consuls were taken to Marseilles and sent to Switzerland. (At this time Dunlop was at the British Consulate in Milan.)

[4] Perhaps two of the several books by Joseph Carmichael published by the Catholic Truth Society. J. & E. Bumpus Ltd were booksellers and publishers at 350 Oxford Street, London. (Though Dunlop was prepared to read books by Roman Catholic apologists, he remained agnostic all his life.)

I am writing myself a little book of philosophy – or religion – which will one day make you scratch your head – when it appears.

Thank you so much for getting me the poetry books.[1] They can come along any time.

I'm sorry you are hard up. I'm in a state of existing on charity. But I don't care. I have done the work, if they won't pay me properly, then they must support me improperly.

All good luck to you, and remembrances to Mrs Dunlop and the children. Frieda sends greetings.

Yours   D. H. Lawrence

1130. S. S. Koteliansky, [6 January 1916]
Text: MS BL; Postmark, St. Merryn 7 JA 16; Spender 30.

Porthcothan, St. Merryn, Padstow, Cornwall
Thursday

My dear Kot,

Well, I am willing to believe that there isn't any Florida – assez, j'en ai soupé.[2] I am willing to give up people altogether – they are what they are, why should they be as I want them to be. It is their affair, not mine: English individualists or not individualists, it is all the same to me. I give it up. Je n'en peux plus.[3] And the same with the world: it is what it is: what has it to do with me, or I with it? I admit it all: you are right: there's no *rapport*.

There is my intimate art, and my thoughts, as you say. Very good, so be it. It is enough, more than enough, if they will only leave me alone.

As for their world, it is like artificial lights that are blown out – one can only remember it. I can't see it or hear it or feel it any more – it must be all blown out to extinction. There is another world, a sort of rarer reality: a world with thin, clean air and untouched skies, that have not been looked at nor covered with smoke. There is another world, which I prefer. And I don't care about any people, none, so long as they won't try to claim attention from me. The world goes on, the old world, very much like a sordid brawl in last night's café-restaurant: like an ugly thing which one remembers in the morning, but which is non-existent. It is non-existent: their wars and lies and foulnesses: last night's sordidness. What has morning got to do with it.

I like being here. I like the rough seas and this bare country, King Arthur's

---

[1] DHL's own MSS; see Letter 1103.
[2] 'enough, I'm fed up with it'.   [3] 'I am at the end of my tether'.

country, of the flicker of pre christian Celtic civilisation. I like it very much.

We are here till March: what then, I neither know nor care. I shall just go where the wind blows me, the wind of my own world. I am not going to urge and constrain any more: there are no people here in this world, to be urged. My dear Kot, it is very nice down here, in Cornwall. Some day you must come and see us.

Yours   D. H. Lawrence

1131. To Katherine Mansfield, 7 January 1916
Text: MS NYPL; Huxley 305.

Porthcothan, St. Merryn, Padstow, Cornwall.
7 Jan. 1916.

My dear Katharine,

I hear Murry has gone to France to see you: good: also that you are well and happy: benissimo!

Give John my love.

I love being here in Cornwall – so peaceful, so far off from the world. But the world has disappeared for ever – there is no more world any more: only here, and a fine thin air which nobody and nothing pollutes.

My dear Katharine, I've done bothering about the world and people – I've finished. There now remains to find a nice place where one can be happy. And you and Jack will come if you like – when you feel like it: and we'll all be happy together – no more questioning and quibbling and trying to do anything with the world. The world is gone, extinguished, like the lights of last night's Café Royal[1] – gone for ever. There is a new world with a new thin unsullied air and no people in it but new-born people: moi-même et Frieda.

No return to London and the world, my dear Katharine – it has disappeared, like the lights of last night's Café Royal.

We Frieda and I – both send our love, for the New Year, the Year 1. of the new world. The same also to Murry. The old year had to die.

But I'm not going to struggle and strive with anything any more – go like a thistle-down, anywhere, having nothing to do with the world, no connection.

Love to you   D. H. Lawrence

---

[1] One of London's most famous restaurants and fashionable meeting-places. DHL portrayed it as the 'Pompadour' in *Women in Love*.

1132. To John Middleton Murry, [9? January 1916]

Text: MS NYPL; Delany 188–9, 264.

Porthcothan – St. Merryn – Padstow – Cornwall

Sunday[1]

Dear Murry,

I meant to write before, but I forgot your address: and also, it is a thing which can only come of impulse, writing to you.

I like Cornwall very much, and I like being here. Only, Oh, my God, the horrible hopelessness of life! We've got to face it out. I feel now pushed to the brink of existence, and there remains only to fall off into oblivion, or to give in, and accept the ruck: or some way out, as yet undiscovered. I feel absolutely run to earth, like a fox they have chased till it can't go any further, and doesn't know what to do. I don't know what to do nor how to go on: like a man pushing an empty barrow up an endless slope. What good is it all. There is nothing but betrayal and denial, nothing at all: no trust, no faith, no hope from anybody, only betrayal and denial.

You ask 'Is there any Florida?' I'm inclined to answer 'No'. There is no Florida, there's only this, this England, which nauseates my soul, nauseates my spirit and my body – this England. One might as well be blown over the cliffs here in the strong wind, into the rough white sea, as sit at this banquet of vomit, this life, this England, this Europe. Out of the disciples, there was one Judas. In modern life, there are twelve Judases in the twelve disciples. They are all Judases, one and all, all Judases. Where is one to turn one's face? What good even is death, when life is nothing but this peaked, traitorous meanness? How can death[2] be great, seeing life such a mean paucity: since they must be counterparts, life and death.

I must own to you, that I am beaten – knocked out entirely. I don't know what to do any more – it seems as if the twilight of all twilights were drawing on, and one could only watch it, and submit: no more hope, nothing further remaining. I could howl with a dog's hopelessness, at nightfall. It seems to be now a case of death, or a miracle. I still believe in miracles – supernatural. I don't believe in human life any more. And failing the miracle, I am finished.

But I'm not going to accept this human life. Foul muck, what have I to do with it.

Yours   D. H. Lawrence

[1] The mood and language of this letter strongly suggest that it was written shortly after Letters 1130 and 1131.
[2] death] life

1133. To Lady Ottoline Morrell, 9 January 1916

Text: MS IEduc; cited in Morrell, *Nation and Athenaeum*, xlvii. 860.

Porthcothan – St. Merryn – Padstow, Cornwall

9 Jan. 1916

My dear Ottoline,

I got all your letters safely, and am very glad you liked Murry. He is one of the very few people I count upon.

We have been here a week, and I like it exceedingly. The sea rages under the black rocks and the western sky is iridescent at evening, so that the water stretches far back into the distance, into the unknown. I have been much happier here. But two days ago another bad cold came on, which makes me feel queer, as if I couldn't see any further, as if all things had come to an end. I suppose things have come to an end, and one must only wait for the new to begin. But it is rather terrible this being confronted with the end, only with the end.

Heseltine is here also. I like him, but he seems empty, uncreated. That is how these young men are. There seems to be no hope for life in the living themselves. But one always believes in the miracle, in something supernatural. I believe in something supernatural, which is not of human life, neither of religion. Except for this, there is only the end.

But the water that is so white and powerful and incomprehensible under the black rocks, that is not of this life. I feel as if there were a strange, savage, unknown God in the foam – heaven knows what god it be.

When will you come and see us. We are here only till March. After that I don't know where we shall be. But come and see us here, because of the sea and the silence and peace and the out-of-the-worldness of it all.

Emma is a good soul, the housekeeper, and a good cook. The house is not too tiny. You would be fairly comfortable. Emma has two illegitimate children. One, the elder, lives at Trevorrid farm, with her parents, the younger lives here. It is a rosy cheeked child of six. Heseltine says a woman with two illegitimate children must be good. Emma is really splendid.

I have written the first part of a short story, but I don't know how to go on.[1] You see one must break into a new world, and it is so difficult. We are going to write, all of us together, a comedy for stage, about Heseltine and his Puma and so on.[2] It will be jolly.

Tomorrow Kouyoumdjian is coming down for a while. I hope we shall like him. He is at any rate more living than poor Philip who really seems as if he were not yet born, as if he consisted only of echoes from the past,

---

[1] Unidentified.   [2] The play – referred to again in Letter 1140 – did not survive.

and reactions against the past. But he will perhaps come to being soon: when a new world comes to pass. Meanwhile conscription hangs over his head like a Sword of Damocles.[1]

One has only to say to one's soul, be still, and let be what will be.[2] One can do absolutely nothing any more, with one's will. Yet still one can be an open door, or at least an unlatched door, for the new era to come in by. That is all.

There are violets here, they smell so sweet. It is quite warm. The wind is at last quiet. Soon my cold will be better, and one can go out and enjoy it all again. – Frieda sends her love to you. She talks of your visit, planning. Remember me to Phillip – is he sad about the conscription? What is he feeling now? Greet the children from me –

Yours   D. H. Lawrence

1134. To Catherine Carswell, [11 January 1916]
Text: MS YU; cited in Carswell, *Adelphi* 170, 210–11.
Porthcothan – St. Merryn – Padstow – Cornwall.
Tuesday.

My dear Catherine,

Never mind about the school: Glasgow seems a God-forsaken place.[3] I am trying to get my sister to leave it.

But I'm sorry about your reviewing, because I believe you enjoyed the bit you had. And one *does not* want to be martyred.[4]

I read *Where Bonds Are Loosed*.[5] It has got some real *go* in it. But it is based on a mistaken idea that brutality is the desideratum. But let us hope the war will cure him of this idea. He seemed in his book to have real courage and vitality, but to be a bit *stupid*. But I forgive stupidity, for strength of feeling. Do keep on knowing him, if you can, and if you really like him, let me know him too. Don't let him slip. Tell me about him, if he is any good, and if you think well, ask him to write to me.

The grave yard poem is *very* good.[6] I *do* wish, however, you didn't use metre and rhyme. It is verse which in spirit bursts all the old world, and yet goes corseted in rhymed scansion. Do leave it free – [...] perhaps not

[1] Heseltine felt under threat from the bill to introduce compulsory military service then being debated in the House of Commons. See p. 495 n. 3.
[2] Cf. A. E. Housman, *A Shropshire Lad*, xlviii.
[3] See Letter 1114.　　　　　　　　　　　[4] See p. 456 n. 3.
[5] The novel by Elliott Lovegood Grant Watson (b. 1885) was published in 1914.
[6] 'I kept sending him poems of mine. There was only one – a Hardyesque poem about a graveyard – that he thought good' (Carswell 42).

this poem: the 'there' rhyme is good, so hard – but even here, do not use *lair*: break the rhyme rather than the stony directness of speech.

The essence of poetry with us in this age of stark and unlovely actualities is a stark directness, without a shadow of a lie, or a shadow of deflection anywhere. Everything can go, but this stark, bare, rocky directness of statement, this alone makes poetry, today. That poem is *very good*, the best yet. My scribblings on it are only impertinent suggestions.

But you know it isn't rhythmed at all, metrically. So why rhyme if you don't rhythm. I mean that for your other poems. This has got its own form as it stands. But in general, why use rhyme when you dont use metrical rhythm – which you don't – you'd lose all reality if you did. Use rhyme *accidentally*, not as a sort of draper's rule for measuring lines off.

The second poem is not good. It is again not created. Do it in free verse accidentally rhymed, and let us see.

I send you the *Spoon River Anthology*.[1] It is good, but too static, always stated, not really art. Yet that is the line poetry will take, a free, essential verse, that cuts to the centre of things, without any flourish.

I like Cornwall very much. It is not England. It is bare and dark and elemental, Tristan's land. I lie looking down at a cove where the waves come white under a low, black headland, which slopes up in bare green-brown, bare and sad under a level sky. It is old, Celtic, pre-christian – Tristan and his boat, and his horn.

I am writing erratically. I am laid up in bed with my wintry inflammation. But this is its last turn – I shall be solid again in a week. Greet Don from me – and Ivy –

Love   D. H. Lawrence

1135. To Lady Ottoline Morrell, [13 January 1916]
Text: MS IEduc; Moore 413–14.

[Porthcothan, St. Merryn, Padstow, Cornwall]
13 Jan. 1915
My dear Ottoline,

The jersey came yesterday, and is *so* nice, so soft and pleasing to feel. I like it very much, and the color is beautiful. I don't want it to be yellow. It suits my beard. It makes me look rather pale, but that is only when I dont wear a coat above it. Buttoned under an open coat, I look like an orange breasted robin in the spring-time. Thank you for it, a thousand times.

[1] By Edgar Lee Masters (1868–1950). Published in 1915, it consisted of free verse epitaphs revealing the secret lives of the persons buried in a cemetery in the midwestern USA.

Kouyoumdjian came on Monday and brought the atmosphere of London, most disturbing. How I loathed that London, that England out there. The only thing to do, truly, is to turn ones back on it.

Heseltine is still here. But he and Kouyoumdjian are most antagonistic, so it is a bit trying. I think one of them will fly away very soon – and after him, the other. I think Heseltine will go first, back to his Puma (the girl, the model). He says he despises her and can't stand her, that she's vicious and a prostitute, but he [will] be¹ running back to her in a little while, I know. She's not so bad, really. I'm not sure whether her touch of licentious profligacy in sex isn't better than his deep-seated conscious, mental licentiousness. Let them fight it out between them. Kouyoumdjian is trying also. I think he is in love with Dorothy Warren, and not at all sure that she will reciprocate.² So he is a little more self-assertive than ever, and tiresome. It is such a bore, about these young people, that they must be so insistently self-sufficient, always either tacitly or noisily asserting themselves. Heseltine silently and obstinately asserts himself, Kouyoumdjian noisily and offensively. But why should they want to assert themselves, nobody wants to obliterate them, or mitigate them. They are quite free: then why assert themselves. They spend their time in automatic reaction from everything, even from that which is most sympathetic with them. It is stupid, it is crass. It is as stupid as the wholesale self-submergence of bygone young men – it is the same thing reversed. Why can't they be simple, fallible like other mortals.

Still, one must be patient, and not dislike them. They will get all right.

It is rather cold now. You must come when it is a little bit warmer. This old farmplace hasn't your Garsington comforts. But do come while we are here – You must know Cornwall.

How is Phillip? I'm afraid the whole temple of Christianised Europe is going to come down on our heads, just now. But I withdraw, I am an outsider.

Frieda sends her love, I mine.

                                                            Yours   D. H. Lawrence

I'm doing my philosophy. It's come at last. I am satisfied, and as sure as a lark in the sky. I shall send it to you when it is finished and typed out.³

---

¹ MS reads 'he be'.
² Dorothy Warren (1896–1954), niece of Lady Ottoline, and friend of Gertler and Catherine Carswell; she met DHL at Garsington. Later she was the owner of the Warren Gallery, where DHL's paintings were exhibited (June–September 1929) and thirteen were seized by the police. m. Philip Coutts Trotter, 1928.
³ Despite this expression of confidence, the 'first half' of the 'philosophy' was not sent until 27 February. See Letter 1189.

1136. To Bertrand Russell, 13 January 1916
Text: MS UT; Moore, *Bertrand Russell* 67–8.

[Porthcothan, St. Merryn, Padstow, Cornwall]
13 Jan 1916.

Dear Bertie,

I have never written to you all the while we have been here, and I've thought about you nearly every day, wondering and wondering what you are doing and how you are feeling; how the lectures are now, and when you begin them, and how you feel about them.[1] Do write and let me know.

I owe you some money. We got those frescoes for 3 guineas.[2] That is, your share, 31/6. Therefore I owe you 8/6. I will send it you, I won't forget.

I like being here *very much.* Cornwall isn't England. It isn't really England, nor Christendom. It has another quality: of King Arthur's days, that flicker of Celtic consciousness before it was swamped under Norman and Teutonic waves. I like it very much. I like the people also. They've got a curious softness, and intimacy. I think they've lived from just the opposite principle to Christianity: self-fulfilment and social destruction, instead of social love and self-sacrifice. So here there is no social structure, hardly, and the people have hardly any social self: only the immediate intimate self. That's why they're generally disliked. And that's why they were wreckers and smugglers and all antisocial things: And that's why the roads are too dodgy to be grasped. And that's why there is such a lovely, intimate softness in the women.

I have suddenly launched off into my philosophy again. Now this time I have got it – my heart is satisfied. I don't want to polish it up, I am so pleased with it. I shall send it you when it is done and typed out, and you must read it with pleasure.

At present Heseltine and Kouyoumdjian are here. I dont know how long they will stay. It is a wee bit painful – these young individualists are so disintegrated: *are* the young more sound than the old? It seems to me they are much more sick.

We've got a jolly old farmhouse, and a good housekeeper. I wish you could come and see us. Come and stay, when your lectures are over, will you. Do come. We shall be here I think till the middle of March – then where, I dont know.

---

[1] Russell's eight lectures, published in November 1916 as *Principles of Social Reconstruction*, were delivered during January, February and March 1916, in the Caxton Hall, Westminster. Writing to Robert Trevelyan about them, Russell said: 'I gather very few people are coming & I am in despair about it' (Clark, *Russell*, p. 268).

[2] See p. 488 n. 3; p. 490 n. 1.

We are just on the sea, looking down into a little cove. The water smashes up the black rocks. It is nice. Then the bare, unformed, urzeitig[1] landscape – there really might be rock-hurling giants and odd pixies. If only it weren't all cut up into fields! If only the Cornish hadn't become foully and uglily Wesleyan. Alas alas!

What is going to become of the world? I wish we were off to Florida. The desert is the only place.

Frieda sends her love, I mine.

Yours   D. H. Lawrence

Write and tell me how things are with you.

1137. To Thomas Dunlop, 15 January 1916
Text: MS Dunlop; PC; Postmark, St Issey 15 JA 16; Huxley 308–9.

Porthcothan – St. Merryn, North Cornwall.

15/1/16

Thank you very much for the slips of MS. also for the 3 little note-books which have arrived safely.[2] There remains only a rather big brown 'Tagebuch' note-book, with verses, which I should like. Have you got it?

Have you received the books I ordered for you from Bumpus in Oxford St?[3]

I've been rather knocked up this last month – how sickening it is.

Yours   D. H. Lawrence

1138. To Lady Ottoline Morrell, [17 January 1916]
Text: MS StaU; cited in Schorer 57.

Porthcothan – St. Merryn – North Cornwall

Monday

My dear Ottoline

A long letter from the Murrys, full of happiness, this morning. They are in France – she has taken a little villa and they are together. You know she is Mrs Bowden.[4] The address is

c/o Madame Bowden, Villa Pauline, Bandol (Var), France.

Also a letter from Bertie – very sad. He says he is living purely from his *will*: which he says is no living: and that his lectures are *not important*. They begin tomorrow.

[1] 'primeval'   [2] See Letter 1103.
[3] See p. 497 n. 4.   [4] See p. 32 n. 3.

You were right about Kouyoumdjian – I dont care for him. I shall ask him to go away. When will you come down? I will ask him to go, if you are coming. I will say that we want his room.

Will you bring Eva,[1] or not? Do, if it is easier for you. But she would have to sleep in the nursery and eat in the kitchen. Would she mind? Would she mind helping Emma? I like Emma. She is Cornish – about 35 – has two illegitimate children one of whom lives with us. But, she is a real decent woman.

I am still not very well – my old wintry sickness and inflammation.

I like Heseltine.

Much love from both of us D. H. Lawrence

The jersey is red like a winter cherry at night, and where the light is on it, yellow like a marigold.

1139. To John Middleton Murry and Katherine Mansfield, [17 January 1916]

Text: MS NYPL; Huxley 309–10.

Porthcothan – St. Merryn, North Cornwall
Monday 17 Jan

Cari miei ragazzi,[2]

I am very glad you are happy. That is the right way to be happy – a nucleus of love between a man and a woman, and let the world look after itself. It is the last folly, to bother about the world. One should be in love, and be happy – no more. Except that if there are friends who will help the happiness on, tant mieux. Let us be happy together.

I am always seedy nowadays – my old winter sickness and inflammation – very weary I get of it – sometimes contemplate my latter end. But it is always darkest before the dawn. The New Year will come. Your spring is a little earlier than ours, that is all. But oh dear it is a long winter, of weather and lovelessness and discontent and sadness and everything: mais cela va finir.[3]

I still like Cornwall. The house is a big low grey well-to-do farm-place, with all the windows looking over a round of grass, and between the stone gate pillars down a little tamarisky lane at a cove of the sea, where the waves are always coming in past jutty black rocks. It is a cove like Tristan sailed into, from Lyonesse – just the same. It belongs to 2000 years back – that pre-Arthurian Celtic flicker of being which disappeared so entirely. The lan[d]scape is bare, yellow green and brown, dropping always down to black

---

[1] Lady Ottoline's maid.   [2] 'My dear old friends.'   [3] 'but that will end'.

rocks and a torn sea. All is desolate and forsaken, not linked up. But I like it.

We are here only till March. Then I don't know where. Heseltine is here – I like him – you will like him – also Kouyoumdjian, whom I don't care for really. But he will go soon.

Let us make some plans for March – let us live somewhere together. You make the plans this time, for us. I am done.

Much love from us to you both.   D. H. Lawrence

1140. To Mark Gertler, 20 January 1916
Text: MS SIU; cited in Moore, *Intelligent Heart* 210–11.

Porthcothan, St. Merryn, Padstow, Cornwall.

20 Jan 1916

Dear Gertler,

I have meant to write to you before, but I've been laid up in bed again with a vile inflammatory cold. Now I am a mere rag, contemplating my latter end.

But it is better being in bed here, than in London. Here I can lie and watch the sea coming in to the little cove, between the black rocks, and bursting in foam high over the yellow-brown cliffs. Which is a very great consolation.

I like Cornwall, it is a bare, forgotten country that doesn't belong to England: Celtic, pre-Christian. There are very rough winds and very fine black rocks and very white bursting seas. And the house is big and silent and forsaken, looking down the lane at the bay.

Kouyoumdjian is here and I don't care for him. He is going away in a few days. Heseltine is here, and I like him. At night we write a play, which is rather fun.[1]

I don't know how long we are to be here – not very long, I feel. Yet I don't know what the next move will be. Out of England, I hope. We hear from Murry and Katharine, that they are both exceedingly happy: they have both found themselves, and each other and the blessed sun also, at last. I am very glad. I hope the spring is going to blossom now for you and Carrington as well.[2]

---

[1] See Letter 1133.
[2] Dora de Houghton Carrington (1893–1932) was a student with Dorothy Brett and Mark Gertler at the Slade, London, and an intimate friend of Lytton Strachey. m. 1921 Ralph Partridge (d. 1960). See *Carrington: Letters and Extracts from her Diaries*, ed. D. Garnett (1970); Noel Carrington, *Carrington: Paintings, Drawings and Decorations* (1978).

I liked her very much at the party. If you could only really give yourself up in love, she would be much happier. You always want to dominate her, which is no good. One must learn to relinquish oneself, not to bother about oneself, but to love the other person. You hold too closely to yourself, for her to be free to love you.

I wonder, if, among the box of books that Murry had of mine, is my *Rainbow* – or both my *Rainbows*, English and American edition both. If so, I wish you would send them me. Also there is a yellow-wrapped book called *The fitness of Environment*, or something such: something about Environment.[1] I wish, one day, when you are taking your walk, you would leave it on Mr Brackenbury, 14A Downshire Hill. It is very near you, and I hate not sending a man's book back.

I will write to you again soon – if we stay here you might like to come down.

Tell me all your news, when you write. Warm greetings to Brett and Carrington. Frieda sends her love, and says she is happy down here. I hope your work goes well: are you reconciled to Eddie?[2]

Yours   D. H. Lawrence

1141. To Amy Lowell, 20 January 1916
Text: MS HU; Unpublished.

Porthcothan, St. Merryn, Padstow, Cornwall
20 Jan. 1916.

My dear Amy,

I have got my poetry MS. books from Italy, and hasten to send you some more verses, in case it is not too late for the anthology.[3] Perhaps you will like some of these. Tomorrow I will send more.

We are here in Cornwall till March: by the sea it is beautiful and wild. But I am ill in bed again. I have been ill a good deal this winter.

Dear Amy, will you hand on to Harriett Monroe the poems you do not want – or save them for me in America. I have got quite enough stuff now for a new book. Do you know who would best publish it in America? I shall

---

[1] Lawrence Joseph Henderson (1878–1942), American biochemist, was the author of *The Fitness of the Environment : An Inquiry into the Biological Significance of the Properties of Matter* (1913).

[2] Edward Marsh who had given Gertler financial support until October 1915 when Gertler broke off their relationship. He was strongly opposed to the war whereas Marsh was a member of the Government which was prosecuting it. (See Hassall, *Marsh*, pp. 370–1.)

[3] *Some Imagist Poets 1916: An Annual Anthology*, which was to appear on 6 May 1916. For DHL's contributions to it, see p. 610 n. 3.

need some money badly by the early summer, for there is nothing in prospect.

It is a pity you are so far off. Do write and tell me about yourself, and your poetry, and America.

If any of this poetry has been published in America, perhaps you will remember. But I don't think it has.

Many greetings from us both   D. H. Lawrence

1142. To J. N. Milnes, [ante 21 January 1916]
Text: MS NYPL; Unpublished.

[Porthcothan, St. Merryn, Padstow, Cornwall]
[ante 21 January 1916]

[Lawrence informed Milnes 'that his novel *Rainbow* is now published in New York' and that Pinker could supply him with 'the publisher's name and price at which published'.][1]

1143. To Lady Ottoline Morrell, [21 January 1916]
Text: MS UT; Moore 416.

Porthcothan – St. Merryn – North Cornwall.
Friday

My dear Ottoline

It is very exciting to hear of your coming on Monday. Kouyoumdjian leaves for London tomorrow. I expect we shall hear from you what time you get into Padstow, and whether you are bringing Eva. The motor will be there to meet you. I shall probably be kept indoors by my cold, especially as it will be evening. But I am better and shall be going out in the daytime.

Do bring me the *Homeric Hymns* if you have got them – I should love them.[2]

Bring also something *warm* for your bed – we are rather short of blankets. Frieda says, bring a nice spirit.

Bring one or two books, will you: *The Possessed*,[3] if you have it, and Petronius in French,[4] if you have it, or something interesting about

---

[1] The existence of a letter to Milnes is established by his letter to J. B. Pinker, 21 January 1916, from 1 Marlborough Road, Woodthorpe, Nottingham. DHL's own letter has not been found.

[2] *Hesiod, The Homeric Hymns and Homerica*, trans. Hugh G. Evelyn-White ('Loeb Library', 1915).

[3] Dostoievsky's novel, trans. Constance Garnett (1914).

[4] Caius Petronius (d. c. A.D. 66), to whom the fragmentary *Satyricon* is attributed. The work portrays, in alternating verse and prose, contemporary Roman life. A French translation (by L. Tailhade) was published in Paris, 1902.

something old, not novels nor verse nor belles lettres, but something a bit
learned: Anglo-Saxon Ballads – like the Seaman, translated[1] – or interesting
Norse literature, or early Celtic, something about Druids (though I believe
it's all spurious) or the Orphic Religions, or *Egypt*, or on anything really
African, Fetish Worship or the customs of primitive tribes: just one or two
books, not more than three, to keep us going down here. (Not Frazer – I've
read him.) I hope this is not a great nuisance – don't bother if there is any
rush.

I hope the weather will be fine. The train journey is *tedious*, especially
from Exeter: so beware of it.

Yours   D. H. Lawrence

1144. To Thomas Dunlop, [22 January 1916]

Text: MS Dunlop; PC; Postmark, St. Issey 22 JA 16; Huxley 310.

Porthcothan
– Sat. 22 Jan

The Tagebuch came today – the letter the other day. You were very
miserable. But whatever possessed you to quote Goethe and 'Reinheit'?
What *does* one mean by Reinheit?[2] Purity lies in pure fulfilment, I should
say. All suppression and abnegation seem to me dirty, unclean. I didn't like
your letter. Why, when you are miserable, do you take the self-abnegating
line? Why not kick a little, in some direction, instead.

I hope you didn't think you had to pay for the books from Bumpus – I
paid for them. Greetings from us – don't get depressed –

Yours   D. H. Lawrence

1145. To Lady Ottoline Morrell, 24 January 1916

Text: MS UT; Moore 416–17.

Porthcothan, St. Merryn, Padstow, Cornwall
24 Jan 1916

My dear Ottoline

I was glad you deferred your visit a little while, really, we were all too[3]
unwell – at least, you were and I am. Maitland Radford says that the pain

---

[1] *The Seafarer*, an Old English poem of 100 lines. A translation was available in *Select Translations from Old English Poetry*, ed. A. S. Cook and C. B. Tinker (Boston and London 1902). Lines 1–64 were translated in A. Stopford Brooke, *English Literature from the Beginning to the Norman Conquest* (1898), pp. 312–13.

[2] 'Purity'.   [3] MS reads 'to'.

and inflammation is *referred* from the nerves, there is no organic illness at all, except the mucous in the bronchi etc are weak. But I have been ill for weeks. I really got the sense of dissolution, that horrible feeling one has when one is really [...] ill. But now, quite suddenly, yesterday and today, there is a change. For weeks it has gone on being ill, feeling more and more dark and deathlike. Then suddenly, yesterday and today, a sort of dawn, a strong dawn. I feel very queer, though, and tender; and my right arm and my right leg and my right side all weak, numbed, like a tiny bit of paralysis, and an effort even to hold a pen to write – but I have turned the corner now, for this year. For the rest of the year I shall be strong, I think.

And you, you must lie still, you must lie very still and give up your body and your mind and your soul, as if they were not yours at all, as if you had no more will. You must loosen all control, undo all bondage and direction, and lie all loosed and gone for a few days. Tell Phillip, he will understand. Then you will get well. Before you can get well you must lie and lapse all unloosed.

Because you must get well and come here, the sea on the wild coast is like the dawn of the world. Oh, it is good, there are no more Englands, no nations, only the dark, strong rocks and the strong sea washing up out of the dawn of the sky. It is the beginning, the beginning only.

You *must* come, it is essential for you to come, in a little time, say in a fortnight, when you have lain quite still and sunk back to the very depths of sleep. Then when you begin to return, when the tide turns toward awakening, then come here, and be here at the beginning of time, with the primeval world that is strong and completely unsaddened. We shall keep your place for you. Come with Phillip, if you can, and Eva also to look after you. And stay some time, at very least a fortnight. It is so beautiful and strong and savage as dawn, unexperienced.

Frieda was sorry she sent you a disagreeable letter when you were ill. But Heseltine and Kouyoumdjian had been telling her the things you said about her – and her and me – so she was cross. But she is not really cross. Perhaps the way we behave to one another she and I makes everybody believe that there is real incompatibility between us. But you know that really we are married to each other – I know you know it.

The things have just come. It is very good of you, indeed. It is what I want, I think, such things as milk casein. We have lost so much, there is much to recover, indeed.

I have got my MS books of poetry from Italy, and am getting ready a book of poetry. I shall dedicate it to you, if you let me.[1] The proofs of my

[1] The book – dedicated to Lady Ottoline – was entitled *Amores* (July 1916). See p. 521 n. 1.

Italian sketches, the book, are coming. I shall send them you in a day or two, the proofs, the duplicate set.

My love to Phillip and to Julian and to you.

Yours   D. H. Lawrence

1146. To J. B. Pinker, 24 January 1916

Text: MS Forster; Unpublished.

Porthcothan, St. Merryn, Padstow, Cornwall
24 Jan. 1916

My dear Pinker,

I have been laid up in bed again these two weeks, contemplating my latter end. But I am getting better now.

I have got my poetry MS books sent from italy, and am putting together a very nice book of poetry, the MS. of which I will send you in about a weeks time. To whom shall we give it in England? Poetry is rather popular now – and particularly in America, where I have some poetic repute. My poetry will sell sooner than my prose, if it is properly marketed.

I am doing the proofs of the Italian Sketches. I know Duckworth will bring them out at a dead season – he always does.

I feel better – soon I shall begin to live, instead of hovering for ever on the borders of Hades.

Yours   D. H. Lawrence

1147. To Amy Lowell, 25 January 1916

Text: MS HU; Unpublished.

[Porthcothan, St. Merryn, Padstow, Cornwall]
25 Jan 1916

My dear Amy,

I sent you some more poems, I should be so glad if they could arrive in time for the anthology. But will you at once *cancel* the last five stanzas from 'Drunk', so that it ends with 'Keep with you the troth I trowed'.[1] Do this for me hastily, Dear Amy, I hate those last five stanzas.

I find I have such a lot of poems, now, and such nice ones. I can make a most beautiful book.

I am still kept indoors by my inflammations but hope soon to be out.

I expect you to write to me *at once* remember, not to delay for a year.

---

[1] As published in *Amores*, p. 57, the poem ends with this line. DHL revised the poem, particularly the ending, for *Collected Poems* (1928). (The original MS is at HU.)

Mrs Aldington said how beautiful your poems for the anthology are – she is going to send them me. I do hope mine will come in time for the anthology, I begin to feel so keen about it.

Yours   D. H. Lawrence

1148. To William and Sallie Hopkin, 25 January 1916
Text: MS NCL; Huxley 310–11.

[Porthcothan, St. Merryn, Padstow, Cornwall]
25 Jan 1916

My dear Sally and Willie,

My *Rainbow* copy was lost, so I had to wait till I could get this.[1] However here it is, with my love. I hope you will like it. A few little passages are left out, but nothing important.

We are here in an old, low, long house, with big, forsaken-feeling rooms. The windows look down at the little cove of the sea, where the white waves come between black rocks. I love Cornwall. It is bare and desolate and like the beginning of the world, the old promethean powers. You must come. I should like you to come when Lady Ottoline Morrell is here – I don't know exactly when she will be down, but in February I think. I should like you two to meet.

I have been ill but am getting better. It was my soul-sickness after London and the state of things. Now I am forgetting everything.

I am doing the proofs of a book of Italian Studies, and preparing a book of poetry, so you will have something else from my pen soon.

Be sure and write me all the news. Much love from Frieda and me to you both – also to the bank clerk, Mistress Enid.[2]

Yours   D. H. Lawrence

1149. To S. S. Koteliansky, [27 January 1916]
Text: MS BL; Postmark, St. Issey 27 JA 16; Zytaruk 64–5.

[Porthcothan, St. Merryn, Padstow, Cornwall]
Thursday

My dear Kot,

Will you please send me a packet of type-writing paper, like this I write on, and also some carbon paper – about eight sheets. We are as usual miles

---

[1] This copy of the American edition (Huebsch, 1915) is now in the Lawrence–Hopkin Collection in the Eastwood Public Library.
[2] See p. 56 n. 4.

from every shop. I enclose a p.o. for 1/6, which I have in my pocket. It is not enough, I know, but it saves my going to St. Merryn. I will owe you the rest.

Will you please send two[1] sets of *Signatures* to

Miss Amy Lowell, Sevenels, Brookline, Mass, U.S.A.

also one set[2] to

A. Hathaway Esq, 258 Garden Avenue, Toronto, Canada.

I have been in bed this last fortnight, but am getting better. The Murrys write that they are still dancing with happiness. I am doing the proofs of a book of Italian Studies, and am preparing a book of poetry. I am very fond of Cornwall still – and Frieda is happy here. You would at last approve: a large house and a very efficient housekeeper.

I had a letter from Gertler. Thank him from me for the books he sent. Tell him I am sorry he is having such a bad time.[3] He must come down here and recuperate when his picture is done.[4] I wish him God-speed with it.

Why don't you write and tell me some news of yourself, Oh tacit one! Best greetings from Frieda and from me.

Yrs   D. H. Lawrence

1150. To Dollie Radford, [27 January 1916]
Text: MS UN; Postmark, St. Merryn 29 JA 16; Nehls, i. 355–7.

Porthcothan – St. Merryn – North Cornwall
Thursday

My dear Dollie,

So long I have been, without writing to you. But I have really felt so seedy and écœuré.[5] Now I am getting better. But it is by fits and starts. Now I've got a neuritis in my arm, and my left hand feels paralysed – but it is all part of the game.

I got your poems, my dear Dollie.[6] They made me sad. They make me think of the small birds in the twilight, whistling brief little tunes, but so clear, they seem almost like little lights in the twilight, such clear, vivid sounds. I do think you make fine, exquisite verse.

---

[1] two] one   [2] one set] two sets
[3] Gertler was in financial difficulties now that he was no longer supported by Marsh (see p. 509 n. 2) and he was despondent over his love affair with Carrington (see *Mark Gertler: Selected Letters*, ed Noel Carrington, 1965, p. 108).
[4] Probably *The Merry-Go-Round*. See p. 531 n. 2.   [5] 'Sick, nauseated'.
[6] *Poems* (Elkin Matthews, 1910).

I like very much the ballad of victory.[1] It makes me think of you: and then, some of the songs the best. 'I could not through the burning day' – and also – 'Because I built my nest so high'.[2] I hear your voice so plainly in these, so like a bird too, they are, the same detachment. I like the April ones, too, the words and the movement, such a delicate glisten of blossom:[3] also the first sonnet ('At Night') – this, and the third sonnet, these are two of the very best.[4]

It is lovely to have poetry, either ones own or that of one's friends. It seems that there, in the poems, at last, living has come to perfection and to an unchanging absoluteness, that is completely satisfying.

I too am doing my poems. The books of MS. came from Italy a week or so ago, and I began to collect for a volume. Now I have nearly done it, and it will be so nice. I shall be so pleased to send you a copy, when it is out. I am doing my Italian Studies, the proofs. Soon I can send you a copy of that.

It was *very* good of Maitland to come down: I was so grateful to him. He says my nerves are the root of the trouble, and I think it is true. I must lie and rest – always lie and rest, at present, I know. I begin to feel ill when I sit up.

I like Maitland so much – he is so sincere and honest. I *do* wish he had more fulfilment in his life. I do wish he really would love a woman, and marry. He only loves you. The rest is all merely superficial, I think.

We still love it down here – but I am nearly always in bed. If I get up and go out I get worse again at once – But I can sit in bed and read or do my poems and look at the sea and see the sun set, so I am not unhappy.

I am not going to trouble any more about anything – one should live and be happy, even if all the rest – or nearly all the rest of the world is slipping painfully to extinction.

We are here till the beginning of March – then where, – I don't know or care. I wish you could have come down. But pray God, in the spring we shall have a nice place and shall be all well and you will come.

Very much love to you from Frieda and me. Our love to Margaret.

Yours   D. H. Lawrence

Mr. Kouyoumdjian would like to come and see you – you remember, you saw him at our house. He is 46 Redcliffe Rd, South Kensington – And I think he would like to bring Dorothy Warren with him. She is beautiful. If you feel you would like to, ask them to tea one day, will you?

DHL

---

[1] *Poems*, pp. 85–90.   [2] Ibid. pp. 117, 120.
[3] A series of six poems entitled 'In April', ibid. pp. 15–25.   [4] Ibid. pp. 29, 31.

1151. To Lady Ottoline Morrell, [27 January 1916]
Text: TMSC NWU; Moore 421–2.

Porthcothan, St. Merryn, N. Cornwall.
Thursday.[1]

My dear Ottoline,

We got all the books: I shall like them all exceedingly: but the Virgil, and that isn't very well translated I think. We are all very glad of them, indeed.

Do you remember that little round picture at the beginning of *Hesiod*, of Dionysos crossing the sea?[2] It is very lovely and delightful, I think. Would you like me to draw it for you to embroider? – a round picture, not too big, Dionysos in a ship with a white sail and the mast a tree with grapes, sailing over a yellow sea, with dark, keen, joyful fish?

Heseltine has got his Puma here: motored over and fetched her from Newquay yesterday. She is a quiet, quite nice little thing really, unobtrusive and affectionate. He is fond of her, as a matter of fact, in spite of what he says.

Let the trouble between you and F[rieda] be forgotten now. Your natures are different and opposite. But why shouldn't opposites exist in a state of peace, like day and night. You will always speak different languages, and stand on opposite shores of the sea. But why not? Why should life be a homogeneity?

I am very much better. The long staying in bed, and the foods, do me good.

Next week I will send you the MS. of the poems.[3] I hope you will like them.

With love from us both,   D. H. Lawrence

1152. To Rufus Hathaway, 28 January 1916
Text: TMSC UT; Unpublished.

Porthcothan, St. Merryn, North Cornwall.
Jan. 28. 1916.

Dear Sir

Thank you for your letter and remittance. Copies of *The Signature* will

---

[1] DHL tells Lady Ottoline that 'next week' he will send her the MS of 'the poems'. On 1 February 1916 he duly dispatched the MS.

[2] The illustration 'Dionysus Crossing the Sea' (from Edward Gerhard, *Auserlesene Griechische Vasenbilder*, 1839–58) is the frontispiece to *Hesiod, The Homeric Hymns and Homerica*. See p. 510 n. 2.

[3] See p. 512 n. 1.

be forwarded to you immediately from London. *The Rainbow* can be obtained from Messrs. Huebsch and Co. Publishers, New York.

Yours faithfully   D. H. Lawrence

R. H. Hathaway Esq.[1]
258 Garden Avenue
Toronto – CANADA.

1153. To Lady Ottoline Morrell, [31 January 1916]
Text: MS StaU; Unpublished.

St. Merryn. N. Cornwall
Monday

My dear Ottoline,

A million thanks for all the books. But they are *too many* – don't please send any more.

Tomorrow I send you the whole MS. of my book of poems.

I am *so much* better, through eating the foods. I am so glad. Are you getting better? Are you getting ready to come?

In haste for the post.

Love   D. H. Lawrence

1154. To J. B. Pinker, 31 January 1916
Text: TMSC Forster; Unpublished.

Porthcothan, St. Merryn, North Cornwall.
31 Jan. 1916

My dear Pinker,

I have done the book of poems, it is all ready except for one poem, 'Snapdragon', which was published in the first *Georgian* Anthology of verse.[2] I've lost my copy of the anthology, and I haven't got the poem anywhere. If you have the first *Georgian* book anywhere, you might have the poem copied out and sent to me here.

About the publication, I am uncertain. Monro, of the Poetry Bookshop,

---

[1] Rufus H. Hathaway (1869–1933), one of the best known Canadian bibliophiles; his extensive collection of Canadian literature is at the University of New Brunswick. Hathaway was a close friend of Mitchell Kennerley, one of DHL's American publishers.

[2] See *Letters*, i. 459 and n.

asked me to give him verses for a *chap-book*.[1] But I dont like six-penny chap-books, and I dont care for Monro. Duckworth is all right, but he doesn't make things go. I dont think he did much with the other book of verse. And I didn't like the form he gave it. Still, I like Duckworth. Then Constable; I dont care for that 'New Poetry Series' of his, it looks so mediocre. The get-up is so insignificant. This book of mine will make about a hundred pages, and it may as well be done nicely. That first book with Duckworths, didn't look cheap, at any rate. – What about Werner Laurie?[2] He does some interesting things. Or John Lane?[3] A book of poetry – and this is really very nice – may become a great asset to us. However, I will let you have the MS. by Thursday or Friday, and we can think about it.

Yours   D. H. Lawrence

I don't want the MS. altered at all from what it is now.

1155. To J. D. Beresford, 1 February 1916
Text: TMSC NWU; Huxley 311–13.

Porthcothan, St. Merryn, Padstow, Cornwall
1 Feb. 1916

My dear Beresford

Thanks for your letter. We heard from Barbara Low that you think of coming back in February. Will you tell me, so that we can leave Emma a few days to make ready for you. I don't know where we shall go. It looks as if we shall have to go to a little place Lady Ottoline Morrell will lend us, for we are very badly off. But I should like to stay in Cornwall. I like it so much. We might afford a cottage, I think.

It is quite true what you say: the shore is absolutely primeval: those heavy, black rocks, like solid darkness, and the heavy water like a sort of first twilight breaking against them, and not changing them. It is really like the first craggy breaking of dawn in the world, a sense of the primeval darkness just behind, before the Creation. That is a very great and comforting thing to feel, I think: after all this whirlwind of dust and grit and dirty paper of a modern Europe. O I love to see those terrifying rocks, like solid lumps of the original darkness, quite impregnable: and then the ponderous, cold light of the sea foaming

[1] See Letter 1037.
[2] T. Werner Laurie established his publishing firm in 1904 (the imprint is now controlled by Bodley Head Ltd). DHL's suggestion is strange since Laurie specialised in fiction (he published Upton Sinclair, for example), biography and somewhat sensational revelations.
[3] John Lane (1854–1925), publisher who, with Elkin Mathews, founded the Bodley Head publishing firm in 1887.

up: it is marvellous. It is not sunlight. Sunlight is really firelight. This cold light of the heavy sea is really the eternal light washing against the eternal darkness, a terrific abstraction, far beyond all life, which is merely of the sun, warm. And it does one's soul good to escape from the ugly triviality of life into this clash of two infinites one upon the other, cold and eternal.

The Cornish people still attract me. They have become detestable, I think, and yet they *aren't* detestable. They are, of course, strictly *anti-social* and unchristian. But then, the aristocratic principle and the principle of magic, to which they belonged, these two have collapsed, and left only the most ugly, scaly, insect-like, unclean *selfishness*, so that each one of them is like an insect isolated within its own scaly, glassy envelope, and running seeking its own small end. And how foul that is! How they stink in their repulsiveness, in that way.

Nevertheless, the old race is still revealed, a race which believed in the darkness, in magic, and in the magic transcendency of one man over another, which is fascinating. Also there is left some of the old sensuousness of the darkness, a sort of softness, a sort of flowing together in physical intimacy, something almost negroid, which is fascinating.

But curse them, they are entirely mindless, and yet they are living purely for social advancement. They ought to be living in the darkness and warmth and passionateness of the blood, sudden, incalculable. Whereas they are like insects gone cold, living only for money, for *dirt*. They are foul in this. They ought all to die.

Not that I've seen very much of them – I've been laid up in bed. But going out, in the motor and so on, one sees them and feels them and knows what they are like.

Hawken was very cross because Heseltine, who is staying with me, chopped down a dead old tree in the garden. I said to him (Hawken), 'I'm sorry, but don't trouble. It was so dead it soon would have fallen. And you may take the wood'.

The young men are all being called up now round here. They are very miserable. There are loud lamentations on every hand. The only cry is, that they may not be sent out to France, to fight. They all quite shamelessly don't want to *see* a gun. I sympathise perfectly with this.

The cursed war will go on for ever.

Don't let us keep you out of your house for one moment. If you want to come in in a week's time, only let us know, and all will be ready for you. We love the house and we love being here. But we can leave at a day's notice.

I have got ready a book of poetry here – quite ready – which I think is a great work to have done.

The Murrys write from France that they are *very* happy: for which I am very glad. They think of coming back in March.

My wife sends warmest greetings to Mrs. Beresford and the child, and to you, in which I heartily join.

Yours   D. H. Lawrence

1156. To Lady Ottoline Morrell, 1 February 1916
Text: Huxley 313–14.

Porthcothan, St. Merryn, Cornwall.
1 Feb., 1916.

My dear Ottoline,

Here I send you the MS. of the poems. It is complete except for that poem 'Snapdragon', which was published in the first *Georgian* Anthology. I will send you that on, and you will insert it in the right place, according to the index, will you? Tell me if you like the poems. You see they make a sort of inner history of my life, from 20 to 26. Tell me if the inscription will do.[1]

...You will find enclosed also three little MS books, from which these poems were chiefly collected. The black book is a new scribble – but the red college note-books – they *are* my past, indeed. Will you let them lie with my other MS. at Garsington? But read the poems first in the typewritten MS., they will make a better impression.

I send you also Petronius.[2] He startled me at first, but I liked him. He is a gentleman, when all is said. I have taken a great dislike to Dostoievsky in the *Possessed*. It seems so sensational, and such a degrading of the pure mind, somehow. It seems as though the pure mind, the true reason, which surely is noble, were made trampled and filthy under the hoofs of secret, perverse, undirect sensuality. Petronius is straight and above-board. Whatever he does, he doesn't try to degrade and dirty the pure mind in him. But Dostoievsky, mixing God and Sadism, he is foul. I will send your books back by degrees. A thousand thanks for them. And that Egyptian book of Mlle. Baillot's is a real pleasure.[3] Please give her my thanks for it.

---

[1] The inscription in the first English edition of *Amores* reads simply 'To Ottoline Morrell'; it appeared in full in the American edition (Huebsch, 1916) as follows: 'To Ottoline Morrell in Tribute to Her Noble and Independent Sympathy and Her Generous Understanding These Poems are Gratefully Dedicated.'

[2] See Letter 1143 and n. 4.

[3] The 'Egyptian book' has been identified as *Egypte* (Paris, 1912) by the renowned French Egyptologist, Sir Gaston Camille Charles Maspéro (1846–1916). For DHL's use of this volume in *Women in Love*, see Delavenay, *D. H. Lawrence: The Man and His Work*, pp. 391–2.

I am getting better – at last I've got a solid core inside me. I've felt so long as if I hadn't any solid being at all. Now I can put my feet on the ground again. But it is still shaky. I believe that milk casein stuff is *very* good, also the Brand's.[1]...When do you think you may be coming down? We had a perfect day on Sunday, when we could see the ships far out at sea, and we were all so happy. But it has gone sad again.

Would you rather have had your title in the inscription? After all, it is to you the inscription is written, not to your social self.

Heseltine is gloomy about conscription. When one thinks out, away from this remoteness, how horrible it is! But there, it is no good: why should one waste oneself?

Frieda sends her love, and I mine. I hope you are feeling better.

Yours,   D. H. Lawrence

1157. To J. B. Pinker, 2 February 1916
Text: TMSC Lazarus; Unpublished.

Porthcothan, St. Merryn, North Cornwall.
2 Feb. 1916

My dear Pinker,

Here is the complete MS. of the poems. I don't want it altered. A duplicate will reach you in a few days, from Lady Ottoline Morrell. That can go to America.

The Proofs of the Italian sketches will all be done by Friday. By the way, won't the book be published in America at all – the Italian Days?[2]

Yours,   D. H. Lawrence

1158. To John Middleton Murry and Katherine Mansfield, 2 February 1916
Text: MS NYPL; Unpublished.

Porthcothan – St. Merryn – North Cornwall.
2 Feb. 1916.

My dear Katharine and Jack,

Of course if you get the cheap *hard* corduroys, true workman's cords, they will smell like Hell for a fortnight – they always do. But it wears off. Also the bracken-frond[3] tint will wear off, and they will go browner. But it is quite true, they will last a life-time.

---

[1] A concentrate of meat juices designed for convalescents.
[2] See p. 398 n. 2.   [3] MS reads 'fond'.

You, John, must have got one of the septic colds one gets in Italy. You must take *great care* with your stomach, and take aperients – some mild salts, like Sale di Montecatini, and take it every morning before breakfast. That is one of the rules for those countries down there.

The 'eclipse' you mention is the old phenomenon of the old moon in the new moon's arms. You often see it at this period of the year. I saw it myself, here, a fortnight ago. But not so well as in Italy. It is caused, I believe, by the earth's reflecting a faint light on to the shadowed, invisible part of the moon. But it is rather lovely, and you don't see it often – practically never in England.

I've been languishing in bed till these last two days. Maitland Radford came down to see me. He says it is inflammation set up by nervous stress, and I ought to go somewhere and be very peaceful. I say all right. But I don't know what I shall do. I don't care very much – *come sarà sarà*. Apart from seediness and detestation of the state of affairs, I am not unhappy here.

We shall be about one more month here, I think, then out into the void. I have no plans. There is rather a beautiful farm house, going down to the sands, to let near here. But it is rather big. Would you like us to live there altogether. Emma, the woman here, is a jewel. She would come with us. Trissie[1] wants to sack her – says she is costly.[2] But she isn't. She's got a child, who lives here. Let me know.

Heseltine is still with us – very nice – will stay if he isn't conscripted. It has been nice living with him – I hope he'll stay on. With Emma to keep house for us, we should be happy, I think.

Just let me know, will you. We might all go to Heseltine's mother's house in Herefordshire, a big house, and pay no rent nor servants. But I don't want somehow. His mother is away.

I think if I hear Beresford is coming back soon, and if I don't hear from you, I shall take a small cottage for Frieda and me, somewhere down here or in Wales.

I have put together a book of poetry. That pleased me.

Cornwall is rather lovely – the black rocks like solid darkness, and great seas like twilight always swinging in. I am afraid it is as Murry says, I am incurably English. I seem as if I can't leave it. But I feel like sulking in one of its remotest caves. I[3] can't go away.

My love to both of you – you shall always be happy. Happiness is the reality. I am happy underneath. But on top – my God, what black sulks.

Love   D. H. Lawrence

The farmhouse with grass in front and the sea so near, is beautiful.

---

[1] Beatrice Beresford.   [2] costly.] dear.   [3] I] But I

1159. To Katharine Clayton, 2 February 1916
Text: MS NCL; cited in Pinto 26.

Porthcothan – St. Merryn – N. Cornwall
2 Feb. 1916

Dear Mrs Clayton,

I was glad to get your letter and to hear that things are going well with you, especially also with Pat. Don't thank me for sending you clients: they are only too glad to have their things as well done as you and Douglas do them.[1] And for heavens sake charge these men full price: they ought to pay double price, though they're my friends: lazy neer-do-wells.

I haven't got anything written lately – have been ill a good deal this winter, and in bed a good deal. The state of this Europe simply kills me – sends me into frenzy after frenzy of rage and misery, so I get ill.

Here down in Cornwall it is better, remote. By this rough sea and these solid black cliffs one forgets, one feels outside of time. We have got a big, delightful old house, low and long, looking down at a cove of the sea. J D Beresford lent it us. It is delightful. I love this bare Cornwall, and the primeval coast. We are here for another month, then where, I don't know.

I am just finishing proofs of those Italian Days which Duckworth is publishing. Do you think the title a very bad one? Can you suggest a better title – you remember those Italian Studies Douglas typed in the autumn. I am utterly at a loss for a title, and I don't think Italian Days very good.

I have got together a number of poems for a book, that is all. I don't quite know what will become of them.

The world is a bad place, my dear Mrs Clayton; there are a few good people, but like Sodom and Gomorrah, not ten to each city – not enough to save the ship, I am afraid.[2]

But one might as well grumble at the weather.

Frieda is happy down here. We have two young friends staying with us, and a very good housekeeper to look after us, so, for the time being, we are untroubled at home. Of course we have very little money, and no prospects of ever having any more, since they suppressed the *Rainbow*. But what will be, will be. It's no good kicking against the pricks.

I often think of you and Connie Garnett. She seems like an old fighter, and her cause is lost. The cause is lost, God knows. But then, the fight itself is worth it, I suppose –

Greetings to Douglas. Love to you from Frieda and me.

Yours   D. H. Lawrence

---

[1] See Letters 1063 and 1215.   [2] See Genesis xviii. 32.

1160. To J. D. Beresford, 3 February 1916

Text: MS UT; Huxley 314–15.

Porthcothan – St. Merryn – N. Cornwall
Thursday 3 Feb. 1916

My dear Beresford,

A thousand thanks for your letter. It is very good of you to write about Trevozan: it looks a *most delightful* house. And of course we can pay some rent. While Heseltine stays with us he will pay half. And the Murrys talk of coming back in March to live with us. Of course they are broken reeds, to depend on. But if they come we should want a bigger house, and we should stick to Emma. I like her very much.

Is the cottage on Constantine Bay that ancient shebeen right on the bay? That pleased me also, very much. I should be quite happy in a tiny cottage. But if Heseltine isn't conscripted, and if the Murrys were to come, it would be too small. However, we shall know about all that in a fortnight. Meanwhile we shall stay peacefully and happily in Porthcothan, till you turn up. It would be nice if we were neighbours for the summer, and possibly for next winter also. I feel if I get fixed up down here I shall stay longer than usual: six months is my usual limit.

If you see Sidgwick, please ask him if he would like my poems:[1] they are very nice, and will make a 100-page book. If he would like them will he talk to Pinker – Talbot House – Arundel St. – Strand – about them. I don't a bit know where to take them to be published. Duckworth is so unimpressive, Constable is a bit cheap, Harold Monro I don't like. Do speak to Sidgwick, if you can, about them: somehow I feel he is a man with some *being*: not a cardboard box, like most of them.

The weather is very grey these last days. But we have always got visitors: Heseltine and his Miss Channing now: Lady Ottoline wants to come in a fortnight – and Dollie Radford: a whole come-and-go.

My respects to Mrs Beresford, and love to the boy.

Yours   D. H. Lawrence

---

[1] Beresford got in touch with his publisher Frank Sidgwick (1879–1939), who replied to him on 5 February (TMS Bodleian Library): 'Many thanks for your letter of the 4th and enclosure from D. H. Lawrence, which I return. I have told him I shall be delighted to read his poems, and that there is great competition to be the last author printed on paper, which is gradually disappearing.' The letter to DHL has not been found; see Letter 1162.

1161. To Lady Cynthia Asquith, 7 February 1916
Text: MS UT; Huxley 315–17.

Porthcothan, St. Merryn, North Cornwall.
7 Feb. 1916.

My dear Lady Cynthia,

I didn't answer your letter about the *Rainbow* because I was ill, and I didn't know what to say. I have been in bed a long time. Maitland Radford came down from London to see me – he is a doctor. He says the stress on the nerves sets up a referred inflammation in all the internal linings, and that I must keep very quiet and still and warm and peaceful. There was a sort of numbness all down the left side, very funny – I could hardly hold anything in my hand. But now, thank heaven, it is all getting better, and I feel my old strength coming back, like a pulse that begins to beat and sounds very deep and strong, as if it went to the very heart of the uncreated darkness. I am glad. I have felt very bad, so nearly disintegrated into nothingness. The Ottoline sent me a lot of things to swallow, which are very good. Now I can walk to the sea again, and all that fever and inflammation and madness has nearly gone. But I feel very queer after it – sort of hardly know myself.

You ask me about the message of the *Rainbow*. I don't know myself what it is: except that the old order is done for, toppling on top of us: and that it's no use the men looking to the women for salvation, nor the women looking to sensuous satisfaction for their fulfilment. There must be a new Word.[1]

Soon, in a few weeks, will come out my book of Italian Studies. I think it is interesting: it contains a plainer statement of a 'message'. I will send it you.

And soon after that, I think a new book of my poems is coming. I got my MS. books from Italy. They are old poems – but good.

The war, the whole world, has gone out of my imagination. I feel like a Sleeper of Ephesus who has waked up, not a 100 years after, but about 5000 years before.[2] This Cornwall is very primeval: great, black, jutting cliffs and rocks, like the original darkness, and a pale sea breaking in, like dawn. It is like the beginning of the world, wonderful: and so free and strong. I feel as if all that Europe were so long ago and so disremembered. It does not exist in me any more.

---

[1] See John i. 1.
[2] According to legend there were seven Sleepers of Ephesus who fled, in the persecution under Decius in A.D. 250, to a cave in Mount Celion. They awoke 230 years later.

We are staying in this house till March 9th, and then I don't know what will happen. I suppose we shall take a tiny cottage somewhere. We have very little money, and there won't come anymore. I dont know what we shall do. But I don't bother. I have lost the faculty just now; perhaps sheer self-preservation. I wish we could go a long voyage, into the South Pacific. I wish that very much. But I suppose it cannot happen. I am afraid now of America. I am afraid of the people. I daren't go there. My will won't carry me either. So I don't know what will happen. The money will last us a month[1] or two. Something in me is asleep and doesn't trouble.

I'm sorry this is all about myself. But I can't talk about general affairs, they are so meaningless, and all I can tell you is just these things about myself. I wish there were miracles – I am tired of the old laborious way of working things to their conclusions. The sea-gulls here are so wonderful, large and white, with strong bent shoulders, in the light of the sun. Why should one care, or *will*.

I suppose there is some sort of a queer, absolved relationship between you and us: abstract. I am afraid you are frightened of the future, with Herbert Asquith in the army, and your young children growing up. But things are not in our will, we can't help what it is. Still there is something beyond, like this sea travelling in from the unknown, and the gulls that cry sharply in the air.

Frieda seems pretty well and happy here – She sends her love.

Yours   D. H. Lawrence

1162. To J. B. Pinker, 7 February 1916
Text: MS UT; Unpublished.

Porthcothan – St. Merryn. – North Cornwall
7 Feb. 1916

My dear Pinker,

Here is a letter from Sidgwick and Jackson.[2] They have done better, this last year, than they have ever done, and mainly through *poetry*. Speak, perhaps first to Duckworth – and then, don't you think Sidgwick might be rather nice?

Yours   D. H. Lawrence

---

[1] month] week
[2] See p. 525 n. 1. Sidgwick and Jackson wrote to Pinker, also on 7 February (TMS Bodleian Library), to express their interest in seeing DHL's poems.

1163. To Lady Ottoline Morrell, 7 February 1916
Text: TMSC NWU; Huxley 317–18.

Porthcothan, St. Merryn, N. Cornwall
7 Feb. 1916

My dear Ottoline

Do not listen to Bertie about going to London. You cannot *really* do anything now: no one can do anything. You might as well try to prevent the spring from coming on. This world of ours has got to collapse now, in violence and injustice and destruction, nothing will stop it. Bertie deludes himself about his lectures. There will come a bitter disillusion. I have a friend who says that they are unimportant, nothing vital: and she is [a] woman who cares tremendously.

The only thing now to be done, is either to go down with the ship, sink with the ship, or, as much as one can, *leave* the ship, and like a castaway live a life apart. As for me, I do not belong to the ship, I will not, if I can help it, sink with it. I will not live any more in this time. I know what it is. I reject it. As far as I possibly can, I will stand outside this time, I will live my life, and, if possible, be happy, though the whole world slides in horror down into the bottomless pit. There is a greater truth than the truth of the present. There is a God beyond these gods of today. Let them fight and fall round their idols, my fellow men: it is their affair. As for me, as far as I can, I will save myself, for I believe that the highest virtue is to be happy, living in the greatest truth, not submitting to the falsehood of these personal times.

It was a beautiful day here today, with bright, new, wide-opened sunshine, and lovely new scents in the fresh air, as if the new blood were rising. And the sea came in great long waves thundering splendidly from the unknown. It is perfect, with a strong, pure wind blowing. What does it matter about that seething scrimmage of mankind in Europe. If that were indeed the only truth, one might indeed despair.

I am reading *Moby Dick*. It is very odd, interesting book: to me interesting, the others can't bear it. I read the *History of the East* – it is a very bad little book.[1] But something in me lights up and understands these old, dead peoples, and I love it: Babylon, Nineveh, Ashiburnipal, how one somehow, suddenly understands it. And I cannot tell you the joy of ranging far back there seeing the hordes surge out of Arabia, or over the edge of the Iranian plateau. It is like looking at the morning star. The world is very big,

[1] Possibly H. R. Hall's *The Ancient History of the Near East: from the Earliest Times to the Battle of Salamis* (1913) – though that is a 'little book' of 626 pages.

and the course of mankind is stupendous. What does a crashing down of nations and empires matter, here and there! What is death, in the individual! I don't care if sixty million individuals die: the seed is not in the masses, it is elsewhere.

I should like you to get me out of the library a history of early Egypt, before the Greeks:[1] a book not too big, because I like to fill it in myself, and the contentions of learned men are so irritating. The text of Mlle. [Baillot]'s book is impossible.[2]

When you feel it is the right time for you to come down here, I hope you will come at once. Frieda will be glad to see you. And these Cornish seas somehow relieve one's soul of mankind.

I wish I were going on a long voyage, far into the Pacific. I wish that very much.

Thank you for the foods that came today. But please when you are badly off, don't spend any more money on me. But I am getting better; I feel the strength striking back into me, like a new strong pulse, with all the power of the uncreated darkness behind.

I can alter the adjectives in the dedication when the proofs come, if still we don't like them. But I like them. I do not believe in this democratic spirit of stripping away nobility.

My love to you: I hope you too are feeling stronger. Frieda sends her love also.

Yours   D. H. Lawrence

1164. To S. S. Koteliansky, 9 February 1916
Text: MS BL; Postmark, St. Merryn 9 FEB 16; Zytaruk, *Malahat* 23–4.

Porthcothan – St. Merryn – Padstow, North Cornwall.
9 Feb. 1916

My dear Kot,

I never thanked you for the paper, and now I am writing for some more. Heseltine typed the whole MS. of the poems,[3] and that used it up. Send me another packet of the same, will you, and some more carbon paper. The last carbon paper was very *bad*, ask if they have some better, will you; I think the blue is really better.

Will you also send to Philip Heseltine, c/o me, two more sets of *Signatures*. I will get a postal order this afternoon, and send it you: for all the things.

---

[1] The 'library' was probably the London Library: see Letter 1231.
[2] See p. 521 n. 3.   [3] *Amores*.

I am much better. Maitland Radford came down to see me. He says that stress on the nerves sets up an inflammation in the lining of the chest, and the breathing passages and the stomach, and that I must be very quiet and very warm and still, and that I mustn't think at all about anything. I lay quite still in bed for two weeks, and kept indoors very quiet another week, now I can walk out and feel something like myself again. My whole left side went numb like paralysis. It is all nerves, Maitland Radford said. Lady Ottoline sent me a lot of things to swallow, and they are really splendid. Soon I shall be a Hercules, a Samson.

I was glad to have your letter. It is a good idea to come down. But leave it about a fortnight longer, because Heseltine and a young woman are here, and they take up the beds. I think they will go in about a fortnights time. Then we should be so glad to see you and Gertler. You would stay as long as possible – this idea of hurrying off in two days is absurd. We are in this house until March 9th: then I suppose we shall find another place in Cornwall. You must come down, it is so different from the rest of England. I am afraid Heseltine will be conscripted – What about Gertler? We must meet soon to talk things over: I want to very much. I shall write to Gertler today – and to you immediately again.

The Murrys continue at a high pitch of bliss. There is no worldly news to tell you. I hope you are cheerful. I look forward to having a talk with you – somehow I feel that things are going to happen now – nice things – to us.

Frieda wishes to be remembered to you.

Yours   D. H. Lawrence

1165. To Mark Gertler, 10 February 1916
Text: TMS SIU; Huxley 319.

Porthcothan, St. Merryn, North Cornwall
10 Feb. 1916

Dear Gertler,

I got the books all right; thanks very much for them.[1] Your letter was gloomy, and I have nothing to say that will cheer you up, otherwise I would have written sooner. Here we sit and watch the sea in the rain. It would be all right if the future were not so beastly just ahead. Heseltine I expect will be conscripted, we shall stay in Cornwall till our money is gone – which will take three or four months – then I think we may as well all go and drown

---

[1] DHL's books from the house in Byron Villas, Hampstead; see Letter 1140.

ourselves. For I see no prospect of the war's ever ending, and not a ghost of a hope that people will ever want sincere work from any artist. You had better make your peace with Eddie.[1] It is a damned life. I curse my age, and all the people in it. I hate my fellow men most thoroughly. I wish there could be an earth-quake that would swallow up everybody except some two dozen people. Meanwhile we've got to watch it that we are not swallowed.

Let me know soon how you are and what you are doing. I, thank God, am better in health, after a long stay in bed. I am really feeling some real strength coming back into me. It is astounding how one slips down the hill and near to the edge of oblivion. How is your picture?[2] How are you? The day must come when work is not so deathly to us; it gets better with me. It used to be, as it is with you, a pure process of self-destruction. But that gets better. I can only work now when I feel well.

I should like very much to see you and Kot. down here. You might come and stay a while when your picture is finished. Don't exhaust yourself too much; it is immoral. You must see this country. Tell me what your possible plans are.

Is there any news of the Cannans? Frieda sends her love. Tell Kot that it rains so heavily I cant go to the post-office today. We stay in this house till the ninth of March.

Let me hear from you immediately.

Yours   D. H. Lawrence

1166. To J. B. Pinker, 10 February 1916
Text: MS Forster; Unpublished.

Porthcothan: St. Merryn: N. Cornwall
10 Feb. 1916

Dear Pinker,

I have not heard from you whether you have received the MS. of the poems sent off to you last week: also of the duplicates from Lady Ottoline Morrell. I forwarded you Sidgwick's letter. I wish you would write to him, or speak to him. I am inclined to think he would be the best man for the book. I sent you his letter to me.

---

[1] See p. 509 n. 2. On 3 February Gertler had admitted to Kot: 'I feel *almost* sorry that I gave up Eddie Marsh! for after all his money was such a help' (Carrington, *Gertler: Selected Letters*, p. 108).
[2] During the early months of 1916, Gertler was 'working hard on a large and *very unsaleable* picture of Merry-Go-Rounds' (Carrington, *Gertler: See Selected Letters*, p. 111). See Letter 1291. The original painting is in the Ben-Uri Gallery, London.

The Edinboro-printers are very slow with the last of the proofs of the Italian Studies.[1] There remain only the last half dozen pages, to come.

Let me know about the poems.[2]

Yours   D. H. Lawrence

1167. To Catherine Carswell, 11 February 1916
Text: MS YU; cited in Carswell, *Adelphi* 211.

Porthcothan – St. Merryn – N. Cornwall
11 Feb 1916

My dear Catherine,

I was glad to hear about your Glasgow triumph:[3] also about Ivy. I must write to her. At any rate, it is well for her to be married, then she can be unmarried when she likes again.[4]

I have been so seedy I thought I was dead. But now I am beginning to feel strong again: life coming in at the unseen sources.

So we are thinking, Heseltine and I, that the only thing to do is to start a private publishing concern, by subscription, to publish any real thing that comes, for the truth's sake, and because a real book is a most holy thing.[5] We could begin with the *Rainbow*, which is likely to give a start, publish at 7/6. Then we can go on with the next as we like. The thing is to be a crusade, to gather the sincere people into one reading circle, and to give them every living book that is born. My dear Catherine, let us bring this off. Tell Ivy, she will help. Out of the very depths of one's despair and death one begins in confident faith.

Are you doing your novel? Have you written any more poetry. Write them as they come, the poems. It is like bearing a child, you can't dictate its form.

I have felt and been so ill that nearly everything has gone out of me but a sort of abstract strength. But I know we can do a lot with our publishing concern. We might look at the girl, Theo, is her name – at her book, soon, if you think it good.[6]

I wish Don would become a rich barrister.

---

[1] *Twilight in Italy* was printed by R. & R. Clark, Limited, Edinburgh.

[2] MS reads 'poem'.

[3] She had been successful in establishing good relations with Donald Carswell's parents who were initially hostile to their marriage (in 1915).

[4] Ivy Low had just married Maxim Litvinoff, then working in London (under the name of Harrison) for the publishers Williams and Norgate.

[5] The result was the venture known as 'The Rainbow Books and Music'; see p. 542 n. 1.

[6] Unidentified.

We stay in this house till March 8th. But I think we shall take another cottage in Cornwall. You might come down and see us later.

I want you to keep the *Spoon River Anthology*.

Give my remembrances to Ivy – I will write to her.

Love from Frieda and me.   D. H. Lawrence

1168. To John Middleton Murry and Katherine Mansfield, 11 February 1916

Text: MS NYPL; Huxley 320.

Porthcothan – St. Merryn – North Cornwall
11 Feb. 1916

My dear Jack and Katharine,

I did answer your letters some ten days ago.[1] They posted it with only a penny stamp, I am very sorry: that may have delayed it. But you will have it now. I have been wondering why you didn't answer. Frieda wrote to Katharine separately, even before my letter: and I'm sure there was nothing censorious in either of us.

I have been thinking with much affection and some longing of you two lately. I feel you are my only real friends in the world. I have really been badly seedy this time. Maitland Radford came down to see me: says it is nervous stress sets up internal inflammations. One feels the slithery edge of oblivion under one's feet. But I am much better now, and can go out again and walk.

We are in this house for 3 weeks longer – until March 8th. What shall we do afterwards? Shall we take a house down here in Cornwall, and keep Emma – she is a most excellent housekeeper – the Beresfords want to sack her. Shall we all live together? Emma is a splendid woman – cheap 5/- a week, because she has a child with her – illegitimate. So far, Heseltine has been here with us all along. We get on very well with him. But I don't know if he would stay on in Cornwall after March. It would perhaps be jolliest if it were us four alone. But that is as it turns out. We can live quite cheaply together. Here it costs us only about £2 a week, F. and me. Heseltine also talks of a publishing scheme. He would combine with you. I myself believe there is something to be done by private publishing. We can set everything going if you come – at least we can try.

I have felt awfully sick and down. But Maitland Radford says I mustn't

---

[1] Presumably Letter 1158.

bother about anything or I shall be worse ill. So I don't trouble. But my soul is a rag.

I shall be very anxious to hear from you – write at once.

Much love from Frieda and me.   D. H. Lawrence

1169. To Bertrand Russell, 11 February 1916
Text: MS UT; Moore, *Bertrand Russell* 69.

Porthcothan – St. Merryn – North Cornwall

11 Feb. 1916

My dear Russell,

I have been thinking about you and your lectures.[1] Are they really a success, and really vital? Are you really glad? – or only excited? I want to know, truly.

I have been very seedy down here – really felt as if I should die – but now am getting better quickly.

What a bitter thing it is, to feel swamped right over by these seas of utter falsehood. One does really die. But one is not dead.

I have been thinking, the only idea is to found a publishing company, that publishes for the sake of the truth. That is the only way. The spoken word nowadays is almost bound to be a lie: because the collective listening ear is a lie. I could never speak truth to 20 collected people.

We must send round circulars for our publishing: begin with *The Rainbow*: publish it at 7/6, by subscription. When we have a sufficient number of names to justify us, we could begin. Then we could go on, print every other month a *real* book, if a real book came. If no real book came, then we would wait till it did. A book is a holy thing, and must be made so again.

Tell me how you are, and how things are with you, and if you agree about the publishing concern.

Yours   D. H. Lawrence

1170. To J. B. Pinker, 12 February 1916
Text: TMSC Lazarus; Unpublished.

Porthcothan, St. Merryn, N. Cornwall.

12 Feb. 1916.

---

[1] Russell had written to a friend on 10 February 1916: 'my lectures are a great success – they are a rallying-ground for the intellectuals, who are coming daily more to my way of thinking.... All sorts of literary & artistic people who formerly despised politics are being driven to action' (*Autobiography*, ii. 59).

My dear Pinker,

Both your letters came this morning. The formal acknowledgement never came, so I wondered merely.

We will see what Constable says,[1] and what Sidgwick says,[2] and then we can decide. If Constable really seems the better, you will agree with him. But I like the idea of Sidgwick: though I see you don't. However, you will let me know their answers, and we can do what seems best then.

Yours,   D. H. Lawrence

1171. To Edward Marsh, 12 February 1916

Text: MS NYPL; Huxley 321–2.

Porthcothan – St. Merryn – North Cornwall
12 Feb. 1916

My dear Eddie,

Cynthia Asquith writes me that somebody says I 'abuse you'. If ever I have abused you to anybody, I am very sorry and ashamed. But I don't think I ever have: though heaven knows what one says. Yet I don't feel as if I had. We have *often* laughed at you:[3] because you are one of those special figures one can laugh at: just as I am, only I'm ten times more ridiculous. But I'm sure we've laughed kindly and affectionately: I know the Murrys and us, we've always laughed affectionately. I did feel rather bitter the way you took the war: 'What splendid times we live in': because the war makes me feel very badly, always. And I may have been furious about that: I must be more restrained. But I don't think I've abused you, apart from the war, which is something special: and even for that I don't think I have.

But whatever I have said, may have said, for I can't remember; I always feel a real gratitude to you, and a kindness, and an esteem of the genuine man. And I'm sorry if ever I've gone against those true feelings for you. I have thought that it was best for us to keep no constant connection, because

---

[1] Constable's decision was communicated to Pinker on 22 February 1916 (MS NYPL): 'We have given Mr. Lawrence's poems most careful consideration, and I am sorry that we do not feel on the whole we can decide to undertake their publication as we could not do so in this instance with the requisite enthusiasm.'

[2] Sidgwick's reply was sent to Pinker on 17 February 1916 (MS Bodleian Library): 'We return herewith Mr. Lawrence's "Amores", which we are sorry to find we cannot offer to publish. We have written our reasons for refusing to Mr. Lawrence himself, and expressed the hope to see another MS. of his poems in due course.' The letter to DHL has not been found; however, see Letter 1188 for DHL's reaction to it.

[3] In her diary for 28 October 1915, Lady Cynthia recalls one such occasion: 'He [DHL] was merciless about poor little Eddie, giving an excellent imitation of his lamenting Rupert Brooke over his evening whisky' (Asquith, *Diaries* 94).

of your position in the government,[1] and of my feelings about the war. But that I do out of respect for your position.

However, if ever I have abused you, though I cant remember, then forgive me: for indeed I am not ungrateful, and I never want to abuse you. If the war makes us strangers, it does not, I hope, make us in the least enemies.

I have been seedy down here, and felt like dying. I must not get into such states.

Next month will appear a vol. of my Italian Sketches, which I will send you. Only don't say, as you said of the *Rainbow*: 'toujours perdrix'.[2] Because you know one suffers what one writes.

And a little later will come a book of poems. I know you don't care much for my verses: but I'll send them along when they appear.

It's been a bad time, this last year. I wish it were ended.

Frieda sends her regards, I mine.

D. H. Lawrence

1172. To C. K. Walton Jameson [ante 14 February 1916]
Text: MS NYPL; Unpublished.

[Porthcothan, St. Merryn, Padstow, Cornwall]

[ante 14 February 1916]

[In reply to an enquiry, Lawrence suggested that Jameson should ask Pinker where he could obtain a copy of the *Rainbow*.][3]

1173. To S. S. Koteliansky, 15 February 1916
Text: MS BL; Postmark, St. Merryn 16 FEB 16; Spender 30–1.

[Porthcothan, St. Merryn, Padstow, Cornwall]

15 Feb. 1916

My dear Kot,

Thank you very much for the paper. I send you a p.o. for 5/-, to pay for it, and for things for which I shall be asking you shortly. And that bold Frieda asked for Kümmel, for which I abused her. But I like Kümmel very much. Don't be jealous of the Ottoline's sendings: they were only vile essences and extracts and plasmon:[4] but they do one good. I am much better, but still a sufferer.

---

[1] See Letter 607 and *Letters*, i. 459n.

[2] DHL's meaning is obscure; but see McDonald, *Phoenix*, p. 755 for another use of the phrase.

[3] Jameson wrote to Pinker from 89 Oakley St, Chelsea, S.W. on 14 February 1916. DHL's own letter has not been found.

[4] A proprietary brand of soluble casein; a nutritive and easily digested preparation for invalids.

If I had the energy I should tirade you about Dostoevsky. He has lost his spell over me: I was bored rather by the *Possessed*. The people were not possessed enough to be really interesting: Stavrogin is a bore. He was only interesting when he bit the old man's ear. Pyotr Stepanovitch was *nearly* interesting. The two most interesting are Varvara and Stepan Trofimovitch – their relation was good and subtle. I thought the *Idiot far* better than *Possessed*, also *Karamazov*.

I could do with Dostoevsky if he did not make all men fallen angels. We are not angels. It is a tiresome conceit. Men want to be Sadists, or they don't. If they do, well and good. There's no need to drag in the fallen angel touch to save ourselves in our own sight. I am most sick of this divinity-of-man business. People are *not important*: I insist on it. It doesn't matter what Stavrogin does, nor whether he lives or dies. I am quite unmoved when he commits suicide. It is his affair. It bores me. People are so self-important. Let them die, silly blighters, fools, and twopenny knaves.

I have sent off to the publishers the MS. of a book of poems. I am once more in the middle of my philosophy. My dear Kot, this time at last I have *got* it. Now you would not tell me, if you read it, that I shall write it again. This time, my dear Kot, I have put salt on its tail: I've caught the rabbit: like the old hare in *Tartarin*.[1] My dear Kot, it is the new word, at last.

I know you don't believe me, but it doesn't alter it.

My dear Kot, I feel anti-social. I want to blow the wings off these fallen angels. I want to bust 'em up. I feel that everything I do is a shot at these fallen angels of mankind. Wing the brutes. If only one could be a pirate or a brigand nowadays, an outlaw, to rob the angels and hang them on a tree. But long-distance guns has stopped all that jolly game.

We are going to look for another house down here. The wind blows terribly, the house shudders, for all its thick old walls. The sea bursts high in towers of foam. We leave here March 8th. I suppose it will be in the next house that you will come and see us. But come before, come here to this house, if you are ready.

Yours   D. H. Lawrence

[1] See *Tartarin de Tarascon* (Paris 1872), I. ii, by Alphonse Daudet (1840–97). The Tarasconnais, who were enthusiastic huntsmen, had killed or frightened off all the game in their locality, with one exception: an old rogue of a hare which had miraculously survived. His name was '*le Rapide*'. (The passage celebrating the unique achievement of '*le Rapide*' forms part of the translated extract from the novel included in Richard Garnett, *International Library of Famous Literature*, xx. 9514–15. See *Letters*, i. 4–6.)

1174. To Lady Ottoline Morrell, 15 February 1916
Text: TMSC NWU; Huxley 322–5.

Porthcothan, St. Merryn, North Cornwall.
15 feb. 1916

My dear Ottoline

We love the counterpane. It is the kind of thing that really rejoices my heart. I am very fond of woollen things too – even more than silk, I think. I don't think the pale blue and black are bad: they make me laugh. I don't know why, but the whole shawl gives me a sudden feeling of laughter. I really like it very much: and so does Frieda. We had puzzled over a word in one of your letters – countrypair, you wrote, I think – and wondered what it *was* you thought of sending us. How jolly it is to have this coloured countrypair. I want to wear it like a Red Indian.

I shall read the history of Egypt and tell you how I like it.[1] I now send you back one or two of your books. The Dostoievsky lay in the window-seat and in the night the rain beat in and spoiled it. I am sorry. Perhaps I ought to buy you another. But you don't like it very much. I *love* the book about St. Francis and Dante – or whatever it is – the Salimbene's biography.[2] I love to see these people as they were when the Christian idea was still only a graft upon their lives, had not entered in their blood. But what times to live in. I should think not two men in a hundred died a natural death then. It is always so interesting to see the original self in man being modified by a big universal idea. One has to recover the original self, now.

I have nearly done the first, the destructive, half of my philosophy. At last it can stand. It is the last word. I am sure it marks the end of a great epoch: at least for me. When this chapter is typed I shall send you as much as is done, for you to read. I feel that probably you won't like it, for a time.[3] But do read it.

Today we have a letter from Bertie: very miserable. He doesn't know why he lives at all: mere obstinacy and pride, he says, keep him alive. His lectures are all right in themselves, but their *effect* is negligible. They are a financial success. But all the people who matter are too busy doing other things to come to listen. He lives only for fussy trivialities, and for nothing else.

That is the whole gist of his letter. I am sorry for him, but my heart doesn't soften to him just yet: I don't know why. I feel he is obstinate in going his own way, and until he ceases to be obstinate, all is useless.

---

[1] In the light of DHL's request (in letter 1163) for a history of early Egypt, this may have been Volume 1 of W. M. F. Petrie's *History of Egypt* (1894).
[2] G. G. Coulton, *From St. Francis to Dante: A Translation of All That is of Primary Interest in the Chronicle of the Franciscan Salimbene (1221–1288)* (1906).
[3] See p. 558 n. 4.

I had a similar despairing letter from the Murrys. Something must have happened to the French mail – the mail to France. I had written them, and so had Frieda. I forgot to tell you, she has £130 a year from her father, he has what he makes. He can make quite a lot by his journalism. It is rather surprising that newspaper editors hold him in such esteem.

About H[eseltine] and Mlle. [Baillot] – I tell him he ought to tell her. I suppose he will. It is queer. He declares he does not like this one, the Puma, but he does really. He declares he wants her to go. But he is really attached to her in the senses, in the unconsciousness, in the blood. He is always fighting away from this. But in so doing he is a fool. She is very nice and very real and simple, we like her. His affection for Mlle. is a desire for the light because he is in the dark. If he were in the light he would want the dark. He wants Mlle. for *companionship*, not for the blood connection, the dark, sensuous relation. With Puma he has this second, dark relation, but not the first. She is quite intelligent, in her way, but no mental consciousness; no white consciousness, if you understand, all intuition, in the dark, the consciousness of the senses. But she is quite fine and subtle in that way, quite, and I esteem her there *quite* as much as I esteem him.

Perhaps he is very split, and would always have the two things separate, the real blood connection, and the real conscious or spiritual connection, always separate. For these people I really believe in two wives. I don't see why there should be monogamy for people who can't have full satisfaction in one person, because they themselves are too split, because they act in themselves separately. Monogamy is for those who are whole and clear, all in one stroke. But for those whose stroke is broken into two different directions, then there should be two fulfilments.

For myself, thank God, I feel myself becoming more and more unified, more and more a oneness. And Frieda and I become more and more truly married – for which I thank heaven. It has been such a fight. But it is coming right. And then we can all three be real friends. Then we shall be really happy, all of us, in our relation.

I am better. I got a cold and my chest was a bit raw, but that is going again. Here the winds are so black and terrible. They rush with such force that the house shudders, though the old walls are very solid and thick. Only occasionally the gulls rise very slowly into the air. And all the while the wind rushes and thuds and booms, and all the while the sea is hoarse and heavy. It is strange, one forgets the rest of life. It shuts one in within its massive violent world. Sometimes a wave bursts with a great explosion against one of the outlying rocks, and there is a tremendous ghost standing high on the sea, a great tall whiteness. I hope it will be more restful by and by, and you will come down here.

I shall send you most of the books back, because we are so wandering.

We have got daffodils and little yellow narcissi, and blue and white violets, on the table, that the children bring us from the gardens. It is really spring. The willow catkins are already silver, very gleaming. We are going soon to look for another house. I wonder where we shall find it. Quite near, I think.

Heseltine is very keen about the publishing scheme. He has sent off a circular to [be]¹ printed at his expense. Do you know, I believe he is one of those people who are born to be conveyors of art: they are next to artists, and they convey art to the world. I shouldn't wonder if he made the publishing scheme a real success in the long run.

I feel quite anti-social, against this social whole as its exists. I wish one could be a pirate or a highwayman in these days. But my way of shooting them with noiseless bullets that explode in their souls, these social people of today, perhaps it is more satisfying. But I feel like an outlaw. All my work is a shot at their very innermost strength, these banded people of today. Let them cease to be. Let them make way for another, fewer, stronger, less cowardly people.

Frieda sends her love – my love to you,   D. H. Lawrence

1175. To Dollie Radford, [15 February 1916]
Text: MS UN; Postmark, St. Merryn 16 FE 16; Nehls, i. 354–5.

Porthcothan, St. Merryn, North Cornwall
15 Jan. 1916 ²

My dear Dollie,

The parcel and your letter came this morning. I am glad to hear of Maitlands job.³

We shall be very glad for you to come down here whenever you like. Philip Heseltine and a girl are staying with us, but there is room for you, and we should all welcome you with joy. So that when you are ready, send us just a word: 'I'm coming', and we will expect you.

I only hope that you will hush the winds a little when you do come: for they are as violent as chaos. Really it is stunning, what with the great, bruising shocks of the wind, the shuddering of the old house, and the incessant heaviness of the sea, we wonder where we are.

---

¹ TMSC reads 'to printed'.
² In error for February 1916.
³ Having returned from France, Maitland Radford had been appointed to a post at Queen Mary's Hospital, Carshalton, Surrey.

We are staying in this house till March 7th or 8th. We shall be looking for another house in Cornwall: I wonder what we shall find. It is rather fun.

The spring is coming. On the table there are blue and white violets, and yellow little narcissi, and daffodils, that the children have brought us from their gardens. This is a bare, bleak country, but it is not cold. One feels the *past* very much, always the darkness of the past, violent and rather passionate. Today scarcely exists here.

I am better: in a way, much better. Still inclined to tremble, and to have pains in my limbs, and a raw chest. But it will pass.

We want to have a scheme of private publishing, that all the books which publishers wont take, shall come out in dignity and conspicuousness. I wonder if it will come off.

The Murrys are still in France. They are very happy there, I believe. But probably they will come home some time in March, and will join us if we find a good house. That will be jolly.

Well, my dear Dollie, we shall expect you to be blown in suddenly one morning, like one of the little flowers one suddenly finds out in the garden. And we shall clap our hands.

Tell Maitland I am getting better. Lady Ottoline sent me a lot of things to swallow, which are strengthening. I am really much better. How is Margaret? Remember me warmly to her.

Our love to you   D. H. Lawrence

I'm glad you like Mrs Aldington.[1] Ask her if she doesn't want a cottage in Cornwall?

1176. To John Middleton Murry and Katherine Mansfield, 17 February 1916

Text: MS NYPL; cited in Murry, *New Adelphi* 196.

Porthcothan – St. Merryn – N. Cornwall
17 Feb. 1916

Dear Katharine and Jack,

Your letters came this morning. We shouldn't bind you: after our experiences, are we such fools? The farmhouse is no more.[2] But we shall look for a furnished place, first in Cornwall, then, if nothing nice here, then in Herefordshire. The Beresford's come back here on March 9th. so we must be housed by then. I will let you know. We will not take anything very expensive, so that if you don't come we can live by ourselves. Probably

[1] See p. 203 n. 3.   [2] See Letter 1158.

Heseltine will stay on with us: if he is not conscripted: and I shouldn't think he will be.

This morning the proofs have come of the circular for the private publishing venture: 'The Rainbow Books and Music'.[1] It looks very well. I will send you a copy when the lot come. We want to begin by doing the *Rainbow* privately – it has got some renown now – then go on and on. No more trivial things. The whole hog.

And no more adhering to society.[2] I am out of the camp, like a brigand. And every book will be a raid on them.

I've just read *The Possessed*. I find I've gone off Dostoevsky, and could write about him in very cold blood. I didn't care for the *Possessed*: nobody was possessed enough really to interest me. They bore me, these squirming sorts of people: they teem like insects.

---

[1] The text of the circular (taken from the copy in the possession of Mr George Lazarus) is as follows:

THE RAINBOW BOOKS AND MUSIC

Either there exists a sufficient number of people to buy books because of their reverence for truth, or else books must die. In its books lies a nation's vision; and where there is no vision the people perish.

The present system of production depends entirely upon the popular esteem: and this means gradual degradation. Inevitably, more and more, the published books are dragged down to the level of the lowest reader.

It is monstrous that the herd should lord it over the uttered word. The swine has only to grunt disapprobation, and the very angels of heaven will be compelled to silence.

It is time that enough people of courage and passionate soul should rise up to form a nucleus of the living truth; since there must be those among us who care more for the truth than for any advantage.

For this purpose it is proposed to attempt to issue privately such books and musical works as are found living and clear in truth; such books as would either be rejected by the publisher, or else overlooked when flung into the trough before the public.

This method of private printing and circulation would also unseal those sources of truth and beauty which are now sterile in the heart, and real works would again be produced.

It is proposed to print first "The Rainbow," the novel by Mr. D. H. Lawrence, which has been so unjustly suppressed. If sufficient money is forthcoming, a second book will be announced; either Mr. Lawrence's philosophical work, "Goats and Compasses," or a new book by some other writer.

All who wish to support the scheme should sign the accompanying form, and send it at once to the Secretary,

PHILIP HESELTINE,
Cefn Bryntalch,
Abermule,
Montgomeryshire.

A pamphlet giving full information of the first seven books and musical works offered will be forwarded in due course.

(An order form was attached to the Prospectus. According to Cecil Gray, Heseltine was responsible for the text above; see *Peter Warlock*, p. 113.)

[2] society] the society

I'll write you some 'notes' on Dostoevsky – you can translate them into your own language, if they interest you.

1. He has a fixed will, a mania to be infinite, to be God.
2. Within this will, his activity is twofold:
    a. To be self-less, a pure Christian, to live in the outer whole, the social whole, the self-less whole, the universal consciousness.
    b. To be a pure, absolute self, all-devouring and all-consuming.
That is the main statement about him.

His desire[1] to achieve the sensual, all-devouring consummation comes out in Dmitri Karamazov, and Rogozhin, and, not so clearly, in Stavrogin.

His desire for the spiritual, turn-the-other-cheek consummation, comes out in the Idiot himself, in Alyosha, partly in Stavrogin.

There is the third type, which represents pure unemotional *will*: this is the third Karamazov brother, and Pyotr Stepanovitch, and the young secretary man at whose house the Idiot first lodges – he who is going to marry the young woman – Gavril, is his name?[2]

The whole point of Dostoevsky lies in the fact of his fixed will that the individual ego, the achieved I, the conscious entity, shall be infinite, God-like, and absolved from all relation i.e. free.

I like *The Idiot* best. *The Idiot* is showing the last stage of Christianity, of becoming purely self-less, of becoming disseminated out into a pure, absolved consciousness. This is the Christian ecstasy, when I become so transcendently super-conscious, that I am bodiless, that the universe is my consciousness. This is the little Idiot prince. It is the ecstasy of being devoured in the body, like the Christian lamb, and of transcendence in the conscious, the spirit.

Karamazov is concerned with the last stages – not nearly so far gone, – of sensuality, of unconscious experience purely within the self. I reach such a pitch of dark sensual ecstasy that I seem to be, in myself, the universal night that has swallowed everything. I become universal, the universal devouring darkness. This is Dmitri Karamazov. This was Dostoevsky's real desire, to obtain this sensual ecstasy of universality. This is why Father Zossima bowed to Dmitri – Zossima is pure Christian, selfless, universal in the social whole. Dead, he stinks.

He was sadish because his *will* was fixed on the social virtues, because he felt himself *wrong* in his sensual seekings. Therefore he was cruel, he tortured himself and others, and goûtait the tortures.

---

[1] desire] major desire, however is
[2] Ganya, who wants to marry Aglaya.

The Christian ecstasy leads to imbecility (the Idiot). The sensual ecstasy leads to universal murder: for mind, the acme of sensual ecstasy lies in *devouring* the other, even in the pleasures of love, it is a devouring, like a tiger drinking blood (Rogozhin). But the full sensual ecstasy is never reached except by Rogozhin in murdering Nastasya. It is nipped in the last stages by the *will*, the social will. When the police stripped Dmitri Karamazov naked, they killed in him the quick of his being, his lust[1] for the sensual ecstasy.

The men who represent the Will, the pure mental, social, rational, absolved will, Stepan Karamazov,[2] and Pyotr Stepanovitch, and Gavril, they represent the last stages of our social development, the human being become mechanical, absolved from all relation. When Stepan talks with the devil, the devil is a decayed *social* gentleman – only that.[3] The mechanical social forms and aspirations and ideals, I suppose, are the devil.

The women are not important. They are the mere echoes and objectives of the men. They *desire* the sensual ecstasy, all of them, even the cripple in the *Possessed* (my hawk, my eagle, she says to Stavrogin). They have the opposite wild love for purity, self-lessness, extreme Christianity. And they are *all* ultimately bound to the social convention – all the 'great' women, that is. The cripple in the *Possessed*, and Nastasya Felippovna,[4] and Dmitri Karamazov's woman, these desire only the sensual ecstasy: but all the while they *admit* themselves the inferior of the other christian ecstasy: which is the social ecstasy.

They are great parables, the novels, but false art. They are only parables. All the people are *fallen angels* – even the dirtiest scrubs. This I cannot stomach. People are not fallen angels, they are merely people. But Dostoevsky uses them all as theological or religious units, they are all terms of divinity, like Christs 'Sower went forth to sow',[5] and Bunyan's *Pilgrims Progress*. They are bad art, false truth.

I will write you more if you want.

Love to you both.   D. H. Lawrence

Don't bind yourselves in the *least* about the house – in fact we will just move as for ourselves, and come if you like, later.

---

[1] his being, his lust] desire
[2] i.e. Ivan Karamazov.
[3] *The Brothers Karamazov*, XI. ix, entitled 'The Devil: Ivan's Nightmare'.
[4] i.e. Filipovna.
[5] Matthew xiii. 3; Luke viii. 5 (R.V.).

1177. To Katherine Mansfield, [17 February 1916]
Text: MS NYPL; PC; Postmark, St. Merryn 18 FE 16; Unpublished.

Porthcothan
– Thursday

Your telegram has just come.[1] Good, we will find a decent sunny house: it will be splendid. I'm sure we shall be happy. There is the publishing scheme – we can do that together. It has begun.

We leave this house on Mar 1st. It means running round during the next week. But there are many available houses – many. I would rather be a bit back from the sea, because of the 'sea-sideness'.

What about your novel – yours and Jacks?[2] – the publishing scheme *must* be made to go. Tell J. I will do the Dostoevsky with him, if he hasn't done it.[3]

Much love from us   DHL

I had written you a letter this morning.

1178. To S. S. Koteliansky, [19 February 1916]
Text: MS BL; Postmark, St. Merryn 19 FE 16; Zytaruk 70.

Porthcothan – St. Merryn, N. Cornwall
[19 February 1916]

[Frieda Lawrence begins]
Dear Kot,

In great triumph they brought the Kümmel *and* the Sherry home – And my cigarettes – But it was as usual too much – I don't think Shatov was a serf or his soul was not that of a serf – But anyhow you are not like him – I thought your belief in Lawrence was like Shatov's in Stavrogin but I dont think it is – He wanted something to believe in and so do you – You used to believe in yourself once but you say you are dead – but I dont think it's true! You dont, do you? Shatov is the most living and real person in the *Possessed* – Stavrogin and Pyotr are more shadowy and unliving, Pyotr is mechanical – Varvara and Stepanovitch are like the Ottoline and Bertie Russell! Exactly! It will be nice if you come – The Murrys will stay with

---

[1] The telegram suggests more than the 'non-committal' response which Murry has described in his version of the plan to live near DHL. See Murry, *Autobiography* 395ff.

[2] Katherine Mansfield was writing the first version of *Prelude* (1918); Murry's novel was *Still Life*.

[3] In August 1916 Murry published a critical study, *Fyodor Dostoevsky*; in December 1916 he wrote an introduction to Dostoevsky's *Pages from the Journal of an Author*, trans. Murry and Koteliansky. DHL is presumably referring to the former.

us for some time. L. is full of plans and feels happy! Miss Channing (Heseltine's friend) will be in London soon (she is *very* pretty) and it would be nice of you, if you saw her – You will like her – I will give her your address – With many thanks for your gifts, we shall have a feast to-night!

With kindest regards   Frieda

[Lawrence begins]

My dear Kot,

Thank you for the Kümmel and the sherry. It grieves me rather, that we should drink up your few wages.

We haven't found a house yet – it rains so much, we can't go out.

It's a good thing somebody believes in me. I am very frightened of the foulness of the world. One feels as if all the time one were dodging the blind, flying tentacles of an octopus. It is hideous.

I understand Nietzsche's child.[1] But it isn't a child that will represent the third stage: not innocent unconsciousness: but the maximum of fearless adult consciousness, that has the courage even to submit to the unconsciousness of itself.

Many warm greetings   D. H. Lawrence

1179. To Bertrand Russell, [19 February 1916]

Text: MS UT; cited in Moore, *Atlantic Monthly* 102.

[Porthcothan, St. Merryn, North Cornwall]
Saturday[2]

My dear Russell,

I didn't like your letter. What's the good of living as you do, any way. I don't believe your lectures *are* good. They are nearly over, aren't they?

What's the good of sticking in the damned ship and haranguing the merchant-pilgrims in their own language. Why don't you drop overboard? Why don't you clear out of the whole show?

One must be an outlaw these days, not a teacher or preacher. One must retire out of the herd and then fire bombs into it. You said in your lecture on education that you didn't set much count by the unconscious. That is

---

[1] A reference to *Thus Spake Zarathustra* (1883–92) by Friedrich Nietzsche (1844–1900): 'Three metamorphoses of the spirit do I designate to you: how the spirit becometh a camel, the camel a lion, and the lion at last a child' (*The Complete Works*, ed. Oscar Levy, 1910–13, xi. 25).

[2] The Lawrences had to vacate Beresford's house on 28 February 1916; the Saturday closest to that date to enable him to write about leaving 'in a week's time' would be 19 February.

sheer perversity. The whole of the consciousness and the conscious content is old hat – the mill-stone round your neck.

Do cut it – cut your will and leave your old self behind. Even your mathematics are only *dead* truth: and no matter how fine you grind the dead meat, you'll not bring it to life again.

Do stop working and writing altogether and become a creature instead of a mechanical instrument. Do clear out of the whole social ship. Do for your very pride's sake become a mere nothing, a mole, a creature that feels its way and doesn't think. Do for heavens sake be a baby, and not a savant any more. Don't *do* anything any more – but for heavens sake begin to *be* – start at the very beginning and be a perfect baby: in the name of courage.

Oh, and I want to ask you, when you make your will, do leave me enough to live on. I want you to live for ever. But I want you to make me in some part your heir.

We have got to clear out of this house in a week's¹ time. We are looking for another house. You had better come and live near us: but not if you are going to be a thinker and a worker, only if you are going to be a creature, an infant. The Murrys are coming to live with us, in April, they say.

Heseltine is starting the publishing Scheme. I shouldn't wonder if he would make something of it, if he isn't conscripted. I feel as if we were all living on the edge of a precipice.

Soon I shall be penniless, and they'll shove me into munitions, and I shall tell 'em what I think of 'em, and end my days in prison or a madhouse. But I don't care. One can still write bombs. But I don't want to be penniless and at their mercy. Life is very good of itself, and I am terrified lest they should get me into their power. They seem to me like an innumerable host of rats, and once they get the scent, one is lost.

My love to you. Stop working and being an ego, and have the courage to be a creature.

Yours   D. H. Lawrence

1180. To Dollie Radford, [21 February 1916]

Text: MS UN; Postmark, St. Merryn 21 FE 16; Nehls, i. 359–60.

Porthcothan – St. Merryn – North Cornwall
Monday

My dear Dollie,

We must leave this house *next Monday*. We are looking for another place.

---

¹ week's] fortnight's

In case we haven't got one, we might go to Maitland's farmhouse at Zennor. Will you ask him for the name and address, and let me have it as soon as possible, so that I can write them if necessary. We have vile weather. But tomorrow we set out to look in the *Redruth* district. I hope we find something nice. The Murrys are coming to live with us in April. I hope we get a *nice* place for you to come to.

                                                                    Love   D. H. Lawrence
        I am a good deal better now.

1181. To John Middleton Murry and Katherine Mansfield,
        24 February 1916
Text: MS NYPL.; Huxley 330–2.

                                                    Porthcothan – St. Merryn – N. Cornwall.
                                                                         24 Feb. 1916

My dear Jack and Katharine,
    Now don't get in a state, you two, about nothing. The Publishing scheme has not yet become at all real or important, to me.
    Heseltine was mad to begin it – he wanted to get *The Rainbow* published. I felt, you don't know how much, sick and done. And it was rather fine that he believed and was so generously enthusiastic. He is the musical one: the musicians he likes are Delius, Goosens, Arnold Bax, and some few others.[1] I believe as a matter of fact they are good, and we are perhaps, outside ourselves, more likely to have good music and bad books, than otherwise.
    This is what is done so far: a circular, or letter, something like that *Signature* one, only bigger and better, is drawn up and 1000 copies are being printed. It is to be sent to everybody we can think of. Heseltine pays for all this.
    It states: that either there is a sufficient number of people to buy books, out of reverence for the books themselves, or else real works[2] will disappear from us: therefore it is proposed to publish by subscription such works as are not likely to have any effect, coming through a publisher, or which are not likely to be published at all in the ordinary way: it is proposed to issue first the *Rainbow*, at 7/6 post free. Will those who wish to partake in the scheme fill in the enclosed form: – Then follows a form for subscription, just to be filled in, and re-addressed to Heseltine at his mother's house in Wales. – I want to announce your book[3] after *The Rainbow*.

---

[1] Eugene Goossens (1893–1962) and (Sir) Arnold Bax (1883–1953).
[2] works] books   [3] Presumably Murry's novel *Still Life*.

He has gone to London, and I haven't yet seen a printed leaflet.[1] When I get one I will send it you.

This is all. You see it is Heseltine's affair so far. I feel that he is one of those people who are transmitters, and not creators of art. And I don't think we are transmitters. I have come to the conclusion that I have no business genius. Heseltines family have just got that curious touch of artistic genius which will make them perfect dealers in art, I believe. His uncle had one of the best collections of pictures in England – Rembrandt Watteau etc – and he was a stockbroker and very rich.[2] That is the style. Heseltine isn't rich. He has £150 a year of his own: his mother gives him something. He will have £600 a year or so when she dies. He is 21 yrs old, and I must say, I am very glad to have him for a friend. He lived here for seven weeks with us, so we know. Now don't think his friendship hurts ours. It doesn't touch it. You will like him too, because he is real, and has some queer kind of abstract passion which leaps into the future. He will be one with us. We must treasure and value very much any one who will *really* be added on to us. I am afraid he may be conscripted.

And now, you two, for Gods sake don't get in a state. I myself am always on the brink of another collapse. I begin to tremble and feel sick at the slightest upset: your letter for instance. Do be mild with me for a bit. Don't get silly notions. I've waited for you for two years now, and am far more constant to you than ever you are to me – or ever will be. Which you know. So don't use foolish language. I believe in you, and there's the end of it. But I think you keep far less faith with me, than I with you, at the centre of things. But faith like everything else is a fluctuating thing. But that doesn't disprove its constancy. I know[3] you will slip towards us [...] again,[4] however you may slip away and become nothing, or even go over to the enemy. It doesn't make any difference. You will in the main be constant to the same truth and the same spirit with me. The personal adherence, the me and thee

[1] DHL received the proof of the circular on 17 February 1916; see Letter 1176. Katherine and Murry were offended because the scheme 'still included the stranger Heseltine'. The strength of their annoyance becomes clear from Frieda Lawrence's letter to Gertler in early March 1916 (MS HU): 'The Murry's wrote very indignant that Heseltine started about these *Rainbow* books without *them*, saying Lawrence was treacherous.' Murry recalled: 'I was piqued that the scheme of publishing our books for ourselves, which I had broached to Lawrence on my return to England [i.e. December 1915] and in which Kotelian-sky alone was included, had been given over to Heseltine without a word to me' (Murry, *Autobiography* 395–6).
[2] John Postle Heseltine (1843–1929), one of the most distinguished collectors of modern times. Trustee of the National Gallery. See the volumes relating to his own collection: *Drawings by Boucher, Fragonard and Watteau* (1900), *Drawings by Rembrandt* (1907), etc.
[3] know] believe   [4] towards us [...] again,] back,

business, is subsidiary to that. We are co-believers first. And in our oneness of belief lies our oneness. There is no *bond* anywhere. I am not bound to agree with you, nor you with me. We are not bound even to like each other: that is as it comes. But we gravitate to one belief, and that is our destiny, which is beyond choice. And in this destiny we are together.

This is my declaration, now let it be enough. As for this publishing business, the whole of the work remains yet to be done. We will fight together when you come. Meanwhile let Heseltine take the vanguard.

We went out looking for a house, and I think we have found one that is good. It is about 7 miles from St. Ives, towards Lands End, very lonely, in the rocks on the sea, Zennor the nearest village: high pale hills, all moor-like and beautiful, behind, very wild: 7 miles across country to Penzance: 25/- a week, eight rooms: a woman there who will clean for us.

We are going next Tuesday from here: address for the time being 'The Tinners Arms, Zennor, St. Ives, Cornwall'. Or just Zennor: it is only seven houses to the church-town; really beautiful. We take the house for four months, I think: March–June inclusive; with the option of staying on, I hope.

You will come at the end of April, when it will be warm. Just at present it is very cold. That icy wind you mention did not touch us at Fiascherino, but if we climbed up the hills, it was there: terrible. It has been blowing here also, and a bit of snow. Till now the weather has been so mild. Primroses and violets are out, and the gorse is lovely. At Zennor one sees infinite Atlantic, all peacock-mingled colours, and the gorse is sunshine itself, already. But this cold wind is deadly.

I have been in a sort of 'all gone but my cap' state this winter, and am very shaky. Also steering in my own direction with nobody to lend a hand or to come along, I feel very estranged. But when we set out to walk to Newquay, and when I looked down at Zennor, I knew it was the Promised Land, and that a new heaven and a new earth would take place.[1] But everything is very tender in the bud, yet. But you will come along, in your own time, soon, I hope. You've escaped the worst of this winter. It has been the worst: one has touched the bottom. Somehow I have a sense of a new spring coming very joyful from the unknown.

My love to you both   D. H. Lawrence

We shall be very badly off soon – and no incomings anywhere. I don't know what we shall do. But I dont bother. It will turn out somehow.

Do let the winter be gone, before Katharine comes to England.

---

[1] place] place there.

1182. To Philip Heseltine, 24 February 1916
Text: MS UT; cited in Delany 203, 404n.

Porthcothan – St. Merryn – N. Cornwall
24 Feb 1916

My dear Philip,

I send you on these papers from No-Conscription league.[1] I sent them another 2/6: they are worthy.

While you are away, I will curse the enemy. That is better than praying for you.

We leave here Tuesday morning for Zennor: The Tinners Arms, Zennor, St. Ives, Cornwall. It is most lovely down there: steep, – pale, stony hills, wild and moorlike, and a tremendous far-spreading sea below, all peacock-colored. I think we can get the house – £1. a week. At any rate we can get cottages, for sure.

Come back soon, free. Then in our retreat we will make the bombs to smite the Philistine. Oh to *bust* up the Philistine – only that.

I feel a new life, a new world ahead, for us – down towards Lands End there. We will be a centre of a new life, a centre of destruction of the old. I believe in the 'Rainbow books and music', quite gaily.

See Bertie Russell, and Beresford, and Gertler, and Kot., and Campbell. When you are coming down again, you can bring a big rug and some things of ours that lie with Gertler.

Much love from all of us to you. Live pleasantly with your mother – my respects to her.

Yours   D. H. Lawrence

1183. To J. D. Beresford, 24 February 1916
Text: TMSC NWU; Huxley 328–30.

Porthcothan – St. Merryn – Padstow – N. Cornwall
24 Feb. 1916

My dear Beresford

I ought to have written to you before about the cottage: but we have been so undecided. We don't like Constantine Bay – it is a fag end of the earth: and I don't like Havlyn very much: and there is no decent house anywhere

---

[1] DHL refers to the No-Conscription Fellowship, whose chairman was Clifford Allen. The organisation 'consisted entirely of men of military age, but it accepted women and older men as associates' (Russell, *Autobiography*, i. 24). Bertrand Russell doubtless drew DHL's attention to the group; in 1916 Russell became acting chairman of the N.-C.F. committee after Clifford Allen's second imprisonment.

else. So Mrs. Lawrence and I made an excursion to St. Ives and Zennor. We can have a house at Gurnard's Head, near Zennor, St. Ives, for £1 a week: I think Heseltine will share it with us: and it is very beautiful down there – so we shall leave here next Tuesday, and go for a week to the Tinner's Arms, Zennor, then move in. Emma will have plenty of time to clean the house; I hope everything will be well.

I don't like these people here. They have got the souls of insects. One feels, if they were squashed, they would be a whitey mess, like when a black-beetle is squashed. They are all *afraid* – that's why they are so mean. But I don't really understand them. Only I know this, I have never in my life come across such innerly selfish people, neither French, German, Italian, Swiss, nor English. I have thought French peasants vile, like hedge-hogs, hedge-pigs. But these people haven't any *being* at all. They've got no inside.

There are very few at Zennor, and they seem decent. I like Emma still. But when we were nice to her, she only became more greedy: she never did anything for us in return. One has to keep them down. They are just like all the rest of people who have no real *being*, but only a static ego, they are the very bottomless pit, if one is to pour any kindness into them. The only thing to do is to use them strictly as servants, inferiors: for they have the souls of slaves; like Aesop.[1]

What are the confessions to make? Chiefly, we stole a bottle of your gin, your good sloe gin. All the while, we hovered in temptation, and I was conscientious. Then last week conscience broke down. Heseltine took a bottle, and I didn't prevent him. We drank it all in one evening, and were very happy. Now I am very sorry to have robbed you, but I will get a bottle of whiskey in place of it.

Then the door of the porch has come to pieces – or nearly to pieces. But that is really the weather. We haven't done anything to it.

Then the cork of one of the hot-water bottles is broken: the screw stopper. Perhaps you could get another in town.

I don't think there is anything else. By good fortune we have not broken much, nor destroyed much.

We are grateful indeed to you for lending us the house. It has been a good time, our staying here; a time of getting well, and of discovering a new world of our own. I only wish you could exterminate all the natives and we could possess the land. The barbarian conquerors were wisest, really. There are very many people, like insects, who await extermination.

It is very cold, terribly cold, and snowy. Don't come back if it keeps so

---

[1] The supposed fabulist was a deformed Phrygian slave of the 6th century B.C.

cold: it is terrible. But the snow doesn't lie. And I pray heaven for a warm wind.

My regards to Mrs. Beresford.

Yours   D. H. Lawrence

1184. To Bertrand Russell, [24 February 1916]

Text: MS McMU; Unpublished.

Porthcothan, St. Merryn, North Cornwall
[24 February 1916][1]

[Frieda Lawrence begins]

Dear Mr Russell.

I want to write you a cross letter – You said to Lawrence that you are not very happy – I dont see how you could be – You told me to say to Lawrence that you loved him – Yet I dont *feel* that you care for him – I dont think you care for any body or if you do it is in a most unsatisfying way – And your belief in your social democratic ideal is *not* vital to you, it seems mostly obstinacy. It is a stale old bun even to you. Lawrence is better and I felt very sure and happy lately of a life that can be lived with meaning and dignity and even happiness – We have found such a nice place and I am looking forward to living there – A few people will come and stay from time to time and I hope you will be one of them – There wont be many I know to my sorrow – I know you have not a high opinion of me but that is because I dont believe in what you put your trust in – And I have a great respect for you ultimately and I wish you would come and stay with us soon for a little while and we would be happy –

Yours sincerely   Frieda Lawrence

Our new address is:

The Tinner's Arms, Zennor, near St. Ives, Cornwall.

[Lawrence begins]

We leave here on Tuesday (29th Feb). Our address is then 'The Tinners Arms, Zennor, St. Ives, Cornwall'. It is very lovely at Zennor. Come down there when you are free, won't you? And give up your London flat when the lease is up.   DHL

---

[1] DHL's intention to leave 'on Tuesday', which appears also in Letters 1182 and 1183, suggests that this letter was probably written on the same date. By 25 February, when the next letter was written, the plan had been changed, and the Lawrences were going to leave 'on Monday next'.

1185. To S. S. Koteliansky, 25 February 1916
Text: MS BL; Postmark, St. Merryn 26 FE 16; cited in Gransden 25.

Porthcothan – St. Merryn – N. Cornwall.
25 Feb. 1916

My dear Kot,

We are leaving here on Monday next, to go to Zennor. The address is: 'The Tinner's Arms, Zennor, St. Ives, Cornwall'.

Zennor is a lovely place far down in Cornwall, towards Lands End: very wild and remote and beautiful. We shall stay for a week in the inn, then I think we shall take a furnished house. There you must come and see us: it will be *much* better than here. The address will always be Zennor. It is a *tiny* place – seven houses.

I go with a strange feeling to Zennor: as if it were in some sort a Promised Land: not territorially, but of the spirit. I feel as if a new heavens and a new earth would come to pass there.

The Murrys will come not till the end of April: they said before, the end of March, but now they put it off for a month, so that the winter may be over, for Katharine's sake.[1] They will, I think, come and live with us.

You will be seeing Heseltine, and talking of the publishing scheme with him. I believe in him, he is one of us. Mind you are nice to him. He is in a very overwrought and over-inflammable state, really.

Here it is very cold. Snow falls, then disappears. But I do wish this black wind would depart again.

I loathe the world outside. How unspeakably foul it is. If only one can sufficiently retire from it, and create a new world, from the spirit. It could be done, with a few people. I think it will come to pass. I think, intrinsically, we can conquer the world. I think, intrinsically, we have conquered the world. I feel victorious, somehow.

But I also feel very shaky, and as if I *must* escape from the contact with this foulness of the world. But I am better in health: only still feel horribly vulnerable and wincing.

The Murrys accused me of being treacherous and not taking them into the publishing scheme.[2] I tell them of course they are included, and they are far more treacherous to me, intrinsically, than ever I shall be to them.

We must add all our strength together, all of us, to win a new world, a new being all together; it is not enough to have being individually, we must have a true being in common.

Yours   D. H. Lawrence

[1] The climate of the south of France was more congenial to her; she suffered from tuberculosis.
[2] See p. 549 n. 1.

1186. To Catherine Carswell, 25 February 1916
Text: MS YU; cited in Carswell, *Adelphi* 211.

Porthcothan – St. Merryn – N. Cornwall
25 Feb. 1916

My dear Catherine,

You didn't answer my last letter[1] – neither has Ivy answered the one I wrote her, asking her if she would like our kitchen table and chairs which I left with Gertler. Has anything untoward happened, or have the letters gone astray? I feel sure Ivy would have answered if she had got my letter. However, just ask her, and tell her to let me know if she'd like those things for her marriage.

We leave here on Monday, to go down to Zennor. Our address is 'The Tinners Arms, Zennor, St. Ives, Cornwall'. Zennor is a lovely place 5 miles south of St. Ives: lovely pale hills, all gorse and heather, and an immense peacock sea spreading all below. We shall stay at the inn for a week, and then, I think, take a furnished house. You must come and see us in the spring. It is quite wild down there.

Did I tell you about 'The Rainbow Books', the publishing scheme. You will get a leaflet. I believe something will come of it, unless the skies fall. And they seem shaky. Oh the world is a foul place. I am so tired of it.

The only thing to do is to save oneself from it, and to build up a new world from within one's soul. I felt, somehow, when we went to Zennor, that a new heaven and a new earth would take place. But to endure the cracking up of the old one is horrible.

But I do think, one must not die without having known a real good life, and a fulfilment, a happiness that is born of a new world, from a new centre. I believe, if we cannot discover a terrestrial America, there are new continents of the soul for us to land upon, Virgin soil. Only one must get away from this foul old world, one must have the strength to depart, and to go where there is no road, into the unrealised.

I think the Murrys will come later and live with us at Zennor. It is always my idea, that a few people by being together should bring to pass a new earth and a new heaven.

Heseltine stayed with us for eight weeks. He is one of us. Ask him to see you, will you – Philip Heseltine, 13 Rossetti Mansions, Chelsea S W. telephone Kensington 6319.

I get so tired, so tired, so tired of the world. It is so foul. But I have real sureness of a new world now. It is time for it to begin.

---

[1] Presumably Letter 1167.

Let us know what you are doing, and how you are. Are you finishing your novel? I shall be glad if you are.

My regards to Carswell. Frieda sends her love, with mine.

D. H. Lawrence

1187. To Lady Ottoline Morrell, 25 February 1916
Text: MS UT; Moore 436–8.

Porthcothan – St Merryn – N. Cornwall.
25 Feb. 1916.

My dear Ottoline

Thank you for the new book.[1] The one on Egypt was very irritating.[2] I read it angrily. Still, it served.

We leave this house next Monday (D.V.). Address us then 'The Tinners Arms, Zennor, St. Ives, Cornwall'. Zennor is lovely – 5 miles S. of St. Ives: lovely pale hills all gorse and heather, and a great peacock-iridescent sea. We can have a house at Gurnards Head for 25/- a week. The Murrys will come in April and share it with us: also Heseltine, if he escapes conscription. So all will be well. They will help us to live cheaply. Heseltine is very good, always paying more than his share. We have got nothing coming in, as yet: but perhaps something will turn up. I shall tell you when we are really in need. Don't mind the money for the bowl. It was very little; and we wanted you to have it – the bowl. As soon as I saw it, so nice and speckled, with its green like a memory of the sea, I said 'Shall we send it to Ottoline'.

The snow falls, and the sheep and lambs are disconsolate, the sea disappears. Then all is white, and the sea leaden and horrible. Then, in an hour, the snow is gone again, the earth is so warm.

When we came over the shoulder of the wild hill, above the sea, to Zennor, I felt we were coming into the Promised Land. I know there will a new heaven and a new earth take place now: we have triumphed. I feel like a Columbus who can see a shadowy America before him: only this isn't merely territory, it is a new continent of the soul. We will all be happy yet, doing a new, constructive work, sailing into a new epoch. Don't let us be troubled.

I send you now the first, the destructive half of my philosophy.[3] Don't read it on a spring day, when the buds are young and tender to unfold. Read it on a black day, when there is a blackness gripping you. Please do this.

I feel my philosophy is real, again a sort of bursting into new seas: when

---

[1] Probably Murray's *Four Stages of Greek Religion* (1912).
[2] See p. 538 n. 1.   [3] See Letter 1189.

it is finished. There remains the new half to write. But I have crossed the ridge, the new world lies before us. We will have a new world to live in.

Heseltine is in a great state of (unjustly) hating the Puma, and looking on Mlle [Baillot] as a white star. He will swing from dark to light till he comes to rest. I believe if he stayed long enough with Mlle *exclusively*, he would hate her: but perhaps not. We can but let him oscillate violently. He is really very good and I depend on him and believe in him. But he is exasperating because he is always in such a state of mad *reaction against* things, all mad reactions. It is a terrible cyclonic state, but he will be worth having with us, oh, very much.

I shall send you your books before we leave here. The 'Countrypair' is still a great joy to us.[1] I *really* don't find any fault at all with the circling of the colours. We lie and discuss them. I know them now in my visual memory.

I wrote to Bertie. I hope he too will come out of the old world.

I loathe the old world – Asquith's speech: about 'Peace Talk', etc.[2] But we will triumph, intrinsically. Myriads of people, all foul. But, a few, ourselves, we will conquer them all, intrinsically.

If you go to London, to[3] stay at all, ask Kotilianski to see you, will you? You will like him. S. Kotilianski, Russian Law Bureau, 212 High Holborn. He is on the telephone Russian Law Bureau.

I am still taking the sanatogen stuffs. I have plenty. I think they are very good. And when one walks, and gets tired, it is splendid to take Brands Essence – Heseltine is sending this also from town. But remember, when you are tired, take a few teaspoonfuls.

Frieda and I have a kind of new being, for each other, which is life.

There is a little Yeats play that is jolly for children – I forget its name – is it *The Tinkers Wedding*? – or is that Synge?[4] But it is something like that.

I want us to be in that Gurnards Head House, then you will come and see us. It is much lovelier there than here.

My love to you   D. H. Lawrence

---

[1] See Letter 1174.

[2] On the previous day, 24 February, the Prime Minister had reiterated in Parliament the Government's 'terms of peace': the restoration of Belgium, security of France and the 'military domination of Prussia wholly and finally destroyed'.

[3] to] ask

[4] *The Tinker's Wedding* (1907) by the Irish dramatist J. M. Synge (1871–1909). 'A Pot of Broth' may have been the Yeats play DHL could not recall: see *Letters*, i. 186 n. 3, 246.

1188. To J. B. Pinker, 25 February 1916
Text: MS UT; cited in Carswell 41.

Porthcothan – St. Merryn – N. Cornwall.
25 Feb. 1916

My dear Pinker,

We are leaving here on Monday to go to 'The Tinners Arms, Zennor, St. Ives, Cornwall'. Address me there, please, after the 28th.

I had a letter from Sidgwick, refusing my poems, also giving an unasked and very impertinent criticism of the MS., together with instructions as to how to write poetry.[1] I wrote and told him his letter was impertinent and foolish and presumptuous.[2] Perish these important fools.

If Constable refuses the MS. also, take no notice.[3] Send it back to me. But send the duplicate to America, will you. The world is so foul, one is almost suffocated. The only thing is to get away into the furthest corner, from the smell of it.

Yours   D. H. Lawrence

1189. To Lady Ottoline Morrell, [27? February 1916]
Text: MS UT; Huxley 328.

Porthcothan, St. Merryn, North Cornwall
Sunday

My dear Ottoline

Here then is the first half of my philosophy:[4] remember not to read it on a spring-like day, only on a winter-dark one.

Thank you for the Gilbert Murray book.[5] I liked it. But I wish he were a little less popular and conversational in his style, and that he hadn't so many

[1] See p. 535 n. 2.
[2] DHL's letter is not in the Sidgwick and Jackson archives at the Bodleian.
[3] See p. 535 n. 1.
[4] Entitled 'Goats and Compasses' but never published. According to Cecil Gray two typescripts were made: DHL destroyed one and Heseltine the other. Gray described the 'philosophy' as 'Lawrence at his very worst: a bombastic, pseudo-mystical, psycho-philosophical treatise dealing largely with homosexuality' (Gray, *Peter Warlock*, p. 114n.). Lady Ottoline also recorded her own impression of it: 'It seems to me deplorable tosh, a volume of words, reiteration, perverted and self-contradictory. A gospel of hate and violent individualism. He attacks the will, love and sympathy. Indeed, the only thing that he doesn't revile and condemn is love between men and women.... I feel very depressed that he has filled himself with these "evening" ideas. They are, I am sure, the outcome of Frieda.... How Lawrence, as I knew him, who seemed so kind and understanding and essentially so full of tenderness, could turn round and preach this doctrine of hate is difficult to understand' (*Ottoline at Garsington* 93).
[5] See p. 556 n. 1.

layers of flannel between him and his own nakedness. But the stuff of the
book interests me *enormously*.

Remember our new address: Zennor, St. Ives, Cornwall. We are there
on Tuesday.

Love   D. H. Lawrence

1190. To Beatrice Beresford, [28 February 1916]
Text: TMSC Moore; Huxley 333–4.

Porthcothan – St. Merryn – N. Cornwall.
Monday.[1]

My dear Mrs. Beresford,

I write at once to assure you that it was *not* the bottle without sloes, which
we drank. It was a bottle with *many* sloes: most of which we ate. I should
have been really distressed if it had been your special bottle. As it is, I am
very sorry we drank this one, and must ask you again to forgive us.

You are quite right about the people too. I wrote in a fit of irritation at
them, they all seemed so *greedy*. But it is true, there is in them, as I felt at
first, a very beautiful softness and gentleness, quite missing in English people
nowadays. And really, I am, we are all *very fond* of Emma; I wish we could
afford to keep her on. I like her presence in the house: which is saying a
great deal. I like her very much, in fact. And I don't think she is really greedy.

But these people, asking their three and four and even five guineas a week,
for a house, *now*, exasperate one past bearing.

We leave tomorrow morning, to catch the 11.0 train in Newquay. I hope
the Gurnard's Head place will turn out satisfactorily.[2] If it does, we shall
be delighted when you and Mr. Beresford and the boy come to stay with
us, only too delighted. But at the present, I feel we are so much at the mercy
of the heavens, that it seems a presumption to ask you. We haven't taken
the house yet, nor anything.

I think you will find everything all right here. I have tried to substitute
everything. There are one or two big cups, which I asked Mrs. Hawke[3] to
bring from Padstow, but she didn't bring them. There will be enough coal
and paraffin to last till you come, and there is a good deal of food in, for
Emma. She will be quite ready for you, I am sure. Poor Emma – I hate to
be unjust to her.

---

[1] Written the day before the Lawrences left on Tuesday, 29 February 1916.
[2] This is the cottage at Higher Tregerthen, Zennor, where the Lawrences took up residence
on 17 March 1916.
[3] Unidentified.

Tell Beresford it is time he ceased to read his reviewers: at his time of life. They are *all* bloody fools; or rather, they are all fools without blood. But he looks as if he were coming into fame and prosperity.[1] Let him not grumble. I shall be begging from him, in three years' time, and he will be treating me handsomely. The old stars, Wells and Co., are setting, you are mounting up. As for me, I am an evanescent rainbow.

I wish we could afford to have Emma, to look after us.

Yours very sincerely   D. H. Lawrence

The snow did not lie here – now it is sunny. I have had another hot cold on the strength of the wind – my beastly health, I hate it.

1191. To Catherine Carswell, 1 March 1916
Text: MS IEduc; Unpublished.

The Tinners Arms – Zennor – nr. St. Ives, Cornwall.
1st March 1916

My dear Catherine,

Your letter at first surprised me, but not upon reflection. Every man must follow his own destiny. That is borne upon me more and more.

I hope Carswell won't be called up. The whole thing is false. But it will be as it will be. At any rate he is your destiny now.

Yours   D. H. Lawrence

1192. To Amy Lowell, 1 March 1916
Text: MS HU; Unpublished.

The Tinners Arms – Zennor – St. Ives, Cornwall.
1st March 1916

My dear Amy,

Thank you very much for your letter, and for all the thought you have taken for me. Constables here have refused my poems: so much the worse for them. Pinker says he will try *Doran* in America. I don't think Pinker is very good at America: and I do put my hopes in your country. We must see what we can do.

Thank you very much also for the money. You are most generous.

---

[1] Beresford's latest novel, *These Lynnekers*, had been published earlier in February 1916; presumably he had told DHL about the favourable reviews of it (e.g. *TLS*, 24 February 1916: 'Mr J. D. Beresford's fiction is enlarging in scope and increasing in power. His new book... is the work of a man with more various knowledge, or at any rate more various interests, than most novel-writers of the day succeed in revealing').

I will let you know how things develop with my poems. All good luck to your new volume;[1] and your lectures.[2]

With regards from my wife and me.

Yours   D. H. Lawrence

1193. To J. B. Pinker, 1 March 1916

Text: MS UNYB; cited in Delany 195.

The Tinners Arms – Zennor – St. Ives, Cornwall

1st March 1916

Dear Pinker

Thank you for your letter. Never mind about the poems.

Some friends of mine want to publish *The Rainbow* here by subscription. I suppose it could be done in conjunction with Paul Ferdinando.[3] I also know nothing of him, but he has a nice and brigand-like name.

Dear old Duckworths, one feels quite mean, going to somebody else, and then coming back upon refusal. On revient toujours à son premier amour:[4] éditeur I suppose one might substitute.

Yours   D. H. Lawrence

The address is Zennor.

Can't you try the poems in America? Has anything happened about *The Rainbow* in America?[5]

---

[1] She was preparing the manuscript of her next book of verse, *Men, Women and Ghosts*, which was published in October 1916 (Damon 346).

[2] Amy Lowell's highly successful lectures on American poets were given in Brooklyn and Chicago. On 24 February 1916, for example, she had lectured on 'The New Poetry: with a Particular Inquiry into Imagism', at the Colony Club, New York. On 18 March she repeated the lecture in Chicago to a full house (100 people were turned away).

[3] Librairie Paul Ferdinando, 11 rue de Châteaudun, Paris.

[4] Charles-Guillaume Etienne (1778–1845), *Joconde ou les Coureurs d'Aventures* (1814), III. i. 24–5 ['Mais l'on revient toujours A ses premiers amours'] 'One always returns to one's first love' ('éditeur' = publisher).

[5] Although DHL had received a copy of *The Rainbow* printed in America by Huebsch (see Letter 1105), the publication of the novel remained hazardous. As late as 3 May 1916 Doran told Pinker (MS NYPL): 'Just now censorship of books is rather keener than it has been for a generation. So very little has been done with THE RAINBOW. It is a great pity that the book offended so violently; otherwise, Lawrence would now be in receipt of a very decent income from it. It is not a question whether you are prudish or I am prudish, but it is really a question of the prudery of the Anglo-Saxon race in general.' Two days later, on 5 May, Doran informed another correspondent that 'they [Huebsch] have not yet published the book and are unable to give any date as to its probable publication in the United States' (MS NYPL). And writing to Pinker on 14 July 1916 (MS NYPL), Doran said that 'the suit against Methuens in England and the change in the administration of the censorship of books in the United States [see DHL's remark on this in Letter 1064] forced Huebsch into an extremely difficult position. Some way or other, he proposes still to publish THE RAINBOW, but before doing so he must have the tacit approval of the censoring official. This he has not been able to secure.'

Amy Lowell has been speaking in America about my poems. She says that[1] Ferris Greenlet authorised me to say to Constable's, that if they published the book of poems in England, then Houghton Mifflins would order[2] 200 copies for America.

1194. To S. S. Kotelansky, 2 March 1916

Text: MS BL; Postmark, Zennor [...] 16; Zytaruk 73.

Tinners Arms, Zennor, St. Ives, Cornwall.

2 March 1916

My dear Kot,

Thank you very much for the Kuprin, which has just come.[3] I shall read it and tell you how I like it, at once.

I enclose a letter from a man for the *Signature*.[4]

It is very rainy here. We live warmly in the inn – and don't bother.

I don't want to write the novel of the young Englishman – he bores me. Forgive me. – Why dont you write your novel of a Jew: the truth, all of it. *That* would be interesting indeed; only save yourself from being sentimental.

Yours   D. H. Lawrence

1195. To Mark Gertler, [4 March 1916]

Text: MS SIU; cited in Moore, *Intelligent Heart* 213.

Tinners Arms – Zennor – nr St. Ives, Cornwall

Saturday[5]

Dear Gertler,

We were glad to hear from you. I am only going to write a note, because we are just driving to Penzance, over the moors. It is a beautiful day, and one drives from this sea, on the north, over to Mount Bay, on the south.

We have been driven almost to Lands End, to get away from the vile people. The next step will be into the sea: or else we shall have to take wings like birds.

When we have really found a house I will write and tell you. This is the best bit of England that I have seen. So you must come down, in spite of the fares.

I am glad you are not going to be a slave to work, any more. One's own

---

[1] She says that] She tells me,   [2] order] take

[3] *The River of Life and Other Stories* by Aleksandr Ivanovich Kuprin (1870–1938), trans. S. S. Kotelansky and J. M. Murry (Dublin, February 1916).

[4] G. E. Stechert and Co., the London firm of book importers and exporters, wrote on 28 February to order 'all the numbers [of *Signature*] that have been Published to Date' (TMS BL).

[5] The Lawrences' move to Zennor on 29 February and DHL's announcement to the Murrys on Sunday, 5 March that he has found a 'two-roomed cottage' establish the date of this letter as Saturday, 4 March, just before they 'have really found a house'.

happiness and good life is the first thing: work is very much the second. I'll be damned if I'll do a scrap of work. I feel as stubborn as a mule. As for people, I am just bored by them all. I only want them to leave me alone. I'll tell you when we have a house.

Yours D. H. Lawrence

**1196. To John Middleton Murry and Katherine Mansfield,
5 March 1916**
Text: MS NYPL; Huxley 334–7.

Tinners Arms, Zennor, nr. St. Ives, Cornwall.
Sunday 5 March 1916

My dear Jack and Katharine,

We have been here nearly a week now. It is a most beautiful place: a tiny granite village nestling under high, shaggy moor-hills, and a big sweep of lovely sea beyond, such a lovely sea, lovelier even than the Mediterranean. It is 5 miles from St. Ives, and 7 miles from Penzance. To Penzance one goes over the moors, high, then down into Mounts Bay, looking at St Michaels Mount, like a dark little jewel. It is all gorse now, flickering with flower; and then it will be heather; and then, hundreds of fox gloves. It is the best place I have been in, I think.

I feel we ought to live here, pitch our camp and unite our forces, and become an active power here, together.

We have been looking for houses. There is nothing satisfactory, furnished. And I am terribly afraid to take a big place. I have very little money, and really, all my sources have dried up.

What we have found, is a two-roomed cottage, one room up, one down, with a long scullery. But the rooms are *big* and *light*, and the rent won't be more than 4/-. It isn't furnished – but with our present goods, we shall need so little. One pays so little in rent.

The place is rather splendid. It is just under the moors, on the edge of the few rough stony fields that go to the sea. It is quite alone, as a little colony.

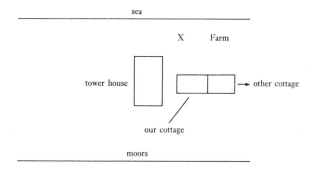

There are two little blocks of buildings, like this ⊟ ☐, all alone, a farm
5 mins. below. One block has three cottages that have been knocked into one,
and the end room upstairs made into a tower room: so it is a long cottage
with 3 doors and a funny little tower at one end. Guy Thorne had it done
for him and then never came.[1] He is a scamp. The other block is at rt. angles,
and is two tiny cottages. But all is sound, done-up, dry-floored, and light.

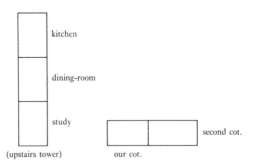

I shall certainly take the little cottage.

What I hope, is that one day you will take the long house with the tower,
and put a bit of furniture in it: and that Heseltine will have one room in
your long cot; and that somebody else will have the second cot: that we are
like a little monastery: that Emma is in your kitchen, and we all eat together
in the dining room of your house: – at least, lunch and dinner: that we share
expenses. The rent will be very little, the position and all is *perfectly lovely*,
Katharine would have the tower-room with big windows and panelled walls
(now done in black and white stripes, broad, and terracotta roof, by Guy
Thorne, alias Ranger Gull), and Jack would have the study below, you two
would have the *very charming* bedroom over the dining room; then there are
2 bedrooms over kitchen and pantry. The tower room is not accessible, save
from Jack's study.

There is a little grassy terrace outside, and at the back, the moor tumbles
down, great enormous grey boulders and gorse. It *could* be so wonderful.
It is about *4* miles from St. Ives.

I don't want you to take it if you feel in the least[2] uneasy: only we shall
take our 2-roomed cottage, if possible, at once, and gladly await you, if you
feel like coming. It would be *so splendid* if it could but come off: *such* a lovely
place: our Rananim.

---

[1] Cyril Arthur Edward Ranger Gull (1876–1923), wrote under the pseudonym Guy Thorne.
Journalist; subsequently a prolific popular novelist. Author of *Miss Malevolent* (1899), *From
the Book Beautiful* (1900), *Back to Lilacland* (1901), etc.
[2] if...least] – only we shall try.

Write and tell me how you feel. It seems to me we *must* strike some sort
of a root, soon: because we must buckle to work. This here is the best place
to live in which we shall find in England, I firmly believe. But we mustn't
go in for any more *follies* and removals and uneasinesses.

This country is pale grey granite, and gorse: there [is][1] something *uhralt*[2]
and clean about it.

I wish you could *fly* over to talk things out: it is so tiresome, this long
distance. I shall be *very glad* when you come back, and we can unite forces.

Much love to you   D. H. Lawrence

Our little cottage is only £5 a year. The three-in-one is £16 a year.

1197. To Edward Marsh, 6 March 1916
Text: MS NYPL; Unpublished.

Tinners Arms, Zennor, nr. St Ives, Cornwall
6 March 1916

My dear Eddie,

Thank you for the cheque for £2.2.6 which came this morning.[3] You
should really keep this, as a crumb from the loaf of debt I owe you.

You asked me what became of the American plan. I didn't go because
I was not well enough – I have been seedy all the winter, and always felt
unequal to the removal. I ought to have sent you your money back.[4] But
my sources are all dried up, so I keep it to live on.

We are just taking a two-roomed cottage down here, £5 a year, so we can
live on very little, doing all our own work.

It is beautiful here: do you know the country? One feels one can hide
here, like a creature outside the pale.

I suppose that before very long we can meet happily again.

Yours   D. H. Lawrence

1198. To Dollie Radford, 6 March 1916
Text: MS UN; Postmark, Zennor [...] MR 16; Nehls, i. 360–1.

Tinners Arms – Zennor – St. Ives, Cornwall
6 March 1916

My dear Dollie,

How are you, and how are the fates behaving? We are here in Maitland's
inn, which is *very* nice indeed. This place is lovely.

[1] MS reads: 'there something'.
[2] 'primeval' ['uralt'].
[3] Probably a share of the royalties from *Georgian Poetry 1913–1915*, ed. Marsh (November 1915). Cf. Letter 699.
[4] See Letter 1048.

We are just taking a two-roomed cottage at £5 a year. It is in a lovely place. We shall furnish it, and there hide, like foxes under the hill.

The wind is very cold. These pale granite hills look blenched, the sea is covered with white lambs of foam, the gorse that has come out seems to try to go in again. How lucky to be a daisy, that can shut so tight.

The grief about our two rooms is that we can't have visitors. But there is a farm just below, where you can sleep, then come up to us. So when we[1] are settled in, you will come.

I am middling well in health. I feel very sick about the war and everything. 'May is the month when kings go forth to war', they used to say. But peoples go forth much earlier.

I had a nice letter from Eleanor Farjeon about *The Rainbow*. She is down at Greatham. I don't want to go there ever again. I don't want to see the Meynells ever again, any of them.

How is Margaret? We have heard nothing of her for a long time?

We are going to be very poor, soon, so we must live very cheaply. Never mind, I don't care, so long as I can live at all, and people will let me alone. We can be perfectly happy in Tregerthan Cottage, if only the world won't stare in at the windows with its evil face.

I hope all is well with you, my dear Dollie. How one's heart always trembles in the balance between cheerfulness and apprehension.

> Frieda sends you her love, I mine.   D. H. Lawrence

We have got our little cottage. Now we shall have to get down the things remaining from Byron Villas. There are some lying at your house, are there not?

1199. To Mark Gertler, 8 March 1916

Text: MS SIU; cited in Moore, *Intelligent Heart* 213.

> Tinners Arms – Zennor – St. Ives – Cornwall
> 8 March 1916

My dear Gertler,

We have taken a little cottage here, two good rooms, £5 a year. It is beautifully situated under the hills and above the sea. We shall furnish it and live there cheaply.

I am going to be very troublesome, and ask you to send our things. I want you to pack up the camp bed. Buy[2] some sacking, about 1½ yds, I expect,

---

[1] we] you   [2] Buy] By

or 1 yd; roll up the mattress and bolster, roll round them the small kitchen rug, (I think it is there), then sew the whole bundle[1] in the sacking, and label it *carefully*. Tie the bed-frame flat, and label that to me,

D. H. Lawrence, Tregerthan, Zennor, St. Ives, Cornwall.

Then write a post card to the nearest *Great Western* depôt – or just call – and ask their goods van to call and collect the things. Send them '*Goods*', 'carriage forward'.

Have the big table also carefully labelled – better tack a label on somewhere. Ask the railway man how much it would cost to send. If it is less than 10/-, then send that with the bed, also perhaps the four chairs. If the man would *advise* you to send the chairs, send them; if not, leave them; they are not *important*. But I should like them if they will come safely and cheaply.

If you have not got all these things with you, call at Dollie Radfords, 32 Well Walk, and see her. She will help.

There remain the Persian rug, the blankets, the bath with *china*, candlesticks, clock, the fender. These I shall ask Dollie Radford to pack, with your help, and Heseltine will bring them with him.

Ask Kot to help you to pack.

Our tiny cottage stands beside another, a big one, with seven rooms (it is really three cottages in one). I want Heseltine or the Murrys to take this (it is £16 a year). Think what a perfect little settlement we could be! It is all alone, just these cottages.

I am sorry to bother you so much. But you will sleep on the camp bed when you come.

I will write to Dollie Radford and Kot and Heseltine.[2]

I'm sure we are going to have a good place and a good time together, down here: a little settlement of us.

Love from us both   D. H. Lawrence

Also please call at Mrs Carswells, Holly Bush House, Holly Mount (you remember I called there one day) and ask her for our *mirror*. Call about 2.30 in the afternoon. Heseltine will bring down the mirror. He will come and see you.

Of the books, I want the dictionary – but you bring that when you come. What else is there? – What other books? I don't want the Hardys.

---

[1] the whole bundle] them
[2] The letter to Heseltine is missing.

568 [8 March 1916]

1200. To Dollie Radford, [8 March 1916]
Text: MS UN; Postmark, Zennor 8 MAR 16; Nehls, i. 361–2.

Tinners Arms – Zennor – St. Ives – Cornwall
Wednesday

My dear Dollie,

We have got our cottage. Now we want our things.

I have written to Gertler – Penn Studio, 13 Rudall Crescent, Hampstead – to ask him to pack the things. Would you help him? Get a hamper from the greengrocer, or a box, for the *china*, *clock*, candlesticks, and the little saucepan. Then roll the Persian rug, blankets, and cushions together. Then there is a mirror, from Mrs Carswells, and an embroidery, framed. Then there is the *fender*. I think there is nothing else. I don't want the fire-irons – unless the poker and the common shovel. Then the Primus stoves – I want them.

All these I want Heseltine to bring when he comes down: he will come next week, probably.

Dear Dollie, I don't know how many of these things are with you, how many with Gertler. Do see him, will you? He is rather a helpless sort. Do see to the packing of the little things, all those things we shall want.

I believe Heseltine will be coming down soon and will bring all these things as his luggage. They are not very heavy. I will ask him to ring you up.

There is a big 3-in-one cottage, £16 a year, beside ours, that I want the Murrys and Heseltine to take – £16 a year. Think what a perfect little settlement of us, above the sea, under the wild hills. How lovely for you to come then and stay a long time. It is going to be *splendid*.

Love to you   D. H. Lawrence

1201. To S. S. Koteliansky, 8 March 1916
Text: MS BL; Postmark, Zennor 9 MAR 16; Zytaruk 74.

Tinners Arms – Zennor – St. Ives, Cornwall
8 March 1916

My dear Kot,

Thank you very much for the Kuprin.[1] He reads awfully well – I think you must have translated him well. But I don't care for him. He is not very significant, I think, and rather vulgar. The Ribnikov story is the only one that really interests me: if *only* he could have created a Japanese, it might have been wonderful. But the Japanese himself is not created: only his attributes, not *he*. It is a pity.

We have taken a little 2-roomed cottage, for £5 a year. We are going to

---

[1] See Letter 1194. One of Kuprin's stories is entitled 'Captain Ribnikov'; it includes a character who is a Japanese spy.

furnish it and live like foxes under the hill. The situation is beautiful indeed, under the moors, above the wide sea. *Do, please*, go and help Gertler to pack up our things to send us: we want them now.

Next to ours is a big cottage, seven rooms, for £16 a year. I want the Murrys to have that – a little settlement. Wouldn't it be good?

I suppose you will be seeing Lady Ottoline this week – go and see her. We are going to be very very poor. So we must live very cheaply indeed.

molti saluti buoni   D. H. Lawrence

1202. To John Middleton Murry and Katherine Mansfield, 8 March 1916

Text: MS NYPL; Huxley 337–8.

Tinners Arms, Zennor, St. Ives, Cornwall
8 March 1916

My dear Jack and Katharine,

We have taken our little cottage for £5- a year and are getting ready to furnish. Of course we shall want *very* little, having the things left from Byron Villas.

Really, you must have the other place. I keep looking at it. I call it already Katharine's house, Katharine's tower. There is something *very* attractive about it. It is very old, native to the earth, like rock, yet dry and all in the light of the hills and the sea. It is only twelve strides from our house to yours: we can talk from the windows: and besides us, only the gorse, and the fields, the lambs skipping and hopping like anything, and sea-gulls fighting with the ravens, and sometimes a fox, and a ship on the sea.

You must come, and we will live there a long long time, very cheaply. You see we must live somewhere, and it is so free and beautiful, and it will cost us so very little.

And don't talk any more of treacheries and so on. Henceforward let us take each other on trust – I'm sure we can. We are so few, and the world is so many, it is absurd that we are scattered. Let us be really happy and industrious together.

I don't know yet what will happen to Heseltine, whether he will be exempted. But I hope you will really like him, and we can all be friends together. He is the only one we can all be friends with.[1]

But if you don't want him to have a room in your house – of course he

---

[1] On the same day as DHL wrote this letter, Heseltine wrote to Robert Nichols (Gray, *Peter Warlock*, p. 116): 'I am not returning to Lawrence; he has no real sympathy. All he likes in one is the potential convert to his own reactionary creed. I believe firmly that he is a fine thinker and a consummate artist, but personal relation with him is almost impossible. At least so it appears at present.'

would share expenses – he could have one elsewhere. Of course he may be kept away indefinitely.

But at any rate, you two come, and we shall be four together. It is cheaper to furnish a little, and pay £16 a year rent, than to pay £75 a year for a furnished place. And I'm sure we can live happily at Tregerthan: Tregerthan, Zennor, St. Ives.

It is still cold. Snow falls sometimes, then vanishes at once. When the sun shines, some gorse bushes smell hot and sweet. Flocks of birds are flying by, to go to the Scilly Isles to nest, and the blackbirds sing in the chill evenings. We got big bunches of wall-flowers in Penzance for a penny – we saw a man plucking them in a field – and they smell very good. But the wind still blows storms with snow out of the sea.

I heard from Campbell – still in the Pity-me sort of voice. He lies in the mud and murmurs about his dream-soul, and says that *action* is irrelevant. Meanwhile he earns diligently in munitions.[1]

Do you think the war will end this year?

Much love from us both   D. H. Lawrence

I suppose you have got my Monday's letter telling you all about the house.[2] Your place has 7 rooms: kitchen, dining room, study, and upstairs, tower-room and 3 bedrooms. It was three old cottages.

Your letter of the 4th has just come – Thursday. Good, all is well between us all. No more quarrels and quibbles. Let it be agreed for ever. I am Blutbruder: a Blutbruderschaft between us all. Tell K. *not* to be so queasy. – Won't Farbman stick to your house?[3] Much love from us both to you two.

DHL

1203. To Katherine Mansfield, [8? March 1916]

Text: MS NZNL; Unpublished.

[Frieda Lawrence begins]

The Tinner's Arms
[8? March 1916][4]

---

[1] Gordon Campbell was Assistant Controller, Ministry of Munitions (1915–18).

[2] Actually Sunday's; see Letter 1196.

[3] Michael S. Farbman (1880?–1933), a Russian journalist living in London, was the author of *The Russian Revolution and the War* (1917), *Russia and the Struggle for Peace* (1918), *Bolshevism in Retreat* (1923). Farbman may have been one of DHL's walking companions in the Lake District in July–August 1914 (see p. 268 n. 2). With his wife Sophie and daughter Ghita, he took over the house at 5 Acacia Road, St John's Wood from Katherine Mansfield on 18 November 1915, and Kot went to live with the family. A few years later when the Farbmans left Kot took over the house, which he occupied until his death. DHL wrote a number of letters to the Farbmans but none has been found.

[4] The contents of the letter suggest a date close to, perhaps the same as, the preceding; the two letters may in fact have been posted together.

Dear Katherine,

We have take our little cottage from which we can shake hands with yours out of the window – Guy Thorne's typist [Lawrence interjects: was to have] had ours and from *your* tower you can used [Lawrence interjects: he was going] to telephone his stuff to her! Lawrence has already quite settled you there, in fact he seemed *more* anxious to make you happy there with all you can wish for than that we should have all we want – It *is* a place one can love unreservedly. Our rooms are such a nice shape – Lawrence has made buttercup yellow curtains with green blobs on them – They are grey granite cottages with *very* thick walls, and *quite* dry – Katherine – I am so looking forward to your coming and to show you this place, meanwhile we are *fed* to such a terrific extent here! Cream and chickens and such good cooking! What about the St John's Wood House? Could'nt a little furniture come cheaply by sea? We might ask – Surely you can let it – I am so anxious now to *live* without any more soulharrassing, we are *friends* and we wont bother anymore about the *deep* things, they are all right, just let's live like the lilies in the field[1] – Lawrence has had a bad time – One has to realise that *nothing* comes from the w[o]rld, *everything* has to come out of oneself – Some of the *wonder* of the world has gone for him – But we will get it again for all that! We will be jolly I can see! I do believe you would be better *here* than there – It wont be long now anyway till you come! This is sandy and *dry* – not at all à l'anglaise! I believe the *Rainbow* scheme is going *well* – But we have'nt heard much, except that a French publisher wanted to print it, he will take a *lot* of these now![2] Did the old Ott[oline] say *horrid* things about me to Jack? I hope he didn't swallow them all – We had a *wet* letter from Campbell – very exasperated! Much love to you both. I am looking forward so very much to your triumphant arrival!

Frieda

[Lawrence begins]

There are lovely stories to hear, about Guy Thorne, alias Ranger Gull, and these cottages. His silk-hat box, mouldy after two years of neglect, hangs in your pantry – and that is all there is of him, save the black and white panels, and orange roof, of your tower room. These black and white panels must be hushed up before you come.

DHL

---

[1] Cf. Matthew vi. 28.   [2] See Letter 1193.

1204. To Lady Ottoline Morrell, 9 March 1916
Text: MS IEduc; Unpublished.

Tinners Arms – Zennor – St. Ives – Cornwall
9 March 1916

My dear Ottoline,

You will be back from London by the time you get this. I wonder how you found it – how was Bertie, and what do you think of his lecture? He is cross with me for another impudent letter I wrote him.

We have taken a little cottage, two rooms and a scullery, for £5- a year. You see I am drawing my horns in, in view of close-prowling poverty. We shall furnish these two nice rooms, and live like foxes in their den, doing our own work.

The situation is lovely: under the hills all wild with gorse and great grey granite boulders, above the wide-stretching sea. Here one will be free to live and to look towards the coming spring, away from the collapsing of the old years.

Next to our cottage is one with seven rooms, quite big, for £16 a year. I want the Murrys to have that. I think they will. Then we shall be a little settlement in the desert. There is a farm just near, where you can have rooms, so all will be very jolly. – The Murrys will come back in April.

Thank you for the book about *Monasteries in the Levant*.[1] I was wanting something to read, and I find this *very* entertaining. But I am not sure that I always believe the Hon. Mr Curzon. One suspects 'Travellers' Tales'.

I shall send you back immediately the *Salimbene*[2] and the *Hesiod*.[3] I *love* Salimbene: I liked the book *very much indeed*. It gives one such a robust belief in life. I don't like Hesiod very much, his virtue is so school-masterish. But the book interested me enormously. 'The Battle of Frogs and Mice'[4] is *so* beautiful, I think, and, in the light of anthropology and the science of religions, these gods become absorbingly interesting. One feels this old stuff in ones bones, very satisfying. Do send me an odd book now and then, just one at a time. Have you got a *Confessions of Augustine*?[5] – or Herodotus,[6] or Thucydides?[7] I will learn Greek when Murry comes.

[1] *Visits to Monasteries in the Levant* (1849; 1916) by Lord Robert Curzon, 14th Baron Zouche (1810–73), a famous traveller.
[2] See p. 538 n. 2.   [3] See p. 510 n. 2.
[4] This parody of the warlike epic (c. B.C. 480) is included in *Hesiod*, pp. 542–63.
[5] St Augustine (354–430), early Christian philosopher, Bishop of Hippo. Author of the great *De Civitae Dei* (*City of God*) in 22 books; his *Confessions* (trans. E. B. Pusey) was available in the Everyman's Library (1907).
[6] Herodotus (c. 484–c. 424 B.C.), Greek historian. His *History* (trans. George Rawlinson) was available in the Everyman's Library (2 vols, 1910).
[7] Thucydides (471–c. 401 B.C.), Greek historian, author of *The History of the Peloponnesian War*. This work was available in numerous translations including one by Richard Crawley in Everyman's Library (1910).

The spring is coming. On Sunday, the gorse, all happy with flower, smelled hot and sweet in the sun, and the lambs were leaping into the air, kicking their hind legs with a wild little flourish. But this morning all was white with snow. This evening, however, in the deep yellow sunset, the birds are whistling, the snow is nearly all gone. Soon the very spring will conquer.

Love from us both   D. H. Lawrence

1205. To Lady Cynthia Asquith, 9 March 1916
Text: MS UT; Huxley 339–40.

Tinners Arms, Zennor, St. Ives, Cornwall
9 March 1916

My dear Lady Cynthia

We have made another move: taken a little cottage for £5 a year, under the moors, above the sea here. It is a splendid place. There we can live like foxes under the hill.

I don't want to come to live near London. I should want to tie tin cans to the coat-tails of the people, to make them look ridiculous.

But Frieda and I might be coming up for a few days soon. She ought to go to the dentist. If we come, and if you are in town, let us have a little carousal somewhere, a real little carousal.

I am bored by calamity. As you say, one's imagination has gone dead to the war, and to all the troubles altogether.

It is all a question of the direction in which one looks. No old world tumbles except when a young one shoves it over. And why should one howl if one's grandfather is pushed over a cliff. Goodbye grandfather, now it's my turn.

I feel the spring coming back, the youth surging in. We were born old, really, all our generation. All the dead, and all the soldiers, and all the good conscientious people, they were born grey-headed. Their hoary old souls in their young bodies: it is time they went down to the halls of darkness! It is time[1] to say goodbye to them for ever, and to turn the other way: like Orpheus when Eurydice sank back into Hell.

If one likes to think of Hell, then one hears a cascade of souls and lives pouring untimely down. But it is not untimely, really, it is timely. Let them go.

If one turns the other way, to think of the spring, one is dazzled, it is so splendid; no matter how much roars over the edge of oblivion, behind one's back.

[1] time] going

The spring is really coming, the profound spring, when the world is young. I don't want it to be good, only young and jolly. When I see the lambs skip up from the grass, into the sharp air, and flick their hind legs friskily at the sky, then really, I see how absurd it is to grieve and persist in melancholy. We can't control the coming and going of life and death. When it is our time to go, we'll go. But when it *isn't* our time to go, why should we fret about those whose time it is. It is our business to receive life, not to relinquish it.

When I look towards the spring, I *do* want to rise up and have done with miseries. It really is our turn to begin to dance round the fountains.[1] This morning the world was white with snow. This evening the sunset is yellow, and birds are whistling, the gorse-bushes are bristling with little winged suns. Many birds go rustling by all day, excitedly, to reach the Scilly Isles, to nest. The new, incoming days seem most wonderful, uncreated. Let the old days trail out and be gone, they are a bore.

So I think, living very cheaply and freely down here, there will be very few old bonds, very few restrictions, one can do pretty much as one likes. I look forward very much to the coming days. I need work hardly at all, we shall want so little, and we can do all the things we want to do.

And I hope, one day, we shall have a gay time with you: I think it is owed to us. You must come to Cornwall for a bit, later on. Do you think you will?

I hope this letter doesn't reach you just when you are supping sorrow with a spoon. But if it does, put the spoon down, that's all.

Herzliche Grüsse from Frieda – D. H. Lawrence

1206. To Bertrand Russell, 9 March 1916
Text: MS UT; cited in Moore, *Atlantic Monthly* 102.

Tinners Arms, Zennor, St. Ives, Cornwall.
9 March 1916

My dear Russell,

Are you still cross with me for being a schoolmaster and for not respecting the rights of man? Don't be, it isn't worth it.

Your lectures are over, are they? What are you going to do now?

We have taken a tiny cottage here, for £5 a year, which we shall furnish. We shall live very cheaply, because we are going to be very poor indeed. But just under the wild hills with their great grey boulders of granite, and

---

[1] fountains.] fountains of delight.

above the big sea, it is beautiful enough, and free enough. I think we can be obscure, and happy, like creatures in a cave.

You must come down to Cornwall some time and have rooms in a farm-house. Will you do that?

One must learn to be happy and careless. The old world never tumbles down except a young world shoves it over, heedlessly. And I'm sure the young world must be jolly. So let us have a good time to ourselves while the old world tumbles over itself. It is no good bothering. Nothing is born by taking thought.[1] That which is born comes of itself. All we can do is to refrain from frustrating the new world which is being born in us.

At the present we only think of getting into our tiny cottage – furnishing, and so on. Later we can dance with the spring-time, very soon.

I hope we shall see you before long.

Yours   D. H. Lawrence

1207. To Captain John Short, 10 March 1916
Text: MS UT; Unpublished.

Tinners Arms, Zennor, St. Ives, Cornwall.
10 March 1916

Dear Captain Short,[2]

It was a pity the weather was so bad yesterday. We quite understood that you could not come out. But I shall be very glad if you can come on Sunday, because we want to move in to the cottage as soon as possible, and nothing can be done till you have been up. The place is full of old timber and lime.

We are very badly off now, because of the war, but if you will do one or two little things to the cottage, I will pay a fair share. Let us make the place properly habitable. It is so small, it needs to be made convenient. And do not fear that I shall be another Guy Thorne.

I am almost sure that my friends will take the other house at £16 a year. They will be coming here in April. So please *don't* let it without first having told me.

Yours Sincerely   D. H. Lawrence

---

[1] Cf. Matthew vi. 27 (A.V.).

[2] John Tregerthen Short (1849–1930), the son of a master mariner, was himself the captain of a steamship, S.S. *Cornwall*, and later – in Cardiff – a shipowner. About 1910 he retired to St Ives, his family home. His grandfather (d. 1873) was named in the title of Sir Edward Hain's *Prisoners of War in France from 1804 to 1814 being the Adventures of John Tregerthen Short and Thomas Williams of St. Ives* (1914). m. Lucy Thomas. (Obituary in *St Ives Times*, 21 November 1930.) Captain Short owned Higher Tregerthen where the Lawrences were to live from 17 March.

1208. To J. B. Pinker, [11 March 1916]
Text: MS Forster; cited in Pinto 26.

Zennor – St. Ives – Cornwall
Saturday 10 March 1916[1]

My dear Pinker,

I suppose we shall go trickling slowly on with dear old Duckworth, till the end of the story. We must take his 15%, I suppose.[2] But can't you have it stated, 20% after the first thousand? I think we *must* have that. But I must say, I *like* Duckworth for sticking to me.

You will tell me about America.

Yours   D. H. Lawrence

1209. To Katherine Mansfield, [11 March 1916]
Text: MS NYPL; Huxley 341–2.

Tinners Arms, Zennor, St. Ives, Cornwall
Saturday[3]

My dear Katharine,

Your letter just come – no more bickering amongst us. And no good trying to run away from the fact that we are fond of each other. We count you two our only two *tried* friends, real and permanent and truly blood kin. I know we shall be happy this summer: *so* happy.

I told you all about the house: the great grey granite boulders, you will love them, the rough, primeval hill behind us, the sea beyond the few fields, that have great boulders half submerged in the grass, and stone grey walls. There are many lambs under your house. They are *quite* tame. They stand and cock their heads at one, then skip into the air like little explosions.

And your tower room is all wood and windows, panelled, with 3 big windows, and cosy as can be.

Don't mind the having to furnish. You can do with *very* little. And I'm sure we shall live on at Tregerthan a long while, years, a tiny settlement all to ourselves. And the war will end before next summer – before the summer that comes after this.

I will make Captain Short – a retired little old captain, soft like a child,

---

[1] 10 March 1916 was a Friday.

[2] The terms which would be included in Duckworth's publication agreement for *Twilight in Italy* and/or *Amores*.

[3] The letter is clearly in sequence with Letters 1196 and 1202; this, together with the mention of Kot's 'Kuprin' (Letter 1194) points to 11 March 1916 as the likely date.

with a mania for fussing – he is the landlord – I will make him put your house thoroughly to rights, before you come.

Much love   D. H. Lawrence

Kot gave me a Kuprin. It reads awfully well. But I *don't* think much of these lesser Russians. Ribnikov is by far the best: but the *Japanese* is not created – he is an object, not a subject.

1210. To Dollie Radford, [11 March 1916]
Text: MS UN; Postmark, Zennor 11 MAR 16; Nehls, i. 362–3.

Tinners Arms, Zennor, St. Ives, Cornwall
Saturday

My dear Dollie,

Your letter has just come. Thank you very much for doing this packing for me. But I think Gertler ought to do the things that are with him.

Are you a little bit cross with me, or only very hurried? I felt before that you were perhaps cross, when you did not answer my letter – the one before this last. I do hope I haven't offended you. If I have, please Dollie, forget it.

I am so looking forward to the little settlement of us under the moors here. I shall love you to come and stay. Poor Miss Abbott, it is a shame she is so ill.[1] I thought you were having another nurse. I don't want you to be bothered with our things, while you are so rushed and oppressed. If only we could all get a real free breathing time! But it will come, in the summer, when foxgloves are out, on Zennor hill. Then we will have a truly happy time, all together.

D. H. Lawrence

Of course Watson's chair is his own.[2]

[Frieda Lawrence begins]

Dear Dollie,

How nice that you want a letter from me! I always think people dont! You are as usual an *angel* to do the packing like that! But then by now I expect a lot from you and yet there always seem *more* hidden wings – Lawrence is better, and when we are settled quietly it will be good, I think he is really better but very upsettable! I feel this place is a legacy of Maitland's – tell him how gratefully I think of him, how is he and how is his work? When

[1] Ernest Radford's nurse (Nehls, i. 584 n. 279).
[2] Herbert Watson, a friend of the Radfords who died of war-wounds in France (Nehls, i. 584 n. 280).

the spring comes, you must be free and come, how is Miss Abbot? We *must* have some nice evenings, the world is so ugly now, that it seems more than ever one's absolute duty to be happy and nice with each other!

With much love   Frieda

1211. To Catherine Carswell, [11 March 1916]

Text: MS YU; cited in Carswell, *Adelphi* 211.

Tinners Arms, Zennor, St. Ives, Cornwall.
Saturday[1]

My dear Catherine,

We have taken a little cottage – with two *good* rooms and a scullery, under the moors here, above the sea – for £5 a year. We shall have to furnish it, of course: but we have a lot of things left. If Gertler or Dollie Radford sends to you for the mirror you gave us, will you let them have it? I should like it so much in the cottage, and somebody will bring it down.

Yours   D. H. Lawrence

1212. To Dollie Radford, 14 March 1916

Text: MS UN; Postmark, Zennor 15 MAR 16; Nehls, i. 363–5.

Zennor, St. Ives, Cornwall
14 March 1916

My dear Dollie,

It is very good of you to do this packing for us. I doubt whether Heseltine will be coming down, so everything must be sent. And I have no answer from Gertler, so he may be away.

I must tell you what things there are.

1. My big persian rug, a small kitchen rug, and a white ragged-edged felt mat: a pair of blankets, a small eider-down quilt, an old coat: tussore curtains: two cushions.
2. *China*, glasses, candle-sticks (two brass), enamel pail, enamel bowl, two primus stoves, a framed embroidery, your Mestrovic *Mother*,[2] and Mrs Carswell's mirror (she *had* it).
3. Fender (I don't want the fire-tongs, or brass shovel), a small saucepan.

---

[1] The reference to Catherine Carswell's mirror in the letter following, 14 March, would explain DHL's writing to her a few days earlier.

[2] Almost certainly a reproduction of the sculpture entitled *The Mother of the Jugovići*, one of the first pieces produced during Ivan Meštrović's 'Vidovdantempel' period, 1907–14. He enjoyed considerable popularity following his appearance at the Rome International Exhibition in 1911 and then his one-man show at the Victoria and Albert Museum in 1915 (see p. 360 n. 2; it is thus likely that reproductions of his work were fairly common in 1916.

4. Camp bed with mattress and pillows.
5. Kitchen table.
6. Kitchen chairs (arm chair and 3 small).

I think the first three lots had better come *passenger* (G[reat] W[estern] R[ailway]). The last three lots will come [...] *goods*. It is probably *not worth while* sending the *chairs*. I should like the kitchen table, but if it will cost *very much* to come, (the man from the G.W.Ry. will advise you), then don't send it: if it will cost more than 8/-.

Do you mind, when the things are ready, asking the railway-man how much he thinks the rugs, china, and fender would cost to come *passenger-train*. If it is very dear, then the rugs can come *goods*. But I value my persian rug. The china must come passenger.

The china is stacked in a *bath*. If it is easy and cheap, send this bath 'goods'. If not, leave it.

My dear Dollie, it seems monstrous asking you to do all this. I wish I could afford to come to town. But oh dear, we are *very poor*.

There is *no hurry whatever*. The captain, our landlord, will lend us all the things we want for as long as we like. Send a post-card when you are ready to your[1] nearest Gt. Western Ry. Office, and they will collect. Don't have Carter Paterson.[2]

Tell Herbert Watson, if he doesn't want that chair, I will buy it back: my nice arm-chair. And when you come, Dollie, you will bring it with you, won't you?

Soon you will have read enough horrors, *House of the Dead*, and so on.[3] Then you will come down here. It is *so lovely*, our cottage, it will seem to you a new earth has come to pass. You will have the camp bed, and all will be jolly. We have been at the cottage all day, till the sun set golden[4] over the sea, and the moor-hills were all strange, shifting purple, and there seemed a new world, full of mystery and sensuous surprise.

I believe you will be our first visitor, a first-comer in spring. I have somehow passed out of the black cloud of the old world, into a new day, fragile and very lovely, inheriting the old Celtic tenderness and subtle wonder. It is very lovely. You will see. The evening star is over the sea, and the moon over the land.

D. H. Lawrence

There may be other things I have forgotten. You will decide whether they are worth sending or not.

---

[1] your] the   [2] A removal firm.
[3] Dostoievsky, *House of the Dead*, trans. Constance Garnett (1915).
[4] golden] all golden

1213. To Lady Ottoline Morrell, 15 March 1916

Text: MS UT; cited in Charles L. Ross, *DHL Review*, viii (Summer 1975), 200.

Tinners Arms, Zennor, St. Ives, Cornwall

15 March 1916

My dear Ottoline,

Thank you for the books from London.[1] They are interesting; but these old fashioned people get on so slowly, their style is so slow. I send you back *Salimbene*, *Hesiod*, and Curzon.[2] You will enjoy Curzon; we liked him very much.

We are busy with our cottage: I am putting up shelves and making a dresser. It is a lovely place. We shall only have to spend about £5, furnishing; and £5 for a year's rent: then we can live very cheaply. I feel I am going to be penniless. We shall do our own work.

The Murrys will be back towards the end of April. I don't think Heseltine will come back to us at all.[3]

Never mind that you don't like my philosophy: it doesn't matter. I am writing nothing just at present. I shall begin when we are settled in our cottage, but I am not quite sure what I shall do. If I can get a manuscript from Germany, I shall go on with that. It is a novel I began three years ago. I should like to go on with it now.[4]

The world will go its own way, and I shall go mine: if only it will let me alone. What I write now I write for the gods. I am useless to this mankind, and this mankind is useless to me. It is no good pretending any more that there is a relation between it and me. If only it will let me alone, and not try to destroy my own inner world, which is real, I don't mind. But my life is not any more of this world, this world of this humanity, and I won't pretend it is.

D. H. Lawrence

1214. To Katherine Mansfield, [16 March 1916]

Text: MS NYPL; PC; Postmark, [...] 16 MAR 16; cited in Delany 218.

Zennor – St. Ives.

– Thursday

[1] Probably those sent in response to the requests in Letter 1204.
[2] See Letter 1204.
[3] See p. 569 n. 1. For a detailed discussion of DHL's involvement in Heseltine's personal relationships and the consequences, see Delany 198–205.
[4] DHL is referring to his unfinished novel 'The Insurrection of Miss Houghton' which was begun in January 1913 (see *Letters*, i. 501 n. 2). After very extensive re-writing it became *The Lost Girl* (1920).

Both letters just come – hurrah! The three-in-one is yours. We go into our mite tomorrow: address '*Higher Tregerthan, Zennor, St. Ives*'. That is your address also. Our landlord is a perfect dear: a little busy old Captain Short. I have *made a dresser* out of old wood he gave me in our house. Also I have made shelves. Today we are off to a sale in St. Ives to buy coco-matting etc. It is wonderful here now, a warm wind, and great white clouds. You should hear the birds at evening, and see the Celtic magic of the dusk.

What about a *housekeeper*? Shall we have one, or not? What about Emma? I hope I shall get enough coco-matting to cover Jack's study.

I will send off the cheques at once.[1]

That will be perfectly splendid, if you come about April 8th. It will leave me time to see that your house is aired and made quite tight. We are so delighted. What a joyful day, when you arrive, and we meet you in St. Ives station, which is on the edge of the sea. I am so frightened that something bad might snatch this from us – but it shant.

Love.   D. H. Lawrence

Shall we have Mrs Powell[2] *every morning*, to work for us, instead of a housekeeper? She would come in from 8.0 till 2.0.

1215. To Katharine Clayton, 16 March 1916
Text: MS NCL; Postmark, Zennor 16 MAR 16; Unpublished.

Tinners Arms, Zennor, St. Ives, Cornwall.

16 March 1916

My dear Mrs Clayton,

Murry asked me to pay this bill for him – he sent me a cheque. Is it three guineas he owes you? Tell me if it is right. He is in France at present, but is coming home in April.

We were so glad to have your letter. I feel like you, that those who face out all this misery will come out clean and strong. But I *do* wish it could end.

I am not writing at all just now, but I shall begin soon. We have taken a cottage for £5 a year, in a most lovely place. We move in tomorrow. The address is Higher Tregerthan, Zennor, St Ives, Cornwall.

Now I must hurry to go to St. Ives to buy coco-matting at a sale. Thank you very much for promising to type for me: I shall send MS. along bravely when I have some: the poor can accept from the poor, happily. For we are very badly off. But nevertheless, life is going to be wonderful.

Love from Frieda and me   D. H. Lawrence

[1] One of the cheques was for Douglas Clayton for typing Murry's MS; see Letter 1215.
[2] Unidentified.

1216. To Dollie Radford, [18 March 1916]
Text: MS UN; Postmark, Zennor 18 MAR 16; Nehls, i. 367–8.

Higher Tregerthen, Zennor, St. Ives, Cornwall.
Saturday.

My dear Dollie,

You see we are living here: it is very jolly.[1] I have been so busy, putting up shelves. I have actually *made* a dresser, a very rough affair. But I am very proud of it.

In answer to your letter of this morning: please *leave* the table (if it is not sent) and the primus stoves, until the Murrys come. We should like the candlestick and cushions, but there is no hurry.

Tell Herbert I would buy back my things, if I were not practically penniless. Ask him if he will let me have the *arm-chair*, the two little *bedroom chairs*, the *Princess lamp*, and the *little wooden bowl*. These I will pay for at once. Then, if he let me have the *mirror* and the *door-mat*, I would pay for those later. I can't afford my dear little desk.

But I will write to him myself, at this moment.[2]

Many thanks, and love from us both

D. H. Lawrence

1217. To Katharine Clayton, 21 March 1916
Text: MS NCL; cited in Pinto 26.

Higher Tregerthen, Zennor, St. Ives, Cornwall
21 March 1916

My dear Mrs Clayton,

Don't be so unmercenary: make out your bill in full, take off the three guineas, and send me the account. I will give it Murry when he comes. He would not wish you to do work for nothing: it is a scandal. They are coming here in three weeks time, to the cottage next door.

Your imaginations are all wrong about the cottage. St Ives is verily famous for wives and cats and children, even now.[3] But we have no fuchsia hedge, no garden. There are three cottages, in a little knot, stand just under a hillside where enormous granite boulders are lodged among the gorse bushes, looking as if they might roll down on us. It is all enormous granite boulders and gorse, above. Below, there are a few bouldery[4] fields with grey-stone hedges,

---

[1] DHL moved into the cottage on 17 March 1916.
[2] This letter has not been found.
[3] Alluding to the nursery rhyme: 'As I was going to St Ives, I met a man with seven wives' etc.   [4] bouldery] rocky

then the sea. There is one farm in the hollow below. But all is rather windswept and grey and primitive. Yet it has a warm southern quality. When the sun shines, it is wonderful beyond words, so rich.

You shall have this cottage for a time, when we are away. That is a promise. Then you can do as you like here. Only the train-fare is dear, the rest is so easy. I should love you to come down.

When we are settled I shall begin to write again. Then I shall send my MS. along to you. However bad the times are, we shall pull through. I feel that this is the worst year: the next will get better. And the wicked *shall* perish, we'll make them.

Send me the account for Murry, and he will settle it when he comes. My regards to Douglas: I wish he were typing a joyous book for me. But let us hope he soon will be. It is misery that makes us ill, makes him have influenza, and me an inflamed chest – nothing but disgusting misery of a vile life.

Love from us both.   D. H. Lawrence

Don't send stamped envelopes any more: it is an insult.

When you and Douglas can come down here, let us know, and we will settle you up. It is no good ruining your health.

1218. To Dollie Radford, [22 March 1916]
Text: MS UN; Nehls, i. 368.

Higher Tregerthen, Zennor, St. Ives, Cornwall
Wednesday[1]

My dear Dollie,

I can't tell you how delighted we are to have the things. We have unpacked and put everything in its place, and now we are beginning to feel shipshape. It is the most splendid little cottage in the world, and I feel we are going to live here for ever. I shall never be able to thank you enough for sending us off all the things: what it must have cost you, in time and energy and expense, I do not like to think. But never mind, you will come down to enjoy it, soon.

One sad thing, I can't find the pendulum of the clock: I *do* hope Murry didn't lose it bringing it to you; that is what I fear. Will you tell me if you remember packing it? If it is lost, I must write to Hollanders, in South Kensington, on the Fulham Rd, where the clock came from, to get me another if they can. The poor clock, it hangs on the wall, and cannot go, like a body awaiting the breath of life.

---

[1] Written on the day when DHL's furnishings from Byron Villas arrived, 22 March 1916.

Also Gertler is defrauding me of my pair of brass candlesticks. They were my mother's, so I want them. I am writing to him now.

I told you the Murrys are coming to the cottage next door. They write so excitedly. They will be in town by the 1st April, and down here by the 8th. You must see them when they are in London. When you come to stay, you will stay in their house, to sleep, and live with us: in fact, we shall all live together. I feel it is going to be so delightful.

Thank you once more for sending these things. Just write me one more post card to tell if you know anything of the missing pendulum, then you will be persecuted no more.

Love from Frieda and me   D. H. Lawrence

Do *please* let me pay packing and Carter Paterson expenses.

1219. To Mark Gertler, 22 March 1916
Text: MS SIU; cited in Moore, *Poste Restante*, p. 45.

Higher Tregerthen, Zennor, St. Ives, Cornwall.
22 March 1916

My dear Gertler,

Today all the things have come, that remain to us from Byron Villas. Thank you very much for keeping them, I hope they were not a great encumbrance to you.

I only miss my pair of brass candlesticks. Did Murry bring them to you? I do hope they are not lost, because they are the only thing that I have kept from my own home, and I really am attached to them. Will you let me know about them, if you can?

We are getting settled in here: it is a most splendid place. The cottage will soon be quite perfect. You must come down and see it soon.

You know the Murrys are coming in about three weeks time, to the cottage next door. Of course their place is much more palatial than ours. But won't it be jolly when we are all here.

Tell Kot I will write to him directly. We have had no place to sit down in lately. Now we are getting shipshape. How are you? What news have you?

Yours   D. H. Lawrence

1220. To Dollie Radford, 24 March 1916
Text: MS UN; Nehls, i. 369–70.

Higher Tregerthen, Zennor, St. Ives, Cornwall.
Friday 24 March 1916

My dear Dollie,

I hope you won't find this trifle too trivial. But it is a bit of Cornwall, of the inner earth. It is 'rose quartz', untouched. I think it is rather a lovely stone. But of course it is not valuable. Never mind, it is true quartz, true crystal of the inner earth, and rosy at that. So forgive its lack of value.

We are getting on famously. We shall be *so* cosy and happy here. We have covered the floor with coco-matting, and today we have been in to St. Ives and made the last purchases: a large green wardrobe-cupboard with mirror, for 37/-, and a chest of drawers, for 16/-: and they are *good* things, splendid. The cupboard had to be hauled up through the kitchen ceiling into the bedroom. In Cornish cottages there are always loose planks left, to lower the coffin when someone dies, because the stairs are so narrow, and the dead must not be tilted about. I was quite frightened when I saw the great hole in the ceiling, and faces peering down. But it is closed up again now, and the green-stained wardrobe holds our clothes, which at last, thank heaven, are hung straight.

It has been a lovely day. There was actually snow this morning. But the sun shone, and it vanished, and the sea has been deep blue, like lapis lazuli, with lovely coloured shadowings, grey and lilac, just like lapis lazuli. If I were a man with money, I should have bought you a necklace of lapis lazuli today, a necklace with small lovely beads. It was 30/-. But it was just your necklace. But I am a man without money.

How are you all? How is Miss Abbott? What is your new nurse like? How are you feeling, in health and spirits? How is Maitland? He didn't answer my last letter.

Do tell me about yourself and answer these questions.

Frieda sends her love, with mine   D. H. Lawrence.

1221. To Captain John Short, [25 March 1916]
Text: MS UT; cited in Delany 218.

Higher Tregerthen, Zennor, St. Ives, Cornwall
Saturday.[1]

Dear Captain Short,

Thank you for your letter and post-card. We bought the cupboard from Benney after all: and with the chest of drawers, the small one, 16/-, it holds all our things, so we are very happy. The things came up through the trap-door, which is not fastened down at all: the planks are loose. So all was easy.

I think the colour-washing ought to be done before the Murrys come: it

---

[1] Dated with reference to the purchase of 'a large green wardrobe-cupboard' and 'a chest of drawers' described in Letter 1220.

is such a hateful business, when one is in the house. I *know* he will like the colours as you and I agreed: dining-room, *red*, as it is; down-stairs tower-room, *cream*; large bedroom, a *pale pink*, cupboards and pantry whitewashed. I think that is all, except those black and white panels in the tower room must be of another colour. I wrote to Mrs Murry, suggesting either pale blue, to go with the orange, or else pale yellow.[1] Perhaps, when she answers, you could let us have the paint, and, if the man were not here, I would put it on.

Then our bedroom needs another wash on the walls. I should like it pale pink, very pale. If this colour is not included in the list of distempers, it can easily be made by mixing white with the salmon. The Murrys large bedroom would be the same as ours.

I suggested in my last letter that Mrs Murry should write to you. I expect she will take the house in her name, as her income is steady, while his fluctuates. So you should hear from her soon: though letters to and from France are very slow indeed. They, the Murrys, will be in England, however, in eight days' time.

There only remains the question of the W. C. The one that stands already is not very satisfactory. Surely it should have a bucket, that it might be emptied quite cleanly. It is a pity it stands there at all, spoiling the only bit of ground. And it would never do to stand another beside it: one might as well, at that rate, live in a public-lavatory. I can see Katharine Murrys face, if she saw two W. C.'s staring at her every time she came out of the door or looked out of the window. It would never do. The one that stands there already spoils entirely the only nice sunny bit of ground where one could sit cosily and have meals out of doors, and spoils the entrance to the cottages. I think there might be a good, simple sand-and-bucket arrangement somewhere at the far end of the Murrys cottages, where the 'conservatory' was[2] going to be, and another somewhere near your cart-shed, where you have put up the fence; and then we have this one removed. Then nothing disagreeable would appear.

We are quite cosy here. The stove upstairs is all right. The piece of piping is perhaps too deep, it wont go into the chimney quite far enough. But it will do all right, to warm and make quite dry the bedroom. We are only waiting for the range in the outhouse here: when is that coming up? We shall be able to cook then. One gets tired of always boiled stuff.

I send you a cheque for £6··5··0, for a *years rent*, and the *bed*, and the *little table*. I don't know if there is anything else I owe you: you must tell me.

---

[1] No letter with these suggestions has been found.   [2] was] is

When the man comes up to the other house, shall I give him coals and coke to make the fires in it, or will you have provided them?

Will somebody see about that damp wall in the red dining-room? It is always quite wet. I suppose it ought to have been concreted over inside.

This is a long letter: but after all, it is only about trifles such as are inevitably necessary.

Mrs Lawrence sends her greetings. We shall be glad to see you again. When we are all settled, we can spend many a jolly hour together, and you can tell us about the merchant service, and Mrs Whittley will be here with her dogs.[1]

Yours Very Sincerely   D. H. Lawrence

1222. To Lady Cynthia Asquith, 25 March 1916
Text: MS UT; Huxley 340–1.

Higher Tregerthen, Zennor, St. Ives, Cornwall
25 March 1916

I'm afraid we can't come to London[2] – no money: What is more, I can't write stories to make money, because I don't want to. Curse the idiotic editors and the more idiotic people who read: shall I pander to their maudlin taste. They bore me.

I should have liked to come up for a few days, for all that, to look at them. And I should have liked us to have some sort of festive meeting.

I dreamed last night, before your postcard came, that I was at some party or other of yours – and that you had other people there, most desolating outsiders. I couldn't describe you the feeling of almost sordid desolateness caused by the established presence of those other people of yours, who are outsiders.

We have got our £5 cottage, and are perfectly happy in it. I have made a dresser, with a cupboard below, and the cups hanging above: also shelves, and a set of bookshelves. We are going to do all our own work, I am going to cover the spring on the hill-side, and clean it, and we can live so cheaply, and I love it. The situation is perfect, with a moor-slope coming down to the back door, and the sea beyond, in the front.

It isn't scenery one lives by, but the freedom of moving about alone.

I wish we could have afforded to come up – Frieda *must* go to the dentist. She is very busy and happy here – we are quite alone.

What news have you? Is Herbert Asquith still free?

Yours   D. H. Lawrence

---

[1] See p. 590 n. 1.   [2] The visit had been contemplated in Letter 1205.

1223. To S. S. Koteliansky, 28 March 1916
Text: MS BL.; Postmark, Zennor 28 MAR 16; Zytaruk, *Malahat* 26–7.

Higher Tregerthen, Zennor, St. Ives, Cornwall
28 March 1916

My dear Kot,

I haven't written before because we have hardly had a place to sit down in. But now the cottage is beginning to be something like ship-shape. It is a warm and cosy place, with great thick walls. But the weather is terrible. All yesterday, a solid blackness over the sea, and masses of snow driving out of it, and a wind that shook the very earth. Today, happily, the snow is almost gone and the wind is stiller. What a life!

As for the man who wants the *Signature*, in America, don't bother with him[1].

I hear from Katharine this morning that they, she and Jack, thought of leaving France *yesterday* (Monday), so they should be in London at least by Wednesday. They don't know where they will stay, in town. But they will not be long there: they will come down here to the cottage next door. I hope to heaven they will get safely across the Channel.

It will be a great blessing when they are safely settled here. I confidently expect the war to end this year, I expect us all to be so happy. We have learned some lessons, let us hope, during these two years of misery, and got rid of a great deal of spleen. Now let us be happy: if only the war will end.

I don't know quite what sort of children's books you would like to translate (was it translation you were thinking of?) Do you mean the *Robinson Crusoe* type: R. L. Stevenson's *Treasure Island* for example. In that list come Captain Marryatt (very good), R. M. Ballantyne, W. H. Kingston, Henty, Ralph Boldrewood, Melville – all these are authors.[2] Then there is the *Little Lord Fauntleroy* type (this was a *very* popular book), authors Frances Hodgson Burnett, Annie S. Swan, Mrs Ewing (oldfashioned and good *Lob lie by the Fire* etc).[3] Then there are the 'school book' series – public-school, like *Tom Brown's Schooldays*.[4]

[1] Unidentified.
[2] Robert Louis Stevenson (1850–94) whose *Treasure Island* (1883) began as a serial in a boys' paper; Frederick Marryat (1792–1848); Robert Michael Ballantyne (1825–94); William Henry Giles Kingston (1814–80); George Alfred Henty (1832–1902); Rolf Boldrewood, pseudonym of Thomas Alexander Browne (1826–1915); and Herman Melville (1819–91): all writers whose works were popular among the young.
[3] Frances Eliza Hodgson Burnett (1849–1924) made her reputation with *Little Lord Fauntleroy* (1886); Annie Shepherd Swan (1859–1943), author of popular stories; Juliana Horatia Ewing (1841–85), author of *Lob Lie-by-the-Fire* (1873).
[4] By Thomas Hughes (1822–96); published in 1857.

Do you mean boys' buoks or girls' books: because they are rather sharply[1]
defined? I think our *boys'* books of adventure are best, like *Treasure Island*,
or books by Henty, or Kingston, or Collingwood.[2] I used to *love* them. And
if I could get hold of a school library list, I could tell you what books were
most popular with my boys: I used to keep the school library.[3] But Barbara
Low could *easily* help you here, she is in a school. I think our *boys books*
are really rather good, and rather fun to translate into Russian.

Will you, when Mudie's sale comes on, please go in and buy me two copies
of my *Trespasser*. They are going at fourpence each. The sale begins April
3rd, I believe – next Monday.

Tell Murry to write me at once: [...] but I will enclose a little note for
him.[4]

I hope soon you will come and see us, here in Cornwall. Greetings from
Frieda.

Yours   D. H. Lawrence

If you see Gertler, ask him if he knows anything of my pair of brass
candlesticks. He has sent only an old copper one, and those brass ones were
old family relics.

1224. To J. B. Pinker, 28 March 1916
Text: MS UT; cited in Carswell 45.

Higher Tregerthen, Zennor, St. Ives, Cornwall.
28 March 1916

My dear Pinker,

I send you the agreement for the poems. Do you think the title *Amores*
is all right? I have a letter from Duckworths about its format. He will make
it Cr. 8vo novel size, and like the *Prussian Officer* in binding. I think that
is rather nice.

We are settled here in our own cottage, to live in poverty and quiet. It
is a beautiful place, and I like it very much. The cottage costs only £5 a
year. So we need not spend much, any more. But the weather is terrible,
blizzards of snow.

Yours   D. H. Lawrence

---

[1] sharply] sharplingly
[2] Harry Collingwood, pseudonym of William Joseph Cosens Lancaster (1851–1922).
[3] Philip Smith, Headmaster of Davidson Road School, Croydon, recalled that DHL's
responsibilities 'included the constant attention bestowed on the details connected with the
school library' (Nehls, i. 87).
[4] The note has not been found.

1225. To Irene Whittley, 31 March 1916
Text: MS UT; Unpublished.

Higher Tregerthen, Zennor, St. Ives.
Friday 31 March 1916

Dear Mrs Whittley,[1]

We have never seen you again, and we confidently expected you to be up here one day. I asked your father to thank you very much for ordering the matting. We have it down, and are much more comfortable.

I believe the Murrys are coming down next Tuesday. They will have to stay at the Tinners Arms until their cottage is ready. I had a wire from them today.

Will you be at Benney's sale at the public hall in St. Ives on Tuesday afternoon. I hope you will, because there are two wicker chairs I think would do splendidly for us, and you will bid for them for me if you are there, won't you? We shall be at the Public Hall at two o clock, and shall look for you. I expect the Murrys will arrive 5.15: then we can drive up together. You must know them soon.

Greetings to you and to Mr. Whittley from my wife and me –

Yours   D. H. Lawrence

I have forgotten your address.

If you were not thinking of going to the sale, and so we shall not see you, won't you walk out here one fine day and have lunch or tea with us, as you prefer?

DHL

1226. To S. S. Koteliansky, [1 April 1916]
Text: MS BL; Postmark, [...] Cornwall 1[...]16; Zytaruk 77.

Higher Tregerthen, Zennor, St. Ives, Cornwall.
Saturday[2]

My dear Kot,

We had a telegram from the Murrys yesterday. They say they will be coming down here early next week. I don't know where they are staying, so I enclose their letter to you.

The letter from Fisher St. was from a man wanting to set some of my verses to music.

---

[1] Irene Tregerthen Whittley (b. 1887) was the daughter of DHL's landlord, Capt. Short. A later letter reveals that she was responsible for preparing Murry's cottage before he and Katherine Mansfield arrived. She was – in 1919 at least – a teacher in Battersea; her husband Percy W. Whittley, served in the Navy during the war and was employed in Barclay's Bank after it. DHL continued to write to Irene Whittley until 1922.
[2] Written on the Saturday before the Murrys' arrival on 5 or 6 April.

I am glad you did not go to the Hutchinsons'.[1] I think they are bad people. I'm sure you are a social success, but I think it is better not to be one. Better be an unsocial success.

Here it is marvellously beautiful, now the fine weather has come. When we are all settled, you will come down, won't you? I am just beginning to feel really better.

Have you read any good books lately? I seem to have nothing but Greek Translations and Ethnology, in my head.[2] Stories don't interest me very much just now.

Yours   D. H. Lawrence

1227. To Lady Ottoline Morrell, 7 April 1916
Text: MS UT; Huxley 342–4.

Higher Tregerthen, Zennor, St. Ives, Cornwall
7 April 1916

My dear Ottoline,

The Murrys have come and we are very busy getting their cottage ready: colouring the walls and painting and working furiously. I like it, and we all enjoy ourselves. The Murrys are happy with each other now. But they neither of them seem very well in health. That will come however.

Our cottage is practically done. At last I am in my own home and feel content. I feel I have a place here. The cottage looks *very nice*. I made a dresser, with cupboard below, and shelves for plates above, also book-shelves. These are painted royal blue, and the walls are pale pale pink, and the ceiling with its beams is[3] white. This is downstairs, a rather low, square room with thick walls. Upstairs looks really beautiful: a good-sized room with a large deep window looking to the sea, and another window opposite looking at the hill-slope of gorse and granite. Your embroidery hangs on the slanting wall of the big window, and the countrypair on the bed is brilliant and gay: it is very nice.

We have only these two rooms, and a long [...] scullery-kitchen with sloping roof at the back. But it is quite enough, there is all the world outside, the sea and the moor-hills quite open. The Murrys like it also.

Frieda wrote to you. I am glad she said what she feels. That is always

[1] St John ('Jack') Hutchinson (1884–1942), barrister; K.C. 1935. He defended Dorothy Warren in the case of the confiscation of DHL's paintings from her gallery (1929). m. Mary Barnes, 1910. The Hutchinsons were close friends of Mark Gertler; Mrs Hutchinson was cousin to Lytton Strachey.
[2] See Letter 1204; p. 593 n. 6.   [3] is] are

best. Then if anything remains, it can begin to grow, free from the weeds.
I do feel that the only thing to try for is a free, natural, unstrained
relationship, without exclusions or enclosures. But it is very difficult.

I did not thank you for Thucydides.[1] He is a very splendid and noble
writer, with the simplicity and the directness of the most complete culture
and the widest consciousness. I salute him. More and more I admire this
true classic dignity and self responsibility.

I have just finished reading Romain Rolland's *Life of Michael Angelo*.[2]
Do you know it? If not, I will give it to you. In its way, I think it is good.
Having reached the same point of overripeness in humble christianity, as
Michael Angelo had reached in proud christianity, Romain Rolland is
understanding. It is *amazing* how plainly one sees, in Michael Angelo, the
transference from the great mediaeval and classic epoch of Power and Might
and Glory to the great modern epoch of Service and Equality and Humility.
Michael Angelo reverted back into the old Catholic form, like Vittoria
Colonna.[3] But he was the new thing as well. Only, it is quite true, he was
more concerned with the End than the Beginning, with the Last Judgment.
What he felt most was the downfall of the old God of Power and Might,
the death of the God, the descent from the Cross, the body in torture. But
he turned his eyes to the Great God of Power and Might, whose sons we
are.

And now Romain Rolland, at the end of the very epoch which Michael
Angelo initiated, looks back and sees only the sorrow and the charity and
the Gethsemane ecstasy. Now it is time for us to leave our Christian-democratic epoch, as it was time for Europe in Michael Angelo's day to leave
the Christian-aristocratic epoch. But we cannot leap away, we slip back. That
is the horror. We slip back and go mad. The world is going mad, as the Italian
and Spanish Renaissance went mad. But where is our Reformation, where
is our new light? Where even is our anathema? They had Savonarola and
Luther,[4] but we only slip wallowing back into our old mire of 'Love thy
neighbour'.[5] It is very frightening. In Michael Angelo's day, Vittoria
Colonna had a choice between Lutheranism, or even 'Free Catholicism', and

[1] See Letter 1204.
[2] Romain Rolland (1866–1944), French musicologist, novelist, biographer and dramatist.
Author of *Michael-Ange* (1905); trans. Frederic Lees, *The Life of Michael Angelo by Roman
Rolland* (1912). It is conceivable that DHL's interest in the book had been kindled by Russell
who, on 10 February 1916, urged another friend to read this 'wonderful book' (Russell,
Autobiography, ii. 60).
[3] Vittoria Colonna (1492–1547), Marchioness of Pescara and poetess to whom Michael Angelo
wrote sonnets and letters.
[4] Girolamo Savonarola (1452–98), Italian religious reformer. He was excommunicated in 1497
and later burnt. Martin Luther (1483–1546), leader of the Reformation in Germany.
[5] Mark xii. 31.

the 'Reactionary Catholicism'. Now there is no choice. There is no choice between new and old, only between old and old. It is so serious that one is hardly moved, one only wonders, and feels outside everything. What is the choice between Oxford and Cambridge, Philip Snowden[1] and F. E. Smith?[2] It is only one old hat or another.

Thank you very much for offering to help us with money. For the present, we can manage. I wish I could always be sure of earning enough to keep us, but I can't. At the Renaissance, Art was holy 'A work of art is an act of faith'.[3] People came from France and Holland and Germany to be present when Michael Angelo's *Last Judgment* was inaugurated.[4] Now art is degraded beneath mention, really trampled under the choice of a free democracy, a public opinion. When I think of art, and then of the British public – or the French public, or the Russian – then a sort of madness comes over me, really as if one were fastened within a mob, and in danger[5] of being trampled to death. I hate the 'public', the 'people', 'society', so much, that a madness possesses me when I think of them. I hate democracy so much. It almost kills me. But then, I think that 'aristocracy' is just as pernicious, only it is much more dead. They are both evil. But there is nothing else, because everybody is either 'the people' or 'the Capitalist'.

One must forget, only forget, turn one's eyes from the world: that is all. One must live [...] quite apart, forgetting, having another world, a world as yet uncreated. Everything lies in *being*, although the whole world is one colossal madness, falsity, a stupendous assertion of not-being.

Murry will read Tylers *Primitive Culture* before I return it.[6] It is a very good sound substantial book, I had far rather read it than *The Golden Bough* or Gilbert Murray.

With affection.

Yours   D. H. Lawrence

[1] Philip Snowden (1864–1937), later Viscount Snowden, statesman. Chairman of the Independent Labour Party (1903–6, 1917–20); M.P. (1906–18, 1922–31); Chancellor of the Exchequer (1924, 1929–31). Lady Ottoline met him in May 1916; she thought him, though 'old-fashioned', 'the one man who can speak and command respect' (*Ottoline at Garsington* 108).
[2] Frederick Edwin Smith (1872–1930), later 1st Earl of Birkenhead. Conservative M.P. (1906–18), and Lord Chancellor (1919–22). On the formation of the first Coalition government in May 1915 he was appointed Attorney-General.
[3] Cf. 'If he still continued his work as a sculptor, he was no longer prompted by faith in art, but by faith in Christ' (Rolland, *Life of Michael Angelo*, p. 130).
[4] Rolland states: 'The inauguration of the "Last Judgement" took place on December 25, 1541. People came from all over Italy, France, Germany, and Flanders to be present' (ibid. p. 123).
[5] danger] being
[6] *Primitive Culture: Researches into the Development of Mythology, Philosophy, Religion, Art and Custom*, 2 vols (1871), by the distinguished anthropologist Sir Edward Burnett Tylor (1832–1917).

1228. To S. S. Koteliansky, [9 April 1916]
Text: MS BL; Postmark, St. Ives 10 APR 16; Zytaruk 77–8.

Higher Tregerthen, Zennor, St. Ives, Cornwall.
Sunday.

My dear Kot,

Thank you very much for the two copies of the *Trespasser*.[1] I must send you a p.o. soon. You sent me back some money a little time since, which I am sure you did not owe me, by any possibility. But I will settle up directly.

The Murrys are here, and we are all very busy getting ready their house. It is rather a nice job, especially when the weather is so beautiful. But we are as yet rather strange and unaccustomed to each other. It is so difficult to reestablish an old footing, after a lapse during which we have all endured a good deal of misery. But I am sure we shall all eventually be happy here.

I am getting really well now, the spring coming back. Soon I shall be like a lion raging after his prey, seeking whom he may devour.[2]

I find Katharine simpler and better, but Murry not much changed in any way.

How are you, and what are you doing? You must be doing something. Frieda sends her regards.

Yours   D. H. Lawrence

1229. To Catherine Carswell, 16 April 1916
Text: MS YU; Carswell, *Adelphi* 211–13, 288.

Higher Tregerthen, Zennor, St. Ives, Cornwall
16 April 1916

My dear Catherine,

I have been on the point of writing to you for some days, but we have been so unsettled, helping the Murrys to get into their cottage.

I am very sorry to hear of you seedy, and with that neuralgia. I have a great horror of pain, acute pain, where one keeps one's consciousness. I always thank my stars that I don't have those pains that scintillate in full consciousness. I am only half there when I am ill, and so there is only half a man to suffer. To suffer in one's whole self is so great a violation, that it is not to be endured.

I think you have been exhausting yourself, making onslaughts on yourself, for a long time now. I hope you will give yourself peace now. One has to withdraw into a very real solitude, and lie low there, hidden, to recover. Then

---

[1] See Letter 1223.
[2] 1 Peter v. 8 ['as a roaring lion, walketh about, seeking…'].

the world gradually ceases to exist, and a new world is discovered, where there are as yet no people.

I am very glad to hear of the novel.[1] I firmly believe in it. I think you are the only woman I have met, who is so intrinsically detached, so essentially separate and isolated, as to be a real writer or artist or recorder. Your relations with other people are only excursions from yourself. And to want children, and common human fulfilments, is rather a falsity for you, I think. You were never made to 'meet and mingle',[2] but to remain intact, *essentially*, whatever your experiences may be. Therefore I believe your book will be a real book, and a woman's book: one of the very few. I often think of the Duse with her lovers, how they were keen and devouring excitements to her, but only destructive incidents, really, even D'Annunzio.[3] I want very much to read your book.

I begin really to feel better, strong again. Soon I shall begin to work. I am waiting for a novel manuscript to come from Germany.[4] But after this last lapse, one is slow and reluctant.

It is queer, how almost everything has gone out of me, all the world I have known, and the people, gone out like candles. When I think of Viola, or Ivy, even, perhaps, the Murrys, who are here, it is with a kind of weariness, as of trying to remember a light which is blown out. Somehow, it is all gone, both I and my friends have ceased to be, and there is another country, where there are no people, and even I myself am unknown, to myself as well.

We have been very busy, doing our cottage, and helping the Murrys. I have made a dresser, which is painted royal blue, and the walls are pale pink: also a biggish cupboard for the food, which looks like a rabbit hutch, in the back place. Here, doing one's own things, in this queer outlandish *Celtic* country, I feel fundamentally happy and free, beyond.

I hope you will be better. Don't talk about me with those others. Frieda sends her greetings.

D. H. Lawrence

[1] Catherine Carswell's novel which DHL first read in MS in June 1914; see Letter 740.

[2] Shelley, 'Love's Philosophy' (1819), l. 7.

[3] Eleonora Duse (1858–1924), a famous Italian actress, noted for her tragic roles. In 1894 she fell in love with Gabriele d'Annunzio; he created tragic roles for her, e.g. *La Gioconda*, 1899; but eventually broke off the relationship and publicised it in his novel *Il Fuoco* (*The Flame of Life*), 1900.

[4] See p. 580 n. 4.

1230. To Dollie Radford, 16 April 1916
Text: MS UN; Postmark, St. Ives 17 AP 16; Nehls, i. 382.

Higher Tregerthen, Zennor, St. Ives, Cornwall
Sunday 16 April 1916

My dear Dollie,

I never thanked you for sending the candlesticks. They arrived safely, and look very twinkling and happy on the mantel-piece.

Oh dear, we are slaving so hard to get the Murrys into their house. They have been here for 12 days now, but they are not nearly done. They have only finished the kitchen and a bedroom, so far. There is still more floor-staining and distempering, and all the furniture to buy. We go to St. Ives to sales, which is rather fun.

I shall be so glad when they are settled in, and we can do jolly things. I am going to learn Greek with Murry. There are so many nice things to look forward to, if only we once get safely housed. Your coming is one of them: I hope you will be here during the spring – next month perhaps.

We are pretty well in health – I am *really much better*, praise the Lord.

I wish they would hurry up with my Italian Sketches: they *are* slow. They say the paper was delayed in transit. My poems are with the printer now. Won't it be good to have another volume out? There is something peculiarly exciting and delightful about a book of verse, more than about prose. I often take down your poems and read one or two over again.

Is Margaret publishing anything? I should like to see it if she is.

I got my Princess Lamp from Herbert – rather broken, alas. But don't tell him. I know he hates being called up. I do wish he needn't go.

The world is soon going to get nicer, isn't it?

Frieda sends her love, I mine.   D. H. Lawrence

1231. To Lady Ottoline Morrell, 18 April 1916
Text: MS IEduc; Moore 447–9.

Higher Tregerthen, Zennor, St. Ives, Cornwall
18 April 1916

My dear Ottoline,

Thank you for the *Storia do Mogor*.[1] I have read one volume, and am

---

[1] Niccolao Manucci, *Storia do Mogor; or, Mogul India, 1653–1708*, trans. W. Irvine, 4 vols, 1907–8. Lady Ottoline was clearly a subscribing member of the London Library which possessed a copy of this work.

very much entertained. I love these odd books. The London Library must be a good thing.

The Murrys are living in their house, and getting more or less settled. But for a pleasant surprise, the policeman came up today with a warrant to arrest Murry, for not joining up. Of course he produced his rejection-certificate. But there seems to be some question as to whether a rejection from the Officers Training Corps is final. I hope it is not serious.

The question of General Conscription seems to be getting more insistent.[1] I shouldn't wonder if it came in. They would give me some sort of clerking to do, I suppose. I would like to see the clerking, when I had done it. They should have more pain than profit out of me. Curse my King and country: and big lumps of society altogether.

But one is impotent, and there is nothing left but to curse. Only, how one hates One's King and country: what a sickening false monster it is! How one feels nauseated with the bloody life, one stodge of lies, and falsehood. I don't care a straw what the Germans do. Everything that is done, *nationally*, in any sense, is now vile and stinking, whether it is England or Germany. One wants only to be left alone, only that. If they will leave me alone in my cottage here, well and good. I hate the whole concern of the nation. Bloody false fools, I don't care what they do, so long as I can avoid them, the mass of my countrymen: or any other countrymen.

I feel the war must end this year. But in one form or another, war will never end now.

It is very beautiful, all the gorse coming out on the hillsides. But one feels behind it all the dirty great paw of authority grasping nearer and nearer of jeopardy. We contemplate all kinds of schemes. But it is like people contemplating schemes who are rolling on board a rotten ship in a storm: the unspoken question all the time, is how long do we hold out.

You never told me if you like *Michael Angelo* by Romain Rolland. I[t] has a good deal of M.A.B.'s poetry at the back – in Italian:[2] it might please you to read it. We have not yet reached a sufficiently advanced stage of house-furnishing to begin to learn Greek. That is one of the schemes. Another is a carpenter's bench, to make chairs. Another is wood carving, to be painted: e.g. Temptation of Eve, with painted apples on a painted tree, and Eve with rabbits at her feet, and a squirrel looking at her, russet,

---

[1] Conscription for all able-bodied men between 18 and 41 came into effect with the passing of the Second Military Service Bill, which received Royal assent on 25 May 1916. It was first introduced in the House of Commons on 27 April 1916.
[2] M.A.B., i.e. Michael Angelo Buonarroti. The poems are printed in the 'Appendix', pp. 174–90; see p. 592 n. 2.

out of the apple tree. Another is an anthology, of short stories, from all the world, and other anthologies.

What do you think of the look of things now, in the world?

I hope you are well. It will never be springtime in the world, for us: but out of the world, the spring might be perfect, but for the gas-fumes that blow in.

D. H. Lawrence

1232. To Philip Heseltine, [ante 22 April 1916]

Text: MS UT; cited in Moore, *Intelligent Heart* 214.

Higher Tregerthen, Zennor, St. Ives, Cornwall
Thursday.[1]

Thank you for the Dionysos, which came this morning.[2] By the same post came Frieda's letter to you, returned by Puma, with a note to the effect that we are both beneath contempt.

I forgot to ask you, when sending the Dionysos, if you would send also the MS. of my philosophy. I should be glad if you would do this. Yesterday your hat turned up: I think it is the last thing I have to send you. My old hat that you took I don't want.

I shall be glad when I have that MS., and this affair is finished. It has become ludicrous and rather shameful. I only wish that you and Puma should not talk about us, for decency's sake. I assure you I shall have nothing to say of you and her. The whole business is so shamefully fit for a Kouyoumdjian sketch.

Please send me the manuscript, and we will let the whole relation cease entirely, and remove the indecency of it.

D. H. Lawrence

1233. To Mark Gertler, 26 April 1916

Text: MS SIU; Huxley 348–9.

Higher Tregerthen, Zennor, St. Ives, Cornwall
Wednesday 26 April 1916

---

[1] It is not possible to assign a particular date to this letter. There is evidence of a rift between DHL and Heseltine from c. 15 March (Letter 1213; see also p. 569 n. 1). A *terminus ad quem* is provided by Heseltine's letter to Delius, 22 April 1916, in which he said: 'When I wrote and denounced [DHL] to his face, all he could say was "I request that you do not talk about me in London"' (Gray, *Peter Warlock*, p. 118). The quotation appears to derive from this letter.

[2] DHL had made the drawing offered to Lady Ottoline in Letter 1151; it had been returned via Heseltine.

My dear Gertler,

I was glad to hear from you that things are going pretty well with you. It looks as if we were all going to be dragged into service one way or another, which is very damnable. But I am becoming fatalistic: it is no use kicking against the pricks. I don't care very much what happens, so long as I get a moderately decent time.

Murry is troubled because it looks as if he were already conscripted: his exemption not final at all. But we know nothing definite yet. They are getting on with their house, which will be very nice indeed. Our cottage is complete, and is a little gem, I think.

It is very lovely here. I am sitting with my back against a boulder, a few yards above the houses. Below, the gorse is yellow, and the sea is blue. It is very still, no sound but the birds and the wind among the stones. A very big seagull just flew up from the east, white like lime-stone, and hovered just in front of me, then turned back in the sky. It seemed like a messenger.

The sun is very hot, it is like summer. Yesterday I saw an adder sleeping on the grass. She was very slim and elegant, with her black markings. At last she was disturbed, she lifted her slender head and listened with great delicacy. Then, very fine and undulating, she moved away. I admired her intensely, and liked her very much. If she were a familiar spirit, she was a dainty and superb princess.

I am much better in health. This last week I have felt really well, as I have not been for many months. So am very glad. And I began a novel.[1] I will only write when I am very healthy. I will not waste myself.

The Murrys are not very well in health. They will get better with the summer. They are not acclimatised here yet. I dont know what will happen to us all, whether we shall be torn away from here or not, by the army needs. I am quite happy here.

I wonder what things of mine remain in your studio: a few books and two primus stoves, I know. Is there anything else? I suppose you couldn't find anywhere the *pendulum* of our little clock that used to hang on the wall in Byron Villas. It has got lost, and so the clock won't go, which is sad.

We need the primus stoves now the summer is coming on, when we don't want fires. I should like my books too. I suppose you could not get a small wooden box from the grocer or somewhere, and send them off by the G[reat] W[estern] R[ailway], addressed to me. If you can't do it, I must ask Mrs Tarry,[2] of 2 Byron Villas, to come up and do it for me: I don't like to ask Dollie Radford any more. Let me know about this, will you.

---

[1] The novel to be published as *Women in Love* (1920).
[2] The Lawrences' neighbour when they stayed at 1 Byron Villas.

The world is so lovely here, one wonders why men want to exert themselves, having wars and so on. It is a great bore. Why wont they let us alone.

All good wishes from Frieda and me.

Yours   D. H. Lawrence

1234. To Lady Cynthia Asquith, 26 April 1916
Text: MS UT; Huxley 346–7.

Higher Tregerthen, Zennor, St. Ives, Cornwall
Wednesday April 26. 1916

My dear Lady Cynthia,

It seems as if we were all going to be dragged in to the danse macabre. One can only grin, and be fatalistic. My dear nation is bitten by the tarantula, and the venom has gone home at last. Now it is dance, mes amis, to the sound of the knuckle-bones.

It is very sad, but one isn't sad any more. It is done now, and no use crying over spilt milk. 'Addio' to everything. The poor dear old ship of christian democracy is scuttled at last, the breach is made, the veil of the temple is torn,[1] our epoch is over. Soit! I don't care, it's not my doing, and I can't help it. It isn't a question of 'dancing whilst Rome burns', as you said to me on the omnibus that Sunday evening – do you remember? It is a question of bobbing about gaily in chaos. 'Carpe diem' is the motto now: pure gay fatalism. It makes me laugh. My good old moral soul is crevé.[2] The poor dear old Ottoline, she has ceased to have any meaning intrinsically, her world is over, her gods fallen and broken to bits. What a funny life!

Will you tell me, if you can, what it would be wisest for me to do, at this juncture. Ought one to attest, and if so, what sort of job can I do? I don't *want* to do anything; – but what will be, will be, and I haven't any conscience in the matter. If I have to serve, all right: only I should like a job that was at least sufferable. Do think a little, and advise me: or ask Herbert Asquith to tell me what I could do. I think it is all rather ridiculous – even when it is a question of life and death; such a scurry and a scuffle and a meaningless confusion, that it is only a farce.

It is very lovely down here, the slopes of desert dead grass and heather sheering down to a sea that is so big and blue. I don't want a bit to have to go away. But it will keep. And the cottage is *very nice*, so small and neat and lovely. There is one next door, the same as this, that you must have when

[1] Matthew xxvii. 51 ['…temple was rent'].   [2] 'worn out'.

the pot bubbles too hard, out there in the world. Will you be coming this way, when you are making your round of visits?

I am still waiting for my book of Italian Sketches to appear. Now there is a strike among the printers in Edinburgh. But it won't be long. It is quite a nice book. I will send you a copy.

I am doing another novel – that really occupies me. The world crackles and busts, but that is another matter, external, in chaos. One has a certain order inviolable in one's soul. There one sits, as in a crows nest, out of it all. And even if one is conscripted, still I can sit in my crow's nest of a soul, and grin. Life mustn't be taken seriously any more – at least, the outer, social life. The social being I am has become a spectator at a knockabout dangerous farce. The individual particular me remains self-contained, and grins. But I should be mortally indignant if I lost my life, or even too much of my liberty, by being dragged into the knockabout farce of this social life.

I hope we shall see you soon. I do think our acquaintance would stand developing – you and Herbert Asquith and Frieda and me. We might have some good times together – real good times, not a bit macabre, but jolly and full. The macabre touch bores me excessively.

Frieda is boiling the washing in a saucepan, I am, for the moment, making a portrait of Taimur-i-lang – Tamerlane, the Tartar: copying it from a 15th century indian picture.[1] – I like it very much.

mila saluti di cuore   D. H. Lawrence

1235. To Mark Gertler, [29 April 1916]
Text: MS SIU; cited in Moore, *Intelligent Heart* 217.

Higher Tregerthen, Zennor, St. Ives, Cornwall.
Saturday[2]

My dear Gertler,

I have written to Mrs Tarry, of 2 Byron Villas, to attend to the sending off of the remaining things, for me. I did not like to trouble Mrs Radford again. I hope Mrs Tarry's coming will not be a nuisance to you. I have asked her first to take the two primus stoves to the ironmonger to be put into order, then to send off all the things together, when they are returned. So you will have no trouble, except that of admitting a stranger.

We are all a little bit blue, looking forward to being compelled to serve. I expect men like Murry and myself will be put into this 'reserve', to do

---

[1] Entitled *Taimur-I-Lang*, the picture is found in *Storia do Mogor*, i, facing p. 98. See p. 596 n. 1. Tamerlane, also called Tamburlaine (c. 1336–1405), the Tartar conqueror.

[2] Dated with reference to the mention of Mrs Tarry in Letter 1233.

some sort of clerking. It is very disgusting, but what will be, will be. So one awaits the 1st June, or whenever it is, with comparative equanimity.[1]

But what in the name of all fortune is Gilbert thinking? Isn't it very likely he will be put smack into the army? What is he going to do, do you know?

It amuses me that Eddie is beginning to rake in his debts. I had better send him a few unpublished stories, that he may pay himself back with them.

It is no use praying to The Lord, because the Lord is the richest man of all. I have got something like £15 between me and complete starvation. Somehow, I don't care. One has had time to be nauseated with all care.

Let me know what is happening to you. I will send you our news.

Yours   D. H. Lawrence

1236. To Barbara Low, 1 May 1916
Text: MS SIU; Moore 449.

Higher Tregerthen, Zennor, St. Ives, Cornwall
1 May 1916

My dear Barbara,

I would write to you oftener, but this life of today so disgusts one, it leaves nothing to say. The war, the approaching conscription, the sense of complete paltriness and chaotic nastiness in life, really robs one of speech.

It is very lovely here, with the gorse all yellow and the sea a misty, periwinkle blue, and the flowers coming out on the common. The sense of jeopardy spoils it all – the feeling that one may be flung out into the cess-pool of a world, the danger of being dragged in to the foul conglomerate mess, the utter disgust and nausea one feels for humanity, people smelling like bugs, endless masses of them, and no relief: it is so difficult to bear.

I have begun the second half of the *Rainbow*. But already it is beyond all hope of ever being published, because of the things it says. And more than that, it is beyond all possibility even to offer it to a world, a putrescent mankind like ours. I feel I cannot *touch* humanity, even in thought, it is abhorrent to me.

But a work of art is an act of faith, as Michael Angelo says,[2] and one goes on writing, to the unseen witnesses.

There is no help, no hope, no anything – was there ever such a bottomless pit. And there *will* be no hope and no help. It is very difficult to continue to hold out in oneself. Yet the truth is all right. Only it is [...] like being

[1] The Second Military Service Act was to come into operation on 24 June 1916; see Letter 1243.
[2] See p. 593 and n. 3.

sunk deep in the sea, with the horrible mass of humanity and universal falseness crushing down on one, to burst one's very veins.

I was very well, but have been seedy again these few days – which explains this letter, partly. Nevertheless, this is the real truth of the case.

We shall be very glad to see you in the summer, if we are still here. I hope you will like Brunswick Square.[1]

saluti di cuore   D. H. Lawrence

1237. To Lady Ottoline Morrell, [5 May 1916]
Text: MS UT; Moore 450–1.

Higher Tregerthen, Zennor, St. Ives, Cornwall
Friday May 1916[2]

My dear Ottoline,

I hope these last events in England and Ireland[3] have not upset you so much that you are ill: it is so long since any of us have heard from you.

One can feel only misery and shame at all that takes place. It is always sad when a big thing, like our democracy, must come to an end. But that it should end so despicably hurts one considerably. The undignified, ludicrous downfall [...] makes us absolutely ashamed and unable to bear up. One is ashamed in one's soul, and that is very hard to bear, to be ashamed in one's very being. In so far as I am a man belonging to my race, my tradition, and my age, I feel pierced to the quick with hopeless shame, and quite, quite hopeless. It is only in my individual self, which struggles to be free of the greater social self, that I live at all. One is at the best only a torn fragment, a torn remnant of a man. It remains only to trust that this remnant is the living essential part, otherwise one is already as good as dead.

When I think of the degenerate and insect-like stupidity of the men now, my heart stops beating. That England should go on destroying herself to fight this chimerical Germany, whilst all the time the Allies, like great insatiable leeches, hang on her body and glut themselves; that she should destroy her own body, tearing her own limbs, wilfully defiling and desecrating herself like an obscene fakir, to make a meaningless war on Germany, for the sake of Allies who gloat and feed like enormous rats on her dismemberment, this one cannot see, and live.

[1] Her new address was to be 10 Brunswick Square.
[2] Dated with reference to his having 'begun a new novel' (cf. Letter 1236) and to the political events mentioned.
[3] In Dublin the Easter rising had begun on 26 April; the rebels surrendered on 2 May; and executions began on 4 May.

There is no mistaking now, that England represents in the world and has represented for 300 years, the great christian-democratic principle; and that Germany represents the Lucifer, the Satan, who has reacted directly against this principle. But the horrible obscene rats that will devour England and Germany both, these are our noble Allies, our greedy-mouthed, narrow-toothed France, our depraved Russia, our obscene little Belgium. And we give ourselves to be eaten by them: Oh God, Oh God, it is too much. Can one do nothing?

I don't believe fundamentally in the Christian-democratic principle. But surely it ought to be saved from the rats. Can we never be shocked into consciousness of our true position? Or are we possessed by a mad, perverse desire to be devoured by rats, like some loathsome fanatic. In the name of common-sense, isn't it worse to be devoured by unclean creatures like our allies, than to admit the frank enmity of Germany.

I don't know what will happen to us particularly. We shall go on here, Murry and I, till we are made to work. One can do no other. I have no conscientious objections. I don't care much who is killed and who isn't, who kills and who doesn't. But oh, I can't stand this unclean and fakir-like mania for self-desecration, which has come over England so strongly: for there is no doubt that the government *does* represent the country.

Write and tell me how you are. I am not very well again. I am glad the Murrys are here with us.

The country is very beautiful, with tangles of blackthorn[1] and solid mounds of gorse blossom, and bluebells beneath, and myriads of violets, and so many [...] ferns unrolling finely and delicately. I have begun a new novel: a thing that is a stranger to me even as I write it. I don't know what the end will be.

I have been reading Mrs O'Shea's life of Parnell.[2] It is *very* poignant, now, when the political life, and Ireland, are so torn. It is my own book, and I should like to give it you, if you haven't read it. In it the passing bell of this present death begins to ring.

                                                With love   D. H. Lawrence

1238. To Dollie Radford, 16 May 1916

Text: MS UN; Postmark, St. Ives 16 MY 16; Nehls, i. 383–4.

                              Higher Tregerthen, Zennor, St. Ives, Cornwall.
                                                            16 May 1916
My dear Dollie,

I wonder why you are silent for such a long time. It is unkind of you.

---

[1] blackthorn] whitethorn
[2] Katharine O'Shea, *Charles Stewart Parnell: His Love Story and Political Life* (1914).

You should just send me a post card of re-assurance now and then, otherwise I am always afraid one member or other of your shaky family is ill. How is Margaret, how is Maitland? Why doesn't Maitland send me a word?

We are pretty well, so are the Murrys. The country here has been, and is, perfectly lovely, with bluebells and primroses, and the sea-pinks now coming out, all along the edge of the sea. I do wish there was peace, so we could have a happy time together. But the state of affairs gnaws one's heart, and one has no rest. Now that Compulsion is inevitable, we are afraid lest we may not be left here with our cottages. We may be forced to do some wretched job. Will you ask Maitland if I ought to see a doctor now, or to get some certificate or other. For I verily don't want to be turned into a clerk or a munitions maker. Though one becomes fatalistic at last. Do ask Maitland, when you see him.

I think I did write and tell him that the scheme for the private publishing of the *Rainbow* has fallen through, there having been 30 answers to 700 pamphlets.[1]

The Italian Sketches are really coming soon. There was a delay on the railway, then a printers strike in Edinburgh. But the sheets are now on their way by sea! Let us hope they are not mined or submarined, poor things.

I have corrected the proofs of my new volume of poems *Amores*, which Duckworth is bringing out. God above knows what the world will say to them. But I shall like very much to give you these poems.

Frieda sends her love, and hopes all is well. We are always on the point of sending you a box of flowers, and then we never know if they would be a nuisance. Shall we send you some?

Remember me very kindly to Margaret. Is there any news of her poems?[2]

My love to You   D. H. Lawrence

1239. To J. B. Pinker, 19 May 1916
Text: MS Forster; Huxley 350.

Higher Tregerthen, Zennor, St. Ives, Cornwall.
19 May 1916

My dear Pinker,

I return here the agreement with Doran: this seems all right, and I am glad.[3]

[1] If DHL wrote to Maitland Radford, the letter has not survived. Heseltine's letter to Delius, 22 April 1916, confirms DHL's remarks: 'The *Rainbow* scheme fulfilled your prophecy and died the death. I got about 30 replies to 600 circulars' (Gray, *Peter Warlock*, p. 118).
[2] *Poems* published in June 1915.   [3] See p. 610 n. 4.

I am half way through a novel, which is a sequel to the *Rainbow*, though quite unlike it.

I have finished and returned the corrected proofs of *Amores* to Duckworth. He tells me he expects the *Twilight in Italy* to be out in a fortnight now.

Yours   D. H. Lawrence

1240. **To Lady Cynthia Asquith, [post 20 May 1916]**
Text: MS UT; Huxley 349.

[Frieda Lawrence begins]

Higher Tregerthen, Zennor, nr St Ives, Cornwall
[post 20 May 1916]¹

Dear Lady Cynthia,

What are you doing? We want to hear from you. Think, we had a shipwreck, practically on our doorstep – in the mist a big Spanish ship – It *was* thrilling² – This is very lovely here and I hope we shall see you soon – The spring is so beautiful here and I have been very happy in this wide open country of air and sea and gorse – L[awrence] has almost finished another novel, it's a much jollier one and wont shock the good people so much – The Murrys are in the next, the towerhouse; we drive miles into Pensance and go to sales and come home hanging on to chairs and cupboards and things – Get lovely things practically for nothing – I had a great 'rumpus' with Lady Ottoline, finally; I told her what I thought of her – All her spirituality is false, her democracy is an autocrat turned sour, inside those wonderful shawls there is cheapness and vulgarity – She wrote how unfeeling Mrs Bonham Carter³ was about the Irish! Oh, those stunts humanity and kindness; they are really for the people whose inside is frozen! How is your young generation? It would be so jolly if you paid us a visit – Would you like some flowers? There are millions here!

Viele herzliche Grüsse   Frieda Lawrence

[Lawrence begins]

Did you not answer my letter because I asked you what to do about Military Service?⁴ Never mind, I don't want to know. I take the question back. We'll

¹ Dated with reference to the shipwreck on 20 May 1916.
² The ship was the *S. Manu*; the shipwreck was recorded in the 'Shipping News': 'St. Ives (Cornwall) May 20 – Spanish S. Manu, Liverpool for Bilbao, ashore four miles west of St. Ives on ridge of rock; decks buckling: fore tank pierced and full of water. Ships standing by, also life-saving apparatus...Crew took to their boats' (*Times*, 22 May 1916). DHL met and conversed in French with some of the crew (see Nehls, i. 384).
³ See p. 63 n. 11.   ⁴ See Letter 1234.

take what comes, and leave what doesn't come. As for the rest I hope I haven't offended you any further – there seems to be a little adder of offence under every bush. But adders are slim and princess-like things, in reality – there are many here.

I feel that things are going to get better soon – in the world.

D. H. Lawrence

1241. To S. S. Koteliansky, 24 May 1916
Text: MS BL; Postmark, St. Ives 25 MY 16; Zytaruk, *Malahat* 27–8.

Higher Tregerthen, Zennor, St. Ives, Cornwall
24 May 1916

My dear Kot,

It is a long time since I have written to you: but you must not be cross with me. One waits, always expecting the happy miracle to happen, when one will rush to write a jubilaeum: but the occasion never comes.

Gertler told me you were joyous when you heard I was doing a novel. That pleased me. It is a novel wherein I am free. It comes very quickly and I am well satisfied. For the rest, there is no news, except that I have finished correcting the proofs of a little vol. of poetry, which Duckworth will bring out in the early autumn. The Italian Sketches will verily *not* be long now.

It is very beautiful here now, with all the flowers out. And we had a great excitement – a Spanish ship on the rocks in the mist on Saturday morning, just below our house. There she still lies, poor thing. They tried to get her off on Saturday evening, but they could not. The hawsers broke as the tugs were pulling, and she had to be left, with her fore deck submerged. I cannot tell you how it made me sad: it seemed a symbol of something, I don't know what. We sat on the cliffs above, watching. And there she lay, in the mist below, with her crew rowing pathetically round, in the small boats. Then they left her alone. She will be a complete wreck.

The Murrys, I think, are going away. They do not like this country, it is too bleak and rocky for them. They want the south side, with trees and gardens and softness. Also the walls of their house are damp. It is a great pity. I love this country, it is big and free. And I love my little cottage. But folk like different things.

I wonder what will happen about compulsion. I suppose they will give me medical exemption. I don't care very much, but I'd rather be left alone.

How are you and what are you doing? Tell me some of your news. Do you think the War is going to end soon? – I do. I wish so very much also that it would. It is enough.

The Murrys want to go to South Cornwall – some 20 miles away.[1] We of course shall stay here.

Greetings from Frieda and from me.

Yours   D. H. Lawrence

1242. To Lady Ottoline Morrell, 24 May 1916
Text: MS UT; Huxley 350–2.

Higher Tregerthen, Zennor, St. Ives. Cornwall.
24 May 1916

My dear Ottoline,

I am sending back Manucci at last.[2] I have read him all, except where, in the last volume, he becomes tiresome and polemical. He was of the greatest interest to me. At last I can understand something of the Indian Mohammedan nature and soul. I become more and more surprised to see how far higher, in reality, our European civilisation stands, than the East,[3] Indian and Persian, ever dreamed of. And one is glad to *realise* how these Hindoos are horribly decadent and reverting to all forms of barbarism in all sorts of ugly ways. We feel surer on our feet, then. But this fraud of looking up to them – this wretched worship-of-Tagore attitude – is disgusting. 'Better fifty years of Europe' even as she is.[4] Buddha-worship is completely decadent and foul nowadays: and it always *was* only half-civilised. Tant pour l'Asie: it is ridiculous to look East for inspiration. I am glad to have read Manucci. One always felt irked by the East coming-it over us. It is sheer fraud. The East is *marvellously* interesting, for tracing our steps *back*. But for going forward, it is nothing. All it can hope for is to be fertilised by Europe, so that it can start on a new phase.

They are fighting hard again, in France, I see. But I feel that the war is nearly over. One seems to have been fighting in the spirit every minute, wrestling with the devil. And I feel that the devil is thrown, in so far as the war is concerned. It will soon be peace, I think. Then for God-knows-what sort of a bout with the devil.

[1] Murry recalled: 'I went on with my search for a cottage and at length found one at Mylor, on a creek of the Truro river, at £18 a year, and a landlord as pleasant as his name, Barnicoat. We lost no time in moving' (Murry, *Autobiography* 417). Murry adds that their preference for south Cornwall was largely a pretext by which they could escape the 'struggle which was wearing us down to the naked nerves'. They moved in June 1916.

[2] See p. 596 n. 1.

[3] the East] the

[4] Tennyson, 'Locksley Hall' (1832), l. 367 ['Better fifty years of Europe than a cycle of Cathay'].

We have had several copies of the *Berliner Tageblatt.*[1] Germany seems queer: she seems to have got over her great anti-christian anti-democratic outburst, her great rage of sheer reaction in which she burst upon us. She seems now like a person who has been in a violent passion, and feels[2] rather strange and vague and a little wistful, not at all beaten or guilty, but like one who has passed through a violent crisis and has come through a little dazed, new and wondering, if self-righteous. So that the war, as it *was*, at all events, has come almost to an end. Whether it will have a new phase, in which *we* shall roll with ecstasy in blood, get our fulfilment out of the hot bath of blood, like the communicants bathing in the sacrifice-blood, God knows. But I think not – I hope not.

Our turn has still to come, nevertheless. But it seems to me *our* real frenzy and passion of positive struggle will be at home, England fighting England. This is what it ought to be, in the fight to a finish. But this is what it won't be, if Col. Churchill and Co. have their own way.[3] We shall all be whipped up like dogs to fasten on the body of Germany.

But I am afraid I bore you *Old-Moore's-Almanack*ing.[4]

Meyrick Cramb has been to see us.[5] He is a pathetic specimen with an odd little wife. He has written a novel,[6] which he talks of sending you. But he is terribly diseased, with his spine and his mouth. Did you know that his father has published three novels? I read one – *Hester Rainsbrook* (Heinemann).[7] It was rather good.

The country is simply wonderful, blue, graceful little companies of bluebells everywhere on the moors, the gorse in flame, and on the cliffs and by the sea, a host of primroses like settling butterflies, and sea-pinks like a hover of pink bees, near the water. There is a Spanish ship run on the rocks just below – great excitement everywhere.

[1] A newspaper probably sent by Frieda's relatives in Germany. (This would no doubt have been noticed by the local postal authorities and thus would have contributed to 'official' suspicion of DHL's loyalty.)

[2] feels] now

[3] Winston S. Churchill had returned as a Lieutenant-Colonel from active service in France; he announced on 9 May that he would resume his parliamentary duties; on 3 June he resigned his commission.

[4] *Old Moore's* was (and remains) the best known and annually published 'prophetic almanac' (originating in the eighteenth century).

[5] Meyrick Cramb (b. 1888) was the son of John Adam Cramb (1861–1913), Professor of Modern History, Queens College, Harley Street, who wrote under the pseudonym of J. A. Revermort. J. A. Cramb was an 'old friend' of Lady Ottoline (see *Ottoline at Garsington* 148).

[6] DHL wrote 'novel' above 'book' and omitted to delete the latter.

[7] *The Marrying of Hester Rainsbrook* (1913). J. A. Cramb's other two novels were *Lucius Scarfield: A Philosophical Romance of the Twentieth Century* (1908) and *Cuthbert Learmont: A Novel* (1910).

Unfortunately the Murrys do not like the country – it is too rocky and bleak for them. They should have a soft valley, with leaves and the ring-dove cooing. And this is a hillside of rocks and magpies and foxes. The walls of their house too are wet from the rain: though this could be put right. So they talk of staying only a short while, then of going, perhaps, to the soft south side, near Penzance or Newlyn, not very far away. I am very sorry they don't like it, because I like this country and my little cottage so much. I think I shall always keep this cottage.[1]

I had the proofs of the poems. I crossed out all the rest of the dedication, leaving only 'To Ottoline Morrell'.[2] I thought you would prefer that, and it was best, seeing people are as they are, so jeering and shallow.

I have got a long way with my novel. It comes rapidly, and is very good. When one is shaken to the very depths, one finds reality in the unreal world. At present my real world is the world of my inner soul, which reflects on to the novel I write. The outer world is there to be endured, it is not real – neither the outer life.

With love from   D. H. Lawrence

1243. To Amy Lowell, 29 May 1916
Text: MS HU; Damon 359.

Higher Tregerthen, Zennor, St. Ives, Cornwall
29 May 1916

My dear Amy,

I got the two copies of the new *Imagiste* on Saturday.[3] It looks very nice, as usual, the book. And I think it is *quite* up to the mark, don't you? It should make a considerable impression. Tell me what the reviewers say, if you have time, will you?

Will Constable publish the book in England? If so I can get another copy or two. If not I must write to America for a couple.

My *Twilight in Italy* and a book of poems *Amores* are both to be published in New York by Doran: at least, I have signed the agreement.[4] I will send you the *Twilight in Italy* when it comes: it is due any day now, here.

[1] cottage] cottage, I think.
[2] For the full dedication see p. 521 n. 1.
[3] *Some Imagist Poets 1916: An Annual Anthology* (Boston and New York, 1916). The book was published on 6 May; it contained the following poems by DHL: 'Erinnyes', pp. 67–9; 'Perfidy', pp. 70–1; 'At the Window', p. 72; 'In Trouble and Shame', p. 73; and 'Brooding Grief', p. 74.
[4] See Letter 1239. *Twilight in Italy* (1916) and *Amores* (September 1916) were both published in New York by B. W. Huebsch. The agreement had been dispatched to Pinker by Doran on 3 May 1916, advising him as follows (MS NYPL): 'I am returning the Lawrence contract

For news, we have always the same: we are gaily ringing our last shilling, for the empty heavens to hear it. We have got a very lovely little cottage *of our own* here, rent £5- a year, looking down on the sea. There are sea-pinks, like little throngs of pink bees hovering on the edge of the land, over a sea that is blue and hard like a jewel. There are myriad primroses spread out so large and cool and riskily, under the shadows, and bluebells trailing under the great granite boulders, and fox-gloves rearing up to look. It is rather a wild, rocky country, of magpies and hawks and foxes. I love it.

The 'Compulsion' comes into force June 24th. I suppose they will leave me alone, because of my health. If only the war would end! It is so bitterly meaningless now.

Have you any news? It is time now that the miracle should happen – the Lord suddenly shouting out of the thunder 'Fous-moi la paix, là bas',[1] like a man just waked up.

Many greetings from my wife and me.

Yours   D. H. Lawrence

1244. To E. M. Forster, 30 May 1916
Text: MS KCC; cited in Delany 226–7.

Higher Tregerthen, Zennor, St. Ives, Cornwall
30 May 1916

Dear E. M.

I was afraid you had gone to Egypt.[2] Alas, I wonder how many of us will keep a thread of real continuity through all this. One after another I feel my friends snap off from the old moorings, and become derelict. England herself seems like a ship adrift, entirely without course or anchorage. We must watch out.

I wonder how much news I have for you! – very little, because I have lost connection with everybody. Ottoline is of course wildly upset about the Compulsion and other anti-democratic things that have come to pass. She thinks the Irish of the late rebellion 'all poets and fine fellows'. I think them mostly windbags and nothings who happen to have become tragically significant in death. I must say the Irish rebellion shocked me – another rent

---

for THE ITALIAN DAYS and the Book of Verse'. The contract for publishing the books was, however, transferred to B. W. Huebsch, as Doran's letter to Pinker, dated 14 July 1916, shows (MS NYPL): 'I have explained the situation to Huebsch, and have told him that unless you opposed the arrangement and the transfer to him, the right to publish AMORES, TWILIGHT IN ITALY, and THE PRUSSIAN OFFICER would be given to him.'

[1] 'Can't you damned well leave me alone down there!'

[2] Forster went to Egypt as a 'Searcher' for the Red Cross in November 1915; he returned to England in January 1919 (Furbank, ii. 20, 52).

in the old ship's bottom. Old Asquith seems fairly often at Garsington – sympathetic. He is derelict now. Bertie wrote to me that 'our ways are separate'. Soit – I never wrote him again. He is going back to *Cambridge* this term: in the autumn is going to America. Lytton Strachey is the chief friend of Ottoline's just now: he is not at all well. – They all, Lytton, Duncan Grant, all that set, got off as 'conscientious objectors'. They are most of them in London as usual, I suppose. Clive Bell and Hutchinson worked for the No-Conscription league. What they will do now, God knows.

For ourselves, we have got a beautiful little cottage here on the Atlantic, for £5 a year. The rent is paid for a year, so we have a roof. And that is about all. We are nearly at our last shilling, and nobody will give me anything for my writings. It is a nuisance, but I don't bother. I become very fatalistic.

We shall be 'compulsed' on June 24th. There is nothing to be done. I shall report in the ordinary way: expect I shall be medically rejected: I have been rather ill all the winter. But if I am 'compulsed', I shall take what comes. I hadn't the strength to go to America: and it was not fated for me to go. I don't believe in America, I believe in it less and less. It is a bad, soulless, mechanical country.

I am expecting any day my book of Italian Sketches to come out. I will send it you if I know where you are. Also Duckworth is doing another little book of poetry of mine, for the early autumn.

I am writing another novel, sequel to the *Rainbow*, but *quite* different. Here in this book I am free at last, thank God, and can move without effort or excitement, naturally. I feel rather triumphant in myself, really. I feel that I have conquered: what I don't know, but *everything*. Nearly everybody has dropped off from me – even Ottoline is *very cool*. It is better to be alone in the world, planté by oneself.

Don't go to India. *All religion is bad*. Don't want to sink and merge and be lost in the background. Come out, rather, and don't have any background. Kick off the whole damned show, admit no authority, play off your own bat. It is time some of us stood alone, and cut ourselves off from the past. The past is too heavy, let it drop into oblivion, all its Gods with it. We have to come out like seeds from a shell, pushing the future out of our uncreated selves, into existence – È fatta la predica.[1]

When you come to England, come and stay here, and forget everything that has been, from the creation up to now. Many warm greetings from Frieda – she will write to you.

D. H. Lawrence

Your letter came an hour ago – it is dated 8/5/16 – 22 days – I hope this will find you all right.

---

[1] 'The sermon is done.'

1245. To Barbara Low, [30 May 1916]
Text: MS SIU; Moore 453–4.

Higher Tregerthen, Zennor, St. Ives, Cornwall
Tuesday[1]

My dear Barbara,

I thought you owed *me* a letter – I'm sure you did: and I was wondering why you didn't write. I wondered also if you had left Brunswick Square, and what your address might be. Can't you find a place in the Suburb?

I am pleased with the Italian book – it looks very nice. I hope it will make me a little money. We are nearly cleaned out to the last quid. Mean life.

This place is *perfectly* lovely. The cottage is tiny –

[Sketch][2]

one room up and one down, with a scullery. The [...] living room is washed pale pink, with a dark blue dresser, and blue bookshelves. The stairs go up at the side, nice and white, the low square window looks out at a rocky wall, a bit of field, and the moor overhead. The fireplace is very nice, the room has a real beauty. Upstairs is a good bedroom with a great window looking down at the sea – which is six fields away.

[Sketch]

There is also a window, as in the living room, at the back, looking over the road on to the hill which is all rocks and boulders and a ruined cottage. It is very lovely, and dear to my heart. I write upstairs, in the big window, and we sit there usually. Upstairs is my Endymion rug from Byron Villas – so it is part sitting room, part bedroom: full of light and beauty.

But the Murrys are going away in a fortnight. They have taken a house near Falmouth. The walls of their cottage are rather damp – though they would be made dry – and they don't like the country. It is too big and exposed to the sky and sea and winds for them. They want to nestle under leaves. We may afford to have two rooms of their cottage – two rather lovely [...] rooms: if I could afford another £5 a year. Then I should have a guest's bedroom, and a perfectly lovely sitting-room, wonderful. It may be done. Then you can sleep there when you come, if you are sure to behave yourself and not stop up all night talking.

---

[1] On 12 June 1916 (Letter 1246), DHL writes that the Murrys 'will probably be moving this week'; by Saturday, 17 June the Murrys were gone (see Letter 1247). Therefore, this letter may be dated 30 May 1916, approximately a 'fortnight' before their departure.

[2] The first sketch is a plan of the ground floor and immediate surroundings; the second is of the upstairs room.

Of course, there is the possibility I may be hooked into the army. I shall have to report myself on June 24th. I am not taking any steps. It bores me all together.

I have married Ursula – yesterday.[1] Two thirds of the novel are written. It goes on pretty fast, and very easy. I have not travailed over it. It is the book of my free soul.

Here it is rather lovely to read. I have just had Dana's *Two Years Before the Mast – very good.*[2] Do you happen to have Melville's *Omoo* or *Typee?*[3] Send me an Everyman *list* one day, will you? I should be grateful. And if you see Mrs Eder, do ask her if she could send the Swinburne Frieda left at her house at Christmas. I love to read him sometimes, and books are really rather precious here. I am just reading *Pickwick* – it's not very good, it doesn't interest me much. I loved Melville's *Moby Dick.* I read Thucydides too, when I have courage to face the fact of these wars of a collapsing era, of a dying idea. He is very good, and very present to one's soul.

Best wishes from us both   D. H. Lawrence

1246. To S. S. Koteliansky, 12 June 1916
Text: MS BL; Postmark, St. Ives 12 JU 16; Zytaruk, *Malahat* 28–9.

Higher Tregerthen, Zennor, St. Ives, Cornwall

12 June 1916

My dear Kot,

I am sorry you had a black mood. What was the cause this time?

I saw in the papers that foreigners – Russians and French – might enlist now.[4] Do you still think of wearing Khaki? Oh abominable!

Of course I shall have to report myself soon. I expect I shall be exempted on the score of health. If not, we shall be comrades in arms. I'd rather be comrades in anything else. But I have ceased to bother over these things.

It does not seem to me so monstrously important, what happens. One will live through it all. One is very tough and resistant inside.

The Murrys have taken a house 30 miles away, on the South side. They

---

[1] In *Women in Love*, Ursula's marriage to Birkin takes place in Chapter XXVII, 'Flitting'.
[2] Published in 1840 by the American writer, Richard Henry Dana (1815–82).
[3] *Typee* (1846) and *Omoo* (1847).
[4] The *Times* (8 June 1916) reported that 'The Army Council have had under consideration for some time proposals for allowing friendly aliens domiciled in this country to join the British Army, and instructions to this effect are shortly to be issued.' Special arrangements had been devised to ensure speedy decisions in the case of applications from Russian Jews.

will probably be moving this week. Then we shall be alone here. But I am very content, really, to be alone. 'Every prospect pleases, and only man is vile', as the hymn says.[1] Not that man is vile – only wearying and confining. It is the most weary thing in this life, this being confined by one's fellow man. But there, that is the fault of taking people seriously. Why should one consider them more important than the horses in the field and the dogs about the farm. The importance of each individual human being has dwindled down to nothing in my soul.

What will you do when you have £50 and are a private gentleman? One cannot exist merely by living on one's means.

Did Farbmann choose a boys' book to translate into Russian? I must tell you we have a beautiful literature for boys, adventurous and romantic. I can read it now, when all other books seem rather tiresome. Fennimore Cooper is lovely beyond words *Last of the Mohicans, Deerslayer*.[2] Do you think they are done into Russian? Then Hermann Melville's *Moby Dick* (Everyman 1/-) is a *real* masterpiece, and *very good* is Dana's *Two Years Before the Mast*. These are books worth preserving in every language. My dear Kot, translate them at once. Dana's *Two Years* you can get for 6d – (Nelsons).

The weather is cold, the country is beautiful. I shrink from asking you down here to the coast – they make such an absurd fuss about foreigners. Oh what fools people are.

I hope your black mood has become a rosy one. Send me all the news – of Horne and Lewis for example.

Many regards from us both.

Yours   D. H. Lawrence

1247. To S. S. Koteliansky, [17 June 1916]
Text: MS BL; Postmark, St Ives 18 [...]; Zytaruk 82.
Higher Tregerthen, Zennor, St. Ives, Cornwall
Saturday

My dear Kot,
    If you feel like sending this man[3] a post card and lending him your copy

---

[1] 'From Greenland's Icy Mountains' by Bishop Reginald Heber (1783–1826).
[2] James Fenimore Cooper (1789–1851), American novelist; *The Last of the Mohicans* (1826), *The Deerslayer* (1841). Cooper later figured prominently in DHL's *Studies in Classic American Literature* (1923).
[3] A fervent but not uncritical admirer of DHL, Douglas King-Page, who had written on 14 June 1916 an eloquent plea for the loan of a copy of the suppressed novel *The Rainbow*. His letter is preserved in the Koteliansky Papers in the BL. See p. 621 n. 2.

of *The Rainbow*, I wish you would. I don't want to answer these people myself.

The Murrys have gone. I told you I had my paper, ordering me to join the colours on the 28th.? Yesterday I had to forward to Murry a similar notice, ordering him to join on the 30th. Our brave boys in Khaki.

There is no news. Remember me to Campbell when you see him.

Many greetings   D. H. Lawrence

1248. To Catherine Carswell, 19 June 1916
Text: MS YU; Postmark, St. Ives 20 JUN 16; cited in Carswell, *Adelphi* 212–14.

Higher Tregerthen, Zennor, St. Ives, Cornwall
19 June 1916

My dear Catherine,

It is such a long while since we have heard anything of you; will you write back quite quickly, and tell me how things are with you and Carswell.

I have no particular news: except that I have to go and join the colours in Penzance on the 28th. I shall go, and take my chance of being accepted. If I must be a soldier, then I must – ta-rattata-ta! It's no use trying to dodge one's fate. It doesn't trouble me any more. I'd rather be a soldier than a school-teacher, anyhow.

I wish I could have sent you my *Twilight in Italy* book. But I expected you to get it for review. Tell me if you liked it. Did you see the idiotic and *false* review in the last *Times Lit. Supplement*?[1] Really, I do object to being treated like that. But oh dear, it wearies me far too much to hope to answer the fool according to his folly.[2]

How are you both, in health? The last time, you were still very far from the mark. I suppose one's soul gets tired, like a clock that won't go. The world is such a blasted burden.

---

[1] The unsigned review entitled 'Italian Sketches' appeared in *TLS*, 15 June 1916, p. 284. The reviewer compares DHL to Ruskin: 'Ruskin has been thought dogmatic, yet his purpose was modest indeed compared with that of Mr Lawrence. He talked about a fresco in a church, where Mr Lawrence soars to the Me and the Not-Me, the Infinite, the One White Flame, the Consummate Self, and drops from the ecstasies of the empyrean but to leap into capitals again with the Great Moloch and the Glory of the Flesh.' The review concludes: 'Mr Lawrence is a writer with some sense of style, and it is disappointing to see a good gift so mishandled.... He might have written a good book about Italy if he had been content to take things simply, and to see no more than he really saw. But he preferred the easier course of discovering the Infinite.'

[2] Proverbs xxvi. 5 ['Answer a fool...'].

But I hope you are better. I remember in your letter you told me about Isabel Carswell.[1] I was very sorry. There is a sort of civilised sordidness in these affairs that is far worse than bestiality. Is she all right now? She ought to go away from Edinboro so that she need not remember.

I remember in your letter also you said how you alternate between a feeling of strength and productiveness, and a feeling of utter hopelessness and ash. I think that is fairly well bound to be, because I think your process of life is chiefly exhaustive, not accumulative at all. It is like a tree which, feeling the ivy tightening upon it, forces itself into bursts of utterance, bursts of flower and fruition, using up itself, not taking in any stores at all, till at last it is spent. I have seen elm trees do this – covered, covered with thick flowering, making scarcely any leaves, taking any food.

But one has to live according to one's own being, and if your method is productive and exhaustive, then it is so. Better that than mere mechanical activity, housework etc. Tell me how the novel has got on. I think that is very important.

As for me, I have nearly done my new novel. It has come rushing out, and I feel very triumphant in it.

The Murrys have gone over to the south side, about 30 miles away. The north side was too rugged for them. And Murry and I are not really associates. How I deceive myself. I am a liar to myself, about people. I was angry when you ran over a list of my 'friends' – whom you did *not* think much of. But it is true, they are not much, any of them. I give up having intimate friends at all. It is a self-deception. But I do wish somebody produced some real work. I am very anxious to see your book.

If I am not conscripted, and Carswell isn't, I think we shall furnish a *nice* room in the Murrys house, and if you would like to come and stay in it, we should be glad. Barbara Low has an old invitation for part of her summer holiday – she is our only prospect in the visitor way. I like her enough.

It is very fine here, foxgloves now everywhere between the rocks and ferns. There is some magic in the country. It gives me a strange satisfaction.

Many greetings from us both to you and Carswell.

D. H. Lawrence

---

[1] Isabel Macquarie Carswell (1887–1974) was Donald Carswell's younger sister. Her distress was caused partly by the death of her brother John Jamieson Carswell (killed at the Battle of Loos) in September 1915 and partly by her parents' strong objections to the man (the son of a gardener) whom she was later to marry, William Marshall Smart (1889–1975). (Smart became Regius Professor of Astronomy at the University of Glasgow in 1937, and, 1949–51, President of the Royal Astronomical Society.)

1249. To S. S. Koteliansky, [29 June 1916]
Text: MS BL; PC; Postmark, Bodmin 29 JUN 16; Zytaruk 83.

Bodmin
– Thursday

I spent last night in the barracks here, like a criminal. Today I have a complete exemption. But – fui!

D. H. Lawrence

1250. To Dollie Radford, 29 June 1916
Text: MS UN; Postmark, Zennor 30 JUN 16; Nehls, i. 387–8.

Higher Tregerthen, Zennor, St. Ives, Cornwall
Thursday 29 June 1916

My dear Dollie,

I have just come back from Bodmin. Yesterday I had to go and 'join the colours' in Penzance. They conveyed me to Bodmin – a distance of fifty or sixty miles. We were kept – thirty poor devils – in the barracks all night, and treated as incipient soldiers. Luckily I got a total exemption – and am home again. But it was a great shock, that barracks experience – that being escorted by train, lined up on station platforms, marched like a criminal through the streets to a barracks. The ignominy is horrible, the humiliation. And even this terrible glamour of camaraderie, which is the glamour of Homer and of all militarism, is a decadence, a degradation, a losing of individual form and distinction, a merging in a sticky male mess. It attracts one for a moment, but immediately, what a degradation and a prison, oh intolerable. I could not *bear* it – I should die in a week if they made me a soldier. Thirty men, in their shirts, being weighed like sheep, one after the other – God! They have such impossible feet. I beg all my stars that I may never see Bodmin again. I hate it so much. I can hardly trust my exemption.

We shall be delighted to see you and Maitland. I think we shall have a room ready for you in the Murrys empty house – won't that be nice! You can *hop* here from Ilfracombe, surely – but wait, it is a bit difficult. Nevertheless, it can be done – via Plymouth. You must come.

If you have got any little box, of wood or tin, whose shape you like – say any box up to the 1-lb of tea size – then if you send it to me I will enamel and paint it for you, and make it lovely, and have it ready when you come. You will just catch the fox-gloves if you come *soon*.

Alas, what a final fall it was when England chose general compulsion to military service. Among the men, there is such a valiant sense of doing what is right, in joining up, overlying a deeper sense of catastrophe. The sense of catastrophe in the midst of that militarism, that Bodmin, that barracks, those khakis and the men to whom khaki is imminent, is really terrifying. It is a sense that men experience when they are transgressing the pure natural right, in the name of some ideal right (the ideal of the fellow man).

I am well merely because I have escaped (unberufen! unberufen!!). If I had not escaped I should be dead.

We shall expect you before long now.

Love from both   D. H. Lawrence

Tell Maitland I shall answer his letter directly.[1]

[Frieda Lawrence begins]

It is time they did away with pro Patria!

Do, come, dear nice Dollie, we can lend you a little cottage, we have taken the Murry's house which is really 2 cottages with a tower built on – it will be primitive but nice!

So you will come on the 14th –

Much love   Frieda

1251. To J. B. Pinker, 30 June 1916

Text: MS Forster; cited in Carswell 58.

Higher Tregerthen, Zennor, St. Ives, Cornwall.
30 June 1916

My dear Pinker,

I agree, it seems to me just as well, to bring out poems hard on the heels of a book of sketches – they support each other. So if the *Amores* are ready by the end of July, let them come then, by all means. At any rate, that will perhaps ensure their appearance in September; this intention to publish in July.

I was going to write to you. I have finished 'The Sisters', in effect.[2] I thought of writing to Duckworth and saying to him, the novel is done in substance, and I could send him the typed MS. in about six weeks' time, and would he give me some money. Duckworth is so decent, I think it is best for him to publish all my books. And I think probably he would give me enough money to get along with. I can manage on about £150 a year, here.

They have given me complete exemption from military service. I have come almost to the end of my stock of money. I think, if I said to Duckworth

---

[1] Unlocated.   [2] To be published as *Women in Love*.

that I would offer him any books I write, during the next year or two, he might keep me going. What do you think?
I have a debt, to you which no doubt I can pay after a time. Settled here at last, I can live cheaply enough. This money business disgusts me. I wish I had two hundred a year, and could send everybody to the devil.
I think the best thing to do would be to make some sort of arrangement with Duckworth. I like him because he treats my books so well; so there is no reason why we shouldn't come to terms, and I give him my writings if he give me enough to live on. I want some sort of business contract like that, to free me from this sense of imminent dependence on a sort of charity.
Tell me what you think. Perhaps I had better write to Duckworth myself, so he will not think I am trying to squeeze money out of him.[1]
                                                              Yours   D. H. Lawrence

1252. To Captain John Short, 3 July 1916
Text: MS UT; cited in Delany 234–5.
                                        Higher Tregerthen, Zennor, St. Ives, Cornwall.
                                                              3 July 1916
Dear Capt. Short,
Perhaps you have heard from Mrs Short that they gave me full exemption from military service, at Bodmin, and that I will take the tower house, if you have made no other arrangement, for the remainder of Mrs Murry's year.
The Mason is here this morning. We have been on the tower roof. There are many fine cracks in the concrete. I believe, however much concrete were put on, it would only crack and leak again. Also, would that roof support any more weight? Is it held up by beams? If so, they will surely rot, seeing they must always be wet: for the roof is always wet.
It seems to me, the only thing to do would be to put another roof over this: a pyramidical slated roof, that could project *over the walls*, and carry the water away by chuting. I don't believe there is any other way of securing that tower, and saving it from rotting. This top is built all wrong. It is built to hold water, not to throw it off. But if the projecting stones, the battlements, were removed, and a low steeple slated roof put on, that would save both walls and ceiling. I am afraid it might be dear – but it is worth it. Under the slates might be a little attic, if you like, with two little windows.
I believe the big wall in the middle house is drying off, and will be all

[1] No such letter has been found.

right, with a little bit of attention. There remains only the leak in the chimney.

I think, if it is dry, we should go and live in the bigger house, and keep this for visitors. I should like to make my home here. Then, if everything is all right by next May, I can take a longer lease.

I was very sorry about the trouble with Mrs Murry.[1] But let us all forget it, now it is over. She is not bad, really, only sometimes she is all out of joint with the world, with herself and everybody else. – But I am sure *we* can always be friendly, you and Mrs Short and Mrs Whitley, and Mrs Lawrence and I. We can be quite happy here.

I really think it is worth while to make that tower house water-tight, even if it does cost rather a lot of money. We will make the place nice when we live there.

Kindest greetings from Mrs Lawrence and myself.

Yours   D. H. Lawrence

P.S. The mason is testing the tower walls. The mortar is very hollow, just laid over the earth between the stones. What a shame it is!

I have cleared your garden thoroughly. The things are growing splendidly. But there is now a good deal of clear space. May I put in broccoli and cabbage plants, when I get them?

DHL

1253. To S. S. Koteliansky, 4 July 1916
Text: MS BL; cited in Gransden 26.

Higher Tregerthen, Zennor, St. Ives, Cwl
4 July 1916

My dear Kot,

I dont know why you send me this cheque:[2] I am sure it belongs far more to you than to me. It reminds me though that I want you to get me a black ribbon for a Smith-Premier No 2 type writer. I will send another 2/6 – I don't know how much they are. I have finished my novel – except for a bit that can be done any time. I am going to type it out myself – or try to.

At present I am working in the hay, helping the farmer. That makes me happy.

---

[1] Perhaps over the Murrys' departure before the year's lease had expired.
[2] Probably from Douglas King-Page, who in his request for *The Rainbow* (p. 615 n. 3), offered to send a cheque for half a guinea to DHL to be paid to a charity of DHL's choice. Presumably Kot lent the man his own copy of the book (as DHL suggested) and King-Page sent the cheque to him; Kot then sent it on to DHL.

You must, if they are really going to 'compel' you militarily, get a job in an office. With your knowledge of English, and other languages, I am sure they would have every use for you. Besides, the war is not going to last much longer. It will end with this year.

But what a mess altogether! I hated my Conscription experience. There is a sense of spiritual disaster underlying this new militarism of England, which is almost unbearable. When one is there, in barracks, with the new Conscripts and the old soldiers, there is a strange sprightliness, a liveliness, almost like a slight delirium, and underneath, this sense of disaster which nobody dares acknowledge. They are not afraid of Germany, or any thing of that: but of their own souls. They feel something has happened to themselves, of their own choice, which is wrong. This sense, of having chosen wrongly, to the last degree, will haunt and pursue my nation like the Erinnyes pursued Orestes[1] – God save us.

But the war will end this year, and the terror will come upon us. Then we must keep our heads, and see what we can do.

I am pretty well, because, for some reason, I feel I have conquered. I felt I conquered, in the barracks experience – my spirit held its own and even won, over their great collective spirit. I always feel ill when I feel beaten.

molti saluti buoni   D. H. Lawrence

Go and see D. King-Page: that is amusing.

1254. To S. S. Koteliansky, [7 July 1916]
Text: MS BL; Zytaruk 86.

Higher Tregerthen, Zennor, St. Ives, Cornwall
Friday[2]

My dear Kot,

Thank you very much for the typewriting ribbon. But it is just twice *too wide* for my machine, which takes a ribbon not more than half an inch wide. I have never seen a ribbon so wide as this. Ought I to *double* it, fold it? – or must I send it back and have it changed? Please let me know. I enclose p.o. for 2/6. I know I owe you various small sums for postage and books.

I hope you will get an interpreter's job – you ought to. I think also that you will. How queer, if they send you to Russia!

---

[1] In Greek mythology, the Erinyes (or Furies) were female avengers of iniquity. Orestes, who slew his mother Clytemnestra, was hounded by them.
[2] Obviously a sequel to the previous letter.

I am glad to hear of the new book with Duckworth.[1] How did you like
working with Gilbert? What, by the way, is he doing about his own military
service? Is he a conscientious objector, or what? What do you think of him
lately? I know Katharine is coming to London. I think – well, she and Jack are
not very happy – they make some sort of a contract whereby each of them
is free. She also talks of going to Denmark! But don't mention to her that
I have told you anything. She has so many reserves. – But really, I think
she and Jack have worn out anything that was between them. – I like her
better than him. He was rather horrid when he was here.
But it wearies me in my soul, this constant breaking with people. – I hope
Katharine will keep steady, and quiet. She needs to be quiet, to learn to live
alone, and without external stimulant.

I shall be glad if you can get a decent job and leave the dirty Bureau and
the obscene Slat.[2] It has lasted long enough.

Yours   D. H. Lawrence

1255. To Barbara Low, 8 July 1916
Text: MS SIU; Moore 458.

Higher Tregerthen, Zennor, St. Ives, Cornwall
8 July 1916

My dear Barbara,

I got my complete exemption because I was able, spiritually, to manage
the doctors. Usually, in a crisis like that, one has a certain authority. I said
the doctors said I had had consumption – I didn't produce any certificate.
I didn't think it fair to Jones.[3] Where is he, by the way, and how is he? Give
me some news of him.

I am pretty well in health – middling. I will tell you all about the barracks

[1] Kot and Gilbert Cannan had collaborated in translating Chekhov's *The House with the
Mezzanine, and Other Stories*. It was published in New York in 1917 and in London as *My
Life and Other Stories* in 1920. The plan for Duckworth to issue the book did not materialise.
[2] R. S. Slatkowsky.
[3] Ernest Jones (1879–1958), physician and psychoanalyst, who founded the London Psycho-
Analytical Society (of which Barbara Low was a founder member) in 1913. This was dissolved
by Jones in 1919 and replaced by the British Psycho-Analytical Society, whose president he
remained until his retirement in 1944. The reference to being 'fair to Jones' suggests that
DHL had a doctor's certificate which he could have produced if necessary. This may have
been issued by Jones to show to the doctors at Battersea Town Hall on 11 December 1915.
(See also Letter 1005.)

experience when you come. I should have died if they had made me a soldier. At this crisis, if they prevented me from being a free agent, I should expire. One fights all the while, in spirit. It is strange, in immediate contact, how one has strength and power. It is in the abstract, against the whole, it is so hard.

It is very beautiful here. We shall have a nice snug room for you. When are you coming? I expect Dollie and Maitland Radford for a few days – a week or so – somewhere about the 20th. When does your holiday begin? Your room will be ready for you. You will be quite a princess, a whole house to yourself. We shall have a happy time, I am sure. We want you to come. We must put our small funds together, and let Tom Berryman[1] drive us out now and then – to Penzance, to Land's End. How splendid! One has been so sad, it is time for a little excursioning and rejoicement.

We have got a few nice books too –

Many greetings – au revoir   D. H. Lawrence

1256. To Dollie Radford, 8 July 1916
Text: MS UN; Postmark, Zennor 10 JUL 16; Nehls, i. 388–9.

Higher Tregerthen, Zennor, St. Ives, Cornwall
8 July 1916

My dear Dollie,

I was *so* sorry to hear of your throat. It must quickly get better. The weather is going to pick up and be glorious. Today is so lovely. I often think of you, how you love blueness: This is the most wonderful bluest place I have ever seen. And the fox gloves are climbing to the top of the steeple. They are so handsome and tanned. You must hurry up. I believe they are Shelley's 'That tall flower that wets its mother's face'.[2] Do you know, the people here call them *poppies*: they don't know any other name: 'them high poppies'. That's like in Italy, where everything was a 'viola'.

We are getting ready for you a snug little room in the Murry's empty cottage. It is so near, we can almost shake hands out of the window. Shall you mind being alone? If so, let Maitland be there. But it will be rather nice. Then Maitland can have a room at the farm below, the Hockings. They are *very nice* people.

We have been helping in the hay. We are very happy in this place, with the people round about. It will be very jolly for you to come.

[1] A relative (perhaps the husband) of Katie Berryman, the shopkeeper in Zennor, whom Frieda described as 'our standby and friend' (Frieda Lawrence, '*Not I, But the Wind...*', p. 87).
[2] Shelley, 'The Question', ll. 13, 15.

Frieda sends her love, and her a rivederci.

D. H. Lawrence

Let us know when we can be expecting you.

Have you got that little book of Trelawneys, on Byron and Shelley?[1] Do bring it, if you have.

1257. To Catherine Carswell, 9 July 1916

Text: MS YU; cited in Carswell, *Adelphi* 214–16.

Higher Tregerthen, Zennor, St. Ives, Cornwall
9 July 1916

My dear Catherine,

I never wrote to tell you that they gave me a complete exemption from all military service, thanks be to God. That was a week ago last Thursday. I had to join the Colours in Penzance, be conveyed to Bodmin (60 miles), spend a night in barracks with all the other men, and then be examined. It was experience enough for me, of soldiering. I am sure I should die in a week, if they kept me. It is the annulling of all one stands for, this militarism, the nipping of the very germ of one's being. I was very much upset. The sense of spiritual disaster everywhere was quite terrifying. One was not sure whether one survived or not. Things are very bad.

Yet I liked the men. They all seemed so *decent*. And yet they all seemed, as if they had *chosen wrong*. It was the underlying sense of disaster that overwhelmed me. They are all so brave, to suffer, but none of them brave enough, to reject suffering. They are all so noble, to accept sorrow and hurt, but they can none of them demand happiness. Their manliness all lies in accepting calmly this death, this loss of their integrity. They must stand by their fellow man: that is the motto.

This is what Christ's weeping over Jerusalem[2] has brought us to, a whole Jerusalem offering itself to the Cross. To me, this is infinitely more terrifying than Pharisees and Publicans and Sinners, taking *their* way to death. This is what the love of our neighbour has brought us to, that, because one man dies, we all die.

This is the most terrible madness. And the worst of it all, is, that it is a madness of righteousness. These Cornish are most, most unwarlike, soft, peaceable, ancient. No men could suffer more than they, at being conscripted – at any rate, those that were with me. Yet they accepted it all: they accepted

[1] *Trelawny's Recollections of the Last Days of Shelley and Byron*, ed. Edward Dowden (1906), a reprint of E. J. Trelawny's *Recollections* (1858).

[2] Cf. Luke xix. 41–4.

it, as one of them said to me, with wonderful purity of spirit – I could howl my eyes up over him – because 'they believed first of all in their duty to their fellow man'. There is no falsity about it: they believe in their duty to their fellow man. And what duty is this, which makes us forfeit everything, because Germany invaded Belgium? Is there nothing beyond my fellow man? If not, then there is nothing beyond myself, beyond my own throat, which may be cut, and my own purse, which may be slit: because *I* am the fellow-man of all the world, my neighbour is but myself in a mirror. So we toil in a circle of pure egoism.

This is what 'love thy neighbour as thyself' comes to. It needs only a little convulsion, to break the mirror, to turn over the coin, and there I have myself, my own purse, I, I, I, we, we, we – like the newspapers today: 'Capture the trade – unite the Empire – à bas les autres'.

There needs something else besides the love of the neighbour: If all my neighbours choose to go down the slope to Hell, that is no reason why I should go with them. I know in my own soul a truth, a right, and no amount of neighbours can weigh it out of the balance. I know that for me, the war is wrong. I know, that if the Germans wanted my little house, I would rather give it them than fight for it: because my little house is not important enough to me. If another man must fight for his house, the more's the pity. But it is his affair. To fight for possessions, goods, is what my soul *will not* do. Therefore it will not fight for the *neighbour* who fights for his own goods.

All this war, this talk of nationality, to me is false. I *feel* no nationality, not fundamentally. I feel no passion for my own land, nor my own house, nor my own furniture, nor my own money. Therefore I won't pretend any. Neither will I take part in the scrimmage, to help my neighbour. It is his affair to go in or to stay out, as he wishes.

If they had compelled me to go in, I should have died, I am sure. One is too raw, one fights too hard already, for the real integrity of ones being. That last straw of compulsion would have been too much, I think.

Christianity is based on the love of self, the love of property, one degree removed. Why should I care for my neighbour's property, or my neighbour's life, if I do not care for my own. If the truth of my spirit is all that matters to me, in[1] the last issue, then on behalf of my neighbour, all I care for is the truth of *his* spirit. And if his truth is his love of property, I refuse to stand by him, whether he be a poor man robbed of his cottage, his wife and children, or a rich man robbed of his merchandise. I have nothing to do with him, in that wise, and I don't care whether he keep or lose his throat, on

---

[1] in] then in

behalf of his property. Property, and power – which is the same – is *not* the criterion. The criterion is the truth of my own intrinsic desire, clear of ulterior contamination.

I hope you aren't bored. Something makes me state my position, when I write to you.

It is summer, but not very summery, such heavy rain. I told you the Murrys had gone away, to South Cornwall. Now she doesn't like that. I believe she is in London at present. She is very dissatisfied with him.

We are keeping on their house for the rest of their year. It is *so* near, that if strangers came, it would be intolerable. So I am buying a very little furniture – it is so cheap and *so* nice here, second hand – to furnish a sitting-room and a bed-room, for the visitors. I think Dollie Radford is coming in about a week's time, then Barbara Low. We get such pleasure, looking at old tables and old chairs: a big round rose-wood table, very large 4 ft 4″ diameter and solid, 10/-: three very nice birch-wood chairs 7/6: an arm-chair 5/-: the sitting-room is furnished: it is an upper room, [?pane]lled,[1] with big windows, and shelves.

It is such a pleasure, buying this furniture – I remember my sermon. But one doesn't really care. This cottage, that I like so much – and the new table, and the chairs – I could leave them all tomorrow, blithely. Meanwhile, they are very nice.

I have finished my novel, and am going to try to type it. It will be a labour – but we have got no money. But I am asking Pinker for some. And if it bores me to type the novel, I shan't do it. There is a last chapter to write, some time, when one's heart is not so contracted.

I think you are not very wise to go to the Hebrides with Carswells people – you would be so much happier with him alone – or with friends.

Greiffenhagen seems to be slipping back and back.[2] I suppose it has to be. Let the dead bury their dead.[3] Let the past smoulder out. One shouldn't look back, like Lot's wife: though why *salt*, that I could never understand.[4]

Have you got a copy of *Twilight in Italy*? If not, I have got one to give you. So just send me word, a p.c.

Frieda sends many greetings.

Yours   D. H. Lawrence

I am amused to hear of Carswell's *divorce* case.

---

[1] MS torn

[2] Maurice Greiffenhagen (1862–1931), painter, whose *Idyll* figures prominently in *Letters*, i. (Catherine Carswell had been in love with him.)

[3] Matthew vii. 22 (A.V.).   [4] Genesis xix. 26.

[Frieda Lawrence begins]

Would you like some nice butter from here? I wish you and Don had come here a little while – We are really happy here! Making hay. I think Don's people will make you cross!

Much love   Frieda

1258. To S. S. Koteliansky, 10 July 1916
Text: MS BL; Zytaruk 87.

Higher Tregerthen, Zennor, St. Ives. Cwl.
10 July 1916

My dear Kot,

I send you here the type-writing ribbon.[1] I am very sorry to give you so much trouble – I do hope you aren't cursing it.

You sound gloomy again in your letter. I suppose it is the army. Don't bother, I feel sure they will give you a decent job, which you will like.

When you see Katharine, tell her to write to us and send us all the news: we are thinking of her, up in London. – You are quite right about her wanderings – she wants to run away from herself – but also from Murry, which complicates matters. I don't know what the upshot will be, how it will end between him and her. To settle that point, of her connection with M., a small sojourn in Denmark might be useful. After that, I do wish she could learn to be still – and alone.

Yours   D. H. Lawrence

1259. To Thomas Dunlop, 12 July 1916
Text: MS Dunlop; Huxley 358–60.

Higher Tregerthen, Zennor, St. Ives, Cornwall
12 July 1916

My dear Dunlop,

I was glad to have your letter and such good news of Mrs Dunlop and the children. We shall like to see the photographs, immensely, to see who is John, and what has become of Paddy and Biddy.[2]

You and I, we seem born to differ. I can never see how my duty to my fellow-man should make me kill another man. Which then is my fellow-man? How shall I distinguish him. And you are quite right, I do esteem individual

[1] See Letter 1254.
[2] 'Biddy' was the Dunlops' daughter, Margaret Dorothea Leda (b. 1913).

liberty above everything. What is a nation for, but to secure the maximum of liberty to every individual. What do you think a nation *is*? – a big business concern? What *is* the raison d'être of a nation – to produce wealth? How horrible! A nation is a number of people united to secure the maximum amount of liberty for each member of that nation, and to fulfil collectively the highest truth known to them. It is by fulfilling the *lowest* truth – that money is honor and glory – that we have come to war and pretty nearly to bankruptcy. If only life were not a horrible wrestling for a limited amount of wealth, we should have none of these disasters. As for equal burdens – if you do not accept the Socialistic 'equal distribution of wealth', how can you accept the conservative retrogressive 'equal distribution of burden'. Each is a pure fiction. Let every man move according to his conscience – and the government which compels a man against his conscience is a dastardly cowardly concern.

You ask about the second half of *The Rainbow*. I have just re-written it, and am typing it out by my own labors. You meanwhile are very busy in Milan, and much happier, I believe. It certainly would be a nice life, if they gave you a *good* job in Milan, and you could have Mrs Dunlop with you, and the children. Then in the big town, the Alps so near, it would be perfect. I am sure you are happier in Italy than you would be in England. Here the whole country seems to be striving to degrade and defile itself with the ugliest doings and the ugliest sayings conceivable. God save us.

As for my finances, they are as bad as ever. I am just asking my literary agent to lend me something. I hate that. But he will make money enough out of me later.

This penuriousness makes me wish I could get the rest of the things I left in Italy with the beloved Felice: sheets, blankets, towels, clothing, and a few nice books. But I feel I can't write for them: and my Italian is all going: and if the Fiori[1] should have happened to use the things, sheets and blankets for example, I should *hate* even to suggest their giving them back. I suppose the Signorina Eva Rainusso[2] said nothing to you of these things?

Have you got any later news of the Cochranes and Huntingdons and the Pearces? For my part, I can only tell you that our dear Ivy has married a poor Russian revolutionary of forty – quite nice-looking, I believe, but of no account.[3] She – Ivy – is already not *too* contented with her new lot. Heaven knows how it will end. I heard last of a man who used to come to see me – a Prince Bibesco, of the Roumanian Legation – seeking her out to

---

[1] the Fiori] they
[2] The schoolmistress at Fiascherino.
[3] See p. 160 n. 3.

tell her *how* he admired her books. How Ivy and Antoine Bibesco – 'Prince
Antoine Bibesco' – will adjust themselves, God knows.

When you have some time to read, I will send you Tylor's *Primitive
Culture*, if you do not already know it. It is a *most* interesting book, better
than *The Golden Bough*, I think.

Remember us both very kindly to Mrs Dunlop when you write. Are you
going to be permanently at Leghorn? Heaven knows when we shall all meet
again.

Kind regards from Frieda.

Yours   D. H. Lawrence

Thank you very much indeed for sending me the manuscripts: though
what they can be, I cannot conceive.[1] My memory gets worse and worse.

1260. To J. B. Pinker, 12 July 1916
Text: MS Forster; cited in Carswell 35.

Higher Tregerthen, Zennor, St. Ives, Cornwall
12 July 1916

Dear Pinker,

Do send me some money then, for I have only six pounds in the world.

I am beginning to type the novel myself. If it becomes too tedious, I will
have it done quicker. But I suppose there is no hurry.

I am glad you take a hopeful view of the financial life of me. Methuen,
for certain, won't want to keep me. What a snake in his boiled-shirt bosom!
To whom will you offer the book, do you think? I call it 'The Sisters'. Do
you think the title is all right?

Thank you very much for keeping me going.

Yours   D. H. Lawrence

1261. To J. B. Pinker, 13 July 1916
Text: MS Forster; Moore 463.

Higher Tregerthen, Zennor, St. Ives, Cwl.
13 July 1916

Dear Pinker,

Thank you for the cheque for £50 received this morning. I hope somebody
will take the novel, and pay you back quick. The only good thing about

[1] They probably included 'The Mortal Coil' to which DHL refers in Letter 1301.

Methuen is his £300. All the rest is vile, and he *cannot* pretend to keep me. Can you not remind him that he published *The Rainbow?* Shall I call the novel *Women in Love.* I'm not good at titles – never know if they're good or bad.

Yours   D. H. Lawrence

1262. To Katherine Mansfield, 16 July 1916
Text: MS NYPL; Moore 464–5.

Higher Tregerthen, Zennor, St. Ives, Cornwall
Sunday July 16th 1916

My dear Katharine,

How do you find Cornwall, after the world? We must come and hear about the world. The *Unknown Pamirs*[1] sound like a trip to our well: but London and Garsington, they are the Darkest Africa.[2]

Will you ask Murry why he did not answer my letter, and why he did not even put a word in with the money he sent on?

We will come to Mylor at your disposal, on a sunny day. The weather is disgusting. Dollie Radford comes here on the 31st; after her, Beresford, and, I expect, Barbara Low. So August is done for. Let us know what day will suit you, between now and the 31st.

We had our first meal – tea in the tower – yesterday. We have furnished it: a large rose-wood table, round, bigger than your round table, dark, old, in the back corner (10/-); three chairs, two of the birch-woods and one all mahogany (2/6 each); a round arm-chair (6/-) all bought from Benney; and our bed. The bed is under the big window. With Friedas tussore curtains at the big window, and half-curtains of the same at the lesser windows, and Endymion on the floor, and plenty of flowers, the room is really very nice. There are no more sales till autumn. It is a great blessing to have a sitting room.

Banfield is supposed to be making the house water tight. I am wrestling with C[aptain] Short to have a small steeple roof, of slate, put on the tower, with gutters to carry the rain. I hope they will make it water tight. We have agreed to keep the house[3] on till the end of your *year.* It is so much easier, and gives us room. I believe Banfield will get it pretty dry. He is rather trustworthy.

The Crambs have been up again.[4] He is bad as ever: wants to call his

[1] An allusion to O. Olufsen's *Through the Unknown Pamirs: The Second Danish Pamir Expedition 1898–99* (1904).   [2] See p. 107 n. 3.
[3] the house] it   [4] See p. 609 n. 5.

next book 'Fin de siècle'. 'They'll never let you', I say. 'Well', he drawls, Cockney, 'if this book gives me any kind of position for holding my own, I shall stick out.' He thinks he is a great author, that he and I are authors-in-arms. They are going away next Tuesday: Ade, Ade! You will be pleased to hear that those red shoes of Mrs Cramb's were ordered specially for her, in Paris, and cost 45/- shillings.

The Westlakes have come: the old Mrs Westlake, a doctor and his wife, and a Madame Motte, a sort of companion. For these four people they have brought four servants, as well as Crowther and his wife.[1] The old woman is invalid. We never see anything of any of them: I have only heard the voices of the maid servants. – The Shorts continue to be completely absent.

I am typing out my novel: in the tower: Tea in the Tower; the Typist in the Tower etc etc. We were going to alter the colour. I like that yellow, but it is a bit trying for the eyes – Put on some *green* – hated it – are going to paint it back to the yellow. I calculate it will take me just *three months* to type my novel. Oh, have you got that flap from the back of the type-writer, that supports the paper? I can't find it anywhere, nor in the rubbish heap. The paper catches without it.

The corn is very high, the hay is cut, the lowlands here are very lovely: that Tremeader[2] corn full of the most beautiful corn-marigolds. Your water-butt has burst. Mrs Powell is having a hard tussel with her new young man (who is aged 42). He is very common, loud, and I believe she hates him. We saw them in Katies.[3] He was treating her, Mrs Powell, to ginger pop and chocolates. Katie is a great dear. The fox-gloves are really wonderful, I regret very much you can't see them, full like honey-combs, with purple wells.

Will you let us know about coming to Mylor. And will you and Jack say which of the books I enumerated, you would like me to bring. I have *Through the Unknown Pamirs*. I will bring that. You must come and see us, if it would not be too much like playing at ghosts, revenants.

Really, one should find a place one can live in, and stay there. Geographical change doesn't help one much. And people go from bad to worse. I think I shall be staring out from Higher Tregerthen when I am a nice old man of seventy.

I read a bit more Maxence.[4] What a stagnant bit of hot mud! Good job he's dead.

[1] Unidentified.
[2] The farm next to DHL's cottage; see Letter 1280.
[3] See p. 624 n. 1.
[4] Unidentified.

How can I get the De Quincey *Lake Poets*, unless I write to London for it.[1] But I will do so: though perhaps not today.

Vale   D. H. Lawrence

1263. To Catherine Carswell, 16 July 1916
Text: MS YU; cited in Carswell, *Adelphi* 216–17.

Zennor, St. Ives, Cornwall
16 July 1916

My dear Catherine,

I think you are right on nearly all your points. I want people to be more Christian rather than less: only for different reasons. Christianity is based on re-action, on negation really. It says 'renounce all worldly desires, and live for heaven'. Whereas I think people ought to fulfil sacredly their desires. And this means fulfilling the deepest desire, which is a desire to live unhampered by things which are extraneous, a desire for pure relationships and living truth. The Christian was hampered by property, because he must renounce it. And to renounce a thing is to be subject to it. Reaction against any force is the complement of that force. So Christianity is based too much on reaction.

But Christianity is infinitely higher than the war, higher than nationalism or even than family love. I have been reading S. Bernard's *Letters*,[2] and I realise that the greatest thing the world has seen, is Christianity, and one must be endlessly thankful for it, and weep that the world has learned the lesson so badly.

But I count Christianity as one of the great historical factors, the has-been. That is why I am not a conscientious objector: I am not a Christian. Christianity is insufficient in me. I too believe man must fight.

But because a thing *has been*, therefore I will not fight for it. Because, in the cruder stage, a man's property is symbol for his manhood, I will not fight for the symbol. Because this is a *falling back*. Don't you see, all your appeal is to the testimony of *the past*. And we must break through the film which encloses us one with the past, and come out into the new. All those who stand one with the past, with our past, as a nation and a Christian people even (though the Christian appeal *in the war* is based on property recognition – which was really the point of my last letter) must go to the war but those who believe in a life better than *what has been* they can view the war only with grief, as a great falling back.

---

[1] *Reminiscences of the English Lake Poets* by Thomas De Quincey (1785–1859); it was available in the Everyman's Library (1907).

[2] *Some Letters of St Bernard*, trans. Samuel J. Eales (1904).

I would say to my Cornishmen 'Don't let your house and home be a symbol of your manhood.' Because it has been the symbol for so long, it has exhausted us, become a prison. So we fight, desperate and hopeless. 'Don't let your nation be a symbol of your manhood' – because a symbol is something static, petrified, turning towards what has been, and crystallised against that which shall be. Don't look to the past for justification. The Peloponnesian war was the death agony of Greece, really, not her life struggle. I am[1] just reading Thucydides – when I can bear to – it is too horrible to see a people, adhering to traditions, fling itself down the abyss of the past, and disappear.

We must have the courage to cast off the old symbols, the old traditions: at least, put them aside, like a plant in growing surpasses its crowning leaves with higher leaves and buds. There is something beyond the past. The past is no justification. Unless from us the future takes place, we are death only. That is why I am not a conscientious objector. The great Christian tenet must be surpassed, there must be something new: neither the war, nor the turning the other cheek.

What we want is the fulfilment of our desires, down to the deepest and most spiritual desire. The body is immediate, the spirit is beyond: first the leaves and then the flower: but the plant is an integral whole: therefore *every* desire, to the very deepest. And I shall find my deepest desire to be a wish for pure, unadulterated relationship with the universe, for truth in being. My pure relationship with one woman is marriage, physical and spiritual: with another, is another form of happiness, according to our nature. And so on for ever.

It is this establishing of pure relationships which makes heaven, wherein we are immortal, like the angels, and mortal, like men, both. And the way to immortality is in the fulfilment of desire. I would never *forbid* any man to make war, or to go to war. Only I would say 'Oh, if you don't spontaneously and perfectly *want* to go to war, then it is wrong to go – don't let *any* extraneous consideration influence you, nor any old tradition mechanically compel you. If you *want* to go to war, go, it is your righteousness.'

Because, you see, what intimation of immortality have we, save our spontaneous wishes? God works in me (if I use the term God) as my desire. He gives me the understanding to discriminate between my desires, to discern between greater and lesser desire: I can also frustrate or deny any desire: so much for me, I have a 'free will', in so far as I am an entity. But

---

[1] am] have

God in me is my desire. Suddenly, God moves afresh in me, a new motion. It is a new desire. So a plant unfolds leaf after leaf, and then buds, till it blossoms. So do we, under the unknown impulse of desires, which arrive in us from the unknown.

But I have the power to choose between my desires. A man comes to me, and says, 'Give me your house.' I ask myself, 'which do I want more, my house, or to fight?' So I choose.

In nearly all men, now, the great desire is *not* to fight for house and home. They will prove to themselves, by fighting, that their greater desire, on the whole, was *not* to fight for their nation, or sea-power, but to know a new value: to recognize a new, stronger desire in themselves, more spiritual and gladdening. Or else they will die. But many will die falsely. *All* Greece died. It must not be so again, we must have more sense. It is cruelly sad to see men caught in the clutches of the past, working automatically in the spell of an authorised desire, that is a desire no longer. That *should not be*.

It upsets me very much to hear of Percy Lucas. I did not know he was dead.[1] I wish that story at the bottom of the sea, before ever it had been printed.[2] Yet, it seems to me, man must find a new expression, give a new value to life, or his women will reject him, and he must die. I liked Madeleine Lucas the best of the Meynells really. She was the one who was capable of honest love: she and Monica. Lucas was, somehow, a spiritual coward. But who isn't? I ought never, never to have gone to live at Greatham. Perhaps Madeleine won't be hurt by that wretched story – that is all that matters. If it was a true story, it shouldn't really damage.

It is a mistake for Ivy to have children (*don't tell her*). For her, that is a clutching at the past, the back origins, for fulfilment. And fulfilment *does not lie in the past*. You should be glad you have no children: they are a stumbling block now. There are plenty of children, and no hope. If women can bring forth hope, they are mothers indeed. Meanwhile even the mice increase – they cannot help it. What is this highest, this procreation? It is a lapsing back to the primal origins, the brink of oblivion. It is a tracing back, when there is no going forward, a throwing life on to the bonfire of death and oblivion, an autumnal act, a consuming down. This is a winter. Children and child-bearing do not make spring. It is not in children, the future lies. The Red Indian mothers bore[3] many children, and yet there *are* no Red Indians. It is the truth, the new-perceived hope, that makes spring. And let

---

[1] he was dead.] him.
[2] 'England My England'; see p. 354 n. 4. Perceval Drewett Lucas (1879–1916) had died of wounds in France on 6 July.
[3] Indian mothers bore] Indians had

them bring forth that, who can: they are the creators of life. There are many enceinte widows, with a new crop of death in their wombs. What did the mothers of the dead soldiers bring forth, in child-bed? – death or life? And of death you gather death: when you sow death, in this act of love which is pure reduction, you reap death, in a child born with an impulse towards the darkness, the origins, the oblivion of all.

Frieda's letter is quite right, about the *difference* between us being the adventure, and the true relationship established between different things, different spirits, this is creative life. And the reacting of a thing against its different, is death in life. So that[1] act of love, which is a pure thrill, is a kind of friction between opposites, interdestructive, an act of death. There is an extreme *self-realisation, self-sensation,* in this friction against the, really hostile, opposite. But there must be an act of love which is a passing of the self into a pure relationship with the other, something new and creative in the coming together of the lovers, in their creative spirit, before a new child can be born, a new *flower* in us before there can be a new seed of a child.

D. H. Lawrence

Thank Ivy very much for her offer. I shall probably send her a bit of MS. What is her address now? I will write to her.

No, I *dont* wish I had never written that story. It should do good, at the long run.

We shall be glad to see you, most glad if you can both come.

Tell me what Ivy's *name* is.[2]

1264. To S. S. Koteliansky, [17 July 1916]
Text: MS BL; Postmark, Zennor 18 JUL 16; Zytaruk 88.

Higher Tregerthen, Zennor, St. Ives, Cwl.
Monday

My dear Kot,

I am so sorry to trouble you again about the type-writer ribbon. The new one has come *this morning*, but it is exactly like the last. I can't possibly put it on my machine. And as it arrived without a word to say who sent it, or anything like that, I am at a loss.

My machine is L. C. Smith and Bros. Number 2. Perhaps I am wrong in calling it a Smith Premier. It takes a ribbon exactly half an inch wide. What then am I to do with a ribbon one-inch wide? All I want is an ordinary half-inch black ribbon. Can you solve the mystery for me?

[1] that] the   [2] See p. 532 n. 4.

Have you any news yet? The weather is bad here, and I am feeling sick: which is all my news. I had a mere note from Katharine at Garsington, to say she is to be back in Mylor today, and will we go and stay. But I am not keen on it.

Barbara is coming to see us in August. Have you seen her lately?

Yours   D. H. Lawrence

Why did you send back the 2/6? I know I owe it you.

1265. To J. B. Pinker, 21 July 1916.
Text: MS Forster; cited in Pinto 27.

Higher Tregerthen, Zennor, St. Ives, Cornwall.
21 July 1916

Dear Pinker,

I gave up typing the novel: it got on my nerves and knocked me up. I've not been well these last few weeks – so much wetness everywhere, I suppose. If I can, I will go to Italy another year.

I shall send you the MS. of the novel to be typed in your office. I am scribbling out the final draft in pencil. I will send it on as I do it, shall I? It is $\frac{4}{5}$ done now. This is the fourth and the final draft.

A man wrote to me from America about a copy of the *Rainbow*.[1] Would it be safe to send the book just ordinarily through the post? Please tell me.

When I have done the novel I shall *only* write stories *to sell*. I hate getting further into debt. Heaven knows what you will think of the novel – I shall soon want some more money: not at once, but very soon. I have got various pieces of *verse* that might sell – in America or here. Is it worth while bothering with them? The *Smart Set* used sometimes to give me £10 for poetry: but I suppose it won't any more, under other management.[2]

Yours   D. H. Lawrence

1266. To Catherine Carswell, [22 July 1916]
Text: MS YU; cited in Carswell, *Adelphi* 291.

Zennor, St. Ives, Cornwall
Saturday[3]

My dear Catherine

I am glad you said you thought it was no good writing to the man

---

[1] Unidentified.   [2] See p. 144 n. 3.

[3] Dated with reference to the previous letter in which, as here, DHL says that he has given up typing the novel.

Silling[1] – I felt it so strongly after reading the poem. He is as dead as his brother Alan – and let the dead bury their dead.[2] – I have never understood till now what that great saying meant.

I think the poem is [...] good – but of death, too deathly. There is not enough of the *opposition* of life to give it form – it falls all over on the side of death and so is viscous, uncreated. The 7th Hoop Epitaph must absolutely be crossed out. 'And yet – there's no great harm in being dead' – that is good. The whole poem is good. It really expresses the horrible and iridescent dissolution of physical death. But as I say – for me – it falls before it reaches the borderline of art, because there is not quite enough *resistance* of life to bring that solid equilibrium which is the core of art, an absolute reached by the sheer tension of life stubborn against death, the two in opposition creating the third thing, the pure resultant, absolved, art.

I've given up typing my novel. Never will I type again. It is that which has made me ill. Here I am seedy in bed again – but not much. I write my novel in pencil and slip along. It won't be long now. I shall send it you when it is typed out. And you will send me yours as soon as it is done.

I think, in a little while we shall go to Italy, and we will [...] live like Aunt Perdy, in the wilderness, and live the life of contemplation. It is those who are married who should live the life of contemplation; together. In the world, there is the long day of destruction to go by. But let those who are single, man torn from woman, woman from man, men all together, women all together, separate violent and deathly fragments, each returning and adhering to its own kind, the body of life torn in two, let these finish the day of destruction, and those who have united go into the wilderness to know a new heaven and a new earth.

What books are you reading?

D. H. Lawrence

1267. To S. S. Koteliansky, [1? August 1916]
Text: MS BL; Zytaruk 89.

Higher Tregerthen, Zennor, St. Ives, Cornwall
Tuesday[3]

My dear Kot,

Many thanks for the ribbon. This is perfect. I suppose all the mistakes came from saying 'Smith Premier'. I am very sorry.

---

[1] Silling and 'his brother Alan' are unidentified.
[2] Matthew viii. 22 (A.V.).
[3] An invitation from Katherine Mansfield to visit Mylor is mentioned in Letter 1264, 17 July 1916; since DHL was 'not keen' to accept, the Lawrences probably delayed their visit for a little time. DHL is writing after their return home.

We have been for the week-end to Mylor. The Murrys have a pretty little villa there – he loves it – Katharine does not care for it. He, as you will know, is declared fit for service at home and abroad, and will be called up on Oct 1st. He is in a bad state, dreading it and hating it, and only hoping to get a job. How devilish this all is!

Let me know when you have some news. Tell me also, if you cannot get the 2/6 back, and I will send it.

Yours   D. H. Lawrence

1268. To Catherine Carswell, 10 August 1916
Text: MS YU; Postmark, St. Ives 10 AU 16; cited in Carswell 59–60.

Higher Tregerthen, Zennor, St. Ives, Cornwall
10 Aug 1916

My dear Catherine,

We shall be very glad to see you and your novel here 'in the autumn' – that is very vague, though; – say *September*.

I feel really eager about your novel. I feel it is coming under the same banner with mine. The 'us' will be books. There will be a fine wild little squadron soon, faring over the world. Nothing shall I welcome so much as books to ride with mine. Oh to see them go, a gallant little company, like ships over an unknown sea, and Pisarro and his people breaking upon a new world, the books, now.[1]

I thought of calling this of mine *Women in Love*. But I don't feel at all sure of it. What do you think. It was 'The Sisters', but May Sinclair having had 'three Sisters' it won't do.[2]

Dollie Radford came and is gone. Barbara Low is here. They make me feel how far off the world is – such stray, blown, sooty birds they seem. It is lovely to bathe and be alive now, in the strong remote days.

Greetings to Carswell – there is no news.

Auf Schönes Wiedersehen   D. H. Lawrence

1269. To Catherine Carswell, 14 August 1916
Text: MS YU; Postmark, Zennor 15 AUG 16; cited in Carswell, *Adelphi* 387.

Higher Tregerthen, Zennor, St. Ives, Cwl.
14 Aug 1916

My dear Catherine

Just a line in answer to your letter to Frieda. I can't come to London – spiritually I *cannot*. But Frieda wants to come, to go chasing her children.

---

[1] Francisco Pizarro (c. 1475–1541) who, as well as conquering the Inca empire of Peru, participated in Balboa's discovery of the Pacific Ocean (1513).

[2] May Sinclair (1863–1942) published a novel called *The Three Sisters* in 1914.

She wants to come when school starts again. That won't be, I am afraid, until September. But *I* cannot come to London – I am *much* too terrified and horrified by people – the world – nowadays. Do you know at all when St. Pauls will be likely to begin?¹ Of course, Frieda would come only for a few days.

Couldn't you call your novel 'The Wild Goose Chase' – It is so nice and gay. Never The Land of the Living, nor the other. And Stanley Weyman once called a book *Wild Geese*.² But say 'The Rare Bird': or 'The Love Bird' (very nice that) or just 'Cuckoo!' (splendid). Do call it 'Cuckoo' or even the double 'Cuckoo, Cuckoo'. I'm sure something bird-like is right. Cuckoo! is so nice, that if you don't like it, I think I must have it instead of *Women in Love*. Then Loose strife is a nice name. Then 'Had' is a good one. 'The Pelican in the Wilderness' is lovely, but perhaps inappropriate: I don't know. 'The Lame Duck' – I'm sure there is a suggestion in the bird Kingdom –– 'The Kingfisher', which I am *sure* is appropriate, or 'Ducks and Drakes'. Write me a post card which one you choose: only *don't* be too seriously-titled.³

We shall be very glad to see you and The Hon. Bird on the 3rd Sept (historic day): The Hon. Bird is the book, which must be a bird: it isn't Carswell: I wish he were coming too.

All the thanks in the world for lending us the house. But I had much rather be Daniel in the lions' den, than myself in London.⁴ I am really terrified.

DHL

Do send the *Times Lit. Supplement*, with the notice of *Amores*, if you can.⁵

1270. To J. D. Beresford, 15 August 1916
Text: TMSC NWU; Unpublished.

Higher Tregerthen, Zennor, St. Ives, Cornwall.
15 Aug. 1916
My dear Beresford

How are things going with you now? I saw somewhere something about a one-act play – I do most sincerely hope it will bring you money, a lovely pot of it.⁶

¹ Frieda's son Montague Weekley attended St Paul's School; she evidently hoped to see him after the term began about 20 September (see Letter 1273).
² Stanley John Weyman (1855–1928) published his novel *The Wild Geese* in 1908.
³ She eventually chose *Open the Door!* (1920).   ⁴ Daniel vi. 16–24.
⁵ *Amores* was appreciatively reviewed in *TLS* on 10 August 1916. The reviewer praised the 'robust sincerity' of DHL's 'poems of passion'; the 'understanding and force' with which he explored 'the love-fever'; the unsentimental poems on the death of his mother; 'the sincere and deliberate fitness of matter to manner'; and concluded that readers will be 'sometimes charmed, sometimes repelled, but always forced to share the experience'.
⁶ *Howard and Son*, by Beresford and Kenneth Richmond, at the London Coliseum, 14 August 1916.

When are you coming here? We have had visitors these last three weeks, which turns our empty Tregerthen into a new world. But soon we shall be quiet again, and very glad to see you, if only you will choose your time. Let me know any time when you feel equal to it: seize an opportunity when somebody is going to Newquay, that makes the journey so cheap and easy. How is Mrs. Beresford? Thank her very much for her invitation to us. But I daren't come out of Zennor. I feel such a terror of the world and its people, that when I get even into a railway train, I almost die of horror. I would rather come to Porthcothan when you and Mrs. Beresford are alone, and there is nobody in sight for miles and miles. There are calls for me to go to London – but I had rather venture among lions and tigers, than amongst my abhorred fellow men, who fill me with untold horror and disgust.

Come while it is nice and warm, and we can have a drive to Penzance, and go among the heather, and pretend we live on the Happy Isles.

I wish Mrs. Beresford would come with you? Is she well enough?

I think it is wise to go to London. I don't think one should [?trust][1] these country doctors, when a child is born. I do hope you have plenty of money, to do the thing without anxiety. Make somebody give you £50.

Yours   D. H. Lawrence

1271. To Barbara Low, [17 August 1916]
Text: MS SIU; Unpublished.

Higher Tregerthen, Zennor, St. Ives, Cornwall
Thursday[2]

My dear Barbara,

I found your bag yesterday, when we went down to bathe at the same place as on Monday. It was splendid also yesterday, waves *mountains* high: but not so hot as the time before. The waves did lift one this time, and fling one to the shore: which was exciting and alarming, among so many rocks.

I hope you got your umbrella also, which I posted immediately in St. Ives. It seems very queer here, to be without visitors: such a silence, I can tell you. The weather is grey and inclined to rain – rained very hard yesterday, in the fore part of the day. The blackberries are ripening every five minutes. Katharine Mansfield writes, in return to our cool letters 'I shall not *dream* of coming to Higher Tregerthen'. Bien! Frieda expects to be in London in

---

[1] TMSC omits a word. (Aden Noel Beresford, b. 24 December 1916.)

[2] Barbara Low was at Higher Tregerthen on 10 August 1916 (see Letter 1268); Letter 1270 gives the impression that she – the last of the visitors – had departed just before Tuesday, 15 August; therefore the Thursday following seems appropriate for the date of this letter.

two or three weeks' time. I don't know whether I shall come or not, I am
sure.

Let us know how you got home – and what success you have, looking for
flats. Give our love to Dollie when you see her – tell her I will write.

D. H. Lawrence

1272. To Barbara Low, [c. 20 August 1916]

Text: MS SIU; cited in Delany 309.

[Higher Tregerthen, Zennor, St. Ives, Cornwall]

[c. 20 August 1916][1]

[Frieda Lawrence begins]

Dear Barbara,

It was so jolly to hear that you miss 'this', and that Londra is
unpallatable – The empty house is not at all nice either, and we miss you
on the martyrised expeditions, I have also a blue yellow and cut *left* knee,
and I do fuss so! Mrs Short said yesterday, (we had tea in the towei) the
only thing Spiers[2] remarked to her was: the man's mad, the man's mad!
'Who?' asked Mrs Short. 'Mr Lawrence' he said, 'mad, quite mad.' 'Do
you mean', politely enquired Mrs Short, 'because he buries himself in the
country like this?' 'No, no he is mad, mad on every point.' Voilà tout! But
its funny! – I am sure a big part of you belongs here into this life, there is
something wild and untamable in you, that I much appreciate and enjoy!
We are worried about William Henry, he is really interesting, we want him
to have a 'lady' what would take an interest in him[3] –

[Lawrence begins]

I like Frieda's suddenly conspiring to marry off poor William Henry. He
is desirous of the intellectual life, and yet he isn't in the least fit for anything
but his farming. Perhaps during the winter I shall get him to go to London
for a few days: then Dollie, and you, and Mrs Eder must look after him a
bit. He is *really* interested in things: but he hasn't enough mental
development, mental continuity. That is the terrible fate of those who have
a high *sensuous* development, and very little mental: centuries of sensuous
culture, and then sprung into mental life, in one generation, and flung into
the seethe of modern intellectual decomposition. He is the *real* Cornish

---

[1] This letter was apparently written shortly after Barbara Low returned to London.
[2] Unidentified.
[3] William Henry Hocking (c. 1882–1955) was a farmer-neighbour of DHL in Higher
Tregerthen. See part of the BBC interview (14 and 22 November 1953) published in Nehls,
i. 365–6. See also 'William Henry' in Delany 309–15.

farmer: those others, of Quiller Couch[1] and Compton Mackenzie and such, are bosh. And he suffers *badly*, and his people hate him – because he *will* take the intellectual attitude, and they want only the vague sensuous non-critical. He ought to live away from them – in one of these cottages. He looks to me as if I could suddenly give him wings – and it is a trouble and a nuisance.

DHL

So if he – William Henry, – *does* come to London for a bit after harvest is over, perhaps Eder might talk to him [...] about things – let him down gently with Christianity etc. But it isn't analysing he wants – it is some real relation with the intellectual life. I must get Catherine Carswell to talk to him a bit. It is really a tragedy, they do hate him and find him an intolerable nuisance at the farm, and he is very plucky, holding to his own half-lights. Why aren't people more harmonious – curse it.

1273. To Catherine Carswell, [21? August 1916]
Text: MS YU; PC; Postmark, St. Ives 2 [...] AUG 16; Carswell 60.

Higher Tregerthen
– Monday

We *love* the 'Bird of Paradise' – that is most beautiful and perfect a title – do not budge a hair's breadth further – the Hon. Bird is christened, we all dance his name-feast. Do, somewhere in the book put the story of the Bird of Paradise – quite tiny. – I am so glad you like the poems.[2]

DHL

[Frieda Lawrence begins]

Yes, I will if it fits stay at your house, it was nice of you to think of it – Then you will come here with me. I think St Paul's begins about the 20th – I will let you know as soon as I can –

1274. To Amy Lowell, 23 August 1916
Text: MS HU; Damon 368–71.

Higher Tregerthen, Zennor, St. Ives, Cornwall
23 August 1916

My dear Amy,
Thank you so much for the cheque for £8, which came today.[3] Those

¹ Sir Arthur Thomas Quiller-Couch (1863–1944), first King Edward VII Professor of English Literature at Cambridge, from 1912; published numerous works of fiction and criticism.
² *Amores.*
³ Each of the six contributors to *Some Imagist Poets* received an equal share of the royalties (Damon 368).

Imagiste books seem to blossom into gold like a monthly rose. I am very glad, too, to hear of the good things the papers are deigning to say. You should see my English critics walking round me in every sort of trepidation, like dogs round a mongoose.

I will ask Duckworths to send you the poems and the Italian Sketches. You know we may only send books abroad, through the publisher or a bookseller. Otherwise, of course, I should gladly autograph them for you.

Thank God they did not make me a soldier. I had to join up, and spent a night in barracks, and then they gave me a total exemption. If they hadn't, I should have been a stretched corpse in a fortnight: that I knew, at four o clock in the morning, on that fatal night in barracks at Bodmin. There is something in military life that would kill me off, as if I were in an asphyxiating chamber. The whole thing is abhorrent to me – even the camaraderie, that is so glamorous – the Achilles and Patroclus business.[1] The spirit, the pure spirit of militarism is sheer death to a nature that is at all constructive or social-creative. And it is not that I am afraid or shy: I can get on with the men like a house on fire. It is simply that the spirit of militarism is essentially destructive, destroying the individual and the constructive social being. It is *bad*. How Aldington will stand it I don't know. But I can tell that the glamour is getting hold of him: the 'now we're all men together' business, the kind of love that was between Achilles and Patroclus. And if once that lays hold of a man, then farewell to that man forever, as an independent or constructive soul.

I am glad you think the war is virtually over. Official London seems to be saying, with much confidence, two more years of it. But nobody knows. God help us if this is going on for two years more. These last two years have made one at least two centuries older. In two years more, we shall have ceased to be human beings at all. Certainly England has spit on her hands and taken hold at last. The whole[2] nation is hanging on tense and taut, throwing all her weight on the rope at last, in the tug of war. It is our tradition – to get our blood up at the eleventh hour. Well, the English blood is up now, the bull-dog is hanging on – alas that it ever need have come to pass. What will be the end, when the war *is* at last over, the mind refuses to consider: but it will be nothing good.

So one's soul knows misfortune and terror. But there is a limit to grief for one's fellow man: one becomes callous, since nothing can be done.

Here we live very quietly indeed, being far from the world. Here we live

---

[1] In the *Iliad* when the hero Achilles refuses to fight, his close friend Patroclus is killed by Hector. Achilles is then roused to vengeance.

[2] whole] old

as if on one of the blessed Isles, the moors are so still behind us, the sea so big in front. I am very much better, much stronger, now. All the winter I was so ill. I hope it won't be so again this year. But I think not. I am busy typing out a new novel, to be called *Women in Love*. Every day I bless you for the gift of the type-writer. It runs so glibly, and has at last become a true confrère. I take so unkindly to any sort of machinery. But now I and the type writer have sworn a Blutbruderschaft.

We go down and bathe among the rocks – not the typewriter, but Frieda and I. Today there were great rollers coming from the west. It is so frightening, when one is naked among the rocks, to see the high water rising to a threatening wall, the pale green fire shooting along, then bursting into a furious wild incandescence of foam. But it is great fun. It is so lovely to recognise the non-human elements: to hear the rain like a song, to feel the wind going by one, to be thrown against the rocks by the wonderful water. I cannot bear to see or to know humanity any more.

Your remoter America must be splendid. One day, I hope to come to see it, when there is peace and I am not poor. We are living on credit as usual. But what does it matter, in a world like this. Hilda Aldington says to me, why don't I write hymns to fire, why am I not in love with a tree. But my fire is a pyre, and the tree is the tree of Knowledge.

I wonder if I have said anything censurous in my letter – I think not. The honeysuckle smells so sweet tonight – what are the flowers in New Hampshire? Often I have longed to go to a country which has new, quite unknown flowers and birds. It would be such a joy to make their acquaintance. Have you still got humming birds, as in Crèvecœur? I liked Crèvecœur *Letters of an American Farmer, so* much.[1] And how splendid Hermann Melvilles *Moby Dick* is, and Dana's *Two Years before the Mast.* But your classic American Literature I find to my surprise, is *older* than our English. The tree did not become new, which was transplanted. It only ran more swiftly into age, impersonal, non-human almost. But how good these books are! Is the *English* tree in America almost dead? By the literature, I think it is.

Remember me warmly to Mrs Russell. Many greetings to you from my wife and me. You will never come back to the England you knew before. But at any rate, when you do come, you must come here.

D. H. Lawrence

Doran is to publish both the books of mine in America.[2]

---

[1] Michel Guillaume Jean de Crèvecoeur (1735–1813), French statesman and agriculturist; emigrated to America in 1754 and published *Letters from an American Farmer* (1782).

[2] See p. 610 n. 4.

1275. To John Middleton Murry, 28 August 1916
Text: MS NYPL; cited in Murry, *New Adelphi* 197–8.

Higher Tregerthen, Zennor, St. Ives, Cwl.
28 Aug 1916

Dear Jack,

Thank you very much for your book on Dostoevsky, which has just come.[1] I have only just looked in it here and there – and read the epilogue. I wonder how much you or anybody else is ready to face out the old life, and so transcend it. An epoch of the human mind may have come to the end in Dostoevsky: but humanity is capable of going on a very long way further yet, in a state of mindlessness – curse it. And you've got the cart before the horse. It isn't the being that must follow the mind, but the mind must follow the being. And if only the cursed cowardly world had the courage to follow its own being with its mind, if it only had the courage to know what its own unknown *is*, its own desires and its own activities, it might get beyond to the new secret. But the trick is, when you draw somewhere near the 'brink of the revelation', to dig your head in the sand like the disgusting ostrich; and see the revelation there.[2] Meanwhile, with their head in the sand of pleasing visions and secrets and revelations, they kick and squirm with their behinds, most disgustingly. I don't blame humanity for having no mind, I blame it for putting its mind in a box and using it as a nice little self-gratifying instrument. You've got to know, and know everything, before you 'transcend' into the 'unknown'. But Dostoevsky, like the rest, can nicely stick his head between the feet of Christ, and waggle his behind in the air. And though the behind-wagglings are a revelation, I don't think much even of the feet of Christ as a bluff for the cowards to hide their eyes against.

You want to be left alone – so do I – by everybody, by the whole world, which is despicable and contemptible to me and sickening.

D. H. Lawrence

1276. To S. S. Koteliansky, 30 August 1916
Text: MS BL; Postmark, Zennor [...] AUG [...]; Zytaruk 90.

Higher Tregerthen, Zennor, St. Ives, Cornwall
30 August 1916

[1] *Fyodor Dostoevsky: A Critical Study* (August 1916).
[2] Murry's concluding sentences read: 'In Russian literature alone can be heard the trumpet-note of a new word: other writers of other nations do no more than play about the feet of the giants who are Tolstoi and Dostoevsky, for even though the world knows it not, an epoch of the human mind came to an end in them. In them humanity stood on the brink of the revelation of a great secret' (p. 263).

My dear Kot,
Do not mind if my letters are far between. I have wondered very often how things are going with you. But I believe, no steps have been taken as yet with regard to Russians in England, have they? Write and give me all your news. Tell me also about Gilbert Cannan and Gertler, and Murry. I suppose Murry has got his job in the Home Office.¹ He sent me his book from London. But I am weary, and I don't want him to write to me any more – at least at present. I don't know what Katharine is going to do – and don't care. They weary me, truly.
We had Barbara here. I do really like her. There is something fierce and courageous in her which wins one's respect. Now we are alone. It is sad, but the world seems wider and freer when one is alone.
I am typing away at my novel, to get it done. I often think of you, and how you laboured at the typing for me, two years ago. I know you hated it. I hope that things will so go, that you get some *real* work to do and *have* to do it: that you have to work *hard*, at something worth doing. It is terrible to have so much inertia as you have.
With greetings from Frieda D. H. Lawrence

1277. To Barbara Low, 1 September 1916
Text: MS SIU; Moore 471–2.
[Higher Tregerthen, Zennor, St. Ives, Cornwall]
1 Sept. 1916
My dear Barbara
I wondered why you were so cross over W[illia]m H[enr]y.² It is true, I still run away from him – and *cannot* ask him to the house. But he was talking to me on Sunday, and sighing for London, to see the search-lights etc. And I realised, with rather a shock, that they truly *hate* him, all the rest: I thought they only *thought* they hated him. So I imagined if he had a few days in London it might help him through the winter, especially if he had a few *people* in his mind. But he wouldn't come up till October, till harvest is fully closed, and before turnip-pulling begins. And I doubt if he'll move at all. I wish one didn't always find a petty tragedy on one's doorstep. – It wasn't that I wouldn't let you see him, here – it was that one *does* avoid him, he *is* rather a burden. He has never been inside the house yet, and for some

¹ Murry was employed at the War Office where he 'was more or less editor of an impressive sheet called *The Daily Review of the Foreign Press*' (Murry, *Autobiography* 428).
² William Henry Hocking.

reason, I cannot invite him. Perhaps it is best to ignore them as much as possible.

I have been in bed for the last three days with a sharp bronchial cold: great crossness on my part, as you can imagine. The mason hasn't turned up to seal the other house: and we've had a sudden deluge of rain. When I go out I expect to find the world darkened with blackberries. I do regret you can't help us to pick some.

Have you found Spiers again? He must be much sicker, psychically, than we have thought.

I wish we were all driving off to Penzance again: this is just such a day. The cinnamon and gold stockings are *very* nice.

                                                   With love from both   D. H. Lawrence

1278. To Lady Cynthia Asquith, 1 September 1916
Text: MS UT; Huxley 365–6.

                                        Higher Tregerthen, Zennor, St. Ives, Cornwall
                                                                          1 Sept 1916

Whether we are alive or not, that is the question. My 'indignant temperament' has done for me, and I am dead to the world. Like the monks of Nitria, I am buried in the desert of Sahara, sit amidst silence like Saint Anthony.[1] Avaunt Woman + + + . –

That is the whole story of the present.

Of the past, or of the world vanquished and forgotten – they gave me a total exemption from military service, otherwise I should be singing with the Cherubim now, instead of sulking amid the sands of Nitria. I had to go to Penzance and join up: was escorted by a little 'Lump' (German word) of a sergeant, with many other condemned wretches, 3 hours journey to *Bodmin*: spent the night in barracks, with the rest, and was let go in the morning. My blood cribbles[2] with fury to think of it. I am no longer an Englishman, I am the enemy of mankind. The whole of militarism is so disgusting to me, that – well well, there is silence after all.

---

[1] DHL alludes to Lord Curzon's *Visits to Monasteries in the Levant* (see p. 572 n. 1): 'The Desert of Nitria is famous in the annals of monastic history as the first place to which the anchorites, in the early ages of Christianity, retired from the world...It was in Egypt where monasticism first took its rise, and the coptic monasteries of St. Anthony and St. Paul claim to be founded on the spots where the first hermits established their cells on the shores of the Red Sea. Next in point of antiquity are the monasteries of Nitria...' (pp. 121–2).

[2] DHL appears to be adapting for his own purpose a Cornish dialect verb meaning 'to fray or wear out by friction'.

But I hate humanity so much, I can only think with friendliness of the dead. They alone, now, at least, are upright and honorable. For the rest – pfui! Here in Nitria there is great space, great hollow reverberating silent space, the beauty of all the universe: – nothing more. The few visionary temptations: heather and blackberries on the hills, a foamy pool in the rocks where one bathes, the postman with barbed letters: they are the disordered hallucinations of temporal reality. Saint Anthony is not deceived by them. In truth there is vast unechoing space where one goes forth and is free.

I send you a bit of the world that has passed away – my book of poems. I suppose you are wearing black clothes for mourning – an ugly thought.[1] I tell you, only the dead are real. For them one should wear a lovely blue. When I go to Penzance again I shall send you a tiny brooch of blue chalcedony. That seems to me the only thing one should wear to the dead, it is so beautiful and immortal. – As for the living, they are really the terrible temptation of temporal reality.

Frieda talks of coming to London for a few days this month. I simply dare not. The thought of the masses of humanity frightens my very soul. I dare not be jostled into them. But before long, when I am stronger than they, I shall come back.

Meanwhile, the monk of Nitria fitfully types out his novel, which is a sequel to the *Rainbow*.

D. H. Lawrence

1279. To S. S. Koteliansky, [4 September 1916]

Text: MS BL; Postmark, St. Ives 4 SP 16; Spender 31.

Higher Tregerthen, Zennor, St. Ives, Cornwall
Monday.

My dear Kot,

Both your letters came this morning. Your 'Dostoevsky evening' gives me a queer contraction of the heart. It frightens me. When I think of London, the Café Royal – you actually there, and Katharine – terror overcomes me, and I take to my heels, and hide myself in a bush.[2] It is a real feeling of

---

[1] Lady Cynthia's brother Hugo, Lord Elcho (1884–1916) had been killed in France in June 1916.

[2] A reference to an incident in the Café Royal in which Katherine Mansfield snatched a copy of *Amores* from some unnamed individuals who were ridiculing DHL's poems in the volume. See Murry's account in *Reminiscences of D. H. Lawrence* (1933), pp. 94–6, and Delany 247–8. DHL used the incident in 'Gudrun at the Pompadour', chap. xxviii, *Women in Love*. See also Antony Alpers, *The Life of Katherine Mansfield* (1980), pp. 215–17.

horror. I dare not come to London, for my life. It is like walking into some
horrible gas, which tears one's lungs. Really – Delenda est Carthago.[1]

I don't believe they will conscript you, in the end. For some reason, I think
they will leave alone the Jews and the Russians. Surely they have got their
mouths as full of conscripted England, as they can chew. I must say I hate
mankind – talking of hatred, I have got a perfect androphobia. When I see
people in the distance, walking along the path through the fields to Zennor,
I want to crouch in the bushes and shoot them silently with invisible arrows
of death. I think truly the only righteousness is the destruction of mankind,
as in Sodom. Fire and brimstone should fall down.[2]

But I don't want even to hate them. I only want to be in another world
than they. Here, it is almost as if one lived on a star, there is a great space
of sky and sea in front, in spirit one can circle in space and have the joy of
pure motion. But they creep in, the obstructions, the people, like bugs they
creep invidiously in, and they are too many to crush. I see them – fat men
in white flannel trousers – pères de famille – and the familles – passing along
the field-path and looking at the scenery. Oh, if one could but have a great
box of insect powder, and shake it over them, in the heavens, and exterminate
them. Only to clear and cleanse and purify the beautiful earth, and give room
for some truth and pure living.

Perhaps after all we shall prevail over the creeping multitudes. The
weather will soon wash them back from these coasts. If only the war ended,
you could come and stay here. *Devise some job* that will let you out of that
Bureau.

Write and tell me what Katharine is doing in London: also Jack. I wrote
to him very disagreeably, and said I wanted him to leave me alone entirely.[3]
But I feel myself relenting, and a little sorrow coming over my heart.

The heather is all in blossom: there are very many blackberries, heavy on
the briars: we got some mushrooms on the cliffs yesterday, small and round
in the close grass: the sea was very beautiful, dark, dark blue, with heavy
white foam swinging at the rocks. If only one had the world *to oneself*! If
only there were not more than one hundred people in Great Britain! – all
the rest clear space, grass and trees and stone! Where is our Rananim? If
only we had had the courage to find it and create it, two years ago. Perhaps
it is not utterly too late.

[1] i.e. 'Carthage must be destroyed', the words which Cato the Elder (234–149 B.C.) is reported
to have used to conclude each of his speeches in the Senate when Carthage was threatening
Rome.
[2] Cf. Genesis xix. 24.
[3] See the last paragraph of Letter 1275.

I'm glad you are not going to Garsington. The place is very bad, really. Don't say anything to the Murrys, of what I say. I think he and she should ultimately stick together – but there is so much in their mutual relationship that must pass away first. Oh dear, how weary things make one.

Greetings from Frieda and me   D. H. Lawrence

1280. To Dollie Radford, 5 September 1916

Text: MS UN; Postmark, St. Ives 5 SP 16; cited in Moore, *Intelligent Heart* 225–6.

Higher Tregerthen, Zennor, St. Ives. Cornwall

5 Sept. 1916

My dear Dollie

I am glad you liked your Jasper and Bridget,[1] who are riding through a dark twilight air. I should have written to you before, but I did not know if you were at home.

I am so sorry these raids come and give you such shocks.[2] I am sure it must be very hurtful to you. What a shame it seems that one's life should be so completely violated. It is my constant wish, that we could be given a star to live on, we who do not want their machines and their gunnery and their barren ugly 'progress'. Even if there were only an island that could be given, to those who wish to be happy amidst happiness: one of the Hesperides! Why oh why have the Hesperides sunk under the Atlantic: I invoke them every time I look at the sea, but they have not risen yet. Perhaps later they will.

I do not think I shall come to London. I could not bear that great town and its people. I must stay in Tregerthen, I am too much afraid of the world to go out. The Weekleys have not written to say they will give Frieda an appointment, to see the children. I do not know what she will do. I suppose she will come up and hunt them out. But I have very little sympathy with her in the business. I think she should leave the children alone, till they are men and women. Then, if there *is* love, if there *is* a connection, it is undeniable: if there *be* no active love, nothing can create it. It wearies me.

The blackberries are ripe: we have made about ten pounds of jam. Also I have got some mushrooms, very nice white ones. We have had many many beans out of both gardens, and peas at last from our little spot – they were very good. But it has been very rainy.

---

[1] Unidentified.
[2] On 2 September 1916, 'thirteen German airships attacked London and the Eastern counties, killing two persons and injuring thirteen. One of the airships was brought down near Enfield' (*Annual Register* [1916]).

William Henry wants very much to come to London, when harvest is over – next month, perhaps. Would you see him, and help to look after him, you and Margaret and Hester – if she is in town?[1] I think it would do him *so much good* – would set him going for the winter. There is a great deal of friction down at the farm: the poor 'rascal and villain'. – You knew that son-in-law, Hollow, was dead – three weeks ago. He went *very* rapidly. Mrs Hocking is just beginning to cheer up a little. – If William Henry came to London, it would not be for long, at the outside a week: so perhaps he could be amused and instructed and *edified* to his heart's content, during that time, if you would see him, and Barbara Low, and the Eders, and Mrs Carswell.

Nothing much has happened here – save that we bought some very lovely bits of purple-pink lustre in Penzance when Barbara was here: a jug with a big bunch of grapes and big vivid green leaves – very nice indeed. It embellishes the tower. Banfield, the mason, has come to make everywhere thoroughly water-tight for the winter: which is a relief. There are some girls staying at Carn. Miss Pilcher, of Tremeader – you know, the next farm – was thrown out of her trap, her pony bolted, her trap smashed up, on Saturday, going to St. Ives. She was not much hurt, but a great sensation in the parish. She drives a pony that is not properly broken in.

The heather is all out on the hills – very beautiful indeed – purple patches. And the young gorse is all in flower again. We have had outrageous rough seas, and of a dark, wine-blue colour. The bracken is withering, the sunsets are tremendous, almost terrible, the autumn is coming in. The corn stands in 'mows' – small ricks, in the field – not carried yet. Of course William Henry is behind. He has not got half his cut yet. It must all be cut by scythe.

Some time, will you ask that man about the restoration of my dear 'George Fox' portrait.[2] I will have it done if I can afford it.

The Murrys are both in London – but I don't know their address there. He, I think, has got some sort of a job in the Home Office. If ever you want to see them, I think if you address them c/o S. Koteliansky, 212 High Holborn, that will get them.

I do hope you won't have any more soul-shattering raids: it is a great shame. Is everything else all right with you and the others?

With love from us both   D. H. Lawrence

Has Maitland got Burnets 'Early Greek Philosophers'?[3] If he has, I should be *so* glad if he would lend it me – I want to refer to it. Perhaps it is at Well Walk – I remember Margaret was reading it there.

---

[1] Dollie Radford's younger and elder daughters. (Hester became Countess Batthyany.)
[2] George Fox (1624–91), founder of the Society of Friends; the portrait has not been identified.
[3] *Early Greek Philosophy;* see p. 364 n. 4.

1281. To Barbara Low, 8 September 1916
Text: MS SIU; Unpublished.

Higher Tregerthen, Zennor, St. Ives, Cornwall
8 Sept. 1916

My dear Barbara,
The atlases came this morning – really a *great* pleasure. I only hope you didn't *buy* the one you gave me. I will write to Collins – noble of him.[1] I *love* maps, these maps of all sorts – I could stare at them for ever. I shan't come to London – I can't. I feel all exposed – and the shock of that great town would almost kill me. I feel a bit queer too, neuralgic, after that last cold – which was a weakening one.
We have made blackberry jelly that hasn't set.
I often think of the chalcedony: it is a symbol of pure space, the most precious of all things. There one is free. You must keep it as a symbol of pure happy freedom – the chalcedony.

with love   D. H. Lawrence

Give my letter to Eder – read it too.

1282. To J. B. Pinker, 9 September 1916
Text: MS Forster; cited in Ross, *DHL Review*, viii. 201.

Higher Tregerthen, Zennor, St Ives, Cornwall
9 Sept 1916

Dear Pinker
I enclose this letter from America.[2] I have got some MS. I left behind in Italy – verse and one or two stories, that want doing up, and then are all right. When I've finished the novel – which is only half done as yet[3] – I will *really* get off some stories, and send them you. I won't be very long with the novel.

D. H. Lawrence

I thought perhaps the *Seven Arts* might be useful – you will know.

1283. To Barbara Low, 11 September 1916
Text: MS SIU; Moore 474.

Higher Tregerthen, Zennor, St. Ives, Cornwall
11 Sept 1916

My dear Barbara
Thank you very much indeed for the Swinburne. I lie in bed and read

---

[1] Vere H. G. Collins of Oxford University Press.
[2] The letter was from Paul R. Reynolds (dated 22 August 1916) enquiring whether DHL would submit stories to *Seven Arts*, a 'little magazine' published in New York, November 1916 – October 1917 (it then merged with the *Dial*). It published two of DHL's stories: 'The Thimble' in March 1917; 'The Mortal Coil' in July 1917.
[3] i.e. *Women in Love* is only half typed.

him, and he moves me very deeply. The pure realisation in him is something to reverence: he is [...] very like Shelley, full of philosophic spiritual realisation and revelation. He is a great revealer, very great. I put him with Shelley as our greatest poet. He is the last fiery spirit among us. How wicked the world has been, to jeer at his physical appearance etc. There was more powerful rushing flame of life in him than in all the heroes rolled together. One day I shall buy all his books. I am very glad to have these poems always by me.

The cake and the book and the sweets all came this morning: what a wealth! The cake *smells* excellent. We must have a tea-party. But I find, when I get to the point, I *cannot* invite anybody to tea. I only want to say 'will you please not come to my tea-party'. So, like the mouse in the fable, we shall eat all the cake ourselves.

My sister from Glasgow sent me shortbread and Herodotus and Heinz pickle and biscuits and oat-cakes: my sister from Ripley sent me water-colour paints (*very nice*) and socks and braces and ties and handkerchiefs. You sent Atlases and Swinburne – then the cake and sweets Frieda ordered. This is the most surprising array I have had for some years: though my two sisters are always faithful.[1] I *do* want to invite the invisible hosts to tea. I will have Swinburne and Shelley and Herodotus and Flaubert: just the four, round the round table in the tower.

When you find rooms, and intend to furnish them, if you do, tell me, and I shall paint you a mirror etc. The mirror I began is now black, with lotus and leaves, very striking and handsome, like terrible night. I will make you one, if you don't live in Brunswick Square.

The heather is already fading on the hill, the wind from the sea is quite cold and strange, one can smell the northern oceans.

                                                        with love   D. H. Lawrence
Do remind Frieda that she pays you for the cake etc. I shall be *so* angry with her if she forgets it, as she is too likely to do.

1284. To S. S. Koteliansky, 12 September 1916
Text: MS BL.; Zytaruk 93.

                                    Higher Tregerthen, Zennor, St. Ives, Cornwall
                                                                    12 Sept 1916
My dear Kot,

Now you have some news, and do not tell me. Why are you leaving the

[1] i.e. his sisters Emily King and Ada Clarke remembered DHL's birthday (11 September).

Bureau, and what are you going to do? Is it merely that you have had enough Slatkovsky, or is it something better? Frieda is coming to London on Saturday, and staying for several days with Dollie Radford, 32 Well Walk, Hampstead. You can always ring her up there. Do not trouble about Saturday. Ring her up on Sunday morning and make an appointment.
We heard from Katharine that she is staying in Brett's studio.
Tell me about your new move.

Yours D. H. Lawrence

1285. To Barbara Low, 16 September 1916
Text: MS SIU; Moore 475.

Higher Tregerthen, Zennor, St. Ives. Cwl.
Sat. 16 Sept. 1916
My dear Barbara
Frieda has set off today for London – I inherit the earth to myself. This man¹ wrote today. I haven't got a copy of *Love Poems*. I said to him, perhaps you might lend him the *Love Poems* and the *Amores*. But don't if you don't want to. – But if you feel like it, do see him and tell me what kind of fish he is.
I hated the Psychoanalysis Review of *Sons and Lovers*.² You know I think 'complexes' are vicious half-statements of the Freudians: sort of can't see wood for trees. When you've said Mutter-complex, you've said nothing – no more than if you called hysteria a nervous disease. Hysteria isn't nerves, a complex is not simply a sex relation: far from it. – My poor book: it was, as art, a fairly complete truth: so they carve a half lie out of it, and say 'Voilà'. Swine! Your little brochure – how soul-wearied you are by society and social experiments! Chuck 'em all overboard. Homer Lane be damned – it is a *complete* lie, this equality business – and a dirty lie.³
I must run for the post.

love D. H. Lawrence
I'll send back the *Review*.

¹ Unidentified.
² Alfred Booth Kuttner, '"Sons and Lovers": A Freudian Appreciation', *Psychoanalytic Review*, iii (1916), 295–317. (This was an expansion of Kuttner's review in the *New Republic*, ii, April 1915; see Draper 76–80.)
³ Homer Tyrrel Lane (1876–1925), an American, had founded (in 1913) a 'Little Commonwealth' on a Dorset farm; it was designed to be a self-governing 'republic' to which delinquent teenagers were sent rather than to a penal institution; 'equality' was an essential feature of its operation. (It was closed down in 1918. See E. T. Bazeley, *Homer Lane and the Little Commonwealth*, 1928.)

1286. To Lady Ottoline Morrell, 26 September 1916
Text: MS UT; Moore 475–6.

Higher Tregerthen, Zennor, St. Ives, Cornwall
26 Sept. 1916

My dear Ottoline

Now I think I should like to see you again, before very long – when this novel is done. Will you come here, or shall we come to Garsington for a little while? – to stay in the bailiffs house, if nobody is wanting the rooms. I only want to finish this novel, which is like a malady or a madness while it lasts. It will take only a week or two.

Arthur Lynch came – and went – bagatelle.[1]

I hear Bertie is working himself deeper and deeper into trouble.[2] Well, I'm only sorry. I don't believe, in these days of hopelessness, in taking up a hopeless cause. One should take up nothing serious unless there is fair chance of success. So with Bertie and with Casement.[3] It is no good turning upon England in direct attack whilst the war lasts, because the English will be against you. But when the war is over, then, in the debâcle, one can hope to shove a stiletto into the stout heart of Britannia.

It is a certain fact, this order of life must go, this organisation of humanity must be smashed. But it is ridiculous to be as innocent as the turtle-dove. Now is time for the wisdom of the serpent.[4] Away with the turtle doves, in with the asps. Secretly, the heart must be bitten out of this old body. It is not martyrdom we seek. I hate those who seek martyrdom. One wants victory. One wants this which *is*, shattered, and the chance to reconstruct according to one's heart's desire. But the day will come. Attendons!

There isn't any particular news. I feel like one who lies in wait and prepares. Heaven send us a favourable issue.

I can see you and Katharine talking together, and can overhear at least a few things you say. But I agree with you, it doesn't matter [...] what

---

[1] Col. Arthur Lynch (1861–1934), M.P. for West Clare, 1909–18; writer of fiction and verse. He had intervened in the Parliamentary debates on 18 November and 1 December 1915 to criticise the suppression of *The Rainbow*.

[2] Russell had been stripped of his lectureship at Trinity College on 11 July 1916 and on 1 September was forbidden by the military authorities to enter any 'prohibited area', obviously to obstruct his plan to lecture in Glasgow, Manchester, etc. under the auspices of the No-Conscription Fellowship.

[3] Roger David Casement (1864–1916), British Consular agent and Irish patriot, was brought to trial on 26 June 1916, convicted of high treason and sentenced to death on 29 June 1916. His appeal was dismissed on 18 July 1916; he was executed on 3 August 1916. For Lady Ottoline's view of these events, see *Ottoline at Garsington* 112–16.

[4] Cf. Matthew x. 16.

anybody says. Sixpence is sixpence, whatever words are on it 'Dei Gratia' etc or 'Diaboli Gratia' – who cares?[1]

Greetings to everybody   D. H. Lawrence

1287. To Mark Gertler, 27 September 1916

Text: MS SIU; Huxley 367–8

Higher Tregerthen – Zennor, St. Ives, Cornwall
27 Sept 1916

Dear Gertler,

I would write, but there seems so much noise, one is afraid to open one's mouth. I was glad to hear such good news of the Roundabout.[2] I want very much to see it, and look forward to having a photograph copy. It seems to me, the stark truth is all that matters, whether it is paint or books or life: the truth one has inside one; and away with their old lies, whether they are of vision or ideas.

I saw the *Daily Mirror* today – the Zeppelin wrecks, etc.[3] How exhausted one is by all this fury of strident lies and foul death. But less and less does the world matter to one – people, and all they say or do, life, all that is out there in the world – it ceases to have any significance. Nothing matters, in the end, but the little hard flame of truth one has inside oneself, and which does not blow about in the draught of blasphemous living. It seems to me, things matter to one less and less and less, till little remains to one but the pure abstraction within one, and that is inviolable.

Still, I know that there are some other people who have the same abstraction, who live finally by the central truth, and by nothing of the loathsome outer world. And in the end, I hope we can add our spirit together, unite in essential truthfulness, in the end, and create a new well-shapen life out of the smashed mess of the old order – I do believe we can, in time. But we have to give ourselves time – heaven knows how long.

This is to tell you – and Kot – that the essential thing is not gone, that is in our relationship. It is only purifying itself and ridding itself of externalities and extraneous things. I will write the same to Gilbert, soon.

---

[1] 'Dei Gratia' ('by the grace of God') preface the monarch's name and title on all British coins. (The words are now abbreviated: 'D.G.')

[2] Gertler's painting, *The Merry-Go-Round*.

[3] On 23–24 September 1916 twelve German airships attacked London and the eastern counties, killing 30 people, and injuring 110, mostly in the metropolitan area. Two airships were brought down in Essex. On 25 September 1916 seven German airships raided eastern and central counties, killing 36 and injuring 27 persons, mainly in the north Midlands.

Our hope is in the central truth, and then in each other. And then we can create a new order of life, in the times after these.

                                                            Yours   D. H. Lawrence

1288. To Katherine Mansfield, 27 September 1916
Text: MS NYPL; Murry, *New Adelphi* 198.
                                    Higher Tregerthen, Zennor, St. Ives, Cornwall.
                                                            Wednesday 27 Sept. 1916
My dear Katharine
    You said I insulted you in my letter – well, I didn't.[1]
    I can only say to you, as I said this time last year, when your brother died – there is a death to die, for us all. As for me, I am Lazarus sitting up very sick in his sepulchre.[2] At last, I think Frieda and I are really at peace with each other, for ever. That too was a fight to the death. But being dead, and in some measure risen again, one is invulnerable.
    Then there is hope too. I know that, in the end, we will turn slap round against this world, and choke it. It is time to be subtle and unified. It is a great and foul beast, this world that has got us, and we are very few. But with subtlety, we can get round the neck of the vast obscenity at last, and strangle it dead. And then we can build a new world, to our own minds: we can initiate a new order of life, after our own hearts. One has first to die in the great body of the world, then to turn round and kill the monstrous existing Whole, and then declare a new order, a new earth.
    This is the hope, and the life of one's soul. And do not doubt – in the end, slowly, subtly, by degrees, we will bring it about, and sing the paean of delivery before we die.
    This is for Murry as well – with my love to both.
                                                            D. H. Lawrence

1289. To Barbara Low, 29 September 1916
Text: MS SIU; Unpublished.
                                    Higher Tregerthen, Zennor, St. Ives, Cornwall
                                                            29 Sept. 1916
My dear Barbara,
    Of course Frieda never paid you for the cake and sweets, so I send on

---

[1] Such a letter has not been found.   [2] Cf. John xi. 1–44.

here the 10/-: also the *Psychoanalytic Review*,[1] for which thank you very much. I can't help hating psychoanalysis. I think it is irreverent and destructive.

Catherine Carswell came yesterday – in rather rainy and very autumnal weather. The world is changing so rapidly, the bracken dying, the blackberries sodden. I do wish one could have a new world, where people could be happy together, and pure in spirit. This world makes one's soul ache with weariness. But I suppose what does not exist, one can create, in some measure. And one *does* want to strangle the world that is.

I hope you are well and fairly peaceful.

DHL

1290. **To Lady Ottoline Morrell, 3 October 1916**
Text: MS UT; Moore 477.

Higher Tregerthen, Zennor, St. Ives, Cornwall
3 Oct. 1916

My dear Ottoline,

I am very sorry you are so knocked up.[2] The state of life does sap ones vitality. If there were a restoring, creating influence equivalent to the destructive, one would not be so bled. One can only be very still and forgetful.

As for my novel, I don't know if I hate it or not. I think everybody else will hate it. But this cannot be helped. I know it is true, the book. And it is another world, in which I can live apart from this foul world which I will not accept or acknowledge or even enter. The world of my novel is big and fearless – yes, I love it, and love it passionately. It only seems to me horrible to have to publish it.

Mrs Carswell has been staying a few days with us. She is well on with a novel that will be a real book. Thank heaven for that. – But there needs a new heaven and a new earth. I shall call my novel, I think, 'The Latter Days'. I will send it you when it is done – and if you are well. But everybody will hate it, save me – most people won't even be able to read it. But that is their look-out. It is enough for me that it is written, in this universe of revolving worlds. – I do hope you will feel better. Let us know.

D. H. Lawrence

1 See p. 655 n. 2.
2 She had a severe attack of influenza (*Ottoline at Garsington* 152).

1291. To Mark Gertler, 9 October 1916
Text: MSS SIU, UCLA; Huxley 368–70.

Higher Tregerthen, Zennor, St. Ives, Cornwall
9 Oct. 1916

My dear Gertler,

Your terrible and dreadful picture has just come.[1] This is the first picture you have ever painted: it is the best *modern* picture I have seen: I think it is great, and true. But it is horrible and terrifying. I'm not sure I wouldn't be too frightened to come and look at the original.

If they tell you it is obscene, they will say truly. I believe there was something in Pompeian art, of this terrible and soul-tearing obscenity. But then, since obscenity is the truth of our passion today, it is the only stuff of art – or almost the only stuff. I won't say what I, as a man of words and ideas, read in the picture. But I *do* think that in this combination of blaze, and violent mechanical rotation and complex involution, and ghastly, utterly mindless human intensity of sensational extremity, you have made a real and ultimate revelation. I think this picture is your arrival – it marks a great arrival. Also I could sit down and howl beneath it like Kot's dog, in soul-lacerating despair.[2] I realise *how* superficial your human relationships must be, what a violent maelström of destruction and horror your inner soul must be. It is true, the outer life means nothing to you, really. You are all absorbed in the violent and lurid processes of inner decomposition: the same thing that makes leaves go scarlet and copper-green at this time of year. It is a terrifying coloured flame of decomposition, your inner flame. – But dear God, it is a real flame enough, undeniable in heaven and earth. – It would take a Jew to paint this picture. It would need your national history to get you here, without disintegrating you first. You are of an older race than I, and in these ultimate processes, you are beyond me, older than I am. But I think I am sufficiently the same, to be able to understand.

This all reads awkward – but I feel there ought to be some other language than English, to say it in. And I don't want to translate you into ideas, because I can see, you[3] must, in your art, be mindless and in an ecstasy of destructive sensation. It is wrong to be conscious, for you: at any rate, to be too conscious. 'By the waters of Babylon I sat me down and wept, remembering

---

[1] A photograph of *The Merry-Go-Round*; see the reproduction of the painting in Carrington, *Gertler: Selected Letters*, facing p. 129.

[2] Kot did not possess a dog: this was a private joke. 'As a young man in Russia he had taught himself to howl like a dog as a measure of self-protection from wolves on his long walks home; and he was willing to howl on demand' (Carswell, *Life and Letters*, p. 89).

[3] To this point the MS is at SIU; the remainder is at UCLA.

Jerusalem.'¹ At last your race is at an end – these pictures are its death-cry. And it will be left for the Jews to utter the final and great death-cry of this epoch: the Christians are not reduced sufficiently. I must say, I have, for you, in your work, reverence, the reverence for the great articulate extremity of art.

Perhaps you are right about sculpture – I don't know – probably you are, since you feel so strongly. Only, somehow, it seems to me to be going *too far* – over the edge of endurance into a form of incoherent, less poignant shouting. I say this, trying to imagine what this picture will be like, in sculpture. But you know best. Only take care, or you will burn your flame so fast, it will suddenly go out. It is all spending and no getting of strength. And yet some of us must fling ourselves in the fire of ultimate expression, like an immolation. Yet one cannot assist at this auto-da-fé without suffering. But do try to save yourself as well. You must have periods of proper rest also. Come down here and stay with us, when you want a change. You seem to me to be flying like a moth into a fire. I beg you, don't let the current of work carry you on so strongly, that it will destroy you oversoon.

You are twenty-five, and have painted this picture – I tell you, it takes three thousand years to get where your picture is – and we Christians haven't got two thousand years behind us yet.

I feel I write stupidly and stiltedly, but I am upset, and language is no medium between us.

With love from Frieda and me   D. H. Lawrence

I am amazed how the picture exceeds anything I had expected. Tell me what people *say* – Epstein, for instance.²

Get somebody to suggest that the picture be bought *by the nation* – it ought to be – I'd buy it if I had any money. How much is it? – I want to know – how much do you want for it.

1292. To John Middleton Murry, 11 October 1916
Text: MS NYPL; Murry, *New Adelphi* 198.

Higher Tregerthen, Zennor, St. Ives, Cornwall.
11 Oct. 1916

Dear Jack,

I've been in two minds whether to write to you, these last few days – wondering whether you are in the 'leave me alone' mood or not. You

---

¹ Psalm 137. 1 (Book of Common Prayer) ['...Babylon we sat down and wept: when we remembered thee, O Sion'].
² (Sir) Jacob Epstein (1880–1959), American sculptor and author who became a British subject in 1911; from 1916 he was best known for his portrait bronzes and abstract sculptures. See his *Let There Be Sculpture* (1940) and *Autobiography* (1955).

understand all right my violent letters, I know. When one says 'I've done with him', well, there is an old 'him' in all of us that must be done away with: an old me, an old you. But then there is a new young me, and a new you, taking place, and that is everything. Terribly and cruelly the old self dies in one, the old world cracks up and falls away piece by piece. But it is all beyond one's will and one's control, one can only writhe and wait for the process to hurry up in one. But then there do come the days when the new self bubbles up and makes one happy. And then I know that what I hate in you is an old you that corresponds to an old me, which *must* pass away, the beastly thing.

I think that one day – before so very long – we shall come together again, this time on a living earth, not in the world of destructive going apart. I believe we shall do things together, and be happy. But we can't dictate the terms, nor the times. It has to come to pass in us. Yet one has the hope, that is the reality.

Frieda and I have finished the long and bloody fight at last, and are at one. It is a fight one has to fight – the old Adam to be killed in me, the old Eve in her – then a new Adam and a new Eve. Till the fight is finished, it is only honorable to fight. But oh dear, it is very horrible and agonising.

I do hope things are all right with you.

D. H. Lawrence

1293. To Catherine Carswell, 11 October 1916
Text: MS YU; cited in Carswell, *Adelphi* 291–2.

Higher Tregerthen – Zennor, St. Ives, Cwl.
11 Oct. 1916

My dear Catherine,

I've had a cold and been seedy since you went, so haven't done anything – novel at a standstill till this very day. I've run on a bit today though, and am feeling much better.

I feel pretty happy inside, too. I believe we shall see some desired things come to pass, before we die. It only needs to be ready, like the Virgins with the lamps.[1]

I do really think we shall see this old order collapsing – even in the outer world – smashing right down. I heard today from my brother in Nottingham – he is an engineer, in the munitions.[2] There seems to come from his letter a strange note, like revolution. I want to have some seed of

[1] Cf. Matthew xxv. 1–13.   [2] George Arthur Lawrence.

a new spirit ready – I know the time is nearly come to sow it. We shall be like Noah, taking all the precious things into the ark, when the flood comes, and disembarking on a new world.

I do hope things will go well and increasingly with you and Carswell – the new world. The novel is the first thing – I feel with mine, that when it is finished, I have knocked the first loop-hole in the prison where we are all shut up. But I shall do it – I feel a bubbling of gladness inside. Frieda and I are in accord – it needs a man and a woman to create anything – there is nothing can be created, save of two, a two-fold spirit. I don't believe in Don as a lawyer – I wish he would discover the unknown truth in himself. I suppose that'll come after the law.

It is wildly blowy here lately – I always expect to read in the paper in the morning that all England is blown clean and bare, and only a few people are hovering winged in the air.

all blessings to you both   D. H. Lawrence

1294. To Dollie Radford, 11 October 1916
Text: MS UN; Postmark, St. Ives 12 OC 16; Nehls, i. 402–3.

Higher Tregerthen, Zennor, St. Ives, Cornwall
11 Oct. 1916

My dear Dollie,

I am so ashamed, to hear that Frieda never wrote to you after being with you. That is too bad. I would have written.

I have had a cold again, and felt seedy and all undone – but now I feel better, feel that there is a new source of strength opened in me. I feel hopes too, of a new heaven and a new earth, here, for us.

The piece of mahogany we have is 34″ × 22″ – rather smaller. But I will look for other things, and see if we can come across something. I *long* to come to your new cottage¹ – it sounds so splendid, and I should like to have a little time *inland*, for a change. Do you think you will be there at Christmas – or about Christmas time. Dear Dollie, I do hope we can have happy evenings, and play charades, as we did in Greatham, when you were King Henry of Rosamund fame.² Do let us plan a time together this winter, and keep to it, when we can really play and be happy.

William Henry would love to come to London, but, since he would be quite alone, I don't think it is fair to ask people to entertain him so much, so I shan't say anything to him about it. He is a queer soul – I have got to

---

¹ Chapel Farm Cottage, Hermitage, Nr Newbury, Berks.
² Rosamond Clifford (d. 1176?), 'Rosamond the Fair', was mistress to Henry II.

know him quite well. If you go right to the root of the matter with him, he is most marvellously understanding. He has thought deeply and bitterly. 'I have always dreamed', he says, 'of a new order of life. – But I am afraid now I shall never see it.' And again 'Yes, there's something one wants, that isn't money or anything like that – But shall I ever get it? – I want it – ' he puts his hand to his chest with a queer, grasping movement – 'I can feel the want of it here – but shall I ever get it? – That's what I begin to doubt. Lately, I begin to doubt it.'

There is something manly and independent about him – and something truly *Celtic* and unknown – something non-christian, non-European, but strangely beautiful and fair in spirit, unselfish.

I am still typing away at my novel. I shall be so glad when it is done. Today I sent a few poems to Hilda Aldington for the new American anthology.[1] My love to Margaret. I shall write again soon. I look forward so much to that time in your cottage – a little joy-time –

with love   D. H. Lawrence

Did Miss Abbott get the £1. note I sent her?

[Frieda Lawrence begins]

Dear Dollie,

I am so sorry I have'nt written before – every day I wanted to – But when I came I found L[awrence] so seedy, the dreary wet outside terrible and I had to nurse L – I never mind the *doing* of things but he is so *depressed* then that it's like a millstone round one's neck – Then Mrs Carswell came for a week-end – But the last four days have been fine – L is better in body and soul, we have been happy in the still, sunny autumn, with the world outside all different kinds of gold – but you know I was so grateful for your generous friendship, your house is such a haven of rest – I enjoyed it thoroughly – The visit meant so much to me about the children, you know; I felt what I had done was *right* for them and for me and the true love, that is, remains and triumphs – It was a great thing for me full of hope for the future – And L. is more at rest and happier – Your cottage fills me with real joy – I do hope it comes off, no 'slip twixt cup and lip' – I think it would be *lovely* if we could come to it fairly soon – It's been so damp and foggy and November and December will be worse – I am sure it would be good for Lawrence to go to a drier place – I am so anxious to get L. *really* well and *it can* be *done* – Is the cottage furnished? You dont say – If not the sending of things does not

---

[1] *Some Imagist Poets 1917: An Annual Anthology* (Boston and New York). Published on 14 April 1917, the volume contains DHL's 'Terra Nuova', pp. 69–75 (retitled 'New Heaven and Earth' when collected in *Look! We Have Come Through!*, 1917).

cost much from here – if you want anything – the piece of mahogany that
you can have is 22 by 34 inches, it would practically do if cut shorter so we
will try and have it made for you – Also we will look out for a sofa – I am
so excited about your cottage – How jolly when you turn up – tell Margaret
I will write to her – Tell Maitland he must come and see L – they ought
to know each other – I thought of Maitland and his health reform – tell him,
I am quite obsessed by the terrible Thames *mud*, when one thinks it could
be a clean and lovely water, and that Lewisham, that mass of ugliness – and
it is *not* poverty but ugly souledness and materialism and stupidity that does
it – I am so disappointed, dear Dolly, about the shawl – As L. knew I didn't
want the other half, he had sent it to his sister for her birthday, but
we will send you something else, from our friend in Penzance – Only you
must wait a bit – So let us know about the cottage – We want to come –

Yours with much love   Frieda

1295. To Amy Lowell, 12 October 1916
Text: MS HU; Damon 385.

Higher Tregerthen, Zennor, St. Ives. Cornwall.
12 Oct. 1916

My dear Amy,

I don't know whether you would get my last letter, which I sent to the
New Hampshire address, and also the two books of mine, which Duckworths
told me they forwarded to you. I hope they reach you safely, and will give
you a little pleasure. You must tell me how you like them.

Hilda Aldington asked me for some things for the new anthology. I sent
several pieces of verse along: don't know what she will think of them. They
are mostly very regular. I must see if Harriett Monroe will publish something
of mine.

I am still typing away at my new novel: it takes a tremendous time: and
the novel itself is one of the labours of Hercules. I shall be glad when it is
done. Then I must really set to and write short stories such as the magazines
may be prevailed upon to publish. Alas, I am afraid I was not born to
popularity.

The winter seems already to have come. The heather on the hills is dead,
the bracken is dry and brown, and blowing away to nothingness. Already
the fowls stand bunched-up motionless and disconsolate under the stacks,
out of the wind, the sky is all grey and moving. One feels like a fowl oneself,
hulking under the lee of the past, to escape the destructive wind of the

present. The atmosphere all over the country is black and painful to breathe, one dare hardly move. Heaven send us happier days.

All good greetings from my wife and me.

D. H. Lawrence

1296. To Katharine Clayton, 13 October 1916
Text: MS NCL; cited in Ross, *DHL Review*, viii. 211.

Higher Tregerthen, Zennor, St. Ives, Cornwall

13 Oct. 1916

My dear Mrs Clayton,

What has happened to you all? – only good things, I hope. But one dreads asking the question nowadays.

We are living quietly here. I got a complete exemption from service on account of health. I hope Douglas did the same. But we are very poor.

I have been typing my novel myself – you know Amy Lowell gave me a type-writer. I have done about two-thirds. But I can't do any more – this typing is bad for me. Shall I send you the rest, as I write it out? – I might not be able to pay you immediately – but before very long. I felt I ought to do it myself – but it upsets me and hurts my nerves, so I give it up.

I do hope and trust things are all right with you and Pat and Douglas. I heard Connie Garnett was rather ill. I hope that isn't true. Poor Connie, I know her world is ended. But there must be a new world, a new heaven and a new earth. There is too much suffering and horror. – The cause that Connie fought for is lost, perhaps, in some ways, lost for ever. But there is hope of a *new* world; no hope of a reformed world.

With every good wish from Frieda and me.

D. H. Lawrence

1297. To S. S. Koteliansky, 15 October 1916
Text: MS BL; Postmark, St. Ives [...] OCT 16; cited in Gransden 26.

Higher Tregerthen – Zennor, St. Ives, Cornwall

15 Oct 1916

My dear Kot

How is the world going with you? Don't take any notice of the Murrys and what they say and do. There is something in them both you have liked, and therefore you like still. What you hate was always there. People are not homogeneous or even coherent. They are dual and opposite. We know the bad things about each other, all of us, pretty thoroughly by now. And they aren't interesting, even though they are true. Murry is a toad – all right. With the toad in him I will have nothing to do any more. If there is a decent creature in him also, and that comes forth, then we will accept that and be thankful. I refuse to see people as unified Godheads any more. They are this and that, different and opposing things, without any very complete identity. Individuality and personality bores me. There is a world I want and seek. Wherever I find a bit of it, I am glad, it goes to make my desired world. So if there is a bit of what to me is true and real in Murry, I am glad of that bit, and all the rest of himself he can take elsewhere. That is how I feel about him, and about people in general. As individuals, they bore me. As pieces of dirt¹ containing bits of true metal, I can accept them.

It has rained heavens hard, and blown great guns, here, for a long time. Today it is better – I feel fairly well. I have felt sick about the world. Now I hardly care. I believe we shall see changes. I believe we shall be able to set our hands to the remaking of the world, before very long. For this that is, will fall to pieces very soon. We can set to to build up a new world of man in a little time, believe me. So be ready – like the Virgins with the lamps. Nil desperandum – this world can go, there shall be another, we will shape its beginnings at least.

With saluti buoni   D. H. Lawrence

[Frieda Lawrence begins]

Dear Kot,

As Katherine does not write to me, I believe you must have told Jack what I said – I am *glad* if you have – I should have had to have it out with them sometimes – It is time that Jack stopped the lies he tells about people to satisfy his own meanness – They are as mean as they can be to everybody, *then* they turn round and say: are'nt people *vile*. And Katherine never opposes Jack's vileness, but rather enjoys it – To me they have been so mean – especially Jack, wherever they have been, they have turned people against me, tried to regard me as a 'quantité négligable'. Well, from my point I am not going to put up with it a minute longer – Only I want to know about you and Jack, I suppose now they put all the blame of his meanness onto *me* – But you know how it is. I dont mind if you repeated every word to them I said – You know I love Katherine, but I blame her when she believes Jack, when she knows better herself – But enough – I always *knew* it all – And I am no angel myself, but they have done me infinitely more

¹ dirt] rock

harm than ever I did to them, so let there be some kind of justice. L[awrence] *loved* Mark's picture. We are very happy in spite of *vile* weather. We both send you kindest greetings.

F.

How are things going with you? Let us be happy or let us look forward to happiness – It will and must come – I feel since London as if I had got real friends in you and Gertler and it makes me very *glad* –

1298. To Edward Marsh, 17 October 1916
Text: MS NYPL; Unpublished.

Higher Tregerthen, Zennor, St Ives, Cornwall

Dear Eddie   17 Oct. 1916

Thank you for the cheque for £4, which has come this morning.

Have you seen Gertler's picture of the *Merry Go Round?* It looks very good, from the photograph.

Yours   D. H. Lawrence

1299. To Katharine Clayton, 21 October 1916
Text: MS NCL; Unpublished.

Higher Tregerthen – Zennor, – St. Ives, Cornwall

21 Oct. 1916

My dear Mrs Clayton

We were very glad to have your letter, and to hear everything was fairly well with you. Thank you a thousand times for offering to type the rest of the novel for me. I know well enough I can trust your generosity. But in the meantime comes a letter from my agent, saying he will have the thing done in his office – and as that will cost nothing, I would much rather he were out of pocket, than that you were. For heaven knows when any more money is going to turn up for me: though we have just enough to scratch along with, and I don't really bother.

The winter is coming, and I don't feel particularly well – seem often to be lapsing into bed. But there, one must not bother.

Warmest greetings from both of us   D. H. Lawrence

1300. To J. B. Pinker, 25 October 1916
Text: MS Forster; cited in Carswell 49.

Higher Tregerthen, Zennor, St. Ives, Cornwall

25 Oct. 1916

Dear Pinker

I send you nearly the whole of the untyped MS. of the novel.[1] I have very nearly finished – only the concluding chapter to do. I shall probably cut it down a little when I have the typescript – the whole novel. It is a terrible and horrible and wonderful novel. You will hate it and nobody will publish it. But there, these things are beyond us.

Yours   D. H. Lawrence

1301. To J. B. Pinker, 31 October 1916
Text: MS YU; Huxley 372–3.

Higher Tregerthen, Zennor, St. Ives, Cornwall

31 Oct 1916

My dear Pinker

I send you the conclusion of the novel *Women in Love* (which Mrs Lawrence wants to be called 'Dies Irae')[2] – all but the last chapter, which, being a sort of epilogue, I want to write later – when I get the typescript back from you. You got the preceding MS. which I sent last week, didn't you?

Don't let them type this too beautifully, so that my first half looks like a ragamuffin, will you.

I send you also a story, re-written from MS. I got a week or two back, from Italy – stuff done before the war – called 'The Mortal Coil'.[3] It is a first-class story, one of my purest creations, but not destined, I fear, like the holy in the hymn, to land – On the golden Strand – Where the ransomed in glory we see.[4] I really grieve when I send you still another unmarketable wretch of fiction. But bear with me. I will write sweet simple tales yet. If only Guy Thorne would lend me his mantle for a week or two, or Lady Russell her muff![5] I wrestle with my Angel, but cannot get him to give me a proper spirit. But patience, patience. We will yet cry Eureka, I have written

---

[1] The last third (DHL says 'half' in Letter 1301) of *Women in Love*, which was in autograph (see Letter 1291).

[2] 'Dies Irae/Dies illa', i.e. 'Day of wrath, O day of mourning'.

[3] See p. 630 n.1.

[4] The hymn is entitled 'Numberless as the Sands of the Sea'; it is No. 444 in the frequently reprinted Sankey's *Sacred Songs and Solos* (n.d.); and it begins: 'When we gather at last over Jordan, / And the ransomed in glory we see'.

[5] Countess Mary Elizabeth Russell, née Beauchamp (1866–1941), novelist and society wit, cousin of Katherine Mansfield. Her second husband, m. 1916, was John Francis Stanley Russell (1865–1931), 2nd Earl Russell, brother of Bertrand Russell. Best known as the author of *Elizabeth and her German Garden* (1898) and other popular works.

the *Smiths of Surbiton*,[1] I have found the philosopher's stone, I am a thrice-blest driveller.

When I have written those stories which are yet unwritten, and they are sold, I shall go to Italy. I am tired of being unwell in England.

The *English Review might* print the 'Mortal Coil'[2] – so might those last Americans who wrote me – the cent-a-worders. – [3]

                                                           Yours   D. H. Lawrence

[1] *The Smiths of Surbiton: A Comedy Without a Plot* (1906) by Keble Howard, pseudonym of John Keble Bell (1875–1928), who also published *The Smiths of Valley View* (1907) and *The Smiths in Wartime* (1917).

[2] The story was refused by Austin Harrison, who wrote to Pinker on 7 March 1917 (MS NYPL): 'As we shall have no room for the next four or five months, I am afraid I must return "The Mortal Coil".'

[3] Many American magazines paid for stories at the rate of one cent per word, but the specific magazine referred to here has not been identified.

INDEX

No distinction is made between a reference in the text or in a footnote.
All titles of writings by Lawrence are gathered under his name.
For localities, public buildings, etc. in London or elsewhere, see the comprehensive entry under
the relevant place-name.
A bold numeral indicates a biographical entry in a footnote.

Index

Authors Society, *see* Society of Authors
Aylwin, Robert Henry, 91
Azzarini, Ezechiele, 106, 109, 118, 125–6

Baden-Baden, 19, 52, 61, 67, 70, 72, 74–5, 76, 88, 175, 177, 179, 184–6
Baillot, Marie Juliette ('Cendrella'), 264, 481, 521, 529, 539, 557
Baker, Harold Trevor, 369, 398
Baker, Karle Wilson, 232
Bale, Edwin, 384
Balfour, Arthur J., 91, 398, 399, 402
Ballantyne, Robert Michael, 588
Bandol, Villa Pauline, 465, 476, 506
Banfield, Mr, 631, 648, 652
Barclay, Florence Louisa, *The Rosary*, 285
Barnes, James Thomas Strachey, 91, 93, 105, 119, 131, 136, 142, 154, 195
Barrie, Sir James M., 120, 128, 195, 208, 213, 224–5
Barrow-in-Furness, 268, 276
Basel, 74, 75
Baudelaire, Charles, 101
Bavaria, 29, 42, 47, 59, 65, 84, 173
Bax, (Sir) Arnold, 548
Bax, Clifford, 407
Baynes, Godwin, 322
Baynes, Ruth, 322
Beardsall, George, 257–8
Beardsley, Aubrey, 117, 118, 157
Bearne, Catherine Mary, 68
Beauchamp, Leslie Heron, 409, 481, 658
Bed of Roses, A, *see* George, W. L.
Bell, Arthur Clive Howard, 16, 435, 451, 612
Bell, John Keble, *see* Howard, K.
Bell, Vanessa, 320
Belloc, Hilaire, 28, 146, 226, 352–3
Bennett, Arnold, 127, 136, 417, 446–7, 479
Benney, Mr, 585, 590, 631
Beowulf, 495
Beresford, Aden Noel, 641
Beresford, Beatrice ('Trissie'), 482, 484, 496, 521, 523, 525, 533, 541, 553, 641
letter to, 559–60
Beresford, John Davys, 13, 435, 472, 482, 485, 487, 490, 494, 497, 523–4, 533, 541, 551, 559, 560, 631; *The House in Demetrius Road*, 497; *Howard and Son*, 640; *These Lynnekers*, 560
letters to, 484–5, 495–6, 519–21, 525, 551–3, 640–1
Beresford, John Tristram, 496, 521, 525, 559
Berliner Tageblatt, 609

Bern, 186
Berry, Matilda, *see* Mansfield, Katherine
Berryman, Katie, 624, 632
Berryman, Tom, 624
Bertie, *see* Russell, B. A. W.
Bet, The, *see* Chekhov, A.
Biart-Bellens, Gustav, 463
Bibesco, Prince Antoine, 17, 63, 453, 458, 462–3, 464, 629–30
letter to, 458
Bible, Acts, 248; 1 Corinthians, 161, 347; Daniel, 640; Ecclesiastes, 62, 478; Genesis, 9–10, 16, 295, 330, 524, 627, 650; Job, 247, 249; John, 526, 658; Judges, 312, 437; 1 Kings, 85, 219, 389; Luke, 107, 109, 271, 362, 544, 625; Mark, 192, 274, 277, 318, 379, 592; Matthew, 37, 92, 223, 271, 277, 381, 404, 408, 414, 544, 571, 575, 600, 627, 638, 656, 662; 1 Peter, 594; Proverbs, 616; Psalms, 101, 125, 252, 660–1; Revelation, 10, 254, 390; 1 Samuel, 105; Song of Songs, 262
Biddy, *see* Dunlop, Margaret Dorothea Leda
Birmingham, University, 440
Birrell, Augustine, 238
Birrell, Francis Frederick Locker, 230, 238, 239, 319–22, 323, 353
Bischoff-Collins, V. H., *see* Collins, V. H. G.
Björkman, Edwin August, 80–1, 82, 144, 174
Blackwood, Lord Basil, 431
Bloomsbury group, 253, 263, 435
Blue Flowers, *see* Gertler, M.
Blue Review, 31, 47, 112, 197
Boccaccio, Giovanni, *Decameron*, 359
Bodenheim, Maxwell, 233
Bodley Head Ltd, 519
Bodmin, 14, 618–19, 620, 625, 644, 648
Bognor Regis, 342
Boissière, Jules, *Fumeurs d'Opium*, 114
Boldrewood, Rolf (Thomas Alexander Browne), 588
Bonham Carter, Sir Maurice, 63
Bonham Carter, Violet, 63, 606
Book of Friendship, The, *see* Ransome, A.
Book of Italy, The, *see* Piccoli, R.
Book of Love, The, *see* Ransome, A.
Bookman, The, 28, 99, 100, 108, 127, 135, 136, 139, 144, 150, 152
Boot, Jesse (Baron Trent), 2, 257
Booth, H., 488
Boots Lending Library, 257

Index

Index

Index

Dante, Alighieri, 538

Daudet, Alphonse, *Tartarin de Tarascon*, 85, 537

Davies, William Henry, 39, 51, 54, 61, 85–6, 92, 118, 136, 341; *Nature Poems and Others*, 136
letter to, 124

Davison, Lawrence H., *see* Lawrence, D. H., *Movements in European History*

Dawn, The, *see* Nietzsche, F. W.

Dax, Alice Mary, 18, 42, 391

Decameron, see Boccaccio, G.

Deerslayer, The, see Cooper, J. F.

Defoe, Daniel, 107; *Robinson Crusoe*, 588

De la Feld, Count, 412

De la Mare, Walter John, 131, 341, 435; *Peacock Pie*, 54
letters to, 54, 56, 83–4

Delius, Frederick, 444, 446, 450, 548, 598, 605

Dentist, *see* Campkin, H. T.

De Quincey, Thomas, *Reminiscences of the English Lake Poets*, 633

Derby, Earl of, *see* Stanley, Edward George

'Derby Scheme', 495, 496

Dewar, George A. B., 47

Dial, The, 212, 653

Dickens, Charles, 62, 74, 95; *Dombey and Son*, 62; *The Pickwick Papers*, 614

'Dionysus Crossing the Sea' (from E. Gerhard's *Auserlesene Griechische Vasenbilder*), 517, 598, *see also* Hesiod, *The Homeric Hymns and Homerica*

Di Rescis, Baroness, 166, 168

'District Visitor, The', *see* Middleton, R. B.

Dombey and Son, see Dickens, C.

Doolittle, Hilda, *see*, Aldington, H.

Doran, George H., Company, 223, 417, 419, 420, 426, 453, 475, 560, 561, 605, 610–11, 645

Dostoievsky, Fyodor, 21, 155, 182, 247, 311, 314, 343, 345, 537, 542–3, 646, 649; *The Brothers Karamazov*, 315, 331, 367, 537, 543–4; *The House of the Dead*, 155, 579; *The Idiot*, 311, 313, 537, 543–4; *Letters from the Underworld*, 247; *Pages from the Journal of an Author*, 545; *The Possessed*, 510, 521, 537, 542–4, 545, *see also* Murry, J. M., *Fyodor Dostoevsky*

Douglas, Lord Alfred, 101

Douglas, George Norman, 31, 44, 82

Douglas, James, 462

Dowson, Ernest, 91, 117–18; 'Non sum qualis', 103–5, 118; *The Pierrot of the Minute*, 118; *Poems*, 117–18

Dream-Songs for the Beloved, *see* Farjeon, E.

Drey, O. Raymond, 404

Drinkwater, John, 16, 136, 155, 447

Driscoll, Louise, 219, 232

Dublin, 10

Duckworth & Co., 6, 26, 29, 43, 65, 98, 117, 131, 132, 133, 135, 144, 152, 165–7, 174, 178, 184, 186–7, 198, 203, 221, 223, 240, 243, 246, 279, 372–3, 398, 405–6, 413–14, 417, 484, 494, 513, 519, 524, 525, 527, 561, 576, 589, 605, 606, 607, 612, 619–20, 623, 644, 665

Duckworth, Gerald, 5, 31, 71, 189–90

Dudley, Dr Emelius C., 229–30, 449

Dudley, Helen, 229–30

Dunlop, John, 191, 477, 498, 628

Dunlop, Margaret ('Madge'), 152, 191–2, 477–8, 497, 628, 630

Dunlop, Margaret Dorothea Leda ('Biddy'), 477, 498, 628

Dunlop, Maurice Hamilton ('Paddy'), 192, 477, 498, 628

Dunlop, Thomas Dacre, 4, 152, 164, 168, 173, 176, 182
letters to, 191–2, 477–8, 497–8, 506, 511, 628–30

Dunn, William, 124

Dürer, Albrecht, 63

Duse, Eleonora, 595

Dymchurch, 70

Early Greek Philosophy, see Burnet, J.

Eastwood, 7, 42, 44, 54, 55, 57, 58, 122, 124, 149, 196

Eastwood and Kimberley Advertiser, 57

Eddie, *see* Marsh, (Sir) E. H.

Eder, Edith, 258, 260, 280, 287, 483, 614, 642, 652
letter to, 491–2

Eder, Dr Montagu David, 1, 258, 260, 279, 287, 317, 483, 643, 652, 653

Edinburgh, 17, 382, 384

Edwards, Agustin, 178

Eekhoud, George, 100

Egoist, The, 131–2, 154, 156, 162, 203, 232–3, 234

Egypte, see Maspéro, Sir G. C. C.

Elcho, Lord Hugo, 649

Elcho, Lord (Hugo Charteris) *see* Wemyss, 11th Earl of

Eliot, George, *Adam Bede*, 101; *The Mill on the Floss*, 101

675

Index

Index

Index

Henderson, Lawrence Joseph, *The Fitness of the Environment*, 509
Henley, William Ernest, 34
Henning, Udo von, 221
Henty, George Alfred, 588, 589
Hepburn, Edith Alice Mary, *see* Wickham, A.
Heraclitus, 364–5
Hermitage (Chapel Farm Cottage, Berks), 316, 476, 478, 481, 663, 664–5
Herodotus, *History*, 572, 654
Heseltine, John Postle, 549
Heseltine, Philip Arnold (Peter Warlock), 12, 13, 18, **442**, 444, 446, 448, 449, 450, 452, 462–3, 465–6, 472, 473, 476, 496, 501–2, 504–5, 507–8, 512, 517, 520, 522–5, 529–30, 532, 533, 539–40, 542, 546, 547, 548–50, 552, 554–7, 558, 564, 567–9, 578, 580, 605
    letters to, 447–8, 480–1, 551, 598
Hesiod, *Hesiod, The Homeric Hymns and Homerica*, 510, 517, 572, 580
Hester Rainsbrook, *see* Cramb, J. A.
Hewlett, Maurice, 3, 212, 213, 224–5
Hilton, Enid, *see* Hopkin, E.
History of Egypt, *see* Petrie, W. M. F.
History of the East, *see* Hall, H. R.
History of the Peloponnesian War, The, *see* Thucydides
Hobson, Harold, **46**, 60, 175, 322
Hocking, Mrs, 652
Hocking, William Henry, 14, **642**–3, 647–8, 652, 663–4
Hockings, the, 621, 624
Hodgson, Ralph, 92–3, 131
Hogarth, Dr Margaret, 407
Holbrook, Muriel May, 77
    letters to, 77, 148–50
Holbrook, William, 77, 148, 149
Hollow, Mr, 652
Holman, Grace, 55
Homer, 298, 618; *Iliad*, 253, 315, 330, 644; *Odyssey*, 253, 315
Homeric Hymns, *see* Hesiod, *The Homeric Hymns and Homerica*
Hood, Thomas, 'The Bridge of Sighs', 108
Hope-Johnstone, John, 288
Hopkin, Enid, 42, 56, 58, 123, 196, 237, 259, 391, 467, 514
    letter to, 76
Hopkin, Henry, 124
Hopkin, Sallie A., 7, 18, 42, 57, 123, 237, 259, 391, 467
    letters to, 41–2, 196, 200, 401–2, 514

Hopkin, William Edward, 7, 18, **42**, 58, 196
    letters to, 56–8, 72, 122–4, 236–7, 258–9, 391, 401–2, 467, 514
Horace, 46, 63, 105; *Odes*, 36, 46, 352
Horne, Maisie, 409
Horne, William K., **205**–6, 210, 213, 220–1, 222, 227, 229, 230–1, 236, 237, 238, 250, 251, 268, 287, 329, 409, 615
Horton, Robert Forman, **477**
Houghton, Mifflin, 223–4, 246, 562
House in Demetrius Road, The, *see* Beresford, J. D.
House of the Dead, The, *see* Dostoievsky, F.
House with the Mezzanine, The, *see* Chekhov, A.
Housman, Alfred Edward, *A Shropshire Lad*, 13, 502
Hovey, Carl, 216
Howard and Son, *see* Beresford, J. D. and Richmond, K.
Howard, Keble (John Keble Bell), *The Smiths of Surbiton*, 670
Howards End, *see* Forster, E. M.
Howitt, Mary, 114
Hudson, Nancy, 360, 393
Huebsch, Benjamin W., 17, 190, 224, 294, 398, 420, **426**, 429, 441, 446, 475, 479, 514, 518, 561, 610–11
Hueffer, Ford Madox (Ford Madox Ford), 31, 75, 132, 232
    letter to, 34
Hughes, Thomas, *Tom Brown's Schooldays*, 588
Hugo, Victor, 34
Humphreys, Ernest Arthur, 91
Hunt, Violet, 8, 34
Huntingdons, the, 120, 133, 139, 168, 173, 192, 629
Hutchinson, Mary, 591
Hutchinson, St John ('Jack'), 591, 612
Huxley, Aldous, 4, 319, **325**, 452, 481, 483
    letters to, 467–8, 471
Huxley, (Sir) Julian Sorell, 264, **481**, 483
Hymnen an die Nacht, *see* Novalis

Idiot, The, *see* Dostoievsky, F.
Idyll, An, *see* Greiffenhagen, M.
Iliad, *see* Homer
Imagism, 203
Imagistes, Des, *see* Pound, E.
Incorporated Society of Authors, Playwrights and Composers, *see* Society of Authors

678

Index

Index

Index

Index

Index

McLeod, Arthur William, 7, 15, **19**, 21, 30, 36, 48
letters to, 22, 27, 47–8, 64–5, 76–7, 86, 89–91, 117–19, 135–7, 138–9, 146–7, 155–6, 162–4, 180–2, 186–7, 188, 193–4, 195, 251, 254–5, 395
MacQueen, William, **319**, 323, 452
Madge, *see* Dunlop, Margaret
Maecenas, Gaius Cilnius, 63
Maeterlinck, Maurice, 26, **181**; *Life of the Bee*, 279
Magnus, Maurice, 31; *Memoirs of the Foreign Legion*, 31
Malory, Sir Thomas, 495, 496; *Morte Darthur*, 492
Man With a Hammer, The, see Wickham, A.
Manchester, 17, 382, 384
Manchester Guardian, 222
Mann, Heinrich, 247
Mann, Thomas, 247
Mansfield, Katherine, 4, 7, 8, 10, 13–14, 17, 31, 45, 46, 50, 51, 53, 110–13, 160–2, 171, 205, 207, 218, 221, 226, 233, 237–8, 240, 246, 252–4, 256, 270, 274, 289, 290, 291, 293, 296, 301, 308, 313, 323, 333, 359, 385–7, 389, 390, 393, 404, 409, 427–8, 464–5, 476, 506, 508, 515, 521, 525, 530, 535, 539, 541, 545, 547–8, 554–6, 567–70, 572, 575, 580, 584–6, 588, 590, 591, 594–7, 599, 604–9, 613–21, 623–4, 627–8, 637–9, 641, 647, 649–52, 655–6, 666–9; *Prelude*, 545
letters to, 451–2, 471–3, 481–2, 499, 507–8, 522–3, 533–4, 541–5, 548–50, 563–5, 569–71, 576–7, 580–1, 631–3, 658
Manucci, Niccolao, 608; *Storia do Mogor*, 596, 601, 608; *Taimur-I-Lang*, 601
Margate, 29, 30, 32, 35, 36, 38, 39, 60, 64, 89, 93, 172
Margueritte, Paul, *Ame d'Enfant*, 100
Marinetti, Filippo Tommaso, **180**, 181–3
Marryat, Frederick, 588
Marrying of Hester Rainsbrook, The, see Cramb, J. A.
Marsden, Dora, 131
Marsh, (Sir) Edward Howard, 2–3, 7–8, 12, 14, 39, 40, 41, 43, 45, 48, 51, 62, 63, 68, 87, 89, 108, 128, 136, 161, 203, 208, 211, 212, 224, 331, 398, 411, 447, 509, 515, 531, 602
letters to, 35–6, 39, 51–2, 53–4, 61, 84–6, 91–4, 102–6, 113, 119–21, 131, 140–2, 144, 152, 154–5, 176–8, 185, 186, 194–5, 198, 199–200, 211–12, 213–15, 384, 399, 400–1, 406, 428–9, 432–3, 535–6, 565, 668
Mary and the Bramble, see Abercrombie, L.
Masefield, John, 131, 136, 176, 254
Mason, A. E. W., 225
Mason, Agnes, 22, 136
Maspéro, Sir Gaston Camille Charles, *Egypte*, 521, 529
Massingham, Harold John, 402
Massingham, Henry William, 402
Masters, Edgar Lee, *Spoon River Anthology*, 503, 533
Mathews, Elkin, 519
Maupassant, Guy de, 244
Maxence, 632
Mayne, Ethel Colburn, 40, 47
Melville, Herman, 588; *Moby Dick*, 528, 614, 615, 645; *Omoo*, 614; *Typee*, 614
Men, Women and Ghosts, see Lowell, A.
Mencken, Henry Louis, 144
Mercure de France, Le, 385, 387
Meredith, George, 146, 177, 180
Meredith, Hugh Owen, 18, **402**, 403–4, 418; *Week-Day Poems*, 425
letter to, 425–6
Merry-go-Round, The, see Gertler, M.
Mĕstrović, Ivan, **157**, 360, 578; *The Mother of the Jugovići*, 578
Methuen & Co., 16, 186–7, 189, 190, 193, 200–1, 207, 211–12, 25, 240–1, 250, 255, 260, 270, 294, 299, 318, 327, 328, 348, 354–5, 356, 357, 364, 370, 372, 402, 406, 480, 630–1; and suppression of *The Rainbow*, 428–31, 434–5, 439–41, 456–8, 462, 561
Metropolitan Magazine, The, 6, 197, 216, 223, 256, 406, 475
Meynell, Alice, **255**, 259, 345–6
Meynell, Monica, *see* Saleeby, Monica
Meynell, Viola, 1, 12, 160, **255**, 256, 258–9, 261, 264, 269, 271, 287, 293, 312, 323, 327, 331, 343, 345, 348, 368, 566, 595
letters to, 299, 373–4
Meynell, Wilfred, **255**, 259, 261, 345–6
Michael Angelo Buonarroti, 130, 592–3, 597, 602; *The Last Judgment*, 593
Middleton, Richard Barnham, 28–9, 34–5, 36, 41, 94–5, 96–7, 101–2, 115, 117, 179; 'The District Visitor', 115; *The Ghost Ship and Other Stories*, 36; *Monologues*, 94–7; *Poems and Songs*, 29
Milan, 78, 88, 93, 124, 135, 139, 629

684

Index

Nichols, Robert Malise Bowyer, **442**, **445**, 448–9, 569; *Ardours and Endurances*, 442, 445, 446; *Invocation*, 442–4 letters to, 442–4, 445–6
Nietzsche, Friedrich Wilhelm, 546; *Die fröhliche Wissenschaft*, 295; *Morgenröte (The Dawn)*, 315, 317; *Thus Spake Zarathustra*, 546; *Will to Power*, 489
Nisbet, James & Co. Ltd, 193, 216, 295
Nitria, Desert of, 648–9
No-Conscription Fellowship, 309, 551, 612, 656
Noelith, 29
Noguchi, Yone, 27, 61
North American Review, The, 26–7, 44
Northcliffe, Alfred Harmsworth (Lord Northcliffe), 357
Northern Newspaper Syndicate, 40, 44, 58, 60, 65, 67
Novalis (Friedrich Ludwig von Hardenberg), 34–5
'Numberless as the Sands of the Sea', 669
Nys, Maria, **325–6**, 360

Obscene Print Act, *see* Obscene Publications Act
Obscene Publications Act, 16, 456
Observer, The, 458
Odyssey, *see* Homer
Old Moore's Almanack, 609
'Old Vicarage, Grantchester, The', *see* Brooke, R.
Olivier, Brynhild, 230, 321–2
Olivier, Daphne, 230, 321–2
Olivier, Margery, 230, 321–2
Olivier, Noel, 230, 321–2
Olivier, Sir Sidney, 321
Olufsen, O., *Through the Unknown Pamirs*, 631, 632
Omoo, *see* Melville, H.
Open the Door!, *see* Carswell, C.
Orage, Alfred Richard, 258, **366**
Orchard, Mrs, 265
Oscar II, 475
Orestes, 107
O'Shea, Katharine, *Charles Stewart Parnell*, 604
Outlines, *see* Collings, E. H. R.
Outlook, 38
Oxford, 32, 291, 319, 355, 428, 461, 472, 593
Oxford University Press, 447, 483
Oxted, 22–3

Paddy, *see* Dunlop, Maurice H.
Padstow, 484, 487, 495, 510, 559
Pages from the Journal of an Author, *see* Dostoievsky, F.
Paget, Miss, 333
Palmer, John Leslie, 254
Papa, *see* Akins, Z.
Paradise Lost, *see* Milton, J.
Parker, W. G., 28, 99
Parnell, Charles Stewart, *see* O'Shea, K.
Partridge, Ralph, 508
Pater, Walter, 111, 138
Peacock, Percy, 409
Peacock Pie, *see* De la Mare, W. J.
Pearsall Smith, Logan, 360
Pearses, the, 120, 133, 139, 146, 149, 168, 173, 175, 629
Penzance, 550, 562, 563, 570, 606, 610, 616, 618, 624, 625, 641, 648, 652
Percy, Esmé, 17, 382
letter to, 384
Peshkov, Zinovii A., **155**, 168
Petrie, W. M. F., *History of Egypt*, 538, 556
Petronius, Caius, *Satyricon*, 510, 521
Phelps, Mary, 404
Phillips, Lisle M., 162
Phillpotts, Eden, 96
'Philosophy of Social Reconstruction', *see* Russell, B. A. W.
Piccoli, Raffaello, 4, 18, **388**, 412; *The Book of Italy*, 384
Pickwick Papers, The, *see* Dickens, C.
Pilcher, Miss, 652
Pilgrim's Progress, *see* Bunyan, J.
P.I.M., 487
Pinker, Eric, 241, 294
Pinker, James Brand, 4–7, 13, 15, 16–17, 31, 38, 44, 45, 58, 60, 64, 66, 67, 81, 83, 98, 135, 165–6, 174, 182, 189, 197, 211, 213, 222, 223, 235, 243, 299, 319, 326, 329, 351, 420, 435, 449, 452, 458, 459, 463, 479, 510, 525, 536, 560, 610–11, 668
letters to, 87, 117, 166–7, 193, 200–2, 206–7, 208, 212, 216, 220, 227–8, 240–1, 245–6, 256, 260, 270–1, 278–9, 293–4, 327, 331, 334, 348–9, 354–5, 356, 357, 358, 364, 369–70, 372–3, 376, 398, 405–6, 410, 412, 417–18, 419, 426, 429–30, 436, 439–40, 446–7, 450–1, 453, 457–8, 464, 475, 478–9, 480, 484, 494, 513, 518–19, 522, 527, 531–2, 534–5, 558, 561–2, 576, 589, 605–6, 619–20, 630–1, 637, 653, 668–70

Index

Index

Rousseau, Jean-Jacques, *Confessions*, 98; *Du Contrat Social*, 312
Royal Literary Fund, The, 3, 9, 223, 224–5, 226, 228
Ruskin, John, 616
Russell, Ada (Dwyer), 207, 210, 211, 224, 235, 245, 645
Russell (Earl), Bertrand Arthur William, 2, 4, 11, 12, 15, 229, 253, 273–4, 276–7, 278, 289, 292, 297, 305, 310, 311, 312, 314, 315, 321, 325, 352, 355, 358–9, 362–3, 366–7, 369, 372, 378–80, 385–9, 392–3, 397, 402, 411, 435, 439, 450, 463, 466, 474–5, 476, 483, 488, 506, 528, 538, 545, 551, 557, 572, 592, 612, 656, 669; 'The Danger to Civilization', 392; 'Philosophy of Social Reconstruction', 361; *Principles of Social Reconstruction*, 505; *War, the Offspring of Fear*, 436
letters to, 282–6, 294–5, 300, 307, 309–10, 327–8, 347–8, 352–3, 356–7, 361, 364–6, 370–1, 376–7, 386–7, 392, 436, 442, 469–71, 490, 505–6, 534, 546–7, 553, 574–5
Russell (Earl), John Francis Stanley, 277, 669
Russell, Countess Mary Elizabeth, 669
Rutherford, Mark (William Hale White), 146
Ryan, Mrs, 440, 441, 446
Rye, 179

S. Manu, 606, 607
Sadleir, Michael, 203
St Anthony, 648–9
St Augustine, *Confessions*, 572
St Bernard, *Some Letters of St Bernard*, 633
St Francis of Assisi, 538
St Helier, Lady Mary, 4, 147, 189
letter to, 147–8
St Ives, 550, 552, 555, 556, 563, 580, 582, 585, 596, 652
St John, 254, 374
St Merryn, 515
Sale of St Thomas, The, see Abercrombie, L.
Saleeby, Caleb W., 340, 342
Saleeby, Mary, 332, 340, 342, 343, 345–6, 351, 353, 362
Saleeby, Monica, 340, 342, 344, 345, 351, 635
Salimbene, 538, 572, 580
San Terenzo, 84, 86, 137
Sands, Ethel, 360, 393
Sanger, Charles P., 411
Sanine, see Artsybashev, M. P.

Sappho, 105, 493
Sardinia, 123
Sargent, John Singer, 418–19
Saturday Review, The, 1
Saturday Westminster Gazette, The, 1, 31, 39, 55, 56, 59, 60, 67, 83, 110, 373
Satyricon, see Petronius, C.
Savage, Henry, 10, 28, 36, 41, 119; 'Carber's Cruise', 73, 98, 116, 180; *Escapes and Escapades*, 35
letters to, 28–9, 34–5, 40, 42–4, 50, 69–71, 72–4, 79, 94–8, 100–2, 113–17, 129–30, 137–8, 152–4, 168–70, 178–80, 192–3
Savarkar, Damodar, 322
Savonarola, Girolamo, 592
Schnitzler, Arthur, 256
Seabrooke, Elliott, 2, 211
Seafarer, The, 511
Secolo, 135
Seven Arts, 420, 653
Severino, 116, 140
Shakespeare, William, *Macbeth*, 37, 107, 108, 129; *A Midsummer Night's Dream*, 339; *Othello*, 162; *Twelfth Night*, 466
Shaw, George Bernard, 13, 97, 236, 366, 402, 430, 444, 449; 'Common Sense About the War', 236
Sheffield, 391, 401
Shelley, Percy Bysshe, 63, 84, 85, 86, 101, 105, 115, 120, 223, 315, 488, 493, 595, 624, 625, 654; 'Love's Philosophy', 595; *Prometheus Unbound*, 488; 'The Question', 624
Short, Captain John Tregerthen, 13, 576–7, 579, 581, 590, 631–2
letters to, 575, 585–7, 620–1
Short, Lucy, 575, 620, 621, 632, 642
Shorter, Clement King, 462
Shropshire Lad, A, see Housman, A. E.
Sicily, 123
Sickert, Walter Richard, 54
Sidgwick and Jackson Ltd, 527, 535, 558
Sidgwick, Frank, 525, 531, 558
Silling, Mr, 638
Silling, Alan, 638
Simon, Sir John, 439, 456–7, 462
Sinclair, May, 267; *The Three Brontës*, 267; *The Three Sisters*, 639
Sinclair, Upton, 519
Sinister Street, see Mackenzie, E. M. C.
Slatkowsky, R. S., 231, 623, 655
Smart Set, 26, 39, 58, 67, 75, 82, 126–7, 132, 144, 166, 187, 197, 202, 209, 305, 637

688

Index

Index